FOUNDATIONS

of MODERN

HARMONY

FOUNDATIONS OF MODERN HARMONY

KAREL JANEČEK

Translated from the Czech by Jana Skarecky
Edited by Anne Carothers Hall

Wilfrid Laurier University Press acknowledges the support of the Canada Council for the Arts for our publishing program. We acknowledge the financial support of the Government of Canada through the Canada Book Fund for our publishing activities. Funding provided by the Government of Ontario and the Ontario Arts Council. This work was supported by the Research Support Fund.

  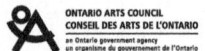 

Library and Archives Canada Cataloguing in Publication

Title: Foundations of modern harmony / Karel Janeček ; translated by Jana Skarecky ; edited by Anne Carothers Hall.
　　Other titles: Základy moderní harmonie. English
　　Names: Janeček, Karel, author. | Hall, Anne Carothers, 1934- editor. | Skarecky, Jana, 1957- translator. | https://isni.org/isni/0000000114576498 | Akademie múzických umění v Praze, issuing body.
Description: Translated from the Czech. | Translation of: Základy moderní harmonie.
　　| Co-published by Nakladatelství Akademie múzických umění. | Includes bibliographical references and index.
Identifiers: Canadiana (print) 20230530753 | Canadiana (ebook) 20230572642 | ISBN 9781771124706 (softcover)
　　| ISBN 9781771126359 (EPUB) | ISBN 9781771126366 (PDF)
Subjects: LCSH: Harmony.
Classification: LCC MT50 J3313 2024 | DDC 781.25—dc23

Cover design by Heng Wee Tan. Interior design by Jakub Kubů. Front cover image by Štěpán Marko.

 Published and distributed outside Czechia by Wilfrid Laurier University Press, 75 University Avenue West, Waterloo, ON N2L 3C5, Canada www.wlupress.wlu.ca/

 Published and distributed in Czechia by Nakladatelství Akademie múzických umění, Malostranské náměstí 12, 118 00 Prague 1, Czechia https://namu.cz/

This edition of *Foundations of Modern Harmony* is published by arrangement with Nakladatelství Akademie múzických umění and Wilfrid Laurier University Press.

First published in 1965 as *Základy moderní harmonie* by Czechoslovak Academy of Sciences / Nakladatelství Československé akademie věd (ČSAV).

© 2024 the Heirs to the Estate of Karel Janeček
Translation copyright © 2024 Wilfrid Laurier University Press

The moral rights of Jana Skarecky and Anne Carothers Hall to be identified as translator and editor of this work have been asserted.

 This book is printed on FSC® certified paper. It contains recycled materials and other controlled sources, is processed chlorine-free, and is manufactured using biogas energy.

Printed in Canada

Every reasonable effort has been made to acquire permission for copyrighted material used in this text, and to acknowledge all such indebtedness accurately. Any errors and omissions called to the publisher's attention will be corrected in future printings.

No part of this publication may be reproduced, stored in a retrieval system, or transmitted, in any form or by any means, without the prior written consent of the publisher or a licence from the Canadian Copyright Licensing Agency (Access Copyright). For an Access Copyright licence, visit http://www.accesscopyright.ca or call toll-free to 1-800-893-5777.

In memory of Otakar Šín

Table of Contents

Introduction 15

Editor's Preface 27

Preface 29

Chapter I – The Harmonic Material of the Tempered Chromatic System
§1. The Tempered Chromatic System and its Notation 39
§2. Premises for the Investigation of Harmonic Material. 41
§3. The Orientation Scheme of Chord-types 43
§4. The Harmonic Scheme of Chord-types. 45
§5. Inversion of a Chord-type. Symmetrical and Asymmetrical Chord-types 46
§6. Types of Two-note Chords 48
§7. Types of Three-note Chords 48
§8. Types of Four-note Chords 51
§9. Types of Five-note Chords 53
§10. The Negative of a Chord-type 54
§11. Types of Six-note Chords 58
§12. The Harmonic Possibilities of the Tempered Chromatic System 62
§13. Types of Multi-note Chords 63
§14. Pitch-systems Contained in the Tempered Chromatic System 64
§15. Conclusions and Prospects. 67

Chapter II – Sonic Characteristics of the Harmonic Material
§16. Consonance and Dissonance 69
§17. Dissonant Elements 70
§18. The Principle of Harmonic Inversion 72
§19. Dissonant Characteristics of Chords. 74
§20. Influence of Consonant Components 76

§21. Family Characteristics of Chords..................................77
§22. Increasing the Dissonant Characteristic..........................80
§23. Merging of Dissonant Characteristics............................83
§24. Semitone Clash of Semitone and Tritone Elements 86
§25. Summary..89

Chapter IIIa – Classification of the Harmonic Material

§26. The Concept of a Harmony in Classical Harmony..................93
§27. Transient Chords..95
§28. Incomplete Harmonies..96
§29. The Formation of New Harmonies................................97
§30. The Concept of a Harmony in Modern Harmony....................98
§31. The Concept of the Characteristic Maximum....................101
§32. The Concept of the Characteristic Nucleus....................102
§33. Consonant Harmonies as Maxima
     with the Negative Dissonant Characteristic...................104
§34. The Characteristic Maximum **6**.............................104
§35. The Characteristic Maximum **2**.............................105
§36. Characteristic Maxima **1** and **01**.......................107
§37. Characteristic Maxima **0, 26,** and **026**.................108
§38. Characteristic Maxima **16** and **016**.....................110
§39. Characteristic Maxima **12** and **012**.....................111
§40. Characteristic Maxima **126**................................112
§41. Characteristic Maxima **0126**...............................115
§42. Characteristic Maxima **166** and **1266**...................117
§43. Characteristic Maxima **112** and **0112**...................119
§44. Characteristic Maxima **1126**...............................120
§45. Characteristic Maxima **01126**..............................123
§46. Characteristic Maxima **11266**..............................125
§47. The Characteristic Maximum **011266**........................127
§48. The System of Characteristic-types...........................128
§49. Connections between Chords with Different Dissonant Characteristics.......130
§50. Boundaries between Characteristic-types......................134

Chapter IIIb – Triadic Combinations

§51. The System of Triadic Combinations 137
§52. True and Partial Combinations; Combination Categories. 138
§53. Basic Triads (Harmonies I). 139
§54. Combination Harmonies II 141
§55. Partial Combinations with Two Components 146
§56. Triadic Combinations III 148
§57. The Triadic Combinations IV 150
§58. Classification of Chords into Combination Categories 152
§59. Representation of Triadic Combinations 153
§60. The Significance of the Combination System. 155

Chapter IV – Disposition of Chords

§61. The Concept of Disposition 157
§62. The Form, Position, and Inner Disposition of a Chord; Pitch Doublings 158
§63. Evaluating the Sound of Dispositions. 159
§64. Disposition of Basic Triads. 160
§65. Evaluating the Sound of Inversions and their Dispositions. 163
§66. Disposition of Consonant Components in Dissonant Chords 164
§67. Disposition of Dissonant Intervals 165
§68. Disposition of Triadic Combinations 169
§69. Disposition of Harmonies II 174
§70. Disposition of Partial Combinations with Two Components;
     Doubled Pitches in Intervals 1 179
§71. Disposition of Triadic Combinations III 183
§72. Disposition of the Triadic Combination IV;
     Softening of Semitone Clashes of Intervals 1 through Disposition 185
§73. Disposition of Chords in a Harmonic Progression. 191
§74. Disposition of Chords and Compositional Practice 194

Chapter V – Expression of Chords

§75. Real and Imaginary Pitches 195
§76. Appearance and Cancellation of an Imaginary Pitch 196
§77. The Counter-canceling Pitch 198
§78. The Dying Away of a Harmonic Imaginary Pitch 199

§79. Compositional Acceleration of the Dying
  Away of a Harmonic Imaginary Pitch...................201
§80. Harmonic Significance of Imaginary Pitches...................202
§81. Chords Expressed by Real Pitches...................204
§82. Chords Expressed by Imaginary Pitches...................207
§83. Composite Expression of Chords in a Single Voice...................208
§84. Composite Expression of Chords in Polyphony...................211
§85. Non-harmonic Tones in Chords of Composite Expression...................214
§86. Time Boundaries between Chords of Composite Expression...................216
§87. Tonal Imaginary Pitches...................221
§88. Incomplete Expression of Harmonies...................224

Chapter VIa – Harmonic Motion: Concepts and Principles

§89. Possibilities of Motion in Music...................227
§90. Possibilities of Harmonic Motion...................228
§91. Links in a Chord Succession...................229
§92. Partial Harmonic Motion...................231
§93. Fundamental Harmonic Motion...................235
§94. Intervals in Fundamental Harmonic Motion; Imaginary Links...................236
§95. Real Links in Fundamental Harmonic Motion...................238
§96. Adjacent Partial and Fundamental Harmonic Motions...................241
§97. Higher-ranked Harmonic Motion or Tonal Motion...................242
§98. The Significance of Cadential Chord Successions...................244
§99. The Principle of the Pure Tonic...................245
§100. Application of the Principle of the Pure Tonic
  in the Tempered Chromatic System...................247
§101. Application of the Principle of the Pure Tonic in the Diatonic System...................249
§102. The Principle of the Leading Tone...................250

Chapter VIb – Harmonic Motion: Functions and their Combinations

§103. The Functional Principle...................251
§104. Establishing the Tonic...................252
§105. Types of Representative Pre-tonic Harmonies...................253
§106. Establishing Possible Representative Pre-tonic Harmonies...................254
§107. The Classical Functional System of Three Members...................256

§108. Šín's Functional System of Five Members 257

§109. Stabilization of Relations between Harmonies of the Functional System; the Minor Dominant..259

§110. Consonant Combinations of Functions (Interfunctions) 260

§111. Dissonant Combinations of Functions....................................264

§112. Functional Ambiguity of Dissonant Combinations 267

§113. Evaluating Functional Components According to their Tonal Significance, Disposition, and Representation 274

Chapter VIc – Harmonic Motion: Function in Harmonic Progression

§114. Harmonic Motion between Functions 277

§115. The Functional Aspect of Chords in a Chord Succession 281

§116. Unitonal, Bitonal, and Polytonal Combinations 284

§117. Local Tonics and Applied Functions 286

§118. Alteration of Functions..289

§119. Modulation..292

§120. Loosening Tonally Functional Relations 295

§121. Non-Functional (Atonal) Music 299

§122. Compositional Order and General Compositional Styling................305

§123. Horizontal Thinking. Voice-leading 309

Chapter VII – Problems

§124. The Concept of Modern Harmony 315

§125. Universal and Artistic Laws 316

§126. The Evolution of Compositional Technique 317

§127. The Natural Foundation of Music Theory 319

§128. The Significance of Experience 321

§129. The Search for Law..324

§130. Static and Kinetic Conceptions of Harmony 326

Chapter VIII – Compositional Practice

§131. Composition and Theory 333

§132. Modern Melody..334

§133. Practical Studies of Chord-types 336

§134. Practical Studies of Characteristic-types and Harmonies 339

§135. Styling Studies on a Given Harmonic Basis 342
§136. Harmonizing a Melody 345
§137. Employing Textural Resources Economically 349
§138. Resolving Dissonant Chords 351
§139. Seeking a Suitable Pre-tonic Combination 355
§140. Functional Chord Successions 356
§141. Functional Variations in a Chord Progression 359
§142. Free Composition 362

Chapter IX – Analytical Practice
§143. A Method of Harmonic Analysis 369
§144. Examining and Evaluating Real Chordal Cross-sections;
      Seeking New Chord Formations 370
§145. Determining Chords from Real and Imaginary Pitches; Rhythmic and Metric
      Distribution of Chords in a Composition; Transient Chords 371
§146. Chordal and Harmonic Character of a Composition; Character of Dispositions
      374
§147. Examining Transient Chords 377
§148. Diatonic Passages; Chromatic Progressions 381
§149. Determining the Compositional Order; Evaluating Melodic Lines 383
§150. The Study of Cadences and Cadential Passages 385
§151. Functional Chord Successions 388
§152. The Formation and Extinction of a Sense of the Tonic 391
§153. The Tonally Functional Plan of a Composition;
      Overall Functional Character 394

Tables and Overviews
I. Comprehensive Survey of Chord-types 397
II. System of Characteristic-types 410
III. Characteristic Maxima by Chord-class 412
IV. Characteristic Nuclei by Chord-class 414
V. Boundaries between Characteristic-types 415
VI. Symbols and abbreviations 418

Table of Contents

Bibliography 423

Sources of Examples from Contemporary Music 427

Zusammenfassung 429

*Karel Janeček: Additional Notes to Some Phenomena
of Harmonic and Tonal Thinking* 453

*Vladimír Tichý: Order, System, Structure, Function
and Mutual Interplay of Theory and Practice* 461
1. On Music Theory. 461
2. Karel Janeček – the Key Figure for Czech Music Theory 467
3. The Path to Foundations of Modern Harmony 473
*4. Foundations of Modern Harmony –
General Overview and Characteristics of the Main Questions* 479
Conclusion 497
References. 499

Subject Index. 503

Name Index. 507

Introduction

It is no exaggeration to say that the present English translation of Karel Janeček's *Foundations of Modern Harmony* by Jana Skarecky and Anne Hall unveils to Western readers one of the true monuments of twentieth-century Eastern European music theory and analysis. The first three chapters will likely always hold a unique fascination for North American readers as a system of atonal chord designation and classification, conceived independently but with equivalent rigor to pitch-class set theory. They hold radically significant insights even for contemporary scholarship – some fifty years after their original publication in Czech and nearly sixty years after their initial piecemeal appearance in *Tempo* and *Rhythm* [Rytmus]. Although the influence of the remainder of the treatise is more difficult to predict, its value is clear as a testament of Janeček's mind-set and most fervent interests, and of post-war Eastern European intellectual accomplishment; I would contend that for those who will access its scope and creative intuition, the entirety of the treatise will continue to influence speculation and investigation in harmonic analysis in many ways.

Janeček was born in Chestokova, Poland in 1903 and raised in the Ukraine, but came to Prague with his parents and studied at the Technical College (1919–21) and at the Conservatory with Jaroslav Křička (1921–24) and then with Vítězslav Novák (1924–27). His most formative scholarly association however was with Otakar Šín, one of the principal composition teachers at the Conservatory in the 1920's and 1930's and a progressive Riemannite who evolved his own application of Riemannian principles to modern harmony. It was most likely Šín who was influential in bringing Janeček back to the Conservatory from his first position in Plzeň (as music teacher and conductor), which he held until 1941, and from Janeček's obituary tribute and the dedication of the *Foundations* it is clear that Šín was a great source of inspiration and direction to his younger colleague. Janeček stayed with the Conservatory through Šín's death in 1943 and through the end of the War, until 1946.

In the post-war "liberation" Janeček sacrificed his profile as a composer for the developing academic opportunities of the new Academy of Performing Arts in Prague (AMU).

There may have been an element of political expediency in this amid Prague's socialist-realist polemics, but ultimately Janeček succeeded in finding an enviable venue for the development of his ideas within Prague's mid-century institutional stability. Following his active role in the founding of the Academy, Janeček progressed faithfully through the ranks from (untenured) lecturer to reader and eventually, having received his doctorate (D.Sc. in Music Theory) in 1956, to Professor of Music Theory in 1961. He became head of the department of Music Theory in 1953, publishing the miscellany *Living Music* [Živá hudba], giving the lectures in "composition theory" (for composers, conductors and opera-directors alike), and later accepting posts of vice-dean, dean and vice-rector. He died in 1974.

Although the discipline of music theory was dropped as a specialization in the early years of the Academy, Janeček was to have many post-graduate students in this area. And so, while he was never a Professor of Composition, many important Czech composers count him among their most influential teachers: Radim Drejsl, Jiří Pauer, Lubomír Železný, Josef Matěj, Viktor Kalabis, Lubor Bárta, Petr Eben, Václav Felix, Vladimír Sommer, Ivan Řezáč, Ivan Jirko, Jaroslav Smolka, Milan Slavický. Among Janeček's students special mention must be made here of the distinguished Czech-Canadian composer, Rudof Komorous, who left Czechoslovakia during the occupation of 1968 and whose promotion, over the years, of Janeček's theories among his students and colleagues at the University of Victoria (British Columbia) and Simon Fraser University has led to this translation of the *Foundations*. Indeed it would seem that without Komorous's vital contact, Janeček's work might have remained indefinitely language-bound to Eastern Europe.

The varied perspectives and levels of presentation in the *Foundations* reflect many of the influences in the Academy and in the larger scholarly circles in Prague at the time, but, as Janeček explains in his *Preface* to the 1965 publication, they are part of a unified and long-sustained attempt to define and relate "static" and "kinetic" aspects of harmony. For this reason such vital theoretical abstractions as the "pure tonic" are treated in meticulous detail, while the essential reasoning in the expansion of Riemann's system from three to five triadic functions and the implications of combined-function sonorities would appear to have been developed elsewhere, and likely in discussion with other authors. The discussion ranges from the elementary and even pedantic to the speculatively sublime within Janeček's comprehensive agenda and the particular framework of issues which he cultivated over the years. North American readers will nevertheless be struck by Janeček's uncanny ability to schematize a wide variety of theoretical issues and by his seemingly relentless affinity for structuralist "classification". Although Janeček dwells little on the necessity for logical formalisms, they are clearly apparent throughout, in the inclusion of "silence" as the "zero" element chord-type, in positing consonant major and minor triads as "negative dissonance" types, and especially in the axiomatic significance of the "dissonant elements" as building blocks in a systematic, combinatorial categorization of more complex structures. His attempted modeling of the "nuclei" and "maxima" of groups of dissonance-related chords on the complete and incomplete "harmonies" of classical tonal theory reveals a more pedagogical dimension in his thinking in which he is concerned (despite his theory's exhaustive complexity) with clarity, musical practicality and accessibility. Finally, a quasi-phenomenological/psychoacoustic discourse emerges throughout *Foundations* in Janeček's meticulous discernment of the dissonant elements in combination and in defining various syntactic effects of harmonic "expression" and "motion". Here, as in the many interpretations of the function and implication of complex sonorities, and even of the philosophical esthetics of tonality, Janeček easily assumes the mantel of the refined and seasoned composer which he is, in explanations and elaborations which attain an equal footing with those of Hindemith and Schoenberg.

Janeček's explanation in *Chapter I* of the orientation scheme follows the natural tendencies of tonal harmony in which the root position, the most compact form, is taken as the basic representation of a harmony. While his system of representing only the intervals (in number of semitones) between tones of the orientation scheme may seem abrupt to Western theorists brought up on the redundant zeros of set theoretic representation, e.g., (014) and (025) for Janeček's 13 and 23, it is interesting to note an early response to Allen Forte's *The Structure of Atonal Music*[1] by Eric Regener which proposes just such an "interval notation".[2] Janeček however is quick to add methodological and pedagogical supplements to the orientation schemes, deriving the "expanded orientation scheme" which shows the intervallic structure of all "rotations" (i.e. harmonic inversions) of a given orientation scheme, and the "harmonic scheme" which provides the most harmonic disposition(s) of any basic form in tertian or alternatively, symmetrical structure – a clear advantage to the composition student who is still learning the most naturally stable and resonant dispositions of complex intervallic structures. While Janeček's strong harmonic consciousness forbids any notion of "inversional equivalency" in which, for example, dominant and half-diminished sevenths (respectively orientation schemes 243 and 233) are subsumed under the same set class (0,2,5,8), chords related by reversal of their orientation schemes (i.e. intervallic inversion such as 13, 31, 34, 43, etc.) are always linked in Janeček's tables of harmonic materials and such chords are, more importantly, always part of the same groups which are determined by "dissonance content" rather than harmonic structure. The orientation scheme tables themselves are primarily pedagogical, presenting common distinctions of symmetrical/asymmetrical, traditional/new, dissonant/consonant, diatonic/chromatic, etc. In his categorization of hexachords Janeček arrives at standard groupings of symmetrical and asymmetrical hexachords whose complements ("negatives" in Janeček's terminology) are transpositions, transposed inversions or of a different type in relation to the original hexachord.

---

1   Allen Forte, *The Structure of Atonal Music* (New Haven: Yale University Press, 1973).
2   For Regener's terminology, see "On Allen Forte's Theory of Chords," *Perspectives of New Music* 13/1 (Autumn–Winter, 1974): 191–212.

While at the outset of *Chapter II* Janeček adapts a vague and Hindemithian definition of dissonance (as harmonic "tension"), the essence of his atonal classification theory is in the formally defined *dissonant elements* and, as he reflects in his *Preface* to the 1965 publication, particularly in the inclusion of the augmented triad as a fundamental dissonance alongside the semitone (symbolized as "1"), whole-tone ("2") and tritone ("6") and their inversions. The elevation of dissonance to the essential distinctive feature for all of harmony has an irresistible logical attraction – of the universe of all three-, four-, five-, six-note, etc. chords, all, except for two (the minor and major triads), contain dissonant elements, and Janeček's theory quickly becomes a typology of different classes and degrees of their combination. Janeček's qualitative descriptions of the dissonant elements, although brief, also demonstrate a refined and compelling harmonic intutition. Elements are compared on the basis of their ability to "fuse," or "pierce" or otherwise attract sensory attention within a harmonic texture; the choice of the distinctive epithet of "warped" for the augmented triad betrays its complex dimensional nature as a dissonant element and, as Janeček contends, its seemingly inevitable suggestion of a deformed major triad. Given its logical integrity and vivid perceptual conception, and, further, its appeal to elements of common-practice intuition, it is not surprising that Janeček's system of chord classification is effective, as doubtless many readers will be able to verify, as a tool in atonal harmonic dictation and aural analysis.

The initial stages of Janeček's classification are enticing in their novelty and simplicity. Sonorities are associated on the basis of radical new criteria, and in the notion of "increased dissonance" a completely new, if somewhat rare, category of relationship is coined – the increase in the preponderance of a specific dissonance type without introducing any other dissonance types. There are thus four possibilities for the inclusion of the semitone dissonance in a chord: as an isolated dissonant element (1), as an "increased" dissonant element (that is, more than one semitone), in "merged" or combined dissonant elements (12, 26, etc.), and in the semitone "clash" of semitones (11).

The seasoned reader may be skeptical even at this early point however, since increased single dissonances engender a greater predominance of consonances which, although unrecognized in the formalism, may have a more distinctive attraction to the ear in these simpler sonorities. At least at this point, this is far overshadowed by the promise and potential of a theory that so rigorously defines and associates atonal sonorities of different cardinalities (in Janeček's terminology, different "chord-classes"). The "merging" (i.e. combination) of dissonant elements is, again, a simple yet powerful logical notion which generates the following field of relations between chords in Janeček's theory (each number represents a group of chords that have only that dissonance or combination of dissonances plus whatever unspecified consonances): sonorities containing only single dissonant elements: 1, 2, 6, 0; two dissonant elements: 12, 16, 01, 26; three dissonant elements: 126, 012, 016, 026; or all four dissonance elements: 0126. There are no two-element 02 or 06 chords, as any combination of an augmented triad with a major second will create a tritone, and any combination of an augmented triad with a tritone will create a major second.

Janeček is uncompromising in his formalization of perceptual intuitions and thus recognizes orientation schemes 11 and 151 as distinct from the normal "merging" of dissonance types. Because of their peculiar concentrations of dissonance they are regarded as "higher order dissonances" which he terms the "semitone clash of semitones" (or just the "clash of semitones") and the "semitone clash of tritones" (or the "clash of tritones") and symbolizes as 11 and 66.

Each dissonant group has one or more maxima – the chord(s) with the most pitches, of the highest "chord-class". Janeček provides two distinct representations for each of the dissonance groups, both showing the subset relations between levels, one graphic and the other in score notation. The latter are more elegant and effective in showing, via common tones, both the exact relation of subsets to the maxima or to the chords in the next upper level, and also the different instances of the same subset in any given level. The 12 collection demonstrates a case of a group with more than one maximum, the six-note **12**[1)] containing the greatest number of whole-tones (4) of any of the 12 sonorities and the four-note **12**[2)] containing the greatest number of semitones (2) of any of the 12 sonorities. The diatonic scale **126**[1)] as one of the maxima of the 126 group demonstrates the ambiguity of the "maximum" concept since it is the chord (i.e. the diatonic scale) of greatest cardinality (7 tones) which manifests the merged 126 dissonance, but the other six-tone maxima (which are all octatonic) all contain significantly more incidences of the 126.

The maxima charts are informative of other interesting relations among such traditional pitch collections as the pentatonic, hexatonic, diatonic, octatonic, whole-tone, harmonic minor, and melodic major and minor scales. The reader is enouraged to play over the maxima charts vertically and horizontally, comparing within and between groups. There are, however, limitations in this aspect of the presentation: firstly in the lack of space (even for Janeček) to represent the subsets of the larger clash families (from Example 29 to Example 40 only the maxima and nuclei are represented) and secondly because the common tone presentation does not allow for varieties of dispositions which, especially in the "higher order" sonorities, might blur the boundaries of dissonance similarity in musical contexts.

In his discussion however, of the differences or "boundaries between characteristic-types" (the dissonances which exist in either of two successive sonorities but which are not common to both) Janeček provides a tantalizing indication of his system's capacity to recognize "progressions" in the dissonance content of chords in succession. The entire set of "boundaries" between pairs of characteristic-types which is presented in *Table V* (with a complete listing of all possible instances of each type) would seem to provide a useful point of departure for a more complete study of this promising aspect of Janeček's system.

As a complement to his system of *characteristic maxima* Janeček formalizes the organizational quality of the triad in his system of *triadic combinations* (*Chapter IIIb*) which is ultimately directed to the notion of combined triadic function in *Chapter VIb*. Again the schematization is exhaustive from the definition of consonant elements (the major and minor triads and the intervals 3, 4 and 5 and their inversions), to the classification of combinations by triadic quality and interval of combination, and by incidence of common tones ("true" combinations combine triads with no common tones and "partial" combinations combine triads with common tones i.e. C E G – E G B), with tabulations of all possible combinations of two, three, and four different triads. In this system Janeček's triads can be complete or incomplete, thus enabling designations in which the complete "true" combinations of two triads have six pitches, while combinations of incomplete triads have five, four, as few as three, and even just two pitches when there is only one pitch from each triad in the combination. Much of the discussion is absorbed in the hypothetical formal logistics of the theory of triadic combination which ultimately Janeček admits is only an alternative to the characteristic maxima when it is reflected in the "concrete disposition" of the music. Nevertheless the fullness of Janeček's exposition of this issue and its central position in the following discussions of chordal dispositions and superimposed functions testifies to how deeply the idioms of stratified triadic organization were ingrained in Eastern European compositional thinking.

The discussion of disposition of chords, although not without a lengthy and normative introduction, emanates from the complexities of the characteristic maxima and triadic combinations. Janeček establishes distinctions of "combination" sonorities, where triadic components are mixed among the registers, versus "non-combination" sonorities, where the triadic components are maintained in distinct registers. He then proposes certain basic tenets of "good" disposition: firstly the relative harmonicity of the major seventh over its inversion, the minor ninth, and, in relation to this, the extreme dissonance of the minor ninth in any dispositions of the major/minor triad (313). Conversely he finds an apparent invariance of "good" dispositions in all inversions of 213 sonorities. The 313 and 213 principles and considerations of the softening effect of intervening octaves between dissonant elements are applied in an exhaustive evaluation of dispositions of two- and even three-triad combinations with comments of "good", "bad" and "very bad", not, obviously, as judgments, but rather as indications of the extent to which each adheres to or contradicts the normal harmonic disposition of dissonance.

In discussing the "expression" of harmonic sonorities, Janeček follows a line of thinking found in earlier writings of Leoš Janáček concerning the capacity of the ear to follow harmonic motion. The North American reader may well hear echoes of Schenker's "motion to inner voices" in Janeček's "imaginary tones", and in particular in harmonic profiles of single-voice melodies, but nothing more comprehensive is attempted by Janeček than the instantaneous impression of harmonies in succession. "Imaginary" tones are felt to continue in the ear until "cancelled" by stepwise motions, and again Janeček asserts interesting practical (but essentially intuitive) principles: that "cancellation" occurs only with half-step motions and descending whole-steps (only under certain conditions with ascending whole-steps) and that descending whole-tone "cancellation" is obstructed by a "counter-cancelling" pitch at a half-step distance in another register. The concept of "cancellation" is accompanied by the notion of the harmonic "dying out" of a tone which is accelerated by superimposed dissonances (more so by minor ninths/major sevenths than by minor sevenths, major seconds and tritones) and relatively "prolonged" (not Janeček's term) by consonances. In accordance with the universal of harmonic formation, lower tones (as quasi-fundamentals) tend to cause higher dissonances to "die out" more easily than vice versa. Janeček does not shy away from perceptual subtleties, distinguishing between the weight of "harmonic imaginary pitches" as opposed to "tonal imaginary pitches" (i.e., sounding pitches that do not belong to the harmony – non-chord tones, passing tones, anticipations, etc.), and considering the tendencies for incomplete chords to be more active in absorbing imaginary (harmonic or tonal) pitches and for the tritone to be the dissonance most easily fused by the ear into the harmonic percept.

The speculations in *Chapter VIa* on principles of harmonic progression offer unique abstractions concerning the impression of "progression" in non-tonal harmony. Janeček pursues a non-triadic and non-harmonic concept of progression based essentially on more tonally neutral effects of common tones; again the categorization and shading which Janeček proposes are impressive. Progressions are "partial" depending on the nature of the "link" (the number of common tones, whether the link is in the bass, etc.) relative to the number of tones in the chord, or "fundamental" where no common tones are found. Links are "direct" via repeated or octave displaced tones between chords, or "indirect" if the octave transfer crosses a step-wise motion in the other voices. "Indirect" octave displacement links which are also part of step-wise motions (but not voice-exchanges) are more substantial than those crossing the step-wise motions and, depending on the structure of the chords involved, various degrees of "fundamental" progression are possible with completely altered dispositions of the same 4-, 5-, or 6-note chord.

With his discussion of "higher-ranked" progressions (the harmonic motion between phrases) and the cadence, Janeček broaches larger issues of tonality and modulation. The cadence is viewed in the terms of classical German organicism as the emblematic harmonic progression of a particular work in which ideal factors of the "pure tonic", the "leading tone" and the "functional" principle interact between the pre-tonic and final tonic sonorities. The principle of the "pure tonic" is that of closure on a pure consonance (major or minor triad) without ("uncancelled") imaginary tones, with one semitone cancellation, and without any pitches in the pre-tonic sonority which could create tritone "false relations" (my term, not Janeček's) with any elements of the tonic triad. Given that only triads have the capacity to suggest pure functional principles of gravitation (as opposed to principles of dissonance tension) the only possibilities in major and minor keys are the perfect authentic and minor plagal cadences.

The system of functional combination assumes a system of five functions which Janeček maintains is implicit in Otakar Šín's work – expanded from the tonic/dominant/subdominant axes of Riemann. The new degrees are the phrygian (P), D♭ F A♭ (in C major), because of the phrygican cadential motion D♭ to C and the lydian (L), B D♯ F♯ which contains the lydian fourth F♯ providing the opposite (deceptive cadential) motion upward to the tonic. The mechanics of combination of these degrees which were anticipated in the system of triadic combination allow for a wide but not unlimited degree of chromatic sonorities given that all functions can be major or minor (+L, −L for example). Because of the principle of the "pure tonic" the functions are not equal; P and L cannot go to T without "tritone" false relations so they are regarded as "auxiliary functions" which can pass to pre-tonic functions (S or D or various combinations with auxiliary functions). Combination functions can be consonant or dissonant. The former, called "interfunctions" (IN), are merely triads on other degrees than the five functional triads. $+IN_3$ is an A major triad in C major or minor – three semitones down (indicated by the subscript) and composed (hence the designation "interfunction") from the minor phrygian (C♯ E) and subdominant (A).

The dissonant combinations are schematized into categories according to whether they combine complete functions or interfunctions, or complete and incomplete functions and interfunctions or even exclusively incomplete functions or interfunctions. With the complete tabulation of functional (and interfunctional) combinations Janeček accesses the structural esthetics of progressions and cadence in the rich style of triadic stratifications for which his theory would appear to have been conceived. Schematic elements from the earlier discussion of (fundamental vs. partial) progressions would seem to carry over to Janeček's considerations of the syntax of functional relations. "Resolution" and "connection" are opposites in their different directions (respectively) to and from the tonic and "transfer" would appear, in progressions not involving the tonic, to be a special case of reducing, via attrition, a combined-function to one of its components. Resolutions can be "simple" (as with triads) or "compound" with more complex (combined-function) sonorities and it is possible (and in most cases compositionally necessary) to have "imperfect" resolutions to the tonic in which the pure triad may be enhanced or (even submerged) with added tones. "Higher-level" progressions cross from "primary" to "auxiliary" functions (or vice versa) while "lower level" progressions remain exclusively within "primary" and "auxiliary" functions.

Vladimír Ladma in more recent work *Harmonic Bindings*[3] seems to have captured a dynamic essence of Janeček's five-function chromatic functionality:

"*Harmonic functions* are groupings from a harmonic variety with extreme properties. They are defined as follows: *Tonic function* is the grouping with the maximum tonicity. *Dominant function* is the grouping with the maximum positive continuity towards the tonic. *Subdominant function* is the grouping with the maximum negative continuity, i.e. the maximum positive continuity in the direction from the tonic. *Phrygian function*, is the grouping with the maximum impulse towards the tonic from above. *Lydian function*, is the grouping with the maximum impulse towards the tonic."

---

3   Vladimír Ladma, "Harmonic bindings," *Traced Ideas,* 1 March 2017, http://www.traced-ideas.eu/music/harmonicbindings.html.

Janeček in *Foundations* does not comment on a dynamic functionality of the different degrees but it would appear to be as vital to his formulations as it was to Riemann's. Whether the listener can discern ascending or descending "impulses", or "positive continuity" to and from the tonic amid the complexities of alterations, superpositions and combination which Janeček proposes would appear to be a crucial test of his five-function system.

Because of Janeček's focus on extended Riemannian harmonic tonality and combined triadic functions, polytonality is regarded as rare and peripheral. The Riemannian notion of the "applied dominant" is active in Janeček's discussion of progression and modulation and is distinguished from the interfunction progressions by its predictable resolutions. Interesting variations of traditional theoretical formulae are seen in the endorsement of minor applied dominants (effective for Janeček for their lack of tritone cross-relations in the minor key) and "applied subdominants" which he finds most effectively in the ascending cycle of fifths. As in modern textbooks, Janeček discusses passages (even complex ones) which can be interpreted alternatively with modulations into different keys or via interfunctions and applied dominants within a single key. Further consideration can be found in *Chapter VIII* of the resolution of complex combined-function chords. Janeček talks about a number of factors in pre-tonic/tonic progressions including the ideal "balancing" of components in a pre-tonic sonority between dominant/lydian and subdominant/phrygian functions, the orienting effect of sequences of chords prior to the pre-tonic sonority, the distinction between "strong" and "loose" linear motions (the latter with dissonant "uncancelled" imaginary tones) to the final sonority and, finally, the value of complex dominants which provide other effective resolutions than those which would appear to be the obvious ones. The reader will find Janeček's examples of these latter effects at the same time impressive and puzzling. The pre-tonic sonorities themselves are rich and superbly crafted chromatic dominants but their resolutions are so plain and empty it can only be assumed that they are theoretical points of harmonic orientation (i.e. "pure tonics") and in real compositional circumstances such highly developed pre-tonic chords could only have equally rich "imperfect" (added-tone) resolutions.

In *Chapter VIc* we encounter a very Schoenbergian discussion of a number of classical issues: the role of auxiliary and interfunctions in providing necessary harmonic variation from the primary functions while gradually weakening the hold of the tonic in preparation for a new key, the notion of "non-functional (atonal) music" where either the gravitational attraction or the distinctiveness of the tonic disappears, but also the possibility of incidental functional relations in music which is pervasively atonal. With the notion of "styling" Janeček seems to touch upon one of his essential concepts of composition, in which the new materials of "modern harmony" function in traditional syntactic and formal idioms of parallel motion, pedals, doublings, chorale-style idioms and imitative contrapuntal techniques, etc.

It is in *Chapter VII* that we see Janeček's remarkable balance of theoretical lucidity and compositional objectivity fuel a larger discussion of abstract disciplinary issues.

A number of significant stances are taken and defined: the relation of "universal law" to creative intuition, the relation of phenomenal experience to theoretical organization, and, most importantly, the dual nature of harmony as static in quality yet kinetic in effect – the ultimate "thesis"/"antithesis"/"synthesis" of the entire treatise, as will be discussed shortly.

The compositional exercises are interesting from a point of view of "atonal" pedagogy and their impeccable compositional crafting in the elaboration of harmonic formulae, the reduction of a four-voice harmonic texture to a more active two-voice texture, conversely, the abstraction of four-voice harmonic "skeletons" from two-voice textures, alternative harmonizations of melodic fragments and bass lines, elementary contrapuntal exercises and (despite their problematic resolutions) voice-leading in complex multi-function sonorities. While limited in their scope and depth in comparison with contemporary North American analysis, the analytical examples of *Chapter IX* provide lucid applications of many of the important functional esthetic principles which Janeček has espoused, including dissonance group relations in chorale-style settings, intentionally harsh dispositions, structural repetition of arbitrary harmonic sequences, significant transient ("passing") sonorities, a loose functional relation clarified through structural repetition, an obliquely resolving dominant seventh, complex linear and functional combinations, intentional functional harmonic ambiguity, and fluctuating modulatory ambiguity. Of special interest for the North American reader are the passages from Czech composers, including Janeček himself, which provide perhaps some of the most revealing insights into the essence of his musical thought.

I hope that Janeček's work will be seen for its value to contemporary research in the perception of harmonic structure and harmonic motion. The issues of complexity in the "boundaries" of higher order (five- and six-tone) sonorities which Janeček discusses at the end of *Chapter IIIa* are essentially those being dealt with in various frameworks by contemporary theorists. Janeček's many other claims concerning the different conditions of "harmonicity" of 313 and 213 sonorities under inversion, the specific linear conditions of "cancellation" and "counter-cancellation" and "indirect links" would similarly seem to represent uniquely verifiable phenomena within contemporary cognitive theory.

It is perhaps not surprising to find, in a work so taken with schematization and tabulation, no real closing summary and perspective. Nevertheless, the discussion in *Chapter VII* of "static and kinetic conceptions of harmony" is clearly the vista toward which Janeček has been climbing from the very opening of the treatise. The concentration on intervallic tension in the opening chapters shifts in *Chapter IIIb* to a classification based upon stratified consonance and considerations of chord disposition and syntactic elements of "expression" or the perceived flow of one sonority into another, and "progression/motion" which is concerned with the distinctiveness of successive sonorities. The notion of "function" takes into consideration fundamental tenets of harmonic tonality and advances an analytical paradigm (the five-function theory after Šín which is particularly adapted to certain Eastern European compositional developments) which attributes degrees of motion and relationship with respect to a central and idealized "pure tonic". Janeček's central thesis is that harmony is "static" in quality and "kinetic" in effect; its superficial tensions are linked to progressions involving fundamental functional relationships. Complex and ambiguous situations are critical to Janeček's theory.

The tension given by the place of the sounding chord in relation to preceding chords likewise represents stimulus toward any motion, not a command for a particular motion. Due to the influence of its harmonic surroundings, the tension of a sounding chord can appear different than when it is judged in isolation; by this means the chord does acquire a property of a new order, however, since functionality and possibility of tension are one and the same. We can verify this at every step, especially in the study of modern harmony. Practical classical harmony, with its well-worn paths, could lead theory to the mistaken conviction that the functional designation of a chord is always determined objectively and unambiguously, and that it allows two interpretations only in modulations.

The tension of functionality for Janeček is the tension of motion to and from the tonic, or in his own words, the "non-tonic quality." Highly valued for Janeček are the unexpected resolutions, of which he provides many examples in *Chapter VIc*; in these, the cues of the superficial tension and functional progression are re-defined in detail but ultimately reaffirm the underlying universal of the "pure tonic". Thus, despite objections to fashionable notions of the relativativity of consonance and dissonance, Janeček's ultimate belief, like Schoenberg's, is in the capacity of tonality to renew itself through creative intuition and artistic ingenuity; and so, while Janeček's journey has been radically different from Schoenberg's we may now see that it is no less significant.

John W. MacKay

Editor's Preface

In his *Preface* to *Foundations of Modern Harmony*, Karel Janeček tells the long saga of the work from his first journal articles in 1931 to the actual writing of the book over seven years in the 1940's to its publication in 1965. The production of this English version of his work has taken almost as many years and has involved several people to be acknowledged here.

Owen Underhill introduced me to Janeček's theory when we collaborated in teaching a course on the theory of 20th century music at Wilfrid Laurier University in 1977. He had learned some of this theory in his studies at the University of Victoria in British Columbia with Rudolf Komorous. In 1980 I became persuaded that Janeček's theory should become more widely available to English-speaking musicians and embarked upon this project, little imagining that it would occupy me, akin to an albatross, for the rest of my academic career and beyond.

I prevailed upon Jana Skarecky, gold medal graduate that year from the B. Mus. program at Wilfrid Laurier, to undertake the translation of Janeček's book. A small grant from the university helped, although it might have been appropriate compensation for translating just one of the nine chapters of this book. When Jana presented me with a typescript of more than 700 pages (this many pages without the musical examples), she warned me that Janeček did not economize in using words. She had done what I asked her to do, which was make as literal a translation as possible, in as perfect English as the original allowed.

I had not anticipated the challenges of translation, having naively assumed that if we had a term in English for a suspension, for example, there would be a corresponding term in Czech. There is, but the same term is used for an appoggiatura. For a book about harmony, that there are in Czech two simple words for "chord", with substantial differences in connotation, provoked long discussions as to which was worse: using *harmony* to mean both "traditional chord" and the whole subject, or asking a musician to read a long book about *simultaneities*. We eventually opted for the former compromise.

Having learned the hard way that there is no such thing as a literal translation, I worked over a period of some 20 years to present Janeček's theory as directly as possible in a style that would be reasonably palatable to North Americans while retaining a certain amount of the flavor of the original. It is tempting to wonder how the course of music theory and even musical composition might have differed had Janeček's work been published at the time it was written, before the publication of Allen Forte's *The Structure of Atonal Music*.

Several people have been especially helpful in my work on the translation. Zdenek Skoumal generously advised me on some passages that seemed difficult in translation. I know that he would have handled some of the terminology differently. Christine Mather helped with the task of putting some of the musical examples into *Finale*. After I had retired and moved to Virginia, John MacKay asked me about the translation, prompting me to visit it again and put it all into a form for him to read. He has championed Janeček's work in his theory journal *Ex tempore* and in his lecturing; he was determined that it be published. I am grateful for Thomas Christensen's interest in the work and his belief in its value.

Finally, I am most grateful to Karen Fiser for her loving support and encouragement through all these years.

Anne Carothers Hall

Preface

1) I began work on *Foundations of Modern Harmony* in 1942 and finished the book in May 1949. Only a relatively small portion of the original texts was used due to my shortening and reworking them in the years 1948–49. This relates mainly to the first three chapters which were revised because they were too extensive in the original version.

I have worked on the problems with which I am concerned in this book since the time of my studies at the Conservatory and its Master School. Some of the results of my reflections were then published as articles in various music journals.[1] The response of other professionals in the field always inspired me to further work. When I was appointed professor of composition at the Prague Conservatory in 1941, I was already thinking about integrating and developing all the material.

At first I was interested only in static harmony, in those aspects of harmony that have to do with isolated chords. In the course of the work, however, I became convinced that kinetic problems, tonal and functional, also had to be resolved. Thus out of what was originally intended to be a guide through contemporary harmonic material grew a systematic harmony illuminating every aspect of harmonic phenomena.

2) *Foundations of Modern Harmony* is not a product of the study of theoretical literature. It is founded on living music, compositional practice, my own thoughts, and my

---

[1] "Moderní harmonie. Souhrnný náčrt" [Modern Harmony. A General Outline], *Tempo* 11 (1931–32): 46–52; "Rozvoj harmonické představivosti jako otázka pedagogická" [The Evolution of Harmonic Imagination as a Pedagogical Question], *Hudba a škola* [Music and School] 4 (1931–32): 33–35, 58–60; "O významu imaginárních tónů v harmonii" [The Significance of Imaginary Pitches in Harmony], *Hudební výchova* [Music Education] 13 (1932): 8–9, 22–25; "Vznik, stavba a ráz nových souzvuků" [The Foundation, Structure, and Nature of New Chords], *Tempo* 12 (1933): 164–172; "Rozvrat diatoniky" [The Breakdown of the Diatonic System], *Tempo* 14 (1935): 151–154, 191–195, 227–231 – 1. Tonality, 2. The Diatonic System, 3. The Structure of the Diatonic System, 4. Chromaticization and Alteration, 5. Combination, 6. Conclusions and Future Prospects, 7. Notation; "Princip harmonické inverse" [The Principle of Harmonic Inversion], *Rytmus* [Rhythm] 8 (1942–43): 54–57; "Harmonické možnosti chromatiky" [The Harmonic Possibilities of the Chromatic System], *Rytmus* [Rhythm] 11 (1947): 21–23; "Systém charakteristických akordů" [The System of Characteristic Chords], *Rytmus* [Rhythm] 11 (1947): 66–69. The last three articles are directly related to *Foundations of Modern Harmony*.

research into harmonic material. It is natural that there should be parallels with the conclusions of other theorists. In any critical work such parallels are inevitable. I was not looking for originality of phrase or presentation, but rather for the simple truth. Consequently, I was bound to arrive at some of the same conclusions expressed elsewhere. In other matters, however, I came up against deeply rooted theoretical assumptions which have been passed on from one book to another.

For example, I consider the prevalent view about the shifting of the boundary between consonances and dissonances to be such an assumption. I have encountered this view in almost every interpretation of modern harmony, and I once supported it myself. I finally realized that with such a bias problems of harmony cannot be resolved honestly. It is precisely the rich diversity of existing dissonances that tempts theorists to think that chords once considered dissonant have now become consonant and that the range of consonances is thus expanding. Although I have studied dissonances thoroughly, I have never converted any of them to consonances. I realized that shifting the boundary between consonances and dissonances was tantamount to admitting that there is no substantial difference in sound between these two categories of chords. The superiority bestowed on consonance by nature would then be fictitious.

This view about the shifting boundary between consonances and dissonances is a typical assumption of modern harmonic theory. A truly "historic" assumption, however, is that the dissonance of a chord is caused simply by the presence of dissonant intervals. I grappled with this problem for a long time and eventually formulated a comparatively clear and simple principle: it is not the presence of dissonant intervals that makes a chord dissonant, but rather the presence of dissonant elements. Dissonant elements include not only dissonant intervals but also the dissonant trichord known as the augmented triad.

The definition of dissonant elements was my starting point in classifying dissonant harmonic material. (In the article *The System of Characteristic Chords*,[2] published in 1947, I presented an earlier version of my classification, which did not yet include the dissonant triadic element.)

3) The actual work on *Foundations* began with a study of the feasibility of classifying harmonic material. Only after sketching a classification of chords according to their sonic character did I proceed to investigate all possible chords in the tempered chromatic system. I was led to this by the realization that theorists with whom I had become familiar were all working under the assumption that the possible chords were virtually unlimited. I studied this assumption, then generally tacitly accepted, and finally concluded that it was not true.

The consequences were far reaching. It became apparent that it was possible to work out a classification of all chords according to character. From this detailed classification, boundaries between character types as well as the extent of individual chord groups could be clearly seen. The all inclusive nature of the classification is demonstrated in this

---

2   Editor's note: See note 1 above.

book, and I believe it to be a basic feature distinguishing the book from other treatises and theoretical systems.

For the detailed investigation of all the harmonic material in the tempered chromatic system it was necessary to establish several new concepts and at the same time to revise thoroughly the range of concepts already in general use. The concepts of the orientation scheme and the negative were the first prerequisites of success; from the concepts pertaining to classical harmony I defined the concept of a chord-type, and as its counterpart I introduced the general concept of a chord's disposition. Only after these foundations had been laid did order begin to emerge out of material which at first appeared hopelessly chaotic and completely unmanageable.

Naturally I did not arrive instantly at a complete understanding of the subject. Progress to a clear and concise exposition of the material was slow and difficult. Every observation, no matter how minute, and every disagreement with generally accepted or deeply rooted views had to be verified from every angle. No wonder then that the individual sections took so long to get finished.

4) The extent of static harmony demanded conciseness. Therefore in the section dealing with harmonic material I mostly present only the bare results, limiting to essentials the explanation of how they were obtained. For example, procedures described in detail for deriving dichords and trichords are not shown as extensively for the higher chord-classes. Surveys of concrete examples of chord-types are not continued past the hexachord class; for the higher classes, reference is made instead to negatives. (A complete list of chord-types is included among the appended tables.) Explanations are of course necessary for newly introduced concepts, and clarifying examples are given for all of these.

Besides condensing the description of static harmony, I limit myself in other ways. For example, I set aside everything pertaining to different tuning systems, on the assumption that equal temperament is the practical foundation of all musical practice today. Even in this respect, *Foundations of Modern Harmony* differs from other treatises. (For example, Paul Hindemith devotes a great deal of space to questions of tuning in his book, *Unterweisung im Tonsatz*.)[3]

Where facts simply need to be stated, I limit myself to stating the facts, as in the description of harmonic material and in the classification of chords according to characteristic-types. Elsewhere I attempt to give exhaustive presentations. I try to avoid speculations of too general a nature. Only the most pressing general questions are dealt with, separately, in the chapter on *Problems* (*Chapter VII*).

In the practical part of the book, dealing with actual composition and analysis (*Chapters VIII* and *IX*), I limit myself to general instructions with specific musical examples. Thus neither the section on composition nor the one on harmonic analysis is an academic harmony textbook.

---

3 Editor's note: Paul Hindemith, *Unterweisung im Tonsatz I–II*, neue, erw. ausg (Mainz: B. Schott's Söhne, 1939–1940).

5) Although I originally intended to deal only with static harmony, I had laid the foundations for kinetic harmony a long time before beginning systematic work on the book. Already in 1932 I had published an article entitled *The Significance of Imaginary Pitches in Harmony*.[4] For me, the concept of the imaginary pitch links static and kinetic conceptions of harmony. Whether or not a chord projects a sense of the tonic is a kinetic property which loses its meaning in static harmony. This property is created by the possibility of a pitch from an earlier chord continuing as an imaginary pitch into a new consonance and interfering with it. (This is shown in the section dealing with harmonic motion.) It is in the combination of dissonant elements in a statically conceived chord that I see the possibilities of these imaginary pitches continuing effectively enough to cause interference; this is especially true of interference by the tritone element.

The discourse on the expression of chords (*Chapter V*), founded on the phenomenon of the imaginary pitch, is placed between the chapters on static and kinetic harmony. A knowledgeable reader will recognize that the concept of the imaginary pitch as I have defined it is entirely different from Janáček's[5] "pseudo-sensed tone" [pacitový tón]; Janáček has in mind a pitch that actually continues to be physiologically perceived rather than one that is only imagined but that can still have a harmonic effect. This hypothetical harmonic effect has been verified in practice.

In the theory of functional chords, I have adopted Otakar Šín's system. Here a few words of explanation are necessary. Only hints of the functional system that I have attributed to Šín were present in his *Complete Theory of Harmony on the Basis of Melody and Rhythm*.[6] Šín did not dare progress explicitly from the classical three member functional system to a five member one. His lydian and phrygian harmonies were not yet seen as independent functional chords. In his obituary, which I wrote at the suggestion of the Czech Academy of Sciences and Arts,[7] I attempted to give an overall picture of his theoretical contribution, freed of the textbook-bound burden. I believe that I am correct in using Šín's name to designate the five member functional system because, although he did not yet dare to speak explicitly of five functional chords, he had arrived at this system in practice, as I trust I showed in the obituary. It is only a small step from Šín's system of meticulously but only outwardly preserved three functional chords to five functional chords.

I have also adopted a second significant contribution of Šín's, namely, the theory of functional combinations. Again there are changes, however. I emphasize the dependence of the functional ranking of a combination on the concrete disposition of the chord; from this I derive a different system of designating combinations. In contrast,

---

4   Editor's note: See note 1 above.
5   Editor's note: The reference is to Leoš Janáček, Czech composer (1854–1928).
6   Editor's note: Otakar Šín, *Úplná nauka o harmonii na základě melodie a rytmu* [Complete Theory of Harmony on the Basis of Melody and Rhythm], 2. vyd., přepracované a rozšířené [2nd ed., revised and expanded] (Praha: Hudební Matice [The Music Association], 1933).
7   Editor's note: Karel Janeček, *Otakar Šín* (Praha: Česká akademie věd a umění [Czech Academy of Sciences and Arts], 1944).

Šín assumed that the functional meaning of combinations was independent of disposition.

6) A book of music theory cannot exist without symbols. This is especially true for the theory of harmony. Just as it is impossible to write about mathematics without using formulae, it is impossible to write about harmony without using symbols. I consider it necessary that this self-evident fact was mentioned in the preface.

Various types of symbols appear in this book. First there are the traditional symbols that are part of common practice (e.g., the functional chord symbols T, S, D), although these may be somewhat modified. Then there are new symbols and supplements to traditional symbols, sometimes numerical, sometimes of another type. Certainly it is not necessary to apologize for the use of traditional symbols. But why to introduce any new ones? The answer is simple: new concepts require new terminology and corresponding new symbols, and well chosen symbols always simplify.

It was relatively easy to create names for the small number of chord-types with which classical harmony was concerned. However, we had to remember not only the name of the chord but also its exact structure. It would be virtually impossible to devise a new name for every modern chord-type. Moreover, such a name would not define anything very specific unless we were given further information about the chord's interval structure. The situation can be greatly simplified by using for the various chord-types numerical designations that express the exact structure of the chord; such new symbols are much less troublesome than new names with long descriptions would be.

Wherever possible, I have attempted to simplify symbols (with such as interfuntions or the various complicating tones). A list of all symbols used in the book is appended, together with brief explanations, examples, and pertinent references.

7) A theory of harmony cannot exist without musical examples. These are enlivened by the welcome inclusion of excerpts from actual compositions. A treatise that haphazardly points out this or that harmonic phenomenon which the author has encountered in musical literature can abound with fortuitous and often highly interesting examples. In a systematic work, however, it is possible to resort to such "living" examples only exceptionally. The problem is that only exceptionally does living music use a single process, a single structure, a single type of disposition, etc. All these are usually interrelated and combined. And in the systematic presentation of material, examples must be simple and clear.

Another reason for a more extensive use of my own examples is that only thus is it possible to demonstrate the variety of effects of changes in disposition or manner of expression.

For these reasons I have used examples from living music only in exceptional cases. Except in the section devoted to harmonic analysis, naturally.

8) As the title suggests, dissonances are discussed in great detail in this book. In contrast to the currently taught systems of harmony, which recognize no precise distinctions among dissonances, I had to weigh and evaluate each dissonance meticulously.

The knowledgeable reader will see from the overall conception of the book that the actual sonic effect is the basis and starting point for the study of static chords. The numbers with which some pages are covered are only symbols, and we must look beyond them to the *living sound*. The vast extent of the material compelled me to give only the most necessary examples in musical notation for the more complex chords; usually I had to be content with the more concise language of symbols.

Emphasis on the actual sonic effect dominates, especially in the chapter on the disposition of chords. I was anxious to show how it is possible to create dispositions that sound beautiful. Wherever this is not possible, I point it out. The sound of every disposition is subjected to criticism, and I do not avoid unfavourable classifications.

It is unproductive simply to stack one pitch on top of another without regard to the resulting sonic effect, in the expectation that the listener will become "accustomed" to it. Sharp dissonances, purposely formed as an important (but often only auxiliary) means of expressing insistent tension, have their place in all good music. Sharp dissonances that are intended to function as consonances, however, represent an embarrassing compositional mistake. This mistake is closely related to the erroneous theoretical attitude about the shifting of the boundary between consonances and dissonances, mentioned above.

9) *Foundations of Modern Harmony* is not a harmony textbook. Knowledge of textbook harmony is expected of the reader. The book is not, however, intended only for composers, but for all musicians who come in contact with new music.

Some problems have been given broader treatment, covering a considerable amount of material belonging to classical harmony. In such cases, a presentation restricted exclusively to phenomena of modern harmony would have been too fragmentary. Such sections are in the chapters on the disposition and expression of chords, and especially in the chapter on harmonic motion. I believe, however, that even a reader familiar with the materials of classical harmony will find some merit in these sections.

The nucleus of the book consists of a *system of modern harmony*, presented in the first six chapters. All that follows is supplementary. However, only through the study of this latter material does the practical usefulness of the preceding theoretical investigations become evident.

10) Finally, a somewhat personal comment remains to be made. I have already mentioned that work on this book was slow and difficult, partly because of the nature of the extensive material. I find some small consolation in the fact that even the eminent Czech theorist Otakar Šín had to struggle for many years in his attempts to resolve the problems of modern harmony. Belonging to the next generation, my own task has been made somewhat easier, especially thanks to his experimental and analytical work, which regrettably was not completed. When I see that I have succeeded in actually bringing this task to an end, I cannot but remember here the one who departed from a work unfinished, although he had devoted to it years of study and searching.

Prague, July 24, 1949. K. J.

Almost fifteen years have passed since the original version of *Foundations of Modern Harmony* was completed. It may be appropriate to record briefly here the subsequent fate of the manuscript.

The book was originally entitled *Modern Harmony*. Under this title it was accepted for publication by the former Czech Academy of Sciences and Arts (Class IV, Arts).[8] It was not published, however, as in the meantime that academy was replaced by the present Czechoslovak Academy of Sciences, where musical science was at first not represented as an independent scientific discipline. The manuscript was returned to me by the original institution. Subsequently, I used the text as a basis for lectures to composers and conductors at the Music faculty of the Academy of Performing Arts in Prague.[9]

Eventually (in 1953) I changed the original title of the book to *Foundations of New Harmony*. Its conclusions were later used to support certain sections of my books *Study of Melodics*[10] and *Musical Forms*.[11]

I published a considerably condensed summary of all the material in *Fundamental Harmonic Problems and their Solutions*, in the annual *Musicology*.[12] Finally, I presented a condensed analytical application of its most important concepts in the book *Harmony Through Analysis*.[13]

---

8   See *Věstník České akademie věd a umění* [Bulletin of the Czech Academy of Sciences and Arts] 59/6 (November–December, 1950): 143–144, where the resolution of a meeting of Class IV (December 12, 1950) is recorded, and where reviews by Alois Hába and František Pícha of *Modern Harmony* are printed.

9   From the founding of the Academy of Performing Arts in Prague (AMU [Akademie múzických umění v Praze]) in 1946, a lecture course *Modern Harmony* was included in the curriculum for majors in composition and conducting. Although in 1950 this course was omitted from the curriculum, I taught its contents in the course entitled *Theory of Composition*. Thus modern harmony has been taught *continuously* at the Music faculty of AMU from its founding to the present day.

10 *Melodika* [Study of Melodics] (Praha: SNKLHU, 1956) – 204 pages, written during 1950–51. This pertains especially to chapters 12, *The Tonal Definition of Melodies*; 13, *The Harmonic Conditionality of Melodies*; 14, *Ornamental and Polyphonic Structure of Melodies*; and 27, *The Formation of Harmonically Conditioned Melodies*.

11 *Hudební formy* [Musical Forms] (Praha: SNKLHU, 1955) – 496 pages, written during 1952–53. This pertains especially to §17, *The Significance of Harmony in Compositional Construction*; §18, *The Functional Significance of Harmony*; §19, *Tonal Aspects of Musical Expression*; and §20, *The Tonal Order of Composition*.

12 "Základní harmonické problémy a jejich řešení" [Fundamental Harmonic Problems and their Solutions], *Musikologie: Sborník pro hudební vědu a kritiku* [Musicology: Annual for Musical Science and Criticism] (Praha: SNKLHU, 1955): 87–129. The study was written at the turn of the year 1953–54. In the concluding remarks of this study, I already refer to *The Foundations of New Harmony* rather than to *Modern Harmony*. It is not merely a brief extract, but a condensed coherent exposition in which I also assert some further ideas. For the phenomena of transposition, disposition, and expression of chords, I use the collective term *inflection of harmonies* here. (The term *inflection* is borrowed from Czech grammar, where it is also used as a collective term for declension, gradation, and conjugation.)

13 *Harmonie rozborem* [Harmony Through Analysis] (Praha: Státní hudební nakladatelství [State Music Press], 1963) – 216 pages. This pertains to chapter VII, *Expanded Chordal and Tonal Possibilities*. In this chapter I further discuss the phenomena of "dominantization", "subdominantization", and "tonicization". The symbols are greatly simplified (made practical). In §67, *Versatile Harmonic and Tonal Analysis*, I present a detailed functional analysis of passages of certain contemporary compositions.

I also had the opportunity to *publish separately* several chapters of the prepared text. At the invitation of editors of the *Musical Horizons* series (1957), I published the *Chapter V – The Expression of Chords*, and I changed the title of the entire work to *Foundations of Tempered Harmony*.[14]

Next I modified the text of the *Chapter II – Sonic Characteristics of the Harmonic Material*, for publication in the annual *Living Music*.[15] This was immediately followed by the *Chapter I – The Harmonic Material of the Tempered Chromatic System*, which was published in the fourth issue of the quarterly *Musical Science*.[16]

As my lecturing at the Music faculty of AMU gave me opportunity to think through the material again and again, certain ideas became further clarified in my own mind, and this led to minor revisions of the original text. As a rule, these revisions were made as opportunity arose to publish certain chapters. *Chapter IIIa – Classification of the Harmonic Material* and *Chapter IIIb – Triadic Combinations* was to undergo more major revisions. Here the question involved the concept of a *harmony*, which I originally considered equivalent to the *characteristic maximum* (at least in modern harmony). The necessary revisions of this chapter were not made until 1963, when I was invited by Dr. Karel Risinger of the newly founded Institute for Musical Science, affiliated with the Czechoslovak Academy of Sciences, to submit the original manuscript for publication by the Academy's publishing house (ČSAV Press [Nakladatelství Československé akademie věd]). On this occasion I also decided on the final title for the book, namely *Foundations of Modern Harmony* [Základy moderní harmonie]. At the same time, some revisions that had been made in chapters published separately were withdrawn in favour of the original wording (e.g., I returned to the original term *imaginary pitch*).

The gradual changes in the title of the book deserve a few words of explanation. When I was writing *Study of Melodics*, I was at the same time sketching the outline for further sections of the theory of composition, of which *Study of Melodics* was to form the first section. It was clear to me that I would present the section on harmonic thinking in a similar manner to that used in *Study of Melodics*. It would be a continuous exposition, illustrating everything necessary primarily by living examples drawn mostly from contemporary musical repertoire. In any area of knowledge, however, "everything necessary" is never equivalent to "everything possible". Good decisions about what is

---

14 *Vyjádření souzvuků: Kapitola ze Základů temperované harmonie* [The Expression of Chords: Chapter of Foundations of Tempered Harmony] (Praha: Svaz čs. skladatelů [Union of Czechoslovakian Composers], 1958) – 56 pages. Here the term *thought pitch* was used instead of the original term *imaginary pitch*. I added an introductory note defining expression in comparison with transposition and disposition, using the collective term *inflection of harmonies*.

15 "Zvukové vlastnosti harmonického materiálu: Kapitola ze Základů temperované harmonie" [Sonic Characteristics of the Harmonic Material: Chapter of Foundations of Tempered Harmony], *Živá hudba: Sborník prací hudební fakulty AMU* [Living Music: Collection of Works by the Music Faculty of AMU] (Praha: SPN, 1962): 69–93.

16 "Harmonický materiál temperované chromatiky: Kapitola ze Základů temperované harmonie" [The Harmonic Material of the Tempered Chromatic System: Chapter of Foundations of Tempered Harmony], *Hudební věda* [Musical Science Quarterly] 4 (1961): 81–119.

necessary and useful, about what is usable or has prospects of being usable at some future time, can *only be made* when one is familiar with the *whole extent of the field in question*, and with all its *possibilities and impossibilities*. For a reliable presentation of the theory of harmonic thinking, one must know not only what is in common use, but also what is ultimately *made possible* by the available material and processes. Thus the first step must be the laying of foundations. And since in *Modern Harmony* I had attempted to clarify all the harmonic material of European music (limited to the chromatic system), I began to see this book as an indispensable starting point for potential future works, even should these be only brief and not exhaustive. I therefore decided to add "foundations" to the title of the book. This is not meant in the sense of "an introduction", "rudiments", or the like. Rather it is meant as a *summary of everything that must be considered* when thinking about any kind of harmonic phenomena, harmonic terminology, harmonic processes, etc., if these thoughts are not to dissolve into inconsequential and useless fantasies. That much to the word "foundations".

I had temporarily given up the designation modern for reasons resulting from the abnormal state of Czech culture in the 1950's. (Instead of "modern" one could equally well say "new"; the designation "tempered" refers to the European tempered chromatic system, seen as the general foundation of all our music.)[17] Today the term "modern" has had its original meaning restored, without the derogatory connotations that accompanied it in the 1950's, when anything even remotely connected with avant-garde attempts in the arts was indiscriminately condemned. Therefore I have returned to the original designation. The reason for returning to my original term "imaginary pitch", rather than continuing to use the later term "thought pitch", is similar: today such a term will no longer lead anyone to suspect it of being a disguised remnant of idealist philosophy.

The history of the manuscript includes not only the changes it has undergone, but also the *responses* it has evoked. Such responses have been *indirect*: they were prompted by the published preparatory studies, excerpts, and ideas in other writings, and by the separately published chapters. Jaroslav Volek devoted the last chapter of his book *The Theoretical Foundations of Harmony from the Perspective of Scientific Philosophy* to my harmonic theory.[18] Subsequently Emil Hradecký concluded his account of the history of modern harmony in his *Introduction to the Study of Tonal Harmony* with an accurate

---

17 Editor's note: As he explained above, Janeček's 1953 title was *Foundations of New Harmony*; his 1957 title was *Foundations of Tempered Harmony*.

18 Jaroslav Volek, *Teoretické základy harmónie z hľadiska vedeckej filozofie* [The Theoretical Foundations of Harmony from the Perspective of Scientific Philosophy] (Bratislava: Vydavateľstvo Slovenskej akadémie vied [Slovak Academy of Science Press], 1954). The last chapter (22, pp. 271–280) is entitled, true to its time, *The Schematicity of Chordal Systematics – The Theoretical Patronage of Formalism in the Twentieth Century*. Here the author concerns himself exclusively with my two published preliminary studies, *The Harmonic Possibilities of the Chromatic System* and *The System of Characteristic Chords*. To this I wrote a response, *A Word about Unscientific Misrepresentation*, in which with my texts I confronted Volek's interpretation of my views; the editors of journal *Musical Horizons* [Hudební rozhledy] at the time, however, did not consider it expedient to print the response.

précis of my summarizing study, *Fundamental Harmonic Problems and their Solutions*.[19] Finally, Karel Risinger in *Leading Personalities in Modern Czech Music Theory* considers my theoretical works, including those on harmony, on the basis of everything that had been published during the previous four decades (since 1924).[20]

This brings me finally to the *literature* dealing with the problems of modern harmony. The appended selected bibliography is of course not exhaustive. I have considered it especially important to draw attention to those works to which I have directly responded in my own work (usually with criticism), and to those works from which I have drawn valuable insights (especially from the historical perspective) or inspiration to further thought. In the new version I completed the original list with my works published after 1949.

Prague, May 22, 1964   K. J.

---

19 Emil Hradecký, *Úvod do studia tonální harmonie* [Introduction to the Study of Tonal Harmony] (Praha: SNKLHU, 1960), 200–203.
20 Karel Risinger, *Vůdčí osobnosti české moderní hudební teorie: Otakar Šín, Alois Hába, Karel Janeček* [Leading Personalities in Modern Czech Music Theory: Otakar Šín, Alois Hába, Karel Janeček] (Praha: SHV, 1963). Because the author could follow my various works only in the order in which they were published, he reacted to the introduction of the harmonic scheme as "a new contribution of this study." He wrote: "By the introduction of the harmonic scheme of chords, Janeček eliminates a certain inadequacy which has so far existed in his system. The inadequacy consisted of the fact that although the orientation scheme clearly described each chord-type, it gave comparatively little information about its musically expressive effect (especially in the case of more complex chords)" (Ibid., 184–185). In reality, the thought process was the reverse: since the harmonic scheme, as it was commonly used in classical harmony, contained some ambiguity, especially in the case of more complex chords, it was necessary to introduce an orientation scheme that would be unambiguous in all cases, although it would be identical to the harmonic scheme only in exceptional circumstances.

Chapter I – The Harmonic Material of the Tempered Chromatic System

§1. The Tempered Chromatic System and its Notation

European music is founded on the diatonic system, the system of pitches in which whole-tones and semitones are arranged in the following series: ... 1 1 ½ 1 1 1 ½ ....

This system was gradually modified and supplemented to become chromatic until finally, through the halving of all the whole-tone distances, the *tempered chromatic system* came into being. The new (inserted) pitches were understood as alterations of the diatonic pitches, so the direction remained diatonic for creative work as well as for theoretical studies.

The tempered chromatic system constitutes the practical material of our music. It allows the fullest possible use of practical consonances – consonances that are not absolutely pure, but that fulfill the practical requirements of music. The tempered chromatic system came into use as a direct result of the demands of the life of music.

Only more recently have attempts been made to establish the tempered chromatic as independent of the diatonic system. In such a conception of the tempered chromatic system, all pitches are equal – the original diatonic ones and those derived from them. Thus the tempered chromatic becomes the twelve-tone system, the basis of twelve-tone music.

For practical reasons, music written in this independent twelve-tone system retains a standard nomenclature and notation of pitch. For example, the pitch lying between C and D we call C♯ or D♭ according to context, even though we are dealing with only one pitch, which is independent of its neighbors C and D. Traditional notation sometimes creates difficulties for readers. This has led some composers to consider each accidental to apply only to the single note immediately following it, thus eliminating natural signs.[1]

The duality of such designations as C♯–D♭, D♯–E♭, etc. could be removed by giving standard names and note symbols to the five pitches that enrich the chromatic system over the diatonic. It would suffice to decide in each case for one of the standard designations, e.g., C♯, E♭, F♯, A♭, B♭. We could do this only if the music in question were completely removed from the diatonic system. It is interesting, however, that not even Arnold Schoenberg, the first and foremost advocate of the twelve-tone system, committed himself to such innovation. In music that adheres to the twelve-tone system less strictly than Schoenberg's, diatonic foundations are often so apparent that even greater difficulties in reading would result, instead of the desired simplification. We therefore decide, following accepted practice, between the pairs C♯–D♭, D♯–E♭, etc. *according to the intervals* (both melodic and harmonic) that these pitches will form with those around them. We give preference to simple and commonly used intervals, preferring, for example, a major second over a diminished third, a major third over a diminished fourth. Thus we would write melodically B–C♯–E (not B–D♭–E), or harmonically A C♯ F♯ B (not A D♭ G♭ B). In short, we give preference to diatonic structures whenever they appear in the music.

Nicolai Obukhov (Obouhow) tried to resolve the discrepancy between a diatonically founded notation and the demands of the twelve-tone system by using a *simplified notation without accidentals*. As a compromise, he notated the original diatonic pitches using the conventional method, but for the derived tones he introduced ×'s instead of black note heads (with the appropriate stems, flags, or beams), and ×'s inside white note heads. These notes were to be read as raised notes; they were written on the same lines and in the same spaces as F♯, C♯, G♯, D♯, and A♯ in conventional notation. Obukhov's proposal found a supporter in Arthur Honegger, who published two piano works using this reformed notation.[2]

Two disadvantages are obvious. First, the new notes are not clearly legible, especially when they are on leger lines, and they are doubtless difficult to write. Second, many diatonic progressions or conventional chords must be notated non-diatonically, for example, G♯ G A♯ G♯ C A♯, which appears at the beginning of one of Honegger's *Esquisses pour piano*, instead of the simple A♭ G B♭ A♭ C B♭. Obukhov also proposed new

---

[1] This style of notation is appropriate for truly atonal music, removed from the diatonic system. In Czechoslovakia it is used by Alois Hába, even in his more recent compositions which have tonal foundations. For example, the *Eighth Quartet, op. 73*, whose first movement is in D, is published with this notation. I used this approach in my earlier works (as late as the *Variations, op. 23*, published in 1949) but later abandoned it. Some composers resort to it only occasionally, when it is convenient. For example, Ernst Toch in his extensive collection of modern etudes for piano used it only in *Zehn Konzert-Etüden, op. 55*, and there only in no. 1–9, abandoning it in no. 10.

[2] Arthur Honegger, *Deux Esquisses pour piano – 1. Large et rapsodique, 2. Allegretto malinconico* (Paris: Durand, 1944). Obukhov's proposal dates from 1919. At the end of the explanatory notes appended to each *Esquisse*, we can read the dubious assurance that "this type of notation does not eliminate a feeling of tonality" ("le sentiment de la tonalité n'est pas aboli par cette notation").

solmisation syllables for the derived notes: Lo (C♯), Te (D♯), Ra (F♯), Tu (G♯), Di (A♯). It is hardly necessary to point out that this new system of notation was never widely adopted.

Another type of reformed notation without accidentals had already been suggested by Auguste Sérieyx at the beginning of the 20th century. In his proposal all accidentals were removed at the expense of *increasing the number of staff lines*; at the same time, all clefs were unified. This simplification, however, only caused greater confusion.[3]

The sounds used in diatonic music, whether it be simple or advanced, pervaded by gradual or abrupt modulations, are the same as those used in the most extreme twelve-tone music. Combinations of sounds that the former type of music dares create are of course much plainer and tamer than those of the latter. Although at the extremes we are dealing with two opposing worlds, it is impossible to establish a precise boundary between them; the one merges very gradually, almost imperceptibly, into the other. One thing, however, unifies them: their common pitch material, collectively known as the tempered chromatic system.

We understand the term *tempered chromatic system* to mean the system of pitches used in both classical and new music, music rooted in tradition as well as that which has broken away from tradition, music which is cautiously conservative as well as that which is courageously avant-garde. The tempered chromatic system contains a number of more specialized sub-systems (the pentatonic, diatonic, whole-tone, etc.) and at the same time completely coincides with the twelve-tone system.

§2. Premises for the Investigation of Harmonic Material

If we want to investigate the harmonic possibilities made available by the pitch-structure of our music, we cannot automatically begin with the traditional, diatonically founded nomenclature and notation. If we are concerned with real possibilities, we must begin with a real basis. Such a real basis can only be an all encompassing system of pitches used in real music, namely, the *tempered chromatic system*. *Intervals*, which are the means for measuring all melodic and harmonic phenomena, rely on this system for their definition.

---

3   The attempt was mentioned by Vincent d'Indy in his *Cours de composition musicale. Livre I*, 3. ed. (Paris: Durand, 1909), 62–63.
    Editor's note: D'Indy's publication was "edited with the collaboration of Auguste Sérieyx according to notes taken in composition classes at the Schola Cantorum in 1897–1898 and 1899–1900." The "unification" of clefs was accomplished by placing the F clef on the fifth line and the C clef always on the third space, so that pitches have the same location in the three clefs – e.g., E is always on the bottom line – and the clefs serve simply to indicate the octave register of pitches. Sérieyx does not combine his proposed staff with his proposed clefs here or in his later publication – *Cours de grammaire musicale* (Paris: Heugel, 1924). In the latter, he shows a six-line staff with lines always a whole-tone apart, but omits any clef (p. 74). Perhaps a more complete exposition of his ideas may be found in his *Peut-on améliorer la notation musicale?* (Paris: Schola Cantorum, 1922).

In the tempered chromatic system there are only twelve different intervals, of which the smallest – the semitone – constitutes a *unit*. When an interval is isolated, its effect is the same whether the semitone is called a minor second or an augmented prime, the whole-tone, a major second or a diminished third, the distance of two whole-tones a major third or a diminished fourth, etc. We can clearly state all intervals as *simple multiples of the semitone unit*. If the semitone is designated by 1, then 2 designates a whole--tone, 3 a minor third, 4 a major third, 5 a perfect fourth, 6 an augmented fourth or tritone, 7 a perfect fifth, etc. (If the whole-tone were considered the unit, we would be forced to work with fractions.)

The precise designation of intervals by number does not keep us from noticing the relation between different seconds (major or minor), different thirds, and other intervals, whenever such a relation appears in music. We can revert to the original interval nomenclature, as long as we acknowledge the principle that all intervals, no matter how they are named, remain simple multiples of the tempered semitone.

Intervals as chords (harmonic intervals) constitute the most rudimentary harmonic phenomena. They are building blocks for higher harmonic structures. We must be precise when dealing with these building blocks, in order to eliminate ambiguity later, when we work with all the harmonic material.

When we speak of harmonic material, we are thinking of concrete harmonic phenomena, of *chords*.[4] Each chord has its harmonic individuality, its own identity. In order to survey effectively the vast amount of available material, we have to arrange it in some appropriate manner and draw related entities together into systematically organized groups. This division into groups can be based on various criteria. For example, we can consider the number of pitches in a chord. By this criterion, we can distinguish various *chord-classes*: two-note chords, three-note chords, four-note chords, etc. The highest class in the tempered chromatic system consists of the twelve-note chord. The total system of classes is completed by structures simpler than the two-note chord: single pitches and silence.

Such differentiation of chord-classes need not prevent us from being aware of relations between chords of different classes, for example, between three-note chords and four-note chords, which are consistently related in classical harmony.[5]

Every chord can be *transposed*, that is, displaced by a certain interval up or down. Transposition changes only the actual pitches of the original chord, while the ratios

---

4   Editor's note: In Czech there are two different terms for chord: *souzvuk* means any group of notes sounding together; *akord* means a chord with harmonic meaning, as triads have meaning in classical harmony. Thus *souzvuk* might be translated as "simultaneity", as "understandable, recognized, harmonically significant chord". It seems unreasonable to ask anyone to read a book about six-syllable *simultaneities*, especially when that word in itself has nothing to do with sound. Therefore, *souzvuk* will be translated as "chord", meaning any group of simultaneous pitches. *Akord* will usually be translated as "harmony", meaning a harmonically intelligible chord, in spite of occasional awkwardness arising from using the same word for both a category of chords and the whole subject of chords.

5   Editor's notes: In classical harmony, seventh chords and incomplete ninth chords (four-note chords) are related to triads (three-note chords).

Chapter I – The Harmonic Material of the Tempered Chromatic System

(intervals) between pitches remain unchanged. (Displacement by an octave is considered to be repetition, not transposition.)

In the tempered chromatic system up to twelve transpositions, including the original, are possible for chords and other structures. Transposition thus considerably reduces the number of possible unique harmonic entities.

Every chord can have a variety of *dispositions*. Disposition is changed when individual notes of the original chord are displaced into higher or lower octaves. Pitches can also be doubled or further multiplied in this process. In contrast to transposition, disposition does not affect the pitch class content of the chord; it does change the order of the pitches and the sequence of intervals.

Combining transposition with changes in disposition enables us to classify individual chords into *chord-types*. Two chords are of the same type not only if they agree in every detail, but also *if they can achieve such agreement* through transposition and/or a change in disposition. Thus the three-note chord C D F is of the same type as its other dispositions – D F C, F C D F, etc.[6] Its transpositions – C♯ D♯ F♯, D E G, etc. – are also of the same type, as are the various dispositions of these transpositions – D♯ F♯ C♯, G E D, etc.

The harmonic possibilities inherent in the tempered chromatic system, with all available variations, are almost endless. If, however, we disregard the variations (the dispositions, transpositions, and eventually also the manner of expression), a comprehensive grasp of this wealth of material does become possible. We must begin by considering the chord-types, and only after that look at the possibilities of their transpositions and concrete dispositions. The broad term *harmonic material* is used to refer to the totality of chord-types – all those that exist, that are possible.

§3. The Orientation Scheme of Chord-types

A musician trained in theory easily recognizes that the chord F A♭ D♭ is a transposition and rotation (different disposition) of the chord C E G. Both F A♭ D♭ and C E G are three-note chords of the same type (major triads), since the disposition F A♭ D♭ can be rearranged to D♭ F A♭, which has the same interval structure as C E G (intervals 4, 3).[7] In classical harmony we arrange the notes of a harmony into ascending thirds in order to recognize its type. When dealing with various chords that appear in modern music, as well as transient chords in classical music, this method is often not useful; in most cases, the notes of the chord cannot be arranged in thirds. Therefore some other more

---

6 Editor's note: Thus *disposition* refers both to rotation (C D F becoming D F C) and to permutation (C D F becoming C F D) and all octave transpositions of pitches including any doubling. Chords are always spelled with pitches in ascending order; in the chord D F C, D is the lowest note.

7 Editor's note: As explained above, 4 and 3 refer to the major third (4 semitones) and minor third (3 semitones) in the triad.

appropriate method must be agreed on, one that is *consistently applicable to every possible chord of the tempered chromatic system*. Working on the assumption that smaller intervals are easier to grasp at a glance, the following two rules can be established for a chord *orientation scheme*:

1. Arrange the notes of the chord in the *smallest possible ambit*.[8]
2. If two or more rotations of the chord yield the same smallest possible ambit, choose the one in which, in ascending order, the intervals are arranged *from the smallest to the largest*.

The orientation scheme of the chord E G C D will therefore be derived from C D E G, as other forms have larger ambits (E–D, G–E, D–C). The orientation scheme of the chord G C D will be derived from C D G, because while these two rotations have the same ambit, the form C D G has the smaller interval at the bottom.

An orientation scheme, then, consists of a series of numbers that correspond to adjacent ascending intervals in the chord. For example, the chord C D E G will be designated as 223, the chord C D G as 25.[9] This orientation scheme designates the chord *unambiguously* and is thus invaluable for comparing chords. Without it, similarity between chord-types can often escape the musician's attention, especially when chords are more complex. The chords G B F A♭ and C E♭ A B seem at first glance to be of different types. By determining the orientation scheme of each, however (F G A♭ B is 213, A B C E♭ is 213), we discover that we are dealing with chords of the same type, known in traditional harmony as the incomplete dominant minor ninth (G B _ F A♭, B D♯ _ A C).

The *complement* of a chord completes the ambit to the distance of an octave.[10] We find the complement by subtracting from twelve the sum of the intervals measured in semitones (the sum of the numbers in the simple orientation scheme). For example, the complement of a chord with the orientation scheme 223 is 5. The completed orientation scheme, with the complement shown in parentheses, is 223(5). We can expand such a completed orientation scheme into the next (higher) octave by the simple repetition of the scheme: 223(5)223. This form will be called the *expanded orientation scheme*. From this we can read all possible rotations of the chord: 223, 235, 352, 522.

The expanded orientation scheme can be used to verify our orientation scheme for a chord. Thus if we expand the assumed orientation scheme 251 into the higher octave, we obtain 251(4)251. (The form 251 does not have the smallest possible ambit, since the complement 4 is smaller than the interval 5 in the scheme. The proper orientation scheme is therefore 142, and we must consider the interval 5 to be the complement, and adjust the scheme accordingly: 142(5).)

---

8   Editor's note: That is, with the smallest possible interval between the top and bottom notes.
9   Editor's note: 223 is read "two-two-three", 25 is read "two-five"; the numbers specify the numbers of semitones in each interval, in ascending order.
10 Editor's note: The reader must keep in mind that in distinction to set theory (Allen Forte) or serialists, Janeček's *complement* is a single interval completing the octave. As explained in §10 below, in Janeček's theory the *negative* is a chord containing all the pitches not in the original chord.

When determining the orientation scheme of a more complex chord, we contract the chord into the compass of an octave, form the expanded scheme, and from that extract the desired simple orientation scheme. For example, the chord C E G B♭ D F♯, contracted into the compass of an octave, is C D E F♯ G B♭ (C); from the expanded scheme 22213 $\boxed{22221}$ 3 we extract its orientation scheme 22221.

The student of theoretical works that deal with modern harmony can appreciate the importance of a system that identifies chords unambiguously. In the absence of such a system, even excellent musicians thoroughly familiar with modern harmonic material are often unaware that two chords differing only by transposition and/or disposition are the same chord-type.[11]

§4. The Harmonic Scheme of Chord-types

Intervals 1 and 2 are preeminently melodic. A melody with these intervals has a sense of flow. On the other hand, a harmonic piling-up of intervals 1 and 2, although it may simplify theoretical orientation, creates tone clusters that mask the chord's harmonic qualities and so make harmonic understanding more difficult. In order to compile a comprehensive inventory of harmonic material, therefore, we must establish a *harmonic scheme* as well as the orientation scheme (which was necessary to obtain the inventory of chords). Since isolated semitones and clusters of whole-tones and semitones can prevent the harmonic understanding of a chord, the following rules can be established for forming a harmonic scheme:

1. Rotate interval 1 to form a major seventh, or at least compound it by an octave to form a minor ninth.
2. Eliminate tone clusters of intervals 2 and 1 so that no interval 2 or 1 is adjacent to any other interval 2 or 1.
3. Give priority to a smaller ambit in the scheme, for theoretical clarity; retain a larger ambit only if it enables the scheme to show the symmetry of a chord distinctly. (See §5 below for symmetrical chords.)

Even following these rules, we are likely to find several possible solutions for the harmonic scheme of a chord. This is especially true for more complex chords. In chords commonly used in classical harmony, it is better to retain the tertian structure in the harmonic scheme, even if this increases the ambit. Similarly, in harmonies that can be arranged into fourths, the quartal structure should be preserved without regard to the

---

11 The practical significance of the orientation scheme of chord-types is discussed in my article "Harmonické možnosti chromatiky" [The Harmonic Possibilities of the Chromatic System], *Rytmus* [Rhythm] 11 (1947): 21–23.

ambit. The harmonic scheme cannot replace the orientation scheme because the variety of chord-types is too great.[12]

The harmonic scheme of the chord F G A♭ B 213 is formed by dispersing the cluster F G A♭ 21: the pitches G A♭ are rotated to A♭ G, and the remaining pitches are placed between them, to give A♭ B F G. The chord is also harmonically understandable as G B F A♭ because it is an incomplete form of the five-note tertian chord: G B D F A♭. In the chord C D E G 223 the cluster C D E 22 must be dispersed: the chord becomes D E G C or E G C D. The chord G♯ A B C E 1214 is written harmonically in thirds as A C E G♯ B, and the chord C D F G 232 in fourths as D G C F.

The orientation scheme is essential for an unambiguous designation of a chord-type, but only the harmonic scheme clearly and graphically expresses the harmonic essence of a chord. It will therefore be necessary to use both. The harmonic scheme will be given in pitch names following the orientation scheme in numbers. In the harmonic scheme, the lowest note of the orientation scheme will be marked with an asterisk for easier verification, for example, 213 G B F* A♭, 223 D E G C*, 1214 A C E G♯* B, 232 D G C* F. Similarly, in notated examples an asterisk beside a note will indicate the lowest note of the orientation scheme.

The foundation of harmonic thinking is still formed by the major and minor triads: 43 C* E G and 34 A* C E. The tertian structure of the five-note chord 1313, for example, will be apparent from its harmonic scheme: A C♯ E G♯ C, which contains one major and two minor triads. If a given chord contains at least one complete major or minor triad, we can show this in the harmonic scheme by placing a square bracket around a major triad ⌊_⌋ and a curved line around a minor triad ⌣. For example:

$$\overgroup{A\,C\sharp\,E}\,G\sharp\,C$$
$$\underbracket{C\sharp\,E\,G\sharp}\,C$$

Since these symbols designate the third of the triad as major or minor, placing them around the fifth (and eventually its rotation, the fourth) will suffice. The triadic contents of the 1313 five-tone chord will therefore become obvious in the harmonic scheme marked as follows:

$$A\,\overgroup{C\sharp\,E\,G\sharp}\,C$$
$$\underbracket{C\sharp\,E\,G\sharp}\,C$$

These symbols will be used in musical examples.

§5. Inversion of a Chord-type. Symmetrical and Asymmetrical Chord-types

The displacement of notes of a chord into various octaves does not create new harmonic entities. Rotations of a chord have the same harmonic content as the original chord; only the disposition is different. However, the process of *inversion* that produces a mirror im-

---

12 Editor's note: Also, there can be more than one harmonic scheme for a chord-type.

age of the original chord's interval structure does produce a new chord.[13] For example, the four-note chord C E F♯ B* 142 inverts to become C F* G B 241.[14] If the inversion is around a note lying half-way between two-notes of a given chord, these two-notes remain in the inversion. The given four-note chord can be inverted around the axis E–F♯ to become B E F♯ A♯, around the axis C–F♯ to become G C D F♯, around the axis E–B to become E A B D♯.[15] The axis can be any other note, for example F♯ (producing C♯ F♯ G♯ B♯) or A♭ (a note not contained in the given chord, producing F B♭ C E). The chord-type of all these inversions is the same.

Inversion can produce a chord-type different from the original only if the original chord is *asymmetrical*. *Symmetrical* chords are always inversions of themselves, so the same chord-type is obtained when a symmetrical chord is inverted. Such symmetrical chords are, for example, the augmented triad 44 C* *E** G♯*, the dominant major ninth 2223 G B *D* F* A, the new chords 1331 F♯ B *D* F B♭*, 13131 C E *G♯ B** E♭* G*, etc. The *axis of symmetry* is shown in italics in the examples.[16] The symmetry of a chord is apparent directly from its orientation scheme, with several exceptions. The orientation scheme of the dominant major ninth (2223) is such an exception. We ascertain symmetry here when we attempt an inversion: the inversion 3222 D F G A B is the same chord-type, as shown by the expanded orientation scheme 2223(3)2223.

A double-headed arrow below an orientation scheme will indicate that the chord is symmetrical ⟵⟶. When the symmetry is not obvious, the scheme may be completed by the complement in parentheses, placed so as to make the symmetry apparent. The symmetry of the five-note chord 2223 becomes obvious when the complement 3 is added below: (3)2223. For the four-note chord 115 D C♯ G C*, the complement 5 below shows symmetry: (5)115. To the four-note chord 224 E G♯ C* D we add the complement 4: (4)224. In the case of the four-note chord 143 C E G B*, symmetrical inversions result from adding the complement 4 above or below, which also proves the symmetry of the chord: (4)143 or 143(4).

---

13 Editor's note: Although *inversion* is often used to refer to rotation, we will use *inversion* only in this sense of mirror inversion.
14 Editor's note: The axis of symmetry is the interval B–C (invariant interval).
15 Editor's note: Inverting around an interval means that the interval stays invariant, i.e. its pitches stay on their places. Orientation scheme is here the starting point. When inverting around E–F♯, these two pitches stay on their positions and the scheme 425 gets inverted into 524 (always read bottom-up). Inverting around C–F♯ only the tone inside the interval changes, the boundaries stay: the scheme 425 changes to 524. Similarly, inverting around E–B, the scheme 425 changes to 524.
  Other theoreticians (e.g. Edward Pearsall), invert around an interval the same way as around a pitch, using an axis through the interval (if necessary, even though a quarter-tone). Inverting in such a manner, only the pitches on the axis stay on their positions, i.e. the boundaries of the interval exchange their positions. The results are the same tone groups but the order of pitches differs from the one generated in Janeček's manner.
16 Editor's note: The axis is so shown when it is a member of the chord, which is not always the case, as in C E G B 143, where the axes of symmetry are between B and C and between F and F♯. Janeček does not mention that every symmetrical chord has two axes a tritone apart.

The harmonic scheme does not involve such complications. It is always constructed so that symmetry is obvious. If necessary, one pitch may be included twice. Thus it is best to write the harmonic scheme of the four-note chord 115 as D G C♯(G) C*.

§6. Types of Two-note Chords

The prime and the octave are not considered to have harmonic value; they are considered "one-note chords". Of the remaining intervals, only one has the same compass as its rotation (6). The rest form five pairs of rotations: 1–11, 2–10, 3–9, 4–8, 5–7. Since rotations as well as other dispositions are considered to have the same harmonic value as the original chord, in the tempered chromatic system we can form only *six* two-note chords that distinctly differ from each other as harmonic entities: 1 (B C or C B), 2 (C D or D C), 3 (E G or G E), 4 (C E or E C), 5 (C F or F C), and 6 (F B = B F = the tritone).

All two-note chords are symmetrical. The orientation scheme of each is the same as the numeric designation of the interval in semitones (1, 2, 3, 4, 5, 6). The harmonic scheme is identical to that of the interval for chords 3, 4, and 6; for chords 5 and 2 it is advisable to use the rotation, and for chord 1 it is necessary (see §4 above). From the rotation of chord 5 it is apparent that it is an incomplete major or minor triad, and the rotation of chord 2 suggests an incomplete tertian four-note chord or an incomplete quartal three-note chord.

The two-note chords 1, 2, 3, 4, and 5 each occur in twelve transpositions, chord 6 in only six transpositions. This exception results from the fact that chord 6 rotated not only contains the same pitches as the original but also has the same compass; thus the number of transpositions normally possible for two-note chords that occur in two different positions each – the original and the rotation – is reduced to half (from twelve to six).[17]

All the two-note chords in the tempered chromatic system are also present in the diatonic system – most of them more than once. Of the various other pitch-systems (sub-systems of the tempered chromatic) the whole-tone system contains the fewest two-note chord-types (only 2, 4, and 6).

§7. Types of Three-note Chords

A three-note chord is formed when any one of the remaining ten pitches of the tempered chromatic system is added to any two-note chord. In this way we can form ten

---

17 Editor's note: By definition, different rotations have the same pitches. If different rotations also have the same interval structure, then what might be a transposition to the level of another note in the chord (F B transposed to B F) turns out to be the same chord. This principle applies to all symmetrical chords whose complement is the same as an interval in the chord, such as the augmented triad 44(4), as will be explained in the following sections.

Chapter I – The Harmonic Material of the Tempered Chromatic System

three-note chords from each two-note chord, but some duplication of chord-types will occur. To avoid duplication, we work out the orientation scheme for each new chord, thus verifying the distinctness of each chord-type. For each three-note chord formed, we must determine the complement. If the complement is smaller than an interval in the chord, the chord is not in its smallest ambit (see the first rule in §3 above). Thus this is not the proper designation for that chord, and we discard it; the proper one will be (or already has been) reached by way of another two-note chord. If the complement is the same as an interval in the chord, then more than one arrangement of the pitches will have the same smallest ambit. We must then rotate the numbers to find the arrangement with the smaller intervals at the bottom (see the second rule in §3 above). By this procedure we arrive at the total number of chord-types possible in the tempered chromatic system.

From the two-note chord 1 (B C), we can form five three-note chords: 11 (B C D♭, ambit 2, complement 10), 12 (B C D, ambit 3, complement 9), 13 (B C E♭, ambit 4, complement 8), 14 (B C E, ambit 5, complement 7), and 15 (B C F, ambit 6, complement 6). The chord 16 (B C F♯) has an ambit of 7 and a complement of 5. As the complement is smaller than the interval 6 in the proposed orientation scheme 16(5), the correct scheme is 51, with an ambit of 6 and 6 as the complement, and this chord will be formed from the two-note chord 5.

From the two-note chord 2 (C D), we can form five three-note chords: 21 (C D E♭, complement 9), 22 (C D E, 8), 23 (C D F, 7), 24 (C D F♯, 6), and 25 (C D G, 5). For the chord 26 (C D A♭, 4) the correct orientation scheme is 42 (A♭ C D), which has a smaller ambit and will be formed from the two-note chord 4.

From the two-note chord 3 (A C), we can form four three-note chords: 31 (A C D♭, complement 8), 32 (A C D, 7), 33 (A C E♭, 6), and 34 (A C E, 5). For the chord 35 (A C F, 4) the correct orientation scheme is 43 (F A C, 5), which has a smaller ambit and will be formed from the two-note chord 4.

From the two-note chord 4 (C E), we can form four three-note chords: 41 (C E F, complement 7), 42 (C E F♯, 6), 43 (C E G, 5), and 44 (C E G♯, 4). For the chord 45 (C E A, 3) the correct orientation scheme is 34 (A C E, 5); it has already been formed from the two-note chord 3.

From the two-note chord 5 (C F), we can form only one three-note chord: 51 (C F G♭, complement 6). The chord 52 (C F G) has an ambit of 7 and a complement of 5 – the same as one of the intervals in the proposed orientation scheme. The correct scheme, however, is 25 (F G C), as it has the smaller interval on the bottom. This chord has already been derived from the two-note chord 2.

From the two-note chord 6, we cannot form any three-note chord not already listed. For the chord 61 (B F G♭) the correct orientation scheme is 15 (F G♭ B); it has already been formed from the two-note chord 1.

The procedure described above is summarized in the following table:

Two-note Chord	Three-note Chords				
1	11 ↔	12	13	14	15
2	21	22 ↔	23	24	(5)25 →
3	31	32	33 ↔	34	
4	41	42	43	44 ↔	
5	51				

Of the nineteen possible three-note chord-types, five are symmetrical; two of these are traditional (known from classical harmony), and three are new. The other fourteen form seven pairs of inversions: one pair of traditional, completely consonant three-note chords; four pairs of traditional incomplete four-note chords; and two pairs of new dissonant three-note chords. All nineteen three-note chord-types are shown in Example 1 in musical notation.

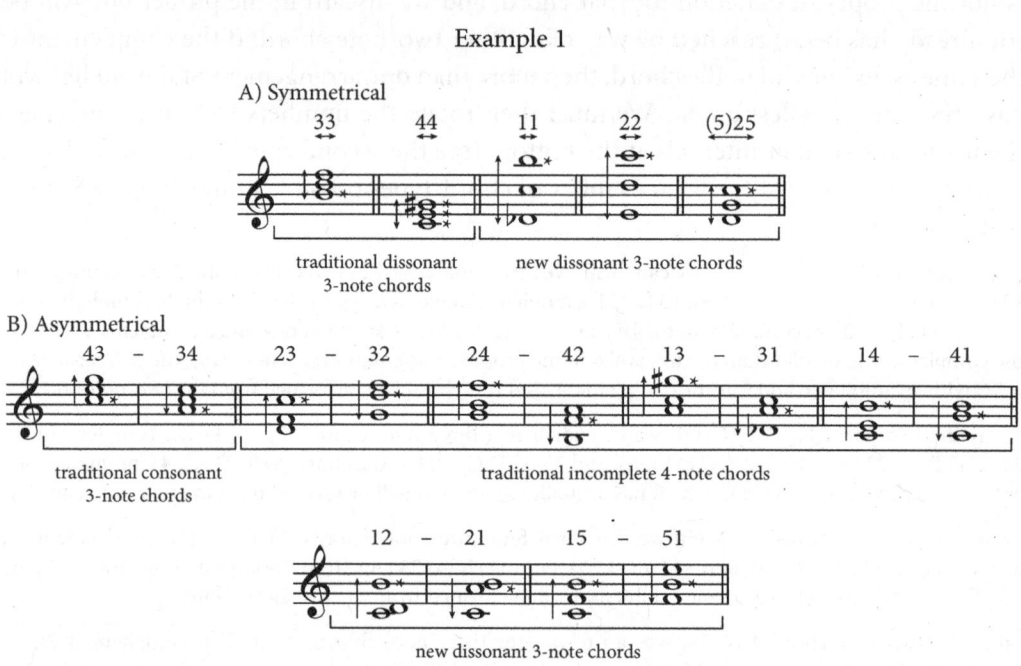

All but one of the three-note chords have three different rotations (the original and two rotations) and twelve transpositions. The chord 44 (the augmented triad) is the exception because its rotations have not only the same pitches but the same interval structure as the original. Since it has one third the number of rotations of the other three-note chords, it has one third the number of transpositions: four instead of twelve.

The chords 11, 44, and 13—31[18] are chromatic. This is apparent from the above table, as they use accidentals that cannot be obtained through using the usual key signatures. All the other three-note chords can be found in the pure diatonic system.[19] This is apparent from the fact that it is possible to write these chords without any accidentals. The frequency with which any given three-note chord appears in the diatonic system is determined by the one of the three intervals in the chord that is least common in that system: 25 appears diatonically five times (determined by interval 2); 23 and 32 four times each (determined by interval 3); 43 and 34 also three times each (determined by 4); 12, 21, 14 and 41 twice each (determined by 1); and 33, 15, and 51 once each (determined by interval 6). The specific location of a three-note chord in the diatonic system is de-

---

18 Editor's note: The long dash signifies the relation of mutual inversion.
19 Editor's note: The pure diatonic system comprises only the seven-note scale described in §1 above.

termined by the location of the one of its intervals that appears in the system least frequently. For example, the diatonic locations of 23 and 32 are determined by the location of minor thirds (interval 3); in D major, the minor thirds are E G, F♯ A, B D, and C♯ E, so the three-note chords 23 will be D E G, E F♯ A, A B D, and B C♯ E, and chords 32 will be E G A, F♯ A B, B D E, and C♯ E F♯.

The term *chromatic* is used here in contrast to *purely diatonic*. Chords that are chromatic in this sense can of course occur in various modified diatonic systems, such as those defined by the melodic, harmonic, and gypsy scales.[20] Some also occur in the whole-tone system. In examining the frequency with which various three-note chord-types occur in different common pitch-systems, the whole-tone system is again found to contain the least variety, as of three-note chord-types it has only 44, 22, and 24—42.

§8. Types of Four-note Chords

From each three-note chord, we can form a four-note chord by adding one of the remaining nine pitches (or to be more precise, pitch-classes). We work out the orientation scheme for each new chord in order to prevent repetition of types. The procedure for drawing up a table is the same as for three-note chords.

From the three-note chord 11 we can form the four-note chords 111, 112, 113, 114, (5)115. (This last chord is symmetrical, as its inversion 511 is of the same type as the original.) From the chord 12 we can form 121, 122, 123, 124; from the chord 13: 131, 132, 133, 134 (the orientation scheme of its inversion will be 314, not 431 – cf. the second rule in §3); from the chord 14: 141, 142, (4)143 (this chord is symmetrical, as its inversion 341 is of the same type as the original); from the chord 15, only the chord 151. From the three-note chord 21 we can form the four-note chords 211, 212, 213, 214; from the chord 22: 221, 222, 223, (4)224 (symmetrical); from 23: 231, 232, 233; from 24: 241, 242; from 31: 311, 312, 313, 314 (which inverts to 134, not 413); from 32: 321, 322, 323; from 33: 331, 332, 333; from 41: 411, 412; from 42, 421.

The procedure is summarized in the following table:

Three-note Chord	Four-note Chords				
11	111	112	113	114	(5)115
12	121	122	123	124	
13	131	132	133	134 (inv. 314)	
14	141	142	(4)143		
15	151				
21	211	212	213	214	
22	221	222	223	(4)224	
23	231	232	233		
24	241	242			

---

20 Editor's note: For these scales, see below, §14.

Three-note Chord	Four-note Chords			
31	311	312	313	314 (inv. 134)
32	321	322	323	
33	331	332	333	
41	411	412		
42	421			

The three-note chords omitted from the table – 25, 34, 43, 44, and 51 – do not produce any four-note chords that are not already included in the table. For example, the four-note chord 251 should be classified as 142, as is apparent from the expanded orientation scheme 25 142 51; this four-note chord has already been formed from the chord 14.

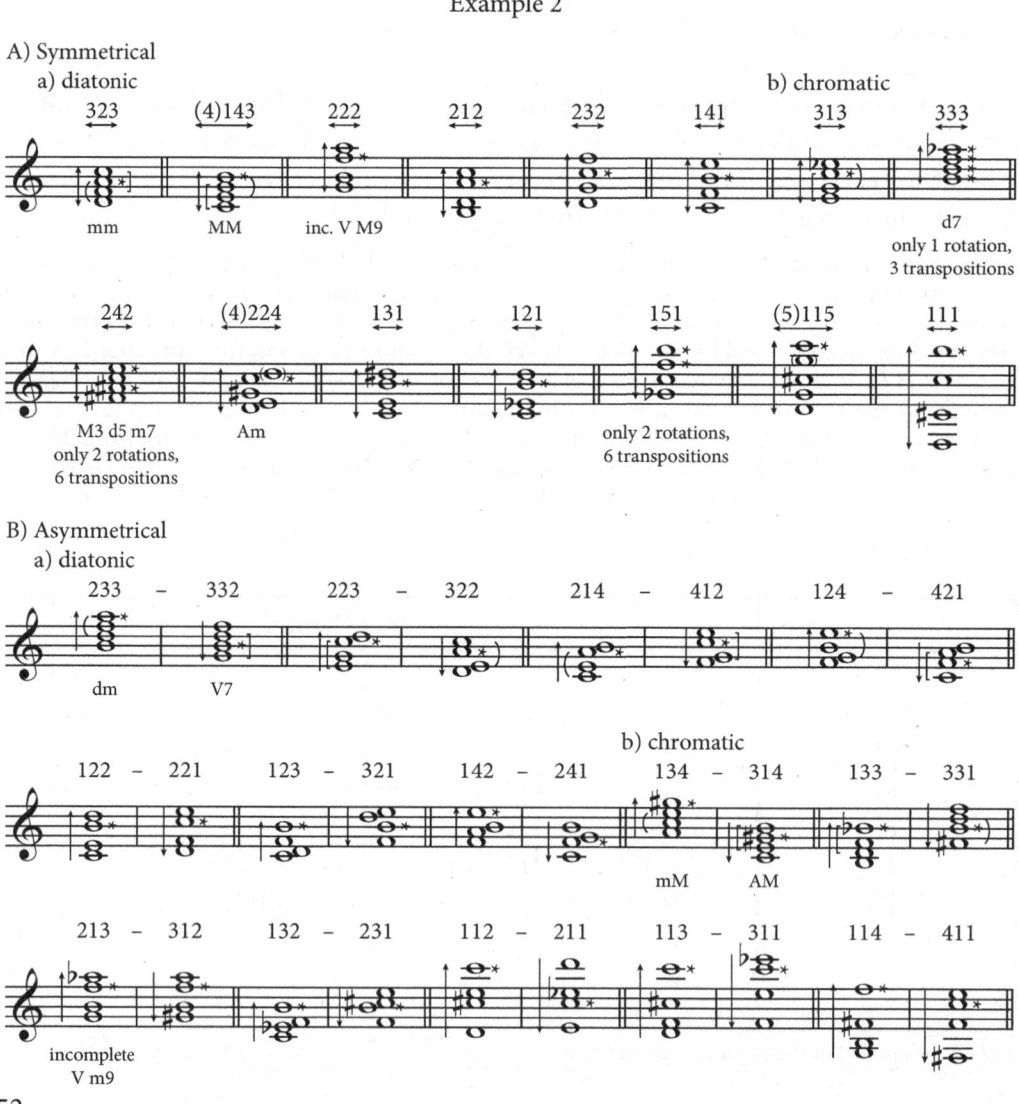

Example 2

Of the forty-three possible four-note chords, fifteen are symmetrical; five of these are traditional complete four-note chords, one is a traditional incomplete five-note chord, and nine are new four-note chords. The other twenty-eight form fourteen pairs of inversions, among which are two pairs of traditional four-note chords and one pair containing a traditional incomplete five-note chord.

All the possible four-note chord-types in the tempered chromatic system are shown in Example 2 in musical notation. The traditional designation for each traditional four-note chord is included.

The chord 333 (diminished-seventh) occurs in three transpositions, the chords 242 and 151 in six transpositions each, and all the other four-note chords in twelve transpositions. Again, chord 333 is an exception because all three of its rotations have the same interval structure as the original, and so the number of possible transpositions is reduced to one fourth – from twelve to three.[21] Chords 242 and 151 are exceptions because their second rotations (in the case of 242, a four-two chord [E F♯ A♯ C]) have the same interval structure as the originals (in the case of 242, a six-five chord [A♯ C E F♯]), and so they have half the normal number of transpositions – six instead of twelve.

All four-note chords that do not appear diatonically are designated as chromatic. The largest number of four-note chord-types can be placed into the modified diatonic system defined by the harmonic scales. The whole-tone system again contains the least variety.

§9. Types of Five-note Chords

From the four-note chords of the chromatic system, we can form 66 five-note chords, as shown in the following table:

Four-note Chord	Five-note Chords			
111	1111	1112	1113	1114
112	1121	1122	1123	1124 (inv. 2114)
113	1131	1132	1133	
114	1141	(4)1142		
121	1211	1212	1213	(4)1214
122	1221	1222	1223	
123	1231	1232	1233 (inv. 2133)	
124	1241			
131	1311	1312	1313	

---

21 Editor's note: As the chord has one fourth the usual number of rotations for a four-note chord (one instead of four), it has one fourth the usual number of transpositions (three instead of twelve).

Four-note Chord	Five-note Chords			
132	1321	1322	1323 (inv. 1332)	
133	1331	1332 (inv. 1323)		
141	1411			
142	1421			
211	2111	2112	2113	2114 (inv. 1124)
212	2121	2122	2123	
213	2131	2132	2133 (inv. 1233)	
221	2211	2212	2213	
222	2221	2222	(3)2223	
223	2231	(3)2232		
231	2311	2312		
232	2321			
311	3111	3112	3113	
312	3121	3122		
313	3131			
321	3211	3212		
322	3221			
331	3311			
411	4111			

All five-note chord-types have twelve different transpositions. Of the forty-three possible four-note chords in the chromatic system, only twenty-eight are included in this table. From the remaining four-note chords we can form five-note chords only of types already given. For example, the chord 1341 could be formed from 134; however, the correct orientation scheme for 1341 is 1313, as becomes evident from the expanded orientation scheme 134 $\boxed{1313}$ 41; this chord has already been formed from the chord 131.

Examples of the five-note chord-types are given in Example 3.

§10. The Negative of a Chord-type

All the pitches of the tempered chromatic system not contained in a given chord can be collectively designated the *negative* of the chord. Such a negative is itself a possible chord. Each chord-type can have only one negative. There are thus pairs of chord-types that are negatives of each other. All the notes in such a pair form a twelve-note chord that includes every pitch of the tempered chromatic system. The negative of a three-note chord will be a nine-note chord, the negative of a four-note chord will be an eight-note chord, etc. Since the negative usually belongs to a different chord-class – has a different number of notes

Chapter I – The Harmonic Material of the Tempered Chromatic System

Example 3

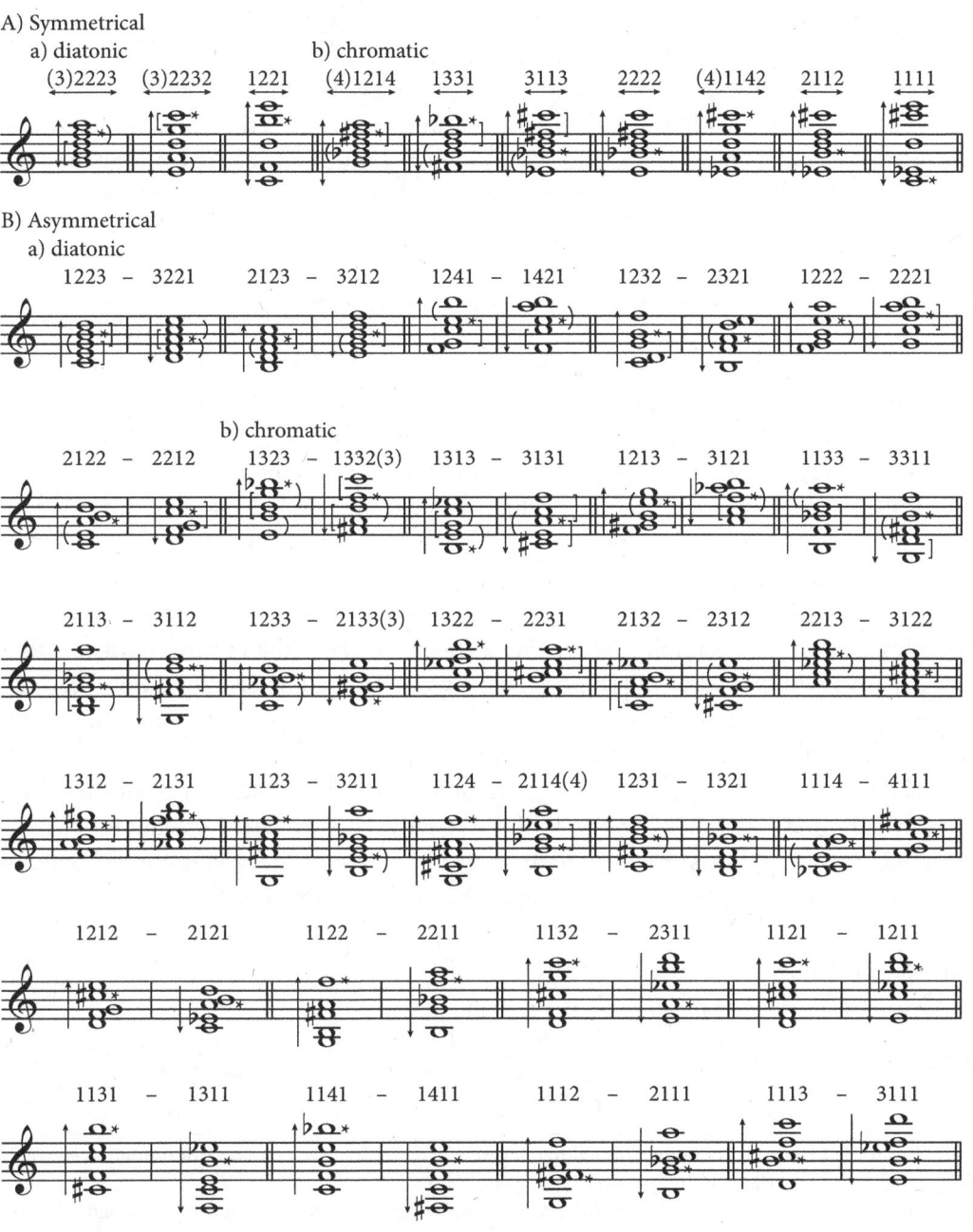

– it will necessarily be a different chord-type and have different sonic qualities from the original chord, which can be called the *positive*.[22] Exceptions can occur only for six-note chords, as their negatives are also six-note chords. A symmetrical chord will have a symmetrical negative, an asymmetrical chord an asymmetrical negative. The negative of an inversion will be the inversion of the negative of the original chord-type, i.e., of the positive.

The number of possible negatives of a certain chord-class is the same as the number of positives in that chord-class. Thus the number of nine-note chords will be the same as the number of three-note chords, the number of eight-note chords will be the same as the number of four-note chords, etc.

The negative of the symmetrical three-note chord B* D F 33 is the symmetrical nine-note chord G B♭ C♯ E A♭ C E♭ F♯* A 11112121. The negative of the asymmetrical three-note chord C* E G 43 is the asymmetrical nine-note chord C♯ D♯ F♯ A B D F A♭* B♭ 11121121; the inversion of this nine-note chord, F♯ G♯ B D F* G B♭ D♭ E♭ 11121211 will then have the negative A* C E 34, which is the inversion of the original three-note chord C* E G 43.

Whenever a chord occurs in a reduced number of rotations compared to other chords of its class, its negative will also have a reduced number of rotations compared to its class, in the same proportion. For example, the augmented triad 44 C* E* G♯* has only one rotation instead of the usual three (one third); its negative 11211211 B E♭ G B♭ D F♯ A* C♯* F* will therefore have only three rotations instead of nine (also one third).[23]

To the number of rotations is related the number of possible transpositions, as has been evident in past examples. Whenever a chord has fewer than twelve transpositions, its negative will also have fewer possible transpositions. For example, both the augmented triad and its negative occur in only four transpositions, the diminished-seventh chord and its negative in three transpositions, etc.[24]

The orientation scheme of the negative of a chord can be derived from that of the original through the following procedure. We write the expanded orientation scheme (see §3 above). Opposite each interval or group of 1's in the orientation scheme, we write its negative counterpart according to the following formula:

opposite:	3	4	5	6	7
write:	1	11	111	1111	11111

and vice versa.

---

[22] Editor's note: i.e. the operations of making negative and making inversion are commutative – give the same result regardless of the order of the two operations.

[23] Editor's note: The rotations beginning four semitones apart can be arranged into the same interval structure as the original (with, by the definition of rotation, the same pitches), as can easily be seen when the pitches are arranged in a scale: the rotations of A B♭ B C♯ D E♭ F F♯ G beginning on A, C♯, and F all have the same interval pattern 11211211.

[24] Editor's note: The augmented triad has one rotation instead of three, so it has a third of twelve, four, transpositions; the diminished-seventh chord has one rotation instead of four, so it has a fourth of twelve, three, transpositions.

Chapter I – The Harmonic Material of the Tempered Chromatic System

We write no interval opposite interval 2. Between each two adjacent intervals of the positive neither of which is interval 1, we write interval 2 in the negative. By this method we obtain the expanded orientation scheme of the negative, from which we then extract the simple orientation scheme according to the chord-class of the negative.

The negative of the six-note chord G♯ C♯ E G C* F♯ 13211 will thus be formed as follows:

1	3	2	11	(4)	1	3	2	11
3	1	2		4	11	3	1 2	4

(with 11 3 1 2 boxed)

Since the negative of a six-note chord is another six-note chord, the simple orientation scheme of the negative must contain five numbers. The result can be verified by using pitches: the orientation scheme of A B♭ B D E♭ F (the pitches missing from the positive) is 11312.

Here is another example:

1	3	1	(7)	1	3	1
3	1	3	11111	3	1	3

(with 11111 3 1 boxed)

The negative of the symmetrical four-note chord 131 must also be symmetrical, which is evident here in the result.[25]

For chords belonging to higher classes, it will sometimes prove advantageous to show not only the chord's own orientation scheme, but also the simpler scheme of its negative. Such *joint orientation schemes of chords* that are negatives of each other can be written as follows:

$$\frac{13211}{11312} \qquad \frac{131}{1111131}$$

(with ↔ arrows above both)

The ⟷ draws attention to the fact that both chords are symmetrical.

---

25 Editor's note: Another example will illustrate the rule about placing 2 in the negative between adjacent intervals of the positive neither of which is 1. The negative of C E G♯ is the scale C♯ D E♭ F F♯ G A A♯ B. Thus, the negative of the augmented triad 44 is Messiaen's mode 3, 11211211.

For brevity, we can designate complex chords belonging to high chord-classes by the orientation schemes of their negatives. In such cases it is obviously necessary to specify that these are negatives: neg. 44, neg. 34, neg. 6, etc. Also, we may use the abbreviation *neg.* in the joint orientation scheme.

§11. Types of Six-note Chords

From the five-note chords in the tempered chromatic system, 80 six-note chords can be formed, as shown in the following table:

Five-note Chord	Six-note Chords			
1111	11111	11112	11113	(4)11114
1112	11121	11122	11123	
1113	11131	11132	(3)11133	
1114	(4)11141			
1121	11211	11212	11213	
1122	11221	11222	11223 (inv. 22113)	
1123	11231	11232 (inv. 21132)		
1131	11311	11312	11313 (inv. 11331)	
1132	11321	(23)11322		
1133	11331 (inv. 11313)			
1141	11411			
1211	12111	12112	12113	
1212	12121	12122	12123 (inv. 21213)	
1213	12131	(3)12132		
1221	12211	12212	(3)12213	
1222	12221	12222		
1223	12231			
1231	12311	12312		
1232	12321			
1311	13111	13112		
1312	13121			
1313	13131			
1321	13211	13212(3)		

Chapter I – The Harmonic Material of the Tempered Chromatic System

Five-note Chord	Six-note Chords			
1322	13221			
2111	21111	21112 ⟷	21113	
2112	21121	21122	(3)21123 ⟷	
2113	21131	21132 (inv. 11232)		
2121	21211	21212 ⟷	21213 (inv. 12123)	
2122	21221	21222		
2131	21311			
2132	21321			
2211	22111	22112	(3)22113 (inv. 11223)	
2212	22121	22122 ⟷		
2221	22211	22212		
2222	22221	22222 ⟷		
2311	23111			
3111	31111	31112		
3112	31121			
3121	31211			
3211	32111			

Of the sixty-six possible five-note chords in the tempered chromatic system, the table shows only forty. From the remaining twenty-six five-note chords, only six-note chords of types already included can be formed. For example, the chord 11241 could be formed from 1124; however, the correct orientation scheme for 11241 is 13112, as becomes apparent from the expanded scheme 1124⟦13112⟧41; this chord has already been formed from the chord 1311.

Eight six-note chords have six-note chords of the same types for their negatives. The other seventy-two types of six-note chords form positive negative pairs of different types; some of the negatives are also inversions. Example 4 gives examples of harmonic schemes of all possible six-note chord-types; in each pair of chords the second chord is negative of the first.

The six-note chord 11411, having only three rotations instead of the usual six (11411, 14114, 41141), has only six transpositions instead of twelve. The chord 13131 has only two rotations (13131, 31313) instead of the usual six, and therefore only four transpositions. The chord 22222 has only one rotation, and therefore only two transpositions. The chords 12312—21321 have only three rotations each (12312, 23123, 31231—21321, 13213, 32132), and therefore only six transpositions each. All the other six-note chords have six rotations and twelve possible transpositions.

59

Example 4

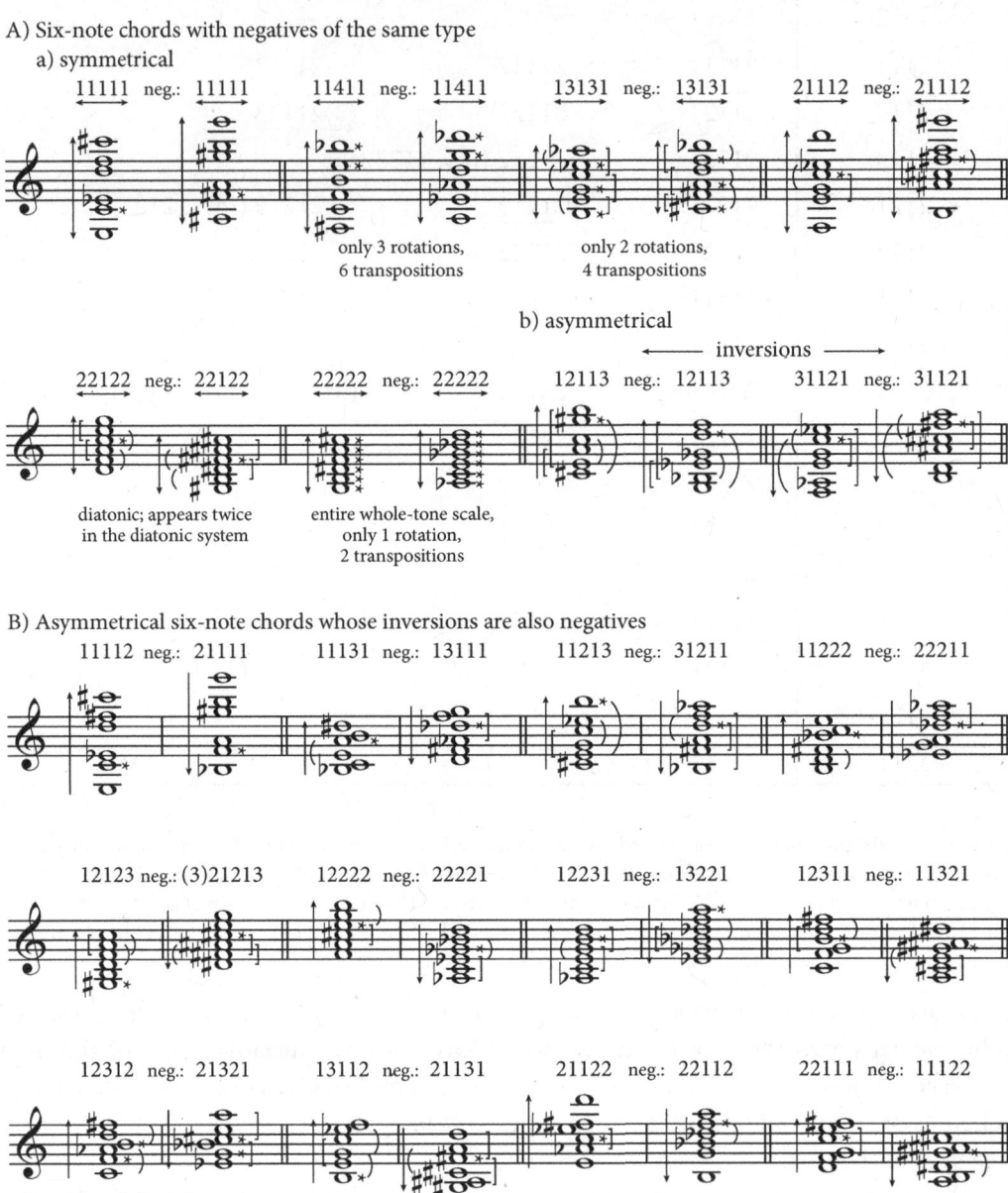

Chapter I – The Harmonic Material of the Tempered Chromatic System

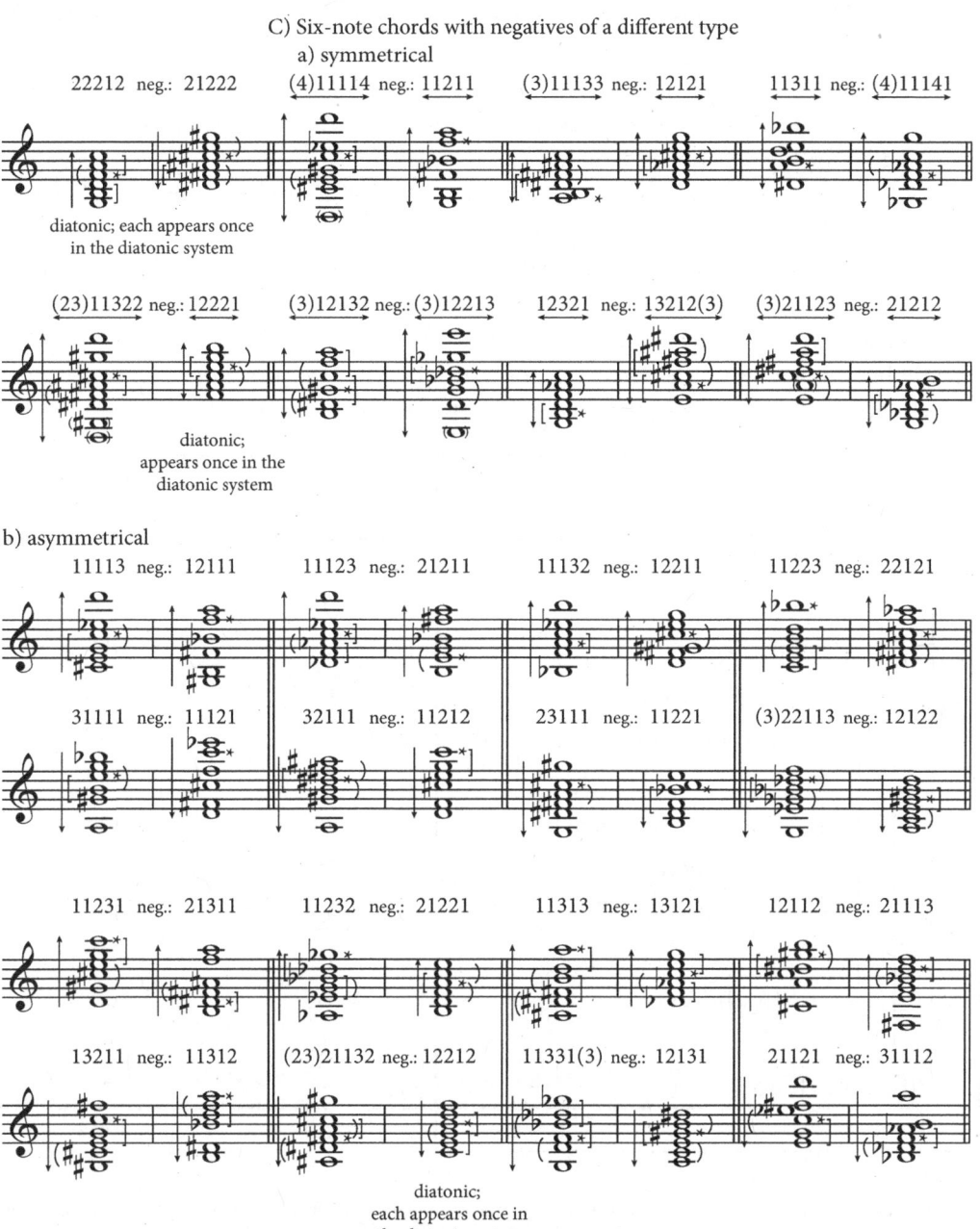

§12. The Harmonic Possibilities of the Tempered Chromatic System

From the tables compiled so far, it is evident that the number of chord-types possible in a chord-class increases with the number of notes. This growth ceases, however, with the six-note chords, which constitute the most extensive chord-class. Following what was said above concerning chord negatives, the number of chords-types possible will decrease again for higher chord-classes.

The following table shows all the harmonic possibilities of the tempered chromatic system, including the number of possible chord-types in each class and the number of possible (i. e. with differring tone contents) transpositions. We cannot simply multiply the number of chord-types by twelve in order to arrive at the number of transpositions, because some chords do not have twelve transpositions. Every such exception has already been noted, and the correct number of possible transpositions has been given. The same exceptions apply to the negatives of these chord-types.

Chord	Number of Chord-types	Number of Transpositions
(silence)	(1)	(1)
(1-note chord)	(1)	(12)
2-note chords	6	66
3-note chords	19	220
4-note chords	43	495
5-note chords	66	792
6-note chords	80	924[26]
7-note chords	66	792
8-note chords	43	495
9-note chords	19	220
10-note chords	6	66
11-note chord	1	12
12-note chord	1	1
Total	350	4083

Square brackets in the table indicate chord-classes that are negatives of each other. Silence and the one-note chord are not included in the totals of chord-types or transpositions, as neither is a chord; they are included in the table only as negatives of the eleven-note and twelve-note chords.

---

26 Editor's note: The original gives 918, and hence a total of 4077.

§13. Types of Multi-note Chords

The chords of higher classes, which collectively can be called *multi-note chords*, are negatives of chords belonging to the corresponding lower classes. Thus the list of chord-types compiled so far can be completed to include every chord-type possible in the tempered chromatic system, by forming the negative for each chord already listed. In this way, we find that there are 66 seven-note chord-types, 43 eight-note chord-types, 19 nine-note chord-types, etc.

The *seven-note chord-class* is subject to conditions similar to those of the five-note chord-class. All seven-note chords can be transposed twelve times. However, although fifteen of the five-note chord-types are diatonic (see §9 above), only one seven-note chord is diatonic: B* E A D G C F 122122 (neg. 2232). This seven-note chord completes the list of diatonic chords, as its pitch material covers the entire diatonic system; it contains all diatonic chord-types of lower classes.

Among the 43 types of *eight-note chords* there are three that do not appear in the usual twelve transpositions:

1. the chord E B♭ E♭ *G* A C♯ F♯* C* 1212121 (neg. 333 G♯* B* D* F*), which has only two rotations (1212121 and 2121212) and three transpositions;
2. the chord G♭ D♭ F B♭* G C E* B 1113111 (neg. 151), which has only four rotations (1113111, 1131113, 1311131, 3111311) and six transpositions;
3. the chord A D♯ G♯ B *D* F (A♭) D♭* G* 1122112 (neg. 242), which likewise has only four rotations and six possible transpositions.

Among the 19 types of *nine-tone chords*, it is B E♭ G B♭ *D* F♯ A* C♯* F* 11211211 (neg. 44) that has instead of nine rotations only three and therefore it occurs in only four transpositions, instead of the common twelve ones.

Among *ten-note chords*, only the negative of the tritone, (G♭) B♭ D♭ F A* C E G B D♯* F♯ (A♯) 111121111 (neg. 6), occurs in only six transpositions because it has only five rotations. The other five ten-note chords, which are the negatives of the two-note chords 1, 2, 3, 4, and 5, all have twelve transpositions.

The *eleven-note chord* is the negative of the one-note chord, or single pitch. Although the tempered chromatic system contains twelve pitches, they are all of the same "type" and so are simply transpositions of each other. Therefore there is only one type each of the one-note and eleven-note chords, although each occurs in twelve transpositions. Orientation schemes are unnecessary in these two cases, as there is no need to distinguish different types within the same class. The eleven-note chord is symmetrical, and contains eighteen major and minor triads (nine of each). Two different harmonic schemes of the eleven-note chord are shown in Example 5 (in this case, the chord is considered to be the negative of G♯). Chordal components found in the first example also appear in the second, although dispersed; similarly, components that are marked in the second example also appear in the first.

Example 5

The *twelve-note chord* is the negative of silence. There is only one, and it cannot be transposed. As with the eleven-note chord, it is unnecessary to use an orientation scheme here. The twelve-note chord is symmetrical, and contains all major and minor triads (twelve of each). Three different harmonic schemes of the twelve-note chord are shown in Example 6.

Example 6

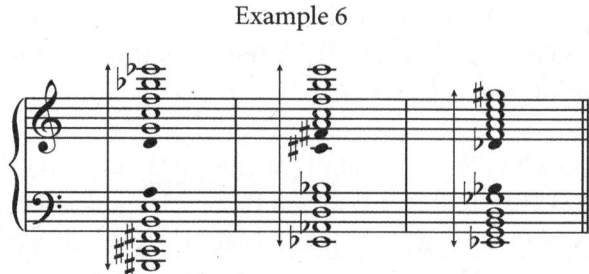

§14. Pitch-systems Contained in the Tempered Chromatic System

The tempered chromatic system contains all pitch-systems that are formed with the semitone as the unit. We can determine the composition of each of these systems the same way we determined that of the multi-note chords that we have already dealt with. There is a specific orientation scheme that applies to each system. Each system can be transposed, as a rule twelve times; exceptions occur where the pitch composition of the system coincides with a chord that has fewer possible transpositions. As there are isolated symmetrical chord-types, as well as asymmetrical pairs that are inversions of each other, there are also isolated *symmetrical pitch-systems*, as well as *pairs of asymmetrical pitch-systems that are inversions of each other*. And as we can speak of negatives of chords, we can also speak of *negatives of pitch-systems*.

Unlike the complex harmonic phenomena known as multi-note chords, these pitch-systems result from a long evolutionary process. They cannot be formed arbitrarily.

The tempered chromatic system contains the following commonly used symmetrical sub systems:

1. *The pure diatonic* system of seven pitches, which is the basis of Western music. When we use the primary pitches (those represented by the white keys on the piano), D functions as the axis of symmetry:

Chapter I – The Harmonic Material of the Tempered Chromatic System

...A B C D E F G...
   2 1 2 2 1 2

The orientation scheme is 122122. The orientation scheme of the negative is 2232.

2. *The tonal (anhemitonic) pentatonic* system of five pitches with no semitones. This is the negative of the pure diatonic system. When the system is constructed from derived (raised) pitches, D (not included) functions as the axis of symmetry:[27]

...F♯ G♯ A♯ C♯ D♯ F♯ G♯ A♯...
   2   2   3   2   3   2   2

The orientation scheme for the pentatonic system is 2232, which is the same as the five-note chord formed from perfect fourths (the second chord in Example 3 above).

3. The *modified*[28] *diatonic* system of seven pitches, defined by the *melodic major and minor* scales. In the transposition showing the ascending scale of A melodic minor and the descending scale of E melodic major, the axis of symmetry is E:

```
    minor                           major
...A  B  C  D  E  F♯  G♯  A  B  C  D  E...
   1  2  2  2  2  1
```

The orientation scheme for this system is 121222. Its negative (E♭ G B♭ D♭* F) is the five-note chord 2223, which is the dominant major ninth (the first chord in Example 3 above).

4. The *modified diatonic* system of seven pitches, defined by the *gypsy major and minor* scales:

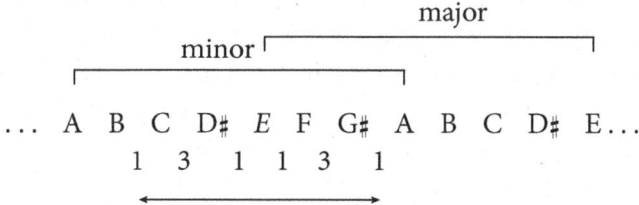

```
    ...A  B  C  D♯  E  F  G♯  A  B  C  D♯  E...
       1  3   1   3   1
```

---

27 Editor's note: Obviously, G♯ also functions as an axis of symmetry: D♯ F♯ G♯ A♯ C♯.
28 Editor's note: Janeček uses a rather emotionally coloured term *deformation*.

The orientation scheme for this system is 113121. Its negative is the five-note chord 1331 (the fifth chord in Example 3 above).

5. The *whole-tone* system of six pitches. In contrast to the other systems, each of which has twelve transpositions, this system has only two:

$$\ldots\text{C D E F\# G\# A\#}\ldots \quad \ldots\text{D}\flat\text{ E}\flat\text{ F G A B}\ldots$$
$$\phantom{\ldots\text{C}}\ 2\ \ 2\ \ 2\ \ 2\ \ 2 2\ \ 2\ \ 2\ \ 2\ \ 2$$

These two transpositions are also *negatives of each other*. (See the symmetrical six-note chords with negatives of the same type in §11 above, Example 4.)

In contrast to the five given symmetrical systems, there is a pair of asymmetrical systems, defined by the *harmonic major and minor* scales:

$$\overbrace{}^{\text{minor}}\ \overbrace{}^{\text{major}}$$
$$\ldots\text{G\# A B C D E F G\# A B C\# D E F G\# A}\ldots$$
$$\phantom{\ldots\text{G\#}}\ 1\ \ 2\ \ 1\ \ 2\ \ 2\ \ 1\ \ 3\ \ 1\ \ 2\ \ 2\ \ 1\ \ 2\ \ 1$$

In the symmetrical systems, the major and minor scales simply represent different rotations of the system, differing only in the location of the lowest pitch. On the other hand, the harmonic major and minor scales belong to different systems, which are inversions of each other.

Several useful precepts become apparent from the arrangement of the various pitch-systems. If a chord belongs to a symmetrical system, then the inversion of the chord belongs to the same symmetrical pitch-system and appears in it as many times as does the original chord. Thus if the major triad 43 appears three times in the pure diatonic system, the minor triad 34 (the inversion of 43), will also appear there three times.

In asymmetrical systems, chords that are inversions of each other appear the same number of times in systems that are inversions of each other. If the five-note chord 1322 G C E♭ F B*, for example, appears once in the harmonic minor (C minor), its inversion 2231 A♭ D E G C* will appear once in the harmonic major (C major).

Since a symmetrical chord is its own inversion, it will appear the same number of times in asymmetrical systems that are inversions of each other. If the symmetrical four-note chord 313 E G C* E♭, for example, appears once in the harmonic minor (E harmonic minor, when E♭ is enharmonically changed to D♯), it will appear also once in the harmonic major (A♭ harmonic major, when E is enharmonically changed to F♭).

It is possible for chords that are inversions of each other to appear the same number of times also in one asymmetrical system (e.g., in the harmonic minor). This happens

Chapter I – The Harmonic Material of the Tempered Chromatic System

when the chord does not contain a pitch that distinguishes the asymmetrical system from one of the symmetrical systems.[29]

We can use the orientation scheme to determine the location of a chord in a particular pitch-system. We start with the expanded orientation scheme of the system, covering a range of two octaves. The orientation scheme of the chord in question must match part of the system's scheme. The intervals in the chord must have as their counterparts in the system either the same intervals or adjacent intervals whose sum is the same. An example is the location of the four-note chord 233 (the diminished-minor) and its inversion 332 (the dominant seventh) in the modified diatonic system defined by the harmonic major and minor scales:

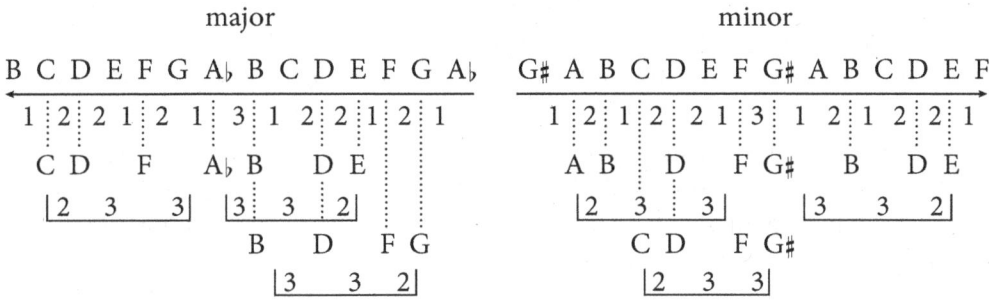

We use the same procedure to determine whether or not a more complex chord contains a given chord-type of a lower class. Instead of the expanded orientation scheme of a pitch-system, we use the scheme of the more complex chord. It is evident that the frequency with which a chord-type appears either in a pitch-system or in a more complex chord is determined by its interval structure.

§15. Conclusions and Prospects

We have now surveyed *all the harmonic material of the tempered chromatic system*. The focus has been only on systems of chord-types and on concrete relations between them. However, what matters in music is of course the *sonic effect*. It will be the tasks of the next chapter to consider the *sonic qualities* of the harmonic material and to build a foundation for a musical investigation.

A fact which is already widely recognized should be noted: *it is possible to make artistic use of all the harmonic material afforded by the tempered chromatic system*. In new music we encounter the most complex chord-types and those unusually rich in sound. At the same time, it is natural that composers tend to avoid the real expression of these

---

29 Editor's note: For example, 14 and 41 each appear twice in the asymmetrical harmonic minor scale: in A harmonic minor, B C E, E F A, C E F, E G♯ A; the chords do not involve D, which distinguishes A harmonic minor from the symmetrical gypsy minor with D♯.

complex chords in particular, finding it too cumbersome, and tend to give precedence to a lighter, more open, composite expression in which not only pitches that are actually sounding have an effect, but also imaginary harmonic pitches.[30]

The fact that multi-note chords are rarely actually sounded in modern music does not mean that they do not exist. Multi-note chords do exist in living music, and their intricate mazes of pitches are an integral part of a particular manner of expression, just as are the crystal-clear dissonances and consonances in classical harmony.

We should further note that, due to the limitations of human perception, the more complex the chord-types become, the less difference we can hear between them. Thus for multi-note chords that tend to be similar in sound, the actual disposition and the specific manner of expression become increasingly important. Composers are aware that the actual disposition of a chord's pitches is often far more significant than the choice of chord-type in the ultimate effect of the sound. *The question of chord-type of multi-note chords is actually secondary.*

For this reason, it has generally sufficed, when dealing with multi-note chords, to refer only to the negatives. Although detailed tables of seven-note, eight-note, and nine-note chord-types could easily be constructed, the necessary information about these chord-types is contained in the tables of their negatives.

---

[30] Imaginary pitches and real and composite expression are discussed in detail in *Chapter V*.

Chapter II – Sonic Characteristics of the Harmonic Material

§16. Consonance and Dissonance

The *sonic characteristics* of the harmonic material determine its musical impact.

The smallest possible structural change in a chord changes its sound impact. A redisposition of pitches, or their transposition, results in a different, sometimes very different sound impact, although the chord-type remains the same; even more striking differences can result through the use of a different manner of expression.[31] Once a particular chord-type is chosen, its degree of roughness can only be adjusted, although sometimes considerably, by an appropriate situation in its harmonic surroundings, by transposition, or by an appropriate manner of expression; it is possible to fuse or fragment the sound, to make it smoother or to sharpen its edges. However, each chord-type has a fundamental sound that cannot be affected by arrangement; should a radical change of character be desired, a different chord-type would have to be chosen. The *fundamental sonic characteristics* of isolated chords, as determined by the chord-types, will be considered here.

First, two distinct categories of chord-types can be distinguished according to the fundamental character of their sound – *consonance* and *dissonance*.

A consonance is any chord-type that under favorable conditions does not arouse tension in the listener. As a rule it has a pleasing sound; it does not, however, create excitement. "Favorable conditions" can refer to a suitable disposition of the chord, its suitable situation in its pitch space, an especially favorable manner in which it is inserted into its harmonic surroundings, etc. It is important to realize that *consonance* is a *potential* quality, not a factual one evident in all circumstances.

---

31 A chord can be *expressed* by the use not only of real (actually sounding) pitches, but also of imaginary pitches in conjunction with real ones; imaginary harmonic pitches are useful, for example, in the representation of harmony in figuration. See *Chapter V*.

In looking for consonances, we must examine the effect of chords under various conditions. If we find that a particular chord-type produces no tension under certain conditions, the chord-type is considered consonant, even though under other ("unfavorable") conditions its effect may be different.

There are only two basic consonances: the major triad (with orientation scheme 43, e.g. C E G) *and the minor triad* (with orientation scheme 34, e.g. A C E). Only these two harmonies can, in some situations (under favorable conditions), occur in such a way as not to arouse tension.

Simpler chords that are components of major and minor triads – their two-note components, and also individual pitches – can have the same effect. We do not, however, consider the components of major and minor triads to be separate consonant harmonies. They are seen as simplified (incomplete) triads; they are only *partial consonances*. This concept is justified by the fact that the omission of pitches does not deprive a more complex chord of the potential essence of its sound, that is, its consonance. Only its family specification (major, minor), or that of its inner structure, is lost. This is not the case when pitches are omitted from chords that are not consonant, nor when chords are enriched by the addition of new pitches.

A dissonance is any chord-type that arouses a sense of unrest and tension in the listener under all conditions, that is, in any disposition and without regard to its place in a chord succession.

There is a great variety of dissonances. Among them can be found sweet-sounding chords and those that are pleasantly exciting, vaguely blurred chords, sharply focused chords and those that are painfully harsh, transparent chords and those that are chaotically cluttered. All have one thing in common: they arouse tension and demand movement.

The great number of possible dissonances makes their *classification* necessary. Although every dissonant chord-type distinctly differs from the others, we can, according to various criteria, group chords that have a similar sound. The two criteria of classification (to which the *Chapters IIIa* and *IIIb* will be devoted) are the *dissonant characteristic* and the *family characteristic*. Other factors, such as the number of pitches, or how these are arranged (symmetrically or asymmetrically), although not without significance, do not contribute as directly and decisively to the actual sonic effect, which is of greatest concern in music.

§17. Dissonant Elements

When individual pitches, and thus individual components of intervals, are systematically omitted from dissonant chords of higher classes, which have a more complex sound, chords of lower classes, which have a simpler sound, result. In this way transparent, simple, *consonant formations* are always eventually reached: three-note chords, two-note chords, or single pitches.³² Thus when certain boundaries are crossed, the complexity and tension (*dissonance*) in the sound disappear. This happens because those components of the chord that cause its complexity or dissonance have been eliminated.

These components can be designated as *dissonant elements*. In traditional harmony, only individual dissonant intervals have constituted such dissonant elements; these have included even two-note chords that would normally be considered consonant, whenever they have been perceived as dissonant because of their musical context (e.g., the augmented fifth which is enharmonically equivalent to the minor sixth, the diminished fourth which is enharmonically equivalent to the major third, etc.). One reason for this has been the desirability of having all dissonant elements belong to the same chord-class, two-note chords. When we start from the tempered chromatic system, however, we cannot accept a different conception of the same interval as an objective characteristic. It is easier and more natural to distribute the dissonant elements among the various chord-classes, should one class (the two-note chords) prove insufficient.

When we simplify complex chords using the method described above, we arrive at the following *four dissonant elements*:

1. the semitone (the interval unit of the tempered chromatic system, interval 1),
2. the whole-tone (2),
3. the tritone (6),
4. the augmented triad (44).

It is clear that we are dealing with three single dissonant relationship between two tones (intervals) and one dissonant relations between three tones (triad). At least one of these dissonant elements can be found in any dissonant chord. All chords that do not contain any of these dissonant elements are consonant.³³

This conception differs from that of traditional harmony (founded on the pure diatonic system) in that here it is not necessary to consider as dissonant all augmented, diminished, doubly-augmented and doubly-diminished intervals; we consider dissonant only those that have the same compass, and therefore the same sound, as the semitone, the whole-tone, the tritone, and their various dispositions (rotations). The interpretation of the augmented triad's dissonance based on a dissonant conception

---

32 We assume, of course, that chords that have been simplified in this way are evaluated as *isolated phenomena*, not as parts of a continuous succession. Only in this way can we speak of simplifying the *real sound* of more complex chords. We perceive a continuous series of chords, a sound is complicated by the lasting effects of the imaginary harmonic pitches; we are then dealing not with a simpler chord but rather with an equally complex one, although it may be of composite expression, having both real and imaginary pitches. See *Chapter V*.
33 Editor's note: It is interesting to compare Janeček's findings with Hindemith's classification of chords – see *The Craft of Musical Composition. Book I: Theoretical Part*, english translation by Arthur Mendel, 4th ed, (New York: Associated music Publishers – London: Schott, 1942), 137.

of the augmented fifth is dropped because we consider the augmented triad itself as a dissonant element. This is correct because its dissonant quality disappears with the removal of any one of its pitches, and therefore any one of its intervals. In the triad C E G♯, we do not need to remove C or G♯ as a component of the augmented ("dissonant") fifth C G♯; removing the E, which is not part of any dissonant interval, is equally effective in eliminating the dissonance. Thus the dissonance of the augmented triad is not caused by the sound of any two of its pitches, but rather by the total sound of all three pitches.

From the single pitch (which in isolation is naturally always consonant) and consonant two-note chords we can progress to the major and minor triads as the richest possible consonant chords. Although in dissonant chords we can designate dissonant elements (the simplest dissonant units, which cannot be further broken down) as the factors that cause dissonance, we cannot do this with consonances. Here the reverse is true: consonance is established and measured by the most complex structures, namely the two consonant triads, major and minor. All simpler chords that are components of these consonances are thus also consonant. Chords that are not entirely coincide with the consonant triads, or to their components, are dissonant. The augmented triad, although all its components are consonances, is dissonant precisely because it can be coincide neither with the major nor with the minor triad.

The augmented triad is the only dissonance that does not contain any intervals that are dissonant in themselves. All other dissonances contain one or more of the intervallic dissonant elements (semitone, whole-tone, tritone); many dissonances of course contain the triadic dissonant element (the augmented triad) as well. The dissonant intervals all appear in the pure diatonic system, whereas the augmented triad cannot be formed unless this system is modified by raising or lowering a pitch.

It may be worth noting that *major and minor triads are the most complex consonant structures that are possible anywhere*, not just in the tempered chromatic system. No other pitch-system, whether containing more or fewer pitches, and no matter how modified, can produce any other equivalent consonant chords of the same class. In contrast, to the great variety of dissonances existing in the tempered chromatic system can be added more dissonances formed in other pitch-systems. Thus the number of dissonances can be increased outside of the tempered chromatic system, whereas the number of consonances cannot.

§18. The Principle of Harmonic Inversion

The material relation of chords that are inversions of each other becomes apparent in their musical effect, that is, in their sound. This is not to say that the inversion is heard as the chord "upside down"; such a thing is not possible. The interval structure of a chord can be determined only by analysis, but each chord has its own direct and independent effect as an individual entity.[34] A relation of mutual inversion between chords, however, is very markedly apparent in their degree of consonance or dissonance. Here the plain and simple principle of harmonic inversion applies: *the inversion of a chord is consonant or dissonant to the same degree as the original chord*. The minor triad is the inversion of the major triad, and they are equally consonant. The diminished-minor chord (B D F A*, 233) is the inversion of the dominant seventh chord (G B* D F, 332), and the degree and character of dissonance are the same for both chords. A similar relation obtains between the augmented-major seventh chord (C E G♯* B, 314) and the minor-major seventh chord (C E♭ G B*, 134), which are mutual inversions; they have the same degree of dissonant tension, although they can be clearly differentiated. The preceding examples are from classical harmony, but modern chords can serve as examples in the same way. For example, the sound of the chord F G E* (12) is related to that of its inversion F D* E (21); the relation between the chord F B E* A (142) and its inversion F B♭ E♭* A (241) is the same. *Thus there are pairs of chords with the same degree and character of dissonance.*

This only applies to *asymmetrical chords*, however. The inversion of a symmetrical chord can never be a different chord-type from the original. Therefore *symmetrical chords have neither consonant nor equally dissonant counterparts*; they are isolated. There is thus no four-note chord that is the sonic counterpart of the diminished-seventh chord (B D F A♭, 333). Likewise, the characteristic musical effect of the dissonant augmented triad (C E G♯, 44) cannot be duplicated by any other chord-type.

The *principle of inversion* as formulated here *applies without exception as long as we are dealing with chord-types*. It is important to be aware of this, as the inversion of a particular disposition can result in a sound that has a very different, even opposite, effect from the original. (Observations and reflections on this subject belong to *Chapter IV*, which deals with the disposition of chords.) When evaluating sonic effects, however, we must rely only on particular dispositions of individual chord-types, since of course an orientation scheme of a chord-type produces no sound. We can obtain undistorted results only when we compare the sounds of chords with *equivalent dispositions* (ideally, optimal disposition). Thus we must not compare the sound of a particular chord-type in a good, well balanced and integrated disposition to the sound of its inversion if the

---

34 This is graphically explained by Čeněk Strouhal in his book *Akustika* [Acoustics] (Praha: Jednota čes. mathematiků, 1902), 192–193: "When we see in the calm surface of a lake the reflection of a house built on the shore, and when we study its vertical dimensions (e.g., the height of individual stories), we do not have the impression that the proportions in the reflection differ from those of the house. This is because in both cases the proportions are perceived in the direction *from the foundations* of the house towards the higher stories. Here aural impressions vastly differ from visual impressions, however. No matter how a triad may be formed, it is *always* perceived *in one direction* only – *from the lower notes to the higher ones*. Thus it happens that in a 'reflected' triad [here designated as "inverted"] what is heard differs completely from the original sound; the 'reflected' triad is not perceived starting with the note from which it has been formed *in a downward direction*, but rather from its lowest note *always in an upward direction*."

disposition of the inversion is poor, fragmented, or unpleasantly acute. Such procedure could even "convincingly" invalidate the principle of inversion.

A further point we must keep in mind when evaluating the sound of inversions is that chord-types that are mutual inversions (and thus of the same quality) *have not been used in music with the same degree of frequency*. Sometimes conspicuous priority has been given to a particular chord-type while its inversion has been neglected; the wider usefulness of the inversion has had to be discovered only later, through new creative activity. This natural aspect of musical evolution, both past and present, has considerably influenced the way in which a sound is evaluated today. We must therefore be alert to free ourselves of habits that result from being engrossed by the music of one particular evolutionary period.

§19. Dissonant Characteristics of Chords

Dissonant elements differ from each other by the measure of their dissonance, their degree of prominence, their impact. These differences are obvious. If we were to try, however, to find some unit of dissonance that together with its multiples could express or at least approximately suggest the tension in the sound of individual dissonant elements and their relations, we would fail. Such a unit, such a primary element, does not exist. We can only look at dissonant elements as separate, *qualitative* rather than quantitative entities of sound. The traditional view is that a chord's dissonance is proportional to the number of dissonant intervals, or rather elements, it contains. This view is unsubstantiated. The error lies in the assumption that we can simply add dissonant components of different qualities. The following will show that the merging of different dissonant elements leads to a remarkable and, for theory, surprising contradiction of the traditional assumption.

Individual dissonant elements represent characteristic sonic qualities, that is, musical qualities. It is impossible to define their effect. It is impossible to say what a semitone represents in terms of quality of sound. This can only be demonstrated, presented to the ear. (The interval between the pitches of a semitone can of course be precisely defined mathematically.) In spite of this, we can attempt to give a *verbal indication*, though never a description, of the *sound of an individual element*, which will approximately express its effect. It is understandable that here we will find it necessary to draw on analogies with phenomena other than sound.

Dissonant elements can be roughly characterized as follows:

1. The semitone (1) is *obtrusively piercing*. Its presence in a more complex chord is unusually noticeable, evoking *acute tension*.
2. The whole-tone (2) is generally *insipid, unobtrusive*. Its presence in a chord causes a certain blurring, and evokes only *mild tension*.
3. The tritone (6) is *pleasantly stimulating*. Its presence in a chord has a *fusing effect*. A chord containing a tritone gives a *unified, coalescent impression*.

4. The augmented triad (44) is *noticeable without being piercing*. Its sound is somewhat *warped*, probably because it eludes the pure diatonic system which has dominated Western music for many centuries and which still influences the perception of music today. The presence of the augmented triad in a more complex chord can immediately be recognized by its *characteristic flavour*.

The dissonant elements themselves are of course also *chords*, albeit greatly simplified. If they can be characterized, then more complex chords can likewise be characterized. However, it would be impossible to devise verbal expressions of the effects of every existing chord-type. That all the more complex dissonant chords *contain dissonant elements* would naturally lead us to suppose that the effect of the chord as a whole will *reflect* the characteristics of the elements it contains. This assumption can be verified by examining the material. Thus it was appropriate in characterizing each dissonant element to draw attention to the effect of its presence on the overall effect of more complex chords. When characterizing a more complex dissonant chord, it suffices, in order to define its dissonance, to state that it contains a particular dissonant element (or elements). Therefore, to arrive at a *dissonant characterization* we must discover which dissonant elements are present in a particular dissonant chord-type; these *mark* the chord-type permanently and unalterably.

There are not many chord-types with single and unmixed dissonant characteristics. These are all shown in example 7.

Example 7

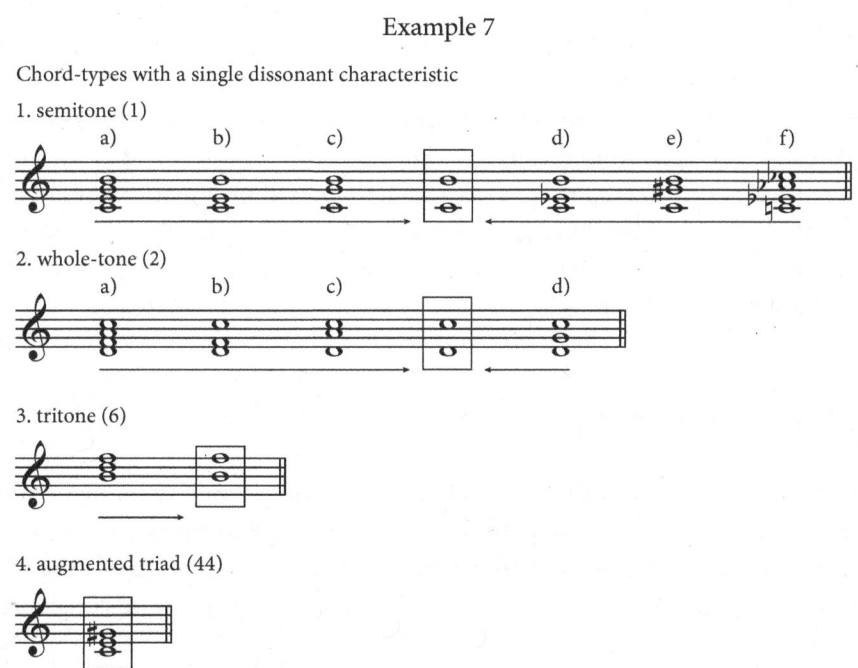

Chord-types with a single dissonant characteristic
1. semitone (1)
2. whole-tone (2)
3. tritone (6)
4. augmented triad (44)

75

The dissonant elements are shown in boxes. The arrows show the direction in which more complex chords are simplified down to their individual elements. The direction of building up chords (i.e., the enrichment of the dissonant elements) is the reverse.

When we follow the changes in effect of adjacent chords with the same dissonant characteristic in the above example, whether we proceed towards their respective element or away from it, we see that the changes are negligible. In the semitone and whole-tone series of chords, the differences in sound between chords with the same dissonant characteristic but shown in the table on opposite sides of the dissonant elements are somewhat greater. A *dividing line* is felt. Classical harmony is correct in considering the three-note chords labeled b and c to be incomplete forms of the four-note chords labeled a. In contrast, the chords 1f in the semitone series and 2d in the whole-tone series are new harmonic formations, or modern harmonies; 1f is a major/minor four-note chord with a common root,[35] while 2d is a quartal three-note chord. In the semitone series, the three-note chords labeled d and e are related to the four-note chord labeled f as, in classical harmony, the three-note chords labeled b and c are related to the four-note chord labeled a. Chords 1d and 1e can be conceived "classically" as well, if we assume that G is omitted in the chord C E♭ B, and that E is omitted in C G♯ B. Even when we conceive the harmonies in this way, however, a dividing line remains between them and the first three harmonies in the same series. This is no longer because new chords are involved, but rather because a new characteristic element (the augmented triad) comes into play (E♭ G B in C E♭ G B and C E G♯ in C E G♯ B). Thus a dividing line is formed both *historically* (by the contrast between classical harmonies and modern harmonies that were not used in the past and are comparatively rare even today) and *materially* (by the inclusion of another characteristic).

The above example shows *all types of two-note, three-note, and four-note chords in which there is only one dissonant element and it is active only once*. It is impossible to form a four-note chord that contains only one tritone and no other dissonant element. The augmented triad is exceptional in that no pitches can be added to it without involving some other dissonant element. All five-note chords contain at least two dissonant elements, the same or different ones.

§20. Influence of Consonant Components

When pitches are added to a dissonant element without changing its dissonant characteristic, new consonant components come into play. Although these do not change the dissonant characteristic, the overall sound does noticeably change, so the influence of consonant components on the sound of a dissonant chord must be considered. The

---

35 Editor's note: That is, a four-note "triad" with both major and minor thirds.

dissonant characteristic is at least supplemented by these consonant components, as can be seen in the chords in Example 7 above.

Moving from the individual dissonant elements in the direction opposite to the arrows, we can see not only that the chords gradually become denser and richer, but also that their dissonant intensity is considerably lessened. From this observation we can derive a general precept: the gradual addition of consonant components to a dissonant element *softens* its dissonance.

Not all consonant components have the same influence. *Full consonances* – major and minor thirds (4, 3) – have a pronounced softening effect. The softening effect of the *open consonance* of the fifth (7 = 5) is perceptible only when the fifth is combined with a full consonance. The quartal three-note chord (D G C) labeled *d* in the whole-tone series of Example 7 is especially instructive in this respect. Its whole-tone dissonant character is softened only by two open consonant components (D G and G C); in comparison with this chord, the chords on the other side of the dividing line (D F C and D A C) have a much fuller sound, as they are influenced not only by the open consonance of the fifth but also by the full consonance of the third.

The open consonance of the fifth and the full consonance of the third function concurrently in both major and minor triads. Dissonant characteristics are substantially softened in chords that contain one of the consonant triads. This is apparent in the chords labeled 1a, 1f, and 2a in Example 7, as all three contain both major and minor triads.

§21. Family Characteristics of Chords

When chords are mutual inversions of each other, they contain the same dissonant elements and the same consonant components: their dissonant characteristics are the same and are softened to the same extent. However, chords that are mutual inversions of each other do differ from each other noticeably, even when dispositions of equivalent value are considered. They do not differ merely in their effect as do any two harmonic entities that are in some way related or at least are not too far removed from each other. The difference lies deeper, even though it may not be very great. This suggests that in addition to the dissonant characteristic, which can be softened to various degrees, chords also possess another important sonic characteristic. This we will designate the *family characteristic*. It is based on the observation that all musical thought and consciousness, and thus also harmonic thought and consciousness, are founded on the major and minor triads. This observation is factually supported by the structure of the tempered chromatic system.

Although the softening consonant components may occur separately in simpler chords, in more complex chords they unite to form major or minor triads. The difference between major and minor triads does not consist in which consonant components they contain, but rather in the manner in which these components are arranged. The relation between major and minor triads also obtains between all other chords that are mutual inversions. Just as the minor triad is the inversion of the major, a more complex (e.g., four-note or five-note) chord containing a major triad will have as its inverted counterpart an equally complex chord containing a minor triad. The relation between two chords that are mutual inversions is best described as the relation of two formations with equal value but contrasting orientation – *positive* and *negative*.

The presence of the major or minor triad in a more complex chord gives the chord as a whole the family characteristic of the respective triad. For example, the character of the chord E G C* D 223 containing the triad C E G is major. The character of the chord D E A* C 322 (the inversion of the previous chord) is minor, because the chord contains the minor triad A C E. Naturally, the family characteristic of a chord can be emphasized or disguised by its actual disposition. It should especially be noted that the family characteristic of a more complex chord is more distinctly perceptible when the characterizing consonant triad is placed as low as possible in the chord, when its notes are not separated from each other by any pitches not belonging to the triad, and when the root is at the bottom.

Since major and minor triads are asymmetrical, chords containing only one of them must also be asymmetrical. More complex chords containing different numbers of these triads (e.g., two major, one minor) will likewise be asymmetrical.

Family characteristics can mutually permeate more complex chords, whereas in simpler chords the family characteristic may not be completely or unambiguously expressed. A chord containing both a major and a minor triad can be said to have a *composite family characteristic*, or to belong to *both families*. A chord that does not contain either consonant triad in its complete form can be referred to as having an *indefinite* or *incomplete* family characteristic, or as belonging to neither family. For example, the symmetrical chord C E G B* 143 contains the major triad C E G and the minor triad E G B; it thus belongs to both families, that is, it has a composite family characteristic, major/minor or minor/major. On the other hand, the chord C D B* 12 belongs to neither family – it has an indefinite family characteristic – since it contains neither a major nor a minor triad.

Asymmetrical chords belonging to neither family can of course be inverted. Such chords that are mutual inversions will differ from each other in their effect in the same way as do chords that are mutual inversions and that do have a definite family characteristic. It should be noted that sometimes an asymmetrical chord belonging to neither family can be supplemented, perhaps only by a single pitch, to become a richer symmetrical chord that contains the inversion of the original. Such an asymmetrical chord will differ only slightly from its inversion. We can see this, for example, in comparing the three-note chords C E B and C G B, which are mutual inversions belonging to neither family; there is as little difference between them as there is between either of them and the four-note chord C E G B, which is symmetrical and belongs to both families. The difference between the sounds of the three-note chords C D B and C A B is equally negligible, because although they are mutual inversions, they both represent the four-note chord C D A B, which contains them both.

For the designation of chords belonging to one of the two opposing families, we can use positive and negative symbols: + (plus sign) for the major family, − (minus sign) for the minor.[36]

A clear differentiation of family is useful especially when dealing with chords of lower classes – four-note and five-note chords. In multi-note chords, the interrelated effects of multiple major and minor components are so pronounced that only the actual disposition, placing one of these triadic components at the bottom, determines the prevailing family characteristic of the chord; however, the characteristic can never be determined so convincingly as in four-note or five-note chords.

The family characteristics of chord-types shown in the examples in *Chapter I* are evident from the square brackets ⌐⌐ designating major triads, the curved lines ⌒ designating minor triads, and in some cases from the absence of both, which indicates chords belonging to neither family.

The following table shows the distribution of family characteristic in all chord-types:

Chord-classes	Number of chords with each family characteristic				Total
	Neither	+	−	±	
2-note	6				6
3-note	17	1	1		19
4-note	28	6	6	3	43
5-note	21	12	12	21	66
6-note	9	9	9	53	80
7-note	1	1	1	63	66
8-note				43	43
9-note				19	19
10-note				6	6
11-note				1	1
12-note				1	1
total	82	29	29	210	350

---

36 Oettingen and later Riemann designate major by the sign + and minor by a zero. Since major and minor are musical opposites, however, it is better to adopt the positive and negative symbols that are already in common use, as was suggested in Czechoslovakia by Čeněk Strouhal in his *Akustika*, 195. Here the former professor of physics at the Charles University in Prague argues with Oettingen. Strouhal writes: "The designation +, −, which alone is correct and clear, being directly connected with logarithmic pitches which are positive in one direction (upward) and negative in the other (downward), has not been introduced because there is a clash here with the entirely inappropriate designation for the pitch a comma higher […] Oettingen places opposite the + sign the index 0, which […] has a completely different meaning mathematically (the exponent zero)."
Helmholtz designated the comma by a dash placed above or below the name of the pitch, depending on whether the pitch was higher or lower by a comma. Helmholtz's symbol is not a minus sign, however, as it is not written in front of the pitch symbol. Moreover, confusion of the two is impossible, as there is no place for considering commas when dealing with chords used in music.

From the table it is evident that the five-note chord-class contains the greatest variety of family. While chords belonging to neither family predominate in the lower classes, only chords with a composite family characteristic are possible in the highest classes.

§22. Increasing the Dissonant Characteristic

The characteristic given by a certain dissonant element can be *increased* by stacking two or more dissonant elements of the same kind on top of each other in a chord. Here we must find out whether such a process relating to the tone material, results in substantial changes in the sound. We would naturally suppose that since the sound of a semitone element and hence the sound of a chord containing it have a piercing quality, the sound of a chord containing two semitone elements would be considerably more piercing. (If we were to consider the quality "piercing" to be measurable, we would almost expect the chord containing two semitones to be twice as piercing.) The supposition that the measure of the dissonant characteristic is linearly dependent on the number of dissonant elements of the same kind that are present, however, is undermined in all actual cases by the principle that has been demonstrated above in §20. When attempting to add another element of the same kind to a chord that contains a dissonant element, new pitches must be used; these then form not only new *consonant components* with the pitches of the original chord, but sometimes also new dissonant elements of a different kind. The new consonant components which come into play bring with them their *softening effect*, while any new dissonant elements lead to the *merging of elements* (which will be discussed below in §23). Thus chords with two or more dissonant elements of the same kind will not be significantly but only slightly more expressive than chords with only one such dissonance. Any addition of pitches to a chord, however, puts the chord in a higher chord-class, so chords that have been enriched in this way always have a fuller, more substantial sound. They need not, however, be higher in tension or energy.

Even the evolution of modern harmonic thought indirectly supports this. The harmonic material used in classic and romantic music needed to be enriched (i.e., increased in dissonance) only slightly in order for it to grow to formidable proportions in a comparatively short period of time. The first impulse of a mild increase in dissonance was sufficient to open the floodgates for the growth of dissonant harmonic material, which then followed of its own momentum. As it is possible to become accustomed to the common use of a chord with one or two dissonant characteristics, it is quite easy to become accustomed to chords in which dissonant elements are multiplied. The number of possible chords is thus increased, although there is no further substantial increase in the measure of dissonance. Differences of sound between complex chords and those that are even more complex are merely a matter of nuance.

Increasing a dissonant characteristic can be followed as an isolated process only in a few specific instances. Usually this process is inseparable from the merging of various characteristics. The same principles apply in such cases, however. Concrete examples of *genuine increases* will be given here.

The *semitone dissonant element* can only be increased once, and in only one way, if merging with other elements is not to take place, as shown in Example 8.

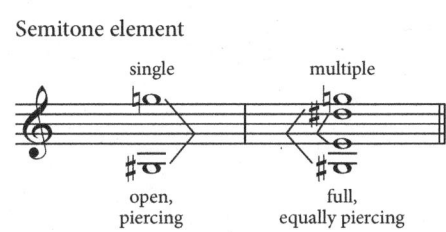

Example 8

When we attempt to find another chord with two semitones, we can arrive at the four-note chord G♯ C B G by adding the semitone C B to the initial semitone G♯ G. Analysis will show, however, that this chord is of the same type as the four-note chord given above:

Example 9

Since Example 9b involves a different disposition from 9a, the sound will also be somewhat different – not quite as good in 9b as in 9a; this difference, which is barely perceptible, results merely from the different disposition and transposition of the same chord-type.

The *whole-tone dissonant element* can be *increased once in two ways and twice in one way*.

Example 10

In looking for other chords with more than one whole-tone element, we only arrive at formations that represent other dispositions and transpositions of chord-types already found.

Example 11

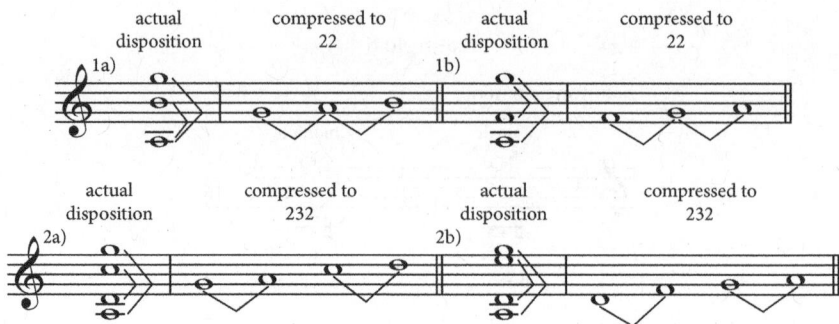

The dispositions of chords 22 and 232 labeled b are different, but their sonic effects have approximately equal value – both are good.

The *tritone dissonant element* can be genuinely increased only once and in only one way.

Example 12

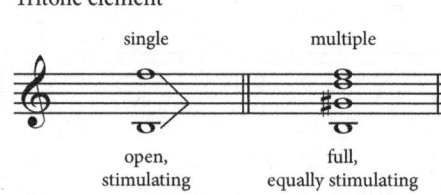

The pitches in all the examples given here are purposely distributed so that the first dissonant interval encloses all the other dissonant intervals. Individual dissonant intervals are marked separately. With each increase, consonant components come into play; these are either all full (involving the third) or both full and open (involving also the fifth). In the case of each element, and of each chord that contains increase of the element, a brief characterization of the effect is noted. The effects of simply increasing the density of chords (progressing from two-note chords to three-note, four-note, and five-note chords) are differentiated from the effects of increasing the dissonant elements. We have shown that none of the increases of two-note elements is accompanied by increased tension, at least not to any significant extent.

When we finally turn to the dissonant element represented by the *augmented triad*, we must conclude that a *genuine increase is impossible*. The addition of any pitch to the augmented triad forms a new dissonant interval. Thus the examples of genuine increases must be limited to simple dissonant elements (two-note chords).

§23. Merging of Dissonant Characteristics

The joint effect of different dissonant characteristics in a chord can be designated as their *merging*. Two, three, or even all four dissonant elements can be merged in a chord. If individual elements are designated by the simple symbols 1 (semitone), 2 (whole-tone), 6 (tritone), and 0 (augmented triad), combinations arising from various ways of merging these elements can be designated by the following compound symbols:[37]

a) combination possibilities of two elements: 12, 16, 01, 26;
b) combination possibilities of three elements: 126, 012, 016, 026;
c) combination possibilities of all four elements: 0126.[38]

Each of these nine combination possibilities can be illustrated by concrete examples of chord-types, of which we can study the sound, and which we can compare with each other, evaluate, and characterize. This indispensable process, demanding detailed and intimate knowledge of the extensive material, knowledge supported by living practice, cannot be described here step by step.

However, the results of this process, which can be verified, are important. The following two *general observations* constitute the most important results of this investigation:

1) *Individual dissonant elements* have their own typical effect on all chord-types in whose formation they are involved, whether they are single or increased. The more *complex* a chord-type is, however, and the more dissonant elements of different kinds it contains, the *less effect* each individual element (whether single or increased) will have. The dissonant characteristics of chords belonging to lower classes are therefore more pronounced than those of higher (and especially the highest) classes. It is practically meaningless to speak of the dissonant characteristic of complex multi-note chords.
2) The use of certain combinations of elements produces a *leap in quality*, so that to the four dissonant elements defining the dissonant characteristic of a chord, these combinations must be added as *factors equivalent to the elements*. The combinations in question are those of a increased semitone element with a whole-tone element (12) or with an increased tritone element (16); these combinations will be designated as the *semitone clash of semitone elements* and the *semitone clash of tritone elements*. (These are discussed further in §24 below.)

We will now examine the behaviour of the individual elements when they are merged with other elements. Since the whole-tone element always has the role of a secondary

---

[37] For simplicity, the augmented triad will be designated by the simple symbol 0 rather than the compound symbol 44.
[38] Editor's note: The form of these symbols is that of orientation schemes, but there is little chance of confusion because of the context in which they are used and because only one of them – 12 – actually designates a chord-type; of course 0 does not appear in orientation schemes. These symbols do not specify the *number* of occurrences of each type of dissonant element in a chord.

component, the observations that follow will be divided into only three groups, according to the three elements involved – the semitone, the tritone, and the augmented triad. The two types of semitone clash will not be dealt with yet.

a) The *semitone element*, whether single or increased, always has a very *piercing effect* in the sound of a chord that contains it. Its presence determines the chord's *basic character* (acute tension). When the semitone is present, all other dissonant elements retreat into the background, and their characteristics assume a merely supplementary role. This may be verified by comparing the sound of chords that contain (besides other elements) the semitone with the sound of chords from which the semitone element is absent. (Of the nine possible combinations of elements given above, only two – 26 and 026 – do not include the semitone. The semitone is, in the main, absent only from chords of lower classes: from 10 of the nineteen three-note chords, from 10 of the forty-three four-note chords, from 3 of the 66 five-note chords, and from only one of the 80 six-note chords.) The dominating effect of the semitone element is especially clear when it merges with the whole-tone element, as shown in Example 13.

Example 13

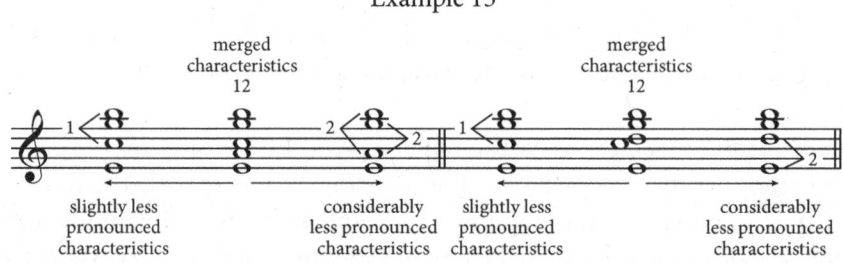

The chord with only the semitone characteristic does not differ nearly as much from the chord with the merged characteristic 12 as does the chord with only the whole-tone characteristic.

b) The *tritone element*, when acting in connection with the other dissonant elements, has a *softening effect*. The tritone characteristic rounds off a sound that has been made acutely tense by the semitone characteristic; it pleasantly colours the grey blur of the chord governed by the whole-tone characteristic and refines the conspicuously penetrating augmented triad. This meliorative effect of the tritone element is very important. It has always been much used, and to great advantage. It has had a far-reaching effect on the evolution of harmonic thought. Whenever composers have had the choice, they have given preference to chords that contain the tritone over chords that do not.

The effect of the tritone element on the character of a chord that already contains other dissonant elements refutes most conclusively the traditional and erroneous claim that dissonances of different qualities can simply be added together. The following musical example shows the minor-minor seventh chord A C E G, characterized only by the whole-tone element, and the major-minor (dominant seventh) chord A C♯ E G and the diminished-minor seventh chord A C E♭ G, both of which contain also the tritone element. Although each of the two latter chords has two dissonant intervals, their effect is softer and more integrated than that of the dull and unrefined minor-minor chord, which has only one dissonant interval, as shown in Example 14.

Example 14

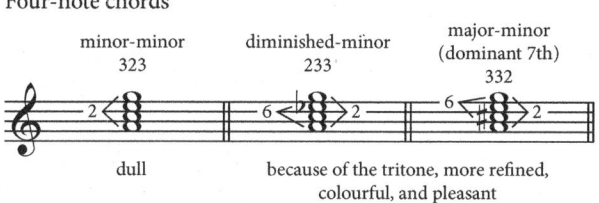

When we compare chords that are characterized only by the semitone with chords that contain the tritone as well, we find the same difference in effect, as shown in Example 15.

Example 15

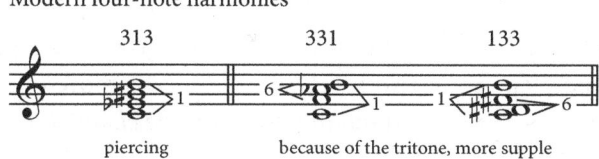

Many chords are influenced by the tritone; of the 43 four-note chord-types, more than half (23) contain the tritone element.

c) The *augmented triad element* (44 or 0), although it represents only a secondary component in connection with other dissonant elements, always contributes distinctly greater *tension* to the sound of a chord. This is especially evident in chords that are not too complex, as for example the four-note chords in Example 16.

Example 16

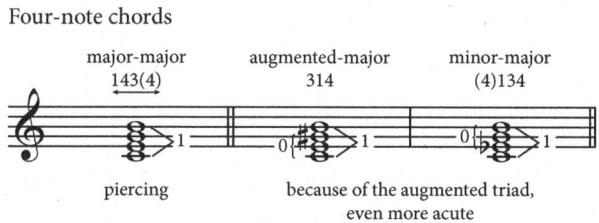

A similar relation is obtained between chords with a merged semitone and tritone characteristic on the one hand, and those that include also the augmented triad characteristic, as shown in Example 17.

Example 17

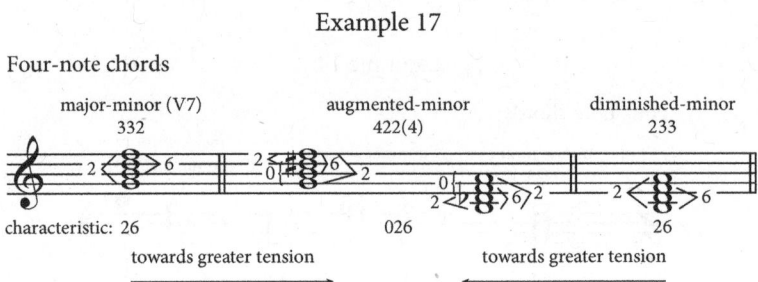

The characteristic 26 represents a mild, pleasantly coloured dissonance, while 026 represents a dissonance with more flavour and more tension (although not piercing). It should be noted that both given four-note chords with the characteristic 026 are of the same chord-type.[39]

§24. Semitone Clash of Semitone and Tritone Elements

We can genuinely increase individual dissonant elements only in isolated instances; usually the increased element is also merged with one or more of the other elements. Thus of the six chords obtained by *doubling the semitone element*, only one represents a genuine increase as shown in Example 18.

Example 18

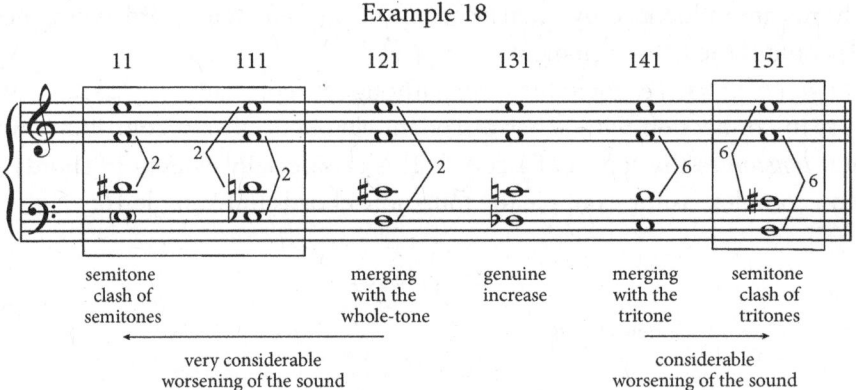

None of the chords shown here is a classical harmony. Chord 131, which makes use of the genuine increase of the semitone element, sounds full and firm although harsh; this is due to the softening effect of its four consonant components, the full consonances

---

39 The following fact is useful for quick orientation: when any note lying a whole-tone away from any note of an augmented triad is added to the augmented triad, the same chord-type always results.

D♭ F, D♭ E, and C E, and the open consonance C F. Close to this chord in sonic value are its nearest neighbours: chord 121, which includes also the here insignificant whole-tone element D E, and chord 141, which includes also the welcome tritone element but has at the same time a preponderance of ineffective open consonant components. The sound of the other chords is considerably worse, that is, harsher; chords 11 and 111 especially are noted for their dissonant harshness.

The pronounced difference in sound between the two groups of chords – 11, 111, and 151 as opposed to 121, 131, and 141 – leads to another observation: the particular way in which elements are merged is another *significant factor in the sound of a chord-type*. The process is no longer that of simple increase, which has been shown essentially not to lead to a sound of increased intensity, nor that of merging, to which the usual principles would otherwise apply. Rather, a *qualitative change* occurs here. Two semitone elements a semitone apart (as in the chord 11) and two tritone elements a semitone apart (as in the chord 151) represent the *intervention of a new factor*. Thus it is necessary to refer to the *semitone clash of semitone elements* and *the semitone clash of tritone elements* as factors *equivalent to the elements themselves*.

Since the clash of semitones is designated by the symbol 11, the clash of tritones can be similarly designated by 66. The compound symbol 11 is at the same time the orientation scheme of the simplest (that is, three-note) chord representing the clash of semitones. The orientation scheme of the simplest chord representing the clash of tritones (151) is too complex, however, and does not immediately and distinctly show that it involves tritones. Therefore we will use instead the simpler symbol 66, preferable because it conveys more information; as the symbol 66 cannot be an orientation scheme (66 = 6, a single tritone), there can be no misunderstanding.

We should further note that in the chord 111 an *increased clash of semitones* occurs: two clashes of semitones are present in this chord (11 + 11). As in increasing the elements themselves, we can observe no substantial worsening of the sound here.

When we systematically *increase the whole-tone element*, we find only two chords that represent a genuine increase as shown in Example 19.

Example 19

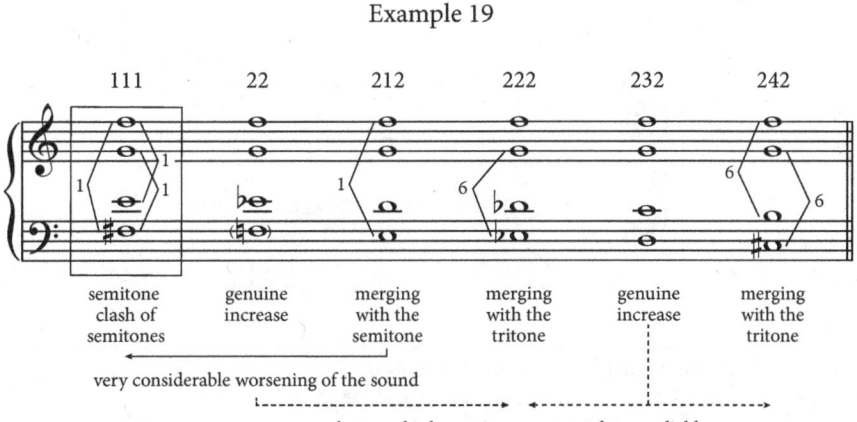

Two of the chords shown are classical harmonies: 222 is an incomplete dominant major ninth, and 242 is a major-minor seventh chord with a lowered fifth (enharmonically C♯ E♯ G B).[40] The chord 111 differs very noticeably from the others in its harshness. It involves whole-tone elements a semitone apart. It is a chord-type already familiar from Example 18, however, where it was identified as representing an increased clash of semitones.[41] Thus there is no need to speak of the semitone clash of whole-tones, as its effect can be obtained by other means.

The *tritone element* can be genuinely increased in only one way, as shown in Example 20.

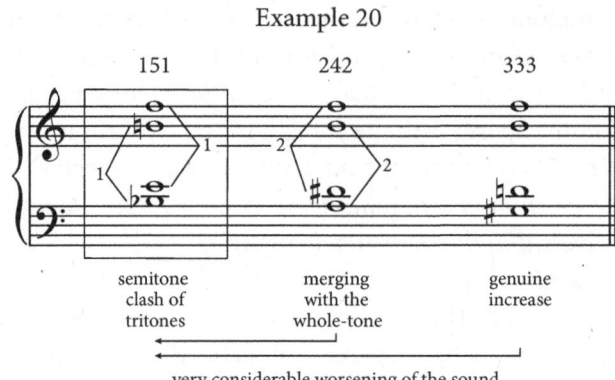

Example 20

The chord 333 is the familiar, long-overused diminished-seventh chord. The chord 242 (B D♯ F A or F A C♭ E♭) appeared in Example 19. The chord 151 appeared in Example 18. It is the simplest chord in which the *semitone clash of tritones* occurs, and so it acts as a representative of this phenomenon. Its sound is very discordant, even if somewhat less so than the sound of chords 11 and 111. Its unpleasant piercing quality is lessened only when it is concealed in a more complex chord, or when its pitches are widely dispersed. (The disposition in Example 18 sounds somewhat better than that in Example 19, as it is more dispersed.)

The increase of the *augmented triad element* is always accompanied by merging as shown in Example 21.

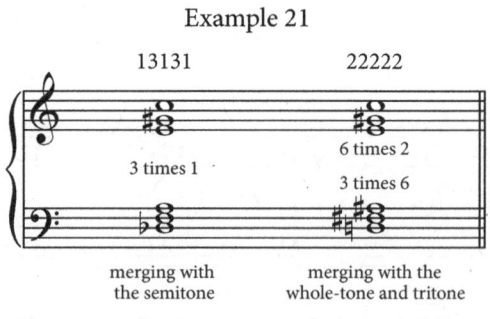

Example 21

---

40 Editor's note: This is the French augmented-sixth chord.
41 Editor's note: That is, C D C♯ D♯ is the same as C C♯ D D♯.

The sonic effects of both these six-note chord-types – the only chord-class in which the augmented triad can be increased – are consistent with their characteristic as well as with their chord-class. Although the chord 13131 contains two augmented triads sounding a semitone apart, the worsening of the sound, which characterized the clashes of semitones or tritones, does not characterize this chord nearly so much. Therefore the clash of augmented triads does not deserve separate evaluation.

From this investigation it follows that, in addition to the dissonant elements, two types of clash, the semitone and the tritone, must be considered. These clashes are *composite phenomena*: they involve increased and merged elements. Unlike its appearance in other situations, the increase of the semitone element here signifies a pronounced sharpening of dissonance. The usual meliorative effect of the tritone element is lost when the tritone is increased, due to the semitone clash. In both types of semitone clash, the *semitone has the leading role*, demanding the most attention.

As was noted above with respect to chord 111, when the semitone clash is increased, there is no substantial worsening of the sound. In this respect, the behaviour of both types of clash is the same as that of the individual elements. It is the presence of a clash in a chord that is fundamentally important, rather than the extent of its increase.

§25. Summary

We have examined here the sonic effects of chords. Familiarity with the entire realm of chords, from two-note chords to the twelve-note chord, in the tempered chromatic system has been assumed. This investigation is significant because it makes possible the next task, namely, the *classification of the harmonic material*. In this task we will now be able to use as support living sound rather than merely structural symbols.

With the prospect of this further classification of the material, it is necessary to limit the number of criteria for classification to the absolute essentials. The fine differentiation of sound that a composer must consider in composing would render the task of classifying the extensive harmonic material completely unmanageable. For this reason we have had to draw conclusions from the actual state of Western music with respect to the pitch-system in common use, and to cast off any restrictive enharmonic encumbrances. We have limited ourselves to four dissonant elements. We have had to delay the evaluation of the sound of actual dispositions, which we will treat separately. Likewise, we have had to concentrate on well-defined, clearly differentiated effects, while overlooking more subtle nuances. (It is sufficient to acknowledge the *presence* of a particular influential component, while the degree to which it may have been increased is considered negligible.) On the other hand, we could not go to the other extreme and ignore significant differences in sound merely for the sake of simple, straightforward results. We have considered families of chords and the two types of semitone clash.

When we understand the sounds of various chord-types and the differences between them, and when we are familiar with the full extent of the harmonic material, we are able to determine with *what frequency* the various individual properties appear, and so to verify their usefulness and justify their selection.

A table showing the distribution of harmonic material according to family characteristic has been given above in §21. The following table shows the *distribution of dissonant characteristics*; the numbers indicate how many chord-types there are with each characteristic:

The Occurrence of the Four Dissonant Elements and the Two Clashes in All the Chords of the Tempered Chromatic System

Characteristic	Number of notes in chords											Totals	
	2	3	4	5	6	7	8	9	10	11	12		
semitone	1	9	33	63	79	66	43	19	6	1	1	321	350
no semitone	5	10	10	3	1							29	
whole-tone	1	9	33	63	79	66	43	19	6	1	1	321	350
no whole-tone	5	10	10	3	1							29	
tritone	1	5	23	50	74	66	43	19	6	1	1	289	350
no tritone	5	14	20	16	6							61	
augmented triad		1	3	12	29	39	35	19	6	1	1	146	350
no aug. triad	6	18	40	54	51	27	8					204	
semitone clash		1	8	28	54	60	42	19	6	1	1	220	350
no semitone clash	6	18	35	38	26	6	1					130	
tritone clash			1	4	15	25	29	17	6	1	1	99	350
no tritone clash	6	19	42	62	65	41	14	2				251	

Individual characteristics do not appear as isolated phenomena; rather, they are interrelated in various ways. It is especially important to realize that when the clash of semitones is present, the whole-tone is present also, and with the clash of tritones the semitone is present also. There are 20 one possible combinations of characteristics, including the individual characteristics.

The following table shows the numbers of all the possible chords that have the specified dissonant characteristics. It includes also consonances (chords with the negative dissonant characteristic). Characteristics are represented by the following symbols: semitone = 1, whole-tone = 2, tritone = 6, augmented triad = 0, clash of semitones = 11, clash of tritones = 66.

Classification of all Possible Chords According to Dissonant Characteristics

Order	Dissonant characteristic	Number of possible chords	Chord-classes represented
1.	negative	5	2–3
2.	1	8	2–4
3.	2	10	2–5
4.	6	3	2–4
5.	0	1	3
6.	12	13	3–6
7.	16	5	3–4
8.	01	5	4–6
9.	26	7	3–5
10.	126	42	4–7
11.	012	1	5
12.	016	1	5
13.	026	3	4–6
14.	112	15	3–6
15.	166	1	4
16.	0126	16	5–7
17.	0112	3	5–6
18.	1126	57	4–8
19.	1266	9	5–8
20.	01126	56	5–9
21.	11266	29	5–8
22.	011266	60	6–12
	total:	350	

It is apparent that a particular characteristic is represented by just one chord-type only in exceptional cases – 0, 012, 016, 166. The similarity of these isolated chord-types and chord-types with related characteristics is shown by arrows. (This is not shown in the case of the augmented triad, 0, as its exceptional nature has been pointed out more than once.) Consequently, to simplify the system, we can add the isolated chord-types to the groups of chord-types with a similar, whether more or less complex, dissonant characteristic.

Some of the groups contain a large number of chord-types. As long as these include chords of higher classes, no problems are likely to arise, as such chords are generally meaningless in practice. This also applies to the most complex characteristics. The extent of the group with the relatively simple characteristic 126 will seem less confusing when we realize that many chord-types in the group are distinguishable by the method used to construct their individual characteristics. Such details will be dealt with in the following chapter.

Chapter IIIa – Classification of the Harmonic Material

§26. The Concept of a Harmony in Classical Harmony[42]

Classical composers did not consider all sonic cross-sections in music to have equivalent value. They considered those cross-sections that acted as harmonic supports for the musical flow to be *harmonies*, that is, significant harmonic formations. Other cross-sections of sound were considered harmonically secondary; their pitch-structures were not nearly as important as those of the harmonies.

A harmony is a phenomenon conditioned by history. We know this because certain common chord-types evaluated as harmonies by classical composers, such as the dominant seventh chord, could formerly (e.g., in Renaissance music) have appeared only in the subordinate role of dependent harmonic formations that had arisen fortuitously.

The concept of a harmony can be generally defined as follows: it is a *harmonically intelligible* group of pitches, *ranked higher* than formations containing fewer pitches, and it is *independent* of its surroundings.

These criteria differ from each other. The first, *harmonic intelligibility*, is the most general; it deals with a wide range of harmonic phenomena. The second criterion, which *ranks* chords according to importance, rests on the observation from compositional practice that certain chords of different classes, especially neighbouring classes (e.g., four-note and three-note) are mutually interchangeable (as the common G B F* 24 = G B* D F 332). The final criterion, *independence*, rests only on the immediate harmonic surroundings in the music; thus it often happens that the same chord-type functions as a harmony in one part of a composition but not in another, depending on the musical texture.

A) *The intelligibility of a harmony*. The requirement of harmonic intelligibility asserts itself in various ways and produces various results according to the evolutionary stage of musical thought and practice. Thus the intelligibility of a chord is not determined

---

[42] Editor's note: In this chapter, Janeček is concerned with the difference between *souzvuk*, "chord" (simultaneity) and *akord*, "harmony" (harmonically intelligible chord).

by the presence of fixed properties, but neither does it depend on the subjective opinion of each casual listener. Of primary importance is the attitude of *composers* towards a particular chord-type. Their works are the basis for determining their attitudes. What is and what is not harmonically intelligible will be revealed by *careful harmonic analysis of compositions of the historical period*. The material for this analysis must be extensive enough; a few compositions do not suffice.

Music employs various processes; the roles of some are opposed, while others complement each other. Harmonic considerations are not the only factor in the formation of chords. Chords are often simply the harmonic result of the development of melodic lines; the requirement of harmonic intelligibility cannot fully apply to such chords, as they are harmonic only secondarily. Thus the first task of this analysis is to eliminate those chord-types in whose formation other considerations than the purely harmonic played a part. In some compositions this will eliminate a large number of chords, perhaps even the majority. The most important factor will be the extent to which a chord is *melodically conditioned*.

Chords have a purely harmonic effect in the following situations:

1) at the end of a composition or section of a composition that is organically brought to a close;
2) when isolated;
3) in a progression in which each new chord is begun by all voices simultaneously;
4) at the beginning of a composition or of a section of a composition, when all voices enter simultaneously.

Thus these are chords that are not both preceded and followed directly by other chords, or, if they are so preceded and followed, they are chords that rhythmically govern the melodic lines of participating voices and so decrease their melodic significance.

B) *The higher-rank of a harmony*. From a chord with a larger number of pitches, a pitch can be deleted to form a chord with fewer pitches. Although this simpler new chord will be different, its similarity to the chord from which it was derived will often be apparent. It will be ranked lower than the original chord; that is, it will be subordinate to it. *We do not consider a chord to be a harmony if it can be derived from a more complex* (i.e., higher-ranked) *chord whose sound has the same essential character*; in such a case the richer and more complex sound is considered the harmony. (Cf. §28 below.)

C) *The independence of a harmony*. In a harmonic progression formed by melodic lines moving in different rhythms, not all chords are equally independent. Some claim the listener's complete attention, overshadowing the rest. Only those that attract more attention, that form harmonic supports in the musical flow, we consider to be harmonies; they are what remains when ornaments are eliminated from a harmonic

phrase so that all voices move at the same time. In this way the independence of harmonies becomes apparent from their *comparative simplicity* (and resulting intelligibility) *in relation to their harmonic surroundings*. (Cf. §27 below.)
The following distinction should be noted:

1) A harmony is the *most complex* formation of certain harmonic qualities; its derivatives have the same sonic essence but are simpler.
2) In contrast, a harmony in relation to its surroundings is the *simplest* formation in a progression of melodically interdependent chords.

In classical harmonic thought, the principles explained here apply without exception.

§27. Transient Chords

Other harmonic formations than harmonies also appear in music; they are not independent and are generally designated *transient chords*. Their structure may or may not be identical to that of harmonies commonly used in a particular style. That these transient chords are not *independent* is apparent *in the continuous musical flow*; here, those components that distinguish transient chords from commonly used harmonies are precisely the components that are subject to specific principles of voice-leading.[43] Transient chords function as temporarily altered or complicated formations closely related to harmonies; these abnormal formations contrast vividly with the harmonies from which they have been derived, ideally by direct juxtaposition. The harmonies are changed or complicated by various *non-harmonic tones*: suspensions and appoggiaturas,[44] passing tones, auxiliary tones, anticipations, and pedal points. According to the type of non-harmonic tone that comes into play, one can speak of suspended and appoggiatura, passing, auxiliary, anticipatory, and pedal chords. Foreign pitches introduce harmonic tension into a chord; this must be relieved by their *resolution*, that is, by the specific voice-leading mentioned above.

In contrast to transient chords, harmonies function as separate entities independent of neighbouring chords. They are independent in that the voice-leading of their component pitches is harmonically free.

Musicians, however, know that in a tonal harmonic phrase, a phrase in which there is a sense of tonality, all harmonies are related to the tonic harmony (whether the primary or a temporary, secondary, local tonic) as their assumed center. In relation to this tonic harmony, whose existence can sometimes only be suspected, certain chord tones appear foreign; they are thus no longer free in terms of voice-leading, and they require

---

43 Editor's note: In other words, the non-harmonic tone that distinguishes a transient chord from a (functional) harmony is characterized by its need to resolve in a certain way; thus the need for F♯ to resolve to G keeps the chord E♭ F♯ B♭ from being heard as a minor tonic in E-flat major, as in m. 27 of Beethoven's *Op. 10/1/II*.
44 Editor's note: The Czech word *průtah*, meaning "delay", refers to both suspensions and appoggiaturas.

resolution. Such chord-tones requiring resolution are the leading-tone, the seventh in a dominant seventh, the added sixth in the subdominant chord, etc. The resolution is required for *tonal* rather than harmonic reasons, that is, it has to do with the prevailing tonic rather than with the chord itself in relation to its immediate harmonic surroundings.

A harmonic phrase or even an entire composition can be composed using harmonies only. Transient chords, however, can occur only in connection with harmonies. A phrase cannot be made entirely of transient chords.

§28. Incomplete Harmonies

The system of classical harmony does not include two-note chords. All two-note chords, however, are contained in three- or four-note chords; therefore classical harmony designates them *incomplete* three or four-note harmonies. With the omission of one or as many as two pitches, the harmony becomes less definite; sometimes it loses some of its characteristic sound. Thus the major third (C E) can be understood according to its context as an incomplete major triad (C E G) or minor triad (A C E), or possibly even augmented triad (C E G♯); in the last case the major third itself does not, of course, contain the dissonant characteristic of the chord it represents. The minor seventh (G F) can be understood as an incomplete dominant seventh chord (G B D F) or diminished-minor (G B♭ D♭ F) or minor-minor seventh chord (G B♭ D F), or possibly even augmented-minor seventh chord (G B D♯ F) or major-minor seventh with diminished fifth (G B D♭ F).

This ambiguity of incomplete harmonies often disappears when their harmonic surroundings are considered. Thus in a harmonic phrase that remains consistently in C major, the seventh G F will definitely represent the dominant seventh chord G B D F and no other. In A-flat major, on the other hand, this same seventh G F will represent only the diminished-minor seventh chord G B♭ D♭ F.

In order to declare a harmonic formation to be an incomplete harmony, its sound must be obviously close in character to that of the complete harmony. This has primarily to do with the *dissonant characteristics* of the chords compared, which must be *essentially the same*. Thus we cannot say that the triad C E G represents an incomplete four-note chord A C E G or C E G B♭, since dissonant components that are not present in the triad play a prominent role in both of these four-note chords: in A C E G the whole-tone A G, and in C E G B♭ the tritone E B♭ and the whole-tone C B♭. We can say, however, that the three-note chord A E G represents the four-note chord A C E G, and that the three-note chord C E B♭ represents the four-note chord C E G B♭, since there is no substantial difference in sound between the related three-note and four-note chords, as they have the same dissonant characteristic.[45]

The introduction of the concept of incomplete harmonies and the differentiation between harmonies and transient chords have made the system of classical harmony

---

45 Editor's note: This paragraph was moved from the beginning of §88.

simple and straightforward. The attempt to establish incomplete harmonies and transient chords as theoretically equivalent to complete harmonies[46] was doomed to failure because it was inconsistent with compositional practice. The system of classical harmony did not result from mere theoretical speculation; rather, it arose through observation and detailed study of living music. And in living music it is easily proved that an incomplete harmony represents a complete one, since the addition of the missing pitch in no way changes the chord's harmonic function.

§29. The Formation of New Harmonies

In a harmonic phrase, transient chords are normally interspersed among complete or incomplete harmonies. Phrases containing only harmonies are less common; no composition of any substantial size can limit itself to harmonies. Transient chords have also been important in introducing dissonant elements, without which the creation of attractive compositions would be impossible.

The melodic origin of transient chords decreases their harmonic significance. This does not mean, however, that their presence in a harmonic phrase passes unobserved. Had they no harmonic effect, it would not matter how they were formed harmonically. It is apparent from composition, however, that their structure is not arbitrary. Each style has defined and established its own circle of transient chords; stepping outside this circle gives the impression that stylistic principles have been seriously violated. It would be unthinkable, for example, for the triple suspension C F♭ F♯ B resolving to C E♭ G C to appear in a classical composition, even if the usual rules for the resolution of non-harmonic tones were obeyed in the same way as in the common progression C F A♭ B to C E♭ G C.

Thus transient chords take part in creating the harmonic character of a composition together with harmonies whose role is that of supporting pillars. Therefore, when at the close of the romantic period the need to create new harmonies was felt, there was no simpler solution than to turn to transient chords, make them independent, and so transform them into harmonies. Thus the two levels of harmonic material, harmonies and transient chords, as found in the music of one period give direction for the evolution of the next one.

The following example shows the process, somewhat abbreviated here, of forming new harmonies

---

46 Such an attempt was made in Czechoslovakia by František Zdeněk Skuherský, *Nauka o harmonii na vědeckém základě ve formě nejjednodušší* [Theory of Harmony with Scientific Foundations in its Simplest Form] (Praha: Fr. A. Urbánek, 1885).

Example 22

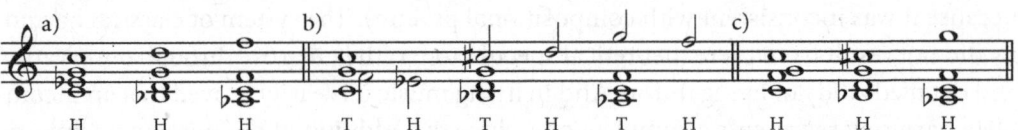

The progression of the three triads in Example 22a is common in classical style. In 22b, the individual harmonies of this progression are decorated with appoggiaturas, creating transient chords, marked "T". Each of these transient chords is properly resolved to form a harmony, marked "H". The transient chords from Example 22b are given the role of harmonies in 22c. The harmonic progression shown in 22c would not be considered the least unusual in modern music, although of course it could never be found in the music of the classical style. To the listener of the classical period it would appear harmonically unintelligible; to a modern listener it might appear unclassical, but it would be intelligible.

§30. The Concept of a Harmony in Modern Harmony

Only a very limited number of harmonies was known in classical harmony. Other chords that appeared were considered either transient chords or incomplete harmonies. Theoretical reasons for such an organization of harmonic material can be given, but it has the valuable practical advantages of simplicity and clarity. Thus when we consider modern harmony, with 350 chord-types at its disposal, it is necessary to organize and classify this extensive material so that it at least begins to be manageable. For practical reasons it is impossible to consider each of the 350 chord-types as an independent harmony.

Experience gained through classical harmony can provide guidelines for classification. The three criteria used for the classification of harmonies in classical music have been mentioned: intelligibility, rank, and independence. The measure of intelligibility today has shifted considerably towards more complex and tonally richer chords, but not so far as to permit all chord-types to be considered potential harmonies. It will be possible to add to the sum of recognized classical harmonies a substantial number of modern harmonies, although for the time being exact numbers will not be given and the measure of intelligibility will not be precisely defined.

It is only natural that even in modern music, besides harmonies, we find harmonic formations that are not independent but rather are conditioned by the melodic progression of voices; these are transient chords. As in classical harmony, these will consist primarily of rich and complex chord-types that can only rarely be used independently in the sense of harmonies.

For understanding the essential harmonic flow of music, the differentiation between harmonies and transient chords is equally crucial in modern and classical harmony. This differentiation affects harmonic theory in a practical sense: it ensures the reducibility of the inexhaustible material to more manageable proportions. The relative degree of this reduction cannot be substantially greater, however, than in classical harmony. In view of the extreme growth of the material, which today includes all the possibilities of the tempered chromatic system, this reduction alone is not sufficient to allow a classification clear and concise enough to make the excessive material reasonably manageable for practical purposes.

Thus we will have to use a second observation verified from classical harmony: various chord-types of similar sound can be drawn together and governed by one representative chord that is ranked higher than the rest.

This has so far been only roughly investigated in practice. We could consistently apply the classical principle regarding representation, and always declare the *most complex* chord-type of a particular character to be a *harmony*. (See above, §26.) We could accept this rigorous process as long as the chords thus designated fulfilled the most fundamental requirement: that they be *harmonically intelligible*. A problem arises, however, when we attempt to build up hierarchies of harmonies and their subordinate chords according to the classical example. It soon becomes evident that the resulting harmonies are often far too complex to be harmonically intelligible at present.

Therefore classical method must be modified: the most complex formations can be considered harmonies only in those groups of related chords in which these formations are still sufficiently intelligible harmonically; elsewhere, it will be necessary to shift the representative rank of harmony to a simpler chord-type that has greater harmonic intelligibility. In contrast to the common classical method of classification, which always places the harmony in the highest class, in modern harmony the harmony may at times belong to one of the lower classes.

The possibilities of modern classification that arise from these considerations are illustrated in Diagram 1.

The classical conception is shown in a. This conception can also be valid in modern harmony, as long as the harmony, the highest ranked representative of the group, is fully intelligible. Intelligibility as a requirement for every harmony necessitates also the situations in b and c, where the harmonies are not border formations[47] in the highest chord-class but rather belong to a lower class; c represents the opposite conception from the classical, as the harmony here is the border formation in the lowest class. *The harmonies in the three groups are aligned.*

---

47 Editor's note: *Border formation* is a chord in the highest or lowest class (i.e., with the most or fewest pitches) in which a particular harmony and its related forms are represented.

Diagram 1

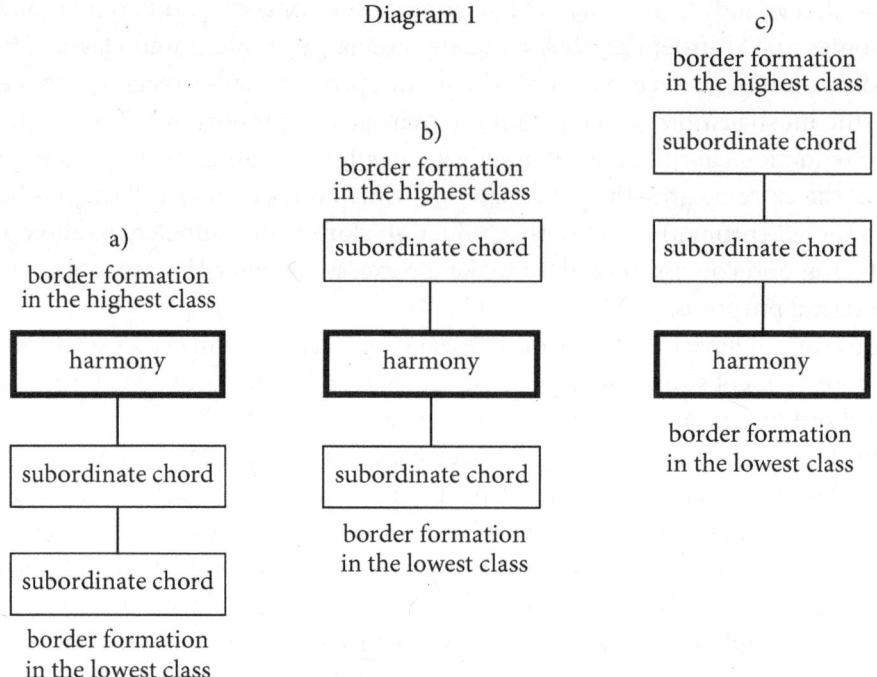

Obviously, the modification does not contradict the classical system of classification, but expands it and makes it more general. The most important aspect of classical practice has been retained, namely, the hierarchical arrangement of chords into sonically-related groups. Within these groups, harmonies are sometimes found in the highest, richest classes, as in the classical conception, but sometimes in lower classes, as long as the sonic essence remains the same; in extreme cases, they are found even in the relatively simplest classes.

In the proposed future system of modern harmonies, differences arising between harmony-types on the basis of chord-class will not be very substantial. Harmonies will belong to classes from three notes up to approximately six notes. Were we to insist that a harmony be always the most complex formation within a particular characteristic, the spread between classical and simple modern harmonies on the one hand and complex modern harmonies on the other would be too great – all the way from three notes to twelve notes.

Modifying the classical conception of harmonies in this way results in a change significant for the derivation of chords that are subordinate to the harmonies: not only can an *incomplete* harmony be formed by omitting pitches, but a *"thickened"* harmony, i.e., one belonging to a higher class, can be formed by adding pitches. (Here the use of a term that was happily introduced in Czechoslovakia by Leoš Janáček is justified.)

Thus we can replace the designation "subordinate chord" in Diagram 1 with the term "incomplete harmony" for a chord belonging to a class lower than that of the harmony, and with "thickened harmony" for a chord belonging to a higher class.

§31. The Concept of the Characteristic Maximum

Although the general requirement of intelligibility justifies shifting the *harmony* (the representative of a group of sonically related entities) from the highest class to lower classes, we cannot establish principles for this procedure that would apply without exception, because compositional practice, widespread and deeply rooted in life, must have the final word. For now, we can only state that certain chords not considered harmonies in classical harmony already have, or soon will have, significance equivalent to representative modern harmonies. Otherwise we can only speak of *potential harmonies*; we can only *presume* that certain chords will eventually achieve the status of harmonies.

Classification is imperative. (We can be content with unclassified material only temporarily – only during the experimental search through the musical repertoire.) Since the concept of the "modern harmony" is so unstable, we cannot use it as a basis for classifying the harmonic material, especially when this includes all the harmonic possibilities of the tempered chromatic system. Therefore we will have to rely on those characteristics that can be *determined objectively*.

The previous chapter dealt with the dissonant and family characteristics of chords. In considering the *dissonant characteristic*, we found groups of chords with related characteristics. These characteristics are objective and verifiable. The chords of each group extend over at least two chord-classes, except, of course, for those groups that contain only one isolated chord-type. (See the second table in §25 above.) The classification of chords according to the number of tones is also an exact procedure. For each group of chords with related characteristics, we can therefore choose (after a discussion) to treat the chord-types of a particular class as representatives of the entire group. The description of the chosen class must be *relative*, not absolute (the highest or lowest class of a particular group, not the three- or four-note class). We will give preference to the class that has *the smallest number* of chord-types with a particular characteristic. Otherwise the classification process would be unnecessarily complicated. The chord-classes at the extremes, the highest and lowest, contain the fewest chord-types; as a rule, the other classes contain a disproportionately large number of chord-types with the same characteristic.

When all the groups with their variously defined characteristics are surveyed (including consonances, whose dissonant characteristic is negative), 51 chords are found in the relatively highest class and 51 in the relatively lowest. There is thus a balance. The chords of the relatively highest class will be chosen as the starting point for the classification according to dissonant characteristic, in keeping with the familiar classical conception of harmonies as representatives of simpler chords. Since a chord that has been given prominence simply because of a practical convention cannot properly be called a "harmony", we create a new term for it: the *characteristic maximum*; this maximum will always be a *chord-type in the highest class*, that is, the *tonally richest* representative of a given dissonant characteristic.[48]

As there are 22 possible dissonant characteristics (including the negative characteristic) and 51 characteristic maxima, it is evident that in some groups of chords with the same dissonant characteristic the highest class contains *several* chords. We will show that only about half the groups are governed by a single characteristic maximum, while as many as six characteristic maxima can be found in the richest groups.

The precise concept of the characteristic maximum is introduced *to take the place of the concept of the modern harmony*, which remains undefined as yet. Certain characteristic maxima will indisputably have the significance of harmonies; we will see that some of them actually are classical harmonies.

Individual characteristic maxima will be designated by **boldface** simple and compound symbols for the corresponding dissonant characteristics. The symbol **6** will thus represent the characteristic maximum with the dissonant characteristic 6, while the compound symbol **126** will represent the maximum with the merged characteristic 126, etc. Whenever more than one maximum with the same characteristic can be distinguished, a superscript number will be added to the symbol, e.g., **126**[1)], **126**[2)], **126**[3)], etc.

Since individual characteristic maxima represent definite chord-types, they can also be designated by their orientation schemes, e.g., **6** = 333, **126**[1)] = 122122, **126**[2)] = 21212, etc.[49] (Further see below, §34, §40, et seq.) The orientation scheme alone does not show that a chord is a maximum; this becomes evident only through analysis. In the same way, we cannot know simply from the characteristic symbols 6, 126, etc., which chord-type with the corresponding characteristic is meant.

§32. The Concept of the Characteristic Nucleus

Beginning with the most complex dissonant formations and progressing towards the simplest, we ultimately reach the border formations known as the dissonant elements. (Cf. §17 above.) If we similarly survey chord-types with a particular dissonant characteristic, from the more complex to the simpler, we likewise reach border formations that are the simplest chord-types of the given dissonant characteristic. They will be designated as *characteristic nuclei*. In the case of single dissonant characteristics, the characteristic nuclei and the individual dissonant elements are identical. The progression from the characteristic maximum to the characteristic nucleus is illustrated in Diagram 2.

---

48 Editor's note: Not all the maxima will be in the highest class, as explained in §40 below. If a lone potential characteristic maximum of the relatively highest class does not contain all the chord-types of lower classes with that characteristic, it does not serve as the only maximum.

49 Editor's note: This last chord, 21212, a segment of the octatonic scale (e.g., C D E♭ F G♭ A♭), is a clear example of the meaning of **126** as opposed to **11266**, as it contains two semitones and two tritones, but not the semitone clash of either interval.

Diagram 2

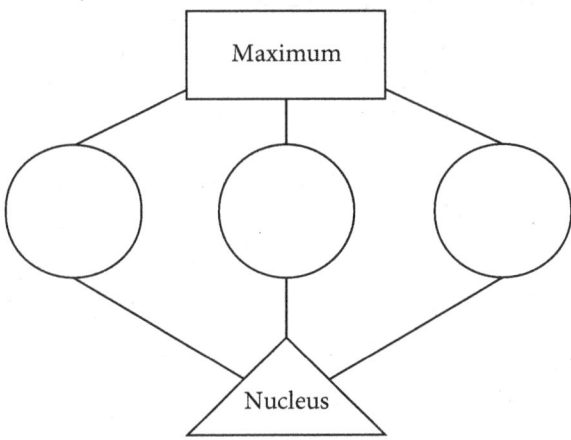

The characteristic maximum represents the most complex chord of a particular characteristic-type, that is, the one belonging to the highest chord-class, while the characteristic nucleus represents the simplest, belonging to the lowest class.[50] Between these two extremes lie the other chord-types with the same characteristic, chord-types that result from simplifying the maximum, or, conversely, from building up the nucleus. Thus they are either incomplete maxima, in the same sense as incomplete harmonies, or thickened nuclei.

In the following diagrams illustrating the regions of sonically related chords, maxima will be shown in boxes, nuclei in triangles, and the other chords derived from the maxima in circles. Some characteristic groups are represented by only one maximum, as in Diagram 2, others by more. The same is true for nuclei. Whenever a chord of a particular characteristic-type cannot be simplified or built up without changing the original character, the maximum and nucleus unite into a single entity.

Diagram 3

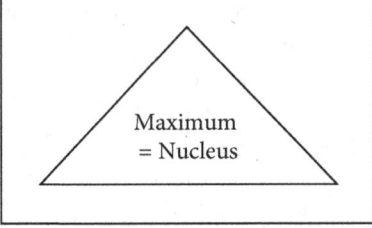

This is true for the four characteristic-types for which there is only one chord-type – 0, 012, 016, and 166. (See the second table in §25 above).

---

50 Editor's note: It will be seen later that different maxima and nuclei for a characteristic-type may be in different chord-classes, that is, not all the maxima, or all the nuclei, for a characteristic-type necessarily have the same number of notes.

§33. Consonant Harmonies as Maxima with the Negative Dissonant Characteristic

The only two consonant harmonies, the major triad 43 and the minor triad 34, have the negative dissonant characteristic. Since there are no more complex chords with the *negative dissonant characteristic*, these are characteristic maxima. Only these two harmonies represent chords of a lower class (two-note chords) that have no dissonant characteristic.

Diagram 4 shows the relation between consonant three-note and two-note chords. In each case, the complement is shown in parentheses below the orientation scheme in order to make the connections between the triad and all its components obvious.

Diagram 4

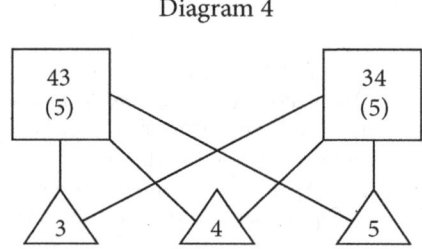

From the diagram it is apparent that the major triad 43 (C E G) contains intervals 3 (E G), 4 (C E), and 5 (C G). These same intervals, 3, 4, and 5, are contained in the minor triad 34 (in A C E: A C, C E, A E).

The two consonant harmonies represent two different characteristic maxima with the negative characteristic. Their *family characteristic* differentiates them from each other. The family characteristic disappears in the component two-note chords (the nuclei), which belong to neither family. (The table in §21 above shows that no two-note chord-type belongs to either family.)

Instead of orientation schemes, we can designate the consonant harmonies by the symbols for family characteristics: + for the major triad, − for the minor triad. (Cf. §21 above and §53 et seq. below.)

§34. The Characteristic Maximum 6

The characteristic-type 6 includes only one characteristic maximum: the symmetrical four-note chord 333, the diminished-seventh chord, i.e. a recognized harmony. Its nucleus is the tritone 6. Only one chord lies between the maximum and the nucleus: the three-note chord 33, which is the diminished triad. The extent of the characteristic-type 6 is illustrated in Diagram 5.

Diagram 5

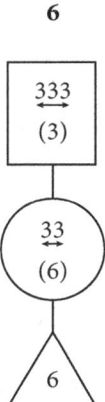

The orientation schemes can be replaced by an actual four-note chord and the three-note and two-note chords derived from it.

Example 23

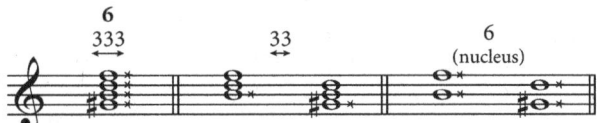

We have already drawn attention to the unusual technical characteristics of maximum **6** (the chord 333) in §8 above, where all four-note chord-types were listed. As a complete chord, this maximum is of no compositional significance in modern harmony. At best it has negative significance – composers avoid it in every way they can. By contrast, its components (the chord 33 and the nucleus 6 itself) are still very much used; they are surprisingly effective representatives of a maximum that has become trite with overuse.

§35. The Characteristic Maximum 2

The dissonant characteristic 2 has a single characteristic maximum, the symmetrical five-note chord 2232. It is a diatonic, more specifically a pentatonic, chord, as it can be formed with the black notes on the piano. It appeared as the second in the survey of five-note chord-types in §9 above (Example 3). Its entire group is shown in Diagram 6.

Diagram 6

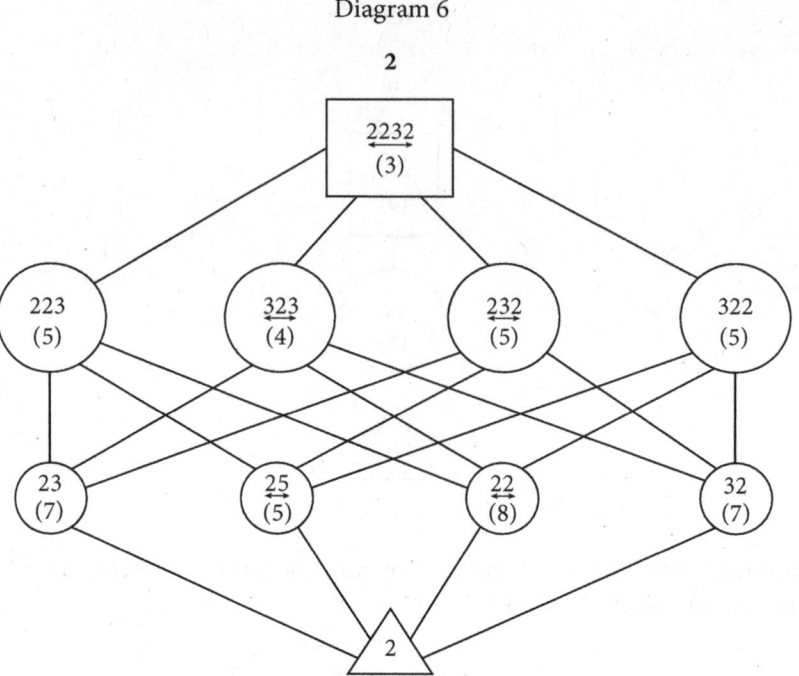

All the chords in the diagram are shown in musical notation in Example 24.

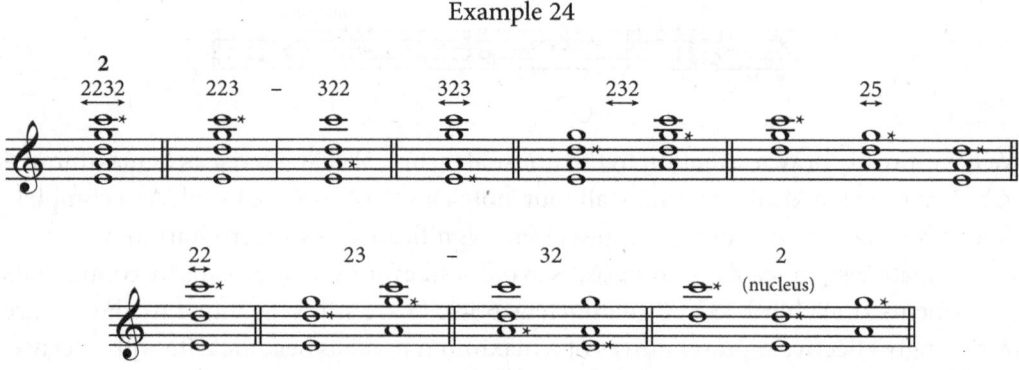

Example 24

When we compare the sounds of the chords, the relation between them is quickly confirmed. The relation between the maximum and its subordinate chords is the same as that between complete and incomplete chords in classical harmony.

The four-note chord 323 is a classical harmony (minor-minor seventh). We perceive the three-note chords 23 – 32 as this same classical harmony type, although incomplete; the same applies to the nucleus 2.[51] We sometimes speak of the maximum (2232) and those of its derivatives that can be arranged in fourths (232, 25) as quartal harmonies. Because

---

51 Editor's note: Depending on the context, 23, 32, and 2 may be understood as incomplete minor-minor or major-minor seventh chords.

the maximum **2** is fully intelligible harmonically, and because of its common use in modern music, we are justified in considering it a *modern harmony*; the other chords that cannot be considered classical complete or incomplete harmonies are incomplete forms of the modern harmony **2**.

§36. Characteristic Maxima 1 and 01

Three maxima represent the characteristic-type 1: **1**¹⁾ is 131, **1**²⁾ is 313, and **1**³⁾ is 143; the characteristic-type 01 is represented only by the maximum **01**, which is 13131. The nucleus of all three maxima **1** is the dissonant element 1 itself; the maximum **01** can be reduced to two four-note nuclei, 134 – 314. The diagrams and musical examples of these two characteristic-types are shown together, as the two types are closely related.

Example 25

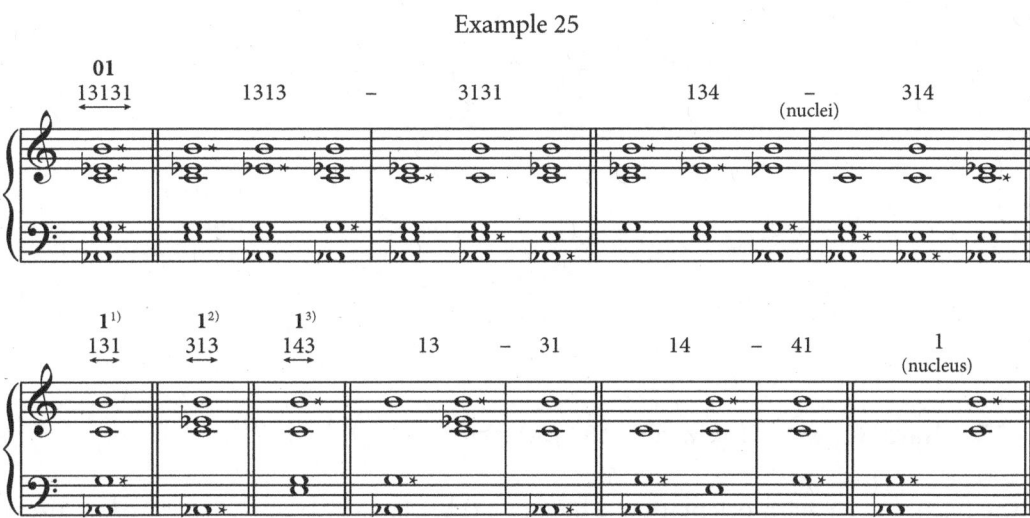

The maximum **01** (the symmetrical six-note chord 13131) occurs in only four transpositions. (See the survey of six-note chord-types above in §11, Example 4.) Each of the chords of lower classes subordinate to it, however, can be transposed twelve times.

The nuclei of the characteristic-type 01, 134 and 314, the minor-major seventh and the augmented-major seventh, are *classical harmonies*, although comparatively rarely used by classical composers. No one can object to conceiving of the chord 1313 as a thickened form of the harmony 134, or the chord 3131 as a thickened form of the harmony 314.[52] Further thickening of 134 and 314, merging the chords 1313 and 3131, which are mutual inversions, leads to the maximum **01** (13131).

---

52 Editor's note: However, the fourth and fifth chords in Example 25, given as examples of 1313 and 3131, are more likely to be heard as thickened forms of the more common 143, the major-major seventh chord.

The maximum **1**³⁾ (143) is a *classical harmony*, the major-major seventh chord, and the other maxima **1**¹⁾ (131) and **1**²⁾ (313) are common enough in modern music to be considered *modern harmonies*.

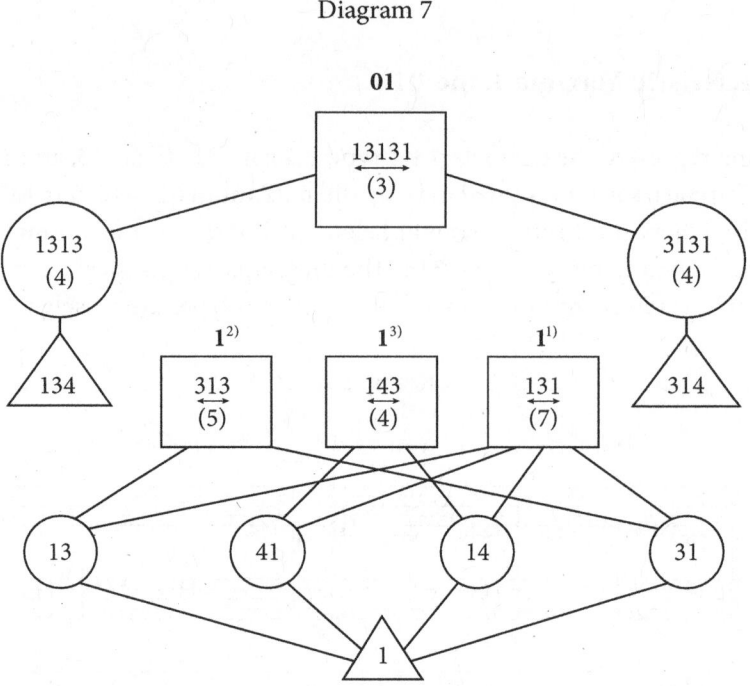

Diagram 7

§37. Characteristic Maxima 0, 26, and 026

The maximum **0**, with orientation scheme 44 (the classical augmented triad), is also a nucleus. It cannot be thickened without the interference of another characteristic, and there is no simpler chord with the same characteristic.

The characteristic-type 26 is represented by two maxima **26**: the symmetrical five-note chord 2223 and the symmetrical four-note chord 242. The first (the dominant major ninth) is *diatonic*, the second (the major-minor seventh with diminished fifth) is *chromatic*.⁵³ The nuclei are three-note chords, since a chord with fewer than three pitches could not contain two dissonant characteristics.

The characteristic-type 026 is represented by one maximum **026**, the symmetrical six-note chord 22222. Its nucleus is the four-note chord 224. The maximum **026** occurs

---

53 Editor's note: A reminder may be in order here. There are two maxima **26**, because both the five-note dominant major ninth and the four-note French augmented-sixth chord contain major seconds and tritones, but the first chord does not contain the second chord, and the addition of any pitch to either chord adds another, different, dissonant element.

in only two transpositions, although the chords subordinate to it occur in the usual twelve transpositions.

Diagrams and musical examples of these characteristic-types are given below.

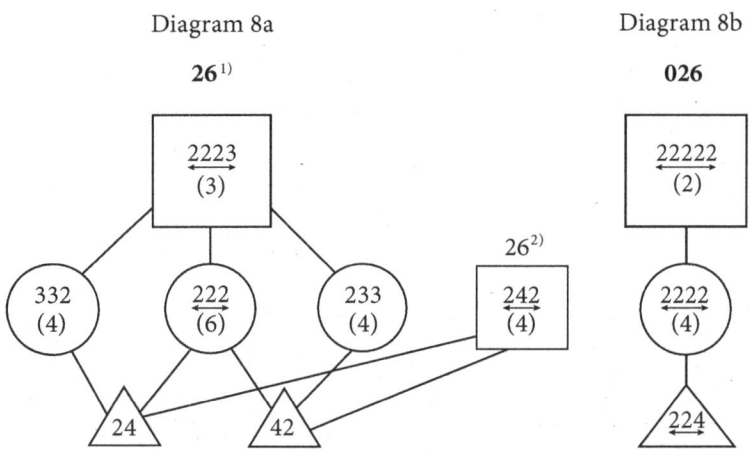

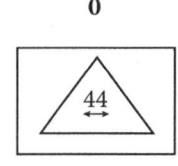

Example 26

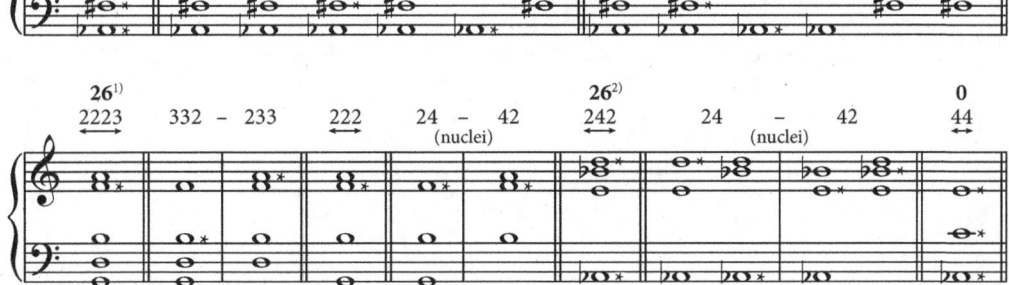

The nucleus of the characteristic-type 026 is 224, a *classical harmony*, the augmented-minor seventh chord (a dominant seventh chord with an augmented fifth). The characteristic-type 26 includes the following familiar classical harmonies: 2223, the dominant major ninth; 332, the dominant seventh; 233, the diminished-minor seventh; and 242, the major-minor seventh with diminished fifth. Thus we can consider all the more complex chord-types with the characteristic 026 to be thickened forms of the harmony 224, and, for the same reason, we can consider all the simpler chord-types with the characteristic 26 to be incomplete harmonies.[54]

§38. Characteristic Maxima 16 and 016

The compound characteristics 16 and 016 are closely related. There is only one maximum **016** (1331). As it can be neither simplified nor thickened without violating its characteristic, it is also a nucleus. There are three maxima **16**: the symmetrical four-note chord 141 and the mutually invertible four-note chords 133—331. Directly subordinate to these are two three note nuclei. Diagram 9 and Example 27 illustrate these two related characteristic-types.

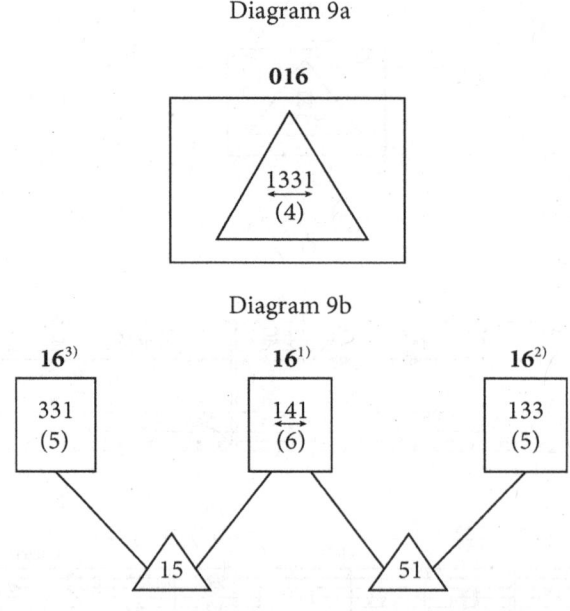

Diagram 9a

Diagram 9b

---

54 Editor's note: The reason for this is the relation of the chords in both groups to classical seventh and ninth chords.

Chapter IIIa – Classification of the Harmonic Material

Example 27

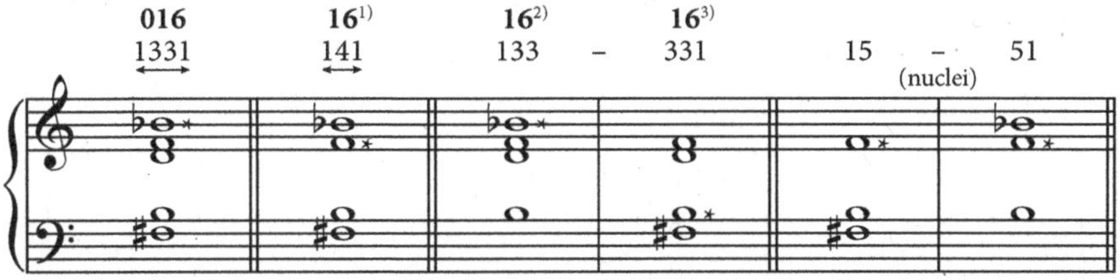

[Musical notation with labels:]
016 — 1331
16¹⁾ — 141
16²⁾ — 133 – 16³⁾ — 331
15 (nuclei)
51

The close connection between the four-note maxima **16** and the five-note maximum **016** is clear from the musical examples, especially since the actual disposition of the chord 1331 (**016**), with other pitches interspersed between the pitches of the augmented triad B♭ D F♯, does not emphasize the characteristic 0. None of the chords shown is a classical harmony. All the maxima appear in modern music so often, however, that they can be considered *modern harmonies*.

§39. Characteristic Maxima 12 and 012

The characteristic-type 12 is represented by two maxima; one is the symmetrical diatonic six-note 22122, the other the symmetrical chromatic four-note 121. Both maxima have the same two three-note nuclei. Closely related to these is the isolated maximum **012**, which is also a nucleus. The subordinate chords for the characteristic-type 12 are shown in the following diagrams and musical example. The illustrations in the example for the chromatic maximum **12²⁾** are based on the nuclei given for the diatonic maximum **12¹⁾**.

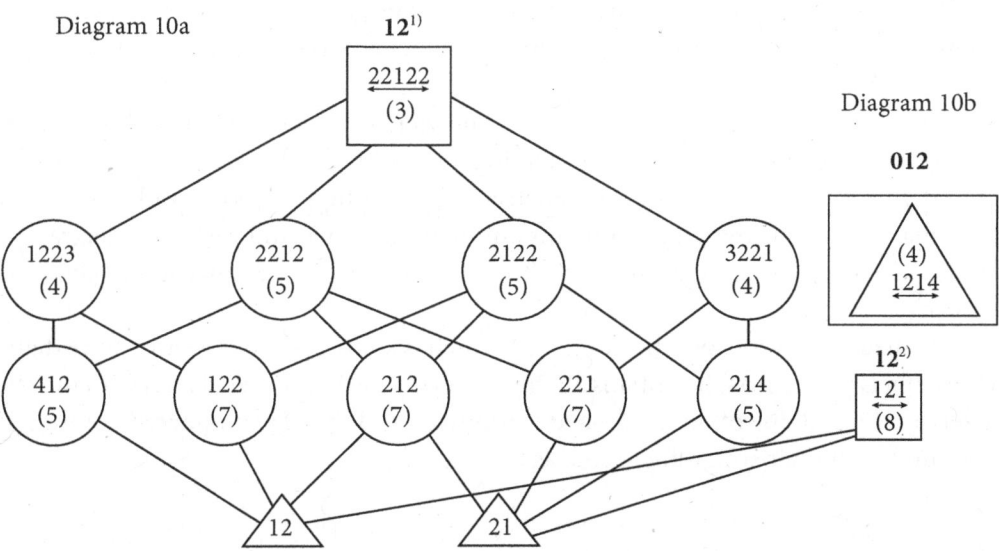

Diagram 10a

Diagram 10b

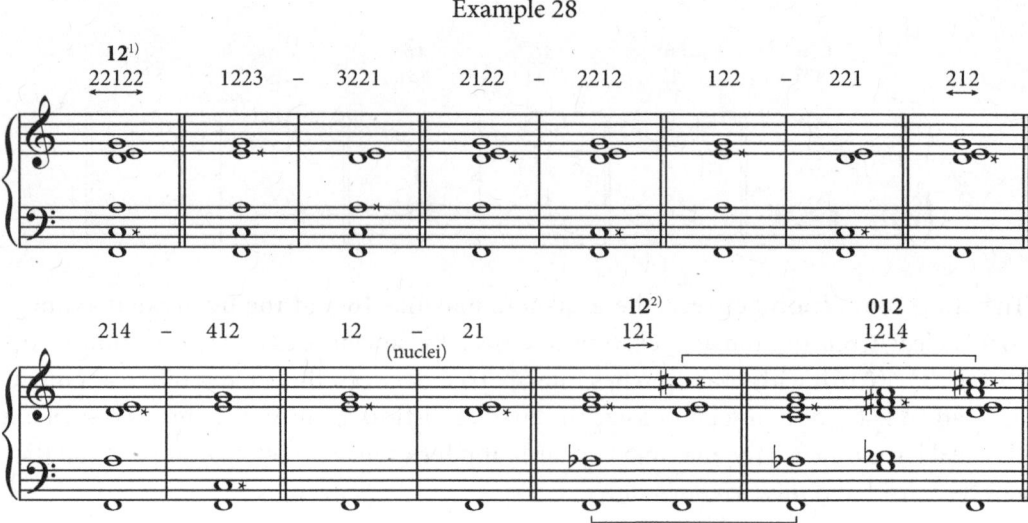

Example 28

We can hear a close connection between the sounds of the maxima **12**[2)] and **012** when we play in immediate succession the chords 121 and 1214 in the transpositions and dispositions marked by brackets.

Again, none of the chords represents a classical harmony. We can consider all the maxima to be *modern harmonies*, as they are harmonically intelligible and frequently appear in modern music as formations independent of their harmonic surroundings.

§40. Characteristic Maxima 126

The characteristic-type 126 includes 42 chords, from four-note chords to a seven-note chord. (See the second table in §25 above.) The chord-type belonging to the highest class, seven-notes, does not represent a characteristic maximum for all the lower chord-types with the characteristic 126, for it does not actually contain all these lower chords. The seven-note maximum plays its role together with five six-note maxima. Similarly, individual characteristic nuclei penetrate through higher chords only into certain maxima. Obviously, the group contains complex relations, and no single diagram can summarize the entire rich diversity of chords. First, only the maxima and nuclei will be shown.

The diatonic seven-note chord 122122, which is equivalent to the entire pure diatonic system, is placed first. It contains all the diatonic chords of lower classes with the characteristic 126. All the other maxima are chromatic and they are numbered according to the number of their subordinate chords.

Chapter IIIa – Classification of the Harmonic Material

Diagram 11

126

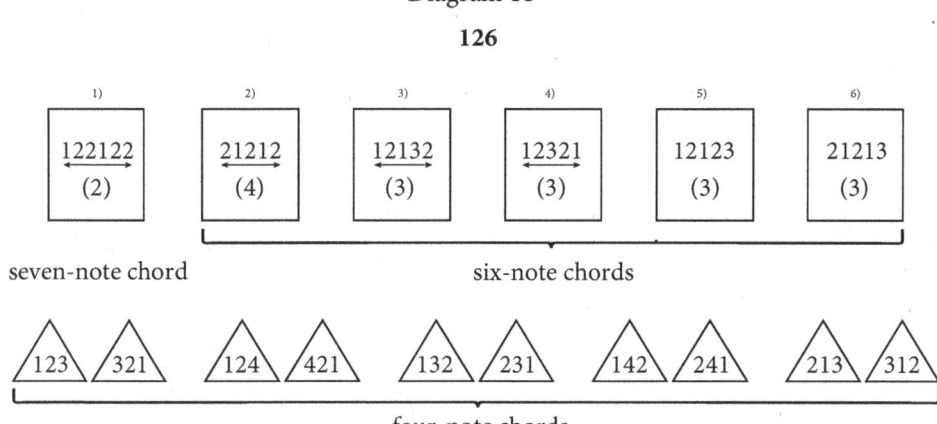

All the subordinate chords with the compound characteristic 126 are shown in the following table:

Orientation Scheme	Characteristic Nuclei				Characteristic Maxima	
six-note chords						
12212(4)		321	124	241	1)	
12221(4)	124	421	142	241	1)	
21221(4)		123	421	142	1)	
21222(3)		321	124	142	1)	
22212(3)		123	421	241	1)	
five-note chords						
1212(6)		123	132	312	2)	5)
1213(5)		124	213		3)	6)
1221(6)		123	321		1)	
1222(5)		124	142		1)	
1232(4)		123	241		1)	4)
1233(3)		123	312		4)	5)
1241(4)		124	241		1)	
1312(5)		142	312		4)	
1323(3)		132			3)	5)
1332(3)		231			3)	6)
1421(4)		421	142		1)	
2121(6)		321	231	213	2)	6)

Orientation Scheme	Characteristic Nuclei			Characteristic Maxima		
2123(4)	123	421		1)	2)	5)
2131(5)	241	213		4)		
2132(4)	421	132	213	2)	3)	
2133(3)	321	213		4)	6)	
2221(5)	421	241		1)		
2312(4)	124	231	312	2)	3)	
2321(4)	321	142		1)	4)	
3121(5)	421	312		3)	5)	
3212(4)	321	124		1)	2)	6)

Only the maxima **126** and their characteristic nuclei are shown in the following musical examples, while other subordinate chords are omitted. Sometimes the same nucleus appears more than once, although each time in a different disposition or transposition.

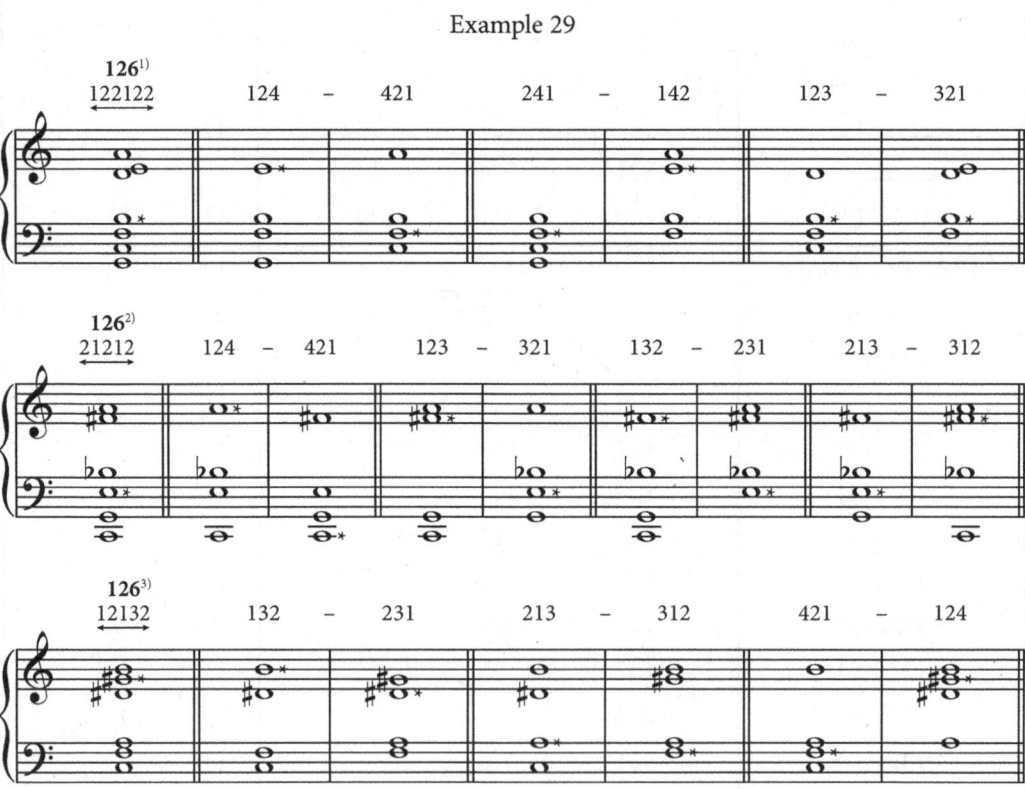

Example 29

Among the chord-types governed by the characteristic maximum **126** only two are classical harmonies: the five-note chord 2133 (the dominant minor ninth, e.g., G B D F* A♭), and the four-note 213 (the same chord incomplete, e.g., G B _ F* A♭). The four-note chord 124 is the dominant seventh chord with a sixth instead of a fifth, a favorite of the romantic composers (e.g., G F B E* [dominant thirteenth] instead of G F B* D); this chord does not of course belong to the system of classical harmonies. The other chord-types heard here may have been introduced by classical composers, at times even emphatically, but always in the role of transient chords rather than harmonies. Since these maxima are not too complex, it is possible to refer to them as *modern harmonies*. The subordinate chords belonging to lower classes are then *incomplete* harmonies.

The maxima **126**[3] (12132) and **126**[4] (12321) represent complete *triadic combinations* (e.g., C F A – D♯ G♯* B = 12132, and C F A♭ – B* D G = 12321). The maximum **126**[1] (122122) is also a triadic combination, although thickened here by an added pitch (e.g., F A C – D G B* – E, or C – D F A – B* E G = 122122). This is further discussed in §51 below.

§41. Characteristic Maxima 0126

Closely related to the characteristic-type 126 is the type 0126, which is represented by three maxima and six nuclei. The maximum **0126**[1] (121222) is equivalent to the modified diatonic system defined by the melodic major and minor scales. (See §14 above.) The maximum **0126**[2] (121221) is composed of the pitches of the harmonic minor scale; the maximum **0126**[3] (122121) is composed of the pitches of the harmonic major. Diagram 12 shows all the chords of this type.

115

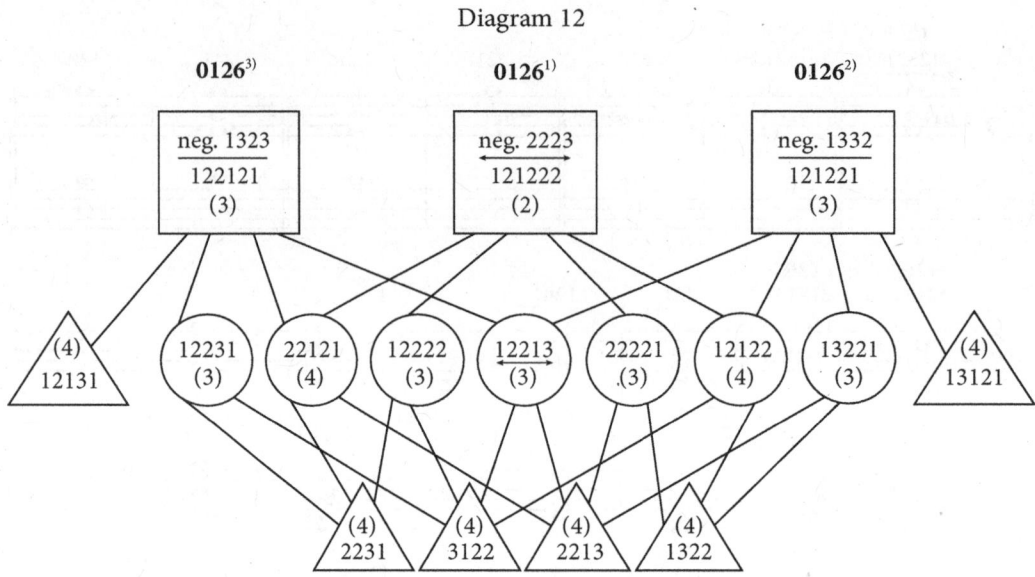

Diagram 12

Only the maxima and nuclei of the characteristic-type 0126 are shown in Example 30.

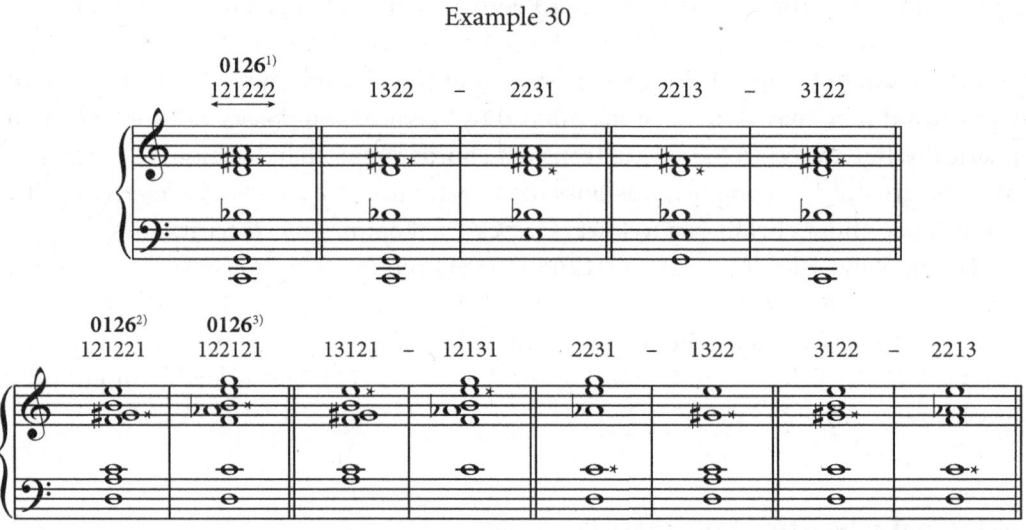

Example 30

Here none of the chords represents a classical harmony any more. The six-note nuclei 13121—12131 represent complete *triadic combinations* that constitute *modern harmonies* already common today; the maxima **0126**[2)] and **0126**[3)] are then considered harmonies thickened by an added pitch. The maximum **0126**[1)] is likewise a triadic combination enriched by an added pitch; in this case, however, it is only this added pitch (B♭ in the example) that completes the characteristic 0; otherwise the combination is diatonic and falls under the diatonic maximum **126**[1]: C E G – D F♯ A. The harmonic qualities of the maximum **0126**[1], intelligibility and a sweet fullness of sound, are especially prominent in the disposition in which the triadic component with the minor seventh (C E G B♭ in the example) is sounding at the bottom.

§42. Characteristic Maxima 166 and 1266

Without including the interval 2, there can only be a single semitone clash of two tritones: only the chord 151 contains two tritones separated by a semitone without also including a whole-tone. Therefore, since there is no simpler chord containing the semitone clash of intervals 6 (four pitches are needed for the two intervals 6), the chord 151 is both nucleus and maximum, like the augmented triad 0 and the maxima **016** and **012**.

The maximum containing the interval 2 and the semitone clash of intervals 6 is more extensive. The simplest chord with this characteristic has five notes, since to the four-note 151, containing the clash of two intervals 6, a fifth pitch must be added to form the interval 2. There are two such five-note chords: 1231–1321. By the gradual addition of pitches, it is possible to progress from these two nuclei via the four six-note chords and the two seven-note chords to the final eight-note chord, which cannot be thickened, and which constitutes the characteristic maximum **1266**.

The maximum **1266** is equivalent to the complete octatonic scale, with alternate whole-tones and semitones; it is the negative of the characteristic maximum **6** (the diminished-seventh chord 333). We can also say that the maximum **1266** consists of two diminished-seventh chords separated by a semitone, as shown in the following analysis of the orientation scheme:

```
     3   3   3
     ∧   ∧   ∧
   1 2 1 2 1 2 1
     ∨   ∨   ∨
     3   3   3
```

The connections between the maximum **1266** and its subordinate chords are shown in Diagram 13a. Diagram 13b is a diagram of the isolated maximum **166**. Since the maximum **1266** is eight notes, it is more easily expressed by the orientation scheme of its negative. Joint orientation schemes (schemes of both the chord and its negative) are shown for both the eight-note chord and the seven-note chords in the diagram.

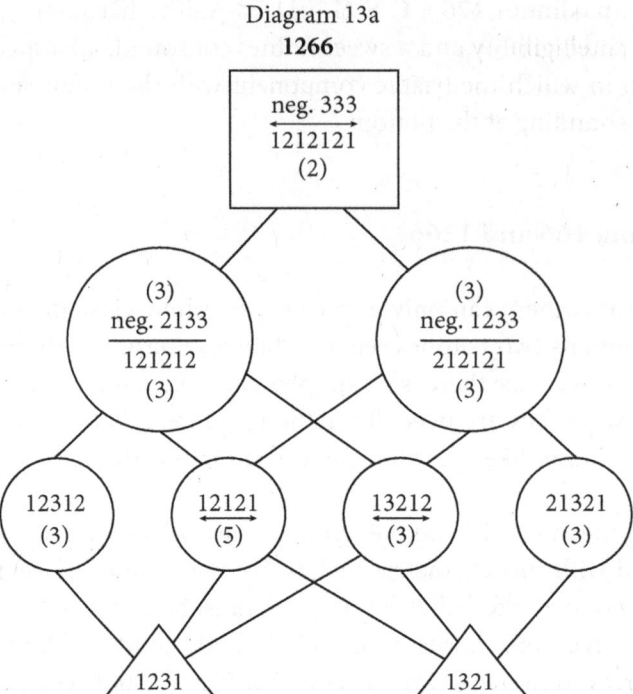
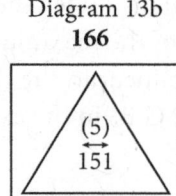

Theoretical relations between chords are perspicuous from their orientation schemes, in that a lower chord is contained in a higher one if the negative of the higher chord is contained in the negative of the lower one. This simplifies the theoretical comparison of chords.

The maximum **1266** has only two rotations: 1212121 and 2121212. Thus it appears in the chromatic system only three times, as does its negative 333, which has only one rotation.[55] Its component chords are not subject to this limitation. As a rule, we can determine the number of times they appear in the original chord by dividing into 12 the number of times the original chord appears in the chromatic system.[56] Example 31 gives an example of the maximum **1266** with its corresponding nuclei, and an example of the maximum **166**.

The maximum **1266** constitutes a rich triadic combination: in this eight-note chord no fewer than three consonant triadic components come into play, with one pitch common to two of the triads. Even lower chords subordinate to the maximum are triadic combinations: complete combinations when they are six-note chords, incomplete when they are nuclei, and thickened when they are seven-note chords.

The difference between the nuclei of the type 1266 and the maximum **166** is small, because the characteristic 2, which enriches the former over the latter, loses its effect because of the overwhelmingly harsh combination of the other dissonant elements.

---

55 Editor's note: As explained earlier, if an 8-note chord, instead of having 8 different rotations, has only 2 – 1/4 the usual number – then the chord has only 1/4 the usual 12 transpositions, or 3.

56 Editor's note: As the maximum appears in the chromatic system 3 times, that is, it exists in three transpositions, its components appear in the maximum 12 ÷ 3 = 4 times. This is because the limited number of transpositions results from the repetition of an interval pattern within a chord (here, 12 appears four times), and the number of repetitions of the pattern determines the number of times a component chord will appear in the larger chord.

Chapter IIIa – Classification of the Harmonic Material

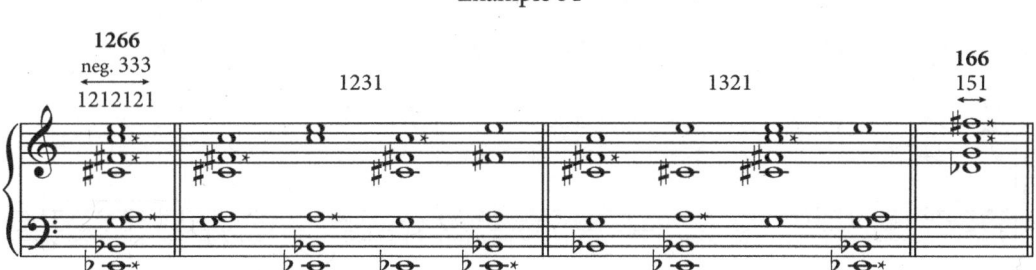

Example 31

§43. Characteristic Maxima 112 and 0112

The clash of intervals 1 without the interval 6 (naturally, the interval 2 cannot be excluded) can be achieved with as few as three pitches, in the chord 11. When new pitches are added to this nucleus, two maxima **112** are eventually reached: 11111 and 21112. The orientation scheme of the nucleus 11 of course appears in all the orientation schemes of the chords thus formed. Since the nucleus is chromatic, all chords derived from it are chromatic.

The simplest chord containing the characteristics 0 (the augmented triad) and 112 is the symmetrical five-note chord 3113. It is the nucleus of the maxima **0112**[1)] and **0112**[2)] (12113 and 31121).

Diagrams 14a and 14b show all the chords belonging to the characteristic-types 112 and 0112.

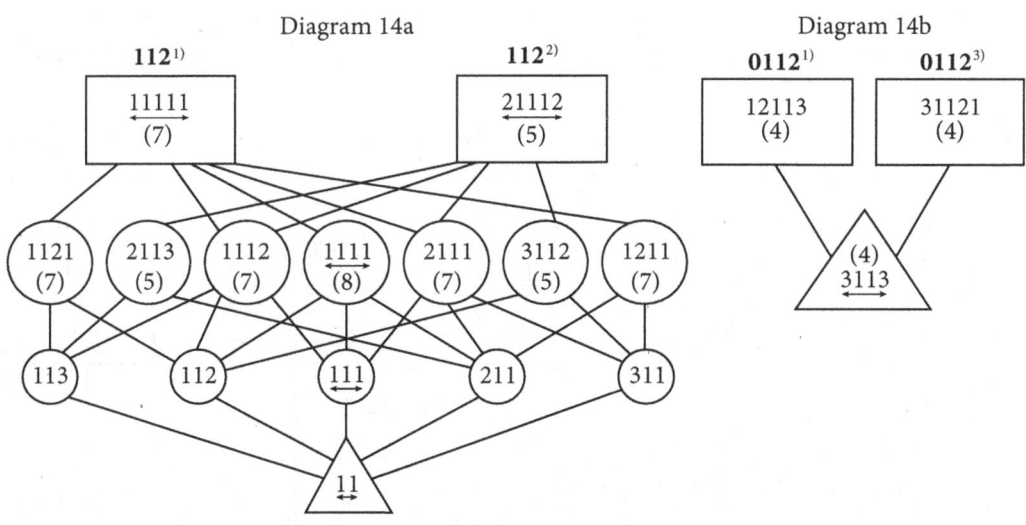

Example 32 shows the maxima **112** and **0112** and their nuclei. These two characteristic-types are closely related, especially in that the acute harshness caused by the clash of semitones is not softened by a tritone.

Example 32

[musical notation with labels: 0112¹⁾ 12113, 0112²⁾ 31121, 3113, 112¹⁾ 11111, 112²⁾ 21112, 11]

Of the three chord-types with the characteristic 0112, the nucleus 3113 is more reasonably considered a modern harmony than is either of the maxima; the two maxima thus represent the harmony in thickened form. In the much richer group of chords with the characteristic 112, on the other hand, it is better to consider the two maxima to be the harmonies.

§44. Characteristic Maxima 1126

The simplest chords with the characteristic 1126 are the three four-note chords 115 and 114—411. The five-note chord 2112 must be added to these nuclei, however, as it also has the characteristic 1126 but cannot be transformed (by the subtraction of a note) into any of these three four-note chords. Thus the maxima **1126** have four nuclei: three four-note chords and a five-note chord. There are five maxima **1126** – one eight-note chord and four seven-note chords. Since there are 57 chords with the characteristic 1126, we cannot show their relations in a single diagram. First, in Diagram 15, we give a general overview of the relations between the maxima **1126** and nuclei of the same characteristic.

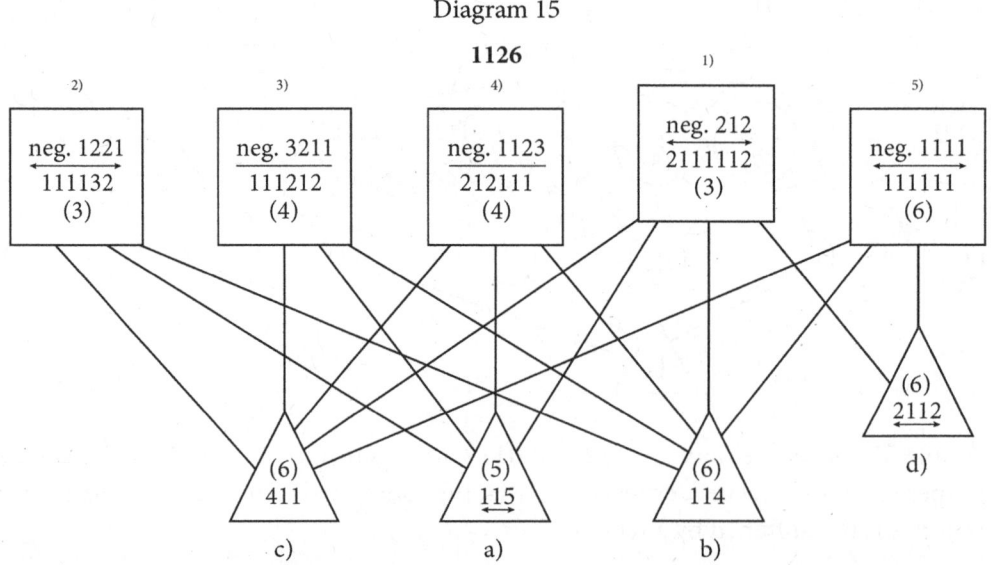

Diagram 15

Chapter IIIa – Classification of the Harmonic Material

The following table shows all the other chords with the dissonant characteristic 1126, with the maxima and nuclei identified by their labels in Diagram 15.

Orientation Scheme	Maxima and Nuclei Represented	Orientation Scheme	Maxima and Nuclei Represented
7-note chords		6-note chords	
neg. 1112(7)	1) a) c) d)	21123(3)	1) a) d)
neg. 1212(6)	1) a) b) c) d)	21132(3)	1) 2) a)
neg. 2111(7)	1) a) b) d)	21211(5)	1) 4) a)
neg. 2121(6)	1) a) b) c) d)	21311(4)	4) b) c)
neg. 2122(5)	1) a) c)	22111(5)	1) a) c)
neg. 2123(4)	1) a) d)	22113(3)	1) c)
neg. 2212(5)	1) a) b)	23111(4)	2) 4) a) b) c)
neg. 3212(4)	1) a) d)	31111(5)	1) 2) a) c)
		32111(4)	1) 4) a) b)
6-note chords		5-note chords	
11112(6)	1) 5) b) d)	1113(6)	1) 2) 3) 5) b)
11113(5)	1) 2) a) b)	1114(5)	1) 2) 4) a) b)
11121(6)	3) 5) b)	1122(6)	1) 5) b)
11122(5)	1) a) b)	1123(5)	1) 2) 3) a)
11123(4)	1) 3) a) c)	1131(6)	3) 5) b)
11132(4)	2) 3) a) b) c)	1132(5)	1) 2) 3) a)
11133(3)	1) b) c)	1133(4)	1) 3) c)
11211(6)	5) b) c)	1142(4)	2) 3) 4) b) c)
11212(5)	1) 3) a)	1311(6)	4) 5) c)
11223(3)	1) b)	2211(6)	1) 5) c)
11232(3)	1) 2) a)	2311(5)	1) 2) 4) a)
11312(4)	3) b) c)	3111(6)	1) 2) 4) 5) c)
12111(6)	4) 5) c)	3211(5)	1) 2) 4) a)
12112(5)	1) d)	3311(4)	1) 4) b)
21111(6)	1) 5) c) d)	4111(5)	1) 2) 3) a) c)
21121(5)	1) d)		

Examples 33–36 show only the maxima **1126** and their nuclei. The symmetrical nuclei 115 and 2112 appear in the maximum **1126**[1] twice, while each of the other nuclei appears once.

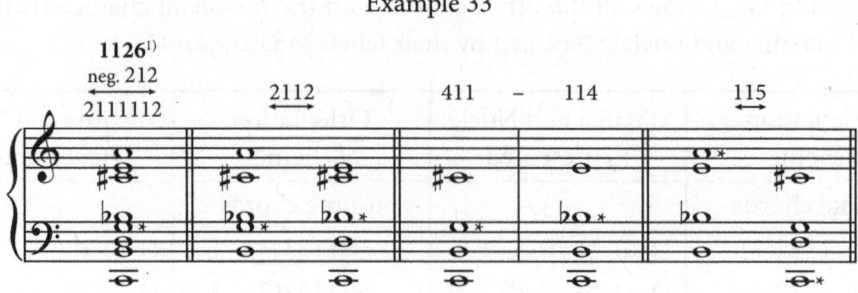

Example 33

Example 34 shows the maximum **1126**[2] and its nuclei:

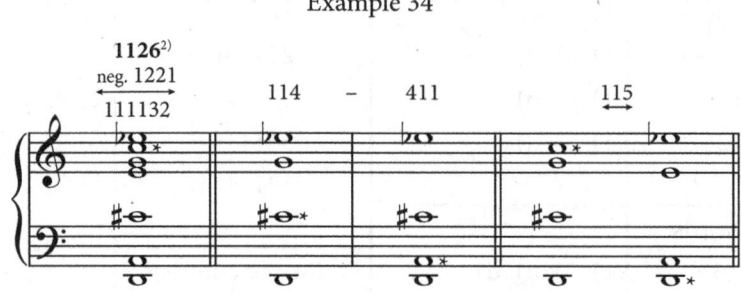

Example 34

The examples of the maxima **1126**[3] and **1126**[4] in Example 35 are chosen so that they have the nucleus 115 in common with the maximum **1126**[2] shown in the previous musical example.

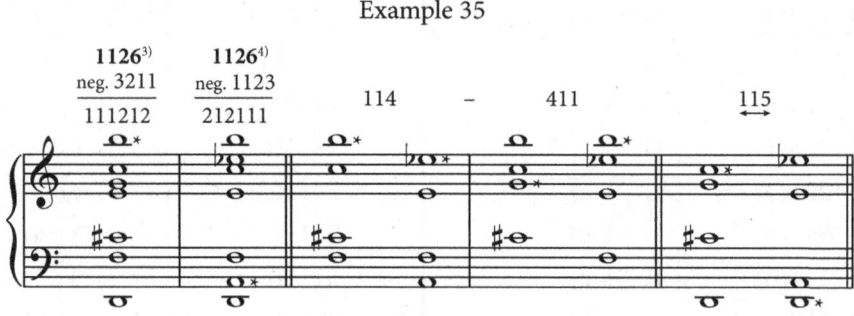

Example 35

As shown in Example 36, the maximum **1126**[5] cannot be transformed into the nucleus 115; it does contain the nucleus 2112, however, as does the maximum **1126**[1].

Chapter IIIa – Classification of the Harmonic Material

Example 36

[musical notation: 1126⁵⁾ 111111, 2112, 114, 411]

Since all the maxima of the characteristic 1126 belong to high chord-classes, it is not advisable to consider them to be harmonies. Nor are the nuclei suitable for this purpose, because of their extreme simplicity and terse sound. In this case *triadic combinations* offer a better interpretation. (See below, §51 et seq.)

§45. Characteristic Maxima 01126

The chords of the characteristic-type 01126 are very closely related to the chords of type 1126. There are 56 such chords (See table in §25), represented by five maxima and six nuclei. Diagram 16 shows the connections between the maxima and the nuclei.

Diagram 16

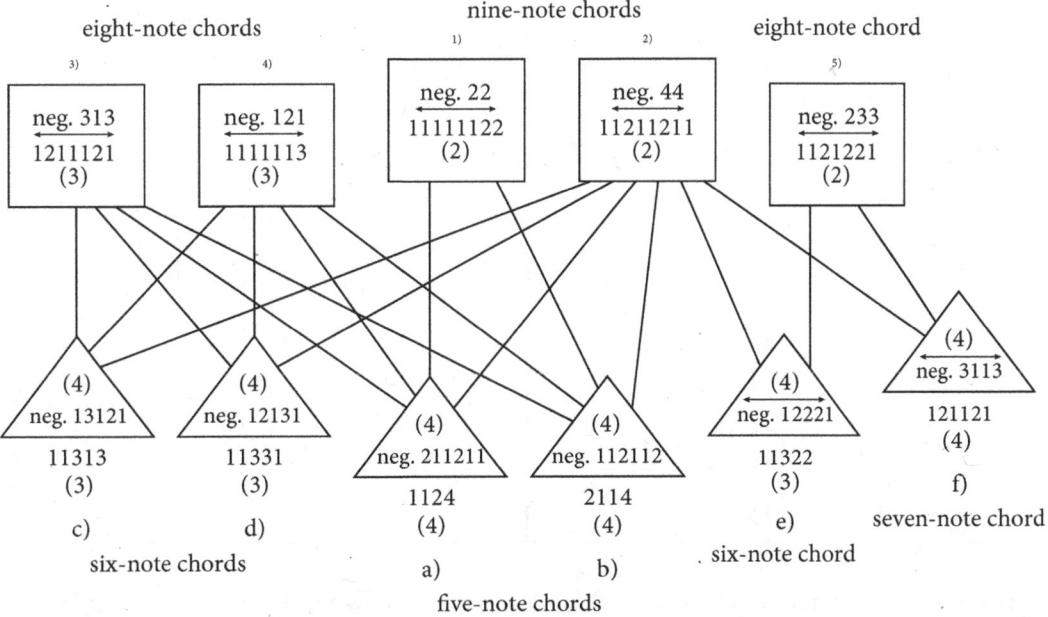

The other 45 chords with the characteristic 01126 are summarized in the following table. Since these are chords of higher classes, they are designated by the orientation schemes of their negatives. The complement is shown with each scheme so that its connections can be more easily verified.

Orientation Scheme of Negatives	Maxima and Nuclei Represented	Orientation Scheme of Negatives	Maxima and Nuclei Represented
8-note chords		7-note chords	
n. 112(8)	1) a) b)	n. 2114(4)	1) 2) a)
n. 122(7)	1) a) b) e)	n. 2211(6)	1) a) b)
n. 134(4)	2) b) c) d) f)	n. 2213(4)	1) 2) b)
n. 211(8)	1) a) b)	n. 2221(5)	1) a) e)
n. 221(7)	1) a) b) e)	n. 2222(4)	1) 2) a) b)
n. 222(6)	1) a) b) e)	n. 2231(4)	1) 2) a)
n. 223(5)	1) a) e)	n. 3112(5)	1) 3) b)
n. 224(4)	1) 2) a) b)	n. 3121(5)	3) 4) a) c)
n. 314(4)	2) a) c) d) f)	n. 3122(4)	1) 2) a)
n. 322(5)	1) b) e)	n. 3131(4)	2) 3) a) d)
		n. 3221(4)	1) 5) e)
7-note chords			
n. 1121(7)	1) 4) a) b)	6-note chords	
n. 1122(6)	1) a) b)	n. 11211(6)	1) 4) a) b)
n. 1124(4)	1) 2) b)	n. 11213(4)	1) 2) 3) 4) b)
n. 1211(7)	1) 4) a) b)	n. 11222(4)	1) 2) b)
n. 1213(5)	3) 4) b) d)	n. 12112(5)	1) 3) 4) b)
n. 1214(4)	2) 4) c) d)	n. 13112(4)	1) 2) 3) b)
n. 1222(5)	1) b) e)	n. 21121(5)	1) 3) 4) a)
n. 1223(4)	1) 5) e)	n. 21122(4)	1) 2) a)
n. 1313(4)	2) 3) b) c)	n. 21131(4)	1) 2) 3) a)
n. 1322(4)	1) 2) b)	n. 22112(4)	1) 2) b)
n. 1331(4)	2) c) d)	n. 22211(4)	1) 2) a)
n. 2112(6)	1) a) b)	n. 31211(4)	1) 2) 3) 4) a)
n. 2113(5)	1) 3) a)		

Only examples of maxima **01126** and their nuclei are shown in Examples 37 and 38.

Chapter IIIa – Classification of the Harmonic Material

Example 37

The maximum **01126**[2] has only four transpositions, so it contains each of its subordinate chords three times, as becomes apparent Example 38.

Example 38

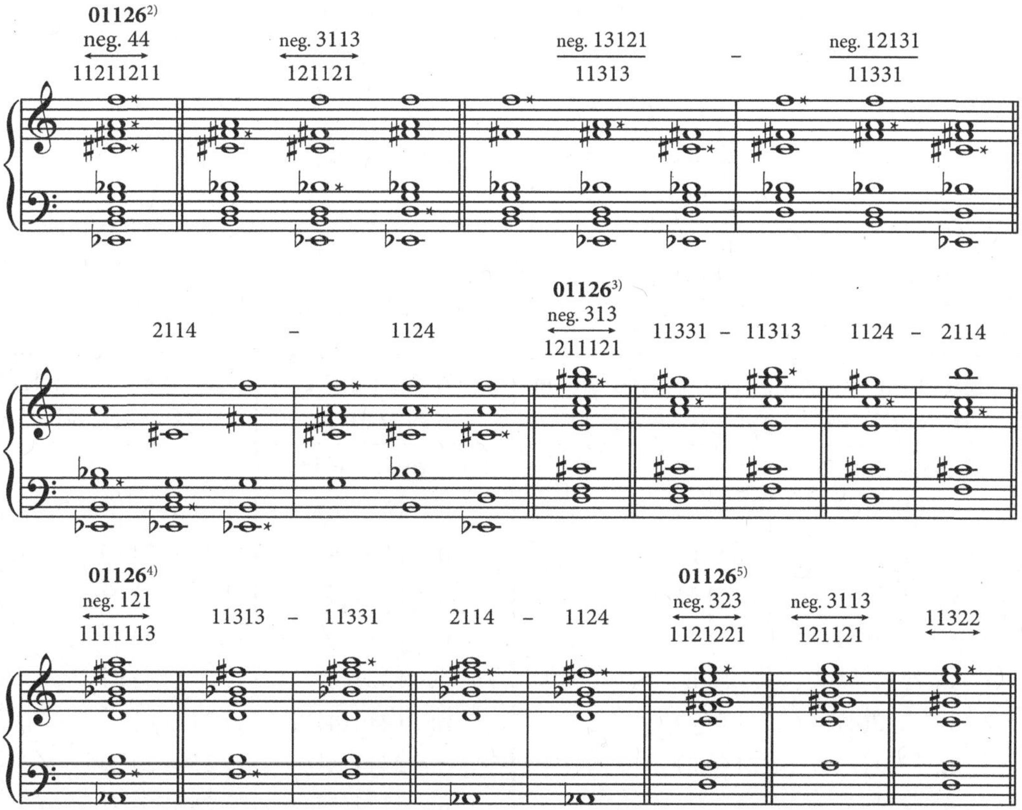

§46. Characteristic Maxima 11266

The characteristic-type 11266 is related to the type 1126. It is distinguished from 1126 by the clash of tritones, which becomes negligible in complex chords already containing the clash of semitones. It also differs only slightly from the characteristic-type 011266, because the characteristic 0 (the triad 44) likewise lacks strength in a complex chord. There are 29 chord-types with the characteristic 11266. Of these, the simplest are the two five-note chords 1141—1411, which constitute the nuclei for the six maxima **11266**. All the maxima are eight-note chords. Diagram 17 shows the relations between the maxima and the nuclei.

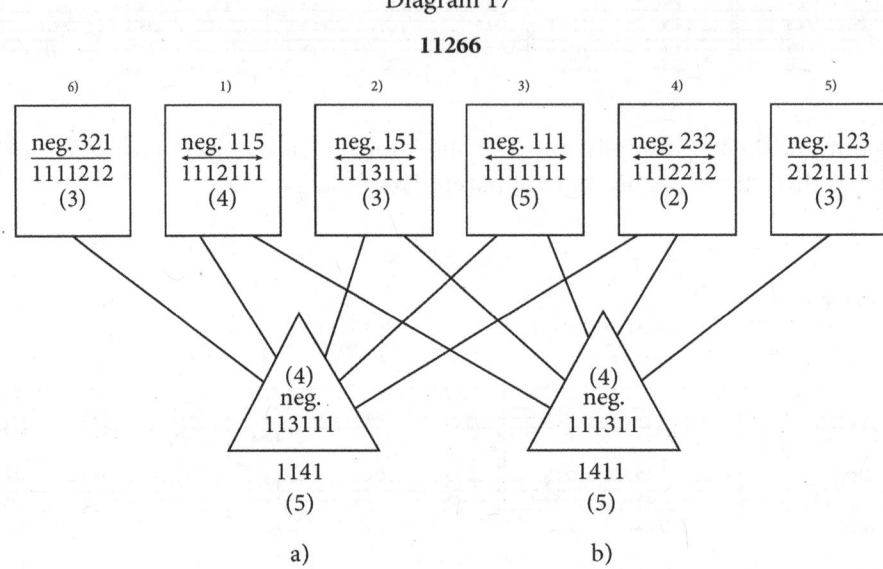

The other 21 chords with the characteristic 11266 are listed in the following table:

Orientation Scheme of Negatives	Maxima and Nuclei Represented	Orientation Scheme of Negatives	Maxima and Nuclei Represented
7-note chords		6-note chords	
n. 1113(6)	3) 5) b)	n. 11131(5)	1) 2) 3) 5) b)
n. 1114(5)	1) 3) a)	n. 11132(4)	1) 3) 4) 5) b)
n. 1132(5)	1) 4) a) b)	n. 11141(4)	1) 2) 3) a) b)
n. 1141(5)	1) 2) a) b)	n. 11311(5)	1) 2) 4) a) b)
n. 1231(5)	2) 5) b)	n. 11321(4)	1) 2) 4) 6) a)
n. 1232(4)	4) 5) b)	n. 11411(4)	1) 2) a) b)
n. 1321(5)	2) 6) a)	n. 12311(4)	1) 2) 4) 5) b)
n. 1411(5)	1) 2) a) b)	n. 13111(5)	1) 2) 3) 6) a)
n. 2311(5)	1) 4) a) b)	n. 23111(4)	1) 3) 4) 6) a)
n. 2321(4)	4) 6) a)		
n. 3111(6)	3) 6) a)		
n. 4111(5)	1) 3) b)		

Musical examples of maxima and nuclei are given in Example 39. The maximum **11266**[2] (neg. 151) occurs in only six transpositions. (See §13 above.) Therefore its subordinate chords appear at least twice in each of its transpositions; it contains each nucleus four times.

Example 39

§47. The Characteristic Maximum 011266

There are 60 chords with the most complex characteristic, 011266. There is only one maximum **011266**, the twelve-note chord. Its subordinate chords include the eleven-note chord; all six ten-note chords; seventeen nine-note chords, that is all except neg. 22 and neg. 44, which were shown in §45 to be maxima **01126**[1] and **01126**[2]; twenty-two eight-note chords; and eleven seven-note chords. The simplest chords with the characteristic 011266 are two six-note chords: a) 11231 (neg. 21311), and b) 13211 (neg. 11312), which are the *characteristic nuclei*. The seven-note and eight-note chords with this most complex dissonant characteristic are listed in the following table.

Subordinate chords of the maximum **011266**	
8-note chords and their nuclei	7-note chords and their nuclei
n. 113 b)	n. 231 b)
n. 114 a) b)	n. 233 b)
n. 124 b)	n. 241 a)
n. 131 a) b)	n. 242 a) b)
n. 132 a)	n. 311 a)

7-note chords and their nuclei
n. 1131 b)
n. 1133 b)
n. 1142 a) b)
n. 1241 b)
n. 1311 a)

Subordinate chords of the maximum **011266**	
8-note chords and their nuclei		7-note chords and their nuclei
n. 133 b)	n. 312 b)	n. 1312 b)
n. 141 a) b)	n. 331 a)	n. 1421 a)
n. 142 b)	n. 332 a)	n. 2131 a)
n. 143 a) b)	n. 411 a) b)	n. 2132 a)
n. 213 a)	n. 412 b)	n. 2312 b)
n. 214 a)	n. 421 a)	n. 3311 a)

The twelve-note chord can only be formed once in the tempered chromatic system, so as a chord-type it cannot be transposed. (Only its various dispositions can be transposed.) The nuclei that are subordinate to the twelve-note chord have the number of rotations usual for their class and so each naturally occurs twelve times. In Example 40, each nucleus is shown twelve times, in different transpositions and dispositions.

Example 40

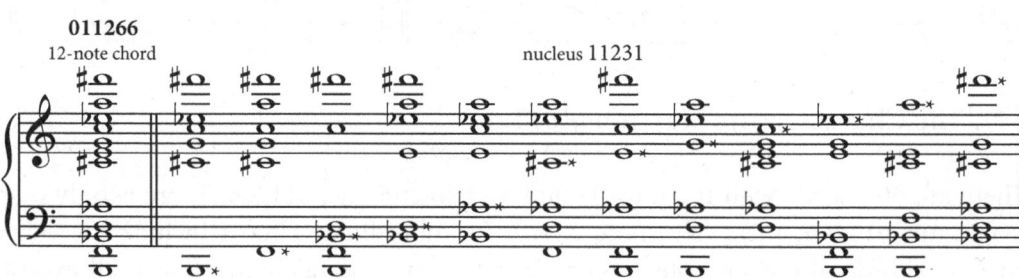

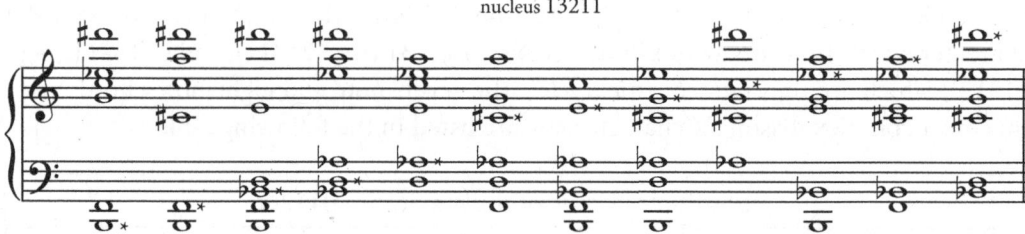

§48. The System of Characteristic-types

All the possible chord-types, as organized in §33–§47 above, are represented in the *system of characteristic-types*, which involves dissonant characteristics and their various combinations. Both the presence and the absence of dissonant characteristics are decisive. The characteristic effect of the absence of al the dissonant elements should be expressedly emphasized. Therefore the consonant chords are also considered to represent a characteristic-type.

The system of characteristic-types covers *all the chord material of the tempered chromatic system*. Every chord-type, if it is not itself a characteristic maximum, belongs to one of the characteristic maxima. A maximum and its subordinate chords are connected both by a common characteristic and by the fact that the maximum contains the entire chord. A chord is not subordinated to a particular maximum simply because the maximum contains all the pitches of the chord, but only when the chord and the maximum have the same characteristic. A similar relation obtains between chords and characteristic nuclei.

Since in some cases there is more than one maximum or nucleus with the same characteristic, it is possible gradually to thicken or simplify certain chords and arrive at several different final results. Such *ambiguity* cannot cross the boundary of the characteristic-type, however. Thus if a chord is subordinate to one of the six maxima **126**, for example, it can also be subordinate to one of the other maxima **126**, but not to a maximum **12** or **1266**. *The differentiation of chord-types according to characteristic-type is therefore of primary importance*; that chord-types also belong to particular maxima or nuclei is only secondary.

The entire system of classifying harmonic material according to dissonant characteristic is founded on the same principle as the system of classical harmony-types. The only difference is that for complex characteristics, the number of individualized characteristic maxima is considerable and the number of incomplete (but nevertheless still complex) lower chords is even larger. Of course a larger number of different chords with the same basic dissonant characteristic *increases the ambiguity* as to which lower chords are related to which higher chords. The connections between subordinate chords and their corresponding characteristic maxima are necessarily *looser* than those between complete and incomplete classical harmonies.

An example can clarify the matter. The five-note chord G B D F A, a classical harmony (the dominant major ninth), is also a characteristic maximum (see §37 above). According to the principles of classical harmony, this chord can be simplified without disturbing its harmonic content only if the ninth G A is retained. In modern harmony, however, this classical restriction need not be considered; the chord can be simplified to B D F A or G B D F, for example, since these retain the dissonant characteristic (26) of the maximum G B D F A; the interval G A represents only one of the component whole--tone intervals, and its removal does not affect the dissonant characteristic.

The *smallest possible difference in sound* between a complete and an incomplete harmony arises when we eliminate only a pitch that forms consonant intervals with the other pitches of the harmony; by eliminating such a pitch we leave undisturbed not only the overall characteristic of the harmony, but also any increased individual characteristics that it might contain. Thus, after the D is eliminated from G B D F A, the original single tritone (B F) and twice replicated whole-tone (G F, G A, B A) remain. The difference in sound between the complete harmony G B D F A and the incomplete harmony G B F A is negligible.

A *greater*, although still inconsiderable, *difference in sound* occurs when we eliminate those pitches whose presence causes the increase of a dissonant characteristic. The *greatest* possible difference in sound (in this sense) is between a characteristic maximum and its corresponding characteristic nucleus; in specific cases, the greater the difference between chord-classes involved, the more obvious will be the difference in sound. The simplest chords with the same characteristic as the five-note chord G B D F A are the three-note chords G B F and B F A. (In a classical interpretation, the three-note chord G B F represents merely an incomplete four-note chord G B D F, and the chord B F A merely an incomplete four-note chord B D F A.)

For the comparison, and thus the classification, of the extensive harmonic material we encounter in new music, it is better in simplifying chords to proceed from those with increased dissonant characteristics to those with the same characteristics singly. This will enable us to form *fewer groups of similar chords*, even if each has numerous members.[57]

Lists of all the characteristic maxima and nuclei are included among the systematic tables at the end of the book, organized according to dissonant characteristic and chord-class.

§49. Connections between Chords with Different Dissonant Characteristics

When forming characteristic maxima, we proceeded by gradually adding new pitches to the simplest initial chord of a characteristic in such a way as not to alter the characteristic. Whenever further thickening became impossible without changing the original characteristic, we had reached the maximum. All chords formed this way while proceeding towards the maximum are of course components of the maximum.

There are two features connecting a subordinate chord with its maximum – a common dissonant characteristics and the fact that the maximum contains the subordinate chord. The second feature can be considered independently from the first: when we add a new pitch to a chord with a certain characteristic, sometimes the resulting chord of a higher class has a different (richer) characteristic. Although the boundary of the original characteristic has been crossed, the newly formed chord is almost as closely connected to the original chord as a maximum would be to its nearest subordinate chord. The more complex and tonally rich are the chords to be compared, the closer will be the connection between them.

Diagrams 18a–e with their corresponding musical examples 41–43 show several such connections, specifically *between characteristic maxima of neighbouring chord-classes*. The dispositions in the musical examples make the outer pitches of the more complex chord enclose the simpler chords.

---

57 Editor's note: The preceding five paragraphs were moved from §88.

Chapter IIIa – Classification of the Harmonic Material

Diagram 18a

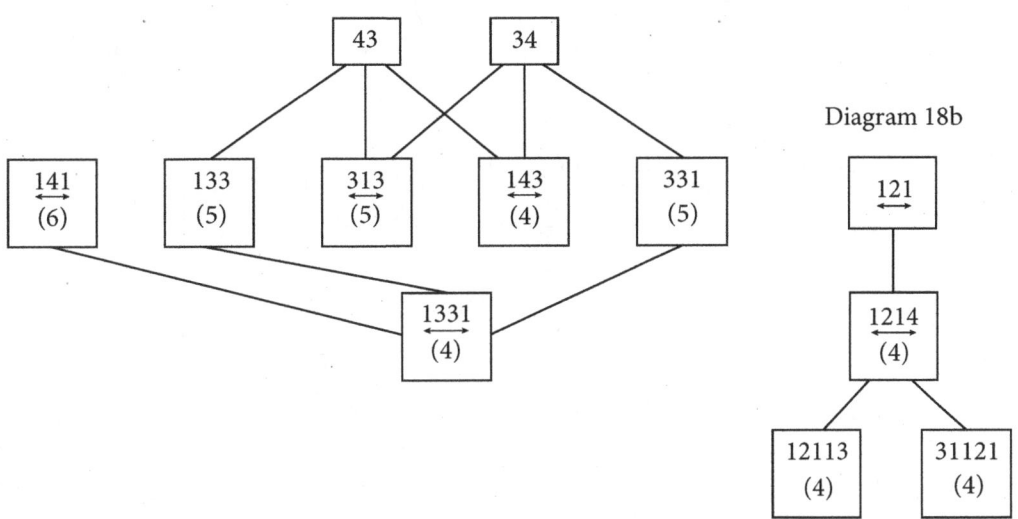

Diagram 18b

Example 41

Diagram 18c

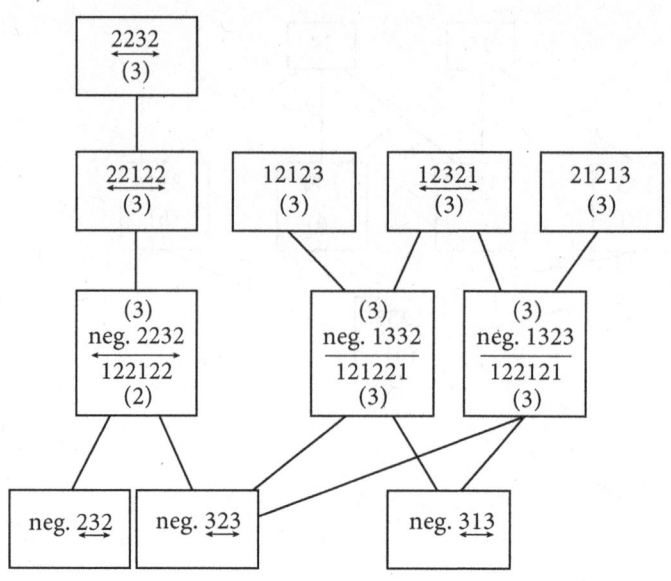

Example 42

Chapter IIIa – Classification of the Harmonic Material

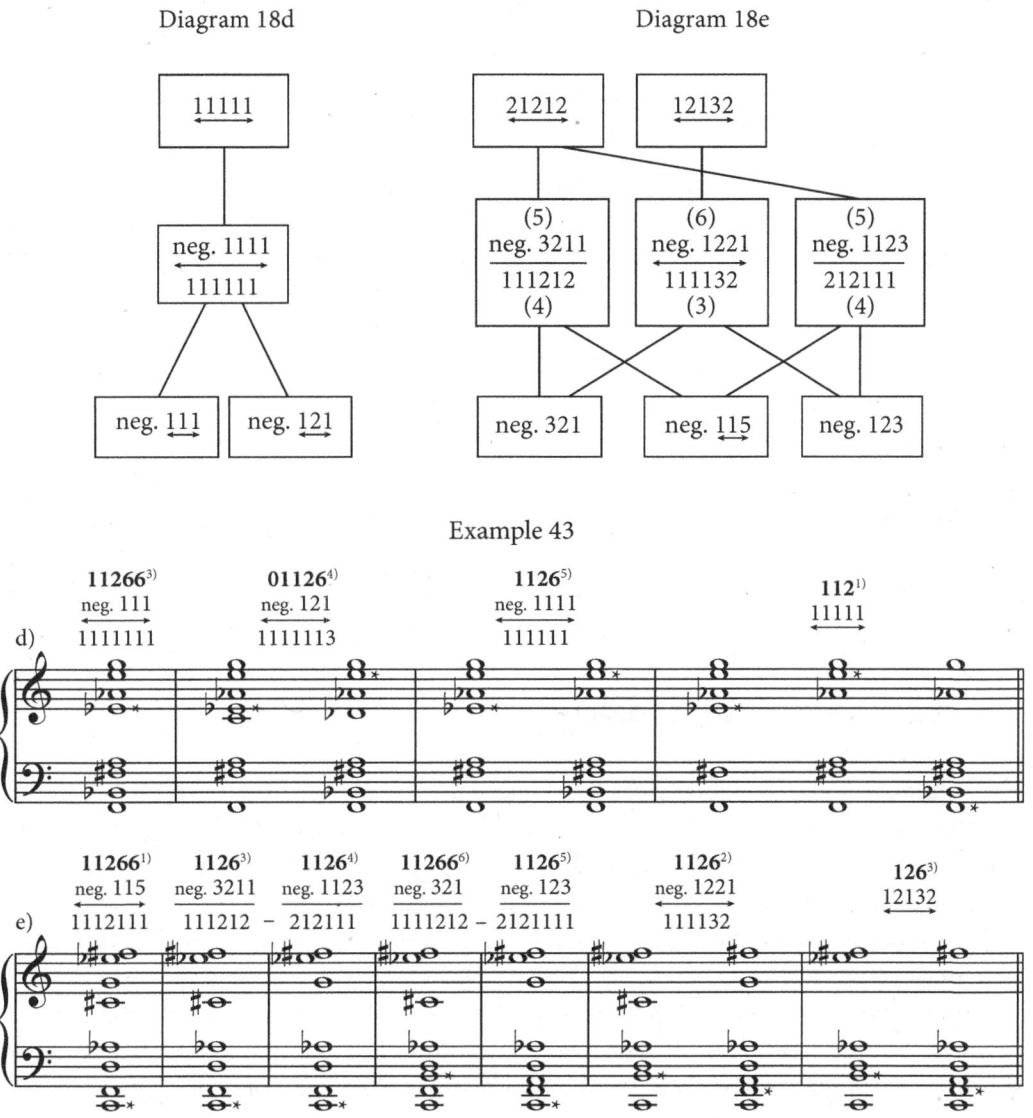

There are the same connections between the subordinate chords of different characteristic-types, so that chains of such overlapping chords (reaching from any two-note chord all the way to the twelve-note chord, or in the other direction) can be formed. Such a chain is shown in Example 44. Both the orientation scheme and the type are shown for each chord; the individual chords are usually incomplete maxima, or simply nuclei.

Example 44

§50. Boundaries between Characteristic-types

The similarity and dissimilarity of chord-types has a real basis in actual pitch material. The more common components there are, both absolutely and relatively, the more apparent will be the similarity between chords. Conversely, the more new sonic characteristics that appear in the chord of a higher class compared to the chord of a lower class, and the more pronounced these characteristics are, the more obvious will be the difference in their sounds.

The relation between the maximum **2** (2232 E A D G* B) and the diatonic maximum **12**[1] (22122 E A C D G* B) serves as an example of a close connection between two chord-types. Since the six-note chord contains the entire five-note chord, the connection between the two is very close despite the difference in characteristic.

The connection between the maximum **6** (333 F* A♭* B* D*) and the maximum **1266** (neg. 333 F A♭ B D G B♭ C♯ E) is looser. This connection is established absolutely by the four pitches of the chord **6**, and relatively by the relation of these four pitches to the eight pitches of the chord **1266**. The difference in sound is much more pronounced: in addition to the intervals 6 that are already contained in the maximum **6**, the maximum **1266** contains new elements: the intervals 2 (F G, A♭ B♭, B C♯, D E) and 1 (F E, A♭ G, B B♭, D C♯), and two clashes of tritones (F B – E B♭, A♭ D – G C♯). Since there is less absolute as well as relative involvement of common components, and the differences in the sounds of the characteristics are more pronounced, the connection between the maxima **6** and **1266** must be looser than that between the maxima **2** and **12**[1].

Chapter IIIa – Classification of the Harmonic Material

The differences in sound between characteristic-types are caused by the differences in the characteristics. These differences vary a great deal. We must not imagine that each maximum with all its subordinate chords is separated from all other maxima by equally pronounced boundaries. The boundary is sometimes obvious, at other times barely perceptible, depending on the number and quality of characteristics that differentiate the chords.

We will refer to the differences in characteristic between chord-types as *boundary differences*, or simply *boundaries*. These differences are distinct and defined. The sounds of any two chords differ in some way; however, this difference may not be attributable to the characteristic. There is no boundary difference between the major and minor triads, for example, although there is an obvious difference in sound; the same is true of the six maxima **126**. The boundaries defined here are those between chords with different characteristics, that is, *between characteristic-types*.

The boundary difference between characteristic-types can be expressed by a symbol formed from the elements that distinguish the characteristics in question. When forming such a differentiating or boundary symbol, first the common elements must be eliminated and then the remaining elements are combined. In types 6 and 16, for example, the common element 6 is eliminated, and the boundary difference is expressed as 1. Whenever two types have no common characteristic elements, the boundary difference is expressed by combining the characteristic elements of both types.

For example, the boundary between types 1 and 2 is 12. This is correct because a chord differs from another chord not only by the characteristics that it does contain, but also by the characteristics that it does *not* contain; in comparison with maximum **2**, maximum **1** is richer because it includes characteristic 1, but less rich because it lacks characteristic 2.

It is important to realize that the elements 11 and 66 contain the simple elements 1 and 6. Thus in forming the symbol for the boundary difference, the symbol 11 must be considered to represent two different elements, 1 and 11; 66 similarly represents the interval 6 as well as the clash 66. Therefore, the boundary difference between the types 2 and 112 is not merely 11, but rather 1, 11. Similarly, the boundary between the types 166 and 1 is 6, 66 rather than merely 66.

As far as *qualitative evaluation of boundary differences* is concerned, essentially the same principle applies as for characteristics in general. (See §19 above.) Of the simple boundary differences 0, 1, 2, and 6, 1 is the most conspicuous. The rules for merging dissonant characteristics generally apply whenever boundaries are doubled (e.g. 26), tripled (e.g. 016), or further multiplied. (See §23 above.) Thus the double boundary difference 26 represents a less pronounced boundary than the single difference 2; a similar relation exists between boundaries 1 and 16, 0 and 06, etc. Although we can speak of single or double boundaries, we must always evaluate actual situations.

A particular boundary difference may not be equally pronounced under all conditions. The characteristic of the chords compared is not the only criterion; the actual chords must be considered, and the *classes* to which they belong. The principle is, the lower the class of the chords compared, the more pronounced and emphasized the boundary. When chords of different classes are compared (e.g., a three-note chord and a five-note chord), the decisive meaning belongs to the chord of the lower class. Thus the triple boundary difference 026 between the characteristic-types 01 and 126 will appear more pronounced when comparing the nuclei (the four-note chords) than when comparing the complete maxima (six- or seven-note chords). However, fluctuation in the definition of the boundaries that results from the classes of compared chords never interferes with the essence of these boundaries.

A table of all possible boundary differences between all characteristic-types is included at the end of the book. Several illustrations are given in Example 45.

Example 45

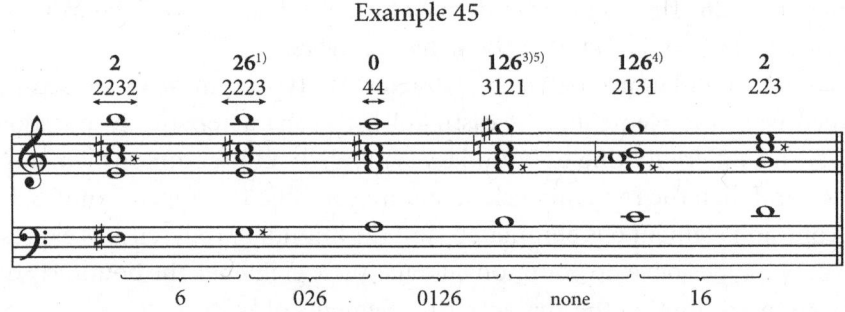

Only boundaries between adjacent chords are marked in the example. However, the example can be used as well to study the boundary differences between any of the chords shown.

Chapter IIIb – Triadic Combinations

§51. The System of Triadic Combinations

All the harmonic material of the chromatic system has been classified according to characteristic-type. This classification is precise and, as to characteristic-types, unambiguous. Within one type governed by several maxima, however, chords may belong to more than one maximum, although the boundary of the characteristic-type is not crossed. There are also relations and gradations of differences between chords of different characteristic-types, as we have just seen in §49 and §50 above.

Classification according to characteristic is advantageous because it is practical. It is not, of course, the only possible means of classification. If it perfectly captured all the sonic qualities of all the chords and all the relations between them, it might be possible to restrict ourselves to this means of classification alone. Although classification according to characteristic is applicable to all chords, it does have one paradoxical flaw, the *rigid precision of the boundaries between characteristic-types*, especially in the case of more complex chords. Precisely defined boundaries between complex chords do not always express the actual situation; sometimes it is difficult to see a definite boundary, as this system demands, between chords of different characteristic-types, and not to see it between chords of the same characteristic-type. Thus it was also necessary to separately study the relations between chords of different types and to consider the nature of the boundaries between them (as in §49 and §50 above). Despite its flaw, we cannot abandon the classification of chords according to dissonant characteristic. The advantages of this system are so obvious that returning to the chaos of unclassified chords would be impossible.

In this chapter we present a complementary system of classification that deals differently with those areas in which the first system is ineffective. This complementary system is the *system of triadic combinations*.

Our basic premise is that major and minor triads are single rather than compound harmonic entities. Although these triads are composed of individual pitches creating intervals that already constitute harmonic formations, these intervals do not represent independent harmonic entities. They are only components of a higher entity, the consonant triad. We thus conceive of the triad as a basic harmonic organism having certain harmonic components that are not themselves independent, rather than as a harmonic formation consisting of independent lower harmonic elements. The justification of such a conception is verified by the dissonant augmented triad 44, as has already been pointed out.

In keeping with this conception, a system is constructed in which higher harmonic formations (dissonant multi-note chords) are perceived as combinations of basic triads, which are considered to be the fundamental entities. This is the combination system. It considers every dissonant chord to be a combination of consonant triads; here, dissonance arises not from the presence of one or more dissonant pairs of pitches, but rather from the interpenetration of two or more consonant triads. By the *juxtaposition* of the triads at various distances from each other we can achieve here what was accomplished by the dissonant characteristics in the system of characteristic-types.

Otakar Šín founded his theory on functional combinations. For him, new chord-types were formed merely as by products in the process of combining basic triads of various *functions*: tonic, subdominant, dominant, phrygian, and lydian. His main interest was in the *combination* of these functional triads. In contrast, for the time being we interpret the higher chord-types as combinations, with no regard for the possible functions of the triads from which they are formed.

§52. True and Partial Combinations; Combination Categories

In the chord summary of §8–§14 the component major and minor triads of every chord listed were shown. The triadic components became the basis for distinguishing chords of different family characteristics. (See §21 above.) Any chord containing at least two basic triads, whether of the same or different family, is a triadic combination. But how can we incorporate chords containing only one triad, or chords belonging to neither family, into the system of combinations? We can apply a principle that we used when subordinating chords to various characteristic maxima, a principle acknowledged in classical harmony: the essence of a chord may remain unchanged even when a subordinate component of the chord is absent. This lets us omit inner pitches in classical dissonant harmonies of tertian structure (e.g., E or G in the chord C E G B), and it lets us omit pitches not essential to the characteristic in our characteristic maxima. Likewise, in triadic combinations we can omit pitches that are not essential to the expression of the combination. Thus in the combination C E G − B D♯ F♯, up to two pitches from either triad, or pitches from both triads, may be omitted, as long as none of the dissonant intervals formed by the combination is lost. The essence of the combination would be disturbed if we omitted either triad entirely, or the pitches C G from C E G and D♯ F♯

from B D♯ F♯; from the remaining consonance E B we could not even attempt to guess the original combination.

According to this view, every dissonant chord can be interpreted as a combination, a *combination harmony*. Because of the rich triadic content of more complex chords, however, the mere presence of certain triads is not a sufficient criterion for classification. The concept of a combination must be more precisely defined. Thus we will distinguish:
1) *true* combinations, in which the component basic triads have no pitches in common, and
2) *partial* combinations, in which the component triads do have common pitches. Naturally, partial combinations outnumber true combinations by far. A true combination can involve no more than four triads, while a partial combination can involve as many as twenty-four; in both cases, the result of combining the maximum number of triads is the twelve-note chord.

Categories of combination harmonies can be differentiated according to the number of basic triads involved. The true combinations can be divided into the following four categories:

I. *uncombined* basic triads,
II. true combinations of *two* basic triads,
III. true combinations of *three* basic triads,
IV. true combinations of *four* basic triads.

§53. Basic Triads (Harmonies I)

The major triad (43) and the minor triad (34), which in the system of triadic combinations we will designate as *harmonies* **I**, are the only two consonant chords. In the system of characteristic-types, these formations are exceptional because neither has a positive dissonant characteristic. In contrast, they are the very foundations on which the system of triadic combinations is built. Although their lack of differentiation by dissonant characteristic is not negligible here, it is secondary. We become aware that they belong together because of their consonant relation only when we see them juxtaposed against the dissonant chords. When considered alone, major and minor triads represent *diametrically opposed* harmonic phenomena, *true opposites*. (For this reason we use signs indicating opposites to express them: + major, − minor) Even though the only difference between them lies in the slight shift of a single pitch (the third of the chord), and they contain the same two other pitches, they are not mere modifications of some common or higher phenomenon. Each is an independent entity; it is impossible to explain one by means of the other. Thus the system of triadic combinations is *dualistic*, founded on two basic phenomena.

In construction, major and minor triads are mutual *inversions*. This can only be ascertained by means of analysis and calculation, not by comparing the general impressions given by the triads. It is impossible to have impressions of sound that are "inversions" of each other in any kind of spatial sense; they can only be different, perhaps diametrically different, polar opposites. (See §18 above.) The overall impression of a chord is more like a colour than a structure. Psychologically, a harmony is a *quality of sound*, not merely an arrangement of pitches. The important fact is that the pitches constituting the harmony are fused into an integrated whole, interpenetrating each other, resulting in a unified impression. If it was not the case, the two basic harmonies would represent even psychologically (i.e. considering their sonic effect) a single phenomenon in two interpretations. Thus the major-minor harmonic duality is the only justifiable attitude of a theory of music founded on psychology.

This dualism of sound, as well as the mutually inverse relation of the consonances established by analysis, can be misleading; it can result in an interpretation of the chords as antithetical in their individual characteristics. The mistake lies in thinking of representative pitches as being inversely related. By representative pitches we mean the roots, whose greater importance becomes obvious in their ability to act as representative pitches; the root of a harmony can represent the entire harmony, as is proven by the music of all ages. In the mistaken dualistic conception, individual pitches in mutually inverse relations in major and minor triads are seen as corresponding to each other; thus the fifth of the minor triad is seen as corresponding to the root of the major triad, and vice versa. If we then hear the root of the major triad as its basic representative pitch, this mistakenly conceived dualistic theory would force us to hear the fifth of the minor triad as its basic pitch.[58] The conflict with practical experience is obvious, and practical experience is always more reliable than theoretical speculation in seeking the psychological essence of the matter.

The basic (representative) pitch of major and minor triads is always the root, the lowest pitch in the tertian scheme (which is also the orientation scheme). It is as if the entire weight of the triad were concentrated in the root; the root reflects the entire triad. We can refer to the fifth, the highest pitch in the orientation scheme, as a *supplementary pitch*; this indicates its considerably lesser importance as well as its dependence on the root, the basic pitch. The third, the middle pitch of the scheme, then becomes the *differentiating pitch*; it is the needle on the balance, determining the family of the triad.

The question of major-minor triadic dualism is complicated by the phenomenon of the *open fifth*, the incomplete major or minor triad. The open fifth lacks a differentiating pitch, a third. Is it then possible to say that major and minor triads are both subordinate to the open fifth? The problem becomes clearer if we realize that because the open fifth is not the highest possible consonant pitch combination, but only one of the possible lower consonances, a two-note chord. It is an incomplete formation, and therefore subordinate.

---

58 Editor's note: That is, since C is the representative pitch of C E G, C is mistakenly understood as the representative pitch of the inversion C A♭ F, where C is not the root but the fifth.

The lower ranking of the open fifth becomes obvious in a harmonic progression. In such a progression the fifth absorbs into itself the differentiating pitch as soon as this pitch appears anywhere nearby, even if it appears as part of another chord. Such an open or empty fifth is then only seemingly empty; it is in fact a triad of composite expression, with two real pitches (those of the fifth) and one imaginary pitch (the third). (See §81 and §85 below.) The fact that from a psychological point of view the fifth does not resist being completed by a third, but rather seeks this out, points to its incompleteness. It does not matter that an incomplete chord can sound effective even on its own.

That we hear both open fifths and thirds as chords is explained by the fact that major and minor triads, in spite of the superiority of their overall impressions, consist of pitches merged together. At the same time, the sound of each of the two-note and one-note components has its own independent effect.

Although a chord consisting of two pitches forming the interval of a third is also an incomplete representation of a basic triad, it is considerably less ambiguous theoretically than the open fifth. It always contains the differentiating pitch, specifying which triad it represents. There can be instability or uncertainty only with respect to the root and the fifth, because the interval of the third can be perceived as being between the differentiating pitch and either the basic pitch (the root) or the supplementary pitch (the fifth). To force the listener to hear as the root a pitch that is not really sounding will always be difficult. As a rule, therefore, the omitted pitch will be the supplementary one, so that the size of the sounding third (3 or 4) will indicate the family of the triad; the interval 4 will thus most likely represent the major triad, the interval 3 the minor triad.

In the system of combinations, the category of harmonies **I** comprises five chords. These are the major and minor triads fully expressed by three different pitches, and all three consonant two-note chords (3, 4, 5). All other chords belong to higher categories.

§54. Combination Harmonies II

It is possible to form twelve true combinations of the second category. They each consist of two complete major or minor triads with no common pitches, and so they are six-note chords. They can all be considered *modern harmonies* (harmonies **II**).

Each combination harmony can of course be designated by its orientation scheme. In order to indicate its triadic structure, however, and thus distinguish it from other six-note chords that are not true combination harmonies, we will use a triadic symbol showing the family of the component triads (major +, minor −), and a numeric symbol indicating the interval formed by their roots. For the numeric symbol we always choose the smallest possible interval: a second rather than a seventh, a third rather than a sixth, etc.

Combination harmonies **II** are *symmetrical* or *asymmetrical* depending on whether they combine two triads of different families or of the same family. Since the major and minor triads are mutual inversions, their full combination as a single chord produces a symmetrical formation. The combination of basic triads belonging to the same family (+ and + or − and −), on the other hand, produces an asymmetrical formation.

Six *symmetrical* harmonies **II** are possible: −1+, +2−, −2+, +3−, −4+, +6− (or −6+, which is identical). There are also six possible *asymmetrical* harmonies **II**: +1+, −1−, +2+, −2−, +6+, −6−; these are three pairs of mutually invertible harmonies, with the pairs +2+, −2− and +6+, −6− also being mutual negatives.[59] The harmonies −2+ and +6− are mutual negatives. The harmonies −4+ and +2− are negatives of themselves.

It is interesting that certain combination harmonies **II** are also characteristic maxima. The harmony −4+ is identical to the maximum **01**, the harmony +2− to the diatonic maximum **12**[1)], the harmony +3− to the maximum **126**[3)], and the harmony −2+ to the maximum **126**[4)].

Example 46 shows all true combination harmonies **II**.

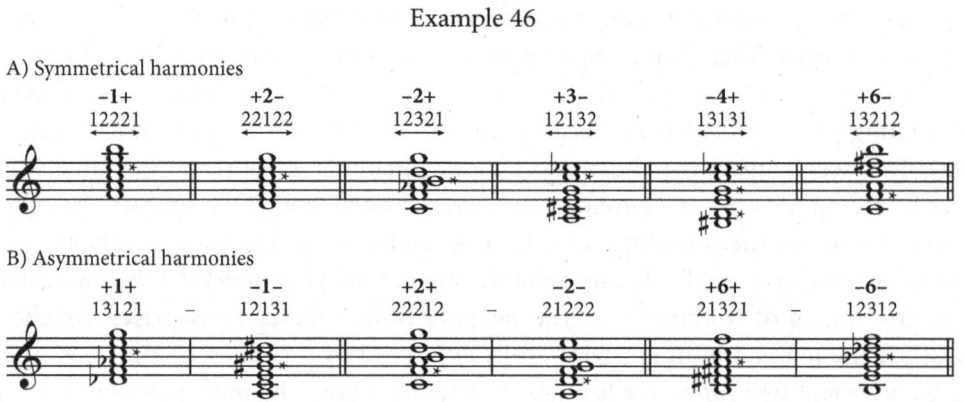

Example 46

The following tables show all the harmonies in category **II**, with their triadic symbols and orientation schemes. Shown with each harmony (or pair of harmonies) **II** are orientation schemes of all its subordinate chords. Not every chord belonging to a lower class and contained in the original harmony is a subordinate chord of the combination – only a chord containing components of both triads in the combination may be so considered.

---

59 Editor's note: For example, +2+ (F A C G B D 22212) and −2− (A♯ F♯ D♯ G♯ E C♯ 21222) are at the same time mutual inversions and mutual negatives.

Symmetrical Combination Harmonies II

	−1+	+2− = maximum 12[1]	−2+ = maximum 126[4]		+6−	+3− = maximum 126[3]	−4+ = maximum 01
harmonies	12221(4)	22122(3) negative of itself	12321(3)	13212(3)		12132(3)	13131(3) negative of itself
			mutual negatives				
five-note chords	1222—2221 1223—3221 1241—1421	2232 1223—3221 2122—2212	1232—2321 1233—2133 1312—2131	1231—1321 1323—1332 2123—3212		1213—3121 2132—2312 1323—1332	1313—3131
four-note chords	323 143 222 141 122—221 124—421 142—241 214—412 223—322	143 212 252 323 122—221 214—412 223—322	131 232 333 123—321 133—331 142—241 213—312 214—412 233—332	151 212 313 323 123—321 124—421 132—231 133—331 233—332		121 242 313 323 124—421 132—231 133—331 213—312 233—332	131 143 313 134—314
three-note chords	22 25 12—21 14—41 15—51 23—32 24—42	22 25 12—21 14—41 23—32	25 33 12—21 13—31 15—51 23—32 24—42	33 12—21 13—31 15—51 23—32 24—42		33 12—21 13—31 15—51 23—32 24—42	44 13—31 14—41
two-note chords	1 2 6	1 2	1 2 6	1 2 6		1 2 6	1

Asymmetrical Combination Harmonies II

harmonies	+1+ 13121(4)	−1− 12131(4)	+2+ 22212(3)	−2− 21222(3)	+6+ 21321(3)	−6− 12312(3)
			mutual negatives		mutual negatives	
five-note chords	1214 1331		2223 2232			
	3121 1421 1312 1313	1213 1241 2131 3131	2221 1232 2212 2123	1222 2321 2122 3212	1321 2133 2132	1231 1233 2312
four-note chords	121 131 141 143 313		212 222 232 323		151 242 333	
	133—331 134—314 214—412		223—322 233—332			
	421 142 312	124 241 213	221 123 421 241 412	122 321 124 142 214	132 213 332 321 421 133	231 312 233 123 124 331
three-note chords	25 33 44		22 25 33		33	
	12—21 13—31 14—41 15—51		12—21 23—32 24—42		15—51 42—42	
	42	24	41 15	14 51	21 13 32	12 31 23
two-note chords	1 2 6		1 2 6		1 2 6	

Chapter IIIb – Triadic Combinations

The domain governed by combination harmonies **II** is much greater than that governed by basic harmonies **I**. Harmonies **I** comprise two triads representing a total of five chord-types, including the triads themselves. (See §53 above.) In harmonies **II**, twelve combination harmonies govern 95 chords (again including the combination harmonies themselves), in the following distribution by class:

12 six-note chords (harmonies **II**),
30 five-note chords,
34 four-note chords,
16 three-note chords,
3 two-note chords,
───────────────
total: 95 chords.

Each of the combination harmonies **II** that is also a maximum (+2-, -2+, +3-, -4+) has more subordinate chords here than in the system of characteristic-types. This is because here a subordinate chord need not preserve the full dissonant characteristic of the original harmony; it is sufficient that it merge any components of the two triads in the combination harmony as long as the result is dissonant. The dissonant characteristic becomes simpler in chords of lower classes.

The four-note chords 143, 232, 323, 223—322, and the three-note chords 22, 25, 14—41, 23—32 are not subordinate to the diatonic maximum **12**[1], 22122, although they do represent the incomplete combination harmony +2-, which also has the orientation scheme 22122. Similarly, neither the four-note chords 121, 242, 313, 323, 133—331, 233—332 nor any three-note chords are subordinate to the chromatic maximum **126**[3], 12132, although a number of three-note chords (see table) and all these four-note chords are contained in the combination harmony +3-, which has the same orientation scheme.

The least difference in terms of subordinate chords occurs with the harmony -4+ and the maximum **01**, which have the common scheme 13131. We can find all the subordinate chords of the characteristic maximum **01** in the combination -4+, as well as all the maxima **1**, their subordinate chords, and the augmented triad 44, which is not one of the subordinate chords of maximum **01**, as it lacks the dissonant characteristic 1. The augmented triad appears in connection with the harmony -4+ as a normal dissonant chord, whose dissonance is given by the combination of two basic triads, minor and major, at the interval 4. It differs from other dissonant chords derived from the combination -4+ in its total lack of the dissonant characteristic 1, which is present in the complete combination harmony three times. We are then justified in saying that in the augmented triad the characteristic 1 is *completely suppressed*. Such elimination of a dissonant characteristic is not unusual in the system of combination harmonies; most of the subordinate chords of lower classes lack one or even two of the dissonant characteristics that are in the combination harmony. Since the harmony −4+ has no single dissonant element other than 1, eliminating that characteristic leaves only the augmented triad with the dissonant combination of intervals 44.

The augmented triad 44 is also subordinate to the harmonies +1+ and −1−.

§55. Partial Combinations with Two Components

As a supplement to the comprehensive inventory of combination harmonies II, we present a summary of partial combinations with two components. These are combinations whose component triads have common pitches. Combinations of two triads with two common pitches form four-note chords, while those with one common pitch form five-note chords. These are not independent combination harmonies equivalent to true combinations; they are merely auxiliary harmonic formations that appear as components in true combination harmonies. We can express them using the same symbols as for true combinations, that is, showing family symbols and the interval between the roots of the two basic triads. In order to distinguish them from true combination chords, we will use one *curved line* to indicate the existence of one common pitch, and two curved lines to indicate two common pitches.

There are twelve partial combinations with two components. In three of these the component triads have two pitches in common. As the two component triads always belong to different families,[60] all three combinations are symmetrical. They are the four-note chords +0̂−, −3̂+, +4̂−, shown in Example 47.

Example 47

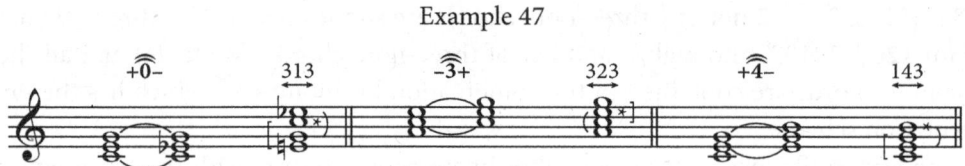

The formations −3̂+ and +4̂− are familiar from classical harmony; only the formation +0̂− is new. These formations can be understood as incomplete true combination harmonies:

+0̂− as +6− or +3− or −4+ or +1+ or −1−,
−3̂+ as −1+ or +2− or +6− or +3− or +2+ or −2−,
+4̂− as −1+ or +2− or −4+ or +1+ or −1−.

---

60 Editor's note: Two consonant triads with two pitches in common either share root and fifth, in which case the thirds (and families) must be different, or they share an interval of a third and, in order to make a different triad, the additional third must be in the opposite position (above or below), making a triad of the opposite family.

Chapter IIIb – Triadic Combinations

We can relate a partial combination to a true combination harmony as follows: we form a major or minor triad by adding to a pitch that is part of only one of the two component triads of a partial combination two new pitches that are not already present. For example, in the formation E G C E♭ (+0–), from the pitch E we can form the triad E G♯ B, making the combination C E♭ G – E G♯ B (the harmony –4+); or from E we can form the triad C♯ E G♯ (making C E♭ G – C♯ E G♯, –1–) or the triad A C♯ E (making A C♯ E – C E♭ G, +6–); then from the pitch E♭, we can form the triad E♭ G♭ B♭ (making C E G – E♭ G♭ B♭, +3–), or the triad B D♯ F♯ (B D♯ F♯ – C E G, +1+), or the triad G♯ B D♯ (G♯ B D♯ – C E G, –4+).

In each of the nine remaining partial combinations, the component triads have only one pitch in common. Shown in Example 48, three of the combinations are symmetrical, since they combine triads of different families.

Example 48

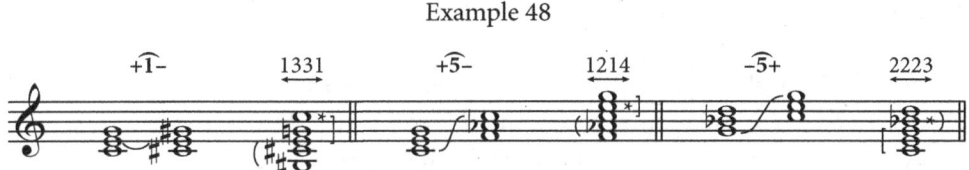

Only the formation +1̂– is modern, while –5̂+ is a dominant major ninth and +5̂– is one of the accessory ninth chords that we occasionally meet in the late Baroque. All three of these five-note chords can be understood as incomplete true combination harmonies, as follows:

$$+\widehat{1}-\text{ as }+1+\text{ or }-1-,$$
$$+\widehat{5}-\text{ as }+1+\text{ or }-1-,$$
$$-\widehat{5}+\text{ as }+2+\text{ or }-2-.$$

The combination +1̂– is identical to the characteristic maximum **016**, the combination +5̂– to the characteristic maximum **012**, and the combination –5̂+ to the diatonic characteristic maximum **26**[1].

In order to form a true combination harmony II from a partial five-note one, we form a major or minor triad by adding an independent third pitch to two pitches that are part of only one of the two component basic triads, without repeating a pitch already present. For example, in the combination G♯ C♯ E G C we use the pitches G C (not part of C♯ E G♯) to form the triad C E♭ G, or the pitches G♯ C♯ (not part of C E G) to form the triad D♭ F A♭; the resulting combination harmonies are C E♭ G – C♯ E G♯ or D♭ F A♭ – C E G, that is, –1– or +1+.

Six other partial combinations, shown in Example 49, form three pairs of mutually invertible *asymmetrical* formations. The combinations +5+ and –5– are known as subsidiary ninth chords, while the combinations +3+, –3–, +4+ and –4– are not considered harmonies at all in classical harmony.

Example 49

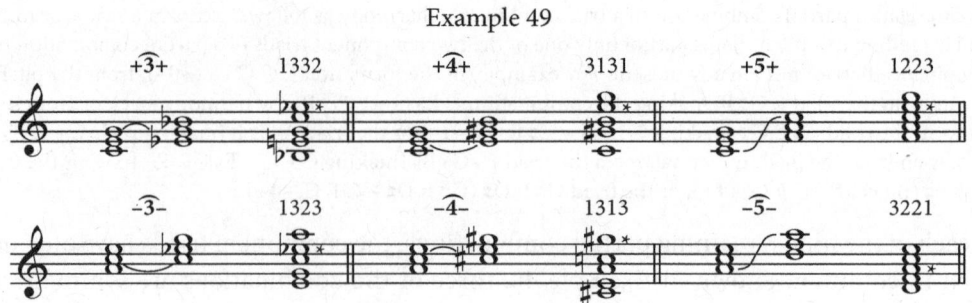

All asymmetrical partial combination harmonies are of course at the same time incomplete true combination harmonies:

+3̂+ and –3̂– are incomplete combinations +3– or +6–,
+4̂+ is an incomplete combination harmony –4+ or –1–,
–4̂– is an incomplete combination harmony –4+ or +1+,
+5̂+ and –5̂– are incomplete combinations +2– or –1+.

We can also discover relations between true and partial combinations by comparing their orientation schemes. Thus the partial triadic combination +3̂+ is part of the true combination harmonies +3– and +6–, since its scheme 1332 is contained in the schemes 12132(3) and 13212(3) of the combination harmonies +3– and +6– respectively. We can deduce that the formation +3̂+ is not contained in any other combination harmony from the fact that its scheme 1332 is not contained in the schemes of any other combination harmonies II: 12221(4), 22122(3), 12321(3), 13131(3), 13121(4), 12131(4), 22212(3), 21222(3), 21321(3), and 12312(3).[61] (When comparing orientation schemes of different classes, we must always consider the expanded orientation scheme or at least include the complement for the chord of the higher class.)

§56. Triadic Combinations III

Three different basic triads can be combined into one chord, with no common pitches in the component triads, in twelve different ways. There are not twelve true combinations III, however, but only eight, because several combinations result in the same chord, as we can verify from their orientation schemes. All true triadic combinations here are *nine-note chords*. As with harmonies II, we will designate combinations III using the family symbols of their component basic triads and the intervals between the roots of these triads; there will be three family symbols and two intervals. Since three asymmetrical triads are being combined, a symmetrical chord can never result (as it could when combining two asymmetrical triads); thus all combinations III are *asymmetrical* and form mutually invertible pairs.

Example 50 presents a summary of all four pairs of triadic combinations III. The fourth pair is shown in three different combinational interpretations. Joint orientation schemes for the nine-note chords and their three-note negatives are shown with

---

61 Editor's note: For more detailed explanation see two last paragraphs of §58.

Chapter IIIb – Triadic Combinations

the combination symbols. An asterisk beside a pitch indicates the lowest pitch of the scheme. An asterisk beside a square or curved bracket (enclosing a component major or minor triad, respectively) indicates the lowest component basic triad in the combination symbol. Thus the triad G B D is the first and lowest component in the combination harmony A C♯ E – A♭ C E♭ – G B D, designated **+1+1+**.

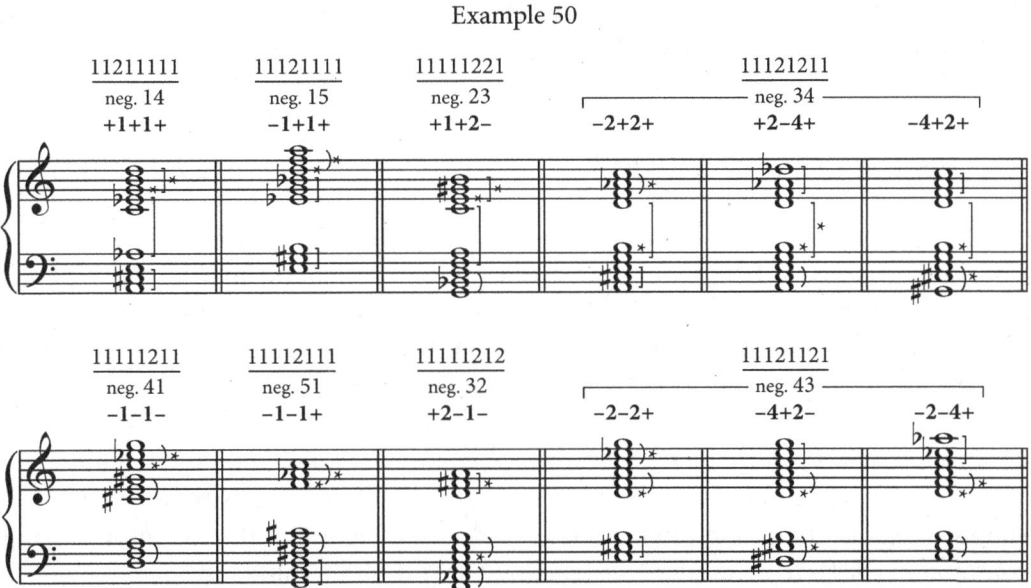

Example 50

None of the triadic combinations is a characteristic maximum. In the system of characteristic-types, all these combination harmonies are derivations of the maximum **011266**.

Combinations **III**, although fewer in number than harmonies **II**, govern a far larger domain. Eight of them are sufficient to represent 217 chords, including the combinations themselves. These are distributed among chord-classes as follows:

> 8 nine-note chords (triadic combinations **III**),
> 33 eight-note chords,
> 63 seven-note chords,
> 67 six-note chords,
> 36 five-note chords,
> 9 four-note chords,
> 1 three-note chord,
>
> 217 chords in total.

We will not present exhaustive lists of orientation schemes of the chords subordinate to combinations **III** here, because that would take too much space.

Individual triadic combinations III can be considered to be *modern harmonies*, similarly to combinations II. However, these are very complex formations, so their harmonic intelligibility must be supported by a suitable disposition. Instead of the term *harmony*, therefore, we will use the less restrictive designation *triadic combination*.

Chords that are subordinate to combinations III can also be understood as *thickened harmonies* II. This applies especially to seven-note chords. Since we are standing on the freer soil of triadic combinations here, it cannot matter if thickening or simplifying chords sometimes leads us to cross a boundary between characteristics.

§57. The Triadic Combinations IV

The triadic combination **IV** contains four basic triads with no common pitches. It is a twelve-note chord. Although only one exists, it is possible to organize it in several different ways (similar to the way combinations neg. 34 and neg. 43 each have three forms; see §56 above). We arrive at the combination **IV** by the merging of two harmonies **II** or the merging of a combination **III** with a harmony **I**. (It is of course possible to form combination **IV** from four triads, harmonies **I**, as defined. We are concerned with finding the different organizational possibilities of combination **IV**, however, and therefore we begin with higher formations that are already themselves combinations.) We cannot simply merge any two chords belonging to the given categories if the condition barring common pitches is to be met and a twelve-note chord is to result.

Example 51

1) Combination **IV** in the arrangement −2−2+2+

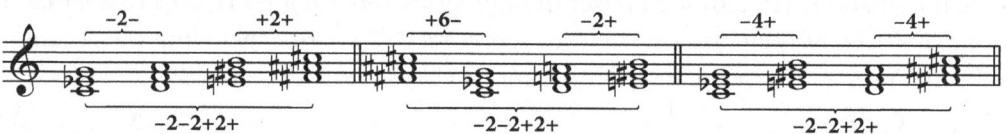

2) Combination **IV** in the arrangement +2−4+2−

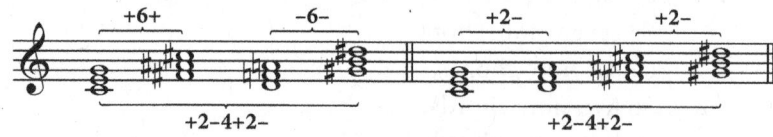

In order for two harmonies II composed of different pitches to produce a twelve-note chord, they must be mutual negatives: the second harmony II must contain all the pitches, and only those, that were not in the first harmony II. According to the tables in §54, there are three pairs of harmonies II that are negatives of each other and two harmonies II that are identical to their negatives. From this we could conclude that merging two harmonies II produces five possible forms of combination IV. In reality the possibilities are not so rich, however: we can form the combination IV in only two different ways. This is shown in Example 51.

When the combination **IV** is to result from the merging of a combination **III** with a harmony **I**, only those combinations **III** can be used whose negatives are harmonies **I**. Harmonies **I** are negatives of combinations neg. 34 and neg. 43, each of which has three possible arrangements. (See Example 50 above.) However, instead of the expected six possible arrangements of the combination **IV** formed from a combination **III** and a harmony **I**, we again have only two arrangements shown in Example 52; these are identical to arrangements formed from merging two harmonies **II**.

Example 52

1) Combination **IV** in the arrangement −2−2+2+

2) Combination **IV** in the arrangement +2−4+2−

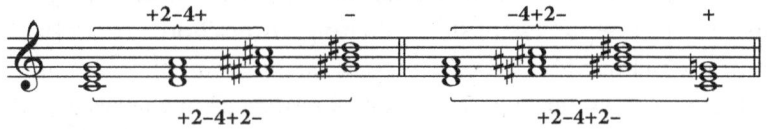

Thus the triadic combination **IV** can be formed from four harmonies **I** in only two ways: as **−2−2+2+** or as **+2−4+2−**.
Only 33 chords belong to the combination category **IV**:

  1 twelve-note chord (triadic combination **IV**),
  1 eleven-note chord (the only one),
  6 ten-note chords (all of them),
  11 nine-note chords: neg. 11, 22, 25, 33, 44, 12—21, 13—31, 24—42,
  10 eight-note chords: neg. 111, 121, 222, 224, 242, 333, 112—211, 213—312,
  3 seven-note chords: neg. 1111, 2112, 2222,
  1 six-note chord: neg. 22222 (= 22222),

  33 chords total.

The triadic combination **IV** is also the maximum **011266**.

§58. Classification of Chords into Combination Categories

We found that the subordination of lower chords to particular maxima of the corresponding characteristic-type is not without ambiguity; the lower chords of any characteristic that is represented by more than one maximum can be understood in several different ways. (See §48 above.) There are similar conditions in the system of triadic combinations. In those categories represented by more than one combination (I, II, III), the subordination of lower chords to particular combinations is not clearly defined; only in category IV is it unambiguous. The farther apart the classes of chord and combination, the greater the ambiguity and uncertainty.

In category I, with only the two triads + and −, a minimal distance is possible between the class of these triads and that of the chord to be classified; it is the distance between two-note and three-note chords, that is, between adjacent classes. Here the ambiguity is limited to the two triads. The variety of possible interpretations is considerably greater in category II, which is represented by twelve harmonies, and which includes everything from these six-note chords to two-note chords. From the tables in §54 above we see that the two-note chord 1 belongs to all twelve combination harmonies; the three-note chord 12 belongs to all except −4+, +6+, and −6− (that is, to nine combination harmonies); the four-note chord 122 belongs to −1+, +2−, and −2−; the five-note chord 1222 only to the two combination harmonies −1+ and −2−. The situation is even more complex in category III, in spite of the fact that it is represented by only eight triadic combinations, since this category extends all the way from nine-note to three-note chords.

The ambiguity in the process of subordinating lower chords to particular combination harmonies is balanced by the *unequivocal classification of chords into combination categories*. Thus, in the system of triadic combinations as in the system of characteristic-types, it is the fact that a chord *belongs to a certain category* (rather than to a certain representative chord of a category) which is significant.

Although chords belonging to lower categories are always also components of higher categories, a chord is always classified in the lowest possible category. We determine the combination category to which a chord belongs in the following way: we divide the pitches of the chord into the smallest possible number of groups such that each group is free of single dissonant intervals and the dissonant triad; the number of groups then indicates the category. For example, we divide the five-note chord G C F* A B 2221 into two groups C F A − G B, the four-note chord D C♯ E C* 112 into three groups D − C♯ E − C or D − C♯ − E C. Our five-note chord thus belongs to category II, but the four-note chord to category III. If we want to determine the particular combination harmony to which a given chord belongs, we must supplement the incomplete groups with new pitches in order to form major or minor triads. In the five-note chord G C F A B, we can complete the group G B in two different ways to produce E G B or G B D, thus forming (with F A C) the true combinations −1+ or +2+. From D C♯ E C it is possible, by completing groups in different ways, to form all eight triadic combinations III.

When only the orientation scheme of a chord is given, we determine to which combination category it belongs by comparing its scheme with the expanded schemes of combination harmonies. We can add several smaller intervals in the scheme of the combination harmony to form a larger interval (this means that we are eliminating pitches from the harmony); part of the scheme of the combination harmony must then be identical to the scheme of the chord in question, if the chord is subordinate to this combination harmony. For example, the scheme 2221 is contained in the schemes of only two triadic combinations **II**: in 12221(4), −1+, and in 22212(3), +2+. The scheme 112 is contained in the schemes of all the triadic combinations **III**. (See the Example 50 above.) Conversely, when using negative orientation schemes for chords of higher classes, we must determine whether the negative scheme of the combination harmony is contained in the negative scheme of the lower chord.

Determining the combination category to which a chord belongs using only its orientation scheme is more difficult. We would have to extract from the scheme the formations 43 and 34, and eventually their components 3, 4, and 5; since in more complex schemes these formations regularly enclose adjacent pitches, error is difficult to avoid. Therefore the category of a chord is better determined from actual pitches. (An orientation scheme can easily be transformed into an example with pitches.) The presence of the group 11 in an orientation scheme indicates that the chord does not belong to the combination category **II**, but rather to a higher category, as the group 11 is unknown in category **II**. On the other hand, there are chords whose orientation schemes do not include the group 11 and that nevertheless belong to higher categories. The six-note chord 22222, whose orientation scheme does not include even the interval 1, belongs as high as category **IV**.

§59. Representation of Triadic Combinations

The difference between the two basic triads is only the third, which determines their family. In harmonies **I**, i.e. triads, family is a *differentiating* feature, that is, secondary rather than essential or fundamental. It is supported also by the fact that the third can distinguish family not when isolated, but only in connection with the other two (or at least one of the other two) pitches of the triad. The isolated pitch of the third cannot be perceived as a third of a triad; an isolated pitch cannot distinguish anything, because it has nothing to distinguish. In contrast, the outer pitches of the triad (the root and the fifth) together can function as the triad even when the third is absent; it may be a triad of indefinite family, but it is still a triad with a specific place in pitch space. Thus the outer pitches of triads (their roots and fifths) have more weight than the central pitch (the third). If we want to use a comparison from the world outside music, we can say that the outer pitches represent the substance of the triad, while the third is only its colour or illumination.

Since the interval between the root and the fifth is the same in both triads, it will suffice to use only one of these pitches to designate the triad (the "substance of the triad"). If the two pitches were of the same weight, an agreement would have to be attained. If one of the pitches weighs more, it would become the one designating the chord.

The misleading logic of mechanically conceived harmonic dualism is a very illustrative example of the complexity that the issue of the root-fifth weight carries. Root was considered to be basic pitch in major, fifth in minor chord. Mutual inversion of the two chords misled theory here to a wrong conclusion completely incomprehensible to practical musicians (See §53).

The relation between the root and the fifth is established by practical music in favour of the root, unequivocally, since the fifth is frequently omitted from triads even in the most exposed places (at cadences), and the root together with the third (or even the root alone) is considered sufficient. Thus it is not arbitrary to speak of the root as the *basic pitch* and of the fifth as the *supplementary pitch*, to which the third is added as the differentiating pitch. The entire triad can be represented by one pitch – the root as the basic pitch.

In combinations, the relation between the pitches of the component basic triads remains the same. Thus *each component triad has its own basic pitch*. Combination harmonies **II** can therefore be represented by two pitches (the basic pitches of their component triads). Similarly, triadic combinations **III** have three basic (representative) pitches, and combinations **IV** have four.

The ambiguity of incomplete combination harmonies also causes ambiguity in their representation. Thus in the five-note chord G C F A B, the representation fluctuates between the possibilities F–G and e–F. (Basic pitches of component major triads are shown in upper case letters, roots of minor triads in lower case letters.) There is a parallel between the variety of representational possibilities and the variety of possible combination harmonies to which a chord could belong. Only complete combination harmonies and certain incomplete combinations of the highest class (closest to the combination harmonies) can be unequivocally represented by basic pitches.

Triadic combinations **II**, **III**, and **IV** that are not realized concretely always have respectively 2, 3, and 4 basic pitches of equal significance. Only in an actual disposition do certain roots assume greater significance than others and thus become the *chief basic pitches*. Only in a specific arrangement of a harmony, therefore, is representation by roots in a certain hierarchy possible. *The component basic triad that is placed lower in the chord always has the greater significance; the basic pitch of this component triad will thus also be the chief basic pitch of the entire combination* **II**, **III**, *or* **IV**. This makes a substantial difference between the individual pitches of triads and the basic pitches of the triadic combinations **II**, **III**, and **IV**. In harmonies **I**, individual pitches have their own value and function as basic, supplementary, or differentiating pitches, regardless of their disposition, whereas the basic pitches of the component triads in combination harmonies of higher categories increase or decrease in significance (becoming either chief or secondary basic pitches) according to their specific disposition. In this respect, the construction of combination harmonies from triads is not parallel to the construction of triads from pitches.

Chapter IIIb – Triadic Combinations

§60. The Significance of the Combination System

The two systems of classification we have used have enabled us to classify all the harmonic material, every possible chord, of the tempered chromatic system. It would be possible to use some other system of classification as well.

The use of two classification systems cannot be justified merely by the fact that musical practice has not yet taken full advantage of the material we are classifying, and has not yet stabilized it to the point where we could rely on one system to shed light on the less obviously perceptible nooks and crannies of each chord. The characteristic system, which we consider generally to be more appropriate and more practical, suppresses certain realities with which the music of some modern composers teems. This is because it ignores the *combination structure of chords*, especially of *multi-note chords*, although this is precisely the structure that tends to be emphasized both by the disposition of chords and by the *voice-leading in chord progressions*. In the layering of triadic components to form higher chord entities, individual characteristics recede into the background; perception of a chord as the juxtaposition of two or three such layers simpler, therefore is more immediate and intelligible than the complex, refined, and often ingeniously obscured combined effect of six or nine individual pitches.

Thus we are faced with an important practical question: when should we classify according to the characteristic system, and when according to the combination system? The following practice is sensible:

a) Chords whose class is too far removed from that of the corresponding triadic combination, especially chords belonging to neither family, are better classified according to dissonant characteristic; for such chords, the combination system is really only possible in the case of partial combinations **II**.

b) Chords that are true combinations, or that closely approach certain true combinations, are classified either according to the characteristic system or the combination system, depending on their concrete disposition.

In situations described in a), classification according to true combinations is not clear enough; thus we choose the characteristic system. In situations described in b), the combination system is appropriate only when the component basic triads are clearly separated from each other; if they are not, if they interpenetrate each other, it is again better to classify according to dissonant characteristic.

For example, if we do not perceive the chord C E G B as a partial combination $\widehat{+4-}$, it is the complete characteristic maximum **1**[3]. The chord C E♭ B D, which does not belong to either family, is the chromatic characteristic maximum **12**[2]; classified according to combination, it is one of the chords of category **II**: +3– (A♭ C E♭ – B D F♯), or +1+ (G B D – A♭ C E♭), or –1– (B D F♯ – C E♭ G). Thus it is simpler and less ambiguous to classify this chord according to characteristic. The chord B C E♭ E G G♯ (13131) can be designated as the characteristic maximum **01**, as long as the components C E♭ G – E G♯ B (or G♯ B D♯ – C E G or E G B – A♭ C E♭) are not clearly separated from each other; otherwise we are dealing with the combination –4+.

We can see from the above that analytical practice will classify according to dissonant characteristic more often than according to combination. The combination system is justified, however, in spite of the more limited opportunities for its use; its elimination would only *seem* to simplify things. This system makes certain chords easy to grasp that would otherwise have to be perceived as complex piles of individual pitches; in situations involving certain dispositions, this latter interpretation would be in sharp contrast to the actual harmonic effect of the chords.[62] Thus the significance of the combination system lies in its ability to supplement effectively, and at times even to replace, the characteristic system where the latter cannot adequately capture the simplified structure of a complex multi-note chord.

---

[62] Editor's note: Precisely one of the great deficiency of Allen Forte's system.

Chapter IV – Disposition of Chords

§61. The Concept of Disposition

In order to make the extensive chord material of the tempered chromatic system manageable, we had to establish the principle that chords with the same pitch-structure and their transpositions were of the same chord-type. This agreed with the generally accepted understanding of chordal phenomena of classical harmony. In order to discern differences in sound between chords of the same type (of the same pitch-structure), we turn to the concept of the *disposition of a chord*. A chord can be disposed or laid out in various ways. Disposition does not touch a chord's pitch content, it simply *arranges* it. (See §2 above.)

Although classical harmony defined in its own way the concept of the chord-type, it did not formulate the complement of this concept, namely the concept of disposition in its most general sense. Instead, it was content with its explanations of chord rotations, positions, and pitch doublings, all of which are aspects of disposition. In the concept of a chord's disposition we include *all processes by which the actual sonic effect of a chord can be modified while the original pitch content remains the same.*

There are two limitations. First, all these changes involve the distribution of pitches within pitch space, affecting the higher or lower placement of the pitch. This means, for example, that it is not enough to change dynamics or instrumentation, to play piano instead of forte, or to use stringed instruments instead of a piano; such a change does not constitute a change of disposition in the harmonic sense. Second, we cannot tamper with the original pitch material forming the chord. No new pitch can be added,[63] just as none can be omitted; we can only arrange the pitch material already given by the chord-type.

Before continuing, it should be noted that the differences in sound between various dispositions of the same chord-type can be as great as or even greater than the differences in sound between different chord-types. We must remember, however, that the essence of a chord's sound (its characteristic) cannot be changed by any change in disposition. It

---

63 Editor's note: Whenever the qualities of chord-types are considered, it is within pitch-class space, while chord dispositions are considered within pitch space.

is impossible to impart to a chord, through disposition alone, a characteristic effect that does not belong to its type.

§62. The Form, Position, and Inner Disposition of a Chord; Pitch Doublings

The *outer* pitches of a chord appear most prominent in its actual sound, since they are its most exposed components, while the *inner* pitches (seen more as supplementary) can be said to play a subordinate role. The *lowest pitch* of the chord determines its *rotation*, the *highest* its *position*. A chord can have as many different rotations and positions as it has pitches: a three-note chord three, a four-note chord four, etc. All the inner pitches determine the *inner disposition* of the chord; according to the disposition of these inner pitches (according to the distances between them), we can speak of inner dispositions that are close (tight), wide, mixed, dispersed, or splintered. The number of possible inner dispositions cannot be specified; it depends on both the distance between the outer pitches and the number of inner pitches.

The number of sounding pitches is not always the same as the number of pitches of the chord-class. Thus in a sounding three-note chord we often find four, five, or even more pitches. This means that certain pitches (more exactly pitch classes) are repeated, that they are doubled (or tripled, or further *multiplied*). Pitches can be doubled in different octaves and also at the unison.

Of course the omission of pitches also affects the sound of a chord. According to our interpretations in *Chapters II* and *IIIa–b*, however, the omission of a pitch produces a different chord, even if this chord can be considered to represent the original one. A three-note chord cannot be realized from only two pitches, because two pitches joined together can only form a two-note chord. A three-note harmony, however, *can be expressed* by two of its pitches, where we perceive the resulting two-note chord as the incomplete form of the harmony. Our entire system of classifying chords is built on this principle. We will discuss the omission of pitches further in the next chapter, which deals with the expression of chords.

In summary: in the disposition of chords, we achieve

1) the *rotation* by assigning to a certain pitch the role of the lowest (bass) pitch;
2) the *position* by placing a certain pitch of the chord into the highest (soprano) voice; and
3) the *inner disposition* by laying out the inner pitches of a chord between the chosen outer pitches; at the same time; we can also
4) *double* certain pitches.

Omission of a tone is outside the considerations of chord disposition.

§63. Evaluating the Sound of Dispositions

Music does not include only chords that sound beautiful, pleasing, and perfect in every way. Even the purest classical music could not exist without harmonic tangles, chordal tensions, or harshness. This is because the harmonic material on which music can draw contains only two consonances but a flood of dissonant chords.

However, almost in spite of themselves, more complex chords flow into consonances, are transformed into them or at least drawn towards them. Thus of the two opposite worlds, consonances have the advantage over dissonances; in spite of being superior in number, dissonances are subordinate to consonances because they are *measured* by them. The more dissonant the environment of consonances, and the more involved the processes by which we approach them, the brighter shines their consonant quality. The relations of consonances to their immediate and more distant harmonic surroundings are responsible for their apparent degree of purity or simplicity. This is also true of dissonances: they are harsher or milder, more or less obtrusive, depending on their harmonic surroundings and on the degree to which we have become accustomed to them from the prior flow of the music.

Composers have always taken into consideration the fact that the *sonic effect of a chord is relative*. The creation of a suitable framework for certain central chords, to give their sounds a clearer profile (whether brighter or otherwise), constitutes a substantial part of a composer's artistic endeavor.

However, the sonic effect of a chord-type can be modified *absolutely* (without the help of its harmonic surroundings) as well as relatively. This is what happens in *disposition*. Various dispositions, achieved through the processes described in §62 above, do not merely represent external changes, but rather determine the *actual sonic effect of the chord*. By changing disposition, we achieve different illumination of chords: they become brighter or darker, their innermost essence (their characteristic) is clearly exposed or concealed, their piercing quality is increased or decreased. A practical study of dispositions enables us to use such changes in sound purposefully.

A change in the sonic effect of a chord-type achieved through disposition is most noticeable if the chord is *isolated* and so cannot be affected by its harmonic surroundings. Therefore the study of dispositions is most successful using isolated chords rather than chord progressions.

The evaluation of the sounds of a chord's different dispositions is a matter of *judgment*. Objective measurement is impossible. Some might demur that the results are based on the subjective opinions, or even the arbitrary whims, of the judge. There would be no sense in trying to objectify the results by the support of an experiment involving a larger group of "judges" whose evaluations would then be statistically processed; it would be impossible to ensure that all the subjects had a well-developed and thoroughly cultivated harmonic sensitivity. A *critical analysis of living music*, both old and new, will serve us much better. Through it we will almost certainly be able to discover the composer's intentions as to sound.

As for these intentions, composers usually strive for good, refined dispositions of chords; when they strive for a barbarously harsh disposition, it tends to be the result of exceptional circumstances, often of programmatic intention or word-painting. However, composers consciously strive for dispositions with a good sound only in the case of chords that are somehow exposed, such as chords that are isolated, or of long duration, or that function as destination; dispositions of chords in a progression are thus not conclusive for verifying evaluations. This is equally true for old and new music. *Modern composers want to create music that sounds beautiful*, even when they make use of sharp dissonances and extremely complex chords in the process.

In the following we will attempt to classify dispositions according to rotation, position, inner disposition, and doubled pitches. Dispositions considered according to these aspects will not always be simply good or bad; there will also be intermediate gradations, that is, dispositions that are better or worse; there will be dispositions whose sound will be of the same value; and, most important, there will be dispositions with enmeshed and conflicting classifications, with both positive and negative evaluations.

§64. Disposition of Basic Triads

The two basic triads, major and minor, each have *three possible rotations* and *three possible positions*. The zero rotation has the root at the bottom: the *five-three chord* (C E G, A C E). The *first rotation* has the third at the bottom: the *six-three chord* (E G C, C E A). The *second rotation* has the fifth at the bottom: the *six-four chord* (G C E, E A C). The evaluation of the sound of these three rotations, as supported by all music almost from the beginning of polyphony, can be expressed quite simply by the following order:

five-three – six-three – six-four.

The superiority of the sound of the five-three chord over the far less satisfying effect of the six-three chord is obvious; the difference between this less good six-three chord and the problematic six-four chord is not so great.

The differences in sonic quality between the rotations of basic triads are pronounced as long as the lowest pitch is sounding low enough (in the third or second octave,[64] or even lower). If the pitch that determines rotation is sounding in the fourth octave or higher, differences in the sonic quality of various rotations are much less pronounced.

Compared to rotations, *positions* have far less significant effect on the sound. The most stable of the three positions is the *basic position*, with the root as its highest pitch (C in the triad C E G); the *position of the third*, with the third (E) as the highest pitch, is

---

64 Editor's note: We are using the system for identifying octaves in which the lowest C on the piano is C_1, and the first octave ascends from C_1 to C_2, which is on the second ledger line below the bass staff (great C). Thus the fourth octave ascends from C_4 (middle C).

less definite; the *position of the fifth* (with G as the highest pitch) has a somewhat open effect.[65]

Those positions and rotations that are determined by the same pitch of the triad can be combined only at the cost of doubling that pitch. Thus a new factor enters into the disposition. For example, a six-three chord in the position of the third (i.e., with the third in the soprano) must have a doubled third (E G C E).

The *inner disposition* with the best and most compact sound is a *close* (*tight*) one, in which the pitches of the triad are as close together as possible. As they are placed further apart, the quality of sound worsens. If we designate as *wide* those inner dispositions where the distances between adjacent pitches are not as small as possible but do not exceed an octave, and as *dispersed* those where the distance of an octave is exceeded, the following order of inner dispositions can be constructed, from best to worst:

tight – wide – dispersed.

Since in a complete triad without doubled pitches there are two intervals (intervals between three pitches) determining the inner disposition, there are instances of variously *mixed* inner dispositions. In such cases, a pitch that is too distant from the other pitches is heard as independent rather than blending with them into a unified sound. Such a greater distance is less significant between the lower two pitches, especially in a five-three chord. In contrast, placing pitches too close together too low (for example, in the second octave or lower) is problematic— the resulting sound is not pleasing.

The link connecting the sounds of the basic pitch and the fifth of the triads is the *third*. If the third is too distant from the other two pitches, not only is it heard independently of them, but its connective properties decrease. The interval between the root and the fifth, when isolated (separated by distance from the other pitches) in the middle or upper register, sounds better as a fourth (5)[66] than as a fifth (7); thus E – – G C is a better arrangement than E – – C G. (The two dashes here indicate a distance exceeding two octaves.)

Following is the order of preference for the doubling of pitches in consonant triads:

---

65 Terminology founded on figured bass is based on the interval between the soprano and the bass. Thus in the case of a five-three chord, the basic position would be referred to as the "octave position" (based on the octave C–C); in the case of a six-three chord, the basic position would be the "position of the sixth" (based on the sixth E–C); in the case of a six-four chord, it would be the "position of the fourth" (based on the fourth G–C). Here, however, we will designate position according to the pitch in the soprano, without considering its interval from the bass (that is, we will consider only the original basic pitch, the original third, and the original fifth).
Editor's note: We point out the possible confusion between the common English designation of "root position" (here called "zero rotation") and Janeček's term of "basic position" which designates a disposition with the root – the basic pitch – in the *highest* voice.

66 Editor's note: Expressed in semitones.

a) for five-three chords: root – fifth – third;
b) for six-three chords: root or fifth – third;
c) for six-four chords: fifth – root – third.

In all three rotations, the pitch that requires the most care is the third. Its doubling is most unpleasantly conspicuous in a six-three chord. A six-three chord sounds worst in the position of the fifth or basic position when its bass pitch (the third) is doubled in a voice other than that adjacent to the bass: E C E G or E C E G C; the position of the third is somewhat better: E – G C E. (The single dash indicates a distance equal to or exceeding one octave.) The most acceptable doubling of the third in the six-three chord is in the bass and tenor: E – E G C.

The dispositions of the basic triads can vary according to rotation, position, inner disposition, and doubled pitches. At the same time, judging the quality of the disposition by these criteria separately can yield *contradictory results*. For example, disposing the triad C E G as C E G C has a positive effect in every respect, as it combines the best rotation (the five-three chord: C at the bottom) with the best position (basic: C at the top), the best sounding inner disposition (tight: pitches as close together as possible), and the best doubling (C – C). The disposition C E C G, while first class in terms of rotation, is less convincing in terms of position (of the fifth), and average in the quality of its inner disposition (wide); the doubling of the basic pitch is again the best possible. [See Example for §64, a.][67] The disposition C – – E – G (C in the second octave, E in the fourth, G in the fifth octave) is substantially worse because of its dispersed inner disposition; this can be corrected by inserting doubled pitches: C – C G C E G C E G. [See Example for §64, b.] Especially bad is the disposition E – C – E G, which not only has a dispersed inner disposition, but also is a six-three chord with the bass pitch doubled in a voice not adjacent to the bass; here the insertion of doubled pitches (for example E – E C G C E G) is not enough of a correction; the problematic doubling must also be removed: E – E C G C G. [See Example for §64, c.] The disposition E – G C G has always been preferred over the disposition E C – C G, which sounds worse because its isolated fifth is unpleasantly penetrating; the equally isolated fourth in the very similar disposition E G – G C does not matter at all. [See Example for §64, d.]

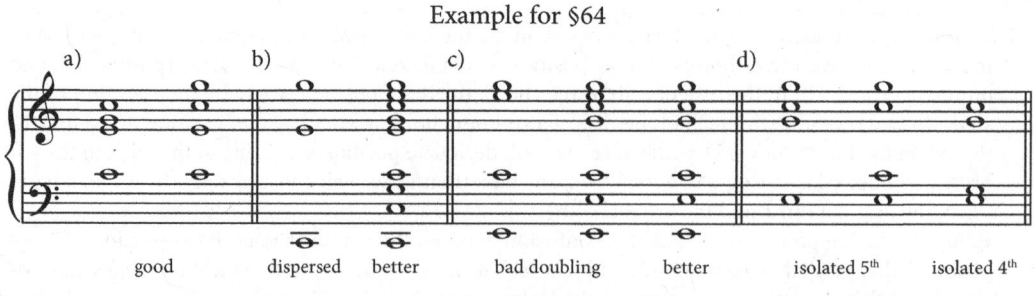

Example for §64

a) good b) dispersed better c) bad doubling better d) isolated 5th isolated 4th

---

[67] Editor's note: This example was not created by Karel Janeček.

§65. Evaluating the Sound of Inversions and their Dispositions

According to the principle of harmonic inversion,[68] mutually invertible chords are equivalent in sonic value. An inverted consonant chord will be a consonant chord, and an inverted dissonant chord will have the same dissonant characteristic as the original chord. (See §18 above.) This principle applies to all chord-types under all conditions. It does not, however, always apply to the concrete dispositions of chord-types.

Through the analysis of dispositions of basic triads, discussed in §64 above, we find that although chords that are inversions of each other are qualitatively equivalent, *inversions of concrete dispositions do vary in sonic quality*. This is true when any of the determinants of disposition are changed by the process of inversion. Inversion changes the *rotation determinant* (the lowest pitch) into the *position determinant* (the highest pitch), and vice versa;[69] if the two determinants are not equivalent in sonic quality the value of the entire inversion changes. Although *distances* between pitches (inner disposition) are not changed by inversion, their *order is reversed*; for example, the disposition "greater distance lesser distance" is changed to "lesser distance greater distance", which as a rule has a different sonic quality; only more or less equivalent distances, roughly symmetrical in their layout (for example, "greater – lesser – greater"), are not changed when inverted, and thus preserve their original sonic quality. The *doubled pitch* of the original chord usually becomes a different doubled pitch in its inversion (for example, the root of a triad becomes the fifth of its inversion).[70] However, doubled pitches retain the same chordal function in inversion when they are in the center of a chord with an odd number of pitches (for example, the third in a triad or the fifth in a complete ninth chord)[71] or when two pitches that are placed symmetrically in a chord are both doubled (for example, in four-note tertian chords, the root and the seventh, or the third and the fifth).[72]

Where differences in disposition do not affect the overall sonic quality of a chord, the principle of harmonic inversion applies without limitations. Thus if it does not matter to the sound which rotation or position we use in a dominant seventh chord, the rotation and position of its inversion, the diminished-minor chord, will likewise not mat-

---

68 Editor's note: We must not confuse *inversion* – the process in which the successive intervals in a chord are taken in the opposite direction in another chord, so a minor triad inverts to a major triad – with *rotation*, which is determined by the lowest pitch of a chord.
69 Editor's note: That is, for example when C G E is inverted about E♭/E to E♭ C G, the original position determinant E (the highest note) becomes the rotation determinant E♭ (the lowest note), and the original rotation determinant C (the lowest note) becomes the position determinant G (the highest note). So a major triad in zero rotation and position of the third becomes through inversion a minor triad in first rotation and position of the fifth. Janeček is here talking about exact inversion of the structure of a chord, keeping all the intervals the same, but taking them in the opposite direction.
70 Editor's note: For example, A A C♯ E, with doubled root, inverts about A to D F A A, with doubled fifth.
71 Editor's note: For example, when C G E G B♭ D♭ with doubled fifth is inverted about D♭ to C♯ E G B♭ G D, the fifth is also doubled in this chord.
72 Editor's note: For example, if A C♯ E G C♯ E is inverted about A, the third and fifth remain doubled: D F B D F A.

ter; differences in inner disposition and doublings of pitches, however, will not always be without effect.

Differences in sonic quality between concrete dispositions of chords and their inversions are especially apparent in the *basic triads*. A five-three triad in the position of the fifth and with a roughly symmetrical inner disposition inverts to a chord with equivalent sonic value. (See Examples 53a and 53b) Otherwise, as a rule inversion produces a different sonic quality. Several examples are shown in the following:

Example 53

§66. Disposition of Consonant Components in Dissonant Chords

From our experience with dispositions of basic triads we can derive precepts for the disposition of consonant components in dissonant chords.

For many dissonant chords, questions of rotation and position are meaningless. We will point out those cases where it is not. The question of doubled pitches is also less important, since the sound of a chord rich in pitch content does not depend on the doubling of pitches, even when its outer pitches are far apart. Thus even with dissonant chords, *inner disposition* is the most important element of disposition. Here we will look at inner disposition where it consists of or includes consonant components.

The task is complicated by the fact that when consonant and dissonant components are sounding together, the sound of certain dissonant components changes as a result of a change in disposition. Thus it becomes necessary, when disposition changes, to determine whether the overall improvement or worsening of sound is due to a change in the disposition of one of the chord's consonant components or one of its dissonant components. The effect of the disposition of dissonant components on the overall sonic quality of a chord will be discussed in §67 below.

In §20 above we pointed out the *softening effect of consonant components* in dissonant chords, and the difference between full consonances (3, 4) and the open consonance (5). Regarding disposition of full consonances, in general the effects of thirds (3, 4) and sixths (9, 8) are about the same when they are functioning together with dissonances. It hardly matters whether they are isolated and thus heard independently or whether foreign pitches are inserted between their pitches. Example 54 shows three chords, each in four different dispositions; all the dispositions are approximately equivalent in sonic value.

Chapter IV – Disposition of Chords

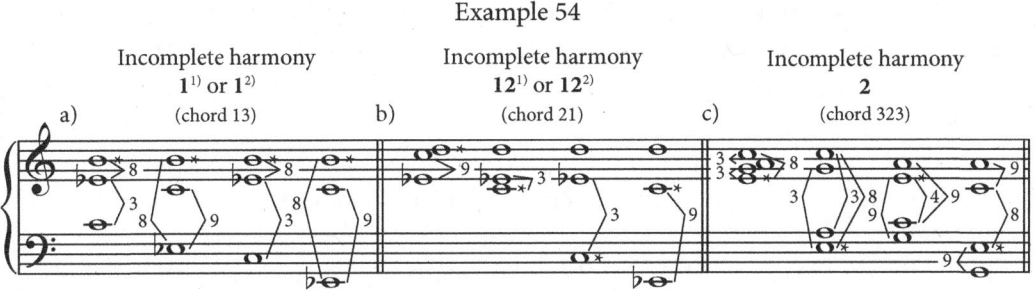

Example 54

All the dispositions in Example 54a have B placed highest, while all the dispositions in 54b have D on top; this is because the presence of the dissonant interval 1 must be considered (C–B, E♭–D). (For further discussion of this, see §67 below.) The extreme distance between the two lowest pitches does not detract from the sound at all.

We observe a conspicuous difference between the two dispositions of the open consonance – 5 and 7 – as long as no foreign pitches are within the interval. A fourth blends with other pitches into a homogeneous sound, while a fifth stands out conspicuously, as we have observed in the consonant triads. The fourth and fifth are shown in Example 55.

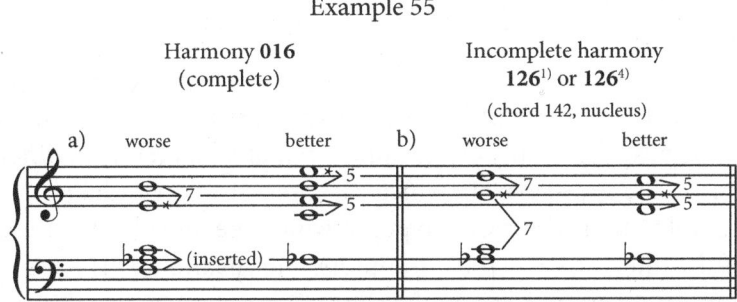

Example 55

It was probably this difference in sound between the fourth and fifth that led theory to build harmonies that have the appropriate pitch content out of fourths rather than fifths. The incomplete harmony **2** sounds more homogeneous in the disposition E A D G than in the disposition G D A E.

A fifth (7) between the lowest pitches of a chord, especially in a low enough register (in the second octave), always has a good sound and does not sound independent from the rest of the chord. In contrast, the intervals 3 or 4 (which usually tend to improve the sound) will be too heavy and unintelligible in such a low register. We have observed these phenomena already in the disposition of consonant triads.

§67. Disposition of Dissonant Intervals

Of the dissonant intervals 1, 2, and 6, only the *semitone* (1) reacts very sensitively to disposition. For intervals 2 and 6 that are isolated (sounding independently), disposition is relatively unimportant, except that the interval 2 placed too low does not have a good sound – it is too thick.

The interval 1 sounds better as a major seventh than as a minor second; compounding it by an octave to form a minor ninth also worsens its sound. *The bottom pitch of the interval 1* (in B–C, the pitch B) functions best when placed in the most conspicuous position in the chord, that is, as its *highest* pitch. This ensures that the interval sounds as a seventh.

For example, the chord A* C D F B 2123 (the incomplete harmony **126**[1)] or **126**[2)] or **126**[5)]) can be arranged so that it sounds more piercing ("bad") or milder ("good"); this depends on the disposition of the C and B, as shown in Example 56.

Example 56

The five-note chord 2123

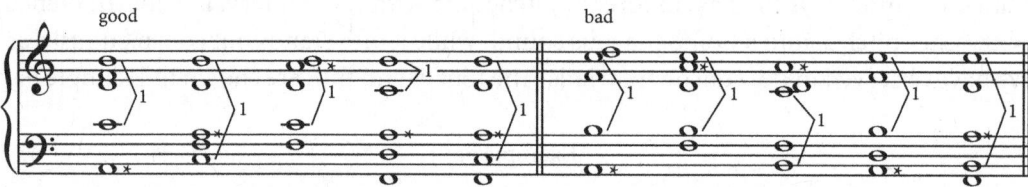

Not all intervals 1 are equally sensitive to changes in disposition. This is because the difference in sound between various dispositions of interval 1 also *depends on the chord-type* involved. We hear the quality of the same interval 1 differently in different dispositions, according to the chord-type in which the interval 1 is sounding.

It will be useful to find such chord-types in which the difference in the effects of the disposition of the interval 1 reach its minimum and maximum. The four-tone chords 313 and 213 are what we search for. In the chord 313, the partial combination harmony $+\widehat{0-}$ (for example, C E♭ A♭* B, shown in Example 57), the interval 1 sounds very bad as a minor second or a minor ninth, while it sounds very good as a major seventh:

Example 57

The four-note chord 313

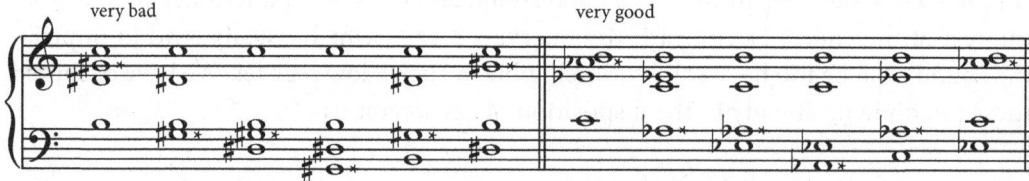

In contrast, in the four-note chord 213 (the dominant minor ninth chord with the fifth omitted – for example, B D♯ _ A C), the differences between various dispositions of the interval 1 are not substantial, as shown in Example 58.

Chapter IV – Disposition of Chords

Example 58

The four-note chord 213

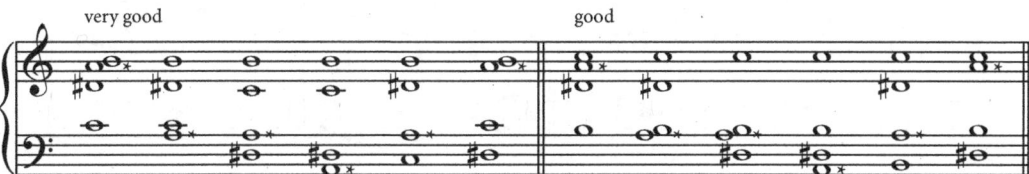

In chord-types closely associated with the chords 313 or 213, a change in disposition will cause a similar change in the sound. In more complex chords containing the chord 313, the difference in sound between various dispositions of the interval 1 will be substantial, while in chords containing 213 it will be negligible. We can verify this by adding a new pitch, for example F♯, to the chords 313 and 213, shown in the preceding examples; the resulting five-note chords will sound much the same in various dispositions as did the original four-note chords.

In chords that are not closely related to the chords 313 and 213, the differences in sound that result from different dispositions can be roughly designated as *average* – not as pronounced as in the chord 313, and not as inconspicuous as in the chord 213. Example 59 shows various dispositions of chords containing one interval 1.

Example 59

In the chord 231, the greater difference in the sonic quality of the dispositions G B♭ F* B and G B F* B♭ is due to the fact that the interval 1 (B–B♭) can be heard as the interval between the major and minor thirds in the triads G B D and G B♭ D (in our chord, D is omitted); thus this chord is related to the "most sensitive" four-note chord 313.

Example 60 shows two progressions wherein each chordal cross-section contains one interval 1; each progression is given in two dispositions.

167

Example 60

If a chord contains two or more intervals 1, we can of course place the appropriate pitch of only one of these intervals 1 highest in the chord. Example 61 shows some good and bad dispositions of such chords.

Example 61

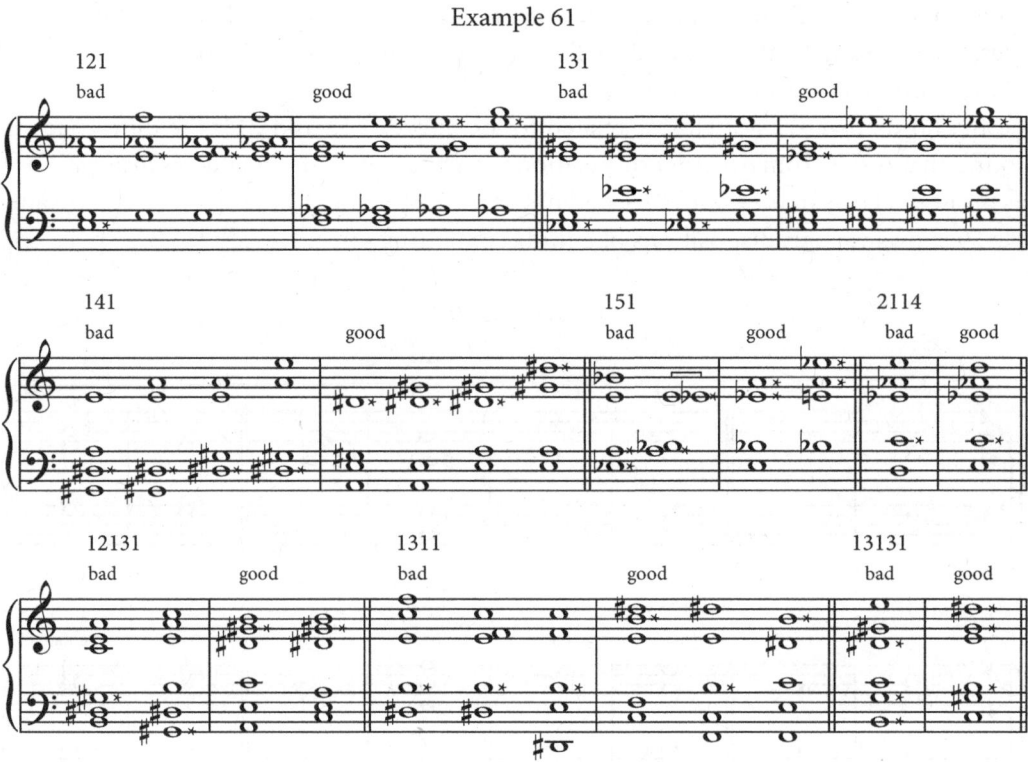

The disposition of the interval 2 is inconsequential as long as it is isolated from the rest of the chord; on the whole, its disposition does not change its sonic quality. This is not true, however, in *clusters of pitches* – chords in which intervals 2 or intervals 2 and 1 are adjacent. A disposition with such clusters always sounds bad, rather confused, unintelligible ("non-harmonic"). In order to improve the disposition, we must separate the clustered pitches from each other, as well as bring the intervals 1 into their good position. Example 62 shows some dispositions of a chord containing clusters:

Chapter IV – Disposition of Chords

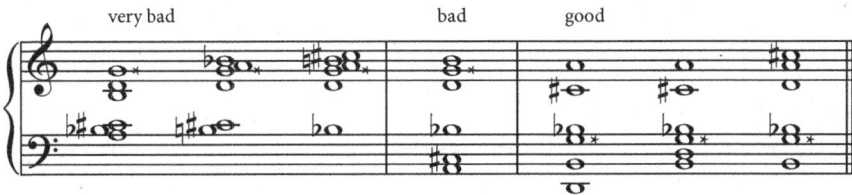

Example 62

The six-note chord 21121

A chord with more than one interval 1, or with a cluster of pitches, can also have a "mixed" disposition; for example, we can place some intervals 1 in their good position and not others; or, although we remove clusters, we can leave intervals 1 in less advantageous positions; or we can adjust the disposition of intervals 1 to achieve a good sound, but not remove all the clusters of intervals 2.

In complex chords, it is not always possible to bring all intervals 1 into their good positions, especially when there are several clashes of intervals 1. It may happen that a complex chord will sound better if we provide a good disposition only for certain intervals 1; it will then be advisable to separate the pitches of the remaining (badly arranged) intervals 1 by a substantial distance (whatever is practical), since this will make them less conspicuous. For example, the bad dispositions D G C E♭ C♯ E or D–E♭ G C E C♯, in which only the interval D–C♯ is in its good position, while the intervals D–E♭, E♭–E, and C–C♯ are positioned less advantageously, can be improved by arranging the pitches as E C E♭ D G C♯. Here the intervals E–E♭, E♭–D, and D–C♯ are all in their good positions, while only the interval C–C♯ is not; the attempt at "improving" this interval also, in the disposition E E♭ D G C♯ C, would give us a chord too sparse in sound, too spread out, with pitches too dispersed.

§68. Disposition of Triadic Combinations

In triadic combinations, the important thing is the *combination structure* of a chord. We are dealing here not simply with six or nine pitches sounding together, but with the organic merging of two or three triads. The individuality of the component basic triads can be emphasized, concealed, or even completely suppressed by the disposition. If we assume a sound homogeneous in colour and dynamics, the component triads can be heard individually only when we separate them from each other and do not allow them to interpenetrate. We will use the term *combination disposition* for a disposition that meets these conditions, and *non-combination disposition* for one that does not.

Combination dispositions and non-combination dispositions are equally justified. A combination disposition makes the triadic structure of a chord vividly audible, while a non-combination disposition conceals or even suppresses this structure. Differences in the sonic quality of various dispositions are determined by the same factors as in characteristic harmonies and chords subordinate to them.

Example 63 presents both combination dispositions and non-combination dispositions, some with a good sound and others with a bad sound. The combination harmony **+3−**, identical to the characteristic-maximum **126**[3], has been chosen for this example. This chord will prove instructive because it contains both the critical groups 313 and 213 (313 twice, and 213 once, as the analysis of the expanded orientation scheme shows: 12132(3)12132. In our example, the pitches of these two groups follow each disposition.

Example 63

The six-note chord

a) Combination dispositions

b) Non-combination dispositions

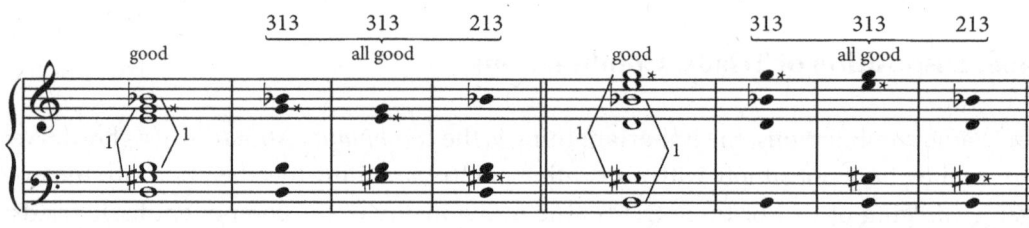

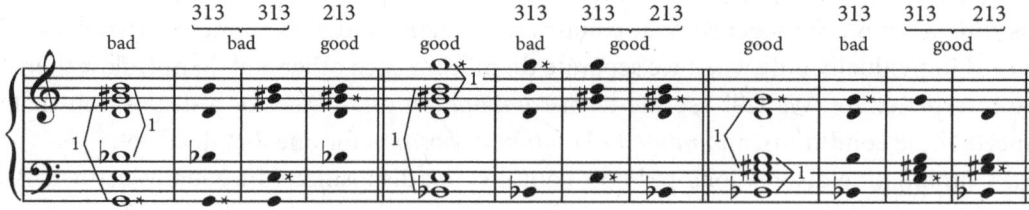

In any concrete disposition of a chord, one of the component triads always has greater weight, so that the other components are so to speak "measured" by it, understood in relation to it. This is related to the absolute place of pitches within pitch space. Judged acoustically, all pitches can have the same sonic significance. When we judge psychologically,[73] however, basing our judgment on the sonic *effect*, we can no longer claim that this is so. Pitches placed higher can have only approximately the same weight as pitches placed lower. We can verify this by comparing different inner dispositions of the same chord. A chord, for example, a consonant triad, has a homogeneous sound if it is compressed into a small ambit, such as an octave. If we increase its ambit, however, its homogeneity will gradually disappear. From a unified, homogeneous chord, individual pitches will emerge as independent entities. This is apparently because the absolute frequency of pitches, their place higher or lower in pitch space, results in differences in the magnitude of their sound, their relative weight; these graphic terms are meant to express the definite sonic quality in our conception of "absolute frequency".

Only pitches of approximately the same weight can be merged into a single harmonic whole. Thus pitches that are too distant from each other must be connected by a bridge of mediating pitches placed centrally enough between the extremes; these may be different pitches (in complex chords), or merely repeated pitches (in simple chords containing few pitches that are widely dispersed). The greater weight of low pitches also lends them a greater harmonic significance; from this grew the Baroque idea that the bass is the foundation of harmonic construction. We can say that we tend to perceive higher pitches as founded on lower (and the lowest) pitches, rather than the other way around.

When we separate component triads from each other spatially in order to hear them individually, the distance between the pitches belonging to the different triadic components of the combination chord also substantially increases. Such a separation results in a distinct gradation in the sonic weight of the components; the component triad that is lowest in the disposition becomes the foundation in relation to which the others are perceived. Thus a specific disposition determines the significance of the individual triadic components; moving from the lowest component to the highest, their significance decreases.

From these reflections, which may seem impractical, we can derive practical precepts for the general disposition of triadic combinations and the evaluation of intervals 1 when not in their good position.

Concerning the general disposition of triadic combinations: *the lowest component basic triad acts as the determinant of the entire combination.* Any higher components, in spite of any independence that they may have or that a composer may have intended them to have, are simply additions to the sound of the chord; according to an expression used by Leoš Janáček, they merely thicken the overall sound. In the chord +6+ (for example, G B D – D♭ F A♭), we can assign the role of determinant to either of the two

---

73 Editor's note: i.e. psychoacoustic point of view.

triadic components: in the disposition D♭ A♭ F – B D G, the D♭ triad has the determining role, while in the disposition G D B – F A♭ D♭ it is the G triad.

It makes no sense to talk about *rotations* of component triads when they do not have the determining role, because the significance of their roots is far outweighed by any of the pitches belonging to the lowest component triad. In those component triads that are determinants for the entire chord, however, we sense clearly the differences in sonic quality between different dispositions. The deciding factor here is whether the lowest pitch of the lowest component triad is its root. Those dispositions in which the determinant, the lowest component triad, sounds as a five-three chord are more definite, more stable, than dispositions in which the determinant sounds in a different rotation. (Cf. combination dispositions in Example 63 above.)

The interval 1 in its advantageous form (as a seventh) is always good. However, interval 1 in its less advantageous forms requires some exploration. The first chord to note is 313 where in reacts the most sensitively to changes in disposition. The group 313 is actually the combination of two triads of opposite family built on a common root: C E G – C E♭ G. The interval 1 arises between the thirds of the two component triads. As explained above in §67, when this interval 1 is arranged as a seventh (E–E♭ = E–D♯), all is well; the disposition sounds good. When the interval 1 is arranged as a second, however (E♭–E), a very bad sound results. Here both critical pitches are part of component triads; in the disposition E♭–E, the minor triad has the greater weight, since it is placed lower. In the disposition C G E♭ – E G C, which has doubled pitches, when the two triads stand as complete and clearly separated counterparts the triad C E♭ G is the determinant. This minor triad remains the determinant even when new pitches are inserted between it and the major triad. Thus a *particularly bad sound results from dispositions in which the determinant (the lowest component triad) is a minor triad from the group 313.* As a rule, therefore, non-combination dispositions (which have no determining triads because their lowest pitches form no basic triad) with the interval 1 in the group 313 in other than its good position will still sound somewhat better than combination dispositions with the interval 1 in the group 313 in other than its good position.

Therefore, in evaluating the sound of the dispositions of more complex chords, especially of triadic combinations, we must find all the groups 313 in the chord and ascertain whether a minor triad belonging to a 313 group is the determinant of the whole chord. If this is so, the disposition is very bad. If it is not so, the disposition may be somewhat better, or even good; this depends on the quality of the dispositions of any other groups 313 in the chord, and on whether or not the chord contains any groups 213 whose presence would improve the sound.

Combination harmonies **II** and **III** are particularly well suited to our study of the sounds of various dispositions. In the examples of combination and non-combination dispositions of the harmony +3– (Example 63 above), analyses of both groups 313 in the chord are given. We can see that the worst dispositions are those in which the determinant is the minor component triad (G B♭ D).

Chapter IV – Disposition of Chords

Let us now explore the second critical group, 213 (the incomplete dominant minor ninth chord). It is insignificant in evaluating the sound of a more complex chord because its interval 1 has a good effect no matter how it is arranged. When the pitches constituting the group 213 are concentrated low, the result may even be a substantial improvement; the effect is especially good when the second pitch of the orientation scheme 213 has considerable weight (for example, A in the chord G* A B♭ C♯).[74]

What is the behaviour of the interval 1 when it is part of both 213 and 313 groups at the same time? It is a valid question. This situation occurs in complex chords (including all combination harmonies III). How then can such intervals 1 be judged, when they are not in their good position? Are they harmless because they belong to groups 213, or do they worsen the sound as components of groups 313? To answer these questions we must evaluate the sounds of a larger number of dispositions of more complex chords. The results verify the validity and the practical significance of the "impractical" ideas introduced above regarding the disposition of weight in the sound according to absolute height.

The conflict between the worsening effect of an interval 1 that is not in its good position in the group 313 and the effect of the same interval 1 in the group 213 is resolved in favour of the group 313 whenever the minor triad of the group 313 is the determinant of the entire chord, or is at least clearly individualized (its pitches concentrated into a coherent whole in which other pitches do not interfere). The sound in this case will be considerably worsened. The worsening will not be as great if the above conditions are not met, and if we can make use of the harmless (and possibly even positive) effect of the group 213. The paralysing effect of very low pitches belonging to the group 213 (particularly the second pitch of this orientation scheme) is especially pronounced when no pitches not belonging to 213 are interspersed between the pitches of this group.

The examples that follow in §69, §70, and especially §71, provide the best demonstration for the above discussion (Exx. 64, 65, and 66). The five-note chord 1213 is the simplest chord in which the critical groups 313 and 213 are merged, and which appears whenever the same interval 1 is contained in these two groups [e.g., when A C C♯ E, 313, is combined with B♭ C C♯ E, 213, in A B♭ C C♯ E, 1213]. This chord can be examined independently, but it has the disadvantages of relative simplicity and transparency of sound. It contains a second interval 1 which is not part of the groups 213 and 313, and which, as its position changes, considerably affects the disposition's sonic quality. As a rule we cannot touch this second interval 1 if we are trying to change the effect of the interval 1 contained in both the groups 313 and 213 (and not in its good position). (The bad disposition C E A* C♯ B♭ becomes the good disposition C E B♭ C♯ A* when the badly arranged interval A–B♭ is arranged in its good position, B♭–A; without this change, the pitches A C E can only be dispersed in the dispositions C E C♯ A* B♭ or C – E C♯ A* – B♭, where the pitches of the group 213 are not, however, sufficiently

---

74 Editor's note: This pitch, A, is, of course, the root of the dominant minor ninth chord.

concentrated.) When more intervals 1 are present in more complex chords, it is easier to ignore their disruptive effects for the very reason that more intervals 1 are present.

§69. Disposition of Harmonies II

To supplement the commentary in §68, we present a summary of dispositions of full triadic combinations II. The various possible *combination dispositions* are arranged in tables. This form of summary gives generalized dispositions that can be modified while retaining the overall arrangement. Although there will be differences in sonic quality between different dispositions of the same basic arrangement, they will not be as great, and they will often be negligible.

The original order of component basic triads, which we will simply designate as *1st* and *2nd*, is established by the triadic scheme of each combination harmony. Thus in the harmony +2− (for example, C E G – D F A), we designate the major triad as 1st and the minor triad as 2nd. The general designation of "1st 2nd" combination disposition represents all dispositions in which the pitches of the first component triad of the scheme are at the bottom and the pitches of the second at the top. The order of pitches within the components, and the extent to which they are dispersed, can vary a great deal.

To enable us to evaluate the sounds of different dispositions, intervals 1 from the pitch groups 313 and 213 are given in separate columns. In the concrete examples of chords, shown below the general triadic schemes, the family of each component basic triad is shown (major by the square bracket, minor by the curved line). The first pitch of the orientation scheme is marked with an asterisk. The semitone intervals in the critical pitch groups 313 and 213 are always given in their disadvantageous position.

The *living sound* of the examples indicated in the tables must be studied (at the piano) in their most diverse variations. In the lower component triad, we mainly vary the *rotation*, then its inner disposition, possibly also various doublings of pitches. In the upper component triad, on the other hand, we first vary the *position*. We then construct the entire combination in several ways so that each time we create a different *distance* between the component triads, from a close mutual cohesion to a striking splitting of pitch space. The sonic effect can also be examined at various dynamic levels (*f, p, pp*); sharp differences in *shading* are possible between the component triads.

Chapter IV – Disposition of Chords

Combination dispositions of harmonies II

Harmonies	Orientation scheme	Number of intervals 1			Combination disposition		Comments
		total	in combinations 313	in combinations 213	good	bad	
−1+ C* E♭ G – D♭ F A♭ 1. 2.	12221 (4)	2	–	–	2. 1.	1. 2.	
+2− C* E G – D F A 1. 2.	22122 (3)	1	–	–	2. 1.	1. 2.	
−2+ C E♭ G – D F#* A 1. 2.	12321 (3)	2	–	1 D–E♭	1. 2.	2. 1.	Disposition 2. 1. is not entirely bad
+6− C* E G – F# A C# 1. 2.	13212 (3)	2	1 C–C#	–	2. 1. 1. 2.		Disposition 1. 2. is worse than 2. 1.
+3− C E G – E♭* G♭ B♭ 1. 2.	12132 (3)	2	2 E♭–E G♭–G	1 G♭–G	1. 2.	2. 1.	
−4+ C E♭* G* – E G# B* 1. 2.	13131 (3)	3	3 B–C E♭–E G–G#	–	2. 1. 1. 2.		Disposition 1. 2. is worse than 2. 1.
+1+ C* E G – D♭ F A♭ 1. 2.	13121 (4)	3	1 E–F	–	2. 1.	1. 2.	
−1− C* E♭ G – C# E G# 1. 2.	12131 (4)	3	1 E♭–E	1 E♭–E	2. 1.	1. 2.	
+2+ C* E G – D F# A 1. 2.	22212 (3)	1	–	–	1. 2.	2. 1.	
−2− C* E♭ G – D F A 1. 2.	21222 (3)	1	–	–	1. 2.	2. 1.	

Harmonies	Orientation scheme	Number of intervals 1			Combination disposition		Comments
		total	in combinations		good	bad	
			313	213			
+6+ C E* G – F♯ A♯* C♯ 1. 2.	21321 (3)	2	–	2 C –C♯ F♯–G	1. 2. 2. 1.	–	all non-combination dispositions without clusters are also good
–6– C* E♭ G – F♯* A C♯ 1. 2.	12312 (3)	2	–	–	–	1. 2. 2. 1.	

From the above table we see that for some harmonies **II** it is impossible to produce a good disposition. The symmetrical harmonies **+6–** and **–4+** and the asymmetrical **–6–** are so afflicted. Bad dispositions are possible for all harmonies **II** except **+6+**; this combination has the advantage that it cannot be "spoiled" even in a non-combination disposition, except when pitch clusters are used. Thus it is understandable that the harmony **+6+** is one of the most sought-after of all combination harmonies. Even composers who generally do not have much interest in combination harmonies occasionally use this harmony. It belongs to the harmonic arsenal of even the least adventurous composers. Because it is so easily usable, however, it is in danger of becoming overused, more so than any other combination harmony. This was the fate of the characteristic harmony **6** (the diminished-seventh chord), which was once so popular and so abused, because everywhere so appropriate, that it has been all but eliminated from the better new music.

That which has been given in excess to the chord **+6+** is lacking in its inversion and negative, the chord **–6–**. The relation between the chords **+6+** and **–6–** demonstrates a fact mentioned earlier, namely, that the principle of harmonic inversion does not always apply to disposition. This is because the interval 1 is insensitive to disposition only in the pitch group 213, and not in its inversion, the pitch group 312; a semitone not in its best position in the group 213 does not worsen the sound, whereas in the group 312 it does. (The chord 312 C E♭ A* C♯ sounds perceptibly worse than its literal inversion, 213 C E B♭* C♯.)

For the 2nd 1st disposition of the chord **–2+**, the comment from our table applies – it is not altogether bad. Here the positive effect of the group 213 apparently comes into play, especially in the disposition D A F♯ – C E♭ G; other dispositions are not as good, for example A D F♯ – E♭ G C, since here the determinant is not in zero rotation.

Of course it is impossible to classify non-combination dispositions of harmonies **II** in any general way, because the mutual interpenetration of their triadic components

Chapter IV – Disposition of Chords

makes the individualization of the triads impossible; instead of two triadic units, we have six pitches that join to form only incidental triadic units in certain situations. For example, in the chord C E G – F♯ A C♯ (**+6–**), it is possible to group certain pitches from the two triadic components into incidental triadic units A C♯ E or A C E, at the cost of not being able to form triadic units from the remaining pitches. We include dispositions containing such incidental triadic units among non-combination dispositions.

Example 64 shows good and bad *non-combination dispositions* of all harmonies **II** in the same order as in the previous table. For harmonies **+6–**, **–4+**, **+6+**, and **–6–**, examples of concrete combination dispositions are shown as well. Our example does not show analyses of the pitch groups 313 and 213; such analyses must be considered, however, in the study of specific dispositions. (Cf. Example 63 in §68 above.)

Example 64

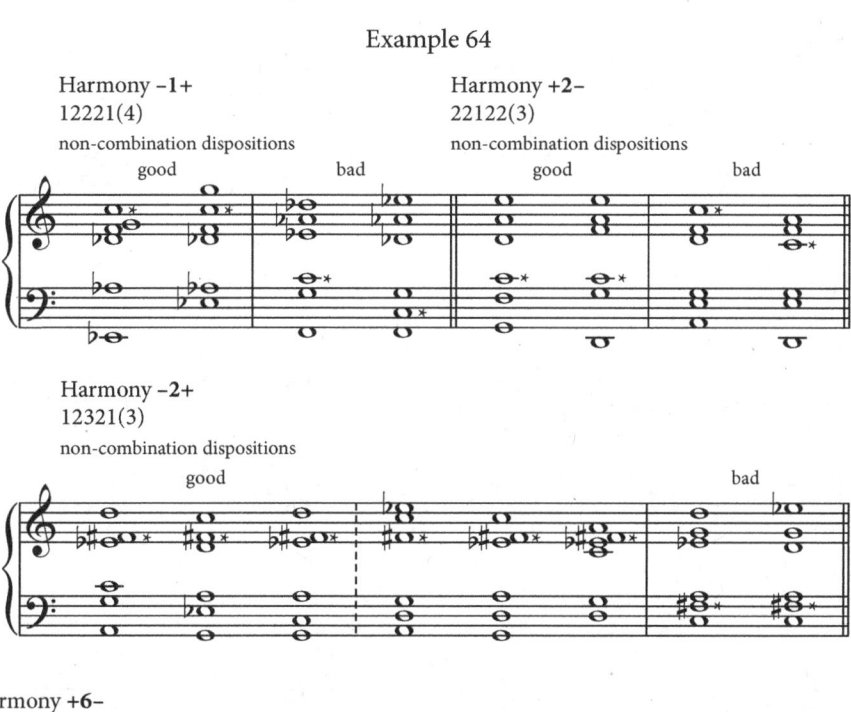

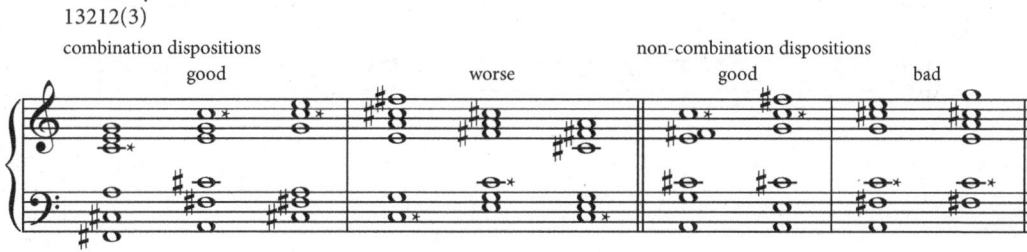

Harmony +3−
12132(3)

Harmony −4+
13131(3)

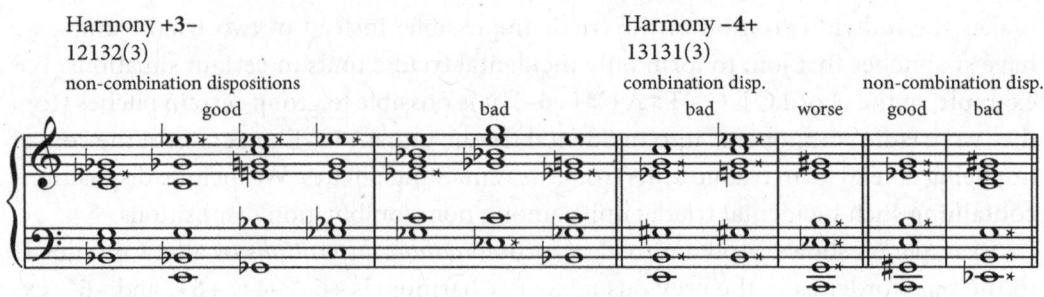

Harmony +1+
13121(4)

Harmony −1−
12131(4)

Harmony +2+
22212(3)

Harmony −2−
21222(3)

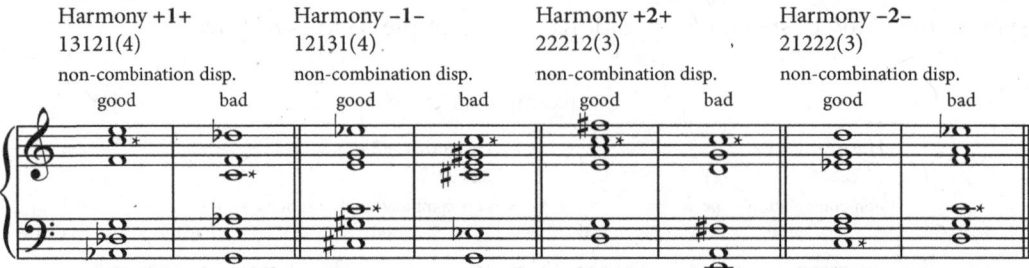

Harmony +6+
21321(3)

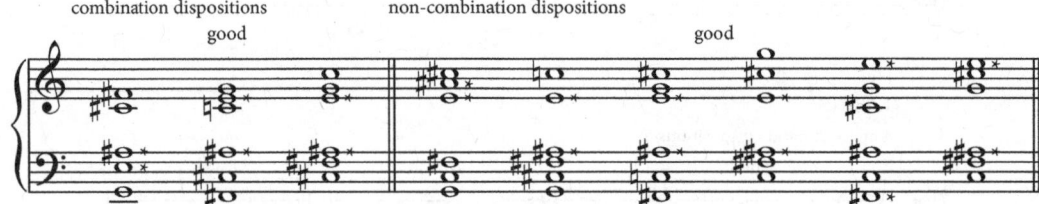

Harmony −6−
12312(3)

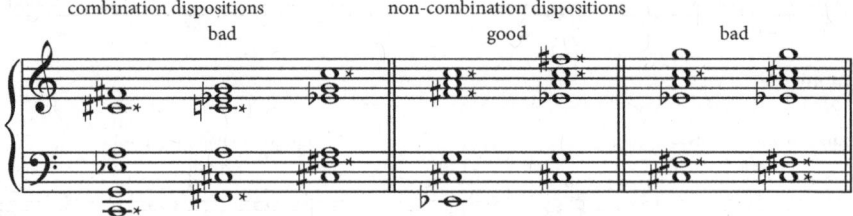

§70. Disposition of Partial Combinations with Two Components; Doubled Pitches in Intervals 1

Classifying dispositions of partial combinations with two components is simpler, not because we are dealing with incomplete harmonies II (five-note and four-note chords), but because the insensitive critical group 213 does not appear in any partial combination with two components. Thus one of the criteria by which we previously classified dispositions is eliminated. It is worth mentioning again that the other critical group, 313, is the combination of two triads with the same root and fifth.

To form actual combination dispositions from partial combinations, we must double those pitches that are common to the combined triads, unless these pitches are placed at the point where the two triadic components *intersect*. For example, in the combination +5– C E G – F A♭ C it is unnecessary to double the pitch C in the good disposition F A♭ C E G or in the bad disposition E G C F A♭; in other dispositions it *is* necessary, however: A♭ C F – G C E (good), G C E – A♭ C F (bad). In four-note chords that are combinations of two basic triads with two pitches in common, we can dispense with the doubling of one or even both of these common pitches: E A C E G, A C E G. Dispositions in which the pitches common to both triads are not doubled and do not form the point of overlap of triads are *non-combination* dispositions, since in such cases the triadic components will interpenetrate each other (C E G A, E G A C).

A summary of all possible combination dispositions of partial combinations with two components follows, again in a table. Combinations with no intervals 1 can be arranged badly only when pitches are stacked into a cluster. This type of bad disposition is not a combination disposition, however, because a cluster of pitches can occur only when the triadic components interpenetrate each other. In the combination –3+ a pitch cluster cannot be formed at all, while in the combination –5+ this can only be done by interpenetration, resulting in a non-combination disposition: G B♭ C D E G.

We have briefly mentioned the necessity of doubling for forming a combination disposition with partial combinations. The difference between combination and non-combination dispositions does not necessarily mean a difference in the value of the disposition; a doubling whose only purpose is to create a combination disposition has no significance for evaluating the sound. A doubling or further multiplication of a pitch that is part of an interval 1, however, appears in a different light, because the arrangement of intervals 1 decisively influences the sonic quality of the disposition of the entire chord. Thus if a pitch that is part of an interval 1 is doubled, a *merging of conflicting effects* can result that is important in evaluating the disposition's sonic quality.

An example will clarify this. We can arrange the interval 1 C–C♯ well (as C♯–C) or badly (as C–C♯); if the interval 1 contains a doubled pitch, however, we can, for example, form not only the good disposition C♯–C–C and the bad disposition C–C–C♯, but also a disposition in which the characteristics of the good and bad dispositions confront each other: C–C♯–C. Such a confrontation of characteristics, such a merging of conflicting effects of various dispositions of the interval 1, when one pitch is doubled, can theoretically have three possible results:

1) the chord as a whole has a good sound as a result of the good arrangement of two of the pitches of the interval 1, regardless of the bad arrangement of two other pitches of the same interval;
2) the chord as a whole has a bad sound as a result of the bad arrangement of two of the pitches of the interval 1, regardless of the good arrangement of two other pitches of the same interval;
3) the chord as a whole has a sound of average quality, as a result of the merging and thus perhaps also the *weakening* of both conflicting effects.

Practical experimentation with a larger number of dispositions (partial combinations with two components are particularly well suited for this, since they contain fewer pitches) will lead us to conclude that in most cases the situation (1) occurs, i.e. that a disposition containing an interval 1 in its good position has a good sound, regardless of whether or not it also contains the same interval 1 in a bad position. This applies roughly to all intervals 1, including those that are sensitive (those that are part of a group 313). Thus we are jutsitified to state that a *good position of the interval 1 overrides the detrimental effect of a bad position of the same interval 1.*

There is a certain instability in the sound of dispositions that contain intervals 1 with doubled pitches; this is caused by secondary features with which we are already familiar – especially position. The bottom pitch of the interval scheme of an interval 1 (in B–C, the pitch B) functions best as the highest pitch in the disposition of the chord; a disposition that ignores this fact may not be particularly bad, but it will never be the best possible. Thus when conflicting effects merge, it is advisable to *double the lower pitch of the semitone scheme,* not the upper. In C–C♯–C, the pitch C can be placed highest, while in C♯–C–C♯ it cannot; when the upper pitch of an interval 1 is doubled in a chord (C–C♯–C♯), it is not even advisable to arrange that chord in such a way that the same interval 1 is in a good position and a bad position at the same time.

Chapter IV – Disposition of Chords

Combination dispositions of partial combinations with two triadic components

Combination	Orientation scheme	Number of intervals 1			Combanation disposition	
		total	in combinations		good	bad
			313	213		
+0− C E G − C E♭ G 1. 2.	313 (5)	1	1 E♭–E	−	1. 2.	2. 1.
−3+ A C E − C E G 1. 2.	323 (4)	−	−	−	1. 2. 2. 1.	−
+4− C E G − E G B 1. 2.	143 (4)	1	−	−	1. 2.	2. 1.
+1− C E G − C♯ E G♯ 1. 2.	1331 (4)	2	−	−	2. 1.	1. 2.
+5− C E G − F A♭ C 1. 2.	1214 (4)	2	−	−	2. 1.	1. 2.
−5+ G B♭ D − C E G 1. 2.	2223 (3)	−	−	−	2. 1. 1. 2.	−
+3+ C E G − E♭ G B♭ 1. 2.	1332 (3)	1	1 E♭–E	−	1. 2.	2. 1.
−3− A C E − C E♭ G 1. 2.	1323 (3)	1	1 E♭–E	−	1. 2.	2. 1.
+4+ C E G − E G♯ B 1. 2.	3131 (4)	2	1 G–G♯	−	−	2. 1. 1. 2.
−4− A C E − C♯ E G♯ 1. 2.	1313 (4)	2	1 C–C♯	−	−	2. 1. 1. 2.
+5+ C E G − F A C 1. 2.	1223 (4)	1	−	−	2. 1.	1. 2.
−5− A C E − D F A 1. 2.	3221 (4)	1	−	−	2. 1.	1. 2.

181

Example 65 shows some of the combinations from the previous table in concrete non-combination dispositions, and the combinations +4+ and –4– also in combination dispositions. To the good non-combination dispositions are added dispositions designated as "also good" that contain doubled pitches in intervals 1; beside each such disposition, an analysis of the pertinent intervals 1 is given. The disposition of the combination –4– designated as "less good" is not in its optimal position; that is, the top note is not the best choice.

Example 65

§71. Disposition of Triadic Combinations III

Triadic combinations **III**, as complete nine-note chords, have the most complex possible characteristic: **011266**. In disposition, we are primarily concerned with intervals 1, which can appear as many as six or seven times in an individual combination **III**. For now we will look at these intervals 1 individually; we will arrange each separately, without regard to the relations between the various intervals 1 in the chord. We will postpone to §72 the classification of dispositions involving semitone clashes of intervals 1 (11) and instructions for possible ways of making the sound of these clashes bearable. Concerning the semitone clashes of intervals 6 (66), we must admit that disposition is incapable of refining their sound. Clashes 66 are not as sharp as clashes 11, however. (See §24 above.)

We can arrange the three triadic components of *combination dispositions* for combinations **III** in six different ways. If we designate the component basic triads as 1st, 2nd, and 3rd, according to their order in the triadic scheme, the possible combination dispositions of each chord **III** can be designated as follows:

| 1st | 2nd | 3rd | | 2nd | 1st | 3rd | | 3rd | 1st | 2nd |
| 1st | 3rd | 2nd | | 2nd | 3rd | 1st | | 3rd | 2nd | 1st |

For harmonies **II**, and for partial combinations with two components, we have classified combination dispositions as good or bad. (See tables in §69 and §70 above.) Here we must say that *all combination dispositions of harmonies* **III** *sound bad*; no complete harmony **III** can be arranged into a combination disposition that sounds good. Of course there are differences between the various dispositions with a bad sound. Example 66 gives two combination dispositions for each chord **III**; the first of these is always the *least bad*, and the second is the *worst* of the six possibilities. Each of the combination dispositions is designated by the order of its triadic components.

Only *non-combination* dispositions of combinations **III** can have a good sound. It is also possible, however, to form an unusually harsh non-combination disposition. Our musical example will therefore show two sample non-combination dispositions for each harmony **III**, one good and one bad. Beside each of the good dispositions is given the analysis of the interval 1 that is not in its optimal position, showing whether it belongs to the group 213 or 313. The difference between good and bad dispositions lies primarily in the fact that good dispositions avoid intervals 1 that are not in their optimal position, while bad dispositions seek them out. An interval 1 that is not in its optimal position occurs at most once in our good dispositions, and only when it is impossible to avoid it by sensible means, that is, while retaining a suitable ambit.

KAREL JANEČEK | *Foundations of Modern Harmony*

Example 66

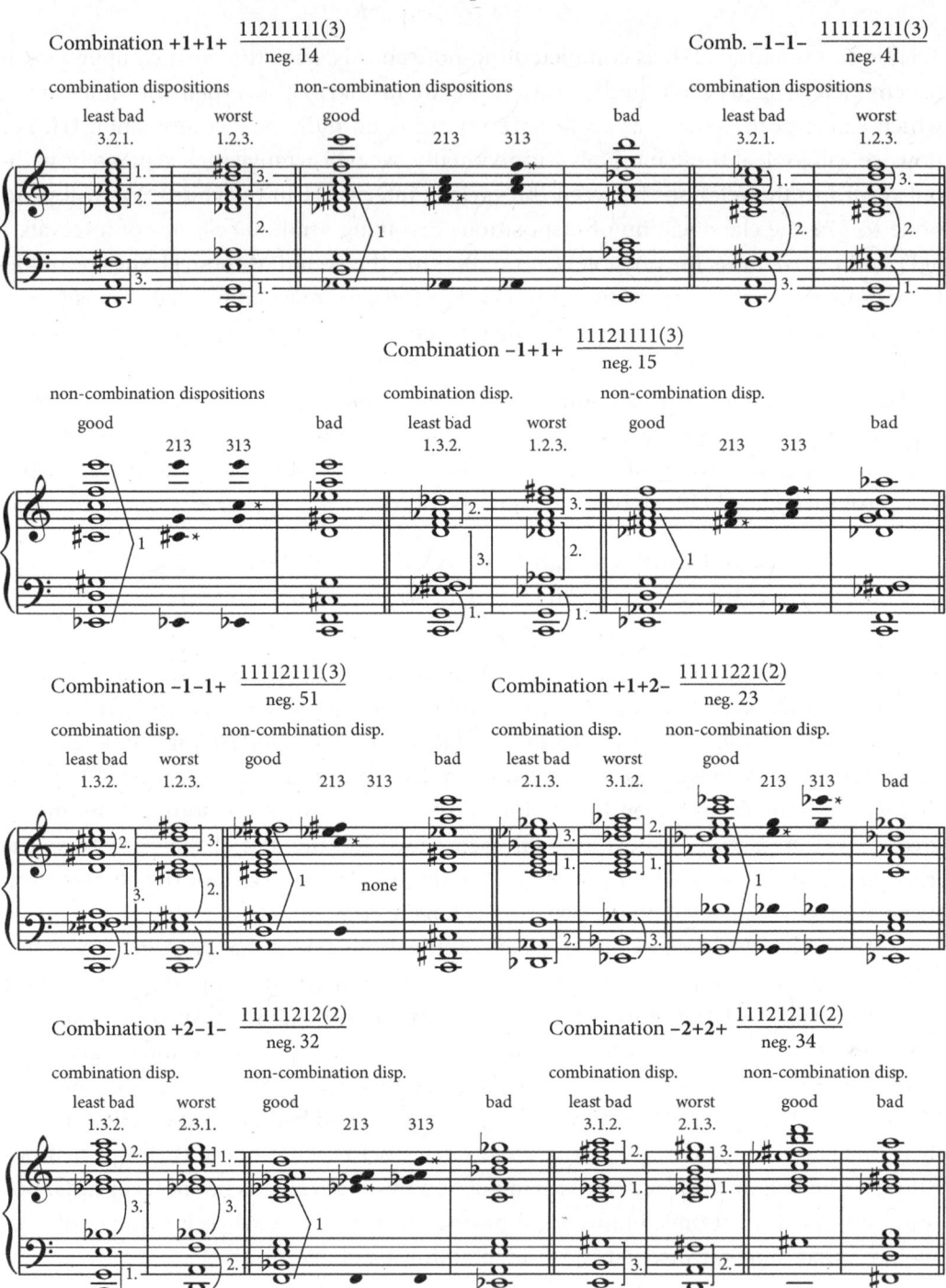

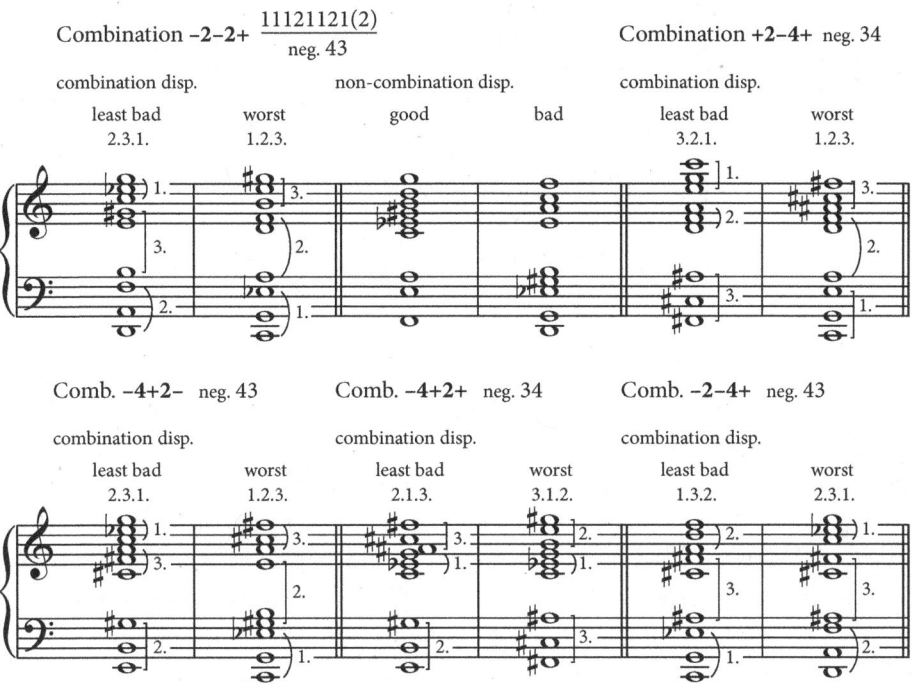

§72. Disposition of the Triadic Combination IV; Softening of Semitone Clashes of Intervals 1 through Disposition

We come to the disposition of the most complex harmonic formation, the combination **IV**, which is a twelve-note chord. As with combinations **III**, *all combination dispositions of the combination **IV** sound bad*. The combination **IV** can be broken down into component basic triads in two ways, arranged either as **+2−4+2−** or **−2−2+2+** (as shown above in §57), so combination dispositions can be constructed from these two sets of triads. Since each of these arrangements contains four members, twenty-four variations of each should be possible; in the case of **+2−4+2−**, however, whose two halves are six-note chords of the same type (**+2−**) half an octave apart, it is possible to form only half the expected number of combination dispositions, namely 12.

Example 67 shows some *combination dispositions* of the twelve-note chord. The two examples of disposition for the arrangement **+2−4+2−**, although their component triads are in a different order, are actually transpositions of the same formation; the second example is a tritone lower than the first.

Example 67

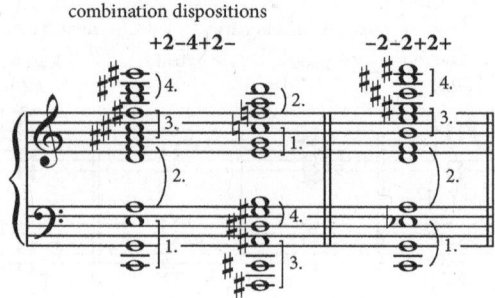

Turning now to *non-combination* dispositions, we first need to be reminded of several facts. Since the complete twelve-note chord contains all the chordal material of the tempered chromatic system, it contains all possible groups 213 and 313, and every interval 1 is part of a group 213 and also of some group 313. Whether the intervals 1 that are badly arranged will have a detrimental effect will depend on the disposition of the pitches that form the pertinent groups 213 and 313. It will certainly be difficult to remove from all intervals 1 that are not in their optimal position the detrimental influence of badly arranged groups 313. Therefore we can conclude that as long as several intervals 1 that are not in their optimal position must be endured in non-combination dispositions of the twelve-note chord, even the best of these dispositions will sound only fairly good.

This invites the question whether it is possible to find a disposition in which all intervals 1 are in their good position. Such a disposition of the twelve-note chord is not practical, because it would cover an ambit of more than ten octaves: C B B♭ A G♯ G F♯ F E E♭ D C♯.[75]

All the intervals 1 that appear in the twelve-note chord are piled up in such a way that none is isolated; each interval 1 clashes with other, immediately adjacent, intervals 1, and thus forms part of a *semitone clash*. The simplest formation with such a clash is 11. Therefore, instead of individual intervals 1 (since intervals 1 do not appear individually, in isolation, here), we can study the sound of individual groups 11 and classify their possible dispositions.

The group 11 is a three-note chord (for example, B C C♯), of which there are six possible dispositions. Which of these are good and which are bad? Which is the best and which is the worst? We can only answer these questions after examining the sound of all the dispositions. We must also discover the effect of the groups 11 in various dispositions when these groups are part of more complex chords.

The summary given in Example 68 shows the results of this investigation. As all the dispositions are built on the pitch C, we are dealing with several different chords 11. The good and bad dispositions of groups 11 could be supplemented by some good and bad dispositions of the more complex groups 111 and 1111; only these can verify our classification. For each disposition, intervals 1 that are in their optimal position are indicated

---

75 Editor's note: Even here, C♯ is above C.

Chapter IV – Disposition of Chords

on the left, and those that are not are indicated on the right. The pitches of the group 11 are designated by the numbers 1, 2, and 3, according to their order in the orientation scheme, and their order in the disposition is given above each chord.

Example 68

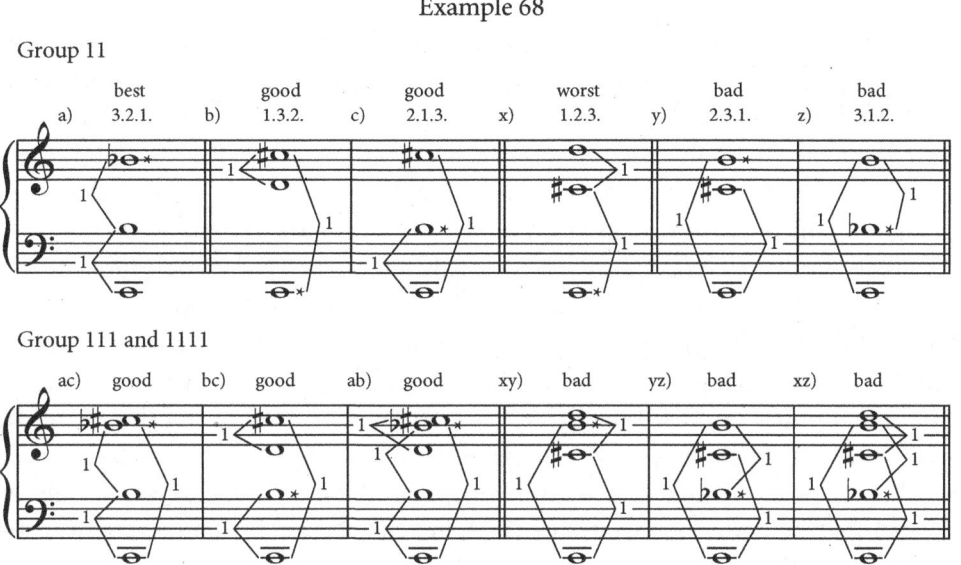

To this we must add those dispositions that sound bad simply because the pitches of the group 11 are insufficiently dispersed.

Example 69

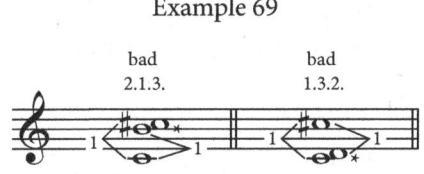

In general the group 11 is best arranged when both intervals 1 are in their good position (Example 68a); the worst is then a disposition in which neither interval 1 is in its good position (Example 69x). The disposition sounds good when the distance between the pitches forming the badly arranged interval 1 is considerably greater than that between the pitches forming the interval 1 that is in its good position (Examples 68b, c); the disposition sounds bad when this is not so (Examples 68y, z). When the pitches of the group 11 are insufficiently dispersed, so there is no significant difference in the distance between the pitches of the interval 1 that is in its good position and the pitches of the interval 1 that is not, the disposition sounds bad.

If we consider the matter on the basis of the previously proposed theory about the weight of pitches according to absolute height (see §68 above), we will find that the results at which we have arrived through experiment are the same as the results at which we had previously arrived through speculation. This verifies the practical value of the theory regarding the weight of pitches. Our speculation can proceed somewhat like this: when two pitches have at least approximately the same weight, they form a homogeneous whole that sounds and functions as a unified entity; pitches that are too distant from each other do not fulfill this condition, and thus cannot function as an effective, unified chord. Thus if a pitch placed very high forms an interval 1 in its bad position with a very distant low pitch, but at the same time forms with a pitch only slightly lower than itself a different interval 1 in its good position, the good effect will outweigh the bad, and the overall sound of the disposition will be good, as demonstrated in our example b. We can consider in a similar way Examples 68c, y, and z.

The twelve-note chord contains not just isolated clashes but a continuous series of them. The sonic quality of the disposition is determined by all the dispositions of groups 11 taken together. The sonic quality is decided not just by the number of intervals 1 that are not in their optimal position, but by the ratio between the number of those that are not and the number of those that are. What matters is whether or not the entire chord contains badly arranged groups 11, and whether or not these groups 11 contain intervals 1 that are badly arranged. Thus it can happen that a disposition containing fewer intervals 1 that are badly arranged is worse than a disposition containing more of them, if these intervals 1 are part of good dispositions of groups 11.

Example 70 shows some non-combination dispositions of the twelve-note chord, with analyses. The angles on the left point out intervals 1 that are in their optimal position, while the angles on the right point out those that are not. One group 11 in Example 70B is shown in brackets, because although its disposition is classified as good, its pitches are not well arranged, as there is insufficient difference between the intervals 1 that are in their optimal position and those that are not.

Chapter IV – Disposition of Chords

Example 70

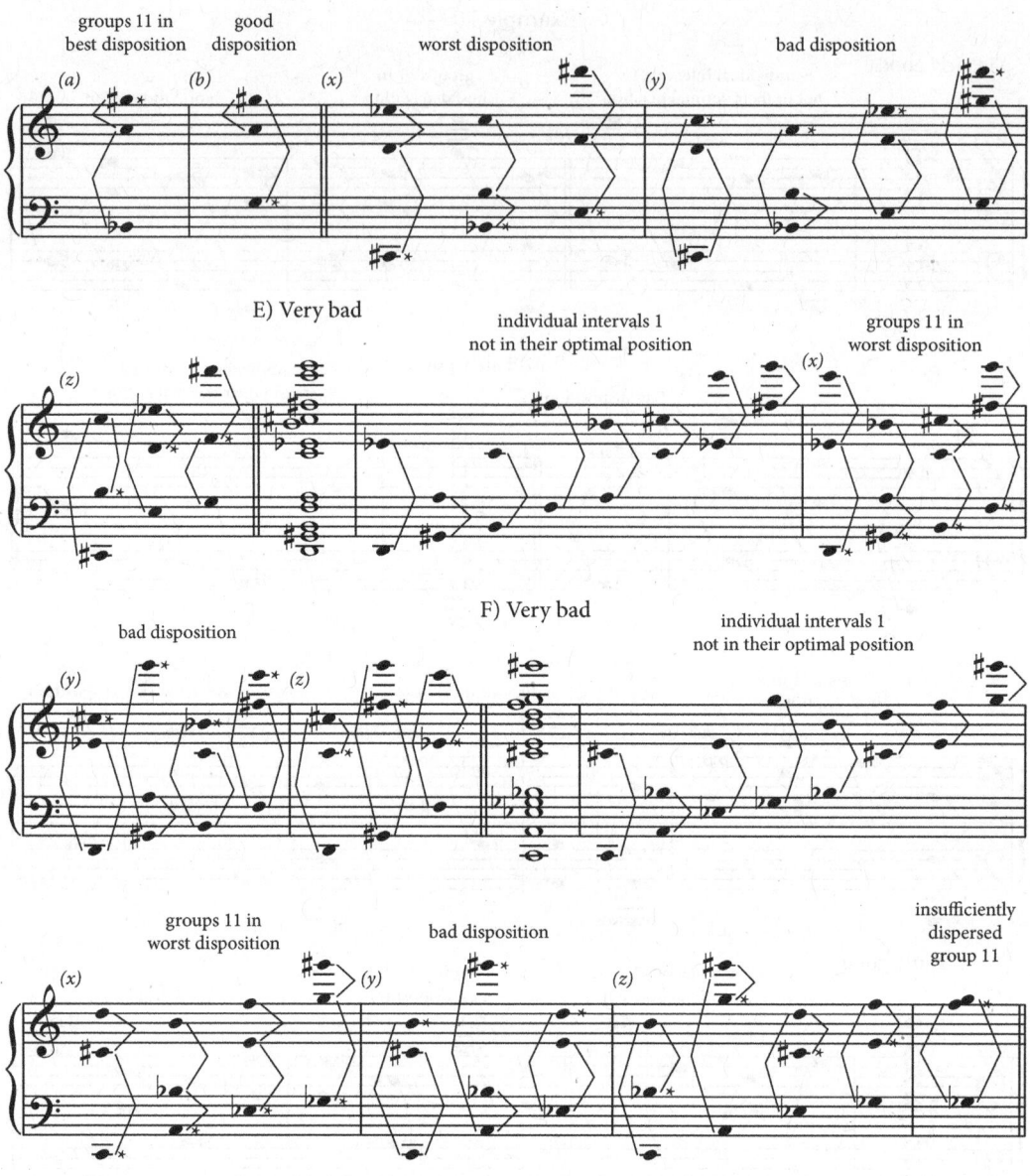

Observations regarding disposition of groups 11 can also be applied to the disposition of the incomplete maximum **011266**, as well as to the maxima **112**, **0112**, **1126**, **01126**, and **11266**.

§73. Disposition of Chords in a Harmonic Progression

We have examined the effect of various dispositions of *isolated* chords. This effect can be perceived differently, however (softened, as a rule), when a chord appears *in a progression*. This is important especially for harsh dispositions of chords. A badly arranged chord becomes acceptable (inconspicuous) when suitably placed in a progression.

The influence of harmonic surroundings and harmonic motion, or of the entire time element (duration), on the effect of a chord with a particular disposition can be understood approximately as follows:

1) The effect of a disposition of a *transient chord* in a continuous chord progression is always less conspicuous than that of an independent chord (a complete or incomplete harmony). Thus it is natural that badly arranged chords occur more often as transient chords. Of all transient chords, *appoggiaturas* are more conspicuous than *passing* or *auxiliary* chords, since the former occur at the moment that the harmony is struck, while the latter occur only after the harmony has sounded.

Example 71 shows two badly arranged chords as independent chords and then as transient chords. The harsh effect of the dispositions is greatly softened, especially in chords that are used as passing chords.

Example 71

Badly arranged four-note chords as independent harmonies (H)

The same chords in the same dispositions, as transient chords (T)

a) appoggiatura b) passing

2) A harsh disposition of a chord is less conspicuous when the voices approach and leave it *most directly*, that is, by melodic intervals 0, 1, or 2. (Movement by interval 0 means that a pitch is repeated or tied.) The voices introducing those pitches whose arrangement causes the harshness of the disposition are especially important. The badly arranged chords E G C F and B♭ F D♭ B are not at all obtrusive in Example 72.

Example 72

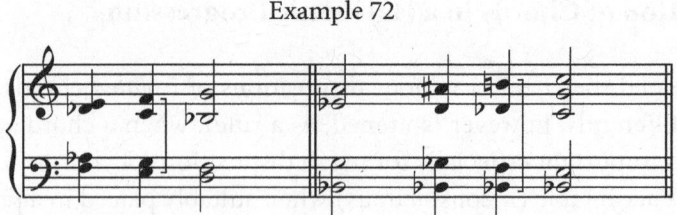

In the second case, the B♭ remains in the bass as a pedal point, so B♭ F D♭ B can be understood as a transient chord.

The same chords, in retrograde order, are found in Example 73.

Example 73

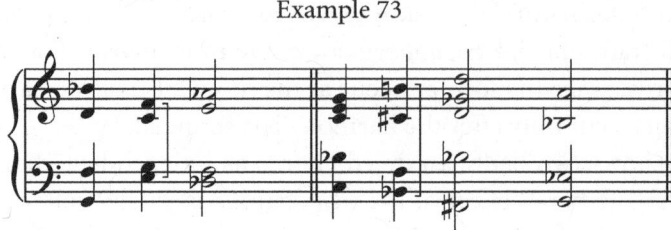

Here it is very difficult to become reconciled to the effect of the chords E G C F and B♭ F D♭ B, since each is approached and left by leap rather then step in some voices, and especially since these voices introduce pitches that cause the bad sound of the disposition (see the bracketed notes). While in the previous example we arrive at the same chords "logically", here we have the impression that we are dealing with a mistake, or with an awkward progression. (We "correct" the examples if we replace the F with A and the B with B♭ in the highest voice.)

The above two methods of handling dispositions are the only two that can effectively soften the harsh sound of badly arranged chords. The following are merely ways in which badly arranged chords can be justified or excused.

3) The harsh effect is slightly softened when a badly arranged chord is immediately preceded by a good disposition of the same transposition of the same chord-type. This process in reverse is less meaningful. Example 74 alternates good and bad dispositions of the chord E G C F:

Example 74

Chapter IV – Disposition of Chords

4) In a composition, a harsh disposition of a chord will usually *recur* several times, or will be excessively *lengthened*, so that the composer can "convince" the listeners that this is not a mistake, an accidental slip of the finger, or an entirely arbitrary choice of chord. Under such circumstances, even a very harsh disposition sounds somewhat better than when the chord is judged in isolation. In Example 75 the chords E G C F and E B F G are used with this principle in mind:[76]

Example 75

Andante

f pesante

Allegretto

pp giocoso

5) When harshly arranged chords appear in a composition in greater numbers, they cease to be exceptions, and thus are not even very noticeable. Badly arranged chords are not so disturbing when they are purposefully *accumulated*. An interesting example of this is Alexander Scriabin's *Prelude for piano, op. 74, no. 4*; in it, chords in good dispositions (a total of 75 chords, including transient chords) sound for the duration of 40 ♩, followed by thirty eight chords in purposely harsh dispositions, for the duration of 33 ♩; the ending of the brief composition is shown in Example 76.

Example 76

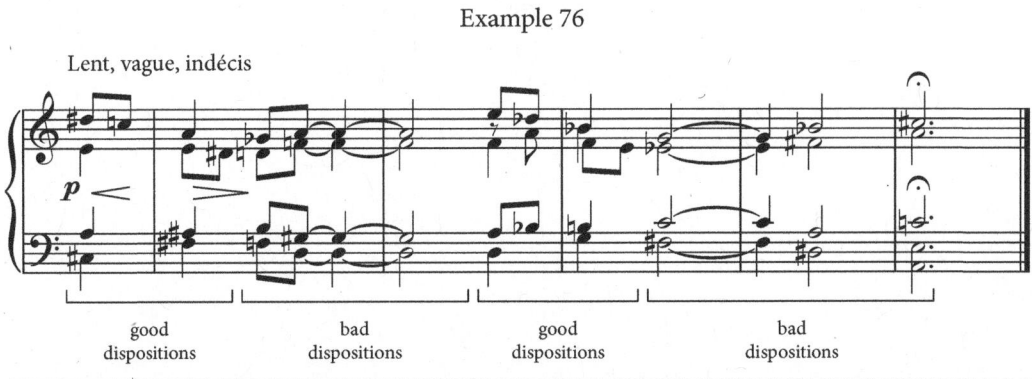

76 Example 75b is from my *Capriccio for piano, op. 13a*, composed in 1932.

The final chord is the most sensitive chord 313 in the worst possible disposition. Not one consonant chord can be found in the entire prelude

§74. Disposition of Chords and Compositional Practice

In considering dispositions of chords, we have been starting with chord-types as given and treating disposition as an act of organization, an act that follows only after the chord-type has been chosen. Compositional practice generally takes a different approach. As a rule, a composer does not think of the chord-type first and only then of its disposition. While the theorist theorizes, generalizes, and analyzes, the composer is creating concrete unified ideas; while the theorist strives to differentiate between various thought processes, the composer searches purposefully for the most effective expressive medium and is not concerned by what means it is reached. For the composer, the search for the right chord-type is inseparable from the search for the right disposition; both take place almost simultaneously. It was this aspect of compositional practice that led certain theorists (in Czechoslovakia, Skuherský and Hába) to merge the two phenomena into an integral whole and thus to make the entire subject unmanageably complicated. The fact that often each chord-type has an immediate and definite disposition in a composer's imagination does not prove that the phenomena are inseparable. Disposition and chord-type remain clearly differentiated and precisely defined concepts, regardless of the fact that their fusion (the chord in disposition) can be realized in one process.

Chapter V – Expression of Chords

§75. Real and Imaginary Pitches

We refer to a pitch that is actually sounding as a *real* pitch. Real pitches constitute the obvious foundation of all harmonic material. Without real pitches, harmony does not exist.

We speak of real pitches even when their actual sound is only assumed. When simply reading through a composition, for example, we consider all those pitches that would actually sound in a live performance to be real. We say that a chord consisting entirely of real pitches has been given *real expression*.

We refer to a pitch that has finished sounding in the real sense, but continues to have an effect, as an *imaginary pitch* (existing only in the mind, rather than actually sounding). Every imaginary pitch must first exist as a real pitch; imaginary pitches are not possible apart from real pitches.

If we play a melody or harmonic progression in which the notes or chords are connected (*legato*), one or several real pitches will sound in any vertical cross-section. If we play the same melody or chord progression with the pitches or chords separated by rests, the pitches sounding immediately before each rest will continue to function for the duration of the rest; this is what we mean by imaginary pitches. The listener does not invent them; rather, they are forced upon the listener, so we are not dealing here with an arbitrary act. The existence of imaginary pitches is determined by the texture.

The duration of a real pitch is determined by how long it sounds. Its beginning and end are objectively established by the composer's notation. The duration of an imaginary pitch does not always have precise limits; it depends on the nature of the harmonic activity that follows the moment of its appearance. In contrast to a real pitch, which simply stops sounding, an imaginary pitch can either be *canceled*, or it can gradually *die away*. Cancellation is due to the intervention of the composer, so it can reliably be determined, while the length of time before an imaginary pitch has died away can only be estimated.

We speak of *harmonic* and *tonal* imaginary pitches, depending on the extent of their effect. Harmonic imaginary pitches are capable of creating or taking part in *creating harmonic formations*. Tonal imaginary pitches cannot do this, since they are weaker, but they can still *influence the tonal design* of a passage in a composition or the composition as a whole. Harmonic imaginary pitches also function tonally, and thus are considered tonal as well as harmonic. However, tonal imaginary pitches are not also harmonic.

Both harmonic and tonal imaginary pitches appear after a real pitch has finished sounding. The harmonic imaginary pitch dies away earlier, however, and is more easily canceled than the tonal imaginary pitch. This means that a harmonic imaginary pitch can continue to function in its weaker form, as a tonal imaginary pitch, after it has been canceled or has died away.

§76. Appearance and Cancellation of an Imaginary Pitch

Whenever any real pitch that is isolated in time – framed by silence – has finished sounding, it is transformed into an imaginary pitch. The appearance of a harmonic imaginary pitch can be prevented by the right melodic progression, however – the same progression that would cancel the effect of a harmonic imaginary pitch already in existence. Thus the following rules for canceling a harmonic imaginary pitch also apply to preventing one's appearance.

A harmonic imaginary pitch is *canceled* by

1) the appearance of a real pitch a *semitone higher or lower*, and
2) the appearance of a real pitch a *whole-tone lower*.

Example 77

In Example 77 the duration of the imaginary harmonic pitch is indicated by a horizontal line of decreasing thickness, while a short vertical line shows the moment of its cancellation. Where this indication is lacking, an imaginary pitch does not appear.

A harmonic imaginary pitch can *sometimes* be canceled by

3) the appearance of a real pitch a *whole-tone above the imaginary pitch*. This applies when the three following conditions are met:
   a) the imaginary pitch that is to be canceled is not emphasized (metrically or by its duration);

b) the pitch that is to do the canceling is longer or more significant metrically than the pitch that is to be canceled; and
c) the pitch that is to be canceled is preceded by at least one lower neighbouring pitch (either a whole-tone or a semitone below).

This is shown in the Example 78.

Example 78

In the first two cases, the unaccented passing note C fulfills all three conditions required for its cancellation, but the preceding B♭ is not canceled. In the third case the appearance of the imaginary pitch D is prevented, but the C does function as an imaginary pitch. In the last case, besides the F♯ (which is left by leap) the C also acts as an imaginary pitch, since although it is unaccented, it is not covered by a lower pitch B or B♭.

We can refer to the cancellation of a harmonic imaginary pitch as a *harmonic cancellation*. As was pointed out above, a harmonic cancellation does not mean a tonal cancellation, since an imaginary pitch that has been canceled harmonically can continue to function as a tonal imaginary pitch. A harmonic cancellation can be *delayed*, as illustrated in the melodic fragments in Example 79.

Example 79

The cancellation can also occur in another voice, as shown in Example 80.

Example 80

We have presented the conditions that prevent the formation or continuation of imaginary harmonic pitches. Thus we have also defined, negatively, the conditions under which it is *possible for such pitches to appear*: they appear or continue wherever the three conditions given above do not prevail—that is, they appear or continue after intervals larger than a second, and sometimes after a rising major second.

§77. The Counter-canceling Pitch

The following precept, derived from earlier as well as modern compositional practice, deals with the duration of imaginary harmonic pitches in polyphony: a harmonic imaginary pitch cannot be canceled by a real pitch appearing a whole-tone above or below if a real or imaginary pitch lying within the whole-tone between the pitch to be canceled and the pitch to do the canceling is in effect immediately preceding the moment of expected cancellation. We will call the pitch that prevents the cancellation in this way the *counter-canceling pitch*.[77] The imaginary pitch is not canceled even when the counter-canceling pitch occurs in a different octave.

A musical example will clarify this.

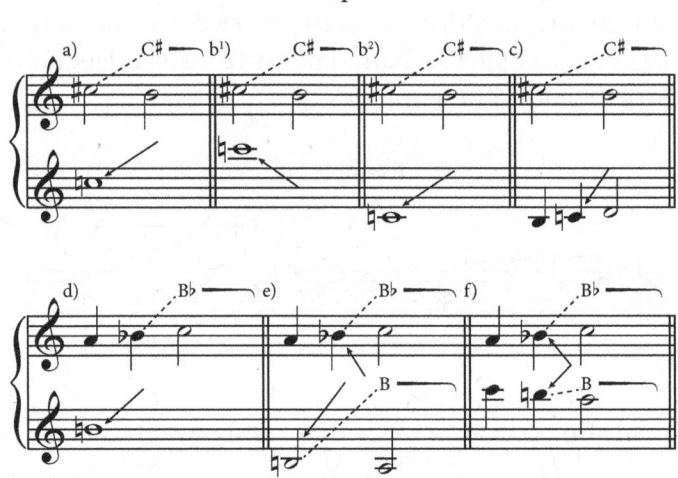

Example 81

In Example 81, counter-canceling pitches are indicated by arrows. The pitch whose effect is to be canceled (in Example 81a–c, the C♯) "steps around" the counter-canceling pitch by the interval of a whole-tone, so the cancellation cannot take place. It would take place if the movement were by semitone instead, towards which end the living sound of the counter-canceling pitch is working. In Example 81e and f, the counter-canceling pitches affect both voices. In view of the acute complications in the sound that arise in such a progression, the imaginary harmonic pitch cannot survive very long; it is condemned to *die away at an accelerated rate*. This is indicated in our examples by a line of decreasing thickness that is bent down at the end.

If the counter-canceling pitch does not appear until the same moment as the pitch that is to do the canceling, it cannot stop the cancellation.

---

77 Editor's note: Janeček's original term is *kritický protirušivý tón*, "critical counter-canceling pitch".

Example 82

Counter-canceling pitches *that appear too late* are indicated in Example 82 and those following by dotted arrows.

In exceptional cases, counter-canceling pitches can be active even in a *single voice*, as shown in the melodic fragments in Example 83.

Example 83

From the examples given in this section, we can see the classical composer's attitude to the counter-canceling pitch, as well as the way in which modern composers make use of this phenomenon. For classical composers, the progressions shown in Example 81 are unacceptable; they are "impurities". The melodic progressions of Example 83 appear equally impossible to them. In contrast, modern composers at times even seek out such two-voice and single-voice progressions, especially if they can use them consistently, rather than only in isolated instances. In the final analysis, both attitudes spring from the same cause: *acute harmonic entanglement*. While classical composers avoided this as stylistically impossible, modernists seek it out as something "unheard", as something that has not yet been used to its full potential. We have here semitone clashes of semitones, which we know as the most acutely pointed harmonic formations of the whole tempered chromatic system. In Example 81a–c, these are the clusters B C C♯ and B C C♯ D, and in 81d–f, the clusters B♭ B C and A B♭ B C; the situation is similar in Example 83.

§78. The Dying Away of a Harmonic Imaginary Pitch

When an imaginary pitch has been created (forced on the listener by the composer) and not harmonically canceled, its effect continues for some time until it dies away. The duration of this effect differs according to the nature of the music that flows in the meantime. It is impossible to determine this duration precisely. On the basis of the harmonic structure of the music, however, instances where the imaginary pitch dies away earlier can be distinguished from those where it dies away later. We can then speak of the dying away as *slow, normal,* or *accelerated.* We will indicate a slow dying away by a horizontal line of decreasing thickness that eventually becomes a dotted line, a normal dying away by a similar but unbroken horizontal line, and an accelerated dying away by a line bent down at the end:

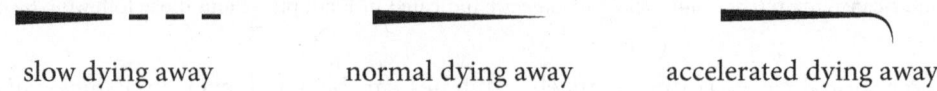

     slow dying away   normal dying away   accelerated dying away

Generally, the simpler the music, and the more transparent its harmonic structure, the longer the life an imaginary pitch will have. A harmonic imaginary pitch lasts longest in real silence; even here there will be differences, however, depending on the complexity of the chord on which the music has stopped.

What has been said about music in general applies to individual harmonic formations as well. We have to evaluate not only chord-types, but also their various dispositions, since these can also cause substantial differences in the sonic effect. From this point of view, harmonic intervals (two-note chords) can be divided into *three groups,* as follows:

1) *Consonances and the tritone.* A harmonic imaginary pitch dies away slowly when preceded by these melodic intervals,[78] as illustrated in Example 84.

Example 84

2) The *whole-tone* as a minor seventh or major ninth, and the *semitone* as a rising major seventh or minor ninth. The dying away of a harmonic imaginary pitch that is preceded by these melodic intervals is normal.

Example 85

3) The *semitone* as a melodically *descending* major seventh or minor ninth. The dying away of an imaginary pitch that follows these melodic intervals is accelerated.

---

78 Editor's note: The intervals under discussion *follow* the real pitch but *precede* the imaginary pitch, because in a line unbroken by silence a real pitch only becomes imaginary when the next pitch sounds.

Example 86

As a rule, a higher pitch followed by a lower pitch dies away more easily than vice versa. This is the reason for dividing semitones into the two categories (2 and 3 above) of rising and falling melodic intervals. All distinctions given here represent only *estimates*, supported by analysis of the compositional technique of earlier as well as contemporary composers.

If several real pitches occur simultaneously or in rapid succession after the appearance of an imaginary pitch, the rate at which the imaginary pitch will die away is determined by the real pitch that would make it die away most quickly. Thus the examples of a slow dying away given in Example 84 can easily be changed into examples of an accelerated, or at least normal, dying away by the addition of a suitable pitch:

Example 87

§79. Compositional Acceleration of the Dying Away of a Harmonic Imaginary Pitch

The life of a harmonic imaginary pitch that has not been canceled can be shortened artificially by compositional devices. A harmonic imaginary pitch dies away at an accelerated rate if it becomes part of a harmonic formation with a more complex sound (and, if possible, dissonant tension), in which most of the pitches are real; at the same time, the simpler the part of the harmonic formation that is expressed by real pitches, the more accelerated the dying away of the imaginary pitch will be. The simplest harmonic formations are of course the two basic harmonies, the major and minor triads. Thus an imaginary pitch that has not been canceled dies away naturally and most easily when a major or minor triad appears with whose real pitches it forms a sharp dissonance or even a badly arranged chord. We see this in Example 88, where the appearance of a consonant triad of real pitches accelerates the dying away of the imaginary pitches.

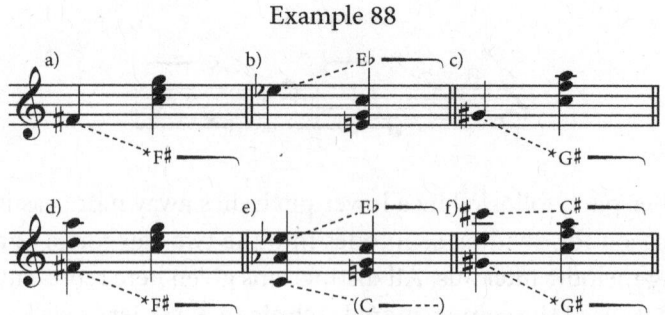

Example 88

To the isolated pitches that linger for a time as imaginary pitches in Example 88a–c are added other pitches in Example 88d–f to form consonant triads; thus a succession of two real consonant triads is formed. According to the classification presented above in §78, the pitches marked with an asterisk in Example 88 would have a somewhat longer duration if what was striving to wipe them out were not a consonant group of pitches. In Example 88e, the harmonic imaginary pitch C dies away slowly, of course, since it is perfectly consonant with the sound of the real pitches of the C triad. It is interesting to compare Example 88b and 88c, in which the lingering imaginary pitches form the same chord-type with the real pitches (C E♭ E G = F G♯ A C); the imaginary G♯ in 88c dies away somewhat faster than the E♭ in 88b, apparently because the specific disposition of the chord-type is worse in 88c than in 88b. A similar relation obtains between 88e and 88f.

An imaginary pitch resulting from the presence of a counter-canceling pitch is subject to an unusually accelerated dying away, as we pointed out above in §77. Thus the conditions under which the counter-canceling pitch comes into play (see §77) are also effective in shortening the life of an imaginary pitch. We will return to this matter when we examine tonal imaginary pitches (see §87 below).

§80. Harmonic Significance of Imaginary Pitches

A rest following a harmony does not cause a harmonic vacuum; rather, the harmonic effect of the chord that has just finished sounding continues. All the real pitches that have just finished sounding (that have not been canceled by newly appearing pitches) continue as harmonic imaginary pitches, just as able to combine to form a harmonic effect as are real pitches. The harmonic effect of a harmonic progression is essentially the same whether the chords are connected in performance (*legato*), or separated by rests (*staccato*), or successively arpeggiated.

Harmonic imaginary pitches can combine with real pitches to form a single harmonic effect. The harmonic effect of a single voice, or the full harmonic effect of two voices, can only be explained by the existence of harmonic imaginary pitches. Similarly, the concept of *latent* (hidden) harmonies can only be explained by the existence of imaginary pitches.

A *single voice* moving by comparatively large intervals represents not only a succession of individual pitches, but also a *progression of chords* each of which is formed by the vertical cross-section of real pitches actually sounding and harmonic imaginary pitches. We can express the harmonic effect of such a single voice as in Example 89.

Chapter V – Expression of Chords

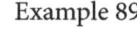
Example 89

On the second staff, real pitches are shown in larger notes, while continuing imaginary pitches are shown in small notes. Eventually, although sometimes belatedly after a delay, all the imaginary pitches are harmonically canceled. The harmonies shown in boxes are heard at the ends of measures; their effect is partially felt already at the beginning of each measure, however (as shown by the arrows pointing back), and is gradually clarified during the course of the measure. Individual vertical cross-sections are partially permeated by neighbouring harmonies.

Similarly, *two voices* represent not merely a succession of two-note chords, but rather a *progression of richer chords* formed by the combination of real pitches and imaginary pitches that have not been harmonically canceled. This harmonic effect of two voices can be shown in a manner similar to that used for the single voice.

Example 90

Again in Example 90 we see how individual harmonies (I II V^7 I over a pedal) become clarified as each measure progresses. We can expect the A_5 at the end of the second measure to die away during the third measure, so that we need no longer be concerned with its resolution, especially since its harmonic function is taken over by the A_4 an octave lower, which is then properly canceled (resolved) in the last measure.

We have chosen the above examples of one and two voices from classical harmony. The process of perception is the same in any style, however. The difference will lie only in the chord-types and their dispositions.

As shown in the examples above, various *possibilities of expressing chords* arise from the supplementary harmonic effect of imaginary pitches. Chords can be expressed

1) by *real* pitches,
2) by *imaginary* pitches, and
3) by *composite* means (with real and imaginary pitches together). The first two methods have a relatively limited usefulness in compositional practice, while the third is rich in possibilities because of its great diversity.

§81. Chords Expressed by Real Pitches

The expression of a chord is *real* when all the pitches that constitute it are real (actually sounding) pitches. As long as a chord of real expression is isolated, no difficulties arise with its disposition: a particular disposition can be chosen for its sonic effect – as the best disposition, or one that is good, or one that is not – without regard for its harmonic surroundings. If several chords follow each other in succession, however, care must be taken *that no imaginary harmonic pitches from a preceding chord interfere with any new chord* (if they are not common to both chords), as this would result in more complex, undesirable chords of composite expression; the pitches of the new chord must cancel all, or at least the majority, of the pitches in the preceding chord. The disposition of the new chord is then not inconsequential, since in choosing it we cannot consider only its own sonic effect, as we could with isolated chords.

Next we present several examples showing successions of more complex chords. Each new chord, as it appears, cancels all the pitches in the preceding chord that are not in the new chord.

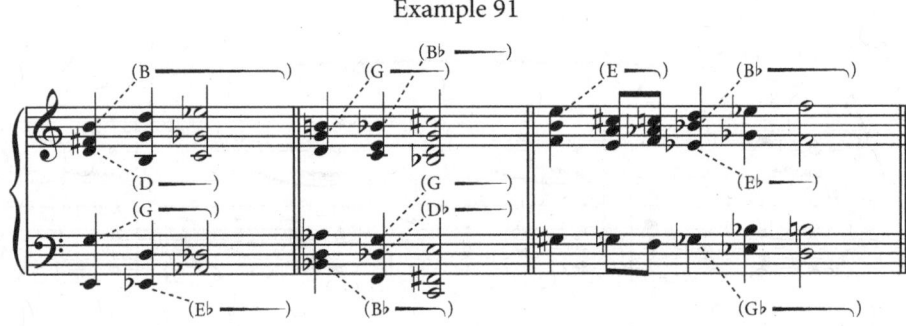

Example 91

Imaginary harmonic pitches remain from the preceding chord, they are also real pitches in the new chord, even if in another octave. Since they do not add pitches to the new chord, they cause no complications for the next chord. They are insignificant, and we show them in brackets.

When a larger number of pitches sounds simultaneously, the position of an isolated imaginary pitch is unstable. An imaginary pitch that continues into a chord that has real sound becomes lost beside the intensely assertive real pitches and always dies away quickly; thus it does not need to be expressly canceled, since any complication it might cause would be very brief. This applies especially to imaginary pitches in the middle of a chord of sounding real pitches; when imaginary pitches are the outer pitches of such a chord, they are somewhat more resistant.

In Example 91, continuing imaginary pitches, as long as they did not reappear as real pitches in another octave and so continue to function, were either canceled by the third harmony (counting from the harmony from which they resulted) or were subject to accelerated dying away. The distinction is insignificant wherever real pitches sound in harmonic blocks, as in the example.

If we construct a chord succession in which each new chord does not cancel all the pitches of the preceding chord, the resulting impression will be similar to that of a succession in which each new chord *does* cancel all the pitches of the preceding one. We can say even about such a succession that its chords have been expressed in a real way and are represented in notation by the notes that are actually written. This applies to the chord successions in Example 92.

Example 92

Pitches marked here with the narrowing line bent down at the end, showing accelerated dying away, are of such short duration that they can be ignored in harmonic analysis. The harmonic blocks that are actually sounding have such a strong impact that the listener cannot at the same time perceive imaginary pitches from chords that have stopped sounding. Pitches that sound as real in another octave are shown in brackets, since it is superfluous to consider them imaginary pitches.

Only *groups of imaginary pitches*, especially when the pitches are *adjacent*, with no real pitches between them, are capable of more pronounced resistance against chords of real expression. We will meet them wherever chords of different registers are involved. Imaginary pitches formed by a chord in a low register cannot be absorbed quickly enough by the pitches of the next chord if it is in a high register, and so a *temporary harmonic complication* results, as a multi-note chord of *composite expression*.

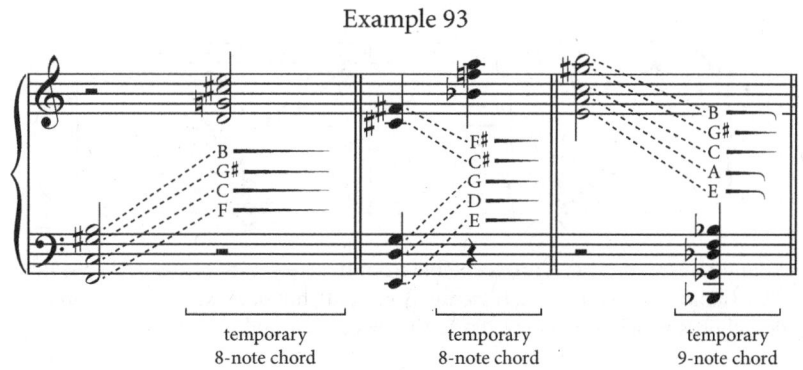

Example 93

temporary
8-note chord

temporary
8-note chord

temporary
9-note chord

Imaginary harmonic pitches continuing from a previous chord are much less conspicuous when *real pitches are interspersed* between them. Even when there are more imaginary pitches (for example four imaginary pitches as opposed to four real pitches), they cannot disturb a *simple real expression* any more significantly.

Example 94

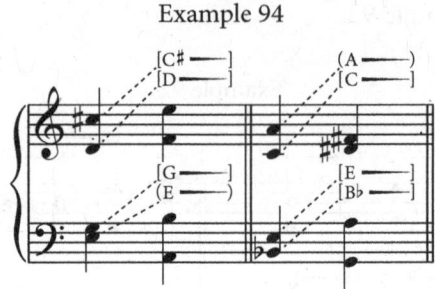

We feel that the new chord in Example 94 is in no way disturbed by any continuing imaginary pitches from the previous chord. Therefore we show these pitches in square brackets. (We use round brackets for pitches in a real, sounding, chord.) There is no essential difference between these harmonic progressions and those in Example 92 above. In both instances we can speak of a simple real expression of chords.

In contrast, the *interference of imaginary harmonic pitches in real consonances is very conspicuous.* Successive but unconnected consonant triads are unsatisfactory from the viewpoint of classical requirements precisely because their sound can never be pure, since they are too obviously complicated by continuing imaginary pitches. We are then no longer dealing with triads, but with more complex (six-note) harmonies in composite expression. If each real triad lasts long enough, the imaginary pitches die away, and the consonance will prevail for the rest of the time. We see this in the series of consonant triads in Example 95.

Example 95

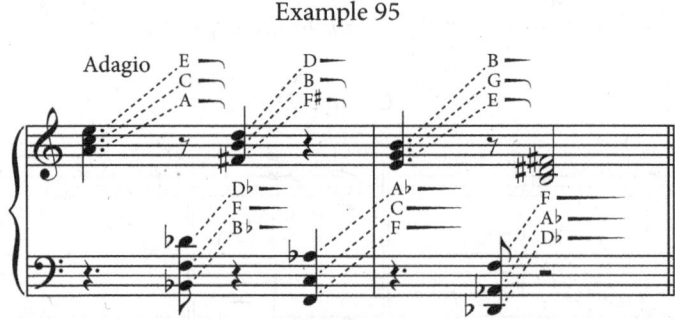

This series lacks any continuity. This is unacceptable from the viewpoint of classical style not only because it represents a functional split in the group (essentially bitonal), but because it forces upon the listener complex combination chords which were not in use in the classical period.

The requirement of school harmony regarding *parsimonious voice-leading* is based on the fact that such voice-leading prevents harmonic imaginary pitches from forming to the extent that they would be difficult to vanquish, and so it prevents the complication of the written chords. The fear of harmonic *cross-relation* springs from the same source, with the counter-canceling pitch playing an additional significant role.

§82. Chords Expressed by Imaginary Pitches

An imaginary pitch can appear only after a real pitch has finished sounding. If a *group of imaginary pitches is to function as a chord*, therefore, this chord must first sound as real pitches, although all the necessary real pitches need not sound simultaneously. When the real pitches sound successively, however, it can happen that in the end the chord cannot function as a complete entity because some of the harmonic imaginary pitches have already died away.

In Example 96 the sound of each chord is interrupted by a rest. For the duration of the rest, the chord is expressed only by imaginary harmonic pitches. Except for the final chord, the duration of each chord is precisely defined by the appearance of the next chord; the final chord (in this case a minor triad) will continue expressed by imaginary pitches without a definite limit. The inserted rests and a staccato performance will lighten even dense chords rich in pitches:

Example 96

It is unthinkable that the listener's mind would fill in the rests with any other chords than those whose real sound has just terminated. Thus the prevailing harmony is always evident, without ambiguity, even during the moments of silence. This is true whether the individual chords are in an advantageous disposition ("well" arranged), or whether their dispositions are "bad", with a piercing sound. Complex and badly arranged chords expressed by imaginary pitches will have a shorter duration than simple (for example, consonant) chords that are well arranged (for example, without semitone or whole-tone clusters); when imaginary pitches form complex and badly arranged chords, they die away faster, and they do so as a group.

When a rest appears after a group of pitches that were not sounded simultaneously (after a melodic figure, for example), the effect of the resulting chord is unified only when the series of pitches is not too long; those pitches that sounded earlier die away easily, especially if they are the complicating elements that make the sound of the resulting more complex chord more piercing. Example 97 clarifies this.

Example 97

In Example 97a the harmonic resultant of the brief figure is a minor triad in six-three rotation (D F♯ B), even though the figure also involves an E♭ that has not been specifically canceled; this pitch, however, which would have enriched the resulting chord into the piercing dissonance D F♯ B E♭, has meanwhile died away at an accelerated rate. The same example also shows the possibility of revitalizing pitches by reintroducing them. In Example 97b, the dissonant four-note chord is heard in a good disposition. Example 97c involves a more complex chord, a six-note chord combining the two triads C E♭ G and B D F♯ in a bad disposition (with clashing semitones F♯ G and B C and the cluster B C D); the chord's nature and disposition result in an accelerated dying away of all its pitches.

In the above Example 97a and c, even after the harmonic imaginary pitches have died away they leave their clearly perceptible shadow "in the air" in the form of tonal imaginary pitches. We realize this because the resulting impression in these instances, even after a longer time lapse when the original chords have been forgotten, is different from the impression that would result from simple progressions or groupings of pitches. Specifically, the B minor triad resulting in Example 97a does not function as a tonic triad because of the E♭ that has died away and the pitch C that has been canceled. Thus the sense and extent of the given figure is different from what it would be if the figure were simpler and arpeggiating only the pitches of a consonant triad. Similarly, the longer silence that would follow Example 97c would not have an entirely neutral effect even if the individual components of the complex chord had already been forgotten; although these components have lost their ability to function as harmonic imaginary pitches, they retain a certain significance as tonal imaginary pitches.

In comparison with the real expression of chords, *expression by imaginary pitches* is only an auxiliary, supplementary system. Chords expressed in this way can only *continue* – they cannot be sounded. In spite of this, expression by imaginary pitches is an important *means of harmonic expression*, used liberally by composers throughout time. The significance of this means of expression has increased especially in modern times, when composers at least on occasion use complex and unusual chords that would have far too heavy an effect if they were expressed by means of a fully real sound.

§83. Composite Expression of Chords in a Single Voice

Chords are most often expressed by *composite* means – by real and imaginary pitches simultaneously. This is the only way that chords can be expressed in a *single flowing voice*;

here no more than one real pitch can actually sound at a given time, while imaginary pitches must suffice for the rest of the chord.

In monophonic texture a chord is expressed basically through *arpeggiation*, either in a straight arpeggio (in one direction) or in a jagged one (with changes of direction). The following example shows two more complex chords of composite expression in a single voice; the arpeggio of the first is straight, that of the second is jagged. Here no pitch cancels the preceding one.

Example 98

However the succession of real pitches must be quick enough that the resulting imaginary pitches do not die away before the complete chord is arpeggiated; it is also necessary from time to time to return to individual pitches in order to renew or revitalize their weakening presence. If we omitted the second B♭ in the second chord of our example, for instance, and played the remaining pitches at a slower tempo, only the four-note chord E♭ A D F would be present by the end of the measure; we would have to consider the B♭ at the beginning of the figure to have died away because of the influence of the lower A, sounded twice.

The differences between good and bad dispositions of chords with composite expression in a single voice are not as great as in the case of chords with real expression. This is demonstrated by our example: the first chord has a good disposition, the second a bad one (sonically disadvanteagous), and yet the effects of these chords are not nearly as different in the composite expression of a single voice as they would be in real expression (shown by whole notes).

A chord that is to have composite expression in a single voice must be arranged with no immediately adjacent pitches a semitone or whole-tone apart, except that a rising step of a whole-tone does not matter if its first pitch is emphasized metrically or by length, or if it is approached by leap, or if it forms the beginning of a melodic phrase. If the arpeggiated chord contains pitches that are a semitone or a whole-tone apart, a chord simpler than the expected one will result, because the semitone and whole--tone intervals prevent the formation of imaginary pitches. Moreover, the result is often harmonically ambiguous. If we want to express in a single voice the six-note chord G B D F♯ A C♯ (the triadic combination −1+), we cannot do so in the following way:

Example 99

Although all the pitches of the supposed six-note chord are shown here, many of them are immediately canceled so they have no harmonic effect. This reduces the six-note chord to one of a lower class, but not without ambiguity. The above example can be understood harmonically in the following ways.

Example 100

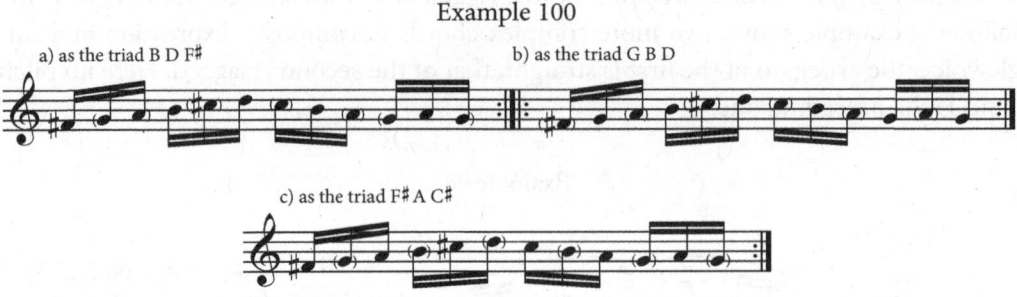

The pitches in brackets are perceived as non-harmonic.

The six-note chord can be expressed in its completeness by a single voice when the intervallic requirements stated above are met, for example as follows:

Example 101

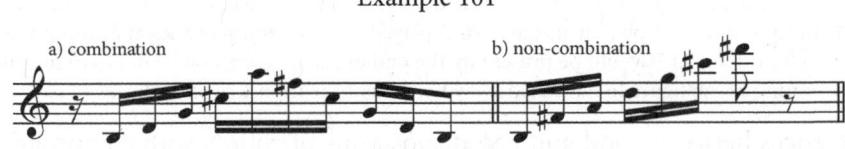

A combination arpeggiation of a more complex chord, if it can be perceived as a triadic combination at all, looks like a succession of component triads or simpler chords. Actually, however, we are dealing with a composite expression of a *single chord*, as in the following example.

Example 102

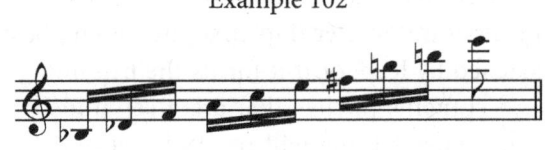

Here we have a ten-note chord containing besides the pitch G the component triads B♭ minor, A minor, and B minor; it is not merely a succession of these triads.

Example 102 is a modern parallel to the arpeggiation of a classical harmony shown in Example 103.

Chapter V – Expression of Chords

Example 103

In order to express in a single voice the chord of Example 102 not as one ten-note chord but as the series of its constituent triads, the voice would have to change direction, as in Example 104.

Example 104

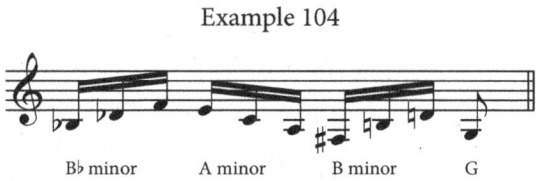

B♭ minor   A minor   B minor   G

§84. Composite Expression of Chords in Polyphony

In *polyphony* more than one real pitch can sound at a time. As the number of voices increases, real pitches prevail increasingly. The harmonic significance of imaginary pitches decreases when enough voices (four or five) are involved, since these imaginary pitches die away quickly even when they are not specifically canceled.

When there is composite expression of chords in polyphony, the differences between good and bad dispositions are again evident. The more voices involved, the more care must be taken that the disposition of the chords is good or at least acceptable. Even so, unfavorable dispositions are more acceptable when their expression is composite than when it is real. Example 105 shows several chords, with a suggested composite expression in two, three, or more voices for each, without non-harmonic tones.

Example 105

A harmony of composite expression must always be understood as the *sum of real and imaginary harmonic pitches*. Thus we cannot say that the melody G–E–B♭ in Example 105d is harmonized by the chord F C♯ B, or the melody B♭–D–F–B♭–F in Example 105f by the chord A♭ E♭ G C; in both cases the chords are given by the sum of the pitches of the melody and accompaniment.

Even in very complex chords, real pitches within separate voices can combine to form consonant intervals or consonant component chords. The chord in question does not thereby become consonant, however, since the listener draws the component consonant chords together into a larger whole that remains dissonant. It does not much matter whether the real pitches that sound simultaneously form component consonances with good dispositions; it is the sonic character of the whole chord that is important, and whether or not the overall disposition of this chord is good or bad. This is shown in Examples 106, 107, and 108.

Example 106

Example 107

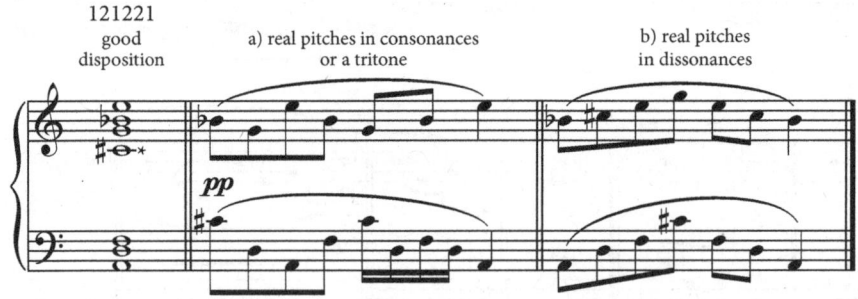

Chapter V – Expression of Chords

Example 108

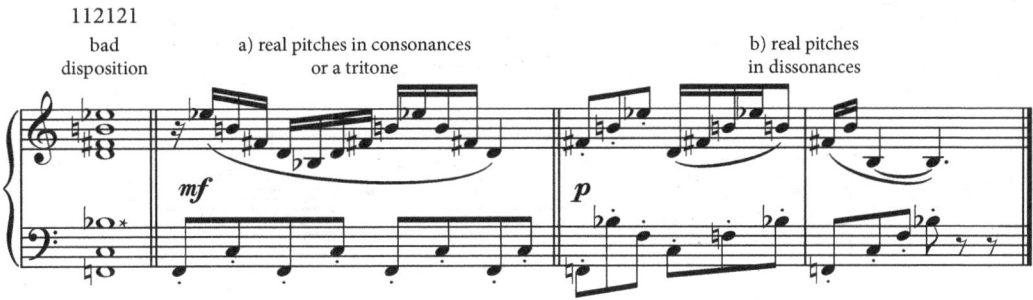

The differences between cases a and b in these examples are negligible. The essential nature of the sound is determined by the chord-type and its overall disposition. In contrast to the cumbersome real expression (shown in whole notes), composite expression always has a lighter effect.

In polyphony, unfoldings of chords can also include *semitones and whole-tones*, even piled up in clusters. The resulting harmonic ambiguity must then be counteracted in another voice; this voice must either involve the same pitches but avoid semitone and whole-tone intervals, or it must introduce one pitch of these intervals at the moment that the other pitch sounds in another voice. This is evident in the following example.

Example 109

The pitches marked "n" can be understood as non-harmonic tones, while the pitches marked "h" must be understood as harmonic. Since we are always dealing with the same pitches (E A B♭ D) alternating between the two voices, they all form part of the intended five-note chord and thus assure that it will be reliably expressed.

It is a matter of sensible economy that the voices share in expressing the intended chord without any superfluous doubling of real pitches. When the number of pitches in the chord that is to be expressed exceeds the number of voices, it is better for different real pitches than doubled ones to sound simultaneously. The doubling of real pitches in two voices makes the voices less distinct and closer to a single voice; this also makes the sound more transparent, which may be the composer's intention. The heightened transparency of two voices with doublings of real pitches is shown in the following example.

Example 110

The doubled pitches are not shown in the suggested chord. The lower voice by itself expresses the complete chord, while the upper voice has a harmonically subordinate role. It is evident from the static effect of this creeping music that we are dealing with a single complex chord, not a chord succession.

§85. Non-harmonic Tones in Chords of Composite Expression

In a single voice, *non-harmonic tones* play an important part; as temporarily real (actually sounding) pitches, they push into the background the harmonic pitches (pitches that are part of the intended chord) that have ceased to function as other than harmonic imaginary pitches. Non-harmonic tones become more significant wherever they are not immediately resolved.

Example 111 shows a chord of composite expression (E♭ G B♭ D) that makes use of non-harmonic tones (C♯, F♯, A, F).

Example 111

Here the pitches of resolution immediately follow the non-harmonic tones shown in brackets.

Delayed resolution extends the effect of the non-harmonic tones and thus increases their significance. This is shown in Example 112.

Example 112

Although the three-note chord D G C lasts for the entire measure, the passage can also be understood, especially at a slower tempo, as a succession of three-note chords (D G C – C E♭ G or D A C – C E♭ G). Since we have only a single voice here, we can also speak of a five-note chord (D G A C E♭), because the delayed resolution of non-harmonic tones complicates the intended simpler harmony for an extended period of time.

Consequently, with a composite expression of chords in a single voice it is advisable to use non-harmonic tones only sparingly and as simply as possible. Excessive accumulation of non-harmonic tones and delay in their resolution complicate the harmony and make it ambiguous; this may of course sometimes be the composer's intention.

Non-harmonic tones are not as disturbing or complicating when there is *more than one voice* as when there is a single voice. Only their excessive simultaneous use in different voices obscures the intended harmony. The Examples 113 and 114 show chords of composite expression in a two voice texture, with non-harmonic tones:

Special attention must be given to those non-harmonic tones that create harmonic complications lasting longer than the pitches themselves. As a rule, the effect of a non-harmonic tone continues until it is resolved (canceled by an adjacent harmonic pitch). Most often, the effect of a non-harmonic tone lasts as long as it is actually sounding; only in the case of a delayed resolution does the effect last longer, although it is always precisely defined by the moment of resolution. However, if at the moment of a whole-tone resolution of a non-harmonic tone a *counter-canceling pitch* sounds in another voice (see §77 above), the non-harmonic tone is not canceled, but rather it *dies away* later, although at an accelerated rate. When a non-harmonic tone is not canceled, the complication continues until the moment when the accelerated dying away is complete. Thus a non-harmonic tone that dies away at an accelerated rate is more significant than one that is normally resolved.

A melody that has such non-harmonic tones that are not canceled is more conspicuous. It is more persistent and self-sufficient, less dependent on harmony, and so it seems to detach itself from other voices and to thrust itself out above them. When harmonizing a melody that occurs at a point of intensity in a composition, modern composers delight in choosing chords that contain the counter-canceling pitch; when the order of these compositional processes is reversed, composers create over a previously chosen harmonic foundation a melodic line in which at least some of the non-harmonic tones are not resolved in the usual way.

Example 115 shows some examples of abnormally resolved non-harmonic tones

Arrows point to counter-canceling pitches. Whole-tone melodic intervals that do not immediately cancel non-harmonic tones (because of a counter-canceling pitch) are shown by square brackets. The first pitch of such intervals intrudes significantly into the currently prevailing harmony, since it serves to enrich this harmony (make it more piercing) even after this pitch itself has ceased to sound. This means that chords are formed not only by pitches that are actually sounding, but also by pitches that without the intervention of the counter-canceling pitch could be considered non-harmonic, vanishing without harmonic trace once they have finished sounding.

The use of counter-canceling pitches is absolutely *not classical*. In classical harmony, such pitches would be technical impurities. However, this is a resource for composers when they want to express particular heaviness, intensity, etc. We find isolated traces of this technique in the neo-romantics; in older music it is exceptional.

§86. Time Boundaries between Chords of Composite Expression

Time boundaries between chords of real expression are unambiguous. This is not the case, however, with chords of composite expression. The fewer voices involved, the more complex the chords, and the more non-harmonic tones, the more ambiguous the time definition of chords becomes. A single voice cannot precisely define the beginning of a chord, and thus the end of the preceding chord, since it cannot introduce more than one pitch of a chord at a time. The more complex the chord, the more time is needed to unfold it; this time is then extended by any non-harmonic tones, which themselves already complicate the harmony. When there are two voices, the conditions are somewhat more favourable.

Ambiguity in defining successive chords when few voices (especially a single voice) are involved results not only from the fact that the pitches of the new chord cannot be sounded simultaneously; it is also due to the harmonic imaginary pitches arising from the preceding chord. Chords that occur in immediate succession sometimes *interpenetrate* each other, so that doubts arise as to whether these are two simpler chords or one more complex chord.

The manner of defining individual chords within the flow of a progression is determined by the texture of the music. From this the listener feels, while the theorist consciously deduces, the intrinsic harmonic activity. We have derived from experience the following three general precepts for distinguishing successive chords from each other, and hence also for defining their time boundaries:

1) Whenever a passage can be understood as a progression of two simpler chords or as one more complex chord, precedence should be given to the former, whether the single chord would be more complex because it would belong to a higher chord-class, or because it would have a more complex dissonant characteristic, or because it would be more richly complicated by non-harmonic tones, etc. Thus our harmonic interpretation of chords of composite expression is always the *simplest possible*; we try to hear chords that have a simpler dissonant characteristic or that are completely consonant, and that are at the same time as uncluttered by non-harmonic tones as possible.

2) Whenever successive chords can be understood metrically in more than one way, the decision should again favour the simpler conception. The conception is *metrically simpler* (more natural because more usual, more familiar) when the chord continues to sound from a stronger to a weaker beat, or to an equally strong beat, for example, from the first to the second beat, or from the first half of the beat to the second half. The syncopated placement of chords, or in general the continuation of chords across a stronger beat, is metrically more complex. When metrical abnormalities such as syncopations are emphasized by repetition, however, or when they appear in some other systematic manner, they can become the norm.

3) Separate rhythmic formations lead to harmonic separation as well. Thus if two distinct rhythmic figures are formed at least partially from different pitch material, they tend to represent two chords rather than one. The contour of the melodic line also plays a significant role here; a change in melodic direction often means a change in harmony.

Differences between musical styles affect the way the time boundaries of chords are defined. In classical music, where the number of chord-types that can be considered harmonies is narrowly defined, in questions of time boundaries between chords we can rely on the definition of familiar, generally understandable, harmonies. This is the main criterion even when there are metrical and other complications. The grouping of pitches into more complex chords is simply not possible in classical music, since such more complex formations were not familiar. In modern music, where practically any chord-type can occur as a harmony, we cannot rely on such limitation of the number of harmonies. In modern music, analysis will be "less comfortable" and the results less definite. No wonder ambiguity regarding the time boundaries of chords is much more common in modern music, and this ambiguity is at times a sought-out expressive device. Several examples follow.

Example 116

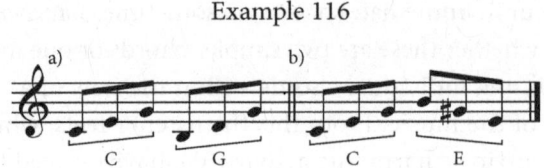

Each single voice formation in Example 116 represents two consonant chords whose time boundaries are shown by square brackets. If we were dealing with a single chord in each case, we would have to interpret the C and E in Example 116a and the G in 116b as non-harmonic; a listener could only be forced to adopt this more remote interpretation if another voice were added – as illustrated in Example 117.

Example 117

Example 117a consists of an appoggiatura six-four chord resolving on to a five-three chord; this progression can be considered a single harmony temporarily complicated by a double appoggiatura. In Example 117b, the four-note chord C E G♯ B is built up gradually (C E G, then C E G B, and finally C E G♯ B). In both cases, the long held pitch in the lower voice contributes to the given interpretation.

For complex harmonies that are rich in pitches and without clearly defined component triads, orientation according to traditional harmonic units is impossible. Thus the first of the above precepts is eliminated, and only the second and third precepts remain. Example 118, involving two different metrical arrangements of the same melodic figure, shows that the metrical placement of a harmonically complex series of pitches is significant.

Example 118

Below each melodic figure, its harmonic content is shown; the small notes indicate harmonic imaginary pitches resulting from the preceding chord. A second, less suitable, harmonic interpretation is given for Example 118a; this second interpretation would correspond to a figure such as the one in Example 119.

Example 119

Although the metrical differentiation between Example 118a and 118b is visible from the notation, it must also be audible. This can be achieved by accenting the first note of each beat, or the listener can be compelled by the music preceding this passage to hear as the harmonic units three notes in 118a and four notes in 118b. If the figure in Example 118 is extracted from musical context, and if it flows without accents, it will be harmonically ambiguous and allow for several interpretations.

Example 120 shows how the harmonic precision of complex figures can be increased by rhythmic differentiation.

Example 120

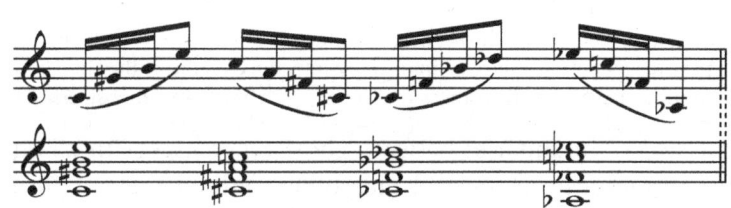

Here the individual chords are defined precisely, because the figures for each chord are separated from each other and the direction of the melodic line changes. Any other harmonic interpretation is scarcely imaginable.

In contrast, the harmonic clarity of a melody suffers when it involves irregular rhythm that avoids repeating a pattern; this is especially true when the melody changes direction frequently. Metrical placement again becomes a significant and reliable factor. In Example 121 we see this from the disjunct single voice:

Example 121

Irregular rhythm helps to clarify meter as long as the essential musical activity has a firm metrical foundation, as it does in our example; here the bar lines are not merely conventionally placed symbols, but rather arise from the rhythm itself. The disadvantage of a single voice lies in the fact that the melodically sketched chords are not clarified until the end of their duration (in our example, immediately before each bar line); this lends considerable harmonic instability to a series of pitches with richer rhythmic variety. For a single chord of somewhat longer duration that serves as the harmonic framework for the evolution of a melodic line, analysis is not difficult; for a succession of chords with shorter durations, however, especially modern ones, as in the given example, their expression in a single voice sometimes becomes doubtful. We recognize this when we compare the previous example with the following one, in which the same chord progression is expressed by two voices.

Example 122

The durations of individual chords are shown here by square brackets. Even if imaginary harmonic pitches from preceding chords sometimes intrude into newly introduced chords, the time boundaries between chords are still definite; not even the differences in durations of chords are an obstacle in this respect.

In general, precision of boundaries between chords increases with a larger number of voices, because harmonies can succeed each other without the complication of interpenetration when a richer texture of more than one voice is involved.

Example 123

We see this from Example 123, where the strong beats clearly define the durations of chords. A sufficiently rich chord (of five notes) prevails in each measure; the semitones between adjacent five-note chords ensure their mutual separation, as does the fact that three or four new pitches sound together on the strong beats.

In the above examples we have seen that the degree of precision in the definition of boundaries between chords within the flow of the music varies a great deal from unambigtuous exactness as far as considerable ambiguity. Our final example shows extreme possible ambiguity in defining the boundaries of harmonies. Even here we can find sections of the melody in which harmonies can be discerned, and which thus represent separable phases of the harmonic activity:

Example 124

A single voice with such an irregular melodic contour is harmonically ambiguous both because its harmonic content is so difficult to discern and because time boundaries between harmonies are not precise. Occasional semitones and whole-tones between "harmonies" that we have laboriously discovered make it possible to interpret certain pitches as non-harmonic, which thus become subordinate to yet another harmony of longer duration, possibly equivalent to the duration of the entire melody.

§87. Tonal Imaginary Pitches

As we stated in §75 above, *tonal* imaginary pitches are unable to combine to create harmonic formations. The difference between harmonic and tonal imaginary pitches is shown in Example 125.

Example 125

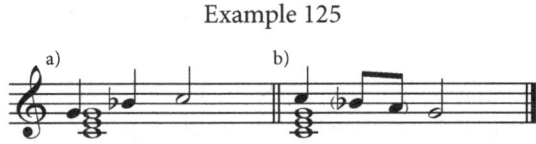

After the B♭ in Example 125a has ceased to sound, it functions as a *harmonic* imaginary pitch; it thus complicates the real triad C E G, transforming it into a four-note chord of composite expression, C E G B♭. The melodic interval of the whole-tone that leads up from the B♭ cannot reliably cancel it, since this B♭ is not preceded by a pitch a semitone or whole-tone lower. (See §76 above.) In Example 125b, although the B♭ is harmonically canceled, it functions as a *tonal* imaginary pitch after it ceases to sound. This pitch does not harmonically complicate the real triad C E G, but it does influence the triad's position within the tonality and any tonal function the triad might have. The triad C E G in Example 125b cannot, therefore, function as a reliable tonic.[79] Of course it cannot do so in Example 125a either; since a harmonic imaginary pitch is stronger, it also functions as a tonal imaginary pitch, as explained in §75 above.

---

79 Editor's note: The Czech term *tónika* refers both to tonic pitch and to tonic triad. We will use *tonic* with the same possibilities of meaning. Usually, as will be clear from the context, *tonic* will refer to the triad.

Because tonal imaginary pitches have a weaker range of influence, harmonies with a complex sound cannot "suffer" from them. Any chord of real or even composite expression, with any dissonant characteristic, has sufficient tension in itself to prevent it from being significantly enriched or otherwise influenced by tonal imaginary pitches; its harmonic tension can only be increased by harmonic means – by new real pitches or harmonic imaginary pitches. The situation is different with consonant major and minor triads. These have no inner tension of their own, so that the least interference, such as that of the imaginary tonal pitch, can disturb their stability and undermine their "security". Thus we need concern ourselves with tonal imaginary pitches only when they intrude into *consonant* harmonic formations. When they appear as components of dissonant formations, we are justified in ignoring them.

The following guiding principles, derived from experience, agree with our observations regarding the effect of particular dissonant characteristics, in isolation or merged:

1) Pitches that form a *tritone* with a pitch belonging to a consonant triad have a very penetrating effect as tonal imaginary pitches. For all intents and purposes, they destroy the stability that is characteristic of a tonic. A tritone relation without merging with a semitone or whole-tone relation can be formed only with the consonant interval of the minor third (which can be interpreted as an incomplete major or minor triad).

Example 126

In Example 126 the minor third B D (possible component of the triads G B D or B D F♯) is strongly influenced by the tonal imaginary pitch F, because although this pitch has been canceled it forms a tritone with the B. Therefore the final third B D cannot be heard as the tonic of either G major or B minor.

2) Pitches that form both a *tritone* with a pitch belonging to a complete consonant triad and a *whole-tone* with another pitch of this triad also have *considerable effect* as tonal imaginary pitches. A pitch forming a tritone with one pitch of a consonant triad and a whole-tone with another pitch [and not forming a semitone with any note of the triad] can only form the tritone with the third of the triad. The pitch B♭ has such a relation to the triad C E G, and A to the triad C E♭ G; thus the tonal imaginary pitch B♭ disturbs the tonic function of the triad C E G, and the tonal imaginary pitch A interferes with the tonic C E♭ G.

3) Pitches that form both a *tritone* with a pitch belonging to a consonant triad and a *semitone* with another pitch of this triad have a penetrating effect as tonal imaginary pitches, and so they undermine the stability of a tonic triad. A tritone and a semitone relation can be formed only with the outer pitches of a complete consonant triad or a perfect fifth. A tritone relation to the root and semitone relation to the fifth disturb

the tonic's stability more than do a tritone relation to the fifth and semitone relation to the root. Thus the tonal imaginary pitch F♯ will disturb the tonic C E G or C E♭ G (or simply C G) more strongly than will the tonal imaginary pitch D♭. This agrees with the experience of classical harmony: in the dominant seventh chord G B D F we only reluctantly alter the seventh F to F♯, while we lower the fifth D to D♭ with no serious detriment to the tonality.

4) Pitches that form a *semitone or whole-tone* with a pitch belonging to a consonant triad, without combination with a tritone, are insignificant as tonal imaginary pitches. A tonic complicated by such pitches retains its unshakable stability. Thus the tonal imaginary pitches D, F, A♭, A, or B cannot affect the tonic C E G; the same is true of the pitches D, F, A♭, and B in relation to the tonic C E♭ G. We can consider the third of the consonant triad of opposite family, built on the same root, to be an exception, especially the third of a major triad in relation to a minor triad; thus the pitch E♭ (D♯) has a certain significance for the triad C E G, and the pitch E (F♭) has even greater significance for the triad C E♭ G.

We can summarize that in general *those tonal imaginary pitches are significant that have a tritone relation to consonances*. This is the same tritone that makes the sound of the chords that contain it more mellow and rounded. It is as if the ear could not relinquish this pleasingly exciting component, even when it is offered in the most minute dose, as a mere tonal imaginary pitch.

The influence of tonal imaginary pitches in older harmony is demonstrated by Example 127.

Example 127

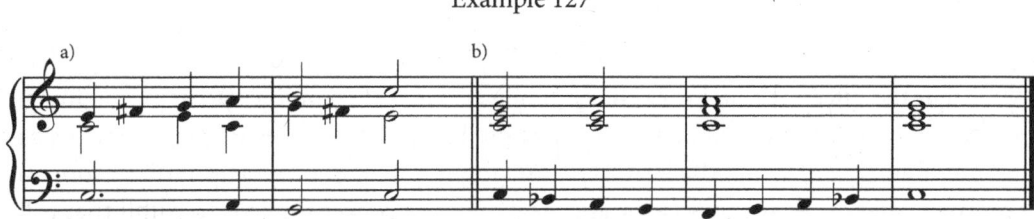

Here the F♯ and B♭ are used as non-harmonic passing tones. Their proper resolution leaves no harmonically active traces, so the final chords are consonances of real expression. Tonal traces do remain, however: the final consonances cannot reliably function as tonics, expressing stability, and rid of all kinetic tension; the tension can only be eliminated, and the final chords thus stabilized, by removing the accidentals (at least the second one in each example). We will then have in Example 127a a convincing authentic cadence in C major, and in Example 127b a plagal cadence.

We have seen that we need not consider tonal imaginary pitches in dissonances, or in a whole-tone or semitone relation to consonances, since they have no significance. What is the situation with their *cancellation* and their *dying away*?

Here it is necessary to note that it is mainly in more complex chords that the tonal imaginary pitches cannot get aword in. Formations with which the pitches that could become tonal imaginary pitches have complex, acutely dissonant relations are naturally the most efficient means for the cancellation of these pitches. The harshest formation in the tempered chromatic system is the chord comprising stacked semitones, in which the replication of the semitone dissonant characteristic leads to the semitone clash of semitones (as in C C♯ D). It will be difficult to retain in our consciousness as tonal imaginary pitches any pitches that form such a chord. This chord, or any more complex formation that contains it, is the most reliable means to effect the *tonal cancellation of imaginary pitches*, so we can state that pitches that are part of a semitone clash cannot function as tonal imaginary pitches. The formation with the semitone clash need not function harmonically; a melodic progression of semitones is sufficient, whether continuous or interrupted, even in a contour of great diversity.

Example 128

In Example 128 the angles mark individual semitones, while the braces show semitone clashes. In melodic progressions like those in this example, the last pitch of the chromatic semitone progression is most significant. In Example 128a this is the F♯, while in 128b it is the F (in this case also because sufficient time has elapsed since the F♯). Thus through the melodic semitone clash, the pitch appearing earlier loses almost all its ability to function as a tonal imaginary pitch. In Example 128c, typical of modern music, the F♯ or A♭ can hardly become tonal imaginary pitches, since these were the first pitches to occur in the semitone clashes (F F♯ G, G A♭ A). In general, this formation is so complex and dissonant that its individual components can no longer assert themselves as tonal imaginary pitches.

Although the effect of tonal imaginary pitches is weaker than that of harmonic imaginary pitches, it lasts longer; tonal imaginary pitches stubbornly *resist dying away*. This is natural if we consider that the harmonic imaginary pitch, in proportion to its more important role, more easily loses a greater degree of the power it needs to fulfill that role, as it is gradually overcome by the continuing activity of the music, whereas even a tiny bit of "energy" in comparison to that needed for real pitches, even a distant "memory" of a previous real existence, enables the tonal imaginary pitch to function.

§88. Incomplete Expression of Harmonies

We have dealt with the phenomenon of the *incomplete harmony* when classifying the chords. Now we will deal with it from the viewpoint of the expression of chords. As stated in §62, omitting tones in a chord is not considered as a change of the chord disposition. Thus we do not say that the chord G B F is a special disposition of the four-note chord G B D F, but rather that the chord G B F constitutes an *incomplete expression* of a richer chord with the same characteristic, such as the four-note chord G B D F or, in the freer modern interpretation, perhaps even the five-note chord G B D F A (see §48 above).

The difference between a harmony of composite expression and a harmony of incomplete expression (an incomplete harmony) is that those components of the harmony that in composite expression are represented by mere imaginary harmonic pitches are in incomplete expression not represented at all; they neither sound as real pitches nor exist as imaginary harmonic pitches. Example 129 shows the difference between various means of expression of a consonant triad.

Example 129

Here the triad C E G is first given real expression, then composite expression, and finally – after the imaginary harmonic pitch E has died away – incomplete expression. The time boundary between the complete harmony of composite expression and the harmony of incomplete expression cannot be established precisely.[80]

Chords with few pitches are inclined to take in spontaneously further components by which they can be enriched. Dissonant chords with few pitches will primarily take in consonant components that do not complicate the dissonant characteristic. Consonant chords with few pitches will take in further consonant components, almost exclusively those that will enable the incomplete harmony to become a complete consonance and nothing more.

In actual situations, it will be important to ask which pitches are suitable to supplement chords that have very few pitches, that is, which pitches have been omitted from the richer "intended" chords that have been incompletely expressed. This question cannot always be answered without ambiguity. (However, the ambiguity itself may be the composer's intention.) Any tonal *imaginary pitches* that happen to exist in such a situation can help us answer the question. *A chord of incomplete expression will be supplemented by any available tonal imaginary pitches to become the simplest possible chord of a higher class.* Tonal imaginary pitches are those that have finished sounding and have been harmonically canceled (i.e. had they not been harmonically canceled, they would at least for a time have constituted a full component of the chord, and the chord's expression would not be incomplete.) Conversely, we can consider as omitted components

---

80 Editor's note: We might argue that in such a situation as this, the chord remains a chord of composite expression as long as the C and G are sounding, because the third, the harmonic imaginary pitch, will not die away in the listener's ear as long as the fifth is sounding.

of a chord neither any pitches that are in obvious conflict with the existing tonal imaginary pitches, nor any pitches that together with the incompletely expressed chord form a more remote or less common chord. Example 130 clarifies this.

Example 130

In each segment of Example 130, the final sound is the two-note chord A♭ C. All other pitches previously introduced are harmonically canceled by semitone or whole-tone melodic progressions. We can use some of these pitches as tonal imaginary pitches to supplement the final real two-note chord. In Example 130a, we can use F, so that we perceive A♭ C as an incomplete triad A♭ C F; the other pitches are not suitable for supplementing the final chord, since they would yield a more complex (more remote, dissonant) chord: A♭ C G or A♭ C E or A♭ C D. We cannot reasonably imagine any pitches not previously used, such as F♯, as being "omitted", since they would conflict with the tonal imaginary pitches; F♯, for example, would strongly conflict with the F. In Example 130b, we can supplement the A♭ C with E♭ or F, but not with the other tonal imaginary pitches (D, G); similarly, we cannot use E or F♯, since they conflict with the pitches that have actually sounded. In Example 130c, we will most likely supplement the A♭ C with E, since no other tonal imaginary pitch yields a more familiar chord with a simpler sound; we will not supplement the final two-note chord with E♭ or F, however, since these pitches would be contradicted by the tonal imaginary pitches D, E, F♯. At the same time, we should not exclude the possibility of perceiving Example 130c as the expression of a chord more complex than three notes; in that case, D, E, and F♯ would be involved in the interpretation.

That we use tonal imaginary pitches to aid us in supplementing real chords of very few pitches does not mean that the role of tonal imaginary pitches as components of incomplete harmonies is as significant as that of real pitches or harmonic imaginary pitches. In harmonic interpretation we resort to tonal imaginary pitches only when the chords formed by real pitches or harmonic imaginary pitches contain too few pitches; the resulting impression is not as ambiguous as it would be were we to use only a fragment of a harmony. We supplement consonant as well as dissonant two-note chords in this way, and at times also three-note or four-note chords, as long as this process results in more complex chords without consequential intensification. This applies especially to *open fifths*, which almost always absorb into themselves a major or minor third, depending on which of these has previously sounded as a real pitch.

Chapter VIa – Harmonic Motion: Concepts and Principles

§89. Possibilities of Motion in Music

The impression of *motion* or any kind of activity in music can arise from the articulation of the time through which the sonic material is spread. This articulation can be achieved by
  a) rhythm,
  b) rhythm and melody,
  c) rhythm, melody, and harmony.

We thus speak of rhythmic, melodic, or harmonic motion. Rhythmic motion can be achieved without the involvement of melodic and harmonic elements, for example on a percussion instrument or on a single repeated pitch. Melodic motion can be achieved only in cooperation with rhythm; harmony is not necessary. Finally, harmonic motion can be achieved only with the participation of rhythm and melody.

Rhythmic motion is produced by the repetition of a single pitch, chord, or sound without definite pitch, in definite time values, among which real silences (rests) may be interspersed. With *melodic motion*, the pitch changes: we proceed from one pitch to another by definite measured or measurable time values. With *harmonic motion*, entire chords change, again in measured time intervals. Thus we proceed from one chord to another; such progressions also involve melodic progressions.

Colour and dynamics can only be secondary aspects of rhythmic, melodic, and harmonic motion. Every sudden or gradual change in colour or strength, whether it involves mere repetition or continuation of a pitch or chord, or progression of different pitches or chords, is tied to a definite division of time.

Any kind of motion, constituting activity taking place in time, *is irreversible*. This means that the progression of formations A B is different from the reverse progression of the same formations, B A. Such retrogression in time is analogous to the process of inversion in pitch space. (See §5 and §18 above.)

§90. Possibilities of Harmonic Motion

There are three types of harmonic motion:
  a) partial,
  b) fundamental,
  c) higher-ranked, i.e., tonal.

Partial harmonic motion is a negligible or not very significant change from one chord to a different one, where the pitch content of the second, although not necessarily its dissonant characteristic, is close to that of the first. Partial harmonic motion involves the progression from a harmony to an adjacent transient chord, or vice versa.

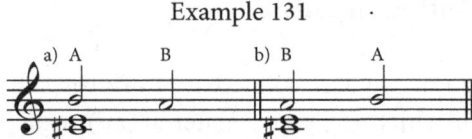

Example 131

In Example 131a, the formation A is an appoggiatura chord, in 131b, a passing chord;[81] in both examples the formation B is an independent harmony.

Fundamental harmonic motion is the progression from one independent chord (harmony) to another, as, for example, in Example 132.

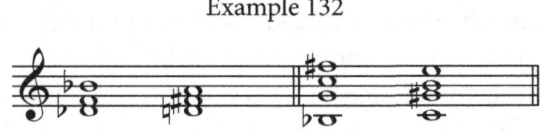

Example 132

Higher-ranked harmonic motion deals with the progression not merely of individual chords, but of entire continuous successions of chords. The fundamental harmonic motion between the last chord of the first continuous group of chords and the first chord of the second group is of greater magnitude, and thus more significant, conspicuous, and pronounced, than the fundamental harmonic motion between the individual chords within each group. This is illustrated by the following diagram:

---

81 Editor's note: As explained in §27 above, Janeček's terms, *appoggiatura chord* and *passing chord*, refer to chords with these non-harmonic tones, not to entire chords with these functions.

A *fn* B *fn* C *fn* D	**fnfn**	E *fn* F *fn* G *fn* H
AA	h-r	**BB**

The letters A, B, C, etc. indicate independent chords; *fn* between each two chords indicates fundamental harmonic motion, **fnfn** the more pronounced harmonic motion between D and E; **AA** is the first continuous succession of independent chords, **BB** the second; "h-r" indicates the higher-ranked harmonic motion between **AA** and **BB**. The fundamental harmonic motion between D and E is also the higher-ranked harmonic motion between **AA** and **BB**, and must therefore represent considerably greater "momentum" than that between the other chords. If **fnfn** and *fn* were of equal weight, the impression of higher-ranked harmonic motion could not arise; the progression A, B,… H would flow together into one indivisible stream. The result would be the same if the fundamental harmonic motion between individual chords had increased significance, which would render it more like the motion between D and E.

§91. Links in a Chord Succession

Tempered chromatics provides twelve different tones. It is within this limited material where all the chord successions occur wheather they are lower (such as triads) or higher chord-classes. Naturally, successive chords often have pitches in common. Common pitches create a *link* between adjacent chords. The link can be *single* when there is only one common pitch, *double* or *multiple* when there are two or more; finally, the link can be *complete* when all the pitches are common, which can occur only when two dispositions of the same transposition of the same chord-type follow each other.

A succession of chords *without a link* can only be realized when the sum of pitch-classes in the two chords does not exceed twelve. Thus for example two three-note chords can be placed together without a link, or a three-note chord and an eight-note chord, but not a three-note chord and a ten-note chord. In a succession of chords without a link, the second chord must be composed of the pitches belonging to the negative of the first chord (See § 10.). The most complex chord that we can approach from another chord without a link is precisely the negative of the initial chord.

A link in a chord succession relates the two chords more closely. Their similarity can be increased until, when the link is complete, *harmonic motion ceases* completely. Our concern here is not merely the number of common pitches, however; the way the links function is also important. We speak of a *direct* link when the linking pitch continues from the first chord to the second, or is repeated in another octave in such a way that it is not a part of, and as it leaps does not cross, a succession of pitches forming an interval 1 or 2. (Voice-leading, as emphasized by classical harmony, is not important here; it is the succession of pitches that is important, regardless of the voices to which they belong. Hence we speak of a "succession of pitches" rather than a "melodic step". A succession of pitches forming an interval 1 or 2 can arise between different voices that may not contain the melodic form of these intervals.) The link is *indirect* or *interrupted* when the common pitch is repeated in another octave in such a way that it *is* a part of, or crosses, one or more successions of pitches forming an interval 1 or 2.

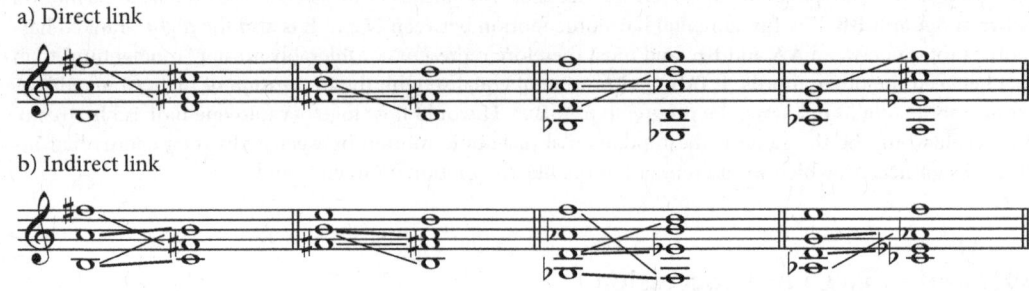

Example 133

a) Direct link

b) Indirect link

Example 133 shows (a) direct and (b) indirect links starting from the same chords; thin lines indicate links, while thick lines indicate successions of pitches forming an interval 1 or 2 that contains the common pitch or is crossed by its leap. There are both single and double links.

The example is only illustrative, to show the differentiation described above. Much more extensive has to be studied and then the following observation be derived:
1) *A direct link is a considerably stronger bond between chords than an indirect link.*
2) *The fewer pitches in the chords, the more effective the link.* Thus the significance of a single link is considerable between three-note chords, less between four-note chords, and only slight between six-note chords.
3) *The lower the link, the more effective it is.*

The differentiation of links into direct and indirect could only be made as a result of the study of actual musical material. When evaluating the greater or lesser continuity of a chord succession, it is the effect of the *succession* that must be judged, not the sonic effect of the chords. A succession that gives an impression of a "great harmonic stride" can be formed as well from chords of lower classes as from those of higher classes. The same is true of a succession intended to give an impression of merely a very slight harmonic shift. The gradations of impression of harmonic motion are captured by analyzing the links according to the simple criteria given above.

We are not concerned here with function, which sometimes plays an important role in creating an impression of harmonic motion, nor with any contradictions that might occur between clearly defined pitch-systems (for example, transpositions of the diatonic system that are remote from each other). Here we have only been concerned with a general understanding of the link, and with establishing the principles relevant to it.

Chapter VIa – Harmonic Motion: Concepts and Principles

§92. Partial Harmonic Motion

The concept of partial harmonic motion must be defined in both directions: we must say what does *not yet* constitute it as well as what *no longer* constitutes it. On one side, partial harmonic motion approaches melodic motion; on the other, it approaches fundamental harmonic motion. This is shown in Example 134a.

Example 134a

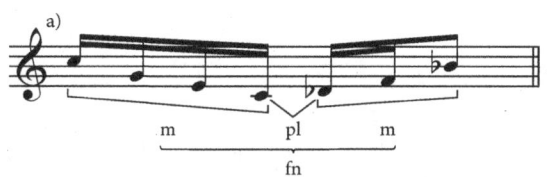

Melodic motion (m) occurs between the pitches within the groups C G E C and D♭ F B♭; however, these individual motions do not change the harmonies C E G or D♭ F B♭. Fundamental harmonic motion (fn) occurs between the complete groups (harmonies) C E G C and D♭ F B♭. Partial harmonic motion (pl) occurs between the pitches C and D♭.

In general, partial harmonic motion can also result from the cancellation of imaginary pitches of the first harmony by real pitches of the second harmony. Thus the fundamental harmonic motion can be broken down into partial harmonic motions pl_1, pl_2, pl_3 as shown in Example 134b.

Example 134b

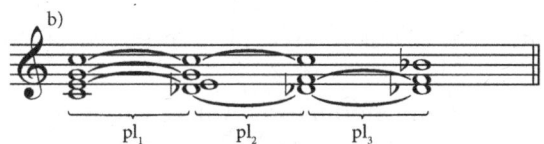

Partial harmonic motion results when melodic motion involves intervals that cancel harmonic imaginary pitches. These intervals are the ascending and descending interval 1 and the descending interval 2; an ascending interval 2 can act as a component of partial harmonic motion only if its first pitch is not emphasized metrically or by duration, and if it is preceded by a pitch lower by an interval 1 or 2. (See §76 above.) Progression by any other interval yields only melodic motion.

Example 135

In each segment of the following example all the pitches form a single chord rather than a succession of chords, so there is only melodic motion. Pitches that have been unresolved melodically continue to function as harmonic imaginary pitches. With the exception of Example 135d, which begins with the complete chord C E G B♭, all the segments begin with incomplete expressions of chords that become complete only after the melodic motion has taken place. Thus for example in Example 135e we have not a succession of the similar chords E♭ G F♯ – E♭ G A F♯, but rather the single chord E♭ G A F♯, which is initially incomplete.

Example 136 illustrates *partial harmonic motion*, which of course also includes melodic motion.

Example 136

A succession of two pitches forming a second is harmonically ambiguous. In Example 136a, we could add one or more held pitches (and thus also voices); this would define the example harmonically and make it more like the following examples. In Example 136b, c, and d, we cannot speak of a single chord that is expressed gradually. Here there are always two different and mutually dependent *chordal cross-sections*; one of these is significant as a harmony, while the second has meaning only as a transient chord.

Besides the close melodic progression of the moving voice, *links* are also important in Example 136. Melodic progression by interval 1 or 2 results in partial harmonic motion only when there is a direct link. Example 136b involves a single link, 136c a double, and 136d a triple link. All the links are direct. Only in a single voice (as in Example 136a), where a link cannot be made by a real pitch, does partial harmonic motion arise without a link.

We speak of partial harmonic motion even when two or three voices move simultaneously, as long as there is a sufficient *counterbalance of the link*. What is counterbalance of the link? The answer reads as follows:
– in a single voice a link is not possible;
– when two voices are involved, there must be a single link;
– when three or four voices are involved, there must be a double link;
– when five voices are involved, there must be at least a triple link; etc.

Thus the motion of *at least half the voices* must be stopped by a direct link. We can go below this minimum only if the significance of the *link is increased by its very low position*, as the classical Example 137 shows.

Example 137

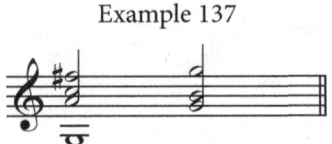

Example 137 shows. Here the chordal cross-sections are made interdependent by a triple melodic progression in intervals 1 or 2, with a single link in the lowest voice. It is the triple suspension or appoggiatura of classical composers, the suspension or appoggiatura of a harmony, especially loved in cadences of slow movements.

In a succession of chordal cross-sections connected by partial harmonic motion, the representative of the harmony will always be the simpler, more intelligible cross-section, the one with less tension. (See §26 above.) If two adjacent chordal cross-sections are equal in this respect, either can be considered the harmony.

This is the case in Example 136b above, where both chordal cross-sections (G E♭ or G E, and G D) are consonant. In 136c, the representative of the harmony is the second cross-section (the consonance C A♭ E♭) while the first represents a transient chord (the dissonance C A♭ D). In 136d, if the D♯ is used at the beginning, we tend to consider the first cross-section (B F♯ A D♯), with its more appealing characteristic 26 as the harmony, rather than the second (B F♯ A E) with its insipid characteristic 2. If D rather than D♯ is the initial pitch in the same example, we must consider the first cross-section (B F♯ A D) to be the harmony, even though it has the same characteristic as the second, because the metrical emphasis on the D, from which the melody rises by an interval 2, prevents the proper cancellation of this pitch by E.

Simultaneous melodic motion in more than one voice without sufficient counterbalance of a direct link will create *fundamental harmonic motion*. Then we can no longer speak of interdependent chordal cross-sections but rather of a succession of independent chords, of *harmonies*. Thus several partial harmonic motions join to form fundamental harmonic motion.

Each measure in Example 138 involves a succession of two chords in fundamental harmonic motion, with the first chord spread out over two chordal cross-sections connected by partial harmonic motion. In group I, the first chordal cross-section represents a harmony (H), and the second a transient chord (T), while in group II the reverse is true; in group III, either interpretation is possible.

Example 138

When evaluating chordal cross-sections it is especially important to pay attention to intervals 1 and clusters 11; chords without these have a simpler and better sound. In music concieved in the system of harmonic functions the *functional aspect* of chordal cross-sections is however also important. In such cases we always consider the cross-section with a simpler or more common tonal function to be the harmony. Thus in the succession of chordal cross-sections E G B – E G C in C major we consider the harmony to be E G C (the tonic), while in E minor we consider the harmony to be E G B (likewise the tonic).

The relative significance or value of transient chord and harmony is not always the same. If the harmony occurs on a stronger beat than the transient chord, the harmony has considerably more significance than the transient chord. If the metrical positions of the harmony and the transient chord are reversed, the significance of the harmony diminishes in favour of the transient chord. The harmonic value of harmonies and transient chords, as affected by varying metrical placement, can be ranked as follows:

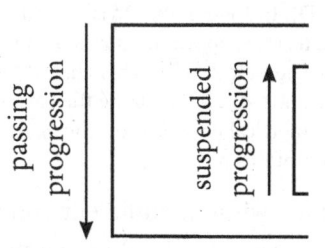

1) harmony on a relatively stronger beat;
2) harmony on a relatively weaker beat;
3) transient chord on a relatively stronger beat;
4) transient chord on a relatively weaker beat.

As long as a progression H T (from a harmony to a transient chord) represents partial harmonic motion, it expresses a considerable decrease in the significance of the chordal cross-sections; since passing tones are usually involved, we will call it a *passing progression*. A progression T H (from a transient chord to a harmony), as long as it also represents partial harmonic motion, conversely represents an increase, although considerably smaller; we will call it a *suspended progression*, since it appears in connection with suspensions or appoggiaturas.

The considerably lesser harmonic significance of the chordal cross-section T in a passing progression H T results in the *melodic aspect* of the motion becoming more pronounced while the partial harmonic motion is shifted into the background *as a mere by-product of the melodic motion*. In a suspended progression (T H), however, partial harmonic motion plays a significant role, so that we feel that a particular melodic progression is compelled by the insistent harmonic requirement. Hence the direction and step of the melody must be subordinated to harmonic principle in a T H progression, while in an H T progression a melody can unfold according to its own melodic inclinations and sometimes can even defy harmonic fetters. This explains the frequent non-harmonic tones left by leap (escape tones) that are found in connection with passing progression.

In each segment of Example 139 the first chordal cross-section represents a harmony, the second (and subsequent ones) a transient chord; there is then fundamental harmonic motion to the next harmony. The upper voice proceeds to the second harmony by an interval greater than 1 or 2. The pitch forming part of the last chordal cross-section before the second harmony then does not meet the requirement for non-harmonic tones – it is not resolved. In spite of this, it cannot be perceived as part of the harmony, because if this were considered an appoggiatura progression T H, the transient chord would be conspicuously simpler and harmonically more intelligible than the harmony. Hence the first two chordal cross-sections must be understood as an H T, that is, as a passing progression, although the passing (or perhaps auxiliary) tones are left by melodic leap. Here the melodic line defies harmonic requirements. Normal melodic progression, fully respecting harmonic principles, would call for a return of the B to A♯ in 139a, a return of the D to C in 139c, and in 139b a leading of the G to the next lower pitch F, even before the introduction of the second harmony.

Example 139

§93. Fundamental Harmonic Motion

Fundamental harmonic motion was defined above as progression from one independent chord (harmony) to another (See § 90). *Every occurrence of fundamental harmonic motion can be broken down into several partial harmonic motions.* Such division may be *deliberately realized* in composition. In a single voice, where several simultaneous partial motions are not possible, an impression of motion from one chord to another (fundamental harmonic motion) only arises in a structure that includes several partial harmonic motions. (See Example 134a in §92 above.) It is possible even in more than one voice, however, to use successively individual partial harmonic motions with the help of *chordal interpenetrations*; by the latter we mean chord formations resulting either from delaying a voice (suspensions), or from a premature unfolding of motion (anticipations). The second and third chordal cross-sections in Example 134b above can be understood as suspended formations.

The link, an important feature of partial harmonic motion, may or may not be involved in fundamental harmonic motion. Naturally, the larger the number of direct links, the closer fundamental harmonic motion will be to partial harmonic motion. While at least half the voices in partial harmonic motion must involve a direct link, there may not be this many direct links in fundamental harmonic motion. As in the former, so in the latter, the *placement of the link* and thus its quality and range are important; a direct link in the lowest voice has a stronger effect than a link between higher voices.

On one side, fundamental and partial harmonic motion meet each other – the difference between them is only one of of degree, since it has to do with the number, and possibly also the position, of the links involved. On the other side there are no limits constraining fundamental motion. Whenever we cannot speak of partial harmonic motion in connection with a succession of two chords (a succession with no link, for example), that succession represents fundamental harmonic motion, regardless of any other relation between the chords involved (their tonal functions, for example). In certain cases, however, fundamental harmonic motion is *also* higher-ranked (tonal) harmonic motion. Thus if in a progression characterized by a larger number of direct links we ask whether we are dealing with partial or fundamental harmonic motion, in a progression lacking direct links we know that we are dealing with fundamental harmonic motion, and *we can try to discover* whether such a progression is also a vehicle of higher-ranked harmonic motion. (Regarding this, see §97 below.)

Questions of particular interest concern intervals in which the pitches of the second chord replace those of the first[82] and the effect of different links in the context of fundamental harmonic motion.

§94. Intervals in Fundamental Harmonic Motion; Imaginary Links

In *Chapter V* we discussed the fact that the progression of voices by intervals 1 or 2 results in the cancellation of pitches from the preceding chord. This need not be the progression of individual voices, however; it is sufficient if an interval 1 or 2 is formed between pitches that sound successively in different voices. Thus we prefer to speak of "replacement of pitches" rather than "voice-leading".

Two successive chords in which the real pitches of the second chord replace the real pitches of the first at intervals 1 or 2 present a pronounced form of fundamental harmonic motion, that is, they can be interpreted in no other way. This of course presupposes that the second chord is constructed from pitches in the negative of the first. (However, not all pitches of the negative have to be used.) Example 140 shows this fundamental harmonic motion.

Example 140

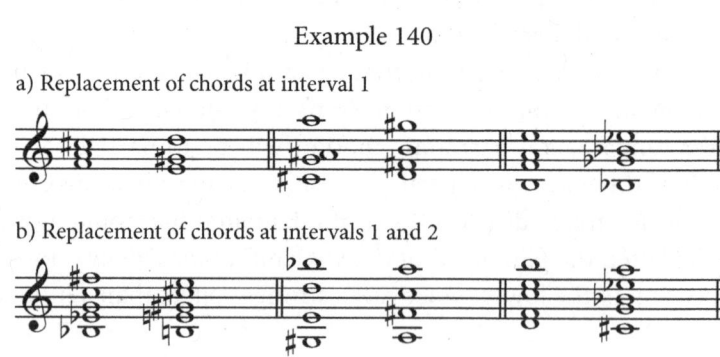

---

82 Editor's note: The next paragraph explains the technical meaning of *replace*.

Replacement at interval 1 causes a closer adhesion between the chords; the *principle of the leading tone* is at work here, a principle that we will discuss further in §102 below.

The appearance of *larger intervals* in the context of pitch replacement between two successive chords can cause complications, because a pitch of the first chord, when not followed by a pitch of the second chord at an interval 1 or 2, at least temporarily has a harmonic function as a part of the second chord. The fewer real pitches sound in the second chord, and the simpler the intervals formed between the imaginary pitch from the first chord and the real pitches of the second, the more effective this harmonic function becomes. Thus in a two-voice or three-voice texture the effect is sufficient for us to speak of a *substitute* or *compensatory fullness of sound*; this is especially true when the imaginary pitch forms part of consonant or only mildly dissonant relations. As the number of voices increases, this phenomenon becomes less significant. Example 141 shows chord successions in which a voice proceeds by a larger interval, thus temporarily supplementing (complicating) the harmony of the second chord.

Example 141

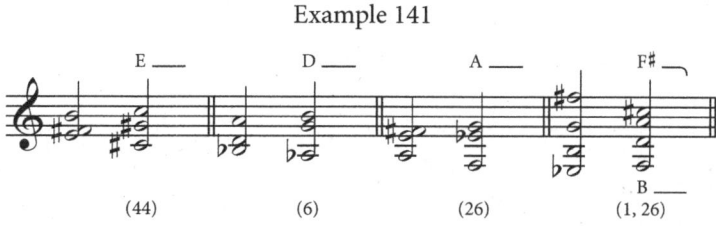

Below each second chord, the dissonant relations of the imaginary pitches to the real pitches are shown in brackets. (Cf. §81 above.)

A real pitch from the first chord intruding into the second chord as an imaginary pitch has the *significance* and *effect of a direct link*. In contrast to a real link, in which there is actual repetition of a real pitch by another real pitch, whether in the same voice or not, we call this an *imaginary link*. As a rule, an imaginary link cannot threaten the full effect of fundamental harmonic motion, since it increases the number of harmonically active pitches in the second chord; that is, with a greater number of direct imaginary links we have a greater number of pitches (the sum of real and imaginary pitches). In a progression of two chords that have the same number of voices, the number of imaginary links can never involve more than half the pitches in the second chord, which is of composite expression. Only where the first chord is lower, and voices leap away from it by larger ascending intervals, the impression of the expected fundamental harmonic motion can be weakened to the extent that the progression represents only partial harmonic motion. Instead of another example, we refer to Example 95 in §81 above.

§95. Real Links in Fundamental Harmonic Motion

In §91 above, we differentiated between *direct* and *indirect* links. In making this differentiation, we were already considering the effect and significance the links would have in a chord succession. Direct links make chords substantially more alike; several direct links can change the expected or planned fundamental harmonic motion into mere partial harmonic motion. In contrast, the influence of an indirect link on the effect of a chord succession is so slight that in most cases it can be ignored, even when several such links are present.

This basic differentiation can be supplemented by some details. There is a difference between a *direct link at the unison*, in which the common pitch is simply prolonged or repeated, and a *direct link at the octave*, in which the common pitch is transferred higher or lower. A purposeful accumulation of direct links at the octave can result in a strong impression of motion, an impression caused by several melodic motions; with direct links at the unison, such an impression cannot arise. This is shown by Example 142.

Example 142

Each segment contains two dispositions of the same chord. *Melodic intervals other than the octave* play a notable role here; we realize this in comparing the examples with a simple transfer of a chord disposition an octave higher or lower. In such octave transpositions, the fact that the dispositions are identical makes any impression of harmonic motion impossible.

The effect of the link varies according to the *number of pitches* in the chords it connects. In chords of lower classes (such as three-note chords), even an indirect link has a conspicuous effect; only in chords of higher classes (for example, five-note or six-note chords) is it negligible. We illustrate this in Example 143 by progressions of two different dispositions of the same chord-type in the same transposition.

Example 143

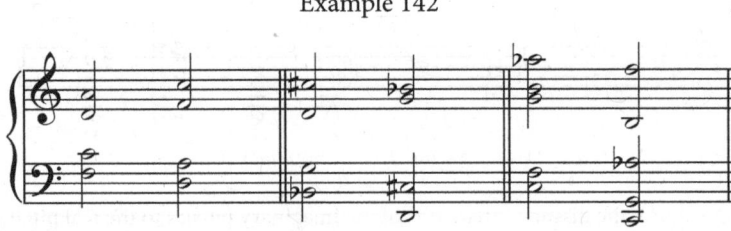

Links are marked in the same way as in Example 133 in §91 above. In Example 143a, although there are only indirect links, the harmonic motion seems very weak because only three-note chords are involved. (Later we will show another situation which gives an impression of such weak motion.) In 143b and especially in 143c the harmonic motion seems very prominent.

In summary: The repetition of the same disposition of the same chord-type in the same transposition, whether in the original octave or a higher or lower one, does not represent harmonic motion; an *impression* of fundamental harmonic motion can arise, however, between two different dispositions of the same chord, especially if it is a more complex chord and if considerable use is made of indirect links.

In distinguishing between direct and indirect links, we have said that an indirect (*interrupted*) link results when the common pitch, as it leaps into another octave, either a) is a part of or b) crosses a melodic interval 1 or 2. The link in situation b) is less significant than that in situation a), especially if chords of lower classes are involved. The effect of the link in situation a) is considerably lessened if the melodic motion in which the pitch common to the connected chords takes part is counteracted by simultaneous motion in the opposite direction (for example, if the step C–D is counteracted by the step D–C in another voice, both of course forming the melodic interval 2). The substantially weakened impression of harmonic motion found in Example 143a is caused also by these circumstances.

An *impression of fundamental harmonic motion* can be evoked by the succession of two chords, if these chords are
1) of different types or represent different transpositions of the same chord-type,
2) of the same type in the same transposition but belong to higher chord-classes or at least contain intervals 1 or 2.

Thus it is not possible to create an impression of fundamental harmonic motion by the succession of two different dispositions of the same transposition of consonant triads or of dissonant three-note or four-note chords that do not contain intervals 1 or 2. (The only such chords are 44, 33, 333.)

To say that it is possible to create the impression of fundamental harmonic motion is not to say that such an impression will result from just any disposition of the chord succession. The same chord succession may represent only melodic (or partial harmonic) motion in one disposition while in another it represents fundamental harmonic motion. This is shown in Example 144.

Example 144

Melodic motion

Fundamental harmonic motion

Especially interesting are those chord successions in which both chords represent the same transposition of the same chord-type. By analogy with common classical chords, we would deduce that such a succession does not represent harmonic motion at all, but simply repetition or continuation. We have already shown in several examples, however, that this is not so. As a supplement to those we present the two examples in Example 145.

Example 145

In both cases we are dealing with triadic combinations **II**. In Example 145a, the first disposition of the harmony **+2+** is better than the second. Does this succession of two dispositions with unequal value give an impression of harmonic motion? We have to answer in the negative because not only is the effect of a worse disposition better when it is part of suitable harmonic motion than when it is isolated (see §73 above), but the replacement of one disposition by another of different value in the simple chords 34, 43, 44, 33, and 333 does not produce an impression of harmonic motion. In 145b, both dispositions of the harmony **+6+** are of equal value. (See the table in §69 above.) In both cases, any impression of fundamental harmonic motion arises from the fact that all the links are *indirect*, and that the chords are considerably *complex*; the *functional differentiation* of the two dispositions also plays a role here, as we will see later. In each case, for comparison, we add another chord (a consonant triad), which we reach by unproblematic fundamental harmonic motion.

Each combination harmony can be repeated in different dispositions in such a way that partial harmonic motion takes place. We present two examples using harmony **+6+**.

Chapter VIa – Harmonic Motion: Concepts and Principles

Example 146

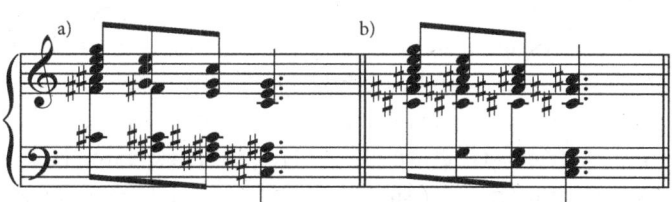

In Example 146a, all are combination dispositions. In 146b, there are combination and non-combination dispositions. Both successions contain many direct links, so only partial harmonic motion takes place here.

§96. Adjacent Partial and Fundamental Harmonic Motions

The difference between fundamental and partial harmonic motion forms the basis for its intrusion into the areas of *rhythm and meter*. The difference between strong and weak beats is also only that of a degree. therefore it is completely natural that a chord formation reached by fundamental harmonic motion will appear weightier than a chord formation reached only by partial harmonic motion or melodic motion. Thus the rhythmic arrangement of adjacent partial and fundamental harmonic motions in a harmonic sentence becomes important in determining the metrical structure of the musical flow.

We cannot speak of metrical phenomena apart from their relation to the concurrent harmonic phenomena. Even in a rhythmic passage without harmonic and melodic activity, the varying significance of time values can be determined without the aid of dynamics, simply from the rhythmic arrangement itself. This means that strong beats can be determined without accents; a strong beat need not have greater force. Accent becomes even less necessary in a richer stream of music, in music with melodic contour and harmonic content. Stress emphasis is just a secondary characteristic of a metrically strong beat. It can only be used to emphasize, or possibly correct, the placement of strong and weak beats determined by the rhythmic values and types of harmonic motion in individual passages.

We are interested here first in the relation between harmonic activity (various types of harmonic motion) and the metrical structure of a musical phrase involving harmony. The final reconciliation of meter and harmony is the same, whether we start with a metrically organized rhythmic passage or with a chord progression with autonomous rhythm.

The harmonic phrase containing successions of independent chords (harmonies) in fundamental harmonic motion and successions of chordal cross-sections connected by partial harmonic motion can be subordinated to a given rhythmic skeleton with regular metrical organization. This can be done by *insuring that fundamental rather than partial harmonic motions end on strong beats*. Fundamental harmonic motion can also be used to approach weaker beats. *Partial harmonic motion is suitable only when moving from a relatively stronger beat to a relatively weaker beat*; otherwise it is contrary to the metrical framework.

From an autonomous progression of chords with prescribed time values but no time signature the metrical structure can be deduced from the time values as well as from the types of harmonic motion between chords or chordal cross-sections. The result may or may not be a regular metrical structure of bars (regularly repeated bars of equal size and type). If we compress a chord progression into regular equal measures even though such a structure is not given harmonically, our creation of rhythm is „unnatural".

The relations described are schematically illustrated by the following example.

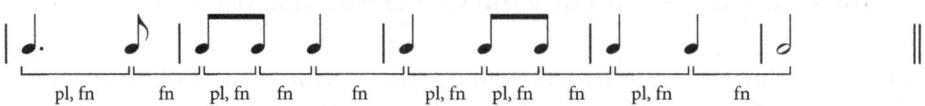

The square brackets marked *pl, fn* indicate that either partial or fundamental harmonic motion can be used between the rhythmic values connected by the brackets; everywhere else, only fundamental harmonic motion can be used (as indicated by *fn*). In the places where partial harmonic motion is indicated, no harmonic motion of any kind need take place – the rhythmic values can represent simply the rhythmic division of the same chord formation, or mere melodic motion.

A different arrangement of adjacent fundamental and partial harmonic motions represents a significant discrepancy between notated, and hence expected, metrical structure and its harmonic realization. It may mean that the meter of the progression is badly notated, or there may be an *intentional conflict between the meter and harmony*, especially if the metrical structure is sufficiently emphasized by other than *metrical* elements (for example, by accents). Both agreement of meter and harmony and conflict between the two are important means of expression, even if they are not immediately obtrusive. We need to differentiate between fundamental and partial harmonic motion because the difference has consequences for meter, among other things.

Relations between harmony and meter are apparent in the music of every style that involves harmony. A favorite older type of interference with regular metrical structure is *syncopation*. A syncopated rhythm cannot be emphasized without involving harmony: harmonic motion either ceases at the moment of syncopation, or it is only partial, because fundamental harmonic motion substantially weakens the effect of a syncopation.

§97. Higher-ranked Harmonic Motion or Tonal Motion

We know from §90 above that higher-ranked harmonic motion is *particularly conspicuous progression* from one chord to another. The conspicuousness of a progression cannot be absolute but rather results from a comparison with surrounding progressions. A progression can become a vehicle for higher-ranked harmonic motion only if the successions in its vicinity (not only its most immediate vicinity) are substantially plainer and unobtrusive. Higher-ranked harmonic motion is at the same time fundamental harmonic motion; it differs from surrounding fundamental harmonic motions only by its greater intensity, by the fact that it stands out.

We can also refer to higher-ranked harmonic motion as *tonal motion*, since as a rule it is used to effect a change of key. By this we do not mean a modulation in the general sense, but an unexpected and sudden modulation, in which, unlike many modulations, functional relations are not important.

Here we are primarily interested in questions about concrete possibilities of higher-ranked harmonic motion. Can any pair of chords connected by fundamental harmonic motion become the vehicle of higher-ranked harmonic motion? How can we overcome the impression created by fundamental harmonic motions already realized and create higher-ranked harmonic motion? Can higher-ranked harmonic motion be created under all conditions?

Our answer to the first question must be that not every pair of chords can become the vehicle of higher-ranked harmonic motion. In §95 above we demonstrated that an impression of fundamental harmonic motion can be created even between two different dispositions of the same transposition of the same chord-type. Such a chord succession, which is "artificial" since it represents no substantial change, cannot under any circumstances become higher-ranked harmonic motion. No matter how ingeniously we vary the same chord and connect varied dispositions of it, we will still be moving in the same sphere; a conspicuous departure arises only with the *interference of new foreign pitch material.*

If we are to override the impression resulting from prior chord successions, we must form, as we have the opportunity, a new conspicuous chord out of material that has not yet been used; further, we must stay with this material for some time, that is, use it in the chord successions that follow. Thus if we move for a certain length of time among chords formed within the basic pure diatonic system, we will override the entire accumulation of chords up to that point, and the fundamental harmonic motions between them, by proceeding to a chord which we extract from a different system; this could, for example, be a system with several lowered pitches, or a system which is remarkably altered in comparison with the previous one. We cannot, however, immediately return to the original pure diatonic system of basic pitches; the following progression must be on the whole inconspicuous. Only in such a way will an impression of terraced accumulation of harmonic successions be created: against the series of former chords the new series will stand as a contrasting entity.

This brings us to the third question. Higher-ranked harmonic motion cannot be formed under all conditions. If we do not from the start limit the choice of connected chords, and if we persist in using fundamental harmonic motions of considerably varied significance, we will be unable to override the results of our prior overindulgence. If higher-ranked harmonic motion represents primarily a change of pitch-system, such a change cannot be effected if from the start we have made full use of, and intermingled the pitches of, the entire tempered chromatic system. The difference between tonal and atonal music lies precisely in the fact that *higher-ranked harmonic motion cannot be used in atonal music*; the impossibility of modulation in atonal music is caused not only by its non-functionality, but also by its inability to support higher-ranked harmonic motion.

To clarify what has been said, we present two musical examples. Both use the same compositional convention, but they use somewhat different pitch material and harmonic content. The first example is structured in such a way that there is higher-ranked harmonic motion between the third and fourth measures. In the second example, although the same chord succession occurs in the same place, there is *no* higher-ranked harmonic motion.

Example 147

The diatonic system, with raised pitches F♯ and C♯, is used in the first three measures of the first example; in the following two measures is an altered diatonic system with lowered pitches E♭ and A♭. In contrast, the second example uses eleven pitches in the first three measures, while in the following two measures the twelfth pitch (A) is added at the very end. After such a beginning, higher-ranked harmonic motion can in no way be realized.

§98. The Significance of Cadential Chord Successions

Of all chord successions, the succession from the penultimate to the final chord – the *approach to the tonic* – is especially important. Various successions within a composition can be corrected and somehow justified by subsequent successions. After the final chord, however, no such thing is possible: the sound of the final (tonic) chord ends up marked by one or more of the chords preceding it, and the unsuitability or simply unusualness of the final chord succession remains as an indelible memory even after the tonic has ceased to sound. Hence it is necessary to take great care with both the choice of the final chord and the manner in which it is approached.

Cadential chord successions then become a natural standard for judging other chord successions, which can be differentiated according to whether they resemble or differ from cadential successions, and to what extent and how they are different.

Three principles can be derived from cadential chord successions:
1) the principle of the *pure tonic*,[83]
2) the principle of the *leading tone*, and
3) the *functional* principle.

The order of these is not arbitrary. The principle of the pure tonic constitutes a general foundation from which it would be possible to derive other and otherwise oriented conventional guiding principles than those reached by music conceived in terms of harmony. The principle of the leading tone represents an auxiliary, supplementary law. Finally, the functional principle follows as a synthesis of the two previous principles; it is the "constitution" of all harmonic music, and it will be discussed in the next chapter.

§99. The Principle of the Pure Tonic

The principle of the pure tonic seems to be the original and most universal law governing cadential chord successions. It can be substantiated whenever a cadence gives the impression of the balancing of forces, of equilibrium, of a calming down with no further subsidiary prospects. This statement also implies our assumption that the final chord will be a consonance, since only a *consonance*, with no inner tension, can be free of kinetic forces.

The principle of the pure tonic is based on the existence of imaginary pitches. It gives further support to our hypothesis regarding imaginary pitches. In searching for a suitable tonic, it is not only the choice of a good disposition (or as good a disposition as possible) of a consonance that is important; we must also take care that no imaginary pitches from preceding chords interfere with the real pitches of the tonic (final) chord, since they would disturb its equilibrium regardless of the pains taken in this chord's construction. Because the final chord is so exposed, we must take into account both harmonic and tonal imaginary pitches (see §87), as they can have equally disturbing effects on the sound of the final tonic.

We discussed in detail in *Chapter V* how harmonic imaginary pitches are cancelled. The introduction of a pitch at a distance of an interval 1 from the preceding pitch reliably cancels the harmonic effect of this preceding pitch. When a pitch is introduced at

---

83 Editor's note: In this context of "pure tonic", *tonic* usually refers to the tonic triad. However, as this is not always the case, we have left the ambiguity of the Czech term *tónika*, which may refer either to chord or to pitch.

the distance of an interval 2, this is no longer so certain – when the new pitch appears an interval 2 higher, the preceding pitch is sometimes *not* cancelled. If we add to this our observation from our study of isolated chords (harmonic statics as compared to harmonic kinetics) about the effect of an interval 6 on the sound of a chord, we conclude that an imaginary pitch forming interval 6 will be especially "welcome" to the sounding chord. Just as the ear likes to eliminate disruptive imaginary pitches that form unpleasantly acute intervals 1, it likes to accept pitches that enrich the sense of the sounding chord, rendering it more pleasing and exciting by means of newly formed tritones. If an imaginary pitch making a tritone has at the same time a relation of interval 2 to another real pitch (especially if it is a whole-tone lower than the real pitch), this interval 2 is no longer powerful enough to "purify" the real chord. If an imaginary pitch making a tritone has at the same time a relation of interval 1 to a real pitch of the chord, a contradiction arises between the excluding power of the interval 1 and the absorbing power of the interval 6, which suggests that the victory of the final triad is not "smooth"; in spite of the interval 1 with its excluding tendencies, the final triad retains a tritone flavour.

Accordingly, the principle of the pure tonic can be expressed as follows: *A harmonic phrase gravitates most naturally to a final consonant chord that is disturbed neither by uncancelled or incompletely cancelled harmonic imaginary pitches, nor by tonal imaginary pitches that form a tritone with the real pitches of the final tonic.* The conditions of this principle can be met by considering the penultimate chord or several chords preceding the ending when searching for the as yet unknown final tonic, as well as by considering the established final tonic when searching for the penultimate chord or several chords preceding the final tonic.

The principle of the pure tonic can be *ignored*, resulting in cadences that are to varying degrees intentionally unsatisfying, partially or even fully open-ended. By increasing the unsatisfying effect of the final chord we ultimately arrive at dissonant final chords, as we can see in modern music. Failing to follow the principle is not a denial of it. *The principle of the pure tonic constitutes the foundation and measure of the concept of harmonic motion, even where the actual motion of chords departs from it in some respect or is absolutely contrary to it.*

Although the principle of the pure tonic is a *kinetic* law, dealing with motion, it arises from *static* laws and is related to them. If we consider both the hypothetical law concerning the continuation of imaginary pitches and the empirical observation concerning the fusing effect of the tritone as components of a universal natural rule of law, we must also consider the principle of the pure tonic as a *universal natural law*. This law is not limited to a particular style, because style is convention; style is a sum of devices, practices, and customs that differ more or less from the characteristics of another style and thus escape universality and all that transcends style. Therefore it will be useful to explore historical music to discover to what extent our principle is applied.

§100. Application of the Principle of the Pure Tonic in the Tempered Chromatic System

Let us now turn to concrete possibilities of approaching a consonance in the tempered chromatic system. We first examine the intervals related to the major triad. The negative of the tonic comprises the material from which the pitches of the chord preceding the tonic may be drawn. No pitch in the negative of the major triad is free of the relation 1 or 2 (or both) to one of the pitches in the final triad. Further, three pitches in the negative form an interval 6 with pitches in the triad. This is shown in Example 148, where pitches of the negative are written as black notes.

Example 148

Of the pitches in the negative only B♭ cannot always be thoroughly cancelled by the triad C E G. B♭ also forms a tritone with the differentiating pitch (the third) of the triad and so can easily be appropriated by the triad. Thus if the triad C E G is to function as a pure final tonic it cannot be preceded by a chord containing B♭, since as a tonal (and sometimes also harmonic) imaginary pitch B♭ would complicate and blur the final real triad.

F♯ and D♭ also form tritones with pitches of the triad C E G. However, these two pitches have the advantage of also forming semitones with other pitches of our triad. D♭, especially, because of its semitone distance from the root (a pitch of great importance and weight), has only a meager hope of interfering substantially with the effectiveness of the pure tonic. In contrast, F♯, forming an interval 1 with the less significant supplementary pitch G (the fifth), is capable of disturbing the final tonic more substantially. Both of these assertions agree with the teachings of classical harmony, where the D♭ represents a fairly common altered fifth of the dominant, while the F♯ is a rare alteration of the seventh of the dominant.

Thus the material from which we can form a good reliable pre-tonic chord is given by the pitches of the tonic's negative (to which we can add certain pitches of the tonic itself), with the exception of the pitch situated an interval 2 lower than the basic pitch (B♭). Also unsuitable are the pitch that forms a tritone with the basic pitch of the tonic (F♯), and to a lesser degree the pitch that forms a tritone with the supplementary pitch of the tonic (D♭).

As in the negative of the major triad, there is no pitch in the negative of the *minor* triad that does not form an interval 1 or 2 (or both) with one of the pitches of the triad. Three pitches of the negative also form an interval 6 with pitches of the triad.

Example 149

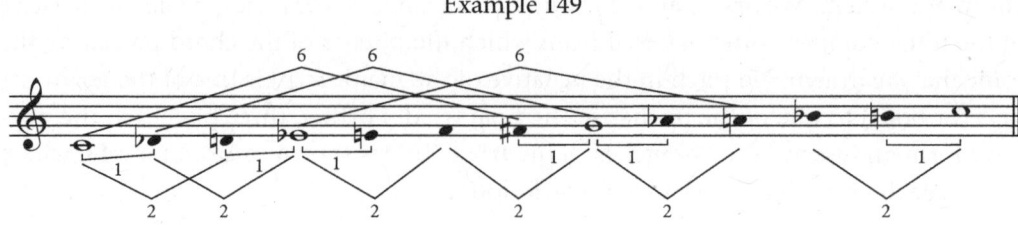

Here again it is B♭ that cannot always be cancelled by the triad C E♭ G. In contrast to the situation with the major triad, however, this pitch does not form a tritone with any pitch of the minor triad. The A forms a tritone relation and also a whole-tone (but not a semitone) relation. F♯ and D♭ are in the same situation as with the major triad, that is, they form 6 and 1 relations.

The presence of B♭ in the pre-tonic chord will not be as disruptive here as in the major triad, because a chord of composite (real and imaginary) expression containing the welcome tritone will not result even if this pitch is not cancelled. An A in the chord preceding the tonic would matter more than a Bb, since although G is adequate to cancel A harmonically, this pitch (A) continues conspicuously in its function as a tonal imaginary pitch by bringing into the triad C E♭ G the welcome tritone E♭–A. The role played in the case of the major triad by the pitch an interval 2 lower than the basic pitch is given here to two pitches, B♭ and A. Thus the material from which a good pre-tonic chord can be constructed is reduced here by one more pitch. Four pitches have been eliminated, which for the tonic C E♭ G are A, B♭, F♯ and D♭.

To summarize: *In an effective pre-tonic chord, we cannot use*
1) pitches that can disturb the tonic as tonal imaginary pitches,
2) in the minor, the pitch an interval 2 lower than the basic pitch of the tonic.

In the major, the pitches specified in point 1 form a major triad at a tritone distance from the tonic (in C major, F♯ A♯ C♯); in the minor they form a minor triad at the same distance from the tonic (in C minor, F♯ A C♯).

In connection with point 2 it should be noted that the pitch an interval 2 lower than the root of a minor tonic should be considered capable of continuing to function as a harmonic imaginary pitch if it is a full-fledged component of the pre-tonic chord. Only when this pitch is a non-harmonic tone does it fail to arouse any special interest. This is demonstrated in Example 150 by the comparison of an authentic (aeolian) cadence and a plagal cadence in a minor key.

Example 150

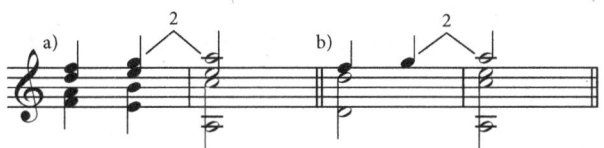

Although the melodic progression of the upper voice is the same in both segments of the example, the role of the G (an aeolian seventh) in the first segment is considerably more significant, and its influence on the final tonic (A minor) is more pronounced than in the second segment, where the G is only a passing tone.

§101. Application of the Principle of the Pure Tonic in the Diatonic System

We have stated that the principle of the pure tonic applies under the assumption that the final chord is a consonance. This is not always the case in modern music. It *is* the case, however, in older music, and even in monophonic music, since the only way a single voice can end is on a single pitch, a one-note chord, which is always consonant. The principle of the pure tonic can be substantiated by examining earlier evolutionary stages. Analysis of the conditions in non-harmonic, monophonic music verifies that this principle prevailed even there.

Monophony, as we know it from notated Gregorian chant, was *diatonic*. Its diatonicism was established either without a key signature or with one accidental, B♭. Possible final pitches (finals) were D, E, F, G, and even C and A. (The *finalis* determined the mode, which is the ancestor of our concept of key.) It is to be noted that B was excluded from the function of finalis. This can be accounted for by our principle of the pure tonic. Even in non-harmonic linear thinking, the tritone (the "diabolus in musica") caused difficulties, as we know from medieval as well as later rules of composition. It was B that could not escape the intruding tritone interval formed with the immovable pitch F. In contrast, F could become a finalis precisely because B was movable in relation to it: "in case of danger" it could be changed into B♭. In fact, it is in the rare lydian mode (on F) that the "characteristic" pitch B is frequently lowered to B♭.

In *polyphony*, as long as it had at its disposal only the pitch material of the pure diatonic system, there were only two practical possibilities for ending – the diatonic system could be directed towards one final major triad or one final minor triad. The reduction of the original possibilities found in a single voice to these two in polyphony can be explained by the requirements of the principle of the pure tonic.

The tritone B–F, which appears in the basic diatonic system, can be safely prevented from interfering with the final tonic by insuring that neither of its pitches is in the tonic. Thus from the six major and minor chords available, the chords containing B or F had to be eliminated as possible tonics in the pure diatonic system. Only two triads were left: C E G and A C E. Thus arose the major-minor dualism of harmonic polyphony.

§102. The Principle of the Leading Tone

Of all single dissonant intervals, the interval 1 has the most acutely pointed effect as a chord. (See §19 above.) Thus it should come as no surprise that when two pitches in a melodic line follow each other at an interval 1 the second pitch quickly and insistently pushes the preceding one into the background (cancels it); the retention of the preceding pitch would cause a violent clash between the two pitches, which is something that perceiving subject ("ear") avoids. Melodic progression by interval 1 is therefore desirable wherever it is important to obliterate the preceding sound reality in order to achieve a smooth flow into the new sound.

If a closing chord progression is to give the impression of coming to rest and reaching its destination, there must be at least one possiblity of the progression by melodic interval 1. If there is no *interval 1*, either one of the chords is incomplete or the progression was not *sufficiently* directed to make a true conclusion.

The principle of the leading tone is founded on melodic progression by interval 1. By *leading tone* in a general sense, we mean a pitch distant by an interval 1 from a component of the terminal chord, the tonic. It can be either an upper or a lower pitch. By *leading tone* in a narrower sense, we mean only the pitch situated an interval 1 lower than the root of the tonic. If for any reason the final chord is expected, the leading tone insistently gravitates to the respective pitch of the tonic.

We see the leading tone as the vehicle of the chord's kinetic energy of the impetus in the chord, as its tendency to flow into the tonic. It is the leading tone that causes the entire pre-tonic chord to gravitate to the tonic. If we speak of the principle of the pure tonic as a *kinetic* law (see §99 above), the same applies to the principle of the leading tone; even here, however, our starting point is a static phenomenon, namely the sonic effect of the interval 1 as a chord.

The gravitation of the pre-tonic chord to the tonic, caused by the leading tone (whether directed upward or downward), can be *increased*, in that there can be more than one leading tone. If we presuppose a consonant final chord (at most a three-note chord), the number of leading tones can reach six – three rising (to the triad C E G: B, D♯, F♯), and three falling (to C E G: D♭, F, A♭). However, increasing the number of leading tones can result in a discrepancy with the requirements of the principle of the pure tonic, as two leading tones (D♭ and F♯ for the tonics C E G and C E♭ G) are among the pitches eliminated from the pre-tonic chord by this principle.

Chapter VIb – Harmonic Motion: Functions and their Combinations

§103. The Functional Principle

The *functional principle* arises from the merged principles of the pure tonic and the leading tone. Application of both these principles results in a particular distribution of tonal functions. We are looking for pre-tonic chords that could serve as a standard for perceiving or judging all other practically possible chord relations.

It follows from the nature of pitch material, namely from its regular layering within pitch space, that opposite every chord formation as well as any of its parts, there can be constituted another formation, situated in the opposite direction in relation to a certain fixed pitch axis. A pitch that is a certain distance above the axis corresponds to a pitch that is the same distance below the axis. Similarly, opposite every chord can be placed another chord, as a rule its simple transposition, sometimes the transposition of its inversion, as a pitch space counterpart. Thus if a suitable pre-tonic chord is found above the tonic, which represents the axis, there is another equally suitable and usable pre-tonic chord the same distance below the tonic. Such suitable pre-tonic chords, always two, together with the tonic, *represent tonal functions*. The tonic is a sound without tension or kinetic tendencies. The pairs of pre-tonic chords are bound to the tonic by their gravitation to it. This can be generally illustrated by the following figure.

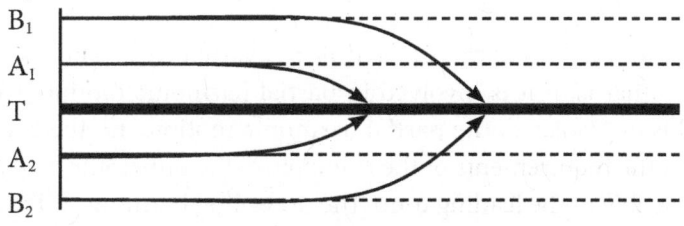

The thick horizontal line T represents the level of the tonic. A_1 constitutes one suitable pre-tonic chord formation, to which the formation A_2 on the opposite side corresponds. Similarly, B_2 below the tonic corresponds to another suitable pre-tonic formation, B_1, above the tonic. The formations A_1, A_2, B_1, and B_2 all gravitate to the tonic, as indicated by arrows.

Once discovered, these functions become the measure for relations between other chords and the tonic, as well as between various non-tonic chords.

The *tonic* is the *axis* of the entire tonally functional system. An essential presupposition of functionality is awareness of the tonic; with the loss of this awareness, the entire functional system vanishes. Any consonant chord can become the axis of a functional system. Once a functional system is formed, it can change in the course of a composition – it can be cancelled and replaced by another. Instead of chords that we have until now generally designated as pre-tonic chords, we can use different and variously combined chords (for example, combinations of chords A_1 and A_2). By means of various deviations and combinations it is possible to shift the original level of the tonic, or to make the awareness of a tonic vanish altogether; the functional system is then either *relocated* or *cancelled*. In the latter case, the music that continues to flow becomes harmonically *functionless*.

We will now examine the concrete possibilities of functional systems. Thereby we will also demonstrate the dependence of the functional principle on the principles of the pure tonic and the leading tone.

§104. Establishing the Tonic

In every functional system, it is first important that the tonic be *established*. A necessary condition for establishing the tonic is that it be *consonant*. If this condition is not met, striving for stability is meaningless.

An *isolated* consonant chord can always assume tonic function, since it has no tension in itself that would impel it to move elsewhere. If it is *part of a chord progression*, however, its tonic function must be supported by the *combination* of the other chords. If this combination conforms to the principles of the pure tonic and the leading tone in relation to the supposed tonic, the stability of this tonic is assured. Unless both principles are adhered to, the chosen consonance cannot assume tonic function. (This is not to say that an awareness of a tonic is not formed. It may be, but the tonic function is assumed by some other chord, possibly one that is not actually in the chord progression.)

A chord cannot be considered isolated if it is varied by or alternates with chordal cross-sections – that is, if it is involved in partial harmonic motion. (See §92 above.) When a chord is not isolated, the partial harmonic motion and the chordal cross-sections must meet the requirements of the principle of the pure tonic, and also, if it can be applied, the principle of the leading tone. The prevailing harmony in Example 151 is the triad A C E. The melody of the highest voice forms with the continually sounding pitches A C E two chordal cross-sections which are more complex.

Example 151

Of these, A E C F (if the sharp in brackets is not used) and A E C D do not affect the final consonant triad with tonal imaginary pitches, so the conditions of the principle of the pure tonic are met. This is not the case with the chordal cross-section A E C F♯, which results if the sharp is applied. Although F♯ (the dorian sixth) is harmonically cancelled, it continues to function as a tonal imaginary pitch, and so the final triad A C E has a pronounced tritone flavour and cannot be considered a reliably established tonic.

In the music of the late nineteenth century, tonics were often intentionally disturbed in this way with the characteristic pitches of church modes, by Rimsky-Korsakov for example. This was probably related to weariness with "reliably established tonics" and to a need for new effects, new "harmonic adventures". Such a disturbance of the tonic, which does not result in a shift to another (transposed) functional system, is possible only when the other chords of the functional system, chords to which we refer generally as pre-tonic, are stabilized and standardized by tradition. Thus our example can represent the key of A minor even with the auxiliary tone F♯, but the tonic A C E is somewhat "exotic", unstable.

As far as the coordination of all the independent non-tonic chords and the tonic is concerned, not only "suitable" pre-tonic chords as established by long use (tradition) can participate in it, but also other chords variously formed or combined from them. As long as the tonic is not implied in advance, however (for example, as an isolated chord of fairly long duration), the other chords must be drawn from the "suitable" pre-tonic chords found on *both* sides of the tonic (according to the figure in §103 above, from A_1 as well as A_2, for example). If only one non-tonic harmony is used, the material from the other harmony must at least flicker in it briefly in the form of non-harmonic tones.

For example, if only the triads C E G and G B D alternate in the key of C major, at least some pitches from the triad F A C (the counterpart of G B D) should sound as non-harmonic tones in the framework of the tonic C E G or the dominant G B D.

§105. Types of Representative Pre-tonic Harmonies

So far we have spoken generally about chords that supplement the tonic to form a functional system as "suitable pre-tonic chords"; under this designation it was possible to imagine chords of the most varied types. Now we face the task of determining these more exactly. We are dealing with chords that should, together with the tonic, constitute the harmonic *representatives* of the key.

In the case of the tonic we stated the obvious requirement that the chord that is to represent the tonic must be consonant. Does the same requirement hold for the other chords of a functional system? Or are dissonant chords also acceptable?

We will first consider these questions in a general sense, without taking into account the concrete possibilities. If the tonic is to represent the area of sonic repose and release of tension, we certainly cannot abandon the requirement of consonance for it. In the case of pre-tonic chords, however, we conversely expect a tendency to gravitate to the tonic; their own inner tension (their dissonance) would only assist them in this mission. Initially, this appears to be correct, but let us examine it more closely. A dissonant harmony is advantageous if it is to lead to the tonic. We are concerned here, however, with representative chords (*two* representative chords at that), which could not only stand alone, but whose pitch material could serve as the basis for forming other chords (whether dissonant or not). The inclination of both representative pre-tonic harmonies towards the tonic must derive from their *relation to the tonic* rather than from their own inner structure, their own tension, their dissonance. It is then better to find, if possible, *consonant* harmonies that, in spite of not having their own sonic tension, gravitate to the tonic and are subordinate to it. In a consonant harmony, the substantial characteristic of gravitating to the tonic is separate from inner sonic tension; a consonant chord is a pure "extract", freed from the secondary characteristic of real dissonance. Thus we conclude, after all, that *consonance is required for representative pre-tonic harmonies*.

Let us step down from the heights of general reflection into the world of concrete phenomena. The *tonic* that we indicated in the figure in §103 above by a single thick line is a *triad*. If we are to determine a certain distance from this triad upward, and then to measure the same distance downward, we need to know from which pitch to measure; we know from §53 above that this must be the *root* as the pitch representing the entire triad. However, a measured distance again yields only a single pitch, which by itself cannot assume the function of a pre-tonic harmony. Thus this again must be the root on which the harmony representing a pre-tonic function is built. Only harmonies **I** (*consonant* triads) have but a single basic pitch. All dissonant chords belong to higher categories, and harmonies of these higher categories have more than one basic pitch of equal significance (see §59 above).

Thus if our task is to find two harmonies equidistant from a certain axis (the tonic), we must look for two harmonies **I**, and so we have resolved the question of chord-type: the representative pre-tonic harmonies can only be *consonant major and minor triads*.

§106. Establishing Possible Representative Pre-tonic Harmonies

Now let us determine the best location for the representative pre-tonic harmonies. If the two (we are assuming only two) representative pre-tonic harmonies are to be mutual counterparts that are distinct from each other, *they cannot have pitches in common*.

There must run a distinct dividing line between them. Were the counterpart of a chord to contain one of that chord's component pitches, that chord would not be a pure pre-tonic harmony, but a derivation, a formation put together from other ("correct") pre-tonic chords. This requirement considerably limits the possibilities for forming further members of a functional system for a given tonic.

The relation between representative pre-tonic harmonies and the tonic is not completely defined by the requirements of the principles of the pure tonic and the leading tone. The concrete possibilities of motion are also important. Since the approach from the pre-tonic harmony to the tonic must represent *fundamental harmonic motion* (see §93 above), we must make certain that the impression of fundamental harmonic motion is created *under all condition*. This impression may not arise if successive triads have two pitches in common (for example, E G B and C E G). Only a single common pitch cannot prevent fundamental harmonic motion. Thus the representative pre-tonic harmony and the tonic may have *no more than one pitch in common*. This further limits the possibilities for representative pre-tonic harmonies.

Because the functional system is symmetrical, the two representative pre-tonic harmonies must have *equal but opposite relations to the tonic*. Thus if one pre-tonic harmony has one pitch in common with the tonic, the second pre-tonic harmony must also have one pitch in common with the tonic. This co-ordination limits the possibilities of representative pre-tonic harmonies even further.

Having laid out these requirements, we can look for actual chords. To make the gradual reduction of possibilities more obvious, for now we will consider only the requirements just presented, and not until later the principles of the pure tonic and the leading tone.

Our search produces the following triadic pairs. The selection was guided by
a) the exclusive acceptability of major and minor triads for each function,
b) the requirement that pre-tonic counterparts have no common pitches, and
c) the requirement that the tonic and any pre-tonic harmony have no more than one pitch in common.

Example 152

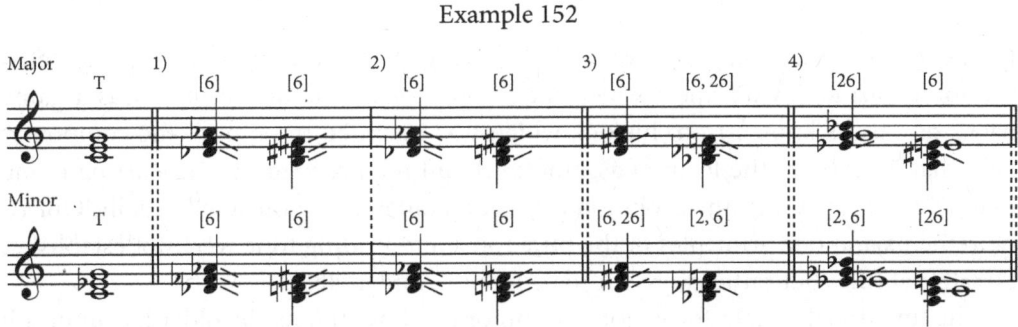

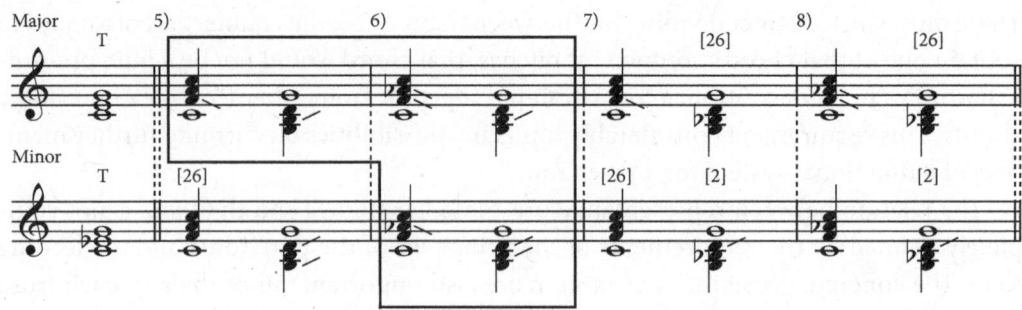

In the example, slanted lines point out leading tones, which rise or fall towards pitches of the tonic. Whole notes indicate the common pitch between the pre-tonic harmony and the tonic. Numerals in square brackets indicate the interval formed by the tonal imaginary pitch (continuing from the pre-tonic harmony) with one of the pitches of the tonic. Thus the [6] above D♭ F A♭ in Example 152-1 means that the D♭ from that triad forms a tritone relation with the G of the tonic C E G; [26] means that one pitch forms two intervals (for example, B♭–C 2, B♭–E 6); [2, 6] means that two different pitches form intervals 2 and 6 respectively (for example, D♭–G, B♭–C). Intervals 1 are not indicated, since they have no part in the formation of tonal imaginary pitches.

These are the only pairs of triads that fulfill the requirements that we established.

If we now consider the principle of the leading tone, we must eliminate from the above possibilities those in which no slanted lines are shown [for at least one of the chords] – in minor, Example 152-5 and 152-7, and in major, Example 152-7 and 152-8. The progressions from F A C to the minor tonic C E♭ G, and from G B♭ D to the major tonic C E G, do not involve leading tones.

If we consider the principle of the pure tonic, we must eliminate all cases where, as indicated by the intervals in square brackets, there is the possibility of continuing tonal imaginary pitches. This leaves only Example 152-5 and 152-6 in the major, and 152-6 in the minor. *These are the only pairs of pre-tonic harmonies that constitute representative harmonies suitable in all respects*, and we have framed them with a heavy line.

§107. The Classical Functional System of Three Members

In the previous section when we were deriving the possibilities for representative pre-tonic harmonies we knew where the sought-for harmonies were. It was a game, based on results known from history, which was intended to point to the component laws that we took in the form of assumptions and requirements as the starting points in our search. In reality, the evolution proceeded differently, non-intellectually. Our requirements and our principles of the pure tonic and leading tone were not established by rational rules but rather were felt to be natural, undeniable.

The functional system for major and minor keys, as attained by older harmonically conceived music, has *three members*. At its center is the *tonic* T (C E G, C E♭ G); situated symmetrically on either side are the *dominant* D (G B D in major and minor), and

the *subdominant* S (in C major F A C or F A♭ C, in the minor only F A♭ C). The system comprises nine pitches: C, D, E♭, E, F, G, A♭, A, B. The other pitches may be used either
  a) as parts of functional systems transposed from other keys, or
  b) as pitches by which the pitch-system as well as individual harmonies are altered.

Classical harmony then speaks of applied harmonies[84] and modulations (a) or of altered harmonies (b).

Other three-note chords than T, D, and S, as long as they were of tertian structure, could be interpreted, according to H. Riemann, as harmonies that *stand in the place* of these primary functions, or, according to the Czech theorist Otakar Šín, as *combinations* of them. Thus for example the triad on the sixth degree of major (A C E in C major) can be interpreted as a modified tonic (a harmony that can stand in the place of the tonic) or as a combination of part of the tonic (C E) and part of the subdominant (A C). According to Riemann and older theorists, more complex harmonies, as long as they were formed from thirds, had the function of their lowest triadic component (for example, C E G B would represent the tonic in C major); according to Šín, they again had a combined function (for example, C E G B would represent a combination of tonic and dominant functions). The advantage of Šín's conception is that it enables us to understand functionally even those chord formations that cannot be arranged into a tertian scheme. Remaining beyond the scope of every theoretical conception, however, were chord formations containing both pitches belonging to the scale and the same pitches altered (for example D, D♭), and such formations appear frequently in new music. Thus it became necessary to expand the classical functional system of three members.

§108. Šín's Functional System of Five Members

According to our study in §106 above, it is possible to form only one pair of representative pre-tonic harmonies that are suitable in every respect, namely the pair S, D. In §107 above, however, we showed that this pair and the functional system of three members derived from it are insufficient, especially for newer music. Thus the functional system must be expanded to include another pair of consonant triads, even if this pair does not meet all the conditions fulfilled by the pair S, D.

The functional system of three members can be expanded to one of five members, assuming that the stability of the tonic is ensured by the S T D system. The stability must be established by the use of the S T D system, as well as by the strength of tradition – that is, by the fact that the relations between the members of the S T D system are familiar, or deeply rooted. If the newly included harmonies have some pronounced virtues not shared by the harmonies of the original more limited system, they will be welcome (because effective) members of the expanded system. What could these virtues be?

---

84 Editor's note: The Czech *mimotonální* means "outside the key". We will use the term *applied* for such functions that relate to other tonics than the main tonic.

According to the overview in §106 above (Example 152), the possibility of tonal imaginary pitches keeps certain harmonies that meet the other conditions from being reliable as pre-tonic harmonies. If we see that most of the harmonies not used in the classical S T D system do not meet the conditions of the principle of the pure tonic, we need to look for a *counterbalance* to this inadequacy *in the principle of the leading tone*. The latter principle applies, of course, to the relations between harmonies in the system of three members, between dominant and tonic and between subdominant and tonic, although not to the maximum extent. In Example 152-1, in major and minor, both assumed pre-tonic harmonies are constructed entirely from leading tones, with rising or falling tendency as shown by the slanted lines. Here the contravention of the principle of the pure tonic is counterbalanced by a *maximum involvement of leading tones* and hence the strongest possible effect of the principle of the leading tone. Thus the classical functional system can be supplemented by the pair of triads of the same family as the tonic and a semitone from the tonic in each direction. The entire functional system of five members is shown in Example 153.

Example 153

For the new members of the expanded functional system we introduce the symbols P and L, corresponding to the terms that Šín used for these harmonies: *phrygian* and *lydian*. Šín derived these terms from characteristic pitches of the phrygian and lydian church modes: in C major and minor, D♭ F A♭ and D♭ F♭ A♭ contain the *phrygian second*, *D♭*, while the *lydian fourth*, *F♯*, is found in B D♯ F♯ and B D F♯.

With a slight variation, we find the same new harmonies in Example 152-2 with the same form in the major and minor (D♭ F A♭, B D F♯). In each mode one of the triads contains one fewer leading tone. This decrease is counterbalanced by something else, however. The flaw of the phrygian and lydian triads as pre-tonic triads lies in their tritone relation to the tonic triad (D♭–G, F♯–C); they thus wrench themselves out of the fundamental principle of the pure tonic. The appearance of tonal imaginary pitches can be prevented, however, and the controlling principle that is being denied thus corroborated, by the group 11, which is complex-sounding, harsh, and hence always unwelcome even as a melodic progression (cf. §87 above). The major phrygian (D♭ F A♭) with the minor lydian (B D F♯) in a progression P L T or L P T outlines this group (D♭–D–C, F–F♯–G, or D–D♭–C, F♯–F–G). Thus we will speak of lydian and phrygian harmonies even when they contain only two leading tones (in C major, B D F♯ instead of B D♯ F♯, in C minor D♭ F A♭ instead of D♭ F♭ A♭).

The status of the new pre-tonic harmonies P and L seems strengthened when they are directly joined to the classical pre-tonic functions D and S. Progressions P D and L S prevent the formation of tonal imaginary pitches in the tonic that follows, because

11 is outlined (D♭–D–C, F♯–F–G); this is even more effective here than in the progressions P L or L P, because the pitch forming the 6 with the basic or supplementary pitch of the tonic is not part of a harmony immediately preceding the tonic. (Cf. §87 above.)

As long as the harmony is of the same family as the tonic, we can use the simple symbols T, D, S, L, and P to identify the harmonies. If the family of the harmonies differs from that of the key, however, we can indicate this by placing the family sign + or in front of the symbol: +T, –L, –S, etc.[85]

The expansion of the classical system of three members into one of five members was not a matter of theory. It had to do with the *loosening of tonal relations* in practical musical thinking, in actual composition. (We will discuss the loosening of the tonal relations established by older music in §120 below.)

In the following we will refer to the functions in the classical system of three members as *primary* functions and to the new phrygian and lydian functional harmonies as *auxiliary* functions.

§109. Stabilization of Relations between Harmonies of the Functional System; the Minor Dominant

It is natural to assume that music evolved historically from harmonic feeling to harmonic thinking – from the unconscious to the conscious, rather than vice versa. The starting point of harmony was the sonic essence of chords, their sound and sense, out of which functional relations and dependencies were discovered only after prolonged examination and searching, more intuitively than by any skill in combining them. The tonic and representative pre-tonic harmonies had to be found. The guiding laws had not yet been discovered, namely, our principles of the pure tonic and the leading tone. When eventually it was found that the results of searching were often the same, frequently used chord progressions could become customary; that is, they could become progressions for whose realization special care, sensitivity, and inventiveness were no longer needed. The progression D T is the prototype of such a progression. With it a composition reliably ends – so reliably that the final tonic, even if it may not actually sound, is expected. Such a transition from intuitive sensory processes through conscious processes to mechanical processes is common in art, affecting the most diverse areas; this is the source of originally unique discoveries becoming commonplace, of mannerism, and of routine manufacturing of all kinds.

In the area of functional relations such stabilization took place especially between the original (primary) representative harmonies in the system of three members. The relation D T appears to practical musicians today self-evident and natural. The inclination of the dominant toward the tonic is one of the most overused harmonic effects. It is like a

---

[85] Šín indicated harmonies of minor family by placing a small circle in front of the symbol (°T, °S); he did not use any specific indication for harmonies of major family. He used the symbols ꜰ for the phrygian and ꜰ for the lydian.

framework of which we have become almost unaware, but by which we still measure and evaluate adjacent harmonic phenomena and those further removed from each other.

With a relation thus stabilized, it is possible that some deviation, created perhaps by mere artistic whim (for the sake of interest), would violate the very guiding principle by means of which this relation was originally sought and found. The relation D T can be varied by complicating the dominant with new pitches (most commonly the seventh) or by altering a particular pitch in the direction of the tonic (thus forming a new leading tone), and also by *moving the dominant further away from the tonic* while possibly *encumbering the tonic with a tonal imaginary pitch*. This last change results from lowering the differentiating pitch of the dominant, for example, in C major and minor by altering the dominant G B D to G B♭ D. This has greater impact in the major than in the minor. In the major it removes the only leading tone and encumbers the tonic (C E G) with the imaginary pitch B♭, which cannot be cancelled harmonically. In the minor it removes only one of two leading tones (although the more effective one), and the tonic sounds without tritone disturbance, in contrast to the major where both whole-tone and tritone relations interfere with the tonic (B♭–C, B♭–E).

The *minor dominant triad* is rarely directly adjacent to the tonic; we must nevertheless consider it in combinations, since only this harmony contains the pitch an interval 2 below the basic pitch of the tonic. When this pitch (B♭ in C major and minor) is not part of some other (transposed) functional system, there is no other way it can be interpreted as part of a harmony in the functional system of five members.

§110. Consonant Combinations of Functions (Interfunctions)

All the harmonies in the functional systems of three and five members are consonant, and so none of them carries the *inner* tension characteristic of dissonances. Only the tonic, however, represents a harmony of complete repose, a harmony without kinetic tendencies. All the other harmonies, although consonant, gravitate toward the tonic and thus give the impression of a *certain tension*. This tension is caused by their relation to the tonic, and so it can be called *outer*. Thus an awareness of the tonic is necessary for outer tension to arise. When an awareness of the tonic is lost, outer tension also disappears, and a consonant harmony can acquire the repose characteristic of the tonic, even if it was not originally tonic. The possible dying away of outer tension, and the related ability of harmonies to become tonic, are important conditions which must be considered with all consonances.

Among the functions in the five-member system, there are gradations of outer tension. The functions S and D have considerably less tension than the functions P and L.

Besides representative pre-tonic harmonies, other consonant harmonies can also be placed against the tonic. In relation to the tonic, these harmonies will also show a certain kinetic tension that will fluctuate according to their position with respect to the

Chapter VIb – Harmonic Motion: Functions and their Combinations

tonic. The tension will be less if the harmony has one or two pitches in common with the tonic, and if the principle of the leading tone cannot come into play in connecting the two. Thus A C E does not have much tension in relation to the tonic C E G, since there are two pitches in common, and the pitch that differs (A) does not form an interval 1 with any pitch of the tonic and so cannot be a leading tone. The harmony E G♯ B has considerably greater tension in relation to the tonic C E G, since these triads have only one pitch in common, and the pitches that are different (G♯, B) form semitones with pitches of the tonic, thus functioning as leading tones (G♯ falling, B rising).

Every consonant harmony that does not represent a primary or auxiliary function can be understood as a *combination structure* made of pitches of these functions. Two or at most three different functions can be combined into a consonant triad. Thus for example the harmony E♭ G B♭ in C major or minor is an incomplete combination of the minor tonic (C E♭ G) and the minor dominant (G B♭ D); if we do not want to accept the validity of a minor tonic in a major key, we can understand the same harmony as the incomplete combination of the major lydian (B D♯ F♯) and the minor dominant. However, we must understand the harmony E G♯ B in C major as the incomplete combination of three functions: the tonic (E), the minor subdominant (G♯ = A♭), and the major dominant (B).

It is worth noting that even the minor phrygian in the major and the major lydian in the minor must be understood as combinations: D♭ F♭ A♭ in C major is D♭ E A♭, and the E is part of the tonic; similarly, B D♯ F♯ in C minor is B E♭ F♯, and the E♭ is taken from the tonic.

We will refer to consonant harmonies that do not represent just single functions (whether primary or auxiliary) as *interfunctional harmonies, interfunctions*. Interfunctions are consonant combinations of single functions. Their symbol will be IN.

Interfunctions can only rarely be understood in their direct relation to the tonic, because this relation is too complex. In most cases it is better to perceive interfunctions in their simple relation to a harmony other than tonic, and only by means of this intermediary harmony to the tonic itself. However, if only for those relatively rare cases when interfunctions do stand in direct relation to the tonic, a suitable system must be invented for identifying them. Here we present three possibilities:

1) The interfunction is designated IN. Its position relative to the tonic can be expressed by a numeral corresponding to the interval by which this harmony is higher or lower than the tonic. If it is above the tonic, the numeral is written in superscript after IN; if it is below, the numeral is written in subscript. The family of the interfunction is indicated by the sign + or – in front of the symbol IN. Thus E G♯ B in C major is +IN^4, and A C E in C minor is –IN$_3$, etc.

2) If it is important to show the type of combination, we can express the interfunction by writing above each other the symbols of its component functions. In front of these symbols family can be indicated by + or –, and following these symbols the number of pitches of each function used in the interfunction can be indicated by a

261

corresponding number of dots. Thus we designate the harmony E G♯ B in C major and minor by the following:

$$+D\cdot$$
$$-S\cdot$$
$$+T\cdot$$

We designate the harmony A C E in C major and minor as $^{+T:}_{+S:}$, and in C minor also as $^{-P\cdot}_{+S:}$ because we perceive the E = F♭ as part of the minor phrygian. If a total of more than three dots is found after the functional symbols, as in the next-to-last example, it means that a pitch is common to two different component functions.

3) Finally, if a precise expression of the combination is important, instead of dots we can write special symbols for individual components of functions. Because each function is represented by a major or minor triad, we will form a general symbol for the harmony in such a way that we will be able to separate it into its various components. For example, the complete consonant triad can be expressed as ⊕; its individual components will thus be ⌣ (the basic pitch), ⌢ (the supplementary pitch), and | (the differentiating pitch, a major or minor third). These symbols can be combined. Thus O represents an open fifth, a chord of the basic and differentiating pitches, and ⌣ the chord of the differentiating and ⌢ supplementary pitches. If the differentiating pitch is omitted from a function, the sign indicating family can be omitted before the functional symbol. We write the symbols indicating pitches or pairs of pitches after the functional symbol in place of the dots in method 2.

The most practical (because the simplest) system of designation is the first one. The advantage of the second and third systems, the precision with which they express the components constituting interfunctions, is overshadowed by the complexity of the symbols and overall lack of clarity. Thus it is advisable to resort to these systems only on those rare occasions when precise expression of the combination is especially important.

We present a survey of all interfunctions in major and minor keys, with symbols in all three systems.

a) Interfunctional Major Triads

Example in C major or minor	Symbol					
	system 1)	system 2)			system 3)	
D F♯ A	+IN²	+S· −L:	or	+S· L· D·	+S| −L⌢	or	+S| L⌢ D⌢
E♭ G B♭	+IN³	−D: −T:	or	−D: +L·	−D⌣ −T⌢	or	−D⌣ +L|

Chapter VIb – Harmonic Motion: Functions and their Combinations

Example in C major or minor	Symbol		
	system 1)	system 2)	system 3)
E G♯ B	+IN⁴	+D· –S· +T·	+D∣ –S∣ +T∣
F♯ A♯ C♯	+IN⁶ or +IN₆	P· –D· L·	P⌣ –D∣ L⌢
A♭ C E♭	+IN₄	–T: or +L· –S: –S:	–T⌣ or +L∣ –S⌢ –S⌢

A C♯ E	+IN₃	–P: +T·
		+S· or P·
		           +S·
			–P⌣ or +T∣
			+S∣ P⌣
			               +S∣

B♭ D F	+IN₂	S· –D:	S⌣ –D⌢
B D♯ F♯	+IN₁ or +L	–T· L:	–T∣ L⌢

b) Interfunctional Minor Triads

Example in C major or minor	Symbol		
	system 1)	system 2)	system 3)
D F A	–IN²	+S: D·	+S⌣ D⌢
E♭ G♭ B♭	–IN³	–D· –D· or L· +L: –T·	–D∣ –D∣ or L⌢ +L⌢ –T∣
E G B	–IN⁴	+D: +T:	+D⌣ +T⌢
F♯ A C♯	–IN⁶ or –IN₆	P· +S· L·	P⌣ +S∣ L⌢

G♯ B D♯	–IN₄	+L: or +L·
		–S· +D·
		            –S·
			+L⌣ or +L∣
			–S∣ +D∣
			             –S∣

A C E	–IN₃	+T: +S:	+T⌣ +S⌢

B♭ D♭ F	–IN₂	+P: or S·
		–D· P·
		             –D·
			+P⌣ or S⌣
			–D∣ P⌣
			             –D∣

C♯ E G♯	–IN¹ or –P	+T· P:	+T∣ P⌢

All consonant harmonies that are not tonics are characterized by a strong tonal *decentralizing force*; by this we mean an inclination toward independence, toward the cancellation or obliteration of their relation to the tonic. This is why a direct relation of interfunctions to the tonic is relatively rare. In an interfunction with a complex relation to the tonic there is always a tendency to simplify the functional relation at the cost of losing awareness of the tonic. Thus the harmony E G♯ B, with its triple functional relation to the tonic C E G, tends to form a simple relation, for example to the harmony A C E, in relation to which it is a plain major dominant. The minor dominant G B♭ D in C major, a rare harmony, is similarly more easily understood, for example, as a subdominant to the interfunctional harmony D F A perceived temporarily as tonic. (We will discuss this further in §117 below.)

A direct relation of interfunctions to the tonic is most effectively enforced by the *immediate adjacency of the tonic*. Where the tonic follows the interfunction, only a direct relation to the tonic can be expected. The triad E G♯ B actually is an interfunction with a triple functional relation to the tonic C E G, as long as this tonic immediately follows it.

§111. Dissonant Combinations of Functions

All dissonant chords, regarded functionally, are *combinations*. Their dissonance is at the same time their *inner (intrinsic) tension*. While with consonant interfunctions the outer tension given by their relation to the tonic can be counted on to die away and vanish if they are prolonged, with dissonances this is not possible. Dissonances can never acquire the absolute repose characteristic of the tonic.

It is impossible to determine the relation of isolated consonances to the tonic from the consonances themselves; for this an *awareness of the tonic*, established by a cooperation of several other functionally differentiated chords, is necessary. The situation is different with dissonances. Since every dissonance is a combination of several consonant components with different functions, as a chordal whole its effect is similar to that of the same components presented successively in time. Therefore, if it is possible to create a certain awareness of the tonic by means of two successive consonances, the same result can be achieved by the sounding together of the same consonances in a *dissonant combination of functions*. If the tonic is not established by two such successive consonances without ambiguity, however, not even their sounding together in one chord will yield a definite awareness of the tonic.

If the minor dominant is included, Šín's five functions contain all the pitches of the tempered chromatic system. Hence every dissonant chord can be understood as a functional combination belonging to any transposed functional system, that is, in relation to any tonic. This possibility is only theoretical, however. In reality, this versatility is limited by the general practical principle that if a phenomenon can be understood more simply it is superfluous to understand it in any more complex way. Thus even from an isolated dissonant chord we can read one or several of the most suitable ways of perceiving it functionally, although theoretically there is always the possibility of several other interpretations. For example, the chord G B D F A♭ D♭, the combination of two major triads a tritone apart (+6+), can be understood as the combination of the dominant and phrygian triads in C major (or F♯ major), or as the combination of the subdominant and lydian triads in D major (or A♭ major). Theoretically it can also be understood as a more complex combination in any other key; for example, in A major it can be the combination of an incomplete minor dominant (pitches G, B from E G B), an incomplete minor subdominant (D, F from D F A), an incomplete major dominant (A♭ = G♯, from E G♯ B) or an incomplete lydian (B, A♭ = G♯ from G♯ B D♯), and an incomplete tonic (D♭ = C♯ from A C♯ E). From this example we see that the more complex interpretations, although theoretically possible, cannot capture the functional essence of the chord; the correct functional interpretation is always the simplest.

Later (in §116 below) we will see that the concepts of bitonality and polytonality are needed to simplify the functional interpretation of individual chords, and that where even these concepts do not result in a simplification, a functional tonal interpretation should be abandoned as impractical (see §120 below).

We can divide dissonant functional combinations into several groups according to the way functional components are used in the chord:

1) The first group comprises *combinations of triads that represent individual functions*. These combinations can be designated by the symbols of the individual component functions, written above each other; for example:

$$\begin{smallmatrix}+D\\-S\end{smallmatrix} = \widehat{E\ G\ B}\ \overline{C\sharp\ F\sharp\ A\sharp}\ \text{(in B major or B minor)},$$

$$\begin{smallmatrix}+P\\+D\end{smallmatrix} = \widehat{A\ C\sharp\ E}\ \overline{G\ B\flat\ E\flat}\ \text{(in D major or D minor), etc.}$$

If any of the functions have pitches in common, the resulting combination will contain fewer pitches; for example:

$$\begin{smallmatrix}+D\\+L\end{smallmatrix} = \overline{D\sharp\ F\sharp\ \underline{B\ D\ G}}\ \text{(C major) is only a five-note chord.}$$

2) The second group comprises the combinations in which *one or more triads representing single functions* are supplemented by *pitches from other functions*. In designating these combinations we write the functional symbol of the function that is fully represented; above or below it we place dots to represent added pitches, or functional symbols with the indications for individual pitches (basic pitch ∪, supplementary pitch ∩, differentiating pitch |, or any pitch may be represented by a dot). For example:

$$\dot{+D} \text{ or } {}^{S\smile}_{+D} \text{ or } {}^{S\cdot}_{+D} = \overline{G\ B\ D\ F} \text{ (C major),}$$

$$\begin{matrix}\dot{S}\\+D\end{matrix} \text{ or } \begin{matrix}+T|\\-S\\+D\end{matrix} \text{ or } \begin{matrix}+T\cdot\\-S\\+D\end{matrix} = \overline{E\ G\sharp\ B\ D\ F\ A\ C\sharp} \text{ (A major).}$$

3) The third group comprises the combinations in which *the triad representing a single function has as its counterpart an interfunctional triad* (one that is itself a combination). We can designate such combinations by the symbols of the individual functions, in conjunction with the correspondingly precise symbol IN for interfunctions. The interfunction can of course be designated by the methods presented in §110 above. For example:

$$\begin{matrix}+D\\+M^4\end{matrix} \text{ or } \begin{matrix}+D\\-S\cdot\\+T\cdot\end{matrix} \text{ or } \begin{matrix}+D\\-S|\\+T|\end{matrix} = \overline{E\ G\sharp\ B\ D\ G} \text{ (C major),}$$

$$\begin{matrix}-S\\+M^2\end{matrix} \text{ or } \begin{matrix}-S\\+S\\-L:\end{matrix} \text{ or } \begin{matrix}-S\\+S\\-L\frown\end{matrix} = \overline{D\ F\sharp\ A\ C\ F\ A\flat} \text{ (C major).}$$

4) The fourth group comprises the combinations in which an *interfunctional triad is supplemented by individual pitches*. The designation is similar to that of the above groups. For example:

$$+\dot{M}^2 \text{ or } \begin{matrix}+S:\\+M^2\end{matrix} \text{ or } \begin{matrix}+S\frown\\+M^2\end{matrix} \text{ or } \begin{matrix}+S:\\-L:\end{matrix} \text{ or } \begin{matrix}+S\frown\\-L\frown\end{matrix} = \overline{D\ F\sharp\ A\ C} \text{ (C major).}$$

5) Finally, the fifth group comprises the combinations in which *no functional or interfunctional harmony is fully represented*. Thus these are chords *belonging to neither family*. (See §21 above.) For example:

$$\begin{matrix}+L:\\+S\cdot\\+T\cdot\end{matrix} \text{ or } \begin{matrix}+L\smile\\+S|\\+T|\end{matrix} = E\ A\ B\ D\sharp \text{ (C major).}$$

Functional specificity is greatest in the first group. In subsequent groups it decreases, so that the combinations in the fifth group can well be perceived as stacks of individual pitches without functional significance. We can reassure ourselves as to the functional significance of such combinations only from their harmonic surroundings, not from the chords themselves. This is because the different possible tonally functional interpretations are approximately equal in complexity, so we cannot find a functional interpretation that would be obviously simpler than the others and which we would then for this reason have to consider better than the more complex interpretations.

Chapter VIb – Harmonic Motion: Functions and their Combinations

§112. Functional Ambiguity of Dissonant Combinations

When we speak of the functional specificity in the first group of dissonant combinations (§111 above), this does not mean that such combinations are always free of functional ambiguity. We will verify this by a closer examination of the relations between the representative harmonies in the functional system of five members.

These harmonies can be combined into ten two-member dissonant combinations, ten three-member combinations, five four-member combinations, and only one five-member combination. Following is a summary of these combination possibilities:

a) Two-member combinations:

D	S	P	L	S	P	L	P	L	L
T	T	T	T	D	D	D	S	S	P

b) Three-member combinations:

S	P	L	P	L	L	P	L	L	L
D	D	D	S	S	P	S	S	P	P
T	T	T	T	T	T	D	D	D	S

c) Four-member combinations:

P	L	L	L	L
S	S	P	P	P
D	D	D	S	S
T	T	T	T	D

d) Five-member combination:

L
P
S
D
T

Each combination can be differentiated into several types according to the families of the triadic components. Two-member combinations can be differentiated in terms of family in four different ways:

+	+	−	−
+	−	+	−

267

With combinations of more members the number of ways of differentiating by family increases quickly. A considerable number of chord-types is thus formed, many of which are equivalent.

Diverse family structure cannot be mechanically prescribed for individual combinations. For example, we must consider that –D is an extremely rare function whose existence must be supported by its harmonic surroundings. In determining tonally functional ambiguity, which is our present task, the function –D can hardly be considered, so we will not deal with it. We will likewise eliminate +S in combination or connection with –T, –P in combination or connection with +T, and +L in combination or connection with –T.

We must eliminate the combinations $\genfrac{}{}{0pt}{}{-D}{-T}$, $\genfrac{}{}{0pt}{}{-D}{+T}$, and $\genfrac{}{}{0pt}{}{+S}{-T}$ because when they precede the tonic they encumber it with continuing imaginary pitches, thus depriving it of its tonic repose.

We eliminate the combinations $\genfrac{}{}{0pt}{}{-P}{+T}$ and $\genfrac{}{}{0pt}{}{+L}{-T}$ because they are incomplete combinations of $\genfrac{}{}{0pt}{}{+P}{+T}$ and $\genfrac{}{}{0pt}{}{-L}{-T}$ (D♭ F♭ A♭ C E G = A♭ D♭ E G C with F omitted, and C E♭ G B D♯ F♯ = G C E♭ F♯ B with D omitted); the differentiating pitch of the secondary functions P and L cannot at the same time be the differentiating pitch of the tonic, since it cannot function at the same time as a leading-tone demanding motion and as a stable pitch of the tonic. As a result of the above restrictions, we can also dismiss the two-member combinations $\genfrac{}{}{0pt}{}{-P}{+S}$ and $\genfrac{}{}{0pt}{}{+L}{-P}$ to connect them directly to either the major or the minor tonic.

Some combinations contain additional functions. For example, the combination $\genfrac{}{}{0pt}{}{-L}{T}$ contains the function +D, and $\genfrac{}{}{0pt}{}{+P}{T}$ contains the function –S:

$$\genfrac{}{}{0pt}{}{-L}{T} = \genfrac{}{}{0pt}{}{\genfrac{}{}{0pt}{}{-L}{+D}}{T} \qquad \genfrac{}{}{0pt}{}{+P}{T} = \genfrac{}{}{0pt}{}{\genfrac{}{}{0pt}{}{+P}{-S}}{T}$$

It is unnecessary to consider a combination as having more members if it can be interpreted as having fewer members. Many such reductions can be made. Seventeen chord-types can be interpreted in two or more different ways as combinations. We present only one example. The functions that can be omitted are shown in boxes. The five-member and four-member combinations represent a three-member combination.

$$\begin{array}{c} -L \\ +P \\ \boxed{-S} \\ \boxed{+D} \\ +T \end{array} = \begin{array}{c} -L \\ +P \\ \boxed{+D} \\ +T \end{array} = \begin{array}{c} -L \\ +P \\ \boxed{-S} \\ +T \end{array} = \begin{array}{c} -L \\ +P \\ +T^{23} \end{array}$$

We can now determine functional combinations whose members are differentiated by family. We present the following results:

---

86 Editor's note: In C, for example, C E G – G B D – F A♭ C – D♭ F A♭ – B D F♯ = C E G – D♭ F A♭ – B D F♯.

Chapter VIb – Harmonic Motion: Functions and their Combinations

a) Two-member combinations:

D + +	S + – –	P + + –	L + – –	S + –	P + –
T + –	T + + –	T + – –	T + + –	D + +	D + +

L + –	P + + –	L + + – –	L + – –
D + +	S + – –	S + – + –	P + + –

b) Three-member combinations:

S + – –	P + –	L + + – – –	P + + –	L +	L + – – –
D + + +	S + –	S + – + – –	D + + +	D +	P + + + –
T + + –	T + –	T + + + + –	T + – –	T +	T + + – –

P + + –	L + + – –	L + + – – –	L + – –
S + – –	S + – + –	P + + + + –	P + + –
D + + +	D + + + +	S + – + – –	D + + +

c) Four-member combinations:

P + –	L + +	L + – –	L +	L + + – – –
S + –	S + –	P + + –	P +	P + + + + –
D + +	D + +	S + + –	D +	S + – + – –
T + –	T + +	T + + –	T +	D + + + + +

d) Five-member combination:
L+
P+
S+
D+
T+

After this preparation we can finally examine tonally functional ambiguity. In the case of two-member combinations (easily grasped at a glance), ambiguity can be determined relatively easily. In the case of complex combinations, however, many interesting ambiguities may be overlooked. A reliable investigation is possible *with the help of general orientation schemes* (See § 3). For each combination group we work out the general orientation scheme on the basis of a concrete example. We then compare the results. If the schemes are identical, the functional combinations are interchangeable and thus *ambiguous*. We have already eliminated any identical schemes that would not signify ambiguity by reducing more complex combinations to simpler ones whenever possible.

We can read from the orientation schemes whether it is *possible to interchange functionally the triadic components in the combination*. This is possible in combinations that have fewer rotations than is normal for their chord-class; such a situation is perceptible in the orientation scheme provided that we include the complement, since the scheme of such a chord consists of two or more repeating components. For example, the scheme 21321(3) breaks into two groups 213. As the combination ${+L \atop +S}$ has just such a scheme, the triad +L can be considered +S, and vice versa. This increases the functional ambiguity of this combination.

Nineteen combinations are *free of functional ambiguity*, that is, they can be related to only one tonic. These are:

a) Two-member combinations:

$$\begin{array}{lll} -S & -P & -L \\ -T = 3221(4) & -S = 1313(4) & -P = 21222(3) \end{array}$$

b) Three-member combinations:

$$\begin{array}{lll} +S & -S & -S \\ +D = \text{neg. } 2232(3) & +D = \text{neg. } 1323(3) & +D = \text{neg. } 1332(3) \\ +T & +T & -T \end{array}$$

$$\begin{array}{lll} +P & -L & -L \\ +S = \text{neg. } 1313(4) & +S = \text{neg. } 232(5) & -S = \text{neg. } 132(6) \\ +T & +T & +T \end{array}$$

$$\begin{array}{lll} +L & -L & -L \\ +P = \text{neg. } 14(7) & -P = \text{neg. } 41(7) & -P = \text{neg. } 1232(4) \\ +T & -T & +D \end{array}$$

c) Four-member combinations:

$$\begin{array}{lll} +P & -P & +L \\ {+S \atop +D} = \text{neg. } 34(5) & {-S \atop +D} = \text{neg. } 31(8) & {+S \atop +D} = \text{neg. } 23(7) \\ +T & -T & +T \end{array}$$

Chapter VIb – Harmonic Motion: Functions and their Combinations

$$\begin{matrix}+L\\-S\\+D\\+T\end{matrix} = \text{neg. } 13(8) \qquad \begin{matrix}+L\\+P\\+S\\+T\end{matrix} = \text{neg. } 4(8) \qquad \begin{matrix}-L\\+P\\+S\\+T\end{matrix} = \text{neg. } 5(7)$$

d) Five-member combination:

+L
+P
+S = eleven-note chord
+D
+T

We see that freedom from ambiguity of tonal function increases as the number of members in the combination rises. Of 27 two-member combinations, only 3 are free from ambiguity; of 33 three-member ones there are 9, of 13 four-member ones 6, and finally the one five-member combination is free of ambiguity.

In the following table, we present a summary of *ambiguous* functional combinations. An orientation scheme is appended to each combination. All functional components are assumed to be complete. The combinations are organized according to chord-class, and within each class they are ordered according to the numerical order of their orientation schemes (or, in some cases, their negative schemes). In designating the combinations, the following ascending order of symbols is preserved, as before: T, D, S, P, L. For combinations whose triadic components can be interchanged, this fact is pointed out by arrows in both the functional symbol and the orientation scheme. A concrete example with a list of corresponding keys is appended to each group of two or three ambiguous combinations.

Summary of Ambiguous Dissonant Functional Combinations

Order	Functional combination		Orientation scheme	Example	Key
1)	−L +D	+P −S	143(4)	G B D F♯	C major C minor F♯ major F♯ minor
2)	+D −T	−S +T	1214(4)	C E♭ G B D	C minor G major
3)	+D +T	+S +T	1223(4)	C E G B D	C major G major
4)	+L +D	+P +S	3131(4)	D♯ F♯ B D G	C major F♯ major

Order	Functional combination		Orientation scheme	Example	Key
5)	−P −T	−L −T	12131(4)	C♯ E G♯ C E♭ G	C minor C♯ minor
6)	+P −T	−L +T	12221(4)	D♭ F A♭ C E♭ G	C minor D♭ major
7)	(−L −S)		12312(3)	F♯ B D F A♭ C	C major C minor F♯ major F♯ minor
8)	−S +D	−L +P	12321(3)	G B D F A♭ C	C major C minor F♯ major F♯ minor
9)	+P +T	+L +T	13121(4)	D♭ F A♭ C E G	C major D♭ major
10)	−P +L +D −S	−L +S	13212(3)	C♯ E G♯ B D G	C minor A♭ major D major
11)	(+P +D)	(+L +S)	21321(3)	D♭ F A♭ B D G	C major C minor F♯ major F♯ minor A♭ major D major
12)	+S +D	+L +P	22212(3)	G B D F A C	C major F♯ major
13)	ıP −S +D	−L +P +D	n. 1231(5)	B D G D♭ F A♭ C	C major C minor F♯ major F♯ minor
14)	−L −S +D	−L +P −S	n. 1321(5)	F♯ B D G C F A♭	C major C minor F♯ major F♯ minor
15)	−L +S +D	+L +P −S	n. 2321(4)	F♯ B D G C F A	C major F♯ major
16)	+L +D +T	−P −S −T	n. 3113(4)	E G C E♭/D♯ F♯ B D G	C major B minor

Chapter VIb – Harmonic Motion: Functions and their Combinations

Order	Functional combination				Orientation scheme	Example	Key
17)	+P +S +D		+L +P +D		n. 124(5)	A C F A♭ D♭ G B D	C major F♯ major
18)	+L −S +T		−P +D −T		n. 131(7)	F A♭ C E G B D♯ F♯	C major e minor
19)	−L −S −T	+L −S +D	−L +P +S		n. 133(5)	F A♭ C G E♭/D♯ F♯ B D	C minor C major F♯ major
20)	−L +P −S +D				n. 151(5)	D♭ F A♭ C G B D F♯	C major C minor F♯ major F♯ minor
21)	+P +D −T		+L +S +T		n. 231(6)	D♭ F A♭ C E♭ G B D	C minor A♭ major
22)	+L +S +D		+L +P +S		n. 233(4)	F A C D♯ F♯ B D G	C major F♯ major
23)	+P +D +T		−P −S +D		n. 331(5)	D♭ F A♭ C E G B D	C major C minor
24)	−L +P +T		−L −P −S +D		n. 15(6)	D♭ F A♭ C E G B D F♯	C major C minor
25)	−L +P −T	+L +P −S +D	−L +P +S +D		n. 51(6)	D♭ F A♭ C E♭/D♯ G B D F♯	C minor C major F♯ major
26)	−L −P −S −T		+L +P +D +T		neg. 1	C F A♭ D♭ F♭/E♯ E♭/D♯ F♯ B D G	C minor C major
27)	+L +P +S +D				n. 6(6)	D G B D♯ F♯ A♭ D♭ F A C	C major F♯ major

273

§113. Evaluating Functional Components According to their Tonal Significance, Disposition, and Representation

When determining the tonally functional ambiguity of functional combinations, we assume that the triadic components in the combination are equally important. However, we have already indicated by distinguishing between primary functions (T, D, S) and auxiliary functions (P, L) that they are not equal. That the auxiliary functions appear later in history justifies the conclusion that they are less significant.

There are considerable differences in average frequency of appearance (and thus also in significance) not only between primary and auxiliary functions as groups but also between individual functions. Setting aside the tonic as a function that does not impel harmonic motion, we can arrange the functions in approximately the following order, from those that appear more frequently and are more significant to those that are rarer and less significant:

$$D..S...P....L$$

The number of dots between the functional symbols indicates more or less difference in their significance.

If we also consider the family differentiation of functions we get approximately the following picture:

$$\begin{array}{c} -P \\ \boxed{+D..+S-S...+P}....+L..-D \\ -L \end{array}$$

Common and significant functions are shown inside the frame, while the rare ones are shown outside. The remoteness of the minor dominant is noteworthy, as we have said.

We emphasize that here we judge individual functions in their *direct relation to the tonic*. Harmonies that represent functions with little tonal significance also occur in relation to other harmonies than tonic; in such situations they are not at all rare. For example, B D♯ F♯ in C major, which in direct relation to the tonic represents the rare function +L, can be understood in relation to the interfunction E G B (–IN[4]) as a common applied +D. (See §117 below.)

We can further evaluate individual components of functional combinations *according to their concrete dispositions*. As emphasized earlier (in *Chapter IV*), components placed *lower* have *greater significance* than components placed higher. Also, a triadic component representing a particular function has a stronger effect when perceived as a *unit* than when its pitches are dispersed or pitches belonging to other functions are inserted between its pitches. Thus, if we want to emphasize a particular functional component in a complex chord, either we place it lowest, or at least we preserve the connections among its pitches while dispersing and intermingling the pitches of other functions.

Because of the importance of disposition, it is advisable, when possible, to write composite functional symbols in such order that their overall arrangement corresponds to the actual disposition. Thus we designate the six-note chord D♭ A♭ F B D G as $^{+D}_{+P}$ in C major but as $^{+P}_{+D}$ in F♯ (G♭) major.

We can emphasize the significance of the lowest component by expressing only this component functionally, while we indicate the other pitches of the chord, even those that represent a particular function, merely by dots. Thus we can express the example in C major given above simply as $+\ddot{P}$, in G♭ major as $+\ddot{D}$. This method of expression is especially appropriate where the upper pitches of the chord do not form a triad with a particular function.

In our considerations in §112 above, we assumed that functions in functional combinations are represented by complete triads. This need not be the case, however. Naturally, those functional components represented by only two pitches or even one pitch are less significant than those that are represented by complete triads. Thus the actual pitch representation of functions also plays a considerable role in the overall functional evaluation of a more complex chord.

We can evaluate every concretely arranged chord according to the three criteria described above – tonal significance, disposition, and representation. Evaluations may differ according to the different criteria. A functional component that is most significant in position may be only partially represented, while a much less significantly placed component is represented fully. Or a component significant because of its position may be remote in the functional hierarchy (for example, +L), while a common and familiar classical function (for example, +S) is made less significant by its position high in pitch space. Such factors are apparent from the functional designation. Thus from the symbol $^{+S}_{+L}$ we see that the absolutely more significant functional +L component +S is placed less advantageously than the component of little significance, +L. In supplementing functional symbols with dots we can take care that individual pitches added below are also indicated below. Thus in the chord F – D G B in C major we will write $+\underset{.}{D}$ rather than $+\dot{D}$. When the symbol is arranged in this way it is apparent that the value of the function +D is lessened.

After considering these matters, we might think that the ambiguity that we investigated in §112 above does not in fact exist. If a difference in disposition results in a difference in the functional conception of a complex chord, then there are no concrete chords whose functional conception is precisely the same. There are always differences in functional conception. For every chord, we can indicate the one of the various possible functional conceptions that fits most closely. But the tonally functional ambiguity resides precisely in the fact that from the various possible conceptions it is not necessary to simply choose the one that appears most natural, the one that suggests itself; a composer may avoid or contradict this most natural functional conception and proceed in the subsequent musical stream in some unexpected way. This was true in classical music, and it is equally true in new music.

Chapter VIc – Harmonic Motion: Function in Harmonic Progression

§114. Harmonic Motion between Functions

So far we have considered harmonic motion according to the general impression given by a chord progression. We have considered the *magnitude* of harmonic motion. Now that we have examined the functional aspect of chords, we can begin to consider the *quality* and *direction* of harmonic motion.

The *quality* of harmonic motion is determined by the *functions represented* by the chords in the progression. Two instances of partial harmonic motion with equal magnitude can differ considerably in quality, depending on the functions involved. (If function is not considered, this difference cannot be theoretically discerned; the difference in effect then seems inexplicable.) In an evaluation that ignores function, the successions of the chordal cross-sections in Example 154a

Example 154a

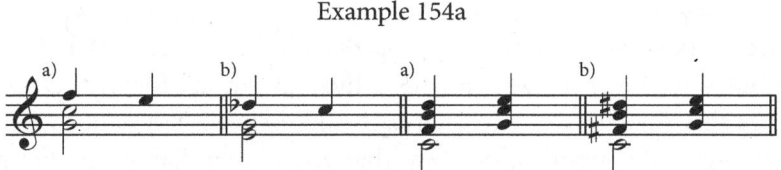

are of equal magnitude, as the only differences are in the sonic quality of the first cross-section (the second is always the same). However, cases *a* represent milder motion, while cases *b* are more extreme; *qualitative differences* are involved here, for which there seem to be no objective premises. If we understand the examples as if they were in C major, however, we see that in cases *a* components of primary functions (S, D) encroach upon the tonic C E G, while in cases *b* components of auxiliary functions (P, L) encroach upon the tonic – hence the differences in effect.

We reach the same conclusion by examining fundamental harmonic motion. In Example 154b,

Example 154b

progressions *a* have a milder effect than the corresponding progressions *b*; the difference in effect is again due to the functions, which are indicated by their symbols.

The differentiation of functions into primary (Pr) and auxiliary (Aux), as in §108 above, and the ordering of functions according to their tonal significance, as in §113 above, provide a basis for *judging the quality of harmonic motion*. We can say roughly that progressions Pr Pr and Aux Aux represent a qualitatively *lower level* of harmonic motion, while progressions Pr Aux or Aux Pr represent a *higher level*. A lower level of harmonic motion gives the impression of something inevitable, unaffected, smoothly flowing, etc. A higher level of harmonic motion conversely surprises us, making a stronger effect. There are also differences in effect within each level, even if they are not as pronounced. Progressions between various combinations $^{Aux}_{Pr}$ of primary and auxiliary functions represent an intermediate level of quality.

We cannot ignore those *unnatural progressions*, whose prototype is the progression D S, that have been tried by classical harmony. Even if the progression represents a lower level of harmonic motion, it still needs to be evaluated as motion whose effect approaches that of higher-level motion. However, the surprising effect of the progression D S, which classical composers tried to avoid, results from the *direction* of the motion rather than from the relation between the functions involved; if the progression D S is surprising or unnatural, its reverse in time, S D, is natural and unobtrusive.

Differences in the effect of harmonic progressions that are equivalent in motion can also be attributed to the *pitch-systems* from which chords are formed. Common experience teaches that the effect of two chords in succession is smoother when these are formed from pitches belonging to the same diatonic system than when they are formed from pitches belonging to different diatonic (or other) systems. The difference between diatonic and chromatic harmonic progressions is of course simply the difference between progressions Pr Pr and Pr Aux or perhaps Aux Pr.

Besides quality, in evaluating harmonic motion we can also speak of a particular *functionally harmonic direction of motion*. Since the tonic is the center of the functional system, with the other functions grouped around it such that they gravitate toward it as the harmonic area of rest, we need to distinguish between harmonic motion directed toward and motion directed away from the tonic. Even in harmonic motion that bypasses the tonic, the direction of the motion makes conspicuous differences in effect. It suffices to recall the difference in effect between the progressions S D and D S.

According to the direction of harmonic motion, we can speak of

a) *resolution*,

b) *connection*, and

c) *transfer*.

By *resolution* we mean harmonic motion directed *toward the tonic*. If we proceed from a single function to the tonic (e.g., G B D – C E G, D T), we speak of a *simple resolution*; in a progression from a functional combination to the tonic (for example, G B D F A – C E G, Ḋ T) we consider the resolution to be *compound*. Finally, if the tonic is complicated in the process of resolution, we speak of an *harmonically imperfect* resolution (for example, G B D – C E G A, D Ṫ).

By the resolution of a *lower* or the *first level* we mean a progression from a primary function or a compound of primary functions to the tonic (for example, F A C D – C E G, Ṡ T); we speak of the resolution of a *higher* or the *second level* whenever auxiliary functions are also involved, to whatever extent (for example, F A C D♯ – C E G, $^{+L}_{+S}$ T).

Although it is possible to reach the tonic through a simple resolution of the second level, as in the progressions P T or L T, after such a resolution the tonic is not stable enough. The tonic is much better reinforced if the chord that resolves into it contains at least some elements of the primary functions D or S. We can call the resolution P T or L T a *weakened* resolution, because the absence of primary non-tonic functions weakens resolution.

By *connection* we mean a progression *to some other function than the tonic*; the starting point may be the tonic itself.[87] A connection is *simple* if both chords involved are *single functions*; if either of the connected chords is a *functional compound*, we speak of a *compound* connection. We refer to a connection of a *lower* or the *first level*, if it involves only primary or only auxiliary functions (for example, S D, T S, or P L); otherwise we are dealing with a connection of a *higher* or *second level* (for example, P D).

A *transfer* is a special type of compound connection. In a transfer we proceed from a complex and hence functionally compound chord to a simpler chord that forms part of the preceding more complex chord (often to a simple function or an interfunctional harmony). At the same time, harmonic imaginary pitches from the first chord generally interfere with the second (simpler) chord, so that often the first chord is essentially merely repeated in composite expression. For example, in the connection G B D F – G B D (Ḋ D in C major), the four-note first chord is transferred to a real triad; however, the triad represents the original four-note chord, since the F cannot be securely cancelled by the G. An example of a transfer in modern harmony is the progression from

---

87 Editor's note: Janeček explains here that *spojení*, "connection", is also used more broadly to refer to any chord succession. However, in English we can restrict the use of *connection* to this narrow meaning of progression to another function than tonic.

the combination harmony **+6+** to any one of its triadic components, for example, from G B D D♭ F A♭ to G B D.

A transfer, which is always compound, can be of the first (lower) or the second (higher) level, according to whether it involves only primary or only auxiliary functions, or both types of functions together.

If resolution gives an impression of relaxation or easing of motion, and connection gives an impression of harmonic change with continuing tension (whether greater or lesser), transfer gives an impression of *harmonic cessation*; a transfer does not disrupt or change any tension that is already present. The term *transfer* was proposed by Otakar Šín, who also defined the concepts of resolution and connection. According to other theorists, it is also possible to speak of resolution to a function other than tonic. We will return to this matter in §117 below.

Resolution and connection can be effected by both fundamental and partial harmonic motion. Transfer usually involves only partial harmonic motion, since partial harmonic motion represents modifications of the same harmony, complete or incomplete.

Resolution, connection, and transfer are illustrated in the following diagram.

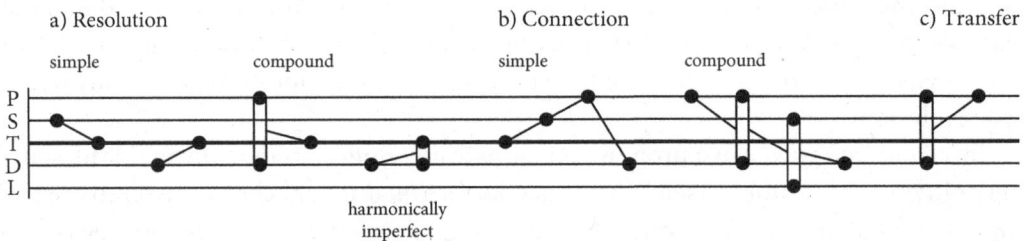

Each function is shown by a horizontal line. Chords of single functions are represented by circles; for compound functions, these circles are joined by two vertical lines. Harmonic motion is indicated by slanted lines.

Example 155 presents harmonic motion in musical notation with functions indicated

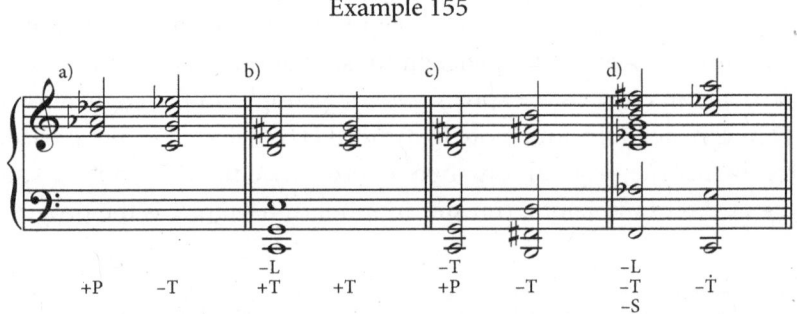

Example 155

Chapter VIc – Harmonic Motion: Function in Harmonic Progression

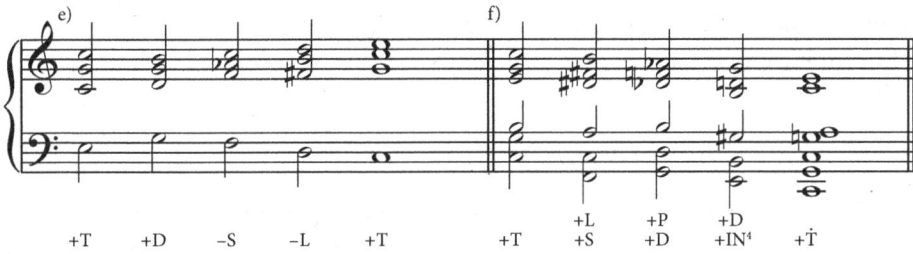

Notes. In Example 155a the resolution is second-level. An awareness of the tonic must be created here by preceding or subsequent chord progressions. As isolated here, the progression D♭ F A♭ – C E♭ G can have a different functional meaning, for example +S –IN³ in A♭ major; then it is no longer a resolution, but a connection. In Example 155b there is partial harmonic motion, a triple rising appoggiatura. In 155c the same six-note chord is resolved in B minor; since the lower voices move, we can call this fundamental harmonic motion. [See §93 above.] In 155d the resolution is harmonically imperfect since the tonic C E♭ G is complicated by the real pitch A; it would be possible to consider this isolated progression a connection in a different key, with the chords having different functional meanings. In 155e all the chords represent single functions, and so they all form simple connections. The cadential resolution is of a higher level. In contrast to 155a, however, the tonic is securely established by the preceding primary functions. The effect of the unnatural or at least unclassical progression +D –S is not inappropriate here, because the very rare simple function –L is used. In 155f, all the chords represent compound functions. The cadential resolution is harmonically imperfect, but after the clear functional meaning of the preceding chords this does not matter.

§115. The Functional Aspect of Chords in a Chord Succession

In §113 above we evaluated functional components of isolated functionally combined harmonies. Already there we could judge chords according to different criteria. In the case of a chord incorporated into a continuous chord succession, the kinetic functional principle, which may or may not be in agreement with the other criteria, comes into play. Here again the *requirement of the simplest possible interpretation* applies. This requirement can be broken down into two component requirements, as follows:

1) We should consider as simpler, and thus more correct, that functional conception of a chord succession in which the *largest number of chords can be subordinate to a single tonic*. Thus for a succession of chords we try to find a functional interpretation in which all the chords represent single functions or functional compounds belonging to a single functional system, for example, to the system in which the last harmony in the series is the tonic. Greater complexity makes a different interpretation, according to which some of the harmonies are subordinate to a different tonic (that is, belong to a transposed functional system), less appropriate if not incorrect.

2) We should further consider as simpler that functional interpretation of a chord succession in which successions of consecutive chords are perceived as *the most common and most intelligible functional progressions*. Thus if it is possible to interpret the progression G B D – C E G as a resolution (D T in C major), we should accept this in-

terpretation instead of some other possible but more complex one (for example IN_2 IN^3 in A minor). The more common the functions in a chord succession, the simpler its interpretation will be.

These two component requirements cannot always be met at the same time. Behind every theoretical interpretation, including the functional one, stands a definite reality, a definite effect and perception. In forming a functional interpretation of a chord succession, it is important to investigate whether, and to what extent, an objectively traceable *awareness of the tonic* has been created and preserved. It makes no sense to perceive a chord in a functional relation to a particular tonic if the awareness of this tonic has been lost, whether or not the tonic has been replaced with another.

An awareness of the tonic is created:

a) by introducing the tonic in a significant place within a harmonic phrase (e.g., at the beginning), emphasizing it (e.g., by length, by prolongation), and following this introduction with a progression of non-tonic chords that strengthen, preserve, or at least do not disturb the sense of the tonic; and

b) by selecting successive non-tonic chords that reliably gravitate toward the tonic; the tonic itself may, although it need not, follow this succession; the introduction of the tonic confirms the concentrated gravitating force of the preceding chords.

When creating an awareness of the tonic by the latter method, we must differentiate between cases where the expected, although not sounded, tonic is defined unambiguously by a chord succession, and cases where the expected tonic can be realized in two or more different ways, *where the chord succession can be directed just before the cadence equally well toward various tonics*. In the latter cases, we can hardly speak of actually creating "an awareness of the tonic". We thus come to the second important reality that forms the foundation of tonally functional harmonic thought – the fact that non-tonic chords are the bearers of *kinetic tension*. If sometimes we cannot state that a particular series of chords has created a definite awareness of the tonic, we must be content with the discovery that the chords contain kinetic tension in themselves, that they gravitate toward a tonic that is unknown to us and objectively indeterminable. (See the following musical examples.)

The *dying away of a sense of the tonic* is related to the indefiniteness of a tonic that has not yet been introduced. The following simple precept applies here: the more complex the harmony and the more extreme the sound of the surrounding music, the more fragile, the more easily lost, will be the awareness of the tonic. A sense of the tonic is more easily lost when the tension of the chords is increased. When this tension is later eliminated by a resolution to a chord that can serve as a suitable tonic for one or two immediately preceding chords, it no longer matters whether this tonic is inappropriate for other chords farther removed in time; if any sense of a tonic had been created by these more distant chords, it has been lost as a result of the subsequent complex chords.

Let us return to the starting point of our commentary. In successions of complex chords with rich sounds and considerable kinetic tension, it is impossible to subordinate to one tonic passages that are too long, even if the theoretical interpretation of the functional relations involved might appear simpler. In such cases it is wiser to comprehend shorter passages, perhaps even just pairs of chords, as functionally separate, if this achieves a simpler interpretation based on simpler and more common functions. Only in harmonically moderate music can we draw together longer successions of chords under the rule of one tonic, since here there is no danger of having a speculatively construed interpretation unsupported by a real sense of a tonic.

Therefore, in harmonically complex music the tonally functional aspect of chords does not have the same role as in uncomplicated music that flows in simple, transparent chords. It is nevertheless advisable to consider the functional aspect of such complex music, even if the investigation often results only in the realization that certain passages of the music are not conceived functionally.

After these general considerations let us examine concrete examples. We will start with the seven-note chord F C A E♭ B D G in a fixed disposition, which we will incorporate into a series of other complex chords.

Example 156

In the first four successions (Example 156A), our seven-note chord is placed next-to last, immediately before the tonic; in the next four successions (156B) it is third from the end, so there is a chord between it and the final tonic. Considerably complex chords have been used most of the time. In all cases, the final tonic is convincing, that is, we feel no need for further harmonic motion. We can see from the functional symbols that the final tonic is established not merely by means of the penultimate chord, but also to a considerable extent by some of the other chords. Naturally, primary functions play the decisive role here, whether they are obvious as triads, hidden in interfunctions, or present as individual dispersed pitches.

Great attentiveness is necessary in examining the functional aspect of the successions in Example 156. It is therefore important that aural verification be carried out "with a fresh mind"; playing through the examples too quickly or for too long tends to dull attentiveness, decreasing our ability to assess critically even the sonic effect, much less the tonally functional effect.

We can experiment with these examples by interchanging the first segments (a) and or the second segments (b) from different successions in Example 156. Most of the time, the final tonic is convincing even after such an exchange. This proves that the functional aspect of complex chords is not so significant. (We have intentionally used dispositions in which component triads are separated from each other and stand out from the overall sound; such dispositions emphasize the functionality of the chords.) If a chord is functionally too remote from the tonic, some other chord will be in a favourable position in relation to this tonic. After exchanging segments, however, the functional comprehension of the chords in the first segment (a) must be adapted to the new tonic of the second segment (b).

It is useful to notice the differences between the functional meaning of each chord in relation to the tonic and the most appropriate ("natural") function of the same chord when isolated. Sometimes there will be agreement, sometimes not. Discrepancies in interpretation point to the functionally decentralizing effect of such a chord in the succession. Thus the second chord in succession B3 (E♭ C G♭ E♭ C E♭ A♭) has a non-tonic function when isolated, most probably +D (in D♭ major), although in relation to the tonic A♭ C E♭ it was properly interpreted as a complication of the tonic. In contrast, the second chord in succession A2 has the natural function $^{+P}_{+D}$ both in isolation and in the given succession.

All the examples were constructed so as to avoid diatonic progressions; therefore, cross-relations, such as B♭–B in different voices between the third and fourth chords of A1, are frequent and not a problem here. In predominantly diatonic (and thus generally also harmonically simple) successions, cross-relations will have an unexpected and sometimes even unpleasant effect.

§116. Unitonal, Bitonal, and Polytonal Combinations

The functional combinations with which we have been dealing so far have all been constructed from functional components belonging to one functional system, one key – they have been *unitonal*. In looking for the simplest functional interpretation it is sometimes helpful to go beyond this limitation. Sometimes it is easier to discern the functional essence of a chord succession by breaking it down into two or more simultaneous functional successions belonging to different (transposed) functional systems. By using two or more systems, we will explain a given succession as *bitonal* (involving two keys) or *polytonal* (involving more than two keys). We will thus understand individual chords as *bitonal* or *polytonal functional combinations*. A dividing line running usually through several compound functional symbols will indicate that individual components belong to different functional systems (keys).

Chord successions arranged as in Example 157 sometimes appear in new music. The concluding tonics of the successions can serve as clues toward establishing the functional meaning of individual chords. The functional aspect of the chord successions appears much simpler, however, if we divide each into two zones and determine an independent functional progression for each. We will thus be able to express the functions in each of these zones very simply; each zone will of course be in its own key, that is, in a different functional system. For the final progression to the tonic we must return to the original unitonal conception.[88]

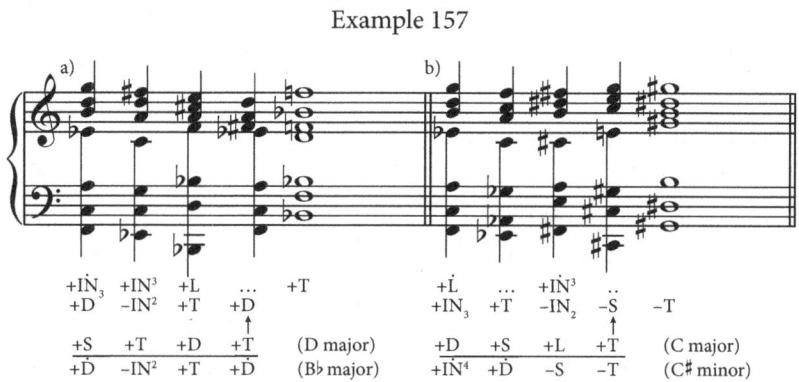

Example 157

The individual chord zones can be played and examined separately. The functional aspect of each component chord is clear. When both zones sound concurrently, however, the functional aspect becomes so complex that we can follow the individual zones only with the aid of dynamic, and possibly also colour, shading; we then follow the zone that is presented more strongly, while the functional aspect of the other zone easily escapes us.

Fully *polytonal* progressions can occur only very rarely, since they presuppose chords that are too complex. Polytonality is more likely to appear in the form of several concurrent zones that are harmonically incomplete or fragmentary, most probably as several melodies not provided with harmony, each of which is in a different key. The functional aspect of the zones is of course most indefinite. The overall impression is probably one of non-functionality. With a suitable disposition of the melodies and with sufficiently contrasting keys the tonal differentiation of the zones can be followed quite well.

As an example of polytonality, we present a passage of three melodies, each of which is created within a different (transposed) diatonic system: the first in D major, the second in E♭ major, and the third in C major.[89]

---

88 Editor's note: The first analysis under each example is the unitonal analysis, in B♭ major for the first progression, in G♯ minor for the second one.
89 The outer voices are from a short composition called *Smutná píseň* [Sad Song] from my 1947 cycle of light piano pieces *Žertem i vážně* [In Fun and Earnestness] (Praha: Melantrich, 1948). The middle voice was added. The dynamic shading of the voices is important here.

Example 158

The chordal aspect is relatively simple, and the disposition of all the chords is good. Cross-relations are characteristic here. The cross-relations between F and F♯ in the outer voices are especially conspicuous, because these pitches create an interval 1 in a bad disposition (as a ninth). Even such a cross-relation is justified, however, if it is emphasized by several repetitions. (Cf. §73 above.)

§117. Local Tonics[90] and Applied Functions

When we discussed harmonic motion between functions (in §114 above), we allowed the *possibility of an imperfect harmonic resolution*; by this we meant a resolution to a complicated, impure tonic burdened by non-tonic elements. We assumed that the tonic character of such a more complex harmony of resolution was preserved by the predominance of tonic components, and that the harmonic surroundings gravitated toward this tonic. Such an impure or complicated tonic can never be the "island of rest" that every tonic ought to be; rather, it has the inner tension characteristic of non-tonic functions. Harmonies that gravitate toward such a tonic nevertheless do subordinate themselves to it, as they would to a pure consonant tonic without inner tension. Thus we can speak not only of dissonant chords (with inner tension) or consonant chords (with outer tension) gravitating toward consonances that are without tension, but also of chords (whether consonant or dissonant) with kinetic tension gravitating *toward dissonances*. A succession of two dissonances, or of a consonance to a dissonance, does not necessarily therefore represent a *connection*, but may under certain circumstances represent a *resolution*, albeit one that is harmonically imperfect.

As a condition for acknowledging the predominantly tonic character of a more complex (dissonant) chord we must require that the surrounding chords "acknowledge" this tonic. In practice this means that the *functional interpretation* attributing the role of a tonic to a dissonant harmony, sonically imperfect, must be *simpler and more intelligible* than an interpretation based on the strict requirement of a pure consonant tonic.

The subordination of chords to a tonic that is sonically imperfect can be not only symbolized and theoretically explained, but also felt. Thus a succession of two dissonant

---

90 Editor's note: The phenomena in this section are often described as *tonicization* by other theorists, especially relating to Schenkerian analysis.

chords of which the first obviously gravitates toward the second cannot be considered a mere connection, that is, a neutral succession giving the effect of mere harmonic change, but rather a resolution (although harmonically imperfect), that is, a *goal-oriented progression*.

The possibility of progression from a non-tonic chord to a complicated tonic opens the way to *simplifying the theoretical interpretation* of chord successions in which the direct relation of individual chords to the final tonic is too complex, in which the final tonic is too remote. If the direct relation to the tonic is complex, it can often be replaced with a simple *indirect* relation via a chord situated closer (ideally the chord immediately following); although this chord retains its original function in relation to the final tonic, it also temporarily acquires a different, most often tonic, function. In contrast to the final tonic, we call such a temporary tonic a *local* tonic. This is not a definitive tonic in the usual sense, since it is *subordinate to the principal tonic*, in relation to which it keeps a non-tonic function.

The chord that we relate functionally to a local tonic eludes the rule of the principal tonic – it does not belong to the principal key. Thus we refer to it as *outside the key*, or *applied*.[91] As a rule applied harmonies have one of the *primary non-tonic functions*, or, in more complex cases, a primary non-tonic function at least plays a predominant role. Classical harmony knew only applied dominants. We can also speak of applied subdominants, however, and of the most diversely combined functions.

According to the system introduced by H. Riemann, and preserved in Czechoslovakia by O. Šín, the function of the chord preceding a local tonic is shown in parentheses. Thus we express the classical progression A C♯ E – D F A – G B D – C E G functionally as follows:

$$(+D) - IN^2 + D + T.$$

The function in parentheses refers to the harmony immediately following, which is understood as a local tonic.

When combinations of functions are involved, the functional relation of the applied harmony toward the part of the following functionally compound chord that represents the local tonic will be shown by an arrow, as in Example 159.

---

91 Editor's note: As was mentioned already in the Editor's note, although Janeček uses only the first term, *mimotonální*, we introduce the more common English term *applied*.

Example 159

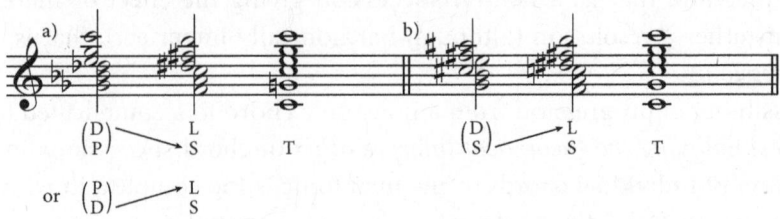

The first interpretation in this example is obviously better, since it relates the applied function to the determinant (the more significant component) of the subsequent compound formation. (See §68 above.)

After an applied chord we can introduce a *harmony other than the corresponding local tonic*, with a possible complication. For example, the progression A C♯ E – G B D – C E G represents D S in D major and D T in C major; the harmony G B D, as the dominant in relation to the final (principal) tonic, also has a temporary subdominant function (in D major). Thus the local tonic is not even heard here. In the normal use of an applied function there are at least two chords outside the key, since the local tonic is also outside the key, belonging to the key in which it is the tonic. Here, however, this second chord outside the key has a non-tonic function. Such a case must then be expressed as follows:

$$\begin{array}{c} D\ T \\ (D\ S) \end{array}$$

A local tonic can be preceded by *more than one chord* that resists direct relation to the principal tonic. We then write the applied functions of these chords inside one set of parentheses. For example, we write the functions of the triadic succession G B♭ D – A C♯ E – D F A – G B D – C E G as follows:

$$(-S +D) -IN^2 +D +T$$

If an applied harmony is followed by a local tonic that is itself an applied non-tonic harmony in relation to the following harmony, we must write separate parentheses for each applied harmony. For example, in the succession E G♯ B – A C♯ E – D F A – G B D – C E G we must write:

$$(+D)\ (+D)\ -IN^2\ +D\ +T$$

Finally we present two harmonically more complex examples with applied functions. In Example 160a, applied chords are strung together in a chain of applied functions; in 160b, the chords proceed in two functional zones (bitonally) and only at the cadence unite in a joint approach to the principal tonic.

Example 160

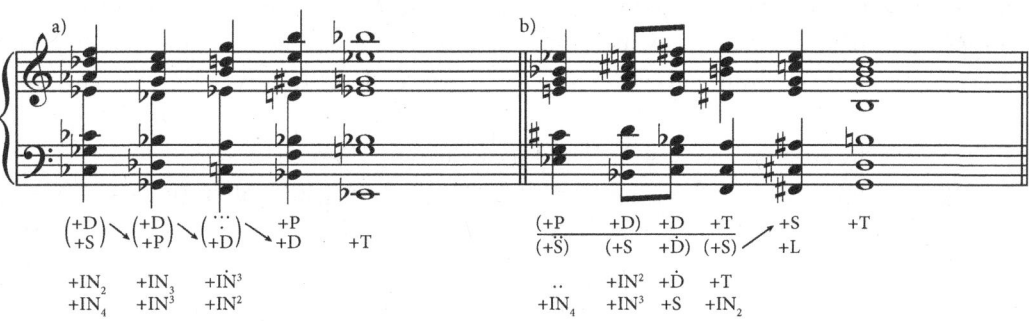

In order to show why it is advantageous here to conceive the chords as applied, we have added a functional interpretation in which the chords are related directly to the principal (final) tonic. The excess of interfunctions in this interpretation demonstrates that a direct relation to the principal tonic is too complex. Also, our musical (non-theoretical) perception does not correspond to such an interpretation.

We can see from the overall effect of the two examples that a unitonal (a) as opposed to a bitonal (b) conception of chords makes no substantial difference in musical effect. This is related to the fact that the functional aspect of complex chords does not have nearly the significance it had in the simpler sounding chords of classical harmony.

§118. Alteration[92] of Functions

In §109 above we mentioned the possibility of a minor dominant. In comparison to the normal dominant, which fully conforms to the principle of the pure tonic, the minor dominant appears as an *altered* formation, whose distinctive feature is its *nonconformance to the principle of the pure tonic*.

We form an alteration by a chromatic change of one of the pitches. Not every such change results in an altered function, however. In the case of the dominant, for example, G B D in C major, an alteration can be formed only by lowering the differentiating pitch B to B♭; semitone changes of the other pitches combine the dominant with other functions, possibly transforming the original dominant function, as in the following example of the dominant

$$\text{G B D in C major: F} \sharp \text{ B D} = -\text{L, G} \sharp \text{ B D} = {}^{+D:}_{-S:}, \text{ G B D} \flat = {}^{P.}_{+D:}, \text{ G B D} \sharp = {}^{+L.}_{+D:}.$$

In C major only the B♭ is a component of no other function than dominant (the minor dominant, of course).

---

92 Editor's note: Janeček uses the narrower term *deformation* to differentiate between chromatically altering a function (*deformation*) and chromatically altering any tone in the tonality. Keeping in mind that in this section, alterations of functions are discussed, we decided to stay with the now deep-rooted term alteration even for the narrower meaning.

Analogous to altering the dominant is *altering the subdominant*. Here a chromatic change of the differentiating pitch is again involved, although this time from its normal minor to the major, for example, in C minor from F A♭ C to F A C. If this altered triad proceeds directly to a minor tonic (+S −T), the principle of the pure tonic is violated, too.

Although the auxiliary functions P and L can also be altered (to +P in the minor and −L in the major) without infringing on any other functions, such alterations are meaningless, since in relation to the tonic they create no new effects. This is because the normal functions P and L already violate the principle of the pure tonic. (See §108 above.)

Thus in practice there are only two altered functions: −D in the major and the minor, and +S in the minor. These are the only cases in which other functions do not become involved, and which, in contrast to their normal form, violate the principle of the pure tonic.

An alteration violates not only the principle of the pure tonic; if these altered functions proceed directly to the tonic (if they are resolved), the principle of the leading tone is also rendered inactive. In the resolution of a −D to a major tonic, or of a +S to a minor tonic, none of the voices can proceed by a semitone (G B♭ D − C E G, F A C − C E♭ G).

The altered functions −D and +S can be useful in

a) a direct relation to the tonic as an effective means of loosening tonal cohesion (further see §120 below), or

b) in an applied relation to a local tonic.

In the second case the altered applied functions can fit into the pitch-system of the principal key and thus help strengthen tonal cohesion. For example, the altered applied dominant of the dominant in C major is D F A, which is at the same time the interfunction $-IN^2 = \frac{+S:}{+D.}$; the normal applied dominant of the dominant in C major, D F♯ A, does not fit into the C major pitch-system.

For a general designation of altered functions, we suggest lower-case letters: d, s.[93] When these are applied altered functions, we place the symbols in parentheses: (d), (s). We then expect the next chord to represent the local tonic. If an altered applied function is used in such a way that the pitch-system representing the principal key is not disturbed, this can be expressed as T——(d)——D; in cases where the pitch-system of the principal key *is* disturbed, the connecting lines on both sides of the parentheses are omitted. The triadic series C E G − E G B − A C E − D F A − G B D − C E G in C major can then be expressed as T——(d)——(d)——(d)——D T. Similarly, the progression F A C − C E G − G B D − D F A − A C♯ E in A major will be expressed by (S) (S) (s) −S +T.

Only the triad G B D appears as an altered subdominant, since only this triad is followed by a minor harmony.

---

93 Editor's note: We will have to remember that while d represents the minor dominant, s represents the *major* subdominant in the minor mode.

Interfunctions $-IN^2$ in the major and $+IN_2$ in the minor occur most frequently as altered applied functions ($-IN^2$ as d, $+IN_2$ as s). Other interfunctions can also be used this way, however, as shown in Example 161.

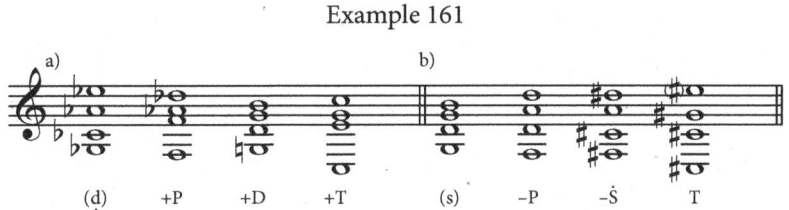

Example 161

Instead of the designation (s) $-P$ in the second segment we can also write $(T\ {-P \atop d})$, since the function d occurs with incomparably greater frequency than s.

In modern music altered functions also occur in functional combinations. An interpretation in which we resort to altered functions (whether isolated or in combinations) seems simpler than an interpretation in which altered functions are perceived as neutral interfunctions.

Example 162 presents altered functions in combinations. A functional interpretation is included with each succession of chords. The component symbols d and s can of course be replaced by the symbols $-D$ and $+S$, and possibly also by the symbol IN with specific family and interval designations.

Example 162

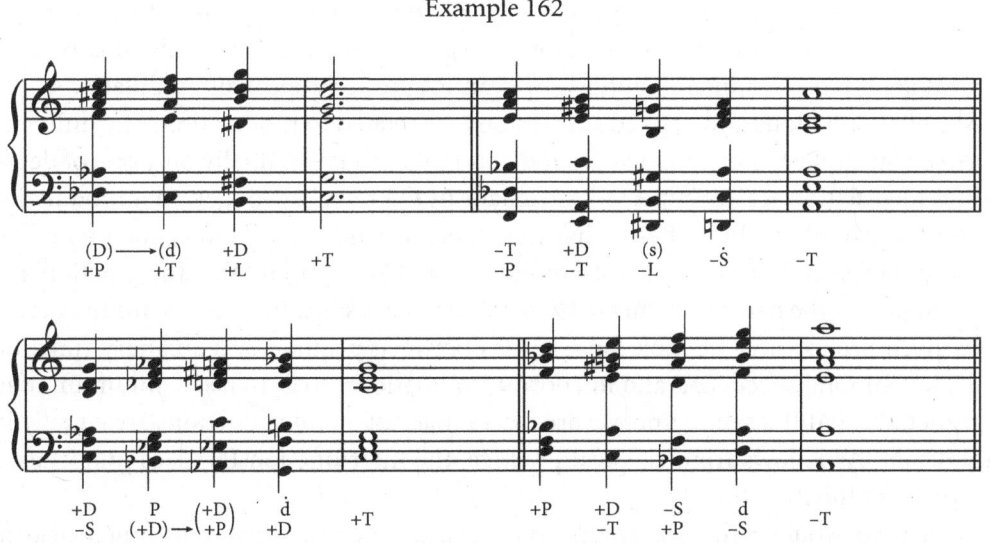

Altered functions are significant primarily when they occur in isolation, rather than in combinations. This is especially true of altered functions that proceed directly to the tonic, because in combinations the tonal decentralization of the altered function can be balanced by other functions. Thus +D or −S can be used to balance d, as we see in the last two segments of Example 162; the cadences are convincing here precisely because of the functions that have not been altered.

§119. Modulation

A harmonic passage with a definite, unambiguous, unchanging tonic cannot last very long. An important aspect of the effect of chord successions is the way they create and strengthen an awareness of the tonic; as soon as an awareness of the tonic is created and strengthened, further functional "striving" of the chords loses its *raison d'être*. Thus *modulation*, the passing to another key and the formation of another tonally functional center, belongs among the indispensable devices of any widely developed harmonic passage that is functionally conceived.

In §97 above we spoke of *higher-ranked harmonic motion*, which we also called *tonal* motion. Higher-ranked harmonic motion and modulation are not identical. Higher--ranked harmonic motion concerns a conspicuous chord succession whose effect overrides less significant surrounding chord successions; it does not matter whether an awareness of a new tonic (remote in relation to the musical stream so far) is created at the same time. In modulation, what matters is the *creation of a new tonal center*, a new tonic, regardless of whether this is accomplished by a conspicuous succession or by one that is unobtrusive, similar to others appearing within the framework of the same key.

It follows from this distinction that modulation in the true sense of the word can occur only in functionally unambiguous music. Unless functional relations between chords are established unambiguously, we cannot properly speak of modulations.

Applied functions and applied successions are related to modulation. The difference between an applied chord succession and a modulation is essentially only one of degree – in a modulation we are expected to remain in the new key longer; in a modulation, a non-tonic or altogether different harmony becomes not a *local* tonic, but a *tonic*.[94] As with applied chord successions, with modulations it is important that the functional interpretation of the harmonic phrase be as simple as possible. In practice this means that in a given progression we look for relations between primary and auxiliary functions both in temporal succession and in chord combinations, so as to use a minimum of interfunctions. (At the same time, we are aware that not all interfunctions are equally insignificant. As follows from classical practice, the interfunction IN^2 is as important as the primary function S.)

Just as we would rather interpret certain chords in a progression of complex chords as applied, and sometimes even resort to a bitonal interpretation (see §116 above), we

---

94 Editor's note: In commonly used terms, here is described the difference between *tonicisation* and *modulation*.

also give precedence to changes of tonal center (modulations) if they result in simpler or more intelligible functional relations.

It is natural that an awareness of the tonic is created when the tonic is actually sounded, if possible in its pure form as a consonance, not harmonically weakened. We see this from the way that tonal stability in chord progressions not beginning with the tonic is achieved only with the introduction of the tonic, albeit belated. However, the tonic can also be defined exclusively by non-tonic functions and their various combinations, in which the tonic is as a rule at least partially involved. Even in a modulation, although it is good if the tonic of the new key is introduced, it is not essential. A modulation without a resolution to the new tonic will be less definite; the new tonal center will be merely assumed.

A modulation in which the new tonic is realized can be illustrated as follows:

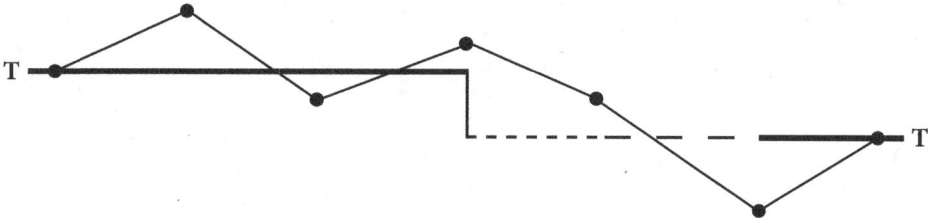

The horizontal line represents the tonic, and the points outside the horizontal line represent non-tonic functions (and at times also their combinations, in which the tonic can be partially involved). The moment when the sense of the original tonic is lost is indicated by the vertical line, and the gradual formation of awareness of a new tonic is indicated by the new horizontal line, dotted at first, then dashed, and finally solid.

A modulation in which the new tonic is not realized in its pure form can be illustrated as follows:

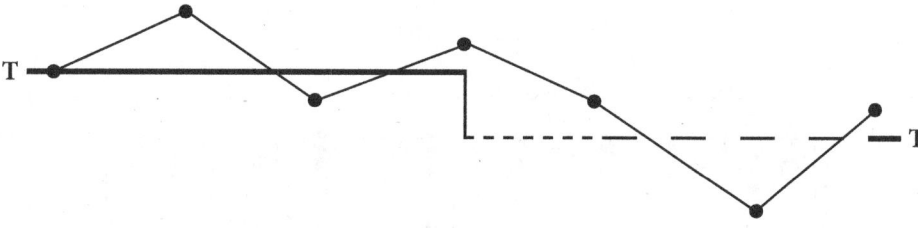

Here the sense of the new tonic is not confirmed. We are conscious of the tonic only from the context of the non-tonic chords that are sounded. Nevertheless, it is possible to follow even such a modulation with another modulation, that is, to abandon the sense of a tonic which has never been sounded.

Example 163 presents both types of modulation.

Example 163

a) Modulation from D major to B minor with real asserted pure tonics

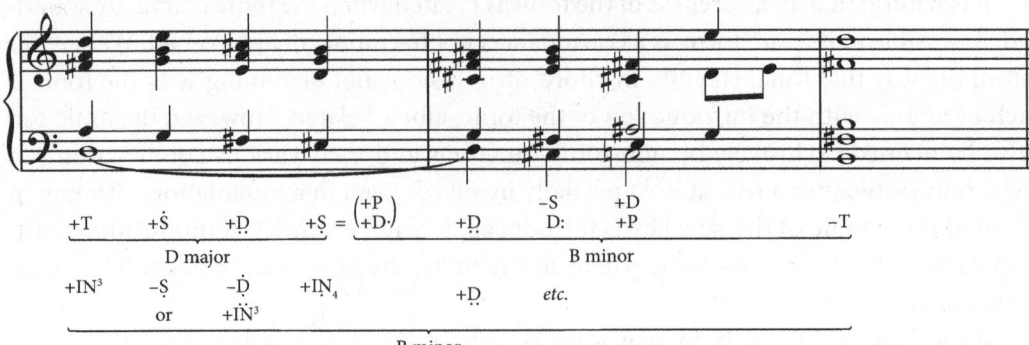

b) Modulation from D major to B minor without real asserted pure tonics

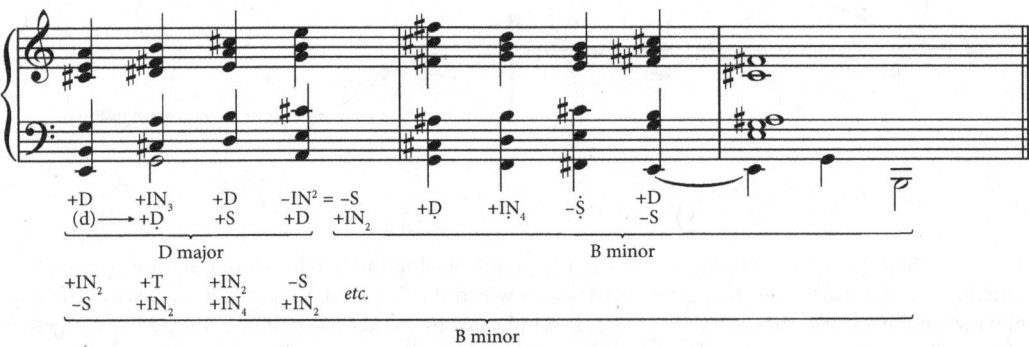

In 163a and 163b modulation is to the most closely related key. The revaluation of a function is shown in the functional interpretation by an equal sign. The second functional interpretation is constructed in relation to the second key (B minor) in order to show that the modulating interpretation is simpler.

Example 164 shows a modulation to a more remote key.

Example 164

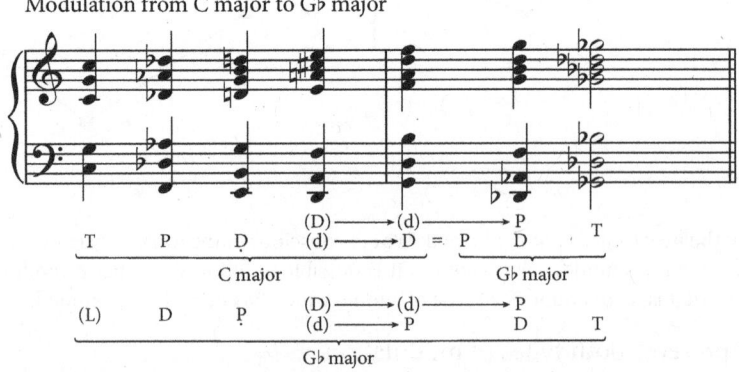

Again two functional interpretations are shown, one that includes a modulation and one that does not. The appliedsuccession (L) D at the start of the second interpretation of our example can also be perceived as $\frac{D}{(T\ P)}$, which makes the second functional interpretation more like the first.

Classical harmony devotes a great deal of attention and care to the problem of modulation. However, as we indicated earlier, in newer music the functional aspect of chords in a succession does not play as great a role as in classical music, and this means that modulation will play a substantially smaller role. What does remain effective, directly affecting the listener, is higher-ranked harmonic motion. Modulation is often significant only as a simplifying device in a functional interpretation, if a reliable functional interpretation is even possible.

§120. Loosening Tonally Functional Relations

The functional significance of chords in a harmonic phrase, and the tonal relations between them, are determined by the principle of the pure tonic, the principle of the leading tone, and the functional principle which is founded on the other two (see §99–103 above). Strict observance of these principles strengthens and clarifies the functional significance of chords and thus increases the cohesion and concentration of the entire harmonic phrase. In contrast, every deviation from the requirements of these principles represents greater or lesser tonal loosening; to this is related the greater (or even complete) ambiguity of the functional significance of individual chords.

On the historical road toward strengthening tonality, the representative pre-tonic harmonies of the three member functional system (see §107 above) were sought and discovered. The diverse ways in which these primary functions can work together constitute one of the most important aspects of the harmonic content of functionally conceived music. Long chord successions are not necessary to establish the functional system (that is, to define a particular harmony as the tonic) clearly and unambiguously. As soon as the tonic and with it a particular transposition of the functional system are established, the role of subsequent chords is limited to confirming harmonic functions that are already known. The excitement that accompanies temporary functional ambiguity regarding newly entering chords naturally disappears, and in its place arises a sense of satisfaction, which after not very long may become tiresome. Chords that sound where a sense of the tonic is still in the process of being formed (for example, at the start of a composition) have a more pronounced effect because they carry important action, *seeking a tonic and defining a particular functional system*. After this goal is reached, the listener's interest in subsequent "less interesting" chords necessarily subsides, since these chords have nothing new to say in a functional sense. Naturally, in such a situation a composer must strive to renew the original full effect of chords and chord successions.

How can such a renewal be achieved? The gravitating force of the functional system that has been established must be shaken off; *the sense of the tonic that has been created must be eliminated*. This can be done by violating the principles of the pure tonic and the leading tone, and the functional principle – that is, by introducing a chord that contradicts these principles.

This brings us to the second task that each composer of functionally conceived music must master: *the disruption of a key*, the elimination of a sense of the tonic that has been formed or is in the process of being formed. Thus the second stage, having the equally important task of concealing or eradicating the functional system, corresponds to the prior stage of creating this system. This second, destructive, task is important because it prepares the ground for a new positive phase, for a possible effective renewal of the process. As soon as the sense of the tonic is eliminated, or at least shaken, the subsequent chords acquire the appeal of novelty (in the tonally functional sense), and the "game" can be repeated – a sense of a new tonic is created, which after a while is removed or disturbed. Such alternation is necessary wherever the direct sensory effect of chords is accompanied by a functional awareness. Thus it is an important compositional task not only to create a sense of the tonic, not only to define a functional system, but also to eliminate the sense of the tonic thus created, to challenge the functional system.

Of the phenomena with which we have dealt, the following have this negative, destructive role:

a) *applied functions*, even when altered, and *modulations*, which in their next phase become carriers of the positive role of creating a sense of a new tonic;
b) the *auxiliary functions* P and L, either isolated or in combinations;
c) *interfunctions*, again either isolated or in combinations with each other or with primary or auxiliary functions; and
d) *bitonality* and *polytonality*.

These phenomena were described in detail above in §117 and §118 (a), §108 (b), §110 (c), and §116 (d).

The alternating phases of tonally functional strengthening and loosening occurred in older music in such a way that the first phase was spread out expansively over time, while the second phase was quite short. In contrast to several chords, frequently repeated in various ways, that strengthened the key, a single chord with a disruptive function sufficed. It seemed necessary that a composition or a section of a composition end with the strengthening phase.

Towards the end of the romantic era, however, we observe an increasing delight in the destruction of key, manifest in the greater frequency and length of tonally loosening phases and the fact that they often involve the end of a composition or of one of its sections. While the classical or early romantic composer tends in codas to depart from the principal key only briefly (by a turning to the subdominant key) but otherwise conscientiously and at length strengthens the fundamental functional system, the late romantic or an impressionist expends a great deal of effort to weaken the principal key and its functional system. The assumption of a tonally clear cadence on the tonic becomes less welcome in the context of refined functional ambiguity, especially at the very end of a composition; the final tonic tends to be burdened with real non-tonic components (for example, an added sixth, characteristic of the subdominant function, such as C E G A in C major). Thus the principle of the pure tonic is violated not only by continuing imaginary foreign pitches, but also by dissonances in real expression. Both the deliciousness and the irritation of impressionist chords go hand in hand with increasing instability of functional tonality. Chord-types with traditionally established functional significance (for example, the dominant seventh chord 332 G B* D F) appear consistently in a different function (for example, G B D F as +Ṡ from D major instead of +Ḋ from C major).

All these examples attest to the fact that composers ceased to *delight* in creating an unambiguously defined sense of the tonic to capture the listener's attention harmonically. However we cannot speak here of complete denial of the functional principle. Its frequent violation results from a reaction to certain classical progressions that respected the fundamental principles of tonally functional harmonic thinking. The chordal and functional abnormalities of the impressionists are essentially only variations of classical chord-types and progressions. Example 165 demonstrates that it is possible to go far even by means of this "tame" route.

Example 165

Here we have the familiar cadence +Ḋ +T in D major. Through gradual modification, we moved from the classical resolution to a mere transfer (see §114 above); at the same time, strength of tradition makes the pre-tonic chord gravitate toward a tonic other than the one to which it is chained "by force". As a rule, such cadences presuppose that the final tonic has already been determined. After such a cadence, the final tonic is unstable, as if in chiaroscuro.

If classical composers defined the chosen transposition of the functional system by a small number of harmonies that they then repeated for a period of time "without further harmonic thinking", composers of the last part of the romantic period were reluctant in their harmonic exposition to point too strongly to the tonic; often already during the first harmonies of a composition they played a "two faced" tonal game. If in spite of this the tonic was sufficiently determined at the end of a composition or of one of its continuous sections, these composers felt a need at the last minute to lighten this tonic tonally, that is, to disturb the connection between it as a ruling element and the other functions dependent on it. Only in this way can we understand those frequent attempts to subvert the prevailing rule of the tonic, such as we find in the final measures of impressionist music. Already in the renowned *The Afternoon of a Faun* by Claude Debussy, in 1894, we feel a distinct suggestion of such an effort. We present the final four measures of this work in Example 166.

Example 166

The precise indication of the functions of chords in the last three measures demonstrates that the final tonic is not reached by resolution of convincing pre-tonic harmony, but rather by a gradual transfer of the functional combination, in which the presence of the function L causes a marked violation of the principle of the pure tonic. From the chord A♯ C♯ E G♯, the A♯ first disappears without resolution, followed by the C♯, also without resolution; only then is the supplementary pitch B of the tonic added to the remaining E and G♯ – not where the A♯ and C♯ previously sounded, however, but elsewhere, so we cannot even speak of a delayed resolution. According to classical conception, the chord A♯ C♯ E G♯ can equally well have the function +S: / +D: in B major or –S in G♯ minor. Thus the influences of established (traditional) functional conceptions of certain chord-types create the centrifugal force of this chord. The stability of the tonic E G♯ B is also shaken by the interfunctions in the first measure of our example.

The reason for the preference for the so called *church modes* is similar. As a rule, alteration is used to "refresh" the primary functions, while use is made of the discrepancy between the classical functional system with its usual presumed tonic and a more remote tonic chosen as if arbitrarily from the diatonic pitches. An example from Vítězslav Novák's harmonization of the second stanza of the Slovak song *Prelecel sokol* [A hawk flew overhead] from his *Slovenské spevy* [Slovak songs] will clarify this.

Example 167

Two functional interpretations are shown in Example 167. The first corresponds to the tonal basis of the entire song (E minor), while the second is founded on the traditional interplay of chords (D major). It hardly needs to be said that the first interpretation is correct. Nevertheless, the theoretical possibility of the second interpretation confirms that the composer was striving to undermine the control of the tonic E G B, not only by introducing an altered (dorian) subdominant several times (marked +S), but also by the artful use of the relation D T from D major in harmonizing the third and fourth measures. The gravitation to the harmony D F♯ A is further strengthened here by the pedal on D. It is noteworthy that the melody of the song is not dorian, so the use of the dorian sixth C♯ is the harmonizer's doing.

The method used by Debussy to weaken the final tonic at the end of *The Afternoon of a Faun* differs from that used by Novák in harmonizing *Prelecel sokol* in that Novák's harmonic intervention conforms to a church mode (dorian). From a harmonic viewpoint, the two methods are essentially in agreement. Characteristic are the intentional violation of general natural guiding principles and the effort to differ from traditional chord progressions by breaking conventional stylistic rules.

§121. Non-Functional (Atonal) Music

From the viewpoint of functional tonality we can distinguish roughly three types of music:
  a) music in which the functional meaning of the chords is definite and unambiguous,
  b) music in which the functional relations are loosened, and
  c) music in which no functional relations between chords can be objectively and reliably determined.

In cases a) and b) it is characteristic that an awareness of the tonic is created, so the tonic is known. In case c) this is not necessarily true. *Non-functional* or *atonal* music, having no tonic, does not rely on harmonic (functional) orientation to the tonic.

In functionally clear music (type a), the expected tonic can be determined from the non-tonic chords on the basis of the principles of the pure tonic and the leading tone. In functionally loosened music (type b), the tonic must actually be introduced and its tonic function emphasized by other means than harmonic, for example, by returning persistently to it or by ending the composition or a section of the composition on it. On the other hand, in non-functional music (type c) any possible tonic must be avoided. Rather than achieving functional loosening by violating the fundamental principles, non-functional music cannot even be given the opportunity to employ these principles. No emphasis or conspicuous precedence can be given to a particular chord, especially a consonant chord, since this could create a weak sense of a tonic.

The following schemes illustrate the three types of tonally functional music:

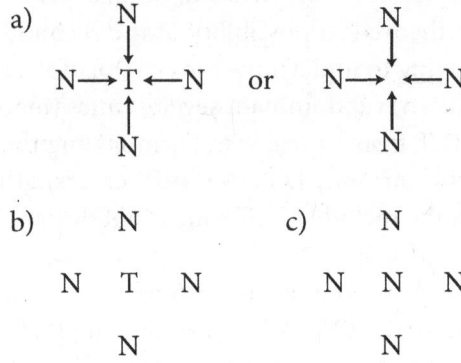

T indicates the tonic, while N indicates non-tonic harmonies. Arrows in diagram a) illustrate the use made of fundamental functional principles: the harmonies N "by their own power" gravitate toward the tonic, and it does not matter if this tonic is not sounded.

From the above description and the diagrams it is clear that if the tonic is omitted in diagram a), the functional significance of the other harmonies does not change. In b), where the tonic has its function so to speak "of its own will" (not determined by the surrounding non-tonic harmonies), elimination of the tonic can result either in a shift of tonic significance to another, originally non-tonic, harmony, or in functional anarchy, that is, non-functionality or atonality. In order to achieve the latter, all harmonies N must be formed in such a way that none of them can assume the T function. We do not create an atonal system merely by removing the tonic from a tonally loosened (functionally not quite definite) system; we achieve atonality only when, after the tonic is eliminated, no other harmony can be considered to be the tonic. Strictly non-functional (atonal) music can be created only when all characteristics that could suggest functional relations are avoided. Thus purely atonal music constitutes the refined product of an entirely negative process against established, deeply rooted laws. In the following we will see that reliable functional relations can be found even in music intentionally created as atonal. This is why certain theorists maintain that atonal music is not possible, and that all music is tonal, even if the loosening of its functional relations is at times extreme.

The classification that we have given is theoretically clear. Nevertheless it is sometimes difficult to decide which functional type is represented by a particular example. Difficulties arise from the fact that some sense of a tonic can be awakened even in opposition to the fundamental functional principles, when at the same time the claim that a sense of the tonic has not been established can be defended. Thus the boundary between types b) and c), especially, is not always firm.

To clarify these theoretical considerations, we present several examples. We will try especially to clarify music of type c), that is, non-functional music.

Chapter VIc – Harmonic Motion: Function in Harmonic Progression

Example 168a

None of the harmonies in Example 168a conforms to the principle of the pure tonic. In spite of this, the final consonances A♭ C E♭ and C E♭ G can be considered to have something of a tonic function. (Pitches that according to the principle of the pure tonic oppose the final tonic are shown in brackets.) By omitting the final harmony (the tonic) in segment a) we achieve a typical non-functional chord succession; none of the harmonies here can assume tonic function. As segment b) involves only consonances, some other harmony (most probably F♯ A C♯) can assume tonic function when the final tonic is omitted; this will not happen through application of the fundamental functional principles, however, but rather through the placement of the harmonies in the way that the original unstable tonic C E♭ G achieved its tonic quality.

Example 168b

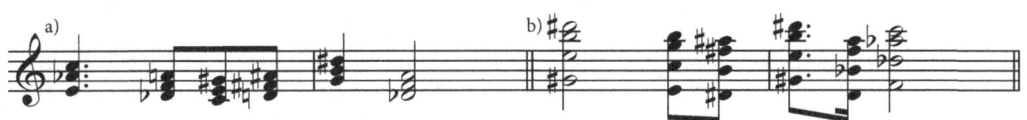

Formations of the same chord-type and disposition in parallel motion of all voices are again used in Example 168b; in this case it is impossible to speak of a tonic. All the chords are non-tonic, and their combination does not point to a tonic that has not been realized. Thus these are typical non-functional atonal progressions.

So far the examples have been characterized by consistent parallel voice-leading. This convention is especially suited to disrupting any functional connections that may have formed and thus to achieving non-functionality. At the same time, strictly parallel voices represent a clear and conventional compositional order that effectively counterbalances the non-functionality.

The following examples of diverse textures do not involve parallelism. They are all conceived as non-functional. However, even in music so conceived, traces of functional relations can often be found; an intended type c) (non-functional) can thus appear as type b (tonally loosened), or even type a).

Example 169

In Example 169 functional relations can be traced only with difficulty, so the two voice passage is non-functional. The manner of harmonic expression also contributes to the non-functionality: the two quickly flowing voices leave behind many imaginary pitches that combine to function as chords; at the same time, boundaries between certain chords of composite expression can be established only provisionally. Where the voices proceed in larger melodic intervals, the chords are better defined. However, nowhere is it possible to speak of chords in a pure combination disposition that would contribute to the functional differentiation of components in complex harmonies; only occasionally do individual triadic components, indicated by braces, gleam through. The full chromaticism contributes to the non-functionality. Pitches of groups 11 (e.g., B♭, B, C) are usually distributed in different voices in immediate proximity, as shown by the dotted frames around such groups. Elsewhere such groups are dispersed. The final chord E♭ F F♯, being a sharp dissonance, moreover in an unfavorable disposition, likewise does nothing to help tonally functional orientation.

In spite of all these characteristics, it is possible in a persistent search for functionality to start with the combination E G B – B D F♯, which sounds immediately before the end; from this it is possible to conclude that we are dealing with a key of B minor that has been extremely complicated ("masked"). To support this opinion, we can refer for example to measure 11, where the determinant F♯ A♯ C♯ represents +D, E G (and earlier E G B) represents –S, and the F is part of L. It is difficult to interpret other sections of the example tonally.[95]

Functionality is suggested more explicitly in the following examples.

Example 170

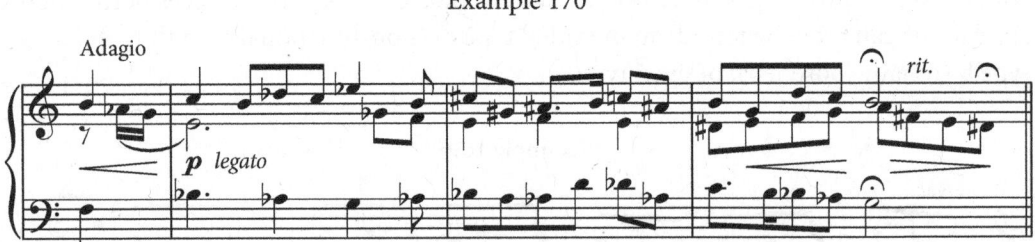

Although Example 170 was conceived atonally, functional relations between chords can nevertheless be felt; in fact the passage as a whole can be tonally classified. At the opening there is the relation (Ḋ) Ḋ between F G B and B♭ E C, after which a complicated tonic A♭ E C from F minor is heard; with good will the whole

---

[95] Example 169 and the following examples 170, 171, and 173 are from my small piano suite *Hlasy ticha* [Voices of silence], *op. 14*, from 1934 (Praha: Hudební matice Umělecké besedy [The Music Association of the Artistic Society], 1935).

passage could be understood in C major (without a close, of course). We cannot eliminate the possibility of some other tonal interpretation, however, such as a cadence in E minor.

Example 171

Although Example 171 was also created as atonal, the structure of its upper voice allows it to be understood in G minor. Pitches not corresponding to the principle of the pure tonic in G minor are shown in brackets.

Example 172

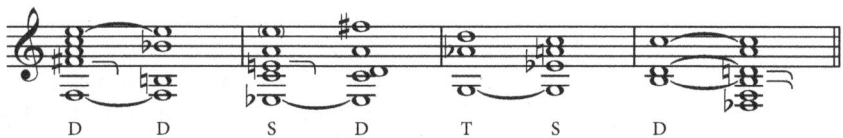

Example 172 is the harmonic interpretation of Example 171. The symbols indicate only the functional skeleton, that is, they draw attention to the most essential functional components of the chords involved. Pitches marked with the symbol  are imaginary and quickly die away.

Example 173

Functionally, Example 173 is especially interesting. This atonally conceived three voice passage ends with an augmented triad (B G E♭) that with continuing imaginary pitches forms the rich chord B E G B♭ C♯ E B♭ E♭. If we listen closely, we can hear the key of B major here, because the tonic of B major can be naturally joined to the final chord. In our example, pitches belonging to functions from B major are placed in boxes, in order

303

to show that we are dealing with the combination of three layers of functions. At the same time, the significance of the tonic, which is not heard in its pure form, is not diminished, and so functional relations are not loosened. According to our classification, this example represents functionally clear music, since the tonic is determined here by the gravitation, in no way weakened, of non-tonic functions toward an expected tonic. Of course if we do not sense the tonic B D♯ F♯, we are dealing with non-functional music.

Example 174

In the non-functionally conceived Example 174, the highest voice describes the melodic contour of B minor. Only the first and fifth chords fully comply with the principle of the pure tonic in B minor. (Pitches that defy this principle are shown in brackets.) Nevertheless, the expected B minor tonic is determined by the given chords reliably enough for the triad B D F♯, added at the end of our example, to function as the natural outcome of the entire progression. It is also possible, however, to feel other functional relations (from other keys) between particular chords; for example, there is a complicated relation T D from F minor between the last two chords.

Finally we add several fundamental practical directions for creating non-functional music. As we have seen from the above examples, strictly non-functional music is not easily created; the subjective attitude – whether the listener can or wants to perceive as functional music originally conceived as non-functional – cannot be ignored.

Non-functional comprehension is aided by:
1) *consistent parallelism* of harmonic formations that appear in diatonic systems rarely or not at all;
2) *full chromaticism*, with semitone progressions divided between voices, or in the case of one voice between different octaves, resulting in frequent cross-relations as well as melodic major sevenths and minor ninths within voices;
3) *non-combination dispositions of chords*; and
4) *limitation of diatonic progressions* to the smallest possible stretches in voices, especially in those that are melodically exposed.

Chapter VIc – Harmonic Motion: Function in Harmonic Progression

§122. Compositional Order and General Compositional Styling[96]

The creative artist does not use material in a naturalistic manner, but rather *styles* it. The result of such styling is *order*, as the antithesis of chaos; by *order* we mean all artistic laws which on one hand grow out of natural assumptions that are universal, given by the material's possibilities, defined by tradition, and on the other hand grow directly from individual creative intervention, that is, from the will of the artist.

Already the fact that from innumerable possible pitches we choose a mere twelve means that we are styling, that we are striving for order. This is similarly true of simplified rhythmic relations (those commonly used in music), of limiting ourselves to particular chords or keys, particular instrumentation, etc.

In contrast to harmony in classical music, which made use of a very limited number of harmonies, harmony in modern music is characterized by a much greater richness. The prevailing order in a work of art is always clearer if the material used is less extensive. In the area of harmony, modern music is at an obvious disadvantage compared to classical music, to the extent that the styling of its hypertrophied harmonic richness is considerably more difficult to manage. Thus it is no wonder that composers concentrate in individual works or in continuous sections of compositions on *purposefully limited* harmonic material.

Such purposeful selection of harmonic material can be realized by three essentially different methods:
1) *limitation to particular chord-types* (and possibly also to certain dispositions);
2) *limitation to a particular pitch-system* or *key*, which also determines the types of individual chords; and
3) *establishing a general compositional styling*; this not only limits the otherwise excessive possibilities of choice of chords, but it also regulates this choice above the limitations established in 1 and 2 above.

These methods can be combined in various ways.

Ad 1) We observe limitation to particular chord-types in musical works of all styles. Here the guide for a particular selection is first natural law (consonance vs. dissonance, good disposition vs. bad disposition), then preferences conditioned by tradition, and finally the creator's own decision. The composer can always adopt a negative attitude that avoids those chord-types or chord successions that should, according to the above, be given precedence. For example, the artist may wish to eliminate all consonances (otherwise surely very "desirable") or consistently avoid established progressions.

---

96 Editor's note: *Stylizace* is the Czech word translated here as "styling" rather than as the more literal "stylization" or "conventionalization". In his book on classical harmony, Janeček defines stylizace as "the arrangement and expression of harmonies" – see Karel Janeček, *Skladatelská práce v oblasti klasické harmonie* [Compositional Practice in the Field of Classical Harmony] (Praha: Academia, 1973), 361–399. In this section Janeček twice equates *stylizační*, also translated here as "styling", with "autonomously artistic". A composer's *stylizace* represents compositional choices made in the "striving for order". In general, the choices described are in the area of what we commonly refer to as musical texture, and when this is clearly the case, then *stylizace* is occasionally translated as "texture".

Ad 2) Classical music selects its chord material from a particular transposition of the diatonic pitch-system, at times of course altering or enriching (chromaticizing) it. Modern composers proceed essentially in much the same way; the difference lies in the fact that instead of the pure or a mildly altered diatonic system, pitch-systems freely formed from chromaticism are introduced. Once a pitch-system is chosen, it is found in only a section of a composition rather than in the composition as a whole. During the course of the composition, then, modulations – changes of pitch-systems – occur. Thus the chromatic system itself, and systems with more than seven pitches (systems very close to the chromatic system) must be fully utilized in the shortest possible segments of time, so that an impression of alternating pitch-systems with fewer pitches cannot result. For example, if we divided the full chromatic system into the pure diatonic system of seven pitches and its pentatonic negative, and separated these two components from each other in time, we could no longer speak of the chromatic system, but rather of the alternation of two more limited pitch-systems. The full chromatic system itself then represents a selection from the richer acoustic possibilities, being a result of hundreds-year evolution of the European music.

Ad 3) Maximum diversity of styling methods within a small stretch represents compositional chaos, as coherence of thought is broken up. Hence even in this area we see in composers both old and new a tendency toward sobriety which sometimes borders on asceticism. A compositional styling, once invented or chosen, is used in a composition for a certain stretch until it is replaced by another. In the realm of styling, the composer's intervention manifests itself to the greatest extent; that is to say, we are dealing here with the most intimate compositional process, although even here we see the pressure and interference of tradition that transcends the personal, and a realization of the requirements of universal evolutionary law.

There is almost always a certain *balance* between the three methods discussed above. One method compensates for what another neglects. The absolute freedom of all elements, that is, the lack of the necessary selection process, leads to incoherence of expression and to confusion. On the other hand, a scrupulous effort to limit maximally all elements results in sterility and boredom. After these general considerations, let us approach the situation we meet in modern music.

In modern music the number of chord-types used has increased. The possibilities of chord progressions have also increased. Richer pitch-systems (representing a richer selection of possibilities), or even the full chromatic system, are vying to take the place of the controlling diatonic system. All this, which is related to the expansion of the functional system from three members to five, can in rare (complex) cases result in a lack of any clarity of the functional aspect, and thus in the practical non-functionality of the music. For compositional coherence, the phenomena that have been mentioned here are *negative, destructive*.

Modern composers resist the danger of amorphism by an *increased interest in general compositional styling*. The weakening of compositional order, caused by expanding the possibilities of what can be used, is balanced by tightened discipline in styling. We can proceed similarly to counter the eventual loss of functionality.

If in music whose tonal functionality is clear enough we can justify extreme sharp dissonance of a particular chord by means of functional logic (that is, by the sounding-together of the most effective chordal representatives of functions), in non-functional music we can transfer this task to the logically consistent assertion of the chosen scheme of styling. Modern composers only rarely realize this fact clearly, but they often resort subconsciously, instinctively, to this method. Of the phenomena that demonstrate this convincingly, we mention frequent *pedal points* and *ostinati*. Many modern chordal liberties would become unintelligible if the composers had not arrived at them by the persistent use of pedal tones or ostinato figures, that is, very simple styling schemes. The same is true of more complex styling processes such as consistent parallel voice-leading, assigning concurrently sounding passages to different pitch-systems (bitonality), etc.

The entire issue can be summarized as follows: *Wherever universal natural law is weaker, autonomous artistic (that is, styling) law is more intensely active; wherever autonomous artistic law of one method is weaker, it is replaced by an artistic law of another method.*

From the viewpoint of practical composition it is important that chords that deviate noticeably from the norm of their immediate context in a composition or section thereof can become acceptable regardless of their possible lack of functional clarity or their non-functionality, and regardless of the lack of clarity or excessive complexity of the pitch-system used. This happens because the composer arrives at the chords *through consistency in the chosen method of styling*. Expressedly we stress here that this applies not only to chords that sound harsh. The relation can also be reversed: a transparent chord surrounded by a predominance of harsh chords can be justified by the same means, in which case the norm is represented by the harsh chords and the deviation by the mild chord.

Some examples will provide clarification. In Example 175 we present two different conceptions, classical and modern, of essentially the same formation.

Example 175

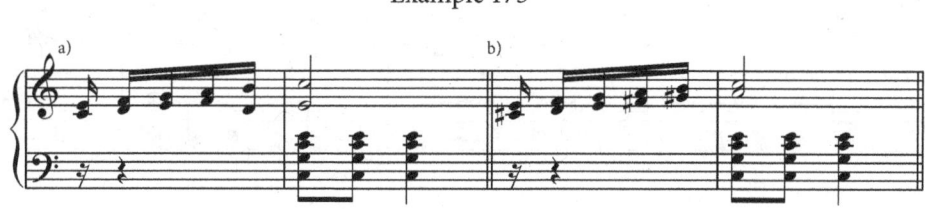

This is a stepwise progression, accompanied by a subordinate voice, and the overall result is a tonic harmony (C major). In Example 175a, the second voice is adjusted to the pitch-system of C major, and the final pitch (E) to the tonic harmony. In Example 175b, both voices consistently proceed in minor thirds even in the cadence, so the sound of the final tonic is complicated by a foreign pitch (A). Thus an autonomous artistic law appears here, a styling plan to which the composer consistently adheres, which works against the requirement of a pure, uncomplicated tonic. Example 175b can only appear in a style that allows for such a complication of the tonic. The difference between 175a and 175b is accentuated by the pitches that do not belong to the C major system; these create a certain tonal loosening.

The increased emphasis that modern music places on the independent assertion of styling law leads to an extension of styling possibilities. Classical composers knew only two types of two-voice parallel motion: thirds and sixths. New music uses two-voice parallel motion in any interval, even in fifths, which classical compositional theory strictly excluded. In Example 176 we present brief passages from Vítězslav Novák's orchestral *Serenade, op. 36*, composed in 1905.

Example 176

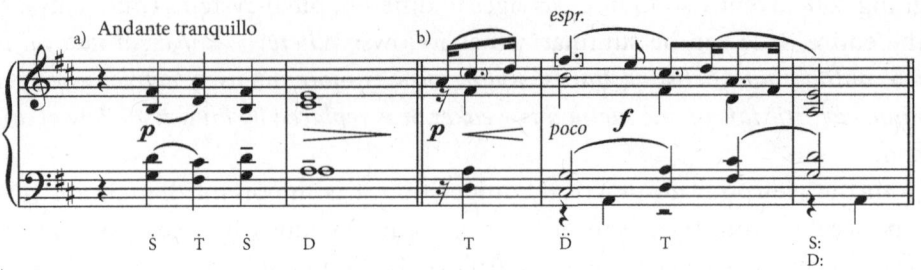

Here two pairs of voices proceed in contrary motion, each pair in parallel fifths. This styling scheme is used consistently in a considerable portion of the first movement (*Preludes*) of Novák's composition, even if some of the pitches forming the fifths are only non-harmonic tones, as shown by the brackets in segment b). Under the pressure of consistency, even unfavourably arranged chord formations may result (in our example, F♯ C♯ D A), or formations not known or accepted by classical harmony as independent harmonies (G A D* E 232 at the end of segment b). In addition to parallel fifths, the D major system helps determine the choice of chords; thus some of the fifths are diminished. The functional aspect of the music is absolutely clear.

Example 177

In Example 177[97] we can see in the pedal tone C♯ a styling justification for the undesirable disposition C♯ G* B D 421 at the beginning of the second and fourth measures. The consistent parallelism at interval 4 of the accompanying inner voices is also responsible for all the chord formations. It is as if the melodic progression D–C in the melody of the second measure ignored the pedal tone C♯, which for a moment has the role of a counter-cancelling pitch (see §77 above). The music of our example cannot be labelled non-functional. The tonal center of gravity is most probably the triad F♯ A♯ C♯, so the key is F♯ major. We thus hear the sharply dissonant chord C♯ G B D functionally as P. The C in the melody of the second measure is part of the function L, whose other pitches (F, A) immediately sound in the inner voices. Here the styling order (autonomous artistic) is conspicuously supported by the functional order. Hence the extreme deviation in sonic effect of the chord C♯ G B D cannot be considered coincidence, an "unforgivable barbarism", a naturalistic error, or the like. That the same chord is introduced twice, and on beats of equal metrical importance, tempers the sonic effect of this chord (cf. §73 above).

---

97 Example 177 is also from *Hlasy ticha* [Voices of silence].

Chapter VIc – Harmonic Motion: Function in Harmonic Progression

Example 178

During the first four measures of Example 178[98] a simple styling method is followed – parallel thirds belonging to the C major system in the two upper voices, and pitches belonging to the G♭ major system in the accompanying voice. Staying within the C major system of course means that the thirds change size.

Tonally, the upper two voices can be interpreted in A minor and the lower voice in B♭ minor (phrygian); the melody of the main voice speaks in favor of A minor, and the persistent return to the basic pitch B♭ in favour of B♭ minor. In the next four measures the styling method is enriched to the extent that an independent melody, forming the natural continuation of the upper melody from the first four measures, is added to the parallel thirds, now relegated to the inner voices. The consistent assertion of a unified styling scheme results in the softening of some chordal harshness. Thus in the first measure, the harsh progression E–D in the melody above E♭ (the counter-cancelling pitch) in the bass, and the progression D♭–C♭ in the bass while a C is sounding, would under other circumstances constitute "impurities" difficult to excuse; we can say that such harshness is only justified by the subsequent musical flow. (The usual procedure is reversed.) At the end of the fourth measure the chord C♭ E G, the first real consonance, does not clarify the sound as we might presume; this is partly a consequence of the styling order used. However, serious harmonic complication is created here by continuing imaginary pitches, so the actual harmonic content at the end of the fourth measure is C♭ F A C E G, in no way a transparent chord. The entire passage is intentionally constructed to be dissonant. However, the chords were not chosen "freely", by unconstrained decisions. Chord-types and their dispositions were determined to a considerable degree by the styling order. From the limited possibilities provided by this styling order, chords with good dispositions were then sought and chosen.

§123. Horizontal Thinking. Voice-leading

We have seen that kinetic harmonic law, defined by tonally functional relations between chords, is counterbalanced by autonomous artistic law, by compositional order. When a particular compositional order is consistent, even chord formations and successions

---

98 Example 178 is the opening of the second movement of my *Sonata for piano, op. 25*, composed in 1944–1945.

that defy the general law are justified, that is, intelligible, not disturbing the flow of the music. So far we have shown how the compositional order is manifest in the overall compositional styling. We must still draw attention to the unusual situation of a higher compositional order. This concerns music in which the decisive factor in forming individual chords and their successions is not merely styling, but *melodic thinking in concurrently flowing passages* (polyphony).

In polyphonically (contrapuntally) conceived music, chord formations and overall harmonic structure result from the melodic development of voices. Harmonic thinking is limited to *controlling* chord-types and dispositions, that is, to a negative role. Each style has its sphere of "natural" harmonic phenomena, the boundaries of which it rarely and only reluctantly oversteps. In a contrapuntally conceived flow of music it is necessary to take care to retain the harmonic character natural to the style. The essential harmonic control eliminates all foreign harmonic phenomena ("impossibilities"). Possible harmonic phenomena, acceptable in the style, are selected not from the point of view of harmonic law, not from a preference for certain harmonies, but exclusively under the pressure of developing melodic passages.

We refer to melodic thinking also as *horizontal thinking*, in contrast to vertical thinking which we understand to mean harmonic thinking, especially when limited to static phenomena – chord-types, their dispositions, expression, etc. Horizontal (melodic) thinking occurs even in essentially *homophonic* phrases if the outer voices have greater melodic significance. This is the source of the fundamental requirement of school harmony regarding a melodically acceptable bass. Example 179 shows that the *melodic lines of the outer voices* play a considerable part in producing the impression of a smoothly flowing chord succession.

Example 179

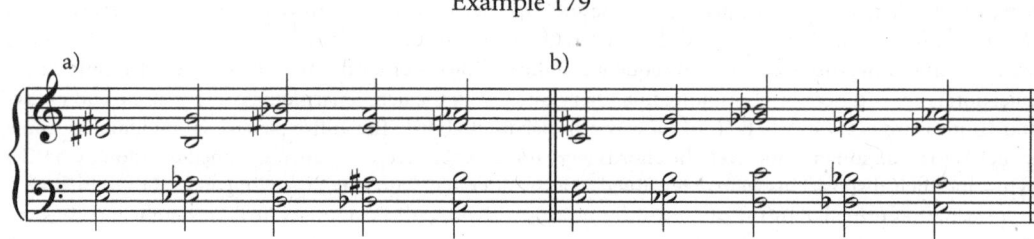

The outer voices proceed identically in 179a and 179b, although the chord content differs. In spite of this harmonic difference the passages are interchangeable (for example, as part of a larger whole), a fact to which every composer can attest. That is to say, this is often how corrections are made, how individual moments are improved, etc. Here the harmonic content, i.e. a definite progression of chords does not play a predominant role; a more significant task is allotted to the melodic lines of the outer voices, since they largely determine the harmonic content.

The significant role of horizontal thinking in creating harmonic content is especially apparent in *non-functional music*. With insufficient functionality, or merely increased functional ambiguity, the leading factor in creating harmony becomes melodic line, as a rule in the two outer voices.⁹⁹ If the outer voices have melodic sense and attract attention as well-arched melodies, or at least as melodies with definite leading, the harmonic effect of the whole recedes into the background, and it becomes possible in the shadow of the prevailing melodic law to accept even those harmonic phenomena unsupported by harmonic law. This applies to chord-types and dispositions as well as to harmonic motion. Especially with the loss of functionality it is important to hold more tightly to melodic law. Non-functional successions of chords expressed by confused voice-leading will always be in danger of sounding incoherent, like an accidental collection of formations that do not belong to each other.

What is true of outer voices regarding melodic voice-leading is also true, to a lesser extent, of inner voices. Even their melodic definiteness and consistency of leading can contribute to the overall unified impression of a harmonic progression. Thus when creating a harmonic phrase it is better to pay attention to good voice-leading even in the inner voices.

In *polyphony*, melodic thinking represents the foundation for harmonic phenomena. Especially in polyphony with ingenious artful *imitation* it is rarely possible to assert independent harmonic law. Here, somewhat as in pre-baroque (non-harmonic) polyphony, harmonic thinking intervenes only in cadential phases, while the rest proceeds linearly. Thus it is useless to look for functional relations between all the chords that arise in music created in this way.

The imitative texture of Example 180¹⁰⁰ allows for the possibility of modern chord formations.

Example 180

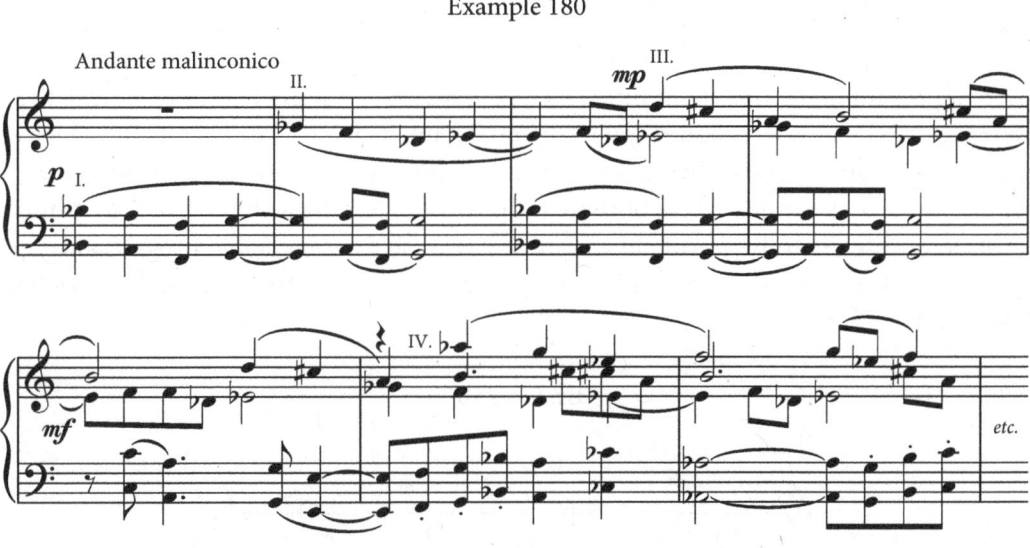

---

99 Paul Hindemith in his book *Unterweisung im Tonsatz I–II*, neue, erw. ausg. (Mainz: B. Schott's Söhne, 1939–1940) places great emphasis on the leading of the outer voices, which he considers to be the carriers of the harmonic phrase (*übergeordnete Zweistimmigkeit*).
100 These are the opening measures of my *Symphony no. 2, op. 30*.

In the imitative four voice texture voice I (the bass) was first formed as a cantus firmus lasting for the first four measures. The imitating voices II, III, and IV were then placed according to the "suitability" of chords. Of primary importance here was good disposition of chords containing the interval 1. In measures 5–7, voice I was composed as counterpoint to the imitative material of the upper voices. We did not consider either the suitability of chord successions or the functional aspect of chords. The imitations are all intervallically exact, so each voice makes use of a different diatonic system. Nevertheless, we cannot consider this harmonic polytonality, because the whole passage, with its obvious non-functionality, is chromatic, and therefore atonal. If a simple functional relation can be felt between certain adjacent chords, this is coincidental rather than intentional; for example, between the first and second beats of the sixth measure the chords E G♭ A (=E F♯ A), G F B A♭ can be heard as (D) D in the key of C.

In creating melodic lines, it is not enough to attend only to the individual voices in isolation; we must attend also to their *melodic combination.* Classical harmony placed especially strong emphasis on purity of voice-leading. Forbidding parallel fifths today of course makes no sense. The simplifying effect of parallel octaves and unisons (one-note chords) remains important, however, since these temporarily reduce the number of voices. Thus voice-leading in octaves or unisons is an irregular procedure that must be justified by a perceptible compositional order. Similarly, progressions of exposed voices by similar (not only parallel) motion to an octave or unison have a disturbing effect in every harmonic phrase, and composers avoid such progressions, especially when fewer voices are involved. By contrast, parallel sevenths, fourths, etc. are common modern progressions.

In melodically (horizontally) conceived music, *parallel motion* of voices temporarily limits the voices' independence. In contrast, independence of voices is intensified by *contrary* or *oblique* motion. Similar motion of voices that are also rhythmically alike always represents a decrease of their melodic independence. Such motion also contains the hidden danger of certain progressions that are not the most suitable. Similar motion approaching the dissonant intervals 1 or 2 gives the impression of technical awkwardness. Such a progression is especially unsuitable when it is not justified by logical consistency (directness) or by the melodic development of the voices. The same is true, to a lesser extent, of the reverse of these progressions: leaving a chord 1 or 2 by similar motion also tends to be unsuitable. Example 181a shows unsuitable progressions approaching dissonances 1 and 2. In 181b the same chords are more suitably approached by contrary motion.

Example 181

As a rule, an excess of progressions of the type in Example 181a testifies to a lack of technical skill, unless a compositional order is being used intentionally. In complex chords in which intervals 1 and 2 are replicated, however, and when more voices are involved, even these progressions do not appear obtrusive or annoying. Especially in inner voices these progressions usually seem harmless.

The melodic progressions in Example 182 are sometimes considered impure.

Example 182

In Example 182a, voices cross in progressing from interval 2 to interval 1. Such a progression (and also 1–2, 1–1, and 2–2), especially at a slow tempo, has an unpleasant effect, because the voices get in each other's way. The same progression would sound better, more intelligible, if we separated the voices by an octave, which would eliminate the crossing. Examples 182b and 182c make use of the counter-cancelling pitch, which must be supported by the compositional order.

What we have presented here and further technical details regarding voice-leading in polyphony belong to the theory of counterpoint. We mention these phenomena in a treatise on harmony only because the weakening of harmonic laws never appears in isolation but is always accompanied by increased intervention of some other law. In practical music it is impossible to dissociate harmonic from melodic phenomena, since they occur simultaneously. Only the center of gravity of their significance shifts at times to one side or the other.

Chapter VII – Problems

§124. The Concept of Modern Harmony

When examining modern harmony, we must constantly look back to the past, because the *connection between the old and the new* could never be completely broken, even when great effort was expended in seeking striking and unusual effects. Thus already in older harmonic expression we find the embryos of typically modern phenomena. Another consequence of this evolutionary connection is the indistinctness of the boundary separating the techniques of consecutive periods. If we assumed a steady evolution, no boundary would exist. In reality, however, evolution does not proceed this way. Instead of steady forward motion we observe sudden running starts followed by periods of relative stability; a discovery is followed by its testing and enjoyment. Further, since the elements of any art are not all of a single type, evolution reaches into a particular area of the artistic arsenal more deeply while it touches others hardly at all. Harmony is one such area, within which we can distinguish individual layers, which again to some degree constitute autonomous areas. Thus we must look for the boundary between different evolutionary stages in that area which is affected by especially penetrating changes during a particular period.

If we follow the evolution of harmonic thought from the time of the baroque until the end of romanticism, we observe gradual changes in tonality, harmonic relations, and styling. In contrast, on the whole the structure of individual chords does not change. The same types of harmonies are used by baroque, classical, and romantic composers.

In modern music, however, apart from further tonal loosening and expansion of possibilities in progressions of harmonies and other styling or rhythmic elements, we find *new unfamiliar harmonies*. This is the most outstanding characteristic of modern harmony. This is why *new harmonic formations* create a natural boundary between old (baroque, classical, and romantic) and modern harmony. We do not consider harmonic composition to be modern if it does not make use of new harmonies that were unknown to classical composers, even if its tonal foundation is unclassically loosened. Conversely, harmonic composition is modern if it contains new types of harmonies, even if it is formed in the pure diatonic system.

This definition of the concept of modern harmony does not absolve us from the responsibility to study phenomena that we know from music without new harmonic formations. Especially in the area of chord successions, the connection with traditional harmonic thought is so strong that we cannot isolate an explanation of successions of new chords from an explanation of successions of traditional chords. Even in other areas, however, we cannot ignore all phenomena belonging to old harmony in order to look exclusively at new formations. If we say that new types of chords appear in a modern harmonic composition, it does not mean that older chord-types could not also be present. Thus the material of modern music does not consist solely of new chord-types; the entire body of traditional chord material also belongs here. When classifying chord-types, we need to notice even consonant triads and familiar, traditional four-note chords, because without them the body of chord-types that appear in modern harmonic composition would be incomplete. All the chapters so far have been worked out in the light of these considerations, especially the first two chapters.

§125. Universal and Artistic Laws

Older music theorists strove to establish a binding and universally applicable system of compositional rules or norms. These efforts could not lead to a positive result, because they were futile. Living creation always broke through all elaborately constructed normative systems and worked its way to a new and different compositional technique, ignoring theorists' rules. The impermanence of theoretical requirements and rules bears witness to the fact that their roots do not reach as deep as theorists might wish.

Now theorists realize more and more that the entire body of working rules represents a law only partially supported by the wider foundation of natural, universal law, while the rest is custom and convention. This realization leads to the formulation of theoretical requirements only as *characteristics of a particular style*; for another style, different requirements apply.

Thus in the area of harmony we speak of classical, baroque, or modern principles. Finally, certain peculiarities are typical only of the procedure of a particular composer, so we can speak of individual stylistic characteristics, and thus of individual principles, as well.

The temporary validity and the changeability of compositional rules, which go hand in hand with changes in procedures, interests, and preferences of composers, do not refute fundamental, permanently applicable natural laws. *Universal natural law*, comprising all acoustic, psychological, and physiological laws, is necessarily valid without change, in spite of all the changes to which *artistic laws* that are a matter of custom or convention are subject; this must be the case because universal law applies even outside the realm of music, or of art in general.

Thus music theory must take into consideration two levels of rules and laws; on one hand it must be based on universal, natural law which transcends art, and on the other hand it must define specifically artistic law. Music theory takes the universal law over from the natural sciences. It then creates artistic law based on artistic practice. Compositional practice tends to become stabilized for a time with certain idioms and procedures, and it is for music theory to capture, classify, and evaluate the essential characteristics of practical gains so established. From the empirical rules obtained by this method it is possible to construct a *theory of a particular style*.

As long as universal law affects the attitude of practical artists, it must be reflected in the results of theoretical investigation. A precept that has been derived from practice can be more far reaching and need not be merely an expression of temporary artistic custom. Thus it is an important task of music theory to define the role of universal law in practical artistic (technical) rules.

§126. The Evolution of Compositional Technique

The constant development of artistic expressive resources means that any stabilizing of technique is only temporary. Efforts always arise to enliven a method that threatens to become a blueprint; thus a varied or new method is sought. This dynamic evolutionary law penetrates all aspects of compositional technique, and it applies in the realm of harmony. Thus it happens that progressions once discovered as possibilities for cadences are revised after a time and replaced by progressions that until then had been tolerated only in the middle of a composition. Such changes in technique can be so penetrating that the resulting phenomena defy not only the stylistic and customary (artistic) laws that prevailed until that time but also general natural laws. That is to say, the law of an artistic work is sufficiently autonomous that a discrepancy with established law in the realm of art is of no consequence to it; neither is a discrepancy with a natural law of any importance, which is at first glance surprising. If we consider that stylistic (artistic) as well as universal natural law must first be sought, and that artistic works arise as the result of artistic creativity even before these laws can be found, the discrepancy between the law of the artistic work and the as yet undiscovered natural law appears natural and even necessary. We assume that the discovery of a natural law is not a matter only for a particular branch of science, but also for practical musicians (in our case, composers) who through their everyday intimate contact with the material can arrive by a different route than science at universally applicable laws. If even after a certain stylistic principle has been established, or after a natural principle has been discovered, an artistic work arises whose law is somewhat or even completely different, it only means that a discrepancy that was possible earlier is recurring.

We will illustrate the matter graphically using one of the basic laws from the realm of visual perception – the law of seeing in perspective. Before the discovery of this law, whose universal natural character (which thus transcends the artistic and stylistic) cannot be doubted, perspective was absent from two dimensional graphic and plastic art; when this law and its practical applications were discovered, perspective naturally began to rule. This did not close the door to further evolution, however, which continued to seek effective resources in breaking this law in the most varied ways. Lack of perspective is possible even today.

In music, directly from the world of chord progressions, we can point to a cadential formula that Riemann called a "Landini sixth".

Example 183

This pre functional formation receded before the prevailing cadential formula D T; in two voices the latter can be expressed by simply reversing the pitches from the above formula.

Example 184

D   T

This did not, however, prevent different and sometimes even contradictory cadences from arising later – and not only as the aftereffect of "old times". We realize that in the case of the cadential formula D T, we are dealing with a practical application of a universal law – the principle of the pure tonic.

The possible artistic defiance of a valid recognized law also creates difficulties for theoretical investigation. Theorists must not lose their heads if they see that living musical creation circumvents, defies, or contradicts a particular law which has been applicable up to that point. We must realize that laws of every order do not exist in order that musical creation meet all their requirements unconditionally, but rather in order to be a *standard for the artistic creative attitude*. A law remains a law, whether an artist submits to it or defies it. If a law of a universal natural character did not exist, the creative artist could not defy it; the artist could not even ignore it, since even in the act of ignoring there must be at least a shadow of realization of that to which we are closing our eyes.

From these considerations it follows that in seeking a particular law we cannot simply amass enough artistic phenomena to which the law we are seeking applies and then mechanically derive the law from them. We cannot do this because if the number and variety of phenomena examined are truly sufficient, no law can be derived, since some phenomena conform to this law while others defy it. The law can be found only by *evaluating*, rather than by merely observing and classifying, the phenomena examined. We must guess at the *inner attitude of the creative artist*, not merely state the artist's procedure.

This means that the result is conditioned by the qualities of the searcher. That is to say, the evaluation of the phenomena examined is a matter not so much of logical intellectual consideration (a thinking mind) as of immediate perception; the phenomena must be "handled", "savoured", that is, *evaluated directly by the senses*. The reliability of the results depends on the examiner's critical conscience.

It cannot be denied that the chapter dealing with chord successions (harmonic motion) belongs among the most problematic chapters of all harmony. In modern harmony, the problems are increased many times by the extent of the material, that is, by the endless variety of actual chord successions. We can manage this task only if we realize the way in which the law of chord succession works – that it is sometimes reflected positively in actually possible chord successions, but other times negatively. Without such a realization, we can reach only the lamentable conclusion that all chord successions are equally possible, that every chord can be followed by any other chord. Such a conclusion is equivalent to an admission of chaos, of an absolute lack of law, of arbitrariness.

§127. The Natural Foundation of Music Theory

Older music theory worked in a pitch-system which it considered to be a fundamental reality, and it built on this foundation. Can a pitch-system be considered to be so fundamental, given by nature, however? Does not the pitch-system itself, as a highly complex organism, result from other less complex parts working together? Did it not originate through the direction of some other phenomenon of a different order?

The above questions and doubts are justified. Today, when we can survey the evolution of music for over two thousand years and follow the gradual rise and transformation of pitch-systems, it is clear that when these were being sought and gradually formed, a directive force whose essence was not (and need not have been) known to the first seekers already played a decisive role.

It was natural that the most ancient theory regarded the pitch-system as the most intrinsic foundation of music. Later, when evolution reached polyphony, and musicians began to savour the first real chordal possibilities, theory retained (again quite naturally) its original standpoint. The fact that chords within a given pitch-system "went along" so wonderfully remained relatively unnoticed. And yet such coherence could not be considered a coincidence. The only explanation can be found in the fact that the as yet unfamiliar excellent chords themselves led to the formation of the pitch-system.

We explicitly say "as yet unfamiliar chords". Although it was impossible to corroborate chordal sweetness by experience, its possible existence was nevertheless given in advance. Individual components of the pitch-system grew precisely from this possibility.

The *sequence chord-system*, at first glance perhaps surprising, appears natural if we realize that even in other areas it is only possible to arrive at phenomena of a higher order by means of phenomena of a lower order; thus for example we proceed from a two-dimensional phenomenon to a three-dimensional, not vice versa. The progression from chord to system does represent a progression from a sonic phenomenon without time (consequently lower) to a phenomenon characterized by extension in time, or concealing in itself at least the possibility of such extension. It is certainly easier to assume that a person "is given" the ability to evaluate sound itself directly, that is, sound not extended in time although already formed into a chord, than to assume as innate the same ability multiplied by time.

Although by a pitch-system we mean simply the collection of pitches from which we can draw in various ways, the original sense and mission of the system lay in the fact that its material (the pitches it established) was spread out over time; first, melodies were formed from it. Unless this material were gathered and arranged on the basis of some law not ruled by flowing time, however, the structure of the system would be just a matter of convention, would depend on fortuitous local customs, etc. The variety of non-European systems at first seems to support this. However, wherever the germs of polyphony appeared, these possibilities were given at least by the existence of intervals of the fifth and the fourth, that is, the basic consonant components constituting phenomena of an order outside time (harmonic). We can then see harmonically "unsuitable" systems as the lower evolutionary degree, as a stage of searching when the directive force of the hidden harmonic law had not yet attained sufficient weight to assert itself significantly.

If we consider that, with no regard to any pitch-system, a greater number of dissonant than consonant chords is possible, we should be right in assuming that a pitch-system formed without considering chordal possibilities could miss some or even all the possibilities for superior chords. The reality is, however, that the *resulting pitch-system is constructed such that all possible superior chord-types* (consonances) *can be realized in it*. It is impossible to believe that this is merely happy chance.

In summary, a pitch-system, whether the diatonic (containing fewer pitches) or the richer chromatic, cannot form the natural or original foundation for music theory. *The system is adapted to fundamental superior harmonic formations and is in fact derived from them.* These superior harmonic formations, *consonances*, form the natural foundation of music theory. Two consonances exist: the major and minor triads. Both our diatonic and chromatic pitch-systems can be constructed from these harmonic formations by their mutual interpenetration, that is, by forming triads having one or two pitches in common. The diatonic system consists of the group S – T – D, for example F A C – C E G – G B D; the chromatic system consists of similar, richer, groups. The intervallic unit of the chromatic system, the semitone, is also given by continuous consonances. It is formed, for example, by the distance between the differentiating pitches of the major and minor triads built on the same basic pitch:

We rely on practical rather than absolutely precise dimensions. Although the semitones E–E♭ or B–C are only approximate twelfths of an octave, this approximation is adequate in practice, as demonstrated by the introduction of equal temperament.

We can consider pitch-systems to be natural if they are founded on natural simple consonant chords. The chromatic and diatonic systems fully meet this condition of being natural. By contrast, the bichromatic (quarter-tone) system is artificial; its unit, the quarter-tone, has no support in the combination of interpenetrating consonances. Although it is possible to see the whole-tone system as a derivation of the natural chromatic system, its structure is so fragmentary that not a single complete consonant harmony can be formed within it; incomplete consonant harmonies (chords 4) are possible, of course.

As for the consonances themselves (major and minor triads), we accept their privileged position as an *assumption* whose justification can be explained by the relevant branches of the natural sciences. For the musician, however, the justification of this assumption is demonstrated by musical creation; it can be fully demonstrated by the analysis of composition together with a reconstruction of the composer's thought.

§128. The Significance of Experience

Branches of music theory are, in contrast to the general term *theory, practical teachings*. This is also true of the study of modern harmony. A characteristic trait of every practical teaching is its close relation to experience and practice.

There are two types of *experience* that no branch of music theory can afford to ignore: (1) individual sensory experience, and (2) the experience of others' compositional practice. By the first we mean the experience of theorist-teachers, as lived through direct contact with the material, whether merely through study or through their own compositional work; we will call this *direct* experience. By the second we mean the experience of other composers, as it can be read from their works; we will call this *indirect* experience. Only by taking into consideration both types of experience can we arrive at observations that are universally rather than just individually applicable. Although direct experience may lead to theoretical originality, without the support and control of indirect experience a theorist may eventually fall into irrelevant eccentricity. Indirect experience is a more reliable support, because the diversity of subjects (composers) provides at least a presumption of objectivity. However, even here there are hazards. Theorists who are not composers may, because of their non-practical viewpoint, overlook what the composer does not overlook; or, conversely, they may attribute significance to phenomena that are compositionally insignificant. For example, music historians untrained in compositional craft often highlight in their analyses of compositions secondary and extra-musical characteristics while ignoring essential characteristics such as the overall compositional plan and the means by which it is realized. The very heart of the effect sometimes escapes even perceptive theorists; only familiarity with compositional work can lead to the uncovering of the actual route by which another composer arrived at such an effect. Thus only a dialectical combination of both types of experience produces reliable results.

Indirect experience must of course be *processed* through because it is the experience of others. For this, a method is needed. As we have said, a requirement that is waived only with great difficulty is the support of direct experience. Without it, the relation of a theorist to the work examined may be similar to that of a reader to a book written in a foreign language, a reader who, although understanding the conceptual content, does not comprehend or feel the expressive shading and finesse, sonic values, emphasis, slurs or irony, etc. In addition to the capacity for lively perception that goes directly to the root of the matter, theorists also need organizational skill to make critical comparisons and discover relations; in a word, theorists must have intellectual as well as critical gifts. Only then can they work through the collection of their own as well as others' experiences, and form from them the support for their own theoretical work. Merely amassing the fruits of experience is not enough. A theorist cannot submit to experience without watchful suspiciousness, a wide view, and a formulating intellect.

We must never lose sight of the fact that not all technical characteristics consistently asserted in a composition necessarily constitute the expression of the composer's own viewpoint, experience, or preferences. We may be dealing with a matter of custom, a stereotype. In such a case we must view the technical apparatus of contemporary composers and then decide the essence of the phenomenon examined.

Which areas of harmony constitute the primary domain that can be worked through on the basis of experience? These are first and foremost areas in which a *static* conception of harmony is valid: the effect and characteristics of chord material, and connected to that, dispositions of chords.

Here especially we see how we must process the results of experience. Experience without criticism and without an organizational method could only arrive at unsystematic and questionable results. It is especially the *disposition of chords* over which theorists lose sleep. Without differentiating between the concepts of chord-type and disposition it would be impossible to clear our way through the confusion of chordal richness, even if the material were poorer than the chromatic system.

That the matter is not as simple as it appears to musicians today is demonstrated by the long groping of evolution, which reaches even into our own times. Composers have always naturally been inclined to hear in every chord, and in every disposition and shading of a chord, a new, individual, and perhaps even unrepeatable harmonic phenomenon.

It was not easy to search for *simplified* relations and to precisely define concepts in the sphere of the apparently unmanageable harmonic material; venerable prejudices that practice had accumulated had to be painstakingly conquered, and precepts of theories derived from practice had to be removed step by step. If finally a clearer and simpler new theoretical conception won out, it was not always certain that further evolution of practice (the multiplication of harmonic material in practical use) would not again repudiate the theoretical gains.

This actually happened in Czech music theory, in connection with the question of chord dispositions. F. Z. Skuherský (*Nauka o harmonii* [Theory of harmony], 1885), and later Alois Hába (*Neue Harmonielehre*, 1927), both biased in favour of new chord possibilities, thought it easier not to consider the generally expressed pitch content of a chord as separate from the concrete disposition of the chord's pitches; rather, they merged the two, contenting themselves merely with stating the chord's concrete disposition. Thus they assumed in this important matter a pre-Rameau, not to say pre-Zarlino, standpoint. A paradoxical situation arose: classical harmony, with fewer chord-types and dispositions, had a clear system of classification, while modern harmony, which was incomparably richer (already according to Skuherský, who allows up to six-note chords), was deprived of the benefit of clear classification.

Whoever realizes what deep changes can be made in chords merely by means of their disposition – and this is even more true of modern chords than of classical chords – will not accuse these Czech authors of idle theorizing unsupported by practice. They were led and misled by practice, by experience. The error that they made is purely theoretical, procedural; it lies in their rejecting the differentiation of two interdependent characteristics of a reality for the reason that they are never separated in practice. (Of course they cannot be: a disposition can never be demonstrated apart from a particular chord, and a chord can be realized in sound only in a particular disposition.)

In summary, although direct and indirect experience have great significance for the building of practical compositional theories, that is, for music theory, this experience must be worked through methodically and critically. An unorganized collection of empirical observations does not form a theory.

§129. The Search for Law

If experience, direct and indirect, is the necessary starting point for music theory, organization and intellectual criticism are essential complements without which a satisfactory (not to say systematic) theory could not be constructed. Let us inspect the essence of this intellectual activity.

From the emphasis we have placed on experiential foundations it follows that by this organizing and critical activity we do not mean unrestrained speculation that forages for a priori laws (unable to reach far enough into practice), originality (which is particularly misplaced in the field of music theory), or astonishing formulations. This is not a game played for the mere joy of the game. On the contrary, the union with experience, and a fundamental utilitarian standpoint, lead the non-speculative theorist to a humble watchful search for connections out of which as if of their own accord arise useful working hypotheses and resulting laws.

Realistic theorists do not invent, they infer; they do not speculate, they organize. They must constantly act as their own critics, must test from various sides even the most apparent and in their opinion objective results in order to verify their objectivity.

Even if our standpoint is non-speculative and realistic, and even if we search for higher laws on an experiential basis, we still cannot deny the possibility and even the justification of other conclusions than our own. The fundamental realistic standpoint must come to this view, because otherwise it would be disputing itself (this may sound paradoxical at first, but it is the case). As soon as theorists leave the experience that is the ground of their starting point – and they must do so – they must seek relations, connections, and the most probable hypothetical phenomena (such as imaginary pitches, tension of chords, the weight of pitches, etc.) and must form a system of imaginary factors (such as tonal functions); all this takes them further and further away from the indisputable experience with which they began. The watchfulness and critical attitude with which they had armed themselves for this journey, however, remain essentially their own. Thus areas of the more general law are at least partially conditioned by the personal disposition, capabilities, horizons, and culture of even the realistic theorist who starts from actual sound, investigates the effects of the sound, and verifies the results of this investigation. Different theorists, then, working conscientiously and independently with the whole personality, even perhaps with the same basic focus, can arrive at different conclusions.

Even under optimal conditions, that is, when the most honest effort is made to work out of experience, and when the work is accompanied by the greatest watchfulness, conclusions of theoretical investigation necessarily drag along with them certain personal characteristics of the worker, so these conclusions cannot be accepted as indisputable dogma. Every theory is at best the latest word, not the final word.

We have said that a method is necessary for working through experiential material. We can imagine the case of the theorist who wants to work alone through the entire body of available experience without considering the work of other theorists. Aside from the lack of economy in such a procedure, there is danger of differing terminology. Something that has already been defined in a certain way and named by other theorists will be unnecessarily defined again and named differently. Such inconsistencies even if they do not concern the essence of the matter are better avoided. If Otakar Šín named the new members of his functional system phrygian and lydian harmonies, it will be better to stay with these terms than to create new ones, as a new term does not change the thing itself. Thus consideration of earlier interpretations will be a useful control at least with regard to such external matters as terminology.

To these general considerations we add several comments pertaining directly to modern harmony. Experience leads the theorist to state that the effects of chords are extremely diverse. The scale of these effects is not practically manageable, since the number of components is given by multiplying together the number of possible chord-types, the number of possible transpositions, and the number of possible dispositions, without taking account of dynamics and colour, which can be combined in a rich variety of ways. Without a suitable method of classification, the theorist retains this view. With all the diversity of effects, however, it is still possible to find common traits, to form groups, to determine characteristics. By this route, harmonic theory arrives at the concepts of chord-type, transposition, and disposition. What appears at first glance as unmanageable confusion produces a clear system. Orderly classification is possible.

Common traits can lead to the designation of a superior phenomenon that cannot be discovered by a sensory search through the material under investigation. Thus an attempt to explain the similarity between the effect of a more complex chord on one hand and that of a series of simpler (perhaps consonant) chords on the other leads us to introduce the concept of harmonic imaginary pitches. It may be possible to find this explanation in some other way, but it will always result from a theorist's interpretive skill.

We come similarly to establish fundamental principles, such as the principle of the pure tonic. The intent of such a principle is that it expresses a relation between phenomena that at first glance seem unrelated. Two or more laws are converted by such a higher principle into a "common denominator".

When transforming primary experiences into principles, and in general when seeking common traits, we cannot continue arbitrarily until we reach some single highest principle. Theorists who do not want to lose the ground from under their feet must realize when they have reached a boundary that they cannot cross. We arrive at establishing common traits which cannot be further explained, that is, which cannot be transformed into other higher traits. The inexplicability of such traits then invites further investigation. Thus, for example, the principle of the pure tonic is directly related to the pleasantly stimulating effect of a tritone in an isolated chord. For the time being, however, we cannot discover the reason for this effect of the tritone element. In a system constructed speculatively, such inexplicability would represent a serious flaw. In a theory that starts from experience and is constructed critically, the inexplicability of certain phenomena is natural. We must consider it a success if we are able to find common traits for at least a few different phenomena, and by such an explanation to simplify, at least partially.

In harmonic theory, the process of generalizing creates not only a system of defined concepts, but also a language of *harmonic symbols*. Just as the meaning of a common trait lies in its explaining certain phenomena and reduces (simplifies) the overall body of phenomena, so the meaning of symbols lies in their capturing the fundamental traits of a particular phenomenon, without regard to secondary traits. Instead of the symbol D, signifying the dominant, we can write G B D (if we are in C major), or even a particular disposition of this triad; by using the symbol, however, we express the dominant generally, for all keys, for all dispositions. The effort of certain theorists to make a symbol capture the phenomenon to which it applies in the greatest possible detail is erroneous because this narrows the general meaning of the symbol. Such detail can be accepted in isolated cases, if there is a specific reason to do so, but not in general.

The system of symbols is valuable especially when it can help capture individual phenomena in *various degrees of generalization*. Thus a chord with a concrete disposition can be designated by its orientation scheme as generalization of the lowest degree, or by the symbol of the harmony type to which our chord is subordinate as generalization of a higher degree, or by the mere characteristic type symbol or combination category symbol as generalization of the highest degree. Similarly, the functional significance of a chord can be expressed by a full functional notation, with all components of the functions precisely indicated, or more generally by a simplified notation pointing out the number of components involved, or even more generally by a notation of only the prevailing function. (Cf. §100 above.) The most general notation, then, expresses only the most essential traits of a phenomenon, for example, its prevailing dominant quality; such a prevailing dominant quality of a chord can be realized by a whole series of concrete chord combinations, not only by the chord we are judging at the moment.

§130. Static and Kinetic Conceptions of Harmony

We can study chords either as isolated harmonic phenomena, without regard to any connections and relations to preceding or subsequent phenomena, or as links in continuous series or chains, where each link has some effect on adjacent links and is influenced by them. In other words, we can conceive of harmonic phenomena *statically* (in repose), or *kinetically* (from the viewpoint of motion). These two standpoints do not, however, represent opposites in the sense that one excludes the possibility of the other that the theory of harmony can be conceived either from the static standpoint or the kinetic one. On the contrary, the *two standpoints complement each other*. Only by their combination can we arrive at a synthesis that captures harmonic phenomena to their full extent. Thus the theorist striving to be objective must be capable of impartiality and investigate harmonic phenomena from both these angles.

In a *static* evaluation of chords we take no account of possible interference from anything lying outside the chord. Although an isolated chord has duration, it does not represent any kind of action, so we need not consider its duration. A chord that is part of a series (a composition), however, can have a different effect from that when it stands isolated; as part of a progression it represents a link within a certain action and is bound together with other similar links that precede or follow it. These surroundings can change the effect of the chord, since through interference from outside, from its surroundings, it can find itself in a different "light". From this it is evident that a one sided static conception of harmony must lead to erroneous conclusions. Static harmony can constitute only part of the theory of harmony.

In a *kinetic* evaluation of chords, we realize fully the significance of the harmonic surroundings, and we investigate the nature and extent of the intervention of these surroundings. We look for phenomena that lie *outside* the chord sounding at the moment; we evaluate *external* forces. At the same time we can hardly imagine a sensible theorist who in this investigation of the external would entirely neglect the effect of the chord that is sounding. External forces influence the chord and modify its effect, but they do not determine it. Thus when we speak of a kinetic conception of harmony, we mean a conception in which the one sided consideration of a chord's internal effect is *complemented* by a look at the harmonic surroundings. A kinetic conception always means a static-kinetic conception.

This almost obvious matter had to be emphasized here because the opinion about the movability of the boundary between consonances and dissonances, prevalent in recent times, and the related underestimation of the sonic effect of dissonant chords, can lead to absolute harmonic kineticism. By this we mean a conception of harmony that tries to ignore chords in themselves, not to notice their intrinsic (internal) sonic aspects. According to such a relativist conception, the effect of a chord is a matter of conditioning, almost a fabrication of theorists. Kinetic theory claims that only the relations between chords are worthy of notice. The absurdity of such a view is apparent from its possible consequences. Thought through, it means that a consonance can be replaced by any dissonance, since the effect of the chord itself is negligible in relation to the significance of external kinetic forces.

The necessity of investigating harmonic material as static follows also from the nature of auditory perception. In contrast to visual perception, where isolated colours, if we consider them analogous to chords, cannot have a pleasant or unpleasant effect (unless we are dealing with idiosyncrasy), but have simply *different* effects, auditory perception is always accompanied by a marked emotional accent, not just by some vague "aesthetic feeling". In the case of auditory impressions we rightly speak of sweetness and irritation, sharpness. We must consider these facts.

Theory of kinetics of harmony (harmonic kinetics) must be built not beside theory of static harmony but directly on its foundations. They have the same material: chords with a certain sonic effect, which can be evaluated and classified.

The fundamental problem of harmonic kinetics is how one chord affects one that follows. What can a chord change about a following one, and what influence can it have? Does only the effect of the sounding chord change, or does it acquire any new traits, when it is influenced by a another (preceding) chord?

According to the developed functional harmony, a chord acquires *functionality* by the influence of its harmonic surroundings. But what is functionality? Is it a new sonic property, something analogous to dissonance or family characteristic? A cursory look at the matter would lead us to think so, but this is not the case.

Consonance and dissonant characteristic are properties given by the pitch content of the chord; the same is true of family characteristic. If a chord has a particular characteristic, this cannot be altered without interfering with its pitch content. This is especially apparent in chords with simple or only slightly complex characteristics. The same is true of family: if a chord is defined in terms of family by the presence of a major triad, it differs conspicuously from, and cannot be interchanged with, a chord whose family is defined by the presence of a minor triad. If the function of a chord is determined by the influence of preceding chords, however, its function (for example, its dominant quality) can be changed into another without any change in its pitch content. (Modulation is founded on this possibility.) Consequently, a defined function of a chord is not an unchangeable property, strictly dependent on the pitch content of chords (of the sounding chord and the preceding chord or chords). Does functionality then perhaps represent a property of a different order, something more general, less specific? Is it necessary to place a defined function (for example "dominantness") into a category different from dissonance or family characteristic?

It is possible to reduce to some general, universal definition the sonic properties (given by pitch content as well as disposition) of isolated chords that are judged statically. Characteristic-types can be grouped together; for example, all chord-types can be divided into a mere two groups – chords without a tritone and chords with a tritone, or consonant chords and dissonant chords, regardless of further differentiation. By means of this generalizing process, it is possible ultimately to arrive at the most general definition of the general properties of chords, for example the definition of the concept of "tension in a chord". (Here it was of course possible to choose another word.) We can say that every chord that contains any dissonant characteristic is distinguished by *tension*; chords without dissonant elements are therefore without tension. Thus by the word *tension* we include all the possible dissonant characteristics. *Functionality*, considering the indefiniteness mentioned above, is just such a superior general characteristic of a chord.

An isolated chord has or may have some tension. A chord in a progression has functionality. Since the concepts "possibility of tension" and "functionality" are so general, it is difficult for music theory to differentiate between these concepts. If we know that the functionality of chords manifests itself in the possibility of tonic or non-tonic quality, just as the possibility of tension manifests itself in tension or lack of tension, it is better to *identify* the concepts of *functionality* and *possibility of tension*. Therefore,

functionality = possibility of tension,
absence of tension = tonic quality, and
presence of tension = non-tonic quality.

We justify these equivalences by the fact that it is hard to find differentiated foundations for an excessively general concept in material provided by both direct and indirect experience. An effort to differentiate come what may would lead to unsubstantiated speculation.

If we now return to our original questions, we must say that the influence of preceding chords does not cause the sounding chord to acquire any new properties unknown in static harmony; the fundamental properties given by pitch content and concrete disposition can only be *modified*, that is, changed somewhat from the original static designation, by the harmonic surroundings. A chord that is without tension when isolated may remain without tension even in a progression (when conceived kinetically); it can also acquire tension, however. This tension (that is, functionality in the sense of a non-tonic quality) is of the same nature as the tension determined by pitch content of other, isolated, chords. It is completely natural that the real (internal) tension can be increased by the influence of other chords but not decreased. An illusory decrease of tension takes place when the tension of surrounding chords is increased by kinetic means while the sounding chord remains unchanged; by this means it becomes tolerable to attribute a tonic function even to dissonant chords (chords with internal tension).

Tension given by the pitch content of chords represents a *stimulus toward motion*; the tension conceals in itself a tendency toward release, resolution. If this tendency is fulfilled by motion, that is, by proceeding to another harmony, a complete release can result, or a partial one, or none at all, depending on how the harmonic motion is realized. The tension in an isolated chord does not represent a command for a particular motion (for motion toward a particular chord), but only a stimulus to any motion; certain real possibilities can then appear as more suitable, of course, and others as remote.

The tension given by the place of the sounding chord in relation to preceding chords likewise represents stimulus toward any motion, not a command for a particular motion. We can verify this at every step, especially in the study of modern harmony. Practical classical harmony, with its well-worn paths, could lead theory to the mistaken conviction that the functional designation of a chord is always determined objectively and unambiguously, and that it allows two interpretations only in exceptional cases – in modulations. (See the musical examples in §115 above.)

We thus summarize that *due to the influence of its harmonic surroundings, the tension of a sounding chord can appear different than when it is judged in isolation; by this means the chord does not acquire a property of a new order, however, since functionality and possibility of tension are one and the same.*

We should point out the concrete method by which tension is changed in a chord that acts as a link in a chord progression. Most conclusive here is the study of progressions of chords belonging to the lowest classes, for example, two-note chords. (See examples in §83 above.) From the dissonant effect that generally manifests itself by tension in real, consonant chords that follow each other in close enough succession, we must deduce that certain components continue from preceding chords. From this originates the *concept of the imaginary pitch*. Increased or changed tension is then nothing other than dissonance between real and imaginary pitches. If a chord of real expression does not determine a particular direction of motion, neither does a chord of composite expression, that is, a chord influenced by preceding chords. If we interpret the actual tension of consonances that have been placed a certain way as caused by continuing harmonic or even tonal imaginary pitches, we cannot consider functional tension, the non-tonic quality, to be anything else than tension caused by the real dissonance of a chord. Any differences between the concepts of *dissonance* and *discordance*, between *consonance* and *concordance*, then vanish. (By *discordance* we mean the tension in a chord not caused by its own content, its dissonance, but rather by its position relative to the tonic. A consonant chord is also concordant if it is the tonic; if it is not, it is discordant. The concepts of concordance and discordance were coined by Carl Stumpf.)

We continue to stress here the *ambiguity of the tendency toward motion* (in terms of direction and goal) in a chord endowed with tension, whatever the source of this tension may be. This does not say that in actual cases conditions are not more favourable for one particular goal or direction than for other goals and directions. These favourable conditions depend on the measure of motion necessary to reach the goal. Most handy are those harmonic formations of resolution that can be reached by only partial harmonic motion. Thus a dissonant formation gravitates most "comfortably" toward another harmonic formation in such a way that it can appear as a mere transient chord. From this follows the frequent conception of new modern chords as appoggiatura/suspension formations, although irregularly resolved, that is, used as independent harmonies.

Another circumstance for a favourable resolution of a dissonant chord, or one that appears dissonant, is consistent use of the traditional (diatonic) pitch-system; a deviation from diatonicism already represents a greater step forward.

In modulations, especially when the tonic of the second key, when it is first introduced, is still tonally unstable, the resolution of a dissonance into the new tonic is more remote; this is because the new tonic represents only a possible tonic, which must still be supported in other ways.

Kinetically "favourable", "privileged" progressions are as possible between chords with internal tension as between chords with external tension.

Possible functions or functional combinations are hidden in every chord: they are *present potentially*. Individual functional components acquire different weights through concrete disposition, and the whole chord's function becomes more defined. Just as the overall sonic effect of a chord can be changed by disposition, its overall functional direction can be changed by the same means. However, the "innate" multi-directionalism (or ambiguity) of the kinetic tendency can manifest itself even with a functionally purposeful disposition by a progression to the least expected, least probable goal. It is this possibility that new music utilizes so richly and consistently. By increasing this to its extremes, music becomes so indefinite that searching for functionality defined in some particular way becomes senseless for practical purposes, and the music becomes non-functional, atonal.

An important question remains: what happens to tension of chords in non-functional music? The exposition of the entire phenomenon of non-functional music is possible only on the assumption that internal and external tension, dissonance and the non-tonic quality, are one and the same. In an absolutely kinetic conception, as we said above, internal tension is not considered; if functionality, the sole remaining carrier of tension, also disappears, tension disappears altogether. According to this conception, non-functional music would then be without any harmonic tension whatsoever, that is, it would be inconsequent and could be interrupted anywhere. Reality is different, however. *Even in non-functional music, chords carry harmonic tension*; the loss of functionality increases the absolute effect of individual chords, which cannot be divested of their tension, since this tension is given by their own pitch content.

In non-functional music, potential directional ambiguity is not limited by a set of established practices (conventions), as in music that deviates less from tradition. Non-functionality consists in the fact that "the most favourable" kinetic possibilities have disappeared, and all possibilities are "equally good".

Chapter VIII – Compositional Practice

§131. Composition and Theory

It is possible to compose without systematic theoretical education. Such a statement is surprising in a theory book that has taken on the task of working through in detail everything connected with harmony in modern music. However, the fact that modern composers mostly work without instruction in this field which is so important for contemporary creation speaks for this thesis.

Composition is a *creative* activity, an activity in which we must distinguish the *conscious* component supported by reason, reflection, combinatorial abilities, or thinking, from the *unconscious*, irrational, intuitive component. Theoretical instruction can be given, and practical training carried out, only in the conscious domain. Novices in composition who have no ideas, who are unable to create directly anything they have not been taught, cannot become composers. Gifted composers are able to create music because they draw on sources whose nature is generally unknown to them.

The sense of a theoretical education lies in the fact that through composers' initial training in traditional styles, the unconscious is constrained and thus exposed to somewhat of a test in resistance. For composers who have come through technical training it is easier to recognize whether they have sufficient creative gifts according to how well they can discover new, personal effects in areas they have not penetrated theoretically. By means of study and training these areas become narrower, and the level of the composers' work rises. Composers who have been insufficiently trained and who thus work mainly on the unconscious level often create music that is not new, and that contains awkwardnesses that have long been tested and rejected. By contrast, trained composers can avoid such groping, because they are conscious of more; if they want to defy some traditional law, for example, they do so in a way that will not appear as lack of skill.

Newly created and applied artistic laws remain only temporarily without theoretical investigation; after a time composers must come to terms with all the phenomena brought by a new style. Thus as late as the beginning of the nineteenth century it was generally considered sufficient if composers were schooled in old vocal counterpoint, as its theory was worked out by J. J. Fux; today it is also necessary to study the instrumental counterpoint of the baroque and later periods. At the end of the last century it was still sufficient to study harmony founded on figured bass, as the Czech harmony text by J. Foerster testifies, for example. Later it became necessary to rely on the system of functions introduced by H. Riemann, and in Czechoslovakia by O. Šín. Now the time has finally arrived for composers to become familiar with a harmonic theory that systematically investigates phenomena which have until now been left to the unconscious inventiveness of composers.

Instruction in theory that systematically shows the entire working process in all detail can bring even uncreative students to the point of being able to "create" examples to the satisfaction of the teacher. Theory is able to provide such detailed instruction only for simple tasks, for "examples", however; here everything is conscious, the students work with their heads. The instruction is *systematic in separating the components* that must be considered, or in *concentrating* on investigation from one angle at a time. It will be a matter of the students' unconscious creative ability to be able to manage in practice a sphere for which they have not yet been theoretically prepared, while consciously concentrating on a different sphere. Only their own creative work allows students to verify their creative talent.

In the realm of modern harmony, such a separation of components can be carried out well. We can concentrate consciously on chord-types and their dispositions, for example, and leave aside, without rational control, relations between harmonies. We can then gradually widen the sphere of rationally controlled phenomena. In every case, the starting point for practical work will be harmonic phenomena that can be judged statically without considering their relation to their surroundings. To these we will gradually add phenomena that are explainable kinetically.

In order that the sphere of the unconscious be as small as possible (which is pedagogically advantageous), work in which kinetic laws play only a slight role will be welcome in the area of static harmony. This will be the case in non-functional music (that is, music fully utilizing the entire tempered chromatic system), in music styled consistently according to some simple order, and in music with independently developed melodic voices.

§132. Modern Melody

The first practical compositional task in modern harmony is the *creation of modern melody*. If we want to create modern melody, we must take care that it differs conspicuously from familiar melodic types, defying traditional melodic laws. This cannot be achieved merely by utilizing the full chromatic system, because even older music knows chromatic melodies. We must intervene in the very structure of phrases, using unusual groupings of intervals.

Of the great number of possible modern melodic types, it is best first to attempt diatonic melodies, and then consistently chromatic melodies. Only then is it advisable to create melodies that represent an intermediate degree between these two types.

It will be better if a *diatonic* modern melody cannot be perceived as if it were in the traditional major or minor. Thus in the diatonic system defined by five sharps we can close on A♯, for example.[101] It will be advisable to use sevenths, ninths, and the tritone (found only once in the diatonic system). These unusual intervals can appear less conspicuously as the span between the outer pitches on which the melodic line changes direction, as shown in Example 186 below. It will be advisable to leave a pitch that is traditionally perceived as a leading tone by an interval larger than a second, that is, not to resolve it. It would also be possible, of course, to use rhythmic formations that do not appear in older music. Examples 185 and 186 present diatonic melodies that differ in character and in which the above advice is heeded.

Example 185

Example 186

A *chromatic* modern melody must be cast in such a way that it does not give the effect of a chromaticized diatonic melody. Thus pitches that wrench themselves out of the diatonic system will need to be led, if possible, in some other way than to the nearest pitch by semitone.

All intervals are of course possible in the diatonic system, if we consider the possibility of enharmonic changes. Thus the chromatic quality of the melody will be given not by individual intervals but by larger groups of pitches. The shorter the diatonically perceivable segments of the melody, the more chromatic the melody will be. The shortest possible chromatic segment is three pitches. (Our table of three-note chords in §7 above shows which groups of three pitches are involved.)

Examples 187 and 188 give chromatic modern melodies that differ in character.[102]

---

101 Editor's note: In referring to "the diatonic system defined by five sharps" Janeček is referring to the pitch collection, but not the tonal relations, of B major.
102 They are from my *String Trio, op. 9*, composed in 1930.

Example 187

Example 188

Segments that can be perceived diatonically are marked by square brackets. These segments often *interpenetrate*. In evaluating diatonic quality, we must consider the enharmonic exchangeability of pitches. It is worth noting that even within diatonic segments, unusual groupings of intervals are used, as in the previous diatonic examples.

We will not present examples of the composite type.

Exercises in the creation of melodies are important in so far as they force students to alter their manner of melodic thinking. To what extent and in what way they will use this in their own composition is a matter of personal disposition and preference. Melodies that we write as exercises, and for which we first establish requirements, cannot constitute spontaneous ideas. It may happen, however, that after we have worked through ("lived through") the material, even freely invented melodies will have non-traditional structures.

§133. Practical Studies of Chord-types

In creating melodies, we also create a certain harmonic content. That is to say, every melody, even when unaccompanied, has its hidden (latent) harmony determined by the action of imaginary pitches. A melody with many semitone and whole-tone steps is harmonically ambiguous because the possibilities for imaginary pitches are slight. By contrast, melodies containing larger leaps, as we attempted them in §132 above, are harmonically more defined. Even in these melodies, it is only by adding a second voice that we can render the harmonic content more precise, especially with respect to time boundaries between chords. In creating melodies, however, harmonic content is a by-product, which is why we did not consider it. We created a melodic line according to certain directives and were not interested in the resulting harmonic effect, which can be studied analytically after the fact.

Now we will attempt *consciously to create passages with a defined harmonic content.* Our harmonic viewpoint will initially be static: we will limit ourselves in the chord-types used, leaving the chord progressions to be governed by unconscious creativity. Thus we can work through in a practical way all chord-types, either individually or in groups. It will only be important to work through chord-types of lower classes.

We will divide the work to be studied into these two basic groups:

1) *A harmonic phrase consisting of real consonances.* Here we will only allow major and minor triads, regardless of whether they constitute primary harmonies or transient chords; thus all chordal cross-sections must be consonant. Those will be our "game rules". Such a phrase can be *diatonic*, as shown in the three-voice Example 189.

Example 189

The occasional six-four chords and parallel fifths reveal that we are not dealing here with the traditional conception of a harmonic phrase. Two chord-types appear – major and minor triads.

In Example 190 we have limited ourselves to a single chord-type, the consonant two note chord 5.

Example 190

The whole is again diatonic. Fifths and fourths alternate. In three voices, one pitch must of course always be doubled.

In the following examples, we abandon rigorous diatonicism. Our procedure can vary. We can first create a melody, and later compose the other voices according to prescribed or chosen chord limitations. We can also construct all the voices of the phrase simultaneously; this second method seems more common in compositional practice.

In Example 191 we first constructed the melody (a diatonic one), to which we added the other three voices such that in every cross-section they would form consonant chords. Square brackets indicate diatonic segments. The real triads that sound everywhere are complicated in some places by continuing pitches from preceding chords. We do not consciously consider this fact. Although the melody is diatonic, the whole is not.

Example 191

Example 192, non-diatonic and three voice, is also constructed solely from real consonances.

Example 192

Here there is greater melodic unrest in the leading of individual voices, as well as harmonic unrest in the continuation of imaginary pitches. The introduction of certain consonant chords is surprising, even harsh.

Work with consonances is important even in modern harmony. There is a considerable difference between the way a modern composer uses old chord-types, including consonant triads, and the traditional way. Parallel fifths often appear in diatonic as well as non-diatonic harmonic phrases, and cross-relations also appear in non-diatonic ones. Even in modern music, however, a harmonic phrase must sound natural. This can be achieved through careful melodic development of voices, consistent assertion of

Chapter VIII – Compositional Practice

a particular styling (cf. §122 above), and balanced distribution of motion – all useful resources even in traditional composition.

2) *A harmonic phrase consisting of real dissonances.* In the case of consonances, we had a small choice of chord-types. With dissonances, the choice of types is copious. Even here, however, we must at first limit ourselves to particular chord-types, or to a particular characteristic-type.

Example 193 presents a harmonic phrase limited to the triad 44 (the harmony **0**).

The phrase is non-diatonic, of course, because the triad 44 is non-diatonic. Where the domain of the triad 44 continues from a real cross-section 44 to simpler chordal cross-sections, 44 occurs in composite expression. Where this is reversed, as in the first measure, a consonance sounds until the triad 44 is unfolded. We cannot always avoid building-up dissonant chords gradually if the phrase is not to sound clumsy.

We can practice with other dissonant chord-types of lower classes in a similar manner. We can also combine several chord-types, so that the phrase is more varied in its chordal cross-sections. Rather than strictly limiting ourselves to one or several chord-types, however, it is better to limit ourselves to a particular characteristic-type.

§134. Practical Studies of Characteristic-types and Harmonies

As with individual chord-types, we can practice with individual characteristic-types. We will base an entire harmonic phrase on one characteristic type or on two related types.

Thus when we are consistently using the dissonant characteristic 2, we will not always use the complete harmony **2** (the five-note chord 2232 – see §35 above), but rather the lower chords subordinate to it. We can cast the phrase in such a way that every chordal cross-section will contain the characteristic 2, as shown in Example 194.

Example 194

In Example 195 a diatonic melody is consistently accompanied by parallel fifths, so a particular styling is conspicuous.

Example 195

All the chordal cross-sections again contain the characteristic 2. The pure diatonic system is infringed upon by the use of both A and A♭.

All the chordal cross-sections in Example 196 are characterized by the compound characteristic 26.

Example 196

By comparing this example with the preceding examples, we can see the effect of the presence of the characteristic 6.

We did not have to consider the disposition of harmonies **2** and **26**. When composing harmonic phrases using chords with the characteristic 1, however, we must be concerned with disposition, since the differences between chords of these types with good and bad dispositions are too distinct. Thus it will be natural if, when using chords with the characteristic **1** or **01** (as in Examples 197 and 198), we establish as our first condition a good (or the best) disposition of all intervals **1**.

Example 197

Example 198

Harmonies **16** and **016** are used in Example 199.

Example 199

Finally, in Examples 200 and 201, we present work with denser harmonies **126**.

Example 200

Example 201

More complex harmonies can be practiced with similarly, and characteristic-types can be variously combined. In such practice the student becomes familiar with the sonic effect of individual types and acquires compositional adroitness. It is better to reserve richer combinations of types for free composition.

§135. Styling Studies on a Given Harmonic Basis

The type of music that we have worked out in our examples up to this point rarely appears in living musical creation. The examples were *technical exercises with a focus on chord-types*. In practical composition, we cannot limit type so strictly. In practice, taking account of particular types or preference for them determines only the overall character of the compositional segment. A particular type of chords characterizes a composition, but only rarely is a composition limited exclusively to one type.

We can supplement the chord studies presented in §133 and §134 above with *practical realizations of given chord successions*. In order to come as close as possible to living practice, we can select the successions from finished music. Our efforts will then be directed toward creating a suitable styling. The excessively stringent limitations to which we submitted earlier will yield to such limitations as those to which composers adhere in practice.

We must first determine chord-types in the passage we choose. If the styling is such that chords occur in real expression, and transient chords are not used, this is simple. We present in Example 202 such a compositional passage from *Three Compositions for String Quartet* by Igor Stravinsky (composed in 1914):

Example 202

Chapter VIII – Compositional Practice

We attempt to create our own music according to this given chord succession, as shown in Example 203.

Example 203

In contrast to the original four voice texture (played *pianissimo, tutti sul tasto*), we have created a transparent two-voice texture. The connection with the model is apparent from the numbers of the segments in this example, which correspond to the numbers of the chords in the original. Occasionally we have also used non-harmonic tones; in the domain of chord no. 14, we have anticipated two pitches (A, F) from chord no. 15.

If the styling of the compositional passage we choose is more complex (in composite expression), we must first construct a simple *harmonic skeleton*. In Example 204 we present the opening of the third movement from the *Suite for piano* by Pavel Bořkovec.

Example 204

The harmonic skeleton of this passage is shown in Example 205.

Example 205

The connection with the model is again shown by the numbers. In the first chord, we ignore the B, since the introduction of A♯ in the lowest voice creates the group 11 (A A♯ B), and the B quickly vanishes. Similarly, in chord no. 7 we ignore the C♯. The details of the musical passage can be perceived differently, as is true also for old music, especially when it is polyphonic as our example is.

On the basis of this skeleton, whose effect is cumbersome, we can create a more lightly styled harmonic phrase. In Example 206 the styling relies on the original styling.

Example 206

Through this type of exercise, the student quickly penetrates the harmonic thinking of contemporary composers. A given harmonic progression can always be transposed, in which case its similarity to the model will be less apparent. We hope we do not have to emphasize that this is not how composition is done; it is merely a useful exercise.

§136. Harmonizing a Melody

If we are creating a newly styled harmonic phrase on a given harmonic basis, we must make sure to give this new phrase a melody. Otherwise our creation would be only a scheme, a harmonic skeleton.

We can also create a harmonic phrase by *harmonizing* a given melody. The less harmonically defined the melody, the more possibilities of harmonization there will be. A melody that already unfolds certain chords can be harmonized by these chords or by more complex chords that contain the unfoldings in the melody, if we do not want to harmonize each pitch of the melody by a different independent harmony. For example, we can harmonize the melodic progression C–E–G–C by the triad C E G, or by more complex chords containing this triad: C E G B♭, A C E G, D♭ F A♭ – C E G, A C♯ E – C E G, etc. By contrast, we can harmonize a melody that has an ambiguous, latent harmony (for example, the descending passage E–D–C–B) equally well with several simple chords (for example, the consonant triads E G B, E G♯ B, D F A, D F♯ A, C E G, A C E, B D F♯, G B D), or with more complex chords; of course, we can also harmonize every pitch with a separate chord.

When harmonizing a melody, we must first outline the *overall harmonic plan*, deciding which chords or which type of chords we will use, and where. In the sphere of classical harmony, as a rule we select certain functions or functional combinations. For a modern harmonic phrase, the functional meaning of chords has far less significance. What is more important here is to realize where it is suitable to use any kind of fundamental harmonic motion at all; our second concern will be to choose types of chords. When beginning to work with new harmonic formations, we do not have to consider at all the functional aspect of chords.

When choosing chords of a particular type, however, we will need to keep in mind the *possibilities of disposition*, especially of chords that contain the dissonant interval 1 (see §67 above), or the group 11 (see §72 above). We prefer to construct such chords by first choosing a suitably arranged interval 1 or group 11, and then filling in the other pitches.

If we want to create a harmonic phrase that flows naturally, we must see to it that even the accompanying voices trace natural simple melodic lines. The closer the texture of a harmonic phrase comes to polyphony, the more natural will be the effect of the chord successions realized in that phrase.

In the following examples we demonstrate new possibilities of harmonization by harmonizing a short melodic passage given in Example 207. The melody contains seven pitches within a range of a fifth, so it is not diatonic.

Example 207

Only with great difficulty could we harmonize this melody with a single chord. Even if we left the accompanying voices unchanged from beginning to end, the progression of the melody would change the harmony for us. For example, when using the triad B♭ D F as accompaniment, in the first measure we can hear this triad with successively resolved non-harmonic tones (C♯, B), but the second measure is already more complex, because to the accompanying B♭, D, F the melody adds G and C, which are not cancelled. Thus the result is the chord succession B♭ D F – B♭ D F G C (2232, the harmony **2**).

The pitch changes introduced by our melody demand to be divided into several chordal regions. We present several different solutions for this task in harmonization.

Example 208

Three chordal regions are found in Example 208, as shown in the appended harmonic skeleton. The harmonic change in the first measure is inappreciable, as we have here merely partial harmonic motion. By contrast, the entry into the second measure represents a considerable harmonic step forward. Square brackets mark dissonant intervals 1 in good disposition. The pitches forming these well arranged intervals are part of the harmonic plan: the C♯ and A at the beginning of the two measures, respectively, lead us to choose the D and B♭ as components of the chords that fall on the strong beats; the final C in the melody then leads to the choice of the D♭ in the second voice.

Example 209

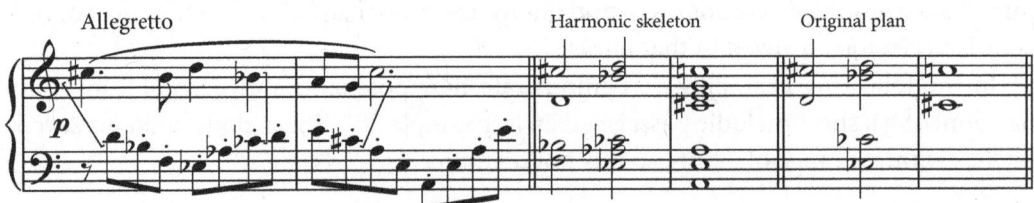

Chapter VIII – Compositional Practice

In Example 209 we again establish three chordal regions. Intervals 1 are chosen so as to be well arranged, as we see from the appended original plan of harmonization. This incomplete harmonic skeleton was only later filled in and worked out in a specific version.

We demonstrate further the gradual building up of texture around a given melody.

Example 210

In Example 210 we again aim for good dispositions of intervals 1. In the first half of the first measure in Example 210c the unfavorably arranged interval B♭–B is heard. In Example 210d this interval changes into a good disposition however, since by the addition of the D in the highest voice it becomes part of the group 213. (See §67 above.)

In Example 211, the accompanying voices proceed in parallel intervals 3.

Example 211

Here the chords are again chosen so that intervals 1 sound in a favourable position. The unfavourably sounding interval 1 between B and C in the second measure is part of a transient chord; the B and C are not introduced simultaneously here, so the interval 1 is "prepared", according to classical terminology. The arrow indicates the resolution of this interval.

In Example 212, the accompanying voices are obviously connected by a particular compositional order, as they consistently proceed in parallel motion.

Example 212

There are only two intervals 1 here, both in good disposition. New chord formations appear compatibly beside classical ones.

We present several more examples of harmonic realizations of the same melodic passage.

Example 213

The dissonant interval 1 B♭–B in the second chord of Example 213a is part of a group 213 (B♭ A♭* D B). At the end of the first measure of Example 213b, the F♯ sounds only briefly with G above it; this interval 1 is not only prepared, but it is also part of a transient chord (the F♯ in the lowest voice is a freely entering auxiliary tone). In Example 213d, half of the chordal cross-sections are consonant. The middle voice has the ostinato figure F♯–E. This is a favorite form for an accompanying voice. (More often the ostinato tends to be the *basis* for creating harmonic as well as melodic content, however; later insertion of ostinato figures is rarer, since it is only rarely possible to use them suitably.)

In all the above examples of harmonization we took care to ensure that the sonic effect of individual chords was good and that there was an overall natural flow. We thus chose chords that were not too harsh, without clashes of intervals 1 and 6, and strove for good dispositions. We led the voices melodically and by the shortest possible path. A practical task defined in this way is pedagogically most useful. It is also possible to practice with harsh chords and provocatively bad dispositions, but the work we have shown here cannot be neglected.

§137. Employing Textural Resources Economically

A particular harmonic content can be realized by different numbers of voices. Two types of problems can arise here: we can either have too many voices for a meager harmonic content, so that we do not know how to occupy them, or we can have too few voices for a rich harmonic content. In the first case we must resort to systematic doubling of pitches in the chords, while in the second case we must take advantage of the harmonic potency of individual voices. Especially in modern harmony, which works mostly with more complex chords richer in pitches, it is important to use a small number of voices economically. We must try to lead voices in such a way that real pitches leave behind as many as possible imaginary pitches that can function harmonically. If complex harmonic content is to be expressed by a small number of voices, it is expedient to combine the voices in such a way that what has been said harmonically by one voice is not redundantly repeated by other voices.

A *two-voice texture* is most suitable for practicing such *economy*. The harmonization can be completed by working out a single accompanying voice. In this way we have worked out some of the examples in §136 above. It is very important that the resulting two voice texture have a sufficiently full sound.

Example 214 demonstrates such economy in the sphere of modern harmony. As our melodic basis we have chosen an evenly-flowing étude melody in a fairly lively tempo. For the accompanying voice in Examples 214a and 214b we always choose a pitch that
1) is not contained in the corresponding half measure segment of the melody, and
2) does not form an unfavourably arranged dissonant interval 1 with any pitch of the corresponding melodic segment.

The first condition ensures that even with relatively little motion in the accompanying voice the partial chord established by the melodic segment is enriched by a new component. The second condition prevents excessive harshness in the created chords. Naturally, pitches are chosen from a melodic viewpoint. By this procedure we can achieve a relatively full sound even in two voices, and with less motion of the accompanying voice.

Example 214

Examples 214a and 214b present two solutions for the same task. In 214c, the accompanying voice is constructed from the pitches we found in 214a and 214b. In 214d, we use two-note chords as accompaniment in the same manner, so the texture involves three voices; the pitches that were used in 214a or 214b are marked with asterisks.

If we want to create richer chords with two voices, we must resort to a styling such as we demonstrated in §135 above, in the example from the *Suite* by Pavel Bořkovec (Examples 204, 205, 206).

We can also construct the accompanying voice so that its real pitches do *not* leave behind imaginary pitches. In such a case it will be advantageous not to double the pitches of the given melody. In the following example the two sample accompanying voices are led consistently in equal small steps in the same direction: in Example 215a chromatically upward, in 215b by whole-tone steps downward. We must try to place such previously chosen pitches according to the rules presented in connection with the preceding example.

Example 215

Practical composition does not adhere strictly to the rules observed in our examples, of course. Isolated deviations cannot disturb the overall effect of a full sound. In the two-voice texture of Example 216[103] both voices were composed simultaneously, so it is not a harmonization of a given melody. The infrequent doubled pitches are marked with asterisks.

Example 216

[musical notation]

By proceeding in large intervals the two voices are striving to create a harmonic content as rich as possible. This is especially true of the lower voice. Thus the opening bass pitches G, D remain in the listener's consciousness for the duration of the full first measure; similarly, the F, D♭ from the opening of the third measure continue as imaginary pitches for a long time after they have actually finished sounding. (The C is immediately cancelled by the D♭.) In contrast to slower harmonic changes in the lower voice, the upper voice brings more rapid changes in quarter- or eighth-note values. If we were to accompany the upper melody by a voice that proceeded mostly in intervals 1 and 2, the harmonic content would not be as rich.

§138. Resolving Dissonant Chords

From a kinetic standpoint, the first practical task of harmony is to resolve dissonant chords. Since in a kinetic conception we consider as dissonant not chords that represent simple (single) functions, but rather functional combinations, we will generally be concerned with compound resolution. (See §114 above.)

Our tasks can be classified according to the dispositions of the given chords. First we can practice resolving chords that are in combination dispositions, or in dispositions in which at least one of the triadic components is clearly isolated. Then we can resolve chords in non-combination dispositions where the pitches of the triadic components (if these components appear at all) are dispersed and interspersed with other pitches.

---

103 This is the opening of the *Preludium* from my *Suite for piano, op. 18*, composed in 1937 (Praha: Hudební matice Umělecké besedy [The Music Association of the Artistic Society], 1939).

In practicing we cannot be content with just one solution. The point of practicing lies in trying to find different solutions. The ideal is to find all the possibilities and then to classify the results.

As an example of a combination harmony we will choose the harmony **+6+** in the disposition G B D – D♭ F A♭. The lower triadic component G B D can represent any one of the pre-tonic functions of the five-member functional system, D or S or P or L. (See §108 above.) The upper component triad then also represents a particular function. The four possible functional interpretations provide four possibilities of resolution into major tonics, as seen in Example 217.

Example 217

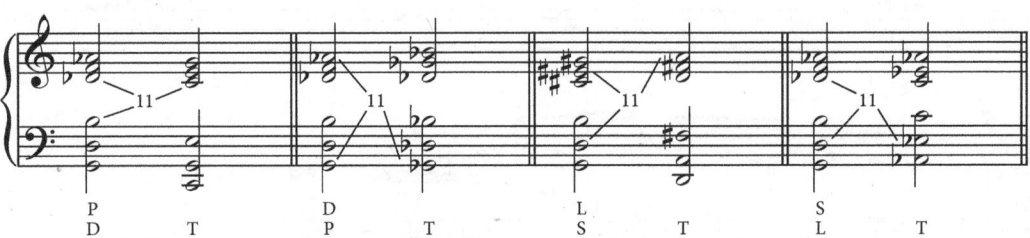

The presence of an auxiliary function is balanced by a primary function; the breaking of the principle of the pure tonic is always tempered by an unfolded group 11 (for example, C D♭ D in the first case); groups 11 are always marked. All four possibilities presented are equally justified; in the given disposition, however, the first one is the most forceful resolution, while the last one is less convincing due to the great weight of the remote function L.

If we want to resolve the partial combination $\widehat{+3+}$ E G♯ B – G B D, we confront the difficulty that when we attribute a particular function to one triadic component, the resulting function of the other component is not single. Thus if we consider the component E G♯ B to be D in A major or minor, the component G B D is the interfunction IN$_2$. (See §110 above.) The interfunction can then break the principle of the pure tonic, since it can contain significant components of functions P, L, or –D, without the necessary counterbalance. (See §118 above.) We present the possible tonics in Example 218.

Example 218

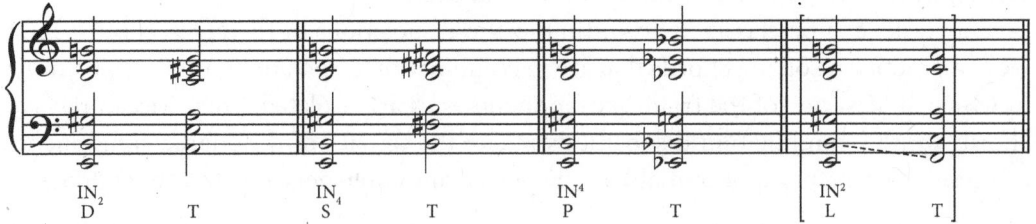

Chapter VIII – Compositional Practice

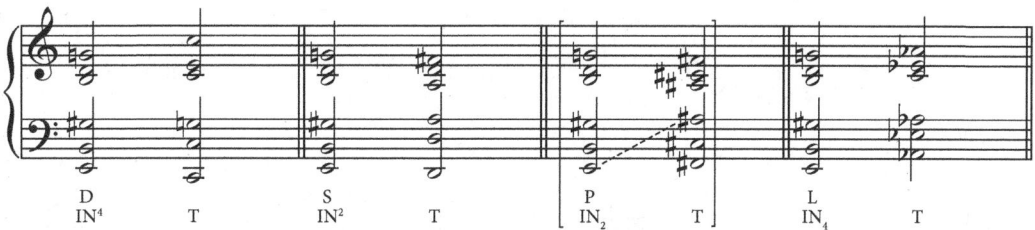

The successions in square brackets lead into unstable tonics; here the principle of the pure tonic is not observed in that the auxiliary functions are not balanced by suitable primary functions, and the pitches that cause a tritone complication of the tonic are not part of the group 11. Tritone relations are indicated by dotted lines.

In all the above examples, we limited ourselves to resolutions into major tonics. We can look for minor tonics in the same way, of course. We can also choose more complex chords.

Let us now turn to the second task, the resolution of chords in whose dispositions triadic components are not separated from each other. Here we can proceed by assigning a particular function to component two-note chords or even to individual pitches; we then find the tonic that corresponds to this function, and we classify the remaining components of the given chord functionally according to this tonic. The following procedure is more practical, however: we work through all the tonics in the chromatic system (C major, D♭ major, D major, E♭ major, etc., and the same in minor), looking for tonics that conform to the principle of the pure tonic; if we find a tritone relation (or a whole-tone relation below the basic pitch of a minor tonic), we ascertain whether or not this relation is softened by an unfolded group 11. An example will clarify this.

We look for tonics into which the chord D F B C♯ can resolve. In each case we present a general functional analysis that justifies our classification.

Major tonics that conform to the principle of the pure tonic are shown in Example 219. Less stable major tonics are shown in Example 220.

Example 219

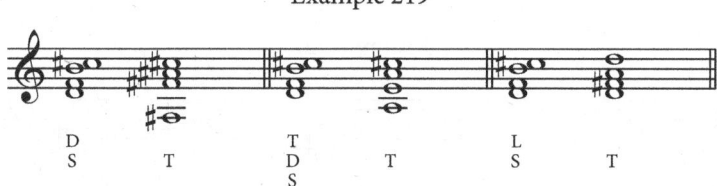

Example 220

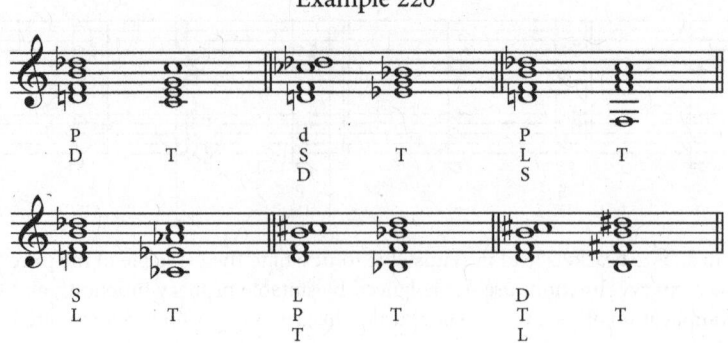

Example 221

Altered dominants d (–D), unless they are balanced by components +D or L, make apparent tonic triads unstable, as shown in Example 221. These remaining major triads cannot be considered possible tonics.

In the same way we can look for possible minor tonics. Here the important factor disturbing the chosen triad's tonic quality will be the presence of altered functions d and s (in A minor, E G B, D F♯ A).[104]

Although the resolution of more complex chords limits the possibilities of complete resolution (see Example 219), the number of triads that cannot be considered tonics is decreased as well (see Example 221).

When dealing with combination harmonies and chords whose dispositions concentrate the pitches of at least one component triad separately, we can look for suitable tonics in the way we have just demonstrated. Thus the chord G B D – D♭ F A♭ can be resolved as in Example 222, in addition to the ways shown earlier.

Example 222

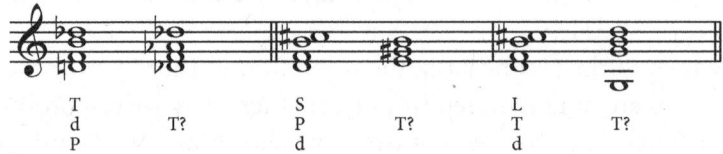

[104] Editor's note: Again a reminder that Janeček uses lower-case letters to indicate alteration – "d" for the minor dominant, "s" for the major subdominant in minor keys – so the lower case does not always indicate a minor triad.

Chapter VIII – Compositional Practice

The functional meaning of the chord being resolved appears complex, as the analyses indicate.

Finally, we remind that a balanced functional structure of a chord is the best guarantee for a strong tonic effect of the triad of resolution. Especially the disruptive altered dominant d must be balanced by a normal dominant or by a major or minor lydian triad. The altered subdominant s in the minor intrudes less strongly into the final tonic; even here, the balancing presence of a normal subdominant or a major or minor phrygian triad is needed.

A strong representation of the tonic in the chord being resolved also weakens the effect of the progression into the tonic. The succession D F♯ B C♯ to D F♯ A D, although containing the resolution of the dominant (C♯) and subdominant (B), is ineffective because the D and F♯ are part of the intended tonic. Thus here we must at least replace direct links by indirect ones. (See §91 above.)

§139. Seeking a Suitable Pre-tonic Combination

The opposite task to seeking a tonic into which a given dissonant chord could resolve is seeking a suitable functional combination (dissonant chord) to precede a previously chosen tonic. Here the possibilities are extensive. In order for such a pre-tonic chord to gravitate reliably toward the chosen tonic, it must contain components of opposite functions: on one side D and L, on the other S and P. Although components of the tonic (especially its differentiating pitch, the third) in the pre-tonic chord relate the chord and the tonic more closely, at the same time they make the move to the tonic tamer, less vigorous, especially when the common pitches function as direct links.

In Example 223 we present several suitable pre-tonic dissonant chords directed to the minor tonic D F A.

Example 223

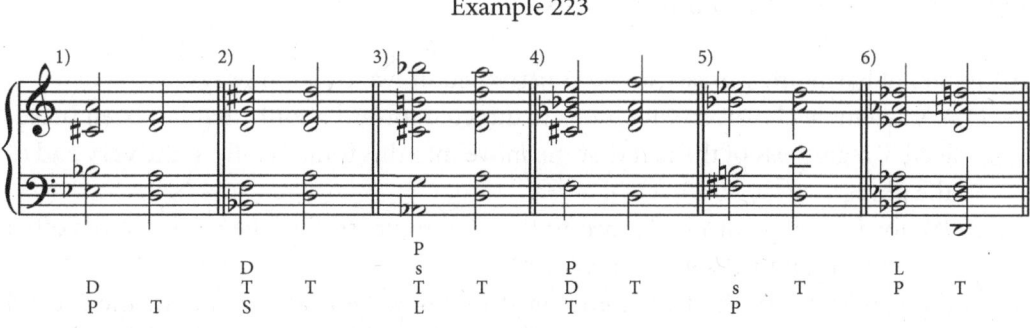

In Example 223.1, the opposing functions P and D are equally involved, with two pitches each. The more significant function D is in a less significant place (higher), while the more remote function P is emphasized by its lower place. – In 223.2, only primary functions are involved; the presence of the tonic (through the differentiating pitch F and the basic pitch D) is not detrimental here, as the other functions are represented clearly enough, and the chord is richer (five notes). The single dominant pitch C♯ counterbalances the complete subdominant (G B♭ D), because tonally it represents a far more important function. (See §113 above.) – In 223.3 we have formed a six-note chord. The somewhat disruptive effect of the B, which stands in a tritone relation to the differentiating pitch F of the tonic and is part of an altered subdominant G B D, is softened by the presence of the B♭; the altered subdominant cannot be fully effective as it is overshadowed by the normal minor subdominant (B♭ as part of G B♭ D), or by the phrygian triad (B♭ as part of E♭ G♭ B♭ or E♭ G B♭). – In 223.4 we have used a five-note chord in a somewhat harsh disposition. (The group 11 F G♭ E* is in a bad, although not the worst, disposition here; it is like Example 68y in §72 above.) Correct resolution justifies even this harshness, however. – Examples 223.5 and 223.6 are more remote, as is evident from the functions. It is interesting that in 223.5 a part of the altered subdominant (the B) intervenes to counterbalance the entire P triad. The functions P and L in 223.6 are not so isolated in reality, since both contain important pitches (C♯, B♭) from the primary functions D and S.

Once found, pre-tonic dissonant chords can be combined into longer successions. In Example 224 we present successions formed from the chords in the preceding example; we have made slight changes in disposition for better (more direct) voice-leading. The reliability and stability of the tonic is always ensured here by two successive chords.

Example 224

This brings us to the point where we can work out continuous chord successions on a functional basis.

§140. Functional Chord Successions

A functional harmonic phrase can be constructed in two different ways:
1) We assemble chords so that they are directed toward a tonic that has been preselected, regardless of the fact that the move into this tonic is only at the very end of the phrase.
2) We form chords with no regard to the final tonic, so that the other chords often conflict with it (are not suitable for it).

In the first method, the final tonic must be known ahead of time. In the second method, this need not be the case; if it *is* known, however, it is possible to defy it consciously, that is, it is possible to form chords that do not constitute suitable pre-tonic formations. In the second method, it often happens that a chord is resolved (imperfectly, of course – see §114 above) into another dissonant chord, which thus acquires the function of a temporary (local) complicated tonic.

We dealt with harmonic phrases of the first type in §139 above (Example 224). We adapt chords to the preselected final tonic; it is unnecessary to consider its concrete disposition. (It is not even advisable to do so, since this would jeopardize the free melodic development of the voices.) In Example 225 we present samples of such short phrases.

Example 225

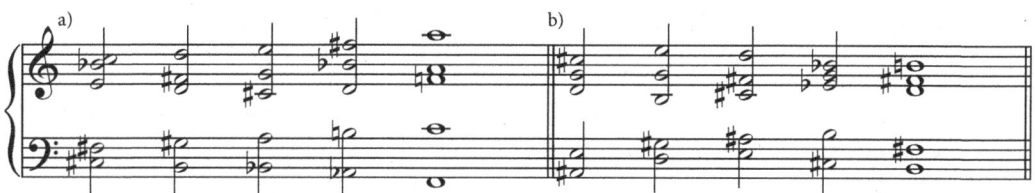

The third chord in Example 225b has a harsh disposition; functionally, however, it is the most definite combination of the entire phrase, since a complete dominant is represented in it. Functional clarity often serves as the excuse for the harsh effect of chords. Each of the chords was constructed such that it could directly and convincingly be resolved into the tonic, which has a different disposition each time. This is shown by Example 226.

Example 226

Harmonic phrases in which all the chords gravitate consciously toward the tonic cannot be too extensive. It is especially important to be economical with length when the chords are very definite functionally. For a harmonic phrase to be as effective as possible, for increased tension and interest, it is better if the dissonant chords that are consciously directed toward the final tonic can be functionally interpreted also in a different way (equally well or even more suitably). We will verify this if we attempt to resolve the individual chords into other tonics. In Example 227 we resolve the first three chords from our phrases in Examples 225a and 225b into other tonics than those originally intended:

Example 227

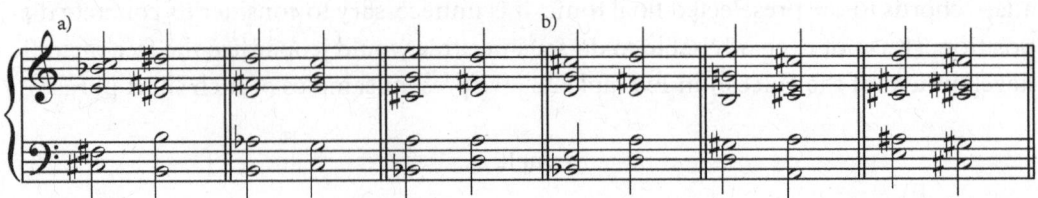

Chords that can be especially favourably resolved into other tonics represent a strong tonally centrifugal element. From here it is only a small step to chords that defy the final tonic completely.

We write the second type of harmonic phrase without considering a preselected tonic, and we examine the relations of individual chords to this tonic only after the fact. We determine the tonic on the basis of the penultimate chord. (See §138 above.) We must continue to pay attention to good voice-leading, however, especially in the outer voices. We present an example of such work in Example 228.

Example 228

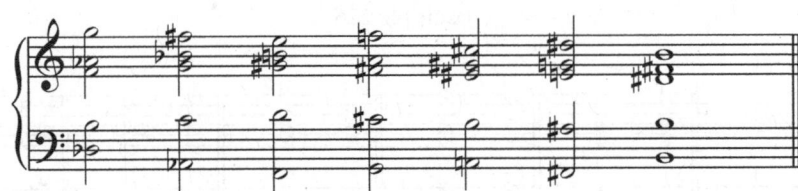

Through analysis carried out after the fact, we find that some chords have a good direct relation to the tonic derived from the penultimate chord, while others do not.

Example 229

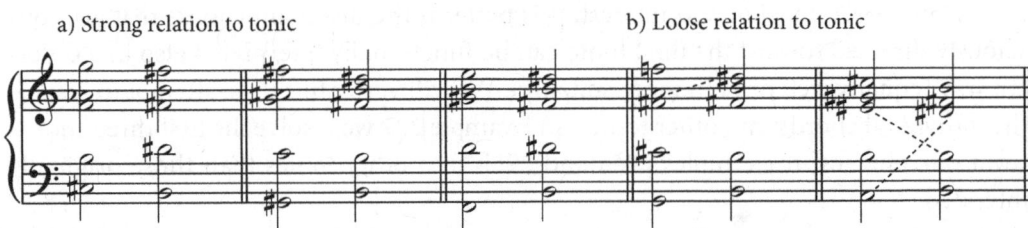

a) Strong relation to tonic   b) Loose relation to tonic

Group b in Example 229 presents connections, since the preceding chord does not make the tonic B D♯ F♯ sufficiently firm; these are shown by the dotted lines indicating tritone relations.

The progression between the fifth and sixth chords of our harmonic phrase in Example 228 can be considered an imperfect resolution in F♯ major. The F♯ major tonic is expressed here only by the pitches F♯ and A♯, while it is complicated by the E, G, and D♯. Thus the chord A B E♯ G♯ C♯ serves as a complicated applied dominant to the complicated local tonic F♯ A♯ E G D♯. (This is the dominant ninth harmony with the sixth D♯ instead of the fifth C♯, well known in romantic music.)

No matter what method was used to work out a harmonic phrase, the phrase can be enriched after the fact by chords that distinctly defy the tonic. In the case of securely determined tonics, such foreign chords have a welcome, refreshing effect – especially immediately before the end of the phrase. For example, we can enrich, or unsettle tonally, the cadence of our harmonic phrase (Example 228) as in Example 230.

Example 230

Especially the second progression in this example represents a deeper interference with the control of the tonic, since the progression from the inserted chord to the tonic comes precariously close to a mere transfer, as shown by the common pitches D♯ and F♯. (See §114 above.)

Practice in working out functional harmonic phrases is important for composers, as it sharpens tonal awareness. Only composers who have mastered the art of determining the tonic can permit themselves to play the dangerous game of disturbing the tonic. Contemporary music is especially sensitive in the extent to which the tonic is determined. Too explicit a definition of the tonic is felt as a trite progression, while deeper interference can fully eradicate a sense of the tonic.

§141. Functional Variations in a Chord Progression

Once formed, a chord succession can be varied in diverse ways. Training in such variation is useful compositional practice. If the pitch content of a chord remains the same, variation occurs only in the chord's disposition. If the pitch content changes, however, the functional orientation of the chord also changes. Here we will be taking note of such functional variations.

Since we are concerned with mere variations, not with a radical functional restructuring of the harmonic phrase, we must not remove the most significant functional component of the chord. We are content with shifting individual pitches or adding new pitches, which vary (complicate) the original function by adding new functional components. With complex chords we carry out functional variations more often by shifting the pitches (for example, in the dominant ninth chord G D B F A♭ we replace the A♭, which in C major belongs to the minor subdominant, by B♭, belonging to the altered dominant in the same key); with simple chords we will more often add new pitches.

The significance of the most important functional component, the one that characterizes the entire chord, is determined by its absolute meaning in the functional system, its representation, and its placement. For example, the component D is more significant than L; a function represented completely by three pitches is more significant than one whose representation is incomplete; finally, a functional component is more significant when it is placed lower.

As a basic exercise, we recommend the variation of a two-chord succession with a single functional meaning, for example the resolution of D into T. In Example 231 we present several variations of the succession D T in C major. We achieve all the variations by adding new pitches to the first chord and then merely doubling pitches in the second, while taking care that there is good voice-leading.

Example 231

In Example 231.1 we added to the original pure dominant a subdominant component (F) and a lydian component (D♯); in 231.2 we added subdominant and phrygian (D♭) components. In classical harmony, such variations are labelled alterations; however, our examples are not classical, in that the original pitch D is used simultaneously with the altered pitches D♯ or D♭. – In Examples 231.3 and 231.4 we used the differentiating pitch of the altered dominant (B♭); considering the significance of the normal dominant (D), this in no way jeopardizes the stability of the tonic. – Not even the addition of three new pitches in Examples 231.5 and 231.6 disguises the fundamental dominant character of the first chord. The dominant still remains the chief functional component. – In 231.7, the lydian components D♯ and F♯ are not balanced by one of the opposite functions (S or P); what is important here is the effect of the added D♯ and the original D sounding simultaneously. If we were to enrich the original triad G B D merely by F♯, we would disrupt much more its relation to the tonic C E G to which it resolves. – In Example 231.8 the bad disposition of the interval 1 (B C) is balanced by the good disposition of the groups 11 (D D♭ C*, B B♭* C); regarding this, see §72 above.

From two chord successions we proceed to successions involving more chords. First we will work out the plain cadence T S D T in C major, as in Example 232. To this cadence, worked out in three voices, we can add a different melody in the highest voice each time, thus varying the single functions of the original chords.

Example 232

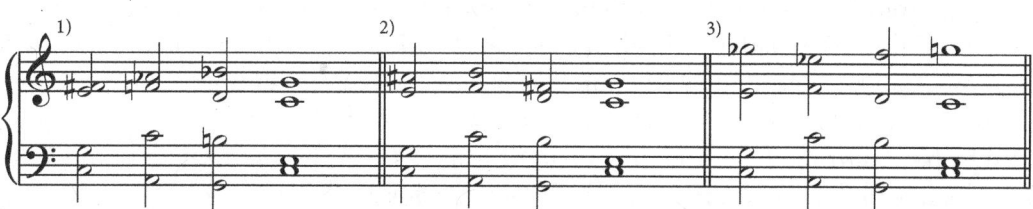

If in creating the added melody we were content to use only pitches contained in the single functions, naturally no functional complications (variations) would result. We have left only the final tonic without interference. The functional components that we added in Example 232.1 are L, –S (or P), d. – In 232.2, we can view the first chord as an applied dominant to the following local tonic. The lydian component F♯ in the dominant can occur without a simultaneous counterbalance, since it is preceded by a pronounced subdominant. – The cadence in 232.3 is almost classical, except that the dominant seventh F does not resolve down.

In Example 233 we present similar variations of a cadence that also involves interfunctions.

Example 233

IN$_2$ IN$_4$ D   T

If we add a melody in the bass to a given chord succession, we interfere more significantly with the functional structure of the chords, because the added pitches, representing new functional components, will have greater weight in relation to the original functional components. In Example 234 we have added a melody in the bass to functional successions realized in the upper three voices:

Example 234

T   S   P   D   T   P –IN^3 S   T

These short examples are related to modern practice of harmonization. Rather than simply realizing the latent harmony of a melody or melodic segment, the contemporary composer often adds a significant functional component that the melody does not even suggest. From a harmonic point of view, the melodic segment then represents a functional addition. The matter will become clearer if we look at all the examples presented as if they had been created by harmonizing a melody. Thus for example the above Examples 231.7 and 231.8 in the variations of the succession D T could also have been created by harmonizing the descending melodic leap C–G; the harmonization of this leap by the succession D T in C major is not to be taken for granted.

§142. Free Composition

The final goal of all the exercises we have recommended here is *free composition*. By this we mean the working out of a composition or a compositional passage on the basis of a spontaneous idea, rather than as a given task. Although immediate ideas and unexpected turns of phrase play a significant part in composition, in its concentration of thoughts and moods good music grows primarily out of an idea that has been considered, that has matured. A unified and coherent whole cannot result just from improvisation.

Music that is not to be a mere technical realization of a given exercise must first arise out of experience, out of a certain mood or state of mind. The music created is then the expression of this mood. The composer's efforts are concentrated on polishing, on working out the original idea technically in the manner most suitable to its character and most effective in translating the composer's experience or mood. The compositional order embodied by music that is created in this way is a reliable guide to the inner pulse of the music. A coldly constructed order that is not founded on experience is worthless for the ultimate effect of the music.

In purely technical compositional work, component tasks can be established. It is possible for example to give a melody that is to be harmonized, or a harmonic basis that is to be worked out by melodic voice-leading. In free composition we must strive to make the music, at least in its main outlines, grow *as a whole, with all its components simultaneously*. The mastery of mature composers is characterized by their ability to think music in an integrated way. Only the details are worked out later, not the entire harmonic or polyphonic structure, for example. Later, any original subsidiary ideas (for example in harmony) that were not so fortunate are corrected, eliminated, or replaced by others more suitable (more prominent, or conversely not so obtrusive). Later, the music that has been created is criticized, and its effect is tested again and again. Later, foreign elements and disruptive or inconsequential impurities are eliminated from the music that has welled up spontaneously. Later, the compositional order that has as if by itself grown out of the original idea is determined, and eventual deviations are adjusted to this order if they disturb the overall organism of the music.

It is impossible to show step by step in a book the gradual growth of music. We can only present the results of our work and comment on them. Our examples are based on a certain presumption of mood, which we briefly indicate whenever possible.

Example 235, the theme from my *Variations, op. 23*, composed in 1942,[105] represents a widely arched melody that steps forth in a stately manner, with a full cadence that dies away into silence. The melody is diatonic (C major), without chromatic weakness, without atonal instability or uncertainty. The harmonic orientation is tonal, and the entry of the tonic is consciously delayed until the very end of the phrase. (We use the above traits to express by circumlocution the atmosphere of the mood from which the phrase originated.)

Example 235

The first measure introduces the original idea (motive). This comprises not just the melody, but the combination of melodic and harmonic components. Even the requested manner of performance (arpeggiated) is characteristic of this idea. Out of the original idea grows an irregular (ten-measure) period with its melodic

---

[105] Praha: Hudební matice Umělecké besedy [Music Association of the Artistic Society], 1949.

climax in the consequent (on the C). The antecedent mainly employs non-tonic functions, all in combinations. In the consequent, the complete tonic flashes through in two combinations (in the eighth and ninth measures). Although the melody ends in the tenth measure, a new three-measure melody (coda-like) is introduced in an inner voice, while the highest voice is accompanimental. The division into period and coda is emphasized by the difference in styling [texture].

The final pitch of the melody (C, in the tenth measure) is not harmonized by the expected tonic, but rather by the combination $\frac{-S}{P}$. B♭, which we avoided from the beginning in order not to disturb the tonic C E G, is introduced in the bass in the second half of the tenth measure. However, B is immediately introduced to counterbalance this B♭, which is remote in C major. An uncomplicated tonic (C G) is first heard in the second half of the eleventh measure, but it is again temporarily complicated by a dominant pitch (D) and a subdominant pitch (A♭), so as *not* to appear without complications *until* the final measure. Thus the harmonic plan of the entire phrase is a search for the tonic. By delaying the entry of the tonic, we encourage the development of the melody. Were the uncomplicated tonic to be introduced earlier, the overall arch of the melody would lose its meaning; the harmonically functional aspect would come into conflict with the melodic plan and frustrate the full effect of the melody.

Example 236 comes from a similar mood, only one somewhat more suffused with lyricism. What is musically important is the open-endedness of the musical flow.

Example 236

The melodic line of the first two measures represents the original idea. This is why it was better to leave it unharmonized. The melody is composed of two not quite equal phrases, and it is clearly tonal (in F minor). The last three measures serve only to fill out the musical flow; they form a transition. An uncombined tonic is used only in the fifth measure, if we do not count the latent tonic in the first measure; everywhere else there are functional combinations. The whole does not modulate. Except for the chords on the second and third beats of the third measure, all chordal cross-sections have a clear, direct relation to the tonic F A♭ C. (All chordal cross-sections can be credibly resolved into the tonic; we discovered this only after the fact – we did not consider such possibilities while working.) In contrast to Example 235, where the music was directed toward a tonic that was constantly being delayed, here the tonic is the starting point; a temporary goal is the complicated dominant in the last three measures. As in Example 235, all chords that appear independently are given good, full-sounding dispositions. The bass G on the second beat of the fifth measure, forming a bad relation with the A♭ in the melody, is passing.

Example 236 is the theme of my *Sonata for piano, op. 25*, composed in 1944–45. The three following examples (237, 238, and 239) are also from this composition. The music in Examples 237 and 238 comes from the world of a different mood. This is painfully tense, unstable, hesitant music. To this mood corresponds the metrical changeability, the non-diatonic line of the main melody (in Example 237 in an inner voice, in Example 238 in the highest voice), and last but not least the intentionally harsh not-too-rich chords (but mostly in good dispositions).

Example 237

Example 238

Functionally, the passages in Examples 237 and 238 are both atonal. As tends to happen, however, even in music so conceived it is possible to uncover functional relations. Example 238 suggests the key of F minor by its persistent return to the chord F A♭ C E; the end of the first measure is a significant deviation.

In Example 239 we present a music transparently styled, clear, and melodious. The melody reaches its climax already at the boundary between the second and third measures. The first two five-measure phrases are open while the third is closed, although only melodically; the expected harmonic goal (D major tonic) has been replaced by a minor subdominant (G B♭ D), which is introduced after a major subdominant (G B D) and is then immediately complicated by a harmony absolutely foreign tonally, F A♭ C. Thus again as a whole this music is not closed.

Example 239

In contrast to the tonally unambiguous melody, the harmony in Example 239 is interlaced with diverse functional twists and turns. The tonic (D major) is suggested twice at the beginning. It does not sound again. The cadences of the first two five-measure phrases do not tie in with the music that follows, so the open endedness of these phrases is emphasized harmonically. The closer we come to the cadence of the melody, the more we try by harmonic devices to lead attention away from the appropriate tonic. The triad (F A♭ C) with which we combine the subdominant at the very end has already been heard twice, in measures 11 and 12. It is worth noting that an inner voice continues its eighth-note figuration in D major here, regardless of the triadic component F A♭ C that has just been introduced. (For the progression of the figure B–C♯–B, the C from the triad F A♭ C functions as a counter-cancelling pitch. Regarding this see §77 above.)

We present a polyphonic example (Example 240) from my *Trio for string instruments, op. 9*, composed in 1930. Here we play with a melodious, widely straddling motive, which also appears in melodic inversion.

Chapter VIII – Compositional Practice

Example 240

Since the essence of the idea lies in this constantly recurring five-pitch motive, we have limited ourselves to the simplest possible harmonic accompaniment, especially since the motive itself is harmonically comprehensive. The passage was composed without tonal orientation.

Many more examples could be presented. It is useful to work out music with types of expression as diverse as possible, music that uses always newer styling resources and is always structured differently and given a different harmonic basis. It is well not to forget bitonality, modulations, and applied functions. We must remember the importance of *melody*, however, since music without a definite melodic line cannot grow to breathe as broadly and cannot even cohere. It is equally important to take care that the compositional order is pure and well-defined, since this increases the cohesion and flow of the music; without a definite ruling compositional order, the music easily becomes scattered, distracted, and lacking in concentration.

We also emphasize that technical dexterity (compositional ease) loses all value if it yields results that are mere repetitions of each other, or are all of the same type (mannered). *Good music must be newly invented.* Thus compositional training cannot consist merely in acquiring working dexterity, but rather it must be the *development of full musical thought*. Well thought-out compositions that have been worked out in a new, independent manner, with the cogency of an artistic personality, cannot be manufactured on an assembly line.

Chapter IX – Analytical Practice

§143. A Method of Harmonic Analysis

Already in our compositional exercises we have pointed out the necessity of temporarily concentrating on a defined group of phenomena (for example, static phenomena), while leaving other matters (for example, problems related to motion) without conscious intervention. We can proceed the same way in harmonic analysis. We can begin to examine static phenomena even before we have mastered the theory of kinetic harmony. However, a comprehensive analysis is only possible after we have exhausted the entire body of theoretical material.

The analysis must be carried out *methodically*. Especially in our first attempts at analysis, we must consider even the smallest and most commonplace details. With more extensive practice, we can work our way to the point where we can orient ourselves quickly and then concentrate our attention only on the unusual, on uncommon deviations, etc.

Our method must proceed from basic harmonic phenomena, that is, from unclassified real chords. We must pay attention to every *chordal cross-section*. From this we can move to phenomena that need not appear in every harmonic phrase: *the differentiation between harmonies and transient chords*, the searching out of imaginary pitches, and *the definition of chords from real and imaginary pitches*. Even before examining the harmony from a kinetic (functional) standpoint, we should note *the compositional order and melodic lines*. Only after this do we get to tracing *functional relations* and all the kinetic harmonic phenomena.

Besides properties that we can determine objectively and unambiguously, in composition we often meet *intentional indefiniteness* that results in indeterminacy of some aspect. This occurs most often in the rhythmic-metric boundary between modern chords in composite expression, and also in the area of functionality. It suffices to point out such indefiniteness; it makes no sense laboriously to devise particular interpretations when other interpretations are equally justified.

Compositional exercises have practical significance especially for composers. Exercises in analysis are essential for all musicians, however, composers and non-composers; it is impossible to understand the harmonic aspect of music merely by reading theoretical reflections.

In the following sections we work through stages of methodical analysis, using examples from contemporary music. It is understood that every passage of a composition can be examined in all its aspects, not merely the one we have chosen for our demonstration. Therefore we will sometimes return to examples.

§144. Examining and Evaluating Real Chordal Cross-sections; Seeking New Chord Formations

As we have said, *real chords* constitute the first reality of every harmonic phrase, so they must be considered first. A description of chords (chordal cross-sections) and determination of their types can be carried out for every harmonic phrase. It will be useful in the first exercise to seek music in which real pitches solely or at least primarily bear the harmony, and in which each chordal cross-section is significant enough to represent a harmony (even if incomplete). In practice this means that primarily music with a larger number of voices moving simultaneously will be suitable for us.

As illustration we present in Example 241 the opening of the *Chorale* from a *Suite for piano* by Pavel Bořkovec.

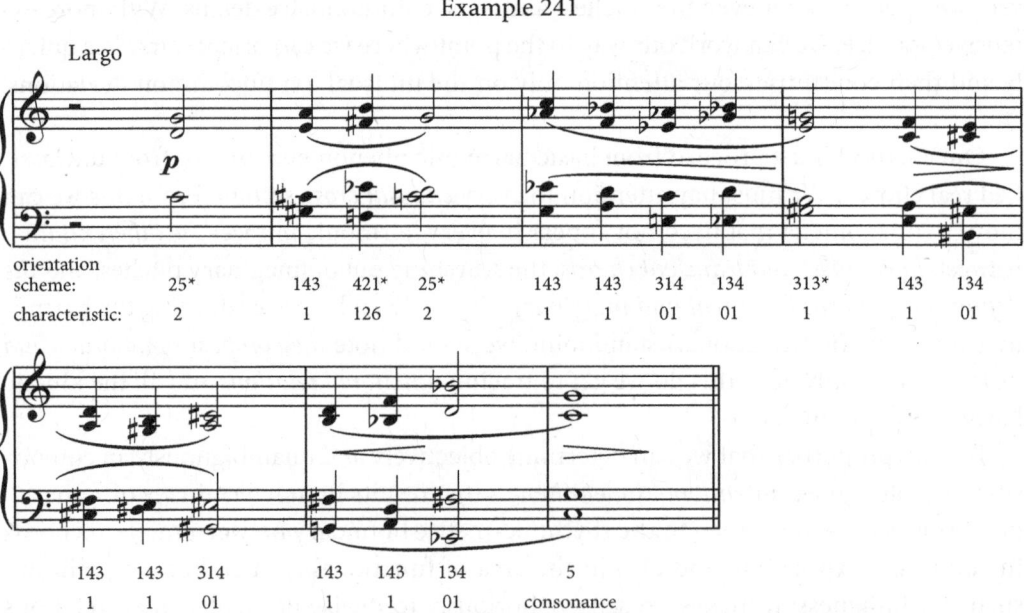

Example 241

Mostly four-note chords are heard here. We have marked with an asterisk new chord formations unknown to classical harmony: these constitute only four chords out of eighteen. Many chord-types return transposed or in different dispositions – most often the four-note chord 143; in all, seven chord-types appear. All the chords represent *harmonies*, complete or incomplete; there are no *transient* chords. The composer was seeking chords with the *characteristic* 1 or 01. Only a single chord (421) is characterized by the tritone. Half the chords have the family characteristic + and − (313 and 143, cf. §55 above), while only three chords belong to neither family – 25, which appears twice, and 5.

Dispositions are intentionally harsh, so the dissonant interval 1 sounds in an unfavourable position as a ninth or a second; where it does sound in a favourable position, as a seventh, this interval does not include the highest pitch, except in the chord G♯ B E G at the beginning of the fourth measure. In the evaluation of chords and their dispositions, we cannot always content ourselves with the classification with which we are theoretically familiar. We must evaluate each chord individually and non-theoretically, by listening. Thus we often find a "beautiful" sound in a disposition that we would theoretically classify as bad. Then we inquire as to the reason for this effect and search for it. In Example 241, the second chord in the second measure (421) has a full ("beautiful") sonority, even though its interval 1 is in an unfavorable position and is not part of the group 213. There are two explanations for the pleasant effect of this chord:

1) the A from the preceding chord was not completely cancelled, so it can be included in the group 213 F E♭* F♯ A; and

2) the chord 421 differs favorably by its rich characteristic 126 from the chords that surround it, the dull chord 25 C* D G and the unfavorably arranged chord 143 G♯* C♯ E A.

The analysis we have presented is only partial.

§145. Determining Chords from Real and Imaginary Pitches; Rhythmic and Metric Distribution of Chords in a Composition; Transient Chords

For the examination of chordal cross-sections in §144 above, we chose music in which there were practically no imaginary pitches and in which it was unnecessary to determine whether chords were harmonies or transient. In actual music, however, we rarely meet a harmonic phrase so conveniently constructed; especially in instrumental music, imaginary pitches play a considerable role in creating harmony. We therefore present, as Example 242, another example from the *Chorale* by Pavel Bořkovec.

We can examine real chordal cross-sections in this passage in the same way as for Example 241 above. In a two-voice texture, these will of course be only two-note chords. However, the real chords only partially bear the harmonic content here. Their examination has meaning only for music that moves slowly, as does our passage. Dissonances 1 are introduced nine times without preparation, by the simultaneous motion of both voices (indicated by the *), and also nine times with preparation, by oblique motion (indicated by the ⁎); these real dissonant intervals are always in a good disposition. The dissonant interval 2 appears only once; the real tritone does not appear at all. Such a distribution of real dissonances is certainly intentional: the composer was seeking dissonances 1. Of the 65 real cross-sections, 46 are consonances. However, the effect of the passage remains thoroughly dissonant.

Example 242

This proves that the real chords we have been examining are only parts of more complex dissonant harmonic formations. We will determine these if we consider the continuing imaginary pitches.

The pitches that we have not incorporated into chords of composite expression in the harmonic content are shown in parentheses in the original. All non-harmonic tones are shown this way, as well as those harmonic pitches that disappear with the introduction of an adjacent harmonic pitch (in the lower voice, B in the fourth measure and F♯ in the sixth measure; these pitches function as full chord components in a different octave in the upper voice). Pitches that we have included in the subsequent chord, although their real sound takes place in the metric region of the preceding chord, are separated out by a square bracket. In measure 5, we eliminated the F♯ from the chord C♯ G A C* E 1332 in this way, and we included it in the subsequent chord B D G F♯* A♯ 1313 in measure 6. From the domain of this chord we eliminated the D♯ and included it in the chord E♭ C D♯ G♯* B 313 in the second half of the sixth measure. We did this because these pitches can be perceived as part of the chords in whose metric regions they actually sound only at the price of excessive (and therefore unnecessary) complication. From the five-note chord C♯ G A C* E 1332 we would have to form the six-note chord C♯ G A C* E F♯ 13212, and from the well arranged five-note chord B D G F♯* A♯ 1313, the badly arranged five-note chord B D G* D♯ A♯ 3131.

The most natural place for boundaries between adjacent chords is on the border between primary metric beats. We draw two or more beats together into the domain of one chord in composite expression only if this does not result in too complex a chord or in one with a bad disposition. Thus if we were to merge the pitch content of the first two beats in the first measure into a single chord, we would get the five-note chord E♭ C♭* F G C 1322, with a badly arranged dissonant interval C♭–C. The complexity and unsuitable disposition of this chord compel us to divide the pitch content into two simpler chords with good dispositions, as we have presented them in the "harmonic content". Although the introduction of the C♭ does not cancel the C, since the C♭ lies in a different octave, the unsuitable disposition of the interval 1 between these pitches prevents the C (which is unsupported by real sound) from interfering effectively and long enough with the chord being formed; the more complex chord therefore breaks up into two chords with a simpler sound. We are not dealing here with a theoretical simplification, with a more comfortable interpretation, but rather with actual harmonic hearing: the music itself demands to be broken down; the music itself resists being drawn together into a single chord. Another motivation for division into two successive simpler chords is the rising whole-tone progression F–G. The G does not cancel the preceding F. This also complicates the resulting harmony, by the harmonically unsuitable component of a second, while division into two chords assigns these pitches to different chord formations, as we see in the written-out harmonic content.

In the second half of the first measure, the pitch content does not have to be divided. All the pitches except the non-harmonic F♯ merge to form the four-note chord C♯ E G♯ C* E 134; although the C and C♯ do not really sound together, they are in a good disposition, so the resulting chord is clear. In the second half of the fourth measure, we have drawn the unfavourably arranged interval 1 between the D and E♭ into one harmony, since the D does not disappear quickly because it is lower. However, we could also have divided this half-measure into two successive chords: D B G* B♭ 313, and C E♭ G B* 134. In the seventh measure we could have drawn together into one well arranged chord the pitch material of the second and third beats: G B♭ D♭ F♯* A 1213. We did not do this, because this division is not the simplest metrically.

In determining chords from real and imaginary pitches, we must constantly consider the possibilities of *transient* chords. By eliminating certain pitches as non-harmonic, we attribute the character of transient chords to the chordal cross-sections involved. According to our interpretation there are four unaccented and three accented transient chords in Example 242. The unaccented transient chords (marked a) were created in the first measure by a regular passing tone (F♯) resolved upward by a whole-step, in the eighth measure by a free passing tone resolved upward by half-step (C♯), in the fifth and sixth measures by premature entry of non-harmonic tones (F♯, D♯) that belong to the following chords (so called "free" or "escape" notes of anticipation). The C♯ in the eighth measure can also be understood as a regular passing tone between the B and D. The accented transient chords (b) were all created by appoggiaturas, belatedly resolved (B♭…B, E…E♭, F♯…G).

We can examine the type and characteristic of the chords at which we have arrived through our analysis in the same way as we did for Example 241. However, we must be aware that chords in composite expression do not have the weight of chords in real expression. A different interpretation changes chord-type and characteristic. In examining the harmonic content we work out, we must never forget the sound of the music we are analyzing.

§146. Chordal and Harmonic Character of a Composition; Character of Dispositions

In the analysis of Examples 241 and 242, we observed that the types and dispositions of chords intentionally formed by the composer determine the impression made by the composition or a passage within it. Determining the overall character of the composition is another task of analysis.

The static harmonic material of a composition is characterized by
a) chord-types,
b) harmonies or characteristic-types of chords, and
c) dispositions of chords. We must judge these three aspects of the harmonic content if we want to characterize and classify the music harmonically.

If we wanted to establish the overall chordal character of a composition absolutely precisely ("pedantically"), we would have to examine all the chordal cross-sections, classify them as harmonies or transient chords, and process statistically all the material thus obtained. For usual analytical practice, however, such a procedure is not profitable. We can resort to it occasionally, when examining shorter distinctive passages, but not in every analysis.

In determining the overall chordal character of a composition, we must first answer the following fundamental questions:

1) Do one or a few chord-types or characteristic-types, one or a few types of disposition, appear exclusively or predominantly in the given passage, or is a great wealth of chords used?
2) Are the expression of chords and their boundaries and metric placement definite and clear at first glance, or are several interpretations possible?

If in answering the first question we discover that the passage being examined is too varied in its chordal aspect, it will be better to forego detailed chordal characterization. In such a case, the overall character is sometimes determined negatively: a particular characteristic (for example the tritone) is consistently or mainly absent from the harmonies. Thus a deliberate lack of a characteristic forms part of the composition's character. It is also possible that certain chord-types that are common elsewhere, such as consonant chords, are not utilized. If even this is not the case, then the music being examined is characterized by unbounded variety and richness, or by distractedness, lack of clarity, and intentional chaos. Even here, however, it is well to notice distinctive deviations, surprising chords that are obtrusive, etc.

If we discover that a passage docilely limits itself to one or a few chord-types, characteristic-types, and/or dispositions, we must examine the chords in more detail. The more harmonically concentrated the music, the simpler and more definite its overall chordal character.

In music in which chords are in composite expression, and in which transient chords play a considerable role, we must proceed prudently. Here the overall chordal characterization depends on correct (natural) determination of chords in composite expression, not only as to their pitch content, but also as to their metric placement. It makes no sense to construct a detailed characterization of a passage whose harmonic material (in composite expression) is indefinite; here it is precisely this chordal ambiguity that constitutes the character. We hope it is unnecessary to remind the reader that chordal definiteness must be apparent at first glance; otherwise we cannot speak about definiteness.

Let us now turn to a practical evaluation of examples.
In Example 241 (§144 above), the chords are represented as follows:

5..................once	314..................twice
421..................once	134..................three times
313..................once	143..................eight times
25..................twice	

Since the numerically prevailing chord-type 143 does not constitute the majority of chords, it does not necessarily characterize the entire harmonic passage. If we consider the characteristic-types (harmonies) in the same example, we see that against one consonance, one harmony 126, and two harmonies 2 stand nine harmonies 1 and five harmonies 01. These last two characteristic-types characterize the entire composition. We have already discussed (in §144 above) the dispositions of the chords in this example.

In Example 242 (§145 above), the supremacy of the characteristic-types 1 and 01 is less apparent.

Example 243

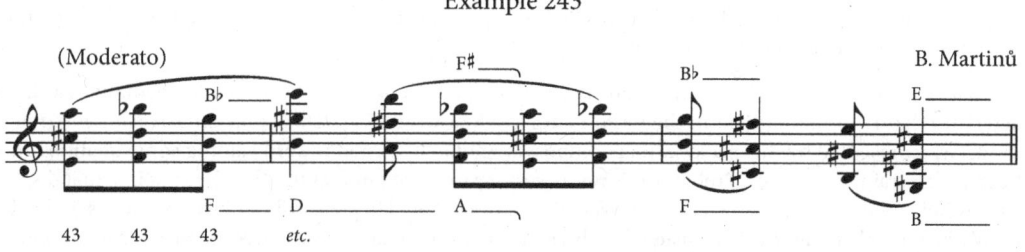

In Example 243 we present a small sample from the opera *Julietta* by Bohuslav Martinů (piano reduction). Only one chord-type appears here (the major triad 43), and in a consistent disposition (as a six-four chord). Thus the chord-type character, and thereby also the harmonic character, of this example is unambiguous. Nevertheless, we cannot recklessly declare the music of the passage to be purely consonant, since there are places in it where continuing harmonic imaginary pitches conspicuously complicate the consonant real sound. Imaginary pitches that continue normally are indicated by a horizontal line after the name of the pitch, while imaginary pitches that die away at an accelerated rate are indicated by a line bent down at the end.

Example 244

In Example 244, the cadence of the final movement (*Fugue*) of the *String Trio, op. 34* by Paul Hindemith, composed in 1924 and dedicated to Alois Hába, we find a different chord-type in each measure, as we can verify from the orientation schemes. The characteristic-types of the chords also change constantly. Here we consider only the chords at the beginning of every phrase, not all chordal cross-sections, because the composer has prescribed a very lively tempo: *sehr lebhafte Halbe*. At first glance, the *exclusion of consonances* is apparent; the simple and mild-sounding dissonant chord 2 is heard only at the very cadence. Common to all the chords except the final one is *harsh disposition*, as pointed out by the square brackets surrounding the pitches of badly arranged intervals 1; the harshness of the dispositions is increased by the frequent *use of counter-cancelling pitches*. The significance of the non-harmonic tones in the melody is thus increased, since these are not quickly and reliably cancelled when resolved by an interval 2. In our example, counter-cancelling pitches are marked by arrows.

The harshness of the sound, which can scarcely be increased with the given instrumental medium, is a characteristic feature of modernism in the period after the first world war. It was only after reaching extreme limits, as represented by this passage, that composers gradually turned toward valuing sonic qualities and began to restrain themselves. Probably it is not necessary to point out that the chords in their actual dispositions in Example 244 are not accidental. Were the chords formed haphazardly and without focus, it would hardly be possible to discover consistent harshness in subsequent analysis; in perfunctory or careless composition, a milder chord in a good disposition would probably slip in despite the composer. The wave of preference of composers for harsh sounds (once "new") has already passed. Composers now prefer to work their way through piled-up ("invented") new chords and attempt to use them as beautiful new sounds, not as repulsive sounds. In this respect, Example 244 represents a standpoint that seems to have been already surmounted. The criticism of its sound is possible because, since its composition, methods have been found and tested by means of which the sound of chords can be "inflected", shaded, or refined.

Chapter IX – Analytical Practice

§147. Examining Transient Chords

In music where the voices move with varied rhythm, besides complete or incomplete harmonies a multitude of *transient chords* arise. The chord-type and disposition of these transient chords help determine the harmonic appearance and effect of the whole, so we cannot omit transient chords in analysis. *Transient chords are always less significant, of course, especially when they are unaccented; their significance increases with their number and duration.*

First we must differentiate between transient chords and harmonies. The following are guides:
1) direct links between chordal cross-sections,
2) the method of leading the moving voices,
3) the sonic quality of consecutive chordal cross-sections connected by partial harmonic motion,
4) the metric placement of chordal cross-sections.

Direct links at the unison, especially, bind together adjacent chordal cross-sections. When we observe voice-leading, we must notice rising *whole-tone progressions*, since not every such progression represents a resolution. We must also remember that the resolution of a non-harmonic tone may be *delayed*.

In evaluating the quality of chordal cross-sections, we pay attention to the general characteristic and also consider familiar classical harmonies. A chordal cross-section with a simpler characteristic will more likely be the harmony than will a neighbouring chordal cross-section with a richer or more remote characteristic; a formation familiar in classical harmony will more probably be the harmony than will a new formation. Often, however, harmonies and transient chords can be differentiated in two or even more different ways.

We present three examples of music rich in transient chords.

Example 245

A. Roussel

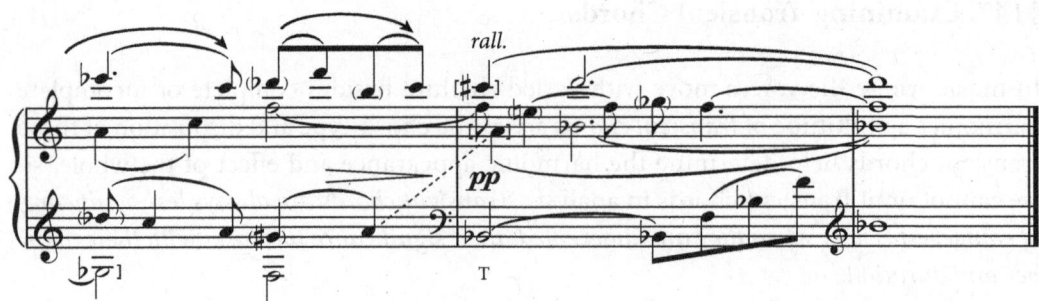

Example 245 is the cadence of the slow movement from the *String Quartet, op. 45*, by Albert Roussel, composed in 1932. This is an authentic cadence D T (F A C E♭ – B♭ D F). These harmonies are continually complicated by non-harmonic tones in such a way that chordal cross-sections always form chord-types that sound good and are familiar from classical harmony. The first harmony does not appear complete as a real sound in any of the cross-sections (on the last eighth of the third measure, only the triad F A C is sounding); the second harmony sounds in the cadence with absolute clarity and completeness. Unaccented non-harmonic tones are shown in round brackets, accented ones (appoggiaturas/suspensions) in square brackets. The resolution of some non-harmonic tones is delayed, as pointed out by arrows.

That transient chords are approximately equivalent in chord-type to the expected harmony F A C E♭ means that some of them can also be interpreted as harmonies, especially when it is possible to find support for such an interpretation in clear functional relations. Thus the first chordal cross-section G♭ B♭ E♭ C represents in B♭ major a minor subdominant with added sixth, a familiar harmony whose location before the dominant is likewise natural. We decided on the harmonic interpretation F A C E♭ – B♭ D F for the following reasons:

1) For the duration of three whole measures, the viola (the third voice) essentially circles around A, alternating upper and lower non-harmonic tones. In the interpretation G♭ B♭ C E♭, the B♭ would be the harmony tone, the A a lower auxiliary, and G♯ a lower auxiliary to the auxiliary tone A. This interpretation would be considerably more remote, even though the long sounding G♭ eventually becomes a harmony tone.

2) Since in the third measure the second voice (violin II) leaves the A without resolution, by leap, we cannot consider it a non-harmonic tone in relation to the harmony G♭ B♭ C E♭. Even if we were to define the harmonic regions in such a way that the harmony G♭ B♭ C E♭ extended over only the first two measures while in the third measure the harmony F A C E♭ were already unfolded, the difficulty presented in the preceding paragraph would apply.

Example 246

Example 246 is a passage from the final movement of the same work. Here we are dealing with the harmony A C♯ E G, which in contrast to the last example is presented in figuration in such a way that the transient chords are often sharply tense and unclassical. Non-harmonic tones are again shown in parentheses; dissonant intervals 1 that have a real sound are indicated by square brackets. Because of the influence of the first three measures, we hear the final chord in the last measure (B♭ C♯ G E G♯) as transient; its lack of resolution, with the persistence of the B♭ and G♯, convinces us, however, that this is a chord with the nature of a harmony. The disposition of the interval 1 G G♯ with an unfavorable sound is noteworthy here; if we have become accustomed to it from the previous play with transient chords, however, it does not have as harsh an effect as if it were isolated. (Cf. §73 above.) The creation of new harmonies, as demonstrated in §29 above, is apparent here from the continuous flow of the music: the chord B♭ C♯ G E G♯, which first flashes by three times as a transient chord, finally becomes a harmony.

In Examples 245 and 246, harmonies familiar from classical harmony were transformed by figuration—in Example 245 into transient chords of old types, in Example 246 into new formations. In spite of the essential similarity (F A C E♭ = A C♯ E G), the transient chords create a perceptible difference in sonic tension.

Example 247

Un poco meno mosso (originally Allegro  = 66) A. Honegger

pp espresssivo

Example 247 is from the first movement of the *Symphony for Strings* by Arthur Honegger, composed in 1941. Here again, numerous transient chords are intentionally created, resulting in sharp chord clashes with dissonant intervals 1, as pointed out by the square brackets enclosing real pitches. Nevertheless, the whole does not have a harsh effect, since these are only transient chords; the prescribed *pianissimo* dynamic level also has a softening influence.

Accented non-harmonic tones are shown in square brackets, unaccented ones in parentheses. In the first measure, the B in the melody is part of the harmony, since it is not resolved; the B that is part of the inner voice figure, on the other hand, has a delayed resolution to the C, and so we write it in parentheses. Thus the complete content of the first measure is B♭ E G♯ C B, not B♭ E G♯ B B.

If we observe the figural accompanying voice in the first two measures without considering its harmonic significance, it appears to be the progression C–B (in whole notes), decorated on both sides by auxiliary tones. If we keep in mind the overall harmonic content of the second measure, however, we cannot consider the C to be non-harmonic (auxiliary); the non-harmonic tones here are B and A♯, as indicated by the brackets. At the same time, the B intrudes into the chord prevailing in the second measure (C F A E) as a weighty complicating factor, since it itself possesses an auxiliary tone (A♯).

In the sixth measure there is a very complicated expression of the five-note chord D F A C E; the E does not surface until the fourth beat, when the real sound of the pitches D, F, and A in the accompaniment has already ceased. In this measure, the counter-cancelling pitch (F, see arrow) occurs in the second resolution of the F♯.

The constant semitone collisions between the melody and the accompanying voices are responsible for the urgently painful, as if pleading, expression of the melody; this is strengthened by the creeping melodic semitones in the inner voice figure. If we play the melody without the accompaniment, the tension completely disappears in many places, and elsewhere it is considerably softened. From this we see that the harmonization of the melody is an integral component of the whole. Music of this type is created as a rule by composing a melody only after a preliminary sketch, at first perhaps only roughly surmised, of a harmonic basis, rather than by "freely" inventing a melody and then harmonizing it.

It is worth noticing that the composer has piled up the greatest chordal harshness on strong beats; the dissonant interval 1 F F♯ at the start of the sixth measure is especially obtrusive, since it is part of the group 313 (D F F♯ A); this group is very sensitive to disposition, and it is precisely here that disposition is used to sharpen the dissonance. (See §67 above.)

In order to determine the *overall chordal character* on the basis of harmonies and transient chords, we need not identify the chord-types of all the chordal cross-sections; it is enough to survey quickly the frequency of occurrence (or simply the presence or absence) of distinctive characteristic components (for example intervals 1, clashes 11, etc.). Example 245 is characterized by mild dissonances, in which a dissonant interval is rare. In Examples 246 and 247, on the other hand, dissonant intervals 1 impress their character on the music as a whole.

The connections between harmonies and adjacent transient chords, and between various transient chords themselves, are always distinguished by a *link*, most often more than one. We see this in all the examples presented. The number of links can be increased by the use of transient chords, even in the moment of transition from the domain of one harmony to the domain of another.

This is the case in Example 245, on the boundary between the third and fourth measures, where the transition from the dominant (F A C) that has prevailed until now to the tonic (B♭ D F) takes place; the link of the F is multiplied here by the continuing (suspended) A joining to create a transient chord. Transient chords inserted in this way increase the sense of continuity in the music; in the example, only the entry of the B♭ in the bass suggests that we have left the dominant which has until now been enveloped in figurations. In Example 247, in the transition from the seventh to the eighth measure there is a progression from the chord A♯ D♯ F♯ D to the chord B D♯ F♯ A C♯. The composer has, however, used links A♯–A♯ and D–D instead of D♯–D♯ and F♯–F♯, by inserting the transient chord A♯ E G♯ B D at the beginning of the eighth measure.

§148. Diatonic Passages; Chromatic Progressions

In determining the overall chordal character of a composition or a passage within a composition, as we have discussed it in §146 above, music that uses too many different chord-types or harmonies (characteristic-types) or types of disposition presents difficulties. To be more precise, we will point out properties whose distribution in the composition may also serve as a basis for the overall harmonic character. These are
1) the extent of occurrence, and the very fact of occurrence, of *diatonic passages* in the composition; and
2) methods of realizing *chromatic progressions*.

Here we are dealing with a general classification of the sound of a composition, not according to the appearance or omission of individual chord-types and dispositions, but rather according to *pitch material*. The best standard of measurement is the traditional pure diatonic system as contrasted with the chromatic system. In our analysis we will note the extent of diatonic passages and how these passages alternate with others. We will note the realization of chromatic progressions in the transition from one diatonic passage to the next: whether or not they are accomplished by means of semitone steps.

The effect of music with long diatonic passages that *are almost uninterrupted* is different from the effect of music with diatonic passages that appear only sporadically and are compressed into narrow time limits. Moreover, the effect of music in which diatonic passages rapidly alternate with chromatic passages will be different if the chromatic progressions are melodic semitones rather than cross-relations piled up at the same time or melodic intervals of ninths and sevenths instead of seconds.

We can identify passages in the overall flow of the music and also in individual voices or voice zones. Thus in the first five measures of Example 244 (§146 above) we do not find a single diatonic chordal cross-section, much less diatonic passages; the non-diatonic quality of the whole is due to the fact that the chords are non-diatonic. In contrast to this, the melody is diatonic throughout. Naturally, we can classify music according to its diatonic passages and chromatic progressions (cross-relations), even where the chordal material is restricted in chord-type and disposition.

The discovery that besides non-diatonic chordal cross-sections in a composition there are only short rapidly alternating diatonic passages is often equivalent to the discovery that the chordal material of the composition is complex; the harmony is agitated, unstable, not anchored, etc. A larger number of seventh or ninth progressions instead of semitone progressions and especially a larger number of cross-relations increase the agitation of the music. Conversely, as a rule long diatonic passages bring a simplification of chordal material and greater stability of harmonic motion.

If we analyze Example 241 (§144 above), we find that out of 18 chords, 11 are diatonic; only two (C D G – G E♭ A♭ C) join to form a single short diatonic passage, however. Thus the music of this example is agitated; the following chromatic progressions and cross-relations contribute to the agitation. The selected pitches from Example 241 are transposed up an octave in Example 248.

Example 248

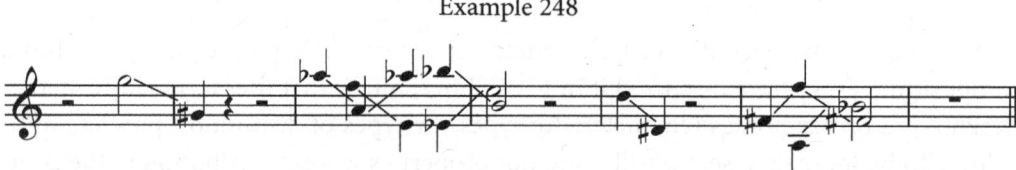

There are similar relations in Example 242 as well (§145 above). Although Example 243 (§146) is characterized unambiguously by a single real chord-type, it is unsettled because only two pairs of the triads can be joined to form short diatonic segments.

In the examples just discussed, we were dealing with chordal cross-sections of the nature of harmonies. A lack of diatonic cohesion between chordal cross-sections of which some represent only transient chords is not reflected so conspicuously in a harmonically unsettled, unstable effect. This is related to the fact that in such cases, chromatic progressions are realized by actual semitone steps (as we see in Examples 245 and 246 in §147 above). Example 247 (§147 above) is more complex in this respect because in it transient chords are joined with complex harmonies by creeping chromatic steps.

Example 249

P. Bořkovec

Example 249 is the beginning of the slow movement of a *Wind Quintet* by P. Bořkovec. Diatonic passages are marked by square brackets above ⌐⌐, even where there is only a single diatonic chordal cross-section. Non-diatonic chordal cross-sections, mostly augmented triads 44, are not marked. Non-harmonic tones are marked by parentheses, and regions of individual harmonies are indicated by braces ⌣⌣. Below the example the characteristic type symbols of harmonies are given. Slanted lines point out semitone progressions between pitches in different octaves (including cross-relations). A piling-up of such progressions always represents great fluctuation in harmonic motion, as we see in the second and sixth measures and in the transition from the third to the fourth measure. In the fourth and fifth measures we find somewhat longer diatonic passages (two to three beats). However, although the music is broken up into small diatonic passages and frequent non-diatonic chordal cross-sections, it is transparent and flows smoothly. This is because all the harmonies are ordinary; not one new formation is to be found among the harmonies.

§149. Determining the Compositional Order; Evaluating Melodic Lines

Harmonic analysis also entails recognizing the *compositional* or *styling* order. (Cf. §122 above.) Compositional order is not always apparent at first glance; we must look for it.

Example 250

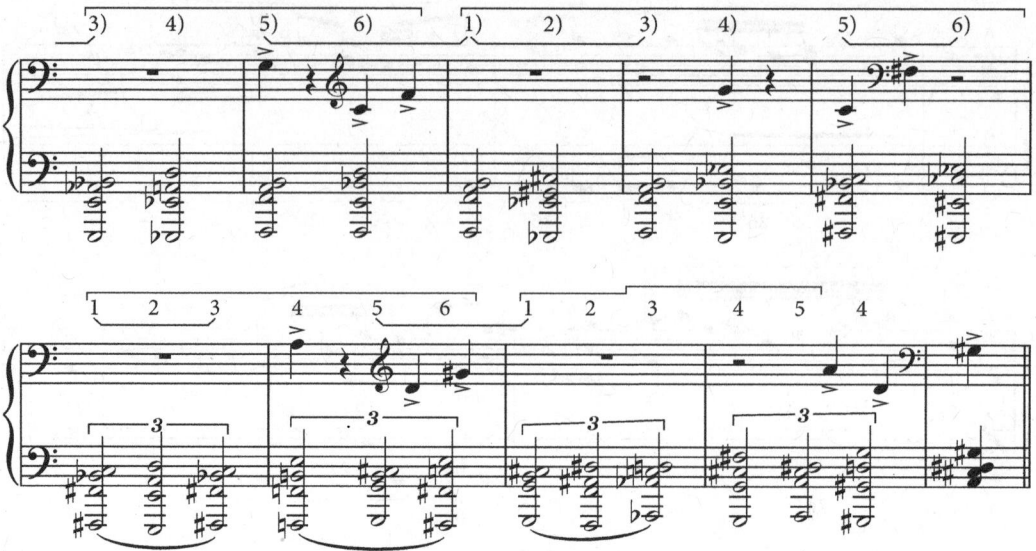

We demonstrate this with Example 250 from the symphonic movement *Pacific 231* by Arthur Honegger, composed in 1923. In keeping with the unsentimental *materialism* of the time the music portrays the journey of a locomotive. Our passage represents the engine as it begins to move. The motion gradually increases, and a melody in its embryonic stage appears over the accompaniment.

The accompanying chords seem at first to be chosen at random; their harshness is given not so much by their pitch content as by their extremely low register. With closer examination we find, however, that their randomness is only illusory. Their basis is a series of six chords, with a swaying motion of the outer voices in the first five measures. In the course of the music that follows, this same series of chords is repeated in the span of three and later two measures, always a semitone higher. In our example the statements of the series are marked with square brackets. Individual chords are numbered, and we have pointed out chords that are the same. The fifth entry of the series is distorted due to a further semitone shift between the second and third chords and the replacement of the sixth chord by the fourth chord, again a semitone higher. The composer disguised this structure by making the fifth chord of the series a semitone transposition of the first chord, thus masking for the listener the boundaries between statements of the series. Individual fragments of the melody in the French horn, con sordino, are distributed such that each time they appear in a different place in relation to the repeating series of accompanying chords.

By finding the compositional order, we generally uncover the *composer's procedure*. From the analysis of our example we see that the composer did not write chords at random. From the way in which he masked the structure, however, we also see that it was important to him that the composition have a naturalistic, unstudied effect.

Looking for the compositional order is related to *evaluating melodic lines*, since, like a particular general styling, a melodically developed voice can act as the stimulus and starting point for the harmonic construction of the music.

In Example 241 (§144 above) the melody of the top voice circles around the G from which it originates and to which it returns. At the same time, it is beautifully arched and lyrical. Although the pitch content and disposition of the chords impress their character on the music, the melody actually carries the musical thought here.

A similarly fully developed melody which seems independent, in that it could exist without accompaniment, can be found in Example 243 (§146 above). Although the melodies in Examples 247 (§147 above) and 249 (§148 above) are also beautifully arched, their gradual development is conditioned by the harmonic component that is created simultaneously. Example 242 (§145 above) involves more the making of a melody from artfully discovered harmonies than an independent spinning out of melodies that disregard the harmony. By contrast, in Examples 245 and 246 (§147 above) transient chords are deliberately formed by the melodic movement of the voices.

In Example 244 (§146 above), the melody consists of a repeating ostinato motive of five pitches; in such cases, as with a pedal point, the accompanying chords have considerable independence and thus can stand in sharp opposition to the pitches of the melody, as we see in this example.

In our most recent example (Example 250), the value of the melodic lines is subordinate; the primary melody (in the upper voice) is in an embryonic stage, from which it extricates itself only later in the composition. Moreover, the contour of the accompanying series is dismally monotonous and meager; this gives the chord series the nature of accompaniment. The center of gravity of the music lies not in the melodic lines, but rather in rhythm, harmony, and color.

In evaluating melodic lines, we also observe the *voice-leading*. We notice especially *parallel* and *similar* motion, and whether or how often two voices approach with such motion octaves and fifths (especially open ones) and dissonances 1 and 2. We do not consider such progressions to be erroneous, but we still notice them, since even modern composers prefer to avoid them. The irregularity is less if non-harmonic tones are involved in such voice-leading. (See for example the inconspicuous parallel fifths E B – F C between the upper voices in the first measure of Example 249 above.) We must of course distinguish between the occasional appearance of unusual voice progressions and their intentional accumulation; in the latter case we are dealing with a particular compositional order.

§150. The Study of Cadences and Cadential Passages

Our first task in analyzing *tonal function* is to examine cadences and in general where the composition leads. If the final sound of the composition is a consonance, we can presume that it has a tonic function, and on that basis we can identify the preceding chords. If the final chord is dissonant, we must first ascertain whether the dissonance is caused by a simple easily recognizable complication of the tonic. If it is, we proceed as with music that ends on a consonance. If the composition remains open ended, that is, if a tonic function cannot be attributed to the final chord, we must determine the functional relations in the same way as in passages in the middle of the composition. (Regarding this, see §151 below.)

We ascertain the tonic quality of the final chord from the relations between several preceding chords. We must not be dissuaded by the centrifugal tendency of certain chords. In modern music we frequently meet an effort to challenge the stability of a previously established tonic, especially immediately before the end of the composition.

As an example of music that flows credibly into the tonic, we recall Example 245 in §147 above. The centrifugal tendencies of certain transient chords (for example, G♭ G♯ E♭ C on the fourth beat of the first measure and F G♯ F D♭ on the third beat of the third measure) cannot conceal the gravitation of a mildly complicated dominant to the tonic, precisely because they are only transient chords.

The cadence of Bořkovec's *Chorale*, the beginning of which we quoted in Example 241 (§144 above), has a different functional effect. In Example 251 we present several of its final measures.

Example 251

Does the composition cadence in C major? Do the last four harmonies not point more to E♭ major, judging by the richly represented functions S and D? If we consider the entire passage, we realize that the key is C major. We see this from the especially distinctive direct relations to the tonic, which is heard three times; two of these times it has no dissonant complication. The chords in the second measure gravitate toward the tonic most reliably, and the tonic follows immediately, although it is complicated by a D. Before the other tonics, whose own real sound is pure, the composer has inserted chords with a different direction. Thus the functional conception of this cadential passage is somewhat loose; a significant (and in such a case also necessary) counterbalance of such looseness is the recurrence of the tonic harmony.

Of the combinations of the five member functional system, the –D interferes most with direct gravitation to the tonic; in Example 251 the interference is from B♭, the minor differentiating pitch. Let us observe how the pitch is used. In the first measure it occurs on the fourth beat in the bass, that is, in a place significant for harmonic effect. The tonic that immediately follows is then problematic. In the penultimate chord E♭ D G♭ B♭, however, B♭ is in the highest voice, a considerably less significant place, and it immediately follows A♭; with good will, we can hear it as a correctly introduced, although unresolved (leaping away) auxiliary note, especially when the simultaneous exchange of pitches in the other voices represents an obvious approach to the pitches of the final tonic. In the rhythmic arrangement in Example 252 the B♭ constitutes only an unaccented non-harmonic tone, whose influence on the final tonic is negligible.

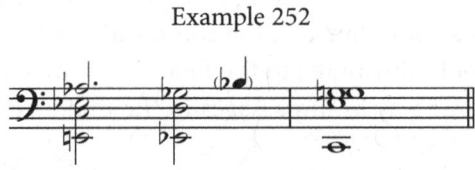

Example 252

Example 253 presents the final measures of the *Fughetta on the name of BACH* by A. Honegger, composed in 1933.[106]

---

[106] It is part of the work *Prélude, Arioso et Fughette sur le nom de BACH* for piano, scored also for string orchestra.

Chapter IX – Analytical Practice

Example 253

A. Honegger

The melody of the highest voice outlines Bach's name (B♭ A C H = B♮). The final major triad constitutes a credible tonic, thanks to the sufficiently clear preceding triads. None of the pre-tonic harmonies is common in classical harmony. Already the first dominant is complicated not by a minor seventh (a subdominant component) but by a major seventh (a lydian component). Immediately before the tonic, auxiliary functions P and L prevail, again quite unclassically.

As our next example of a cadential passage we present in Example 254 several measures from the *Third String Quartet, op. 66*, by Vítězslav Novák, composed in 1939.

Example 254

Vít. Novák

Relative to the tonic D♭ F A♭, reached in the *Più lento* and then further emphasized, we easily determine the functional components of the preceding chords. However, the D♭ major tonic does not follow from the preceding harmonic stream unambiguously. The chordal cross-section D G F A♭ B in the sixth measure, aiming elsewhere than to the tonic (most probably to C E♭ G), is noteworthy; it is only a transient formation, however, as shown by the resolution of the B to C. Both auxiliary functions, P (D♮) and L (G) are in the lowest register.

The functional essence of the passage can be captured by the schematically simplified progression given in Example 255.

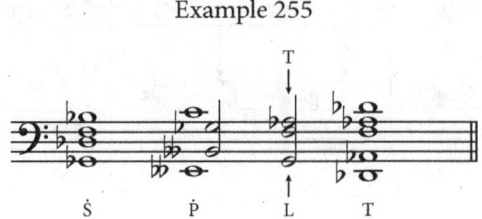

Example 255

Three different functions are to be found here: S, P, and T. Between the last two is a transient chord formed by a double anticipation (F, A♭) as a functional component of the tonic, and by an auxiliary tone (G) as a component of the function L. This final cadence is rather unusual (unclassical) in that it employs the dominant component only discreetly, as the complicating pitch C in the function P. We can also understand the note of anticipation A♭ as part of the function D, although its functional effect is greatly weakened by the simultaneous sounding of the indisputably tonic pitch F.

§151. Functional Chord Successions

A particular transposition of the functional system, determined by the final chord, can only rarely serve as the basis for the functional direction of chords in the entire composition. As a rule, modulations – changes of functional system – occur in the course of the composition. We must then determine the functional meaning of chords according to other, temporary, tonics.

In the course of a composition, the most suitable tonics are first a *consonant chord* and second a *not too complicated dissonant chord*. Chords containing the dissonant element 6 are least suitable as tonics; they can only serve as briefly prevailing local tonics, as we know from using applied dominants in classical harmony.

A discovered or expected tonic is naturally surrounded by non-tonic chords. It depends on the nature of the non-tonic functional combinations whether the expected tonic can be the center of a temporarily prevailing functional system, or whether we must look for a different transposition of the functional system. The relative *simplicity of the functional combinations* and their *harmonic intelligibility* are the decisive factors.

It is natural that in the sphere of modern harmony, the auxiliary functions P and L will have greater significance than in classical harmony. Even in a modern harmonic phrase, however, we will always give precedence to an interpretation that limits these functions as much as possible.

As an example of the functional analysis of a composition, we give in Example 256 a passage from the *Arioso* from Honegger's *Prélude, Arioso et Fughette*.

Example 256

The *Arioso*, a chaconne on the theme BACH, begins with the consonant triad E♭ G♭ B♭, which constantly returns. Nothing is more natural than to consider this consonant harmony to be the tonic (E♭ minor). We then perceive subsequent chords functionally in direct relation to this tonic, and indirectly as applied chords; the interpretation shown in our example is the simplest, even though auxiliary functions, in fact, the most remote function L, play the greatest role in it. Thus the functional harmonic structure of the composition acquires a conspicuously non-traditional character. The melody that enters in the third measure, which is counterpoint to the constantly recurring four-measure cantus firmus, does not change the functional essence of the first four chords. The third chord, C♯ E G♯ C, defies the principle of the pure tonic most strongly, not only by the C♯ (an interval 2 below the basic pitch of the tonic E♭), but also by the C (forming a tritone with the differentiating pitch of the tonic, G♭). Because it is an applied chord, its disruptive influence is not so momentous. The final chord of the series, D F A B, gravitates insistently back to the original tonic E♭ G♭ B♭.

We present in Example 257 an example of music whose functional aspect is considerably more complex. This is the beginning of the *Trio-Divertimento for oboe, clarinet, and bassoon*, by Iša Krejčí.

Example 257

Iša Krejčí

The music at first appears non-functional. If we listen more closely to this lightly sparkling, humorously frolicking musical stream, however, we discover its overall functional orientation: C major. Although the triad C E G is never completely sounded, in the fifth measure the bassoon traces C G, to which it returns in measures 7 and 8. If we return to the *Molto allegro* opening in octaves, we will be convinced that the totality of these pitches is directed toward the C major tonic.

The four measure opening could also serve as a suitable approach to the tonics of D major, F♯ major, A♭ major, or B♭ major, in that it would not violate too flagrantly the principle of the pure tonic. (A tritone relation to the differentiating pitch of the tonic would cause a problem with other tonics, for example, B–F in D♭ major, C♯–G in E♭ major, etc.) The following table compares the possibilities. After the names of the pitches of the functions, the duration of these units is shown by the number of quarter-note beats during which they sound.

Chapter IX – Analytical Practice

Key	Representation of non-tonic functions			
	D	S	P	L
C major	B G D (6)	A F A (4)	C♯ (1)	E♭ (2)
D major	A C♯ A (4)	B G D (6)	E♭ G (3)	F C♯ (2)
F♯ major	F C♯ (2)	E♭ B D (7)	B G D (6)	A F A (4)
A♭ major	E♭ G (3)	F C♯ (2)	A C♯ A (4)	B G D (6)
B♭ major	A F A (4)	E♭ G (3)	E♭ B (6)	A C♯ A (4)

We see from the table that the opening four measures do gravitate functionally with greatest insistence toward C major, considering the strong representation of primary functions and the weak representation of auxiliary functions. Although the total number of primary functions is the same for C major and D major, in C major the most effective function D is represented more strongly.

Functional symbols referring to individual pitches or pitch groups in Example 257 indicate the functional aspect of the *Presto*. We have left without indication places that are functionally uncertain. The A♯ in the eighth measure is immediately suppressed by the B, so that it dies away quickly, even though it is not expressly cancelled; thus its influence, unfavorable for the key of C major, is only fleeting.

When evaluating functionally music in which the tonic is insufficiently emphasized, we must proceed carefully. It is better to leave such a passage without a functional interpretation than laboriously to construct an interpretation that could as well be replaced by several other interpretations based on different keys.

§152. The Formation and Extinction of a Sense of the Tonic

We will make the functional interpretation of complex music more reliable if we consider not only the theoretically possible transpositions of the functional system but also the *sense of the tonic* as it is actually formed and dies away again. Even when considering classical or traditionally directed music, we must sometimes concede that an actual sense of the tonic is not formed quickly. Romantic composers often intentionally created a musical flow in such a way that a secure sense of the tonic would only emerge after a long delay. Ambiguity or uncertainty means that the sense of the tonic is not established.

If we consider the music of Example 256 (§151 above) from this standpoint, we must say that a sense of the tonic is formed right at the beginning, by means of the consonance E♭ G♭ B♭; we hear this harmony as a tonic simply because it is consonant. The sense of this tonic is undermined rather than confirmed by the harmonies that follow, since they are applied auxiliary functional combinations. The decentralizing significance of these non-tonic harmonies is not powerful enough to suppress the sense of the tonic E♭ G♭ B♭ completely because this tonic soon returns.

The sense of the tonic in Example 257 (§151 above) is a different matter. Although we have ascertained through detailed theoretical analysis that the first four measures gravitate insistently toward the tonic

C E G, we still cannot say that the music of these four measures alone could evoke in us a *sense* of this tonic. It is only the introduction of the real pitches C, G in the fifth measure that evokes a sense of this tonic. From the seventh measure to the end of the passage presented, however, sufficient care is not taken to maintain the sense of this tonic. The functional components indicated do not suffice for the task.

Composers sometimes directly play with the instability and uncertainty of the tonic. We present two examples of this.

Example 258

Example 258 is a passage from the opera *Julietta* by B. Martinů (piano reduction). The first two measures are securely in G minor. The formation of a sense of the tonic is supported here by several appearances of the tonic G B♭ D. The disruptive quality of the F and E in the first measure is immediately balanced by the sounding E♭ and F♯. After the tonic is thus introduced, however, it is gradually ejected. At first this happens only inconspicuously, by means of the C♯, then by the altered dominant D F A and the altered subdominant C E G. On the other hand, the C♯ and the two occurrences of the triad D F A lead to the formation of a sense of D F A as tonic, which is also ejected, however, by the triad C E G. Only in the final two measures can we speak of the actual reign of the D minor tonic.

We have indicated the gradually increasing and decreasing sense of the tonics G B♭ D and D F A by thick, thin, and dotted lines.

Example 259

Chapter IX – Analytical Practice

Example 259 is the final passage of the first movement from the *Suite for string orchestra and gong, op. 18* by František Pícha. The entire passage is strictly diatonic with the pitch-system of the key of G major, although the composition begins in C major. To the listener's surprise, the composer finishes on the six-three chord D F♯ B, that is, in B minor. Of all the real consonances that appear in the passage, the tonic B D F♯ is represented most strongly, for a duration of 25 quarter-notes. However, the actual *sense* of the tonic B D F♯ is very weak. In the first six measures we are unaware of this tonic. Although from the seventh measure on our attention is drawn somewhat more to the triad B D F♯, we still cannot conceive it as tonic. Only in the last four measures do we tend toward the tonic B minor, or B phrygian, although even here we are not dealing with just a single tonal direction; thus we are uncertain until the last moment as to how the composer will end the passage.

The natural tonal center of gravity in the first eight measures of this example is the G major tonic G B D. Functional symbols are presented on the basis of this, ignoring temporarily complicating pitches. With the entry into the ninth measure (from D to S), the G major tonality begins to break down; the sense of the tonic G B D begins to disappear. This occurs not because of any interference with the original diatonic pitch-system, but rather because of unusual harmonic progressions (D S, S –IN⁴, S –IN⁴),[107] consistent omission of the previous tonic, and excessive lingering (in the fourth measure from the end) on the new tonic.

---

107 Editor's note: Janeček has D S, S –IN⁴, –IN⁴ S.

The whole example shows how the sense of the tonic can be eliminated even without higher-ranked harmonic motion and without modulation in the classical sense.

Of course it is only possible to follow changes in the sense of the tonic in music that is functionally clear enough. In non-functional or functionally indefinite music, it is well to be content with pointing out those places where some sense of the tonic is formed; the rest is better left with no functional interpretation.

§153. The Tonally Functional Plan of a Composition; Overall Functional Character

Unless the composition we are examining is thoroughly non-functional, we can read its *tonally functional plan* from the functional structure of individual areas. This involves considering the cohesiveness or contrast (tonal remoteness) between passages, the distribution and length of functionally indefinite and ambiguously directed passages, the occurrences of particular functions and functional combinations, how long particular transpositions of the functional system prevail (that is, the duration of the sense of particular tonics), etc. The results of our investigation can then be drawn together into the *overall functional characterization* of the composition.

The first tonally functional trait we must notice for every composition is its *overall tonal location*, its *main key*. The classical requirement that a composition begin and end in the same key is generally respected even in very much freer modern music. Thus our Examples 241 (§144 above) and 251 (§150 above), presenting the beginning and end of Bořkovec's *Chorale*, point clearly to an overall framework of C major. Similarly, the C major that we found at the beginning of the *Trio-Divertimento* by Iša Krejčí in Example 257 (§151 above) is confirmed by the ending of the composition, which is given in Example 260.

Example 260

The stability or security of the main key can then be expressed objectively by the relation between the duration of this key, which is naturally extended especially at the beginning and at the end of a composition, and other keys, including functionally indefinite areas. Of course in modern music the main key plays a considerably lesser role in the overall tonal aspect of the composition than it does in classical music. Often such a "framework" key will be only symbolic.

A second important tonal characteristic of a composition is the *relation between the main key and secondary keys*. In older music, secondary keys were as a rule closely related. The modern composer, however, delights in juxtaposing very remote keys and the main key. What concerns us in practice is which keys we should consider closely related, and which remote.

The remoteness of keys can be most simply expressed by the difference in signature: C major – A minor = 0, C major – G major = 1♯, C major – B major = 5♯, etc. We can also say that the keys of functions S and D and the relative minors or majors of the functions T, S, and D are closely related, while the keys of the functions P and L are remote.

The pitch content of the sections of the music in different keys is also important. We can build a wall of great contrast between areas in related keys, by making one area strongly chromatic while leaving the other in an undisturbed diatonic system, for example.

In order to classify a composition according to functional properties, we must consider the *involvement of particular functions*. The tonally detailed functional aspect of the music differs completely according to whether primary functions (independently or in combination) or also auxiliary functions occur in it. Especially the appearance of the remote function L is a sensitive measure of how modern and non-traditional the composer's thinking is. We can say roughly that the more the remote functions P and L are employed, or the less definite the overall functional basis of the music, the further removed that music will be from its classical foundation. By contrast, closeness to classical models in harmony is expressed by a clear prevalence of primary functions (see Example 245 in §147 above, or the beginning of Example 259 in §152 above).

Different tonally functional properties of a composition are sometimes *contradictory*. Thus a composer may favour primary functions (that is, think in a traditionally verified manner) with respect to particular chords and chord progressions, while seeking great fluctuations (remote keys) for the overall plan of the composition. Conversely, the overall tonal concentration of another composition is accompanied by unusual ("courageous") chord successions (as for example in Example 256 in §151 above.)

Practical musicians must train themselves in the analysis of modern music to the point that they can reliably and easily characterize the tonally functional aspect of a composition, since besides the chordal aspect this also is an expression of the composition's stylistic direction. In routine analysis, we embark on a detailed examination of all functional relations only in exceptional circumstances. Therefore we point out here only those traits that must be traced even in a perfunctory overall analysis. Details of tonal function, especially those that can only be ascertained by studious and careful searching, can always be incorporated within the trait of tonally functional indefiniteness, or non-functionality. If we say about the first four measures of Example 257 (§151 above) that they are non-functional (atonal), we will not be actually wrong; their functional direction, which must be verified by the subsequent course of the music or by the final cadence, is in a practical sense indefinite, and non-functionality is essentially simply functional indefiniteness.

Different kinds of tonally functional thinking can be intentionally used to create contrast within the framework of the same composition; it is impossible to decide by theoretical analysis to what extent such an effort to achieve variety disturbs the overall stylistic unity of the composition and its very coherence. We recognize a defect of this type only non-intellectually, intuitively. The *conscious recognition of differing stylistic traits* in passages within the composition is always helpful, however. Thus the ability to analyze a composition harmonically, both generally and in detail, is part of the essential technical equipment of a music critic.

Tables and Overviews

I. Comprehensive Survey of Chord-types

For each orientation scheme, its complement to octave is given. With the examples of harmonic schemes, asterisk is used to mark the lowest tone of the orientation scheme. Symmetry in a chord is marked both in the orientation scheme and in its negative by ⟷ . In the "characteristic" column, bold is used for characteristic maximums; otherwise they are subordinate chords and their affiliation with a maximum is marked by numbers like [1)] [2)] [3)]. In the "family" column, + is the symbol for a major, – for a minor chord, and + – for a chord of both families; no-family chords are not marked by any symbol. The number ot partial major and minor triads can be observed in the examples of harmonic schemes where major triads are enclosed within square brackets ⌊—⌋ , and minor ones within curved lines ⌣ . With more complex chords (from nine-tone chords up), this marking is dropped and in the "family" column numbers of partial major (+) and minor (–) triads are listed instead. In the "comments", mutually inverse orientation schemes are pointed out (if not obvious allready in the positive orientation scheme) as well as the characteristic maxima and their nuclei, the true and partial combinations, the instances of limited transpositions, and with six-note chords also their relations to their six-tone negatives.

Orientation scheme	Harmonic scheme	Negative	Characteristic, maximum	Family	Category	Comment
silence		12-note chord				
1-note chord	C	11-note chord				
2-note chords		10-note chords				
1(11)	C B*	11111111	1[1) 2) 3)]		II	nucleus
2(10)	D C*	11111112	2		II	nucleus
3(9)	A* C	11111121	(consonance)		I	nucleus
4(8)	C* E	11111211	(consonance)		I	nucleus
5(7)	G* C	11112111	(consonance)		I	nucleus
6(6)	F* B*	11121111	6		II	nucl., only 6 transp.
3-note chords		9-note chords				
11(10)	D♭ C B*	11111111	112[1) 2)]		III	nucleus
12(9)	C D B*	21111111	12[1) 2)]		II	nucleus
13(8)	A C G#*	12111111	1[1) 2)]		II	
14(7)	C E B*	11211111	1[1) 3)]		II	
15(6)	C F B*	11121111	16[1) 3)]		II	nucleus
21(9)	C A* B	11111112	12[1) 2)]		II	nucleus
22(8)	E D C*	11111122	2		II	
23(7)	A C G*	11111221	2		II	
24(6)	G B F*	11112211	26[1) 2)]		II	nucleus
25(5)	D G C*	11121112	2		II	
31(8)	C G#* B	11111121	1[1) 2)]		II	
32(7)	A E* G	11111212	2		II	
33(6)	B* D F	11112121	6		II	
34(5)	A* C E	11121211	**consonance**	–	I	harmony –
41(7)	C G* B	11111211	1[1) 3)]		II	
42(6)	B F* A	11112112	26		II	nucleus
43(5)	C* E G	11121121	**consonance**	+	I	harmony +
44(4)	C* E* G#*	11211211	0		II	harmony, nucl., only 4 transp.
51(6)	F B* E	11112111	16[1) 2)]		II	nucleus
4-note chords		8-note chords				
111(9)	C B* D C#	1111111	112[1) 2)]		III	

Tables and Overviews

Orientation scheme	Harmonic scheme	Negative	Characteristic, maximum	Family	Category	Comment
112(8)	D C♯ E C*	2111111	112[1) 2)]		III	
113(7)	D F C♯ C*	1211111	112[1) 2)]		III	
114(6)	G F♯ B F*	1121111	1126[1) 2) 3) 4) 5)]		III	nucleus
115(5) ↔	D G C♯ C*	1112111	1126[1) 2) 3) 4)]		III	nucleus
121(8) ↔	C E♭ B* D	1111113 ↔	12[2)]		II	maximum
122(7)	C E B* D	2211111	12[1)]		II	
123(6)	C D F B*	2121111	126[1) 2) 4) 5)]		III	nucleus
124(5)	F G B E*	2112111	126[1) 2) 3) 5)]	–	II	nucleus
131(7) ↔	C E B* D♯	1111131 ↔	1[1)]		II	maximum
132(6)	C E♭ F B*	1221111	126[2) 3) 5)]		II	nucleus
133(5)	B D F B♭*	1212111	16[2)]	+	II	maximum
134(4)	A C E G♯*	1211211	01	–	II	nucleus, inv. 314
141(6) ↔	C F B* E	1111311 ↔	16[1)]		II	maximum
142(5)	F A B E*	1122111	126[1) 4)]		II	nucleus
143(4) ↔	C E G B*	1121211 ↔	1[3)]	+ –	II	max., +4–
151(5) ↔	F♯ C F* B*	1113111 ↔	166		II	max., nucl., 6 transp.
211(8)	E C* E♭ D	1111112	112[1) 2)]		III	
212(7) ↔	C A* D B	2111112 ↔	12[1)]		II	
213(6)	G B F* A♭	1211112	126[2) 3) 4) 6)]		II	nucleus, chord least sensitive to disposition of interval 1
214(5)	C E A* B	1121112	12[1)]	–	II	
221(7)	D F C* E	1111122	12[1)]		II	
222(6) ↔	G B F* A	1111222 ↔	26[1)]		II	
223(5)	E G C* D	1112221	2	+	II	
224(4) ↔	D E G♯ C*	1121122 ↔	026		III	nucleus
231(6)	F B* C♯ E	1111221	126[2) 3) 6)]		II	nucleus
232(5) ↔	D G C* F	1112212 ↔	2		II	
233(4)	B D F A*	1122121	26[1)]	–	II	
241(5)	C F* G B	1112211	126[1) 4)]		II	nucleus
242(4) ↔	F♯ A♯* C E*	1122112 ↔	26[2)]		II	max., only 6 transp.
311(7)	F E C* E♭	1111121	121[1) 2)]		III	
312(6)	E♭ F B* D	2111121	126[2) 3) 4) 5)]		II	nucleus

Orientation scheme	Harmonic scheme	Negative	Characteristic, maximum	Family	Category	Comment
313(5) ↔	E G C* E♭	1211121	**1**[2)]	+ −	II	max. $\widehat{+0-}$, chord most sensitive to disposition of interval 1
314(4)	C E G♯* B	1121121	01	+	II	nucleus, inv. 134
321(6)	F B* D E	1111212	126[1) 2) 4) 6)]		II	nucleus
322(5)	D E A* C	1112122	2	−	II	
323(4) ↔	D F A* C	1121221	2	+ −	II	$\widehat{-3+}$
331(5)	F♯ B* D F	1112121	16[3)]	−	II	maximum
332(4)	G B* D F	1121212	26[1)]	+	II	
333(3) ↔	B* D* F* A♭*	1212121	6		II	max., only 3 transp.
411(6)	F♯ C* F E	1111211	1126[1) 2) 3) 4) 5)]		III	nucleus
412(5)	F G C* E	2111211	12[1)]	+	II	
421(5)	C F* A B	1112112	126[1) 2) 3) 5)]	+	II	nucleus
5-note chords		7-note chords				
1111(8) ↔	C* E♭ D C♯ E	111111	112[1)]		III	
1112(7)	B* D C♯ E C	211111	112[1) 2)]		III	
1113(6)	B* D F C♯ C	121111	1126[1) 2) 3) 5)]		III	
1114(5)	B♭ E A* C B	112111	1126[1) 2) 4)]	−	III	
1121(7)	D F C♯ E C*	311111	112[1)]		III	
1122(6)	G B F♯ A F*	221111	1126[1) 5)]		III	
1123(5)	D C♯ E G C*	212111	1126[1) 2) 3)]	+	III	
1124(4)	D G♯ C♯ E C*	211211	01126[1) 2) 3) 4)]	−	III	nucleus, inv. 2114
1131(6)	B E♭ B♭ D A*	131111	1126[3) 5)]		III	
1132(5)	D F C♯ G C*	122111	1126[1) 2) 3)]		III	
1133(4)	B B♭ D F A*	121211	1126[1) 3)]	+ −	III	
1141(5)	C F B E B♭*	113111	11266[1) 2) 3) 4) 6)]		III	nucleus
1142(4) ↔	C F♯ B E B♭*	112211	1126[2) 3) 4)]		III	
1211(7)	A F A♭ E* G	111113	112[1)]		III	
1212(6)	A C D G♯* B	211113	126[2) 5)]		III	
1213(5)	F G♯ B E* G	121113	126[3) 6)]	+ −	II	
1214(4) ↔	A C E G♯* B	112113	012	+ −	II	maximum, nucleus, $\widehat{+5-}$
1221(6) ↔	C B* D F E	111132	126[1)]		III	
1222(5)	F G B E* A	222111	126[1)]	−	II	

Tables and Overviews

Orientation scheme	Harmonic scheme	Negative	Characteristic, maximum	Family	Category	Comment
1223(4)	C E G B* D	221211	12[1]	+ −	II	$\overgroup{+5+}$
1231(5)	C F♯ B* D F	111321	1266	−	II	nucleus
1232(4)	C D G B* F	212211	126[1) 4)]	+	II	
1233(3)	A D F G♯* B	212121	126[4) 5)]	−	II	inv. 2133
1241(4)	F C E* G B	113211	126[1)]	+ −	II	
1311(6)	F C E B* E♭	111131	1126[4) 5)]		III	
1312(5)	F A B E* G♯	132111	126[4)]	+	II	
1313(4)	E G C E♭ B*	121131	01	+ −	II	$\overgroup{-4-}$
1321(5)	B D F B♭* E	111312	1266	+	II	nucleus
1322(4)	G C E♭ F B*	122211	0126[1) 2)]	−	III	nucleus
1323(3)	E G C E♭* A	122121	126[3) 5)]	+ −	II	$\overgroup{-3-}$, inv. 1332
1331(4) ↔	F♯ B D F B♭*	113121	**016**	+ −	II	maximum, nucleus, $\overgroup{+1-}$
1332(3)	F B D G B♭*	121221	126[3) 6)]	+ −	II	$\overgroup{+3+}$, inv. 1323
1411(5)	F♯ C F B* E	111311	11266[1) 2) 3) 4) 5)]		III	nucleus
1421(4)	F A C E* B	112311	126[1)]	+ −	II	
2111(7)	D F E C* E♭	111112	112[1) 2)]		III	
2112(6) ↔	A F* A♭ B G	211112	1126[1) 5)]		III	nucleus
2113(5)	E G C* E♭ D	121112	112[2)]	+ −	III	
2114(4)	E A♭ C* E♭ D	112112	01126[1) 2) 3) 4)]	+	III	nucleus, inv. 1124
2121(6)	C E♭ A* B D	111123	126[2) 6)]		III	
2122(5)	C E A* B D	221112	12[1)]	−	II	
2123(4)	D F A* C B	212112	126[1) 2) 5)]	+ −	II	
2131(5)	A♭ C F* G B	111231	126[4)]	−	II	
2132(4)	F A* C E♭ B	122112	126[2) 3)]	+	II	
2133(3)	A* C D♯ F♯ B	121212	126[4) 6)]	+	II	inv. 1233
2211(6)	B G B♭ F* A	111122	1126[1) 5)]		III	
2212(5)	D F G C* E	211122	12[1)]	+	II	
2213(4)	A C E♭ G* B	121122	0126[1) 2) 3)]	−	III	nucleus
2221(5)	G C F* A B	111222	126[1)]	+	II	
2222(4) ↔	E B♭* D F♯ C	112222	026		III	
2223(3) ↔	G B D F* A	121222	**26**[1)]	+ −	II	maximum, $\overgroup{-5+}$
2231(4)	E♭ D E G C*	112221	0126[1) 3)]	+	III	nucleus

Orientation scheme	Harmonic scheme	Negative	Characteristic, maximum	Family	Category	Comment
2232(3) ↔	G C* E A D ↔	122122	2	+ −	II	maximum
2311(5)	G C* F♯ D F	111221	1126[1) 2) 4)]		III	
2312(4)	B E♭ F A* D	211221	126[2) 3)]	−	II	
2321(4)	B A* D F E	112212	126[1) 4)]	−	II	
3111(6)	D F B* E E♭	111121	1126[1) 2) 4) 5)]		III	
3112(5)	F E G C* E♭	211121	112[2)]	+ −	III	
3113(4) ↔	A C G♯ E* G ↔	121121	0112[1) 2)]	+ −	III	nucleus
3121(5)	A C F* A♭ B	111213	126[3) 5)]	+ −	II	
3122(4)	F A C♯* E G	221121	0126[1) 2) 3)]	+	III	nucleus
3131(4)	C G♯ B E* G	112131	01	+ −	II	+4+
3211(5)	E A* C E♭ D	111212	1126[1) 2) 4)]	−	III	
3212(4)	F E G B* D	211212	126[1) 2) 6)]	+ −	II	
3221(4)	D F A* C E	112122	12[1)]	+ −	II	−5−
3311(4)	G B* D F♯ F	112121	1126[1) 4)]	+ −	III	
4111(5)	F E G C* F♯	111211	1126[1) 2) 3)]	+	III	
6-note chords		6-note chords				
11111(7) ↔	E C* E♭ D F D♭	11111 ↔	112[1)]		III	= neg., maximum
11112(6)	E C* E♭ D F♯ C♯	21111	1126[1) 5)]		III	inv. = neg.
11113(5)	C♯ E G C* E♭ D	12111	1126[1) 2)]	+ −	III	
11114(4) ↔	C♯ E G♯ C* E♭ D	11211 ↔	01126[1) 4)]	+ −	III	
11121(6)	D F♯ C♯ F C* E♭	31111	1126[3) 5)]		III	
11122(5)	B D B♭ E A* C	22111	1126[1)]	−	III	inv. = neg.
11123(4)	C E G B* D C♯	21211	1126[1) 3)]	+ −	III	
11131(5)	E A* C D♯ B B♭	13111	11266[1) 2) 3) 6)]	−	III	inv. = neg.
11132(4)	F C E* G B♭ F♯	12211	1126[2) 3)]	+	III	
11133(3) ↔	G B D F♯ F* A♭	12121	1126[1)]	+ −	III	
11141(4)	F♯ C E* G B F	11311 ↔	11266[1) 2) 4)]	+ −	III	
11211(6) ↔	G B F♯ B♭ F* A	11114 ↔	1126[5)]		III	
11212(5)	D F C♯ E G C*	32111	1126[1) 3)]	+	III	
11213(4)	C♯ E G C E♭ B*	31211	01126[1) 2) 3) 4)]	+ −	III	inv. = neg.
11221(5)	B D F B♭* E C	23111	11266[1) 3) 4) 6)]	+	III	
11222(4)	E C F♯ B D B♭*	22211	01126[1) 2)]	−	III	inv. = neg.

Tables and Overviews

Orientation scheme	Harmonic scheme	Negative	Characteristic, maximum	Family	Category	Comment
11223(3)	C E G B D B♭*	22121	1126[1]	+ −	III	inv. 22113
11231(4)	D G♯ C♯ E G C*	21311	011266	+ −	III	nucleus
11232(3)	G D F♯ A C F*	21221	1126[1] [2]	+ −	III	inv. 21132
11311(5)	B E B♭ E♭ A* D	11141	11266[1] [2] [3]		III	
11312(4)	D♭ F C E G B*	13211	1126[3]	+ −	III	
11313(3)	B E G C E♭ B♭*	13121	01126[2] [3] [4]	+ −	III	nucleus, inv. 11331
11321(4)	B B♭ D F A* E	12311	11266[1] [2] [4] [5]	+ −	III	inv. = neg.
11322(3)	C♯ G D F A C*	12221	01126[1] [5]	+ −	III	nucleus
11331(3)	E B D* G B♭ E♭	12131	01126[2] [3] [4]	+ −	III	nucleus, inv. 11313
11411(4)	F♯ C F B E B♭*	11411	11266[1] [2]		III	= neg., only 6 transp.
12111(6)	G B F♯ B♭ F* A	11113	1126[4] [5]		III	
12112(5)	A F G♯ B E* G	21113	1126[1]	+ −	III	
12113(4)	C♯ E A C G♯* B	12113	**0112**[1]	+ −	III	= neg., maximum
12121(5)	D F G♯ C♯* E G	11133	1266	+ −	III	
12122(4)	A C E G♯* B D	22113	0126[1] [2]	+ −	III	
12123(3)	D F A C G♯* B	21213	**126**[5]	+ −	III	inv. 21213 = neg., maximum
12131(4)	A C E G♯* B D♯	11331	0126[3]	+ −	II	nucleus, −1−
12132(3)	A C♯ E G C* E♭	12213	**126**[3]	+ −	II	maximum, +3−
12211(5)	C F♯ B* D F E	11132	11266[1] [3] [4] [5]	−	III	
12212(4)	C E G B* D F	21132	126[1]	+ −	III	
12213(3)	G♯ C♯ E G* C B♭	12132	0126[2] [3]	+ −	III	
12221(4)	F A C E* G B	11322	126[1]	+ −	II	−1+
12222(3)	F A C♯ E* G B	22221	0126[1]	+ −	III	inv. = neg.
12231(3)	A♭ C E G B* D	13221	0126[3]	+ −	III	inv. = neg.
12311(4)	C G B* D F♯ F	11321	11266[1] [2] [4] [6]	+ −	II	inv. = neg.
12312(3)	C F* A♭ B D F♯	21321	1266	−	II	inv. = neg., −6−, only 6 transp.
12321(3)	C F A♭ B* D G	13212	**126**[4]	+ −	II	maximum, −2+
13111(5)	G F♯ D F A♭ D♭*	11131	11266[1] [2] [3] [5]	+	III	inv. = neg.
13112(4)	F B* E G C E♭	21131	01126[1] [2] [3]	+ −	III	inv. = neg.
13121(4)	D♭ F A♭ C* E G	11313	0126[2]	+ −	II	necleus, +1+
13131(3)	G♯ B* E G* C E♭*	13131	**01**	+ −	II	= neg., maximum, −4+, only 4 transp.

Orientation scheme	Harmonic scheme	Negative	Characteristic, maximum	Family	Category	Comment
13211(4)	G C E♭ F♯ B* F	11312	011266	+ −	III	nucleus
13212(3) ↔	C F* A D F♯ B	12321 ↔	1266	+ −	II	+6−
13221(3)	E G B D F♯ A♯*	12231	0126[2)]	+ −	III	inv. = neg.
21111(6)	B♭ F* A G♯ B G	11112	1126[1) 5)]		III	inv. = neg.
21112(5) ↔	F E G C* E♭ D	21112 ↔	**112[2)]**	+ −	III	= neg., maximum
21113(4)	F♯ E G B♭ D* F	12112	01126[1) 3) 4)]	+ −	III	
21121(5)	E G C* E♭ F♯ D	31112	1126[1)]	+ −	III	
21122(4)	E A♭ C* E♭ F♯ D	22112	01126[1) 2)]	+	III	inv. = neg.
21123(3) ↔	E A C* D♯ F♯ D	21212 ↔	1126[1)]	−	III	
21131(4)	C♯ E A* C F B	13112	01126[1) 2) 3)]	+ −	III	inv. = neg.
21132(3)	A D F* A♭ C G	12212	1126[1) 2)]	+ −	III	inv. 11232
21211(5)	B E* G B♭ F♯ A	11123	1126[1) 4)]	−	III	
21212(4) ↔	B G B♭ D♭ F* A♭	21123 ↔	**126[2)]**	+ −	III	maximum
21213(3)	E♭ G♭ D F A C*	12123	**126[6)]**	+ −	III	inv. 12123 = neg., maximum
21221(4)	B D F A* C E	11232	126[1)]	+ −	III	
21222(3)	E G B D* F A	22212	126[1)]	+ −	II	inv. = neg., −2−
21311(4)	B♭ D* F A E G♯	11231	126[4)]	+ −	III	
21321(3)	B D♯ F♯ A* C F	12312	1266	+	II	inv. = neg., +6+, only 6 transp.
22111(5)	E G C* F♯ D F	11122	1126[1)]	+	III	inv. = neg.
22112(4)	B G B♭ D♭ F* A	21122	01126[1) 2)]	−	III	inv. = neg.
22113(3)	E♭ E G B D* F♯	12122	1126[1)]	+ −	III	inv. 11223
22121(4)	D F A♭ C* E G	11223	0126[1) 3)]	+ −	III	
22122(3) ↔	D F A C* E G	22122 ↔	12[1)]	+ −	II	= neg., maximum, +2−
22211(4)	A F A♭ D♭* G E♭	11222	01126[1) 2)]	+	III	inv. = neg.
22212(3)	C F* A B D G	21222	126[1)]	+ −	II	inv. = neg., +2+
22221(3)	G B D F* A C♯	12222	016[1)]	+ −	III	inv. = neg.
22222(2) ↔	G* B* D♯* F* A* C♯*	22222 ↔	026		IV	= neg., maximum, only 2 transp.
23111(4)	F♯ D F A♭ C* G	11221	1126[2) 4)]	−	III	
31111(5)	A G♯ B E* G B♭	11121	1126[1) 2)]	+ −	III	
31112(4)	B D F♯* A C B♭	21121	01126[1) 3) 4)]	+ −	III	
31121(4)	F A♭ E G C* E♭	31121	**0112[2)]**	+ −	III	= neg., maximum

Tables and Overviews

Orientation scheme	Harmonic scheme	Negative	Characteristic, maximum	Family	Category		Comment
31211(4)	B♭ F♯ A D* F A♭	11213	01126[1) 2) 3) 4)]	+	−	III	inv. = neg.
32111(4)	B♭ A C E* G B	11212	1126[1) 4)]	+	−	III	
7-note chords		5-note chord		+	−		
111111(6)	C♯ E B* D F C E♭	1111	**1126**[5)]	0	0	IV	maximum
111112(5)	D F C♯ E G C* E♭	2111	1126[1)]	1	1	III	
111113(4)	C♯ E G C E♭ B* D	1211	01126[1) 4)]	2	2	III	
111121(5)	F♯ A C F* A♭ B G	3111	11266[3) 6)]	1	1	III	
111122(4)	C E♭ G B* D F C♯	2211	01126[1)]	1	1	III	
111123(3)	B D G B♭* D♭ E C	2121	1126[1)]	2	2	III	inv. 211113
111131(4)	B♭ D♭ A* C F B E	1311	011266	2	2	III	
111132(3)	C♯ E A D G C* E♭	1221	**1126**[2)]	2	2	III	maximum
111211(5)	G B E* F♯ B♭ F A	4111	11266[1) 3)]	0	1	III	
111212(4)	D F C♯ E G C B*	3211	**1126**[3)]	2	1	III	maximum
111213(3)	D C♯ F C E G♯ B*	3121	01126[3) 4)]	2	2	III	
111221(4)	G F♯ A C F B E*	2311	11266[1) 4)]	2	2	III	
111222(3)	C F♯ B D B♭ E A*	2221	01126[1)]	1	2	III	
111231(3)	F B E B♭ E♭ G D*	2131	011266	3	2	III	
111311(4)	G C F♯ B F B♭ E*	1411	11266[1) 2)]	1	1	III	
111312(3)	A♭ C F* G B D F♯	1321	11266[2) 6)]	1	2	III	inv. 111321
111321(3)	B♭ D F A B E G♯*	1231	11266[2) 5)]	2	1	III	inv. 111312
112111(5)	G B F♯ B♭ C F* A	1114	11266[1) 3)]	1	0	III	
112112(4)	F C♯ E G C E♭ B*	2114	01126[1) 2)]	1	2	III	
112113(3)	B G B♭ D F♯ A F*	1214	01126[2) 4)]	3	3	III	
112121(4)	B D F B♭ C♯ E A*	3311	011266	2	2	III	
112122(3)	D F A C♯ E G C*	3221	01126[1) 5)]	3	2	III	
112131(3)	G♯ B E G* C E♭ A	3131	01126[2) 3)]	3	4	III	inv. 121131
112211(4)	C F♯ B D F B♭* E	1142	011266	1	1	III	
112212(3)	G B D F♯ A C F*	2321	11266[4) 6)]	3	2	III	
112221(3)	F A C E G B D♯*	2231	01126[1) 2)]	2	3	III	
112222(2)	E♭ G B D F A C♯*	2222	01126[1) 2)]	1	1	IV	
112311(3)	C F B E G B♭ E♭*	1421	011266	2	2	III	
113111(4)	C F♯ B F B♭ E* A	1141	11266[1) 2)]	1	1	III	

405

Orientation scheme	Harmonic scheme	Negative	Characteristic, maximum	Family +	Family −	Category	Comment
113121(3) ↔	E♭ G B♭ D F♯ A C♯*	1331 ↔	01126[2]	3	3	III	
113211(3)	C♯ F♯ A C F B E*	1241	011266	2	2	III	
121111(5)	A F G♯ B E* G B♭	1113	11266[3) 5]	1	1	III	
121112(4)	C B D G B♭ F♯* A	2113	0112[1) 3]	2	2	III	
121113(3)	F A♭ C E B* E♭ D	1213	0112[3) 4]	2	2	III	
121121(4) ↔	D♯ F♯ B D F B♭* D♭	3113 ↔	0112[2) 5]	3	3	III	nucleus
121122(3)	G B D♯ F♯ A D* F	2213	0112[1) 2]	3	2	III	
121131(3)	G C♯ E* A C F A♭	1313	0112[2) 3]	4	3	III	inv. 112131
121211(4)	G C E♭ F♯ B* D F	1133	011266	2	2	III	
121212(3)	G B D F B♭* D♭ E	2133	1266	2	3	III	
121221(3)	D F A C E G♯* B	1332	**0126**[2]	2	3	III	maximum
121222(2) ↔	E G B♭ D F♯* A C	2223 ↔	**0126**[1]	2	2	III	maximum
122111(4)	C F B E* G B♭ A	1132	11266[1) 4]	2	2	III	
122112(3)	F A D♯ G♯ B D* G	2132	011266	1	2	III	
122121(3)	F A♭ C E G B* D	1323	**0126**[3]	3	2	III	maximum
122122(2) ↔	B* E A D G C F	2232 ↔	**126**[1]	3	3	III	maximum, only diatonic 7-note chord, it fills pure diatonic
122211(3)	D♭ F A C E* G B	1322	0112[1) 2]	3	2	III	
131111(4)	C F B* E G D♯ F♯	1131	011266	2	2	III	
132111(3)	D A C♯ F♯ C F* B	1312	011266	2	3	III	
211111(5)	C♯ E A* C E♭ B D	1112	1126[1]	1	1	III	
211112(4) ↔	C♯ E B♭* D F♯ C E♭	2112 ↔	0112[1]	1	1	IV	
211113(3)	E C* D♯ F♯ A D F	1212	1126[1]	2	2	III	inv. 111123
211121(4)	G B♭ F♯ A D* F E	3112	0112[1) 3]	2	2	III	
211122(3)	C B D G* B♭ E A	2212	1126[1]	2	3	III	
211211(4)	F C♯ E A* C E♭ B	1124	0112[1) 2]	2	1	III	
211212(3)	A C F* A♭ B D G	3212	1126[1]	2	2	III	
211221(3)	A D F* A♭ D♭ G B	2312	011266	2	1	III	
212111(4)	F E A* C E♭ B D	1123	**1126**[4]	1	2	III	maximum
212112(3)	A D* F G♯ B E G	2123	1126[1]	2	2	III	
212121(3)	C D♯ F♯ B D F A*	1233	1266	3	2	III	

Orientation scheme	Harmonic scheme	Negative	Characteristic, maximum	Family +	Family −	Category	Comment
212211(3)	B E G B♭ D* F A	1232	11266[4) 5)]	2	3	III	
221111(4)	E♭ B D F A* C♯ E	1122	0112[6)1)]	1	1	III	
221112(3)	G C* F♯ A D F E	2122	1126[1)]	3	2	III	
221121(3)	B D G B♭ D♭ F* A	3122	0112[6)1) 2)]	2	3	III	
221211(3)	E A C E♭ G* B D	1223	0112[6)1) 5)]	2	3	III	
222111(3)	G C F♯ D F B♭* E	1222	0112[6)1)]	2	1	III	
311111(4)	D F C♯ E A* C E♭	1121	0112[6)1) 4)]	2	2	III	
8-note chords		**4-note chords**					
1111111(5) ↔	D B♭ C♯ E A* C E♭ B	111 ↔	**11266**[3)]	1	1	IV	maximum
1111112(4)	D F C♯ E G C E♭ B*	211	0112[6)1)]	2	2	IV	
1111113(3) ↔	G♯ B D G B♭ F♯ A (D) F* (A♭)	121 ↔	**01126**[4)]	3	3	IV	maximum
1111121(4)	B D F B♭ C♯ E A* C	311	011266	3	3	III	
1111122(3)	D F A C♯ E G C* E♭	221	0112[6)1)]	3	3	III	
1111131(3) ↔	E G B E♭ F♯ B♭ D* F	131 ↔	011266	4	4	III	
1111211(4)	C F G♯ B E* G B♭ F♯	411	011266	2	2	III	
1111212(3)	G B D F B♭* D♭ E C	321	**11266**[6)]	3	3	III	maximum
1111221(3)	F A C E G B D♯* F♯	231	011266	3	3	III	
1111222(2) ↔	G♯ C♯ E B♭ D F♯ C* E♭ (A♭)	222 ↔	0112[6)1)]	2	2	IV	
1111311(3) ↔	A♭ E♭ G B♭ D F♯* A C♯ (G♯)	141 ↔	011266	3	3	III	
1112111(4) ↔	F B♭* D♭ E C D♯ F♯ B	115 ↔	**11266**[1)]	2	2	III	maximum
1112112(3)	F A E G♯ B D♯ G D*	421	011266	2	3	III	
1112121(3)	D F C♯ E G♯ C G B*	331	011266	4	3	III	
1112122(2)	G B♭ F♯ A D F C E*	322	0112[6)1)]	4	3	III	inv. 1112221
1112211(3)	F B E G B♭ E♭ A D*	241	011266	3	3	III	
1112212(2) ↔	G C F♯ A D F B E*	232 ↔	**11266**[4)]	4	4	III	maximum
1112221(2)	C E B D G B♭ F♯ A*	223	0112[6)1)]	3	4	III	inv. 1112122
1113111(3) ↔	G♭ D♭ F B♭* G C E* B	151 ↔	**11266**[2)]	2	2	III	max., only 6 transp.
1121111(4)	B♭ F♯ E C F A♭ B E*	114	011266	2	2	III	
1121112(3)	C B G B♭ D F♯ A F*	214	011266	4	3	III	
1121121(3)	F A C E G♯ B E♭* G	314	0112[6)2)]	4	5	III	
1121122(2) ↔	F C♯ E G A C E♭ B*	224 ↔	0112[6)1) 2)]	3	3	IV	
1121211(3) ↔	E A C E♭ G♯ B D G*	143 ↔	011266	4	4	III	

Orientation scheme	Harmonic scheme	Negative	Characteristic, maximum	Family +	Family −	Category	Comment
1121212(2)	G B D F B♭ D♭ E A	332	011266	3	4	III	inv. 1122121
1121221(2) ↔	D A C F A♭ B E G*	323 ↔	01126 [5)]	4	4	III	maximum
1122111(3)	D G C♯ F♯ A C F* B	142	011266	3	3	III	
1122112(2) ↔	A D♯ G♯ B D F (A♭) D♭* G*	242 ↔	011266	2	2	IV	only 4 transp.
1122121(2)	G C D♯ F♯ B D F* A	233	011266	4	3	III	inv. 1121212
1211111(4)	E G C E♭ F♯ B* D F	113	011266	3	3	III	
1211121(3) ↔	F C E A♭ B* E♭ G B	313 ↔	01126 [3)]	4	4	III	maximum
1211112(3)	C E G♯ B D G* B♭ D♭	213	011266	3	3	IV	
1211211(3)	A C♯ F A♭ C E* G B	134	01126 [2)]	5	4	III	
1212111(3)	F A E A♭* C E♭ B D	133	011266	3	4	III	
1212121(2) ↔	E B♭ E♭* G A* C♯ F♯* C*	333 ↔	1266	4	4	IV	max., only 3 transp.
1221111(3)	B♭ D♭ F A C E* G B	132	011266	3	3	III	
2111111(4)	F C♯ E A* C E♭ B D	112	01126 [1)]	2	2	IV	
2111112(3) ↔	B D G* B♭ C♯ E A C	212 ↔	1126 [1)]	3	3	III	maximum
2111121(3)	D♯ F♯ A D F G♯ C* E	312	011266	3	3	IV	
2111211(3)	B G B♭ D* F♯ A F E	412	011266	3	4	III	
2112111(3)	D A D♭ F* A♭ C G B	124	011266	3	2	III	
2121111(3)	E C D♯ F♯ B D F A*	123	11266 [5)]	3	3	III	maximum
2211111(3)	C♯ E A C E♭ G* B D	122	01126 [1)]	3	3	III	
9-note chords		3-note chords					
11111111(4) ↔	C D♯ F♯ B D F B♭* D♭ E	11 ↔	011266	3	3	IV	
11111112(3)	G E♭ F♯ A D F C♯ E C*	21	011266	4	4	IV	
11111121(3)	F♯ A C F G♯ B E G D♯*	31	011266	5	5	IV	
11111122(2) ↔	C♯ E A B* D F G C E♭	22 ↔	01126 [1)]	4	4	IV	maximum
11111211(3)	D F A C♯ E G♯ C* E♭ G	41	011266	5	5	III	−1−1−
11111212(2)	F A♭ C E* G B D F♯ A	32	011266	5	5	III	+2−1−, inv. 11111221
11111221(2)	G* B♭ D F A C E G♯ B	23	011266	5	5	III	+1+2−, inv. 11111212
11112111(3)	G B D F♯ A C♯ F* A♭ C	51	011266	4	4	III	−1−1+
11112112(2)	F A C E♭ G B* D F♯ C♯	42	011266	4	4	IV	inv. 11112211
11112121(2) ↔	C* E♭ G B♭ D F♯ A C♯ E	33 ↔	011266	5	5	IV	
11112211(2)	E♭ B♭ D F A C♯* E G B	24	011266	4	4	IV	inv. 11112112
11121111(3)	E G♯ B E♭ G B♭ D* F A	15	011266	4	4	III	−1+1+

Tables and Overviews

Orientation scheme	Harmonic scheme	Negative	Characteristic, maximum	Family +	Family −	Category	Comment
11121112(2) ↔	G C F♯ B D F B♭ E* A	25 ↔	011266	5	5	IV	
11121121(2)	E♭ A♭ C E G B D* F A	43	011266	5	6	III	−2−2+, −4+2−, −2−4+, inv. 11121211
11121211(2)	G B* D F A C E G♯ C♯	34	011266	6	5	III	−2+2+, +2−4+, −4+2+, inv. 11121121
11211111(3)	A C♯ E A♭ C E♭ G* B D	14	011266	5	5	III	**+1+1+**
11211211(2) →	B E♭ G B♭ D F♯ A* C♯* F*	44 ↔	**01126**[2])	6	6	IV	max., only 4 transp.
12111111(3)	D♭ A C F A♭ B E* G B♭	13	011266	5	5	IV	
21111111(3)	E C E♭ B D G* B♭ C♯ A	12	011266	4	4	IV	
10-note chords		2-note chords					
111111111(3) ↔	F A♭ C* E♭ G D F♯ A C♯ E	<u>1</u>	011266	6	6	IV	
111111112(2) ↔	G♯ B E* G B♭ D F♯ A C F (A♭)	<u>2</u> ↔	011266	6	6	IV	
111111121(2) ↔	B♭ D F A C♯ A♭ C E G* B	<u>3</u> ↔	011266	6	6	IV	
111111211(2) ↔	G♯ B D♯ G B♭ D F♯ A D♭ F* (A♭)	<u>4</u> ↔	011266	7	7	IV	
111112111(2) ↔	(E) G B D F♯ A♯ D♭ F A* C E (G)	<u>5</u> ↔	011266	7	7	IV	
111121111(2) ↔	G♭ B♭ D♭ F A* C E G B D♯* (F♯) (A♯)	<u>6</u> ↔	011266	6	6	IV	only 6 transp.
11-note chord	(F♯) A♯ C♯ E G B D F A* C E♭ G♭ (B♭)	1-note chord	011266	9	9	IV	
12-note chord ↔	G♯ C♯ F♯ B E A D G C F B♭ E♭	silence	**011266**	12	12	IV	maximum, −2−2+2+, +2−4+2−, only 1 transp.

II. System of Characteristic-types

In the the "characteristic" column, the marks determining the characteristic-types are given, in the the "characteristic maxima" and the "nuclei" there are the relevant orientation schemes (sometimes with a more detailed verbal description). The last column indicates the numbers of sections where the individual types are discussed.

Characteristic	Characteristic maxima	Characteristic Nuclei	§
+ −	43—34 (major–minor)	3, 4, 5	33
0	44 (augmented)	44	37
6	333 (diminished)	6	34
2	2232 (pentatonic)	2	35
1	131[1], 313[2], 143[3]	1	36
01	13131	134—314	36
26	2223[1] (diatonic), 242[2] (chromatic)	24—42	37
026	22222	224	37
16	141[1], 133[2]—331[1]	15—51	38
016	1331	1331	38
12	22122[1] (diatonic), 121[2] (chromatic)	12—21	39
012	1214	1214	39
126	122122[1] (diatonic), 21212[2], 12132[3], 12321[4], 12123[5]—21213[6]	123—321, 124—421, 132—231, 142—241, 213—312	40
0126	$\dfrac{\text{neg. }2223^{1)}}{121222}, \dfrac{\text{neg. }1332^{2)}}{121221} - \dfrac{\text{neg. }1323^{3)}}{122121}$	1322—2231, 2213—3122	41
166	151	151	42
1266	$\dfrac{\text{neg. 333}}{1212121}$	1231—1321	42
112	11111[1], 21112[2]	11	43
0112	12113[1]—31121[2]	3113	43

Characteristic	Characteristic maxima	Characteristic Nuclei	§
1126	$\dfrac{\text{neg. }212^{1)}}{2111112}$, $\dfrac{\text{neg. }1221^{2)}}{111132}$, $\dfrac{\text{neg. }3211^{3)}}{111212} - \dfrac{\text{neg. }1123^{4)}}{212111}$, $\dfrac{\text{neg. }1111^{5)}}{111111}$	$\underset{\leftrightarrow}{115}$, 114—411, $\underset{\leftrightarrow}{2112}$	44
01126	$\dfrac{\text{neg. }22^{1)}}{11111122}$, $\dfrac{\text{neg. }44^{2)}}{11211211}$, $\dfrac{\text{neg. }313^{3)}}{1211121}$, $\dfrac{\text{neg. }121^{4)}}{1111113}$, $\dfrac{\text{neg. }323^{5)}}{1121221}$	1124—2114, $\underset{\leftrightarrow}{11322}$, 11313—11331, $\dfrac{\text{neg.}3113}{121121}$	45
11266	$\dfrac{\text{neg. }115^{1)}}{1112111}$, $\dfrac{\text{neg. }151^{2)}}{1113111}$, $\dfrac{\text{neg. }111^{3)}}{1111111}$, $\dfrac{\text{neg. }232^{4)}}{1112212}$, $\dfrac{\text{neg. }123^{5)}}{2121111} - \dfrac{\text{neg. }321^{6)}}{1111212}$	1141—1411	46
011266	12-note chord	11231—13211	47
all 22 characteristic-types	all 51 maxima	all 51 nuclei	

III. Characteristic Maxima by Chord-class

Chord-class	Orientation schemes of Maxima	Characteristic
3-note chords	43–34	+ –
	44	0
4-note chords	333	6
	131[1)], 313[2)], 143[3)]	1
	242[2)]	26
	141[1)], 133[2)]—331[3)]	16
	121[2)]	12
	151	166
5-note chords	2232	2
	2223[1)]	26
	1331	016
	1214	012
6-note chords	13131	01
	22222	026
	22122[1)]	12
	21212[2)], 12132[3)], 12321[4)], 12123[5)]—21213[6)]	126
	11111[1)], 21112[2)]	112
	12113[1)]—31121[2)]	0112
7-note chords	neg. 2232[1)] / 122122	126
	neg. 2223[1)] / 121222, neg. 1332[2)] / 12121 — neg. 1323[3)] / 122121	0126
	neg. 1221[2)] / 111132, neg. 3211[3)] / 111212 — neg. 1123[4)] / 212111 neg. 1111[5)] / 111111	1126

Chord-class	Orientation schemes of Maxima	Characteristic
8-note chords	$\overleftrightarrow{\text{neg. 333}}$ / 1212121	1266
	$\overleftrightarrow{\text{neg. 212}}^{1)}$ / 2111112	1126
	$\overleftrightarrow{\text{neg. 313}}^{3)}$ / 1211121 , $\overleftrightarrow{\text{neg. 121}}^{4)}$ / 1111113 , $\overleftrightarrow{\text{neg. 323}}^{5)}$ / 1121221	01126
	$\overleftrightarrow{\text{neg. 115}}^{1)}$ / 1112111 , $\overleftrightarrow{\text{neg. 151}}^{2)}$ / 1113111 , $\overleftrightarrow{\text{neg. 111}}^{3)}$ / 1111111 , $\overleftrightarrow{\text{neg. 232}}^{4)}$ / 1112212 , $\overleftrightarrow{\text{neg. 123}}^{5)}$ / 2121111 , $\overleftrightarrow{\text{neg. 321}}^{6)}$ / 1111212	11266
9-note chords	$\overleftrightarrow{\text{neg. 22}}^{1)}$ / 11111122 , $\overleftrightarrow{\text{neg. 44}}^{2)}$ / 11211211	01126
12-note chord	12-note chord	011266

IV. Characteristic Nuclei by Chord-class

Chord-class	Nuclei	Characteristic
2-note chords	3, 4, 5	+ or –
	6	6
	2	2
	1	1
3-note chords	44 ↔	0
	24—42	26
	15—51	16
	12—21	12
	11 ↔	112
4-note chords	134—314	01
	224 ↔	026
	123—321, 124—421, 132—231, 142—241, 213—312	126
	151 ↔	166
	115, 114—411	1126
5-note chords	1331 ↔	016
	1214 ↔	012
	1322—2231, 2213—3122	0126
	1231—1321	1266
	3113 ↔	0112
	2112 ↔	1126
	1124—2114	01126
	1141—1411	11266
6-note chords	11322, 11313—11331 ↔	01126
	11231—13211	011266
7-note chords	neg.3113 ↔ 121121	01126

V. Boundaries between Characteristic-types

Boundary	Relations of Characteristic-types
0	1 : 01, 12 : 012, 16 : 016, 126 : 0126, 26 : 026, 112 : 0112, 1126 : 01126, 11266 : 011266
01	0 : 1, 2 : 012, 6 : 016, 26 : 0126, 026 : 126
012	0 : 12, 2 : 01, 6 : 0126, 26 : 016, 16 : 026
0126	0 : 126, 1 : 026, 2 : 016, 6 : 012, 01 : 26
016	0 : 16, 2 : 0126, 6 : 01, 26 : 012, 12 : 026
02	0 : 2, 1 : 012, 6 : 026, 01 : 12, 16 : 0126, 016 : 126
026	0 : 26, 1 : 0126, 01 : 126, 12 : 016, 16 : 012
06	0 : 6, 1 : 016, 2 : 026, 01 : 16, 12 : 0126, 012 : 126, 112 : 01126, 0112 : 1126
1	0 : 01, 2 : 12, 6 : 16, 26 : 126, 026 : 0126
12	0 : 012, 1 : 2, 6 : 126, 16 : 26, 016 : 026
126	0 : 0126, 1 : 26, 2 : 16, 6 : 12, 01 : 026
16	0 : 016, 1 : 6, 2 : 126, 12 : 26, 012 : 026
2	1 : 12, 6 : 26, 01 : 012, 16 : 126, 016 : 0126, 166 : 1266
26	0 : 026, 1 : 126, 2 : 6, 01 : 0126, 12 : 16, 012 : 016
6	1 : 16, 2 : 26, 01 : 016, 12 : 126, 012 : 0126, 112 : 1126, 0112 : 01126
11	12 : 112, 012 : 0112, 126 : 1126, 0126 : 01126, 1266 : 11266
0, 11	12 : 0112, 012 : 112, 126 : 01126, 0126 : 1126, 1266 : 011266
01, 11	2 : 0112, 26 : 01126, 026 : 1126
012, 11	0 : 112, 6 : 01126
0126, 11	0 : 1126, 6 : 0112
016, 11	2 : 01126, 26 : 0112, 026 : 112
02, 11	1 : 0112, 01 : 112, 16 : 01126, 016 : 1126, 166 : 011266
026, 11	1 : 01126, 01 : 1126, 16 : 0112, 016 : 112

Boundary	Relations of Characteristic-types
06, 11	12 : 01126, 012 : 1126, 126 : 0112, 112 : 0126
1, 11	2 : 112, 26 : 1126, 026 : 01126
12, 11	0 : 0112, 6 : 1126
126, 11	0 : 01126, 6 : 112
16, 11	2 : 1126, 26 : 112, 026 : 0112
2, 11	1 : 112, 01 : 0112, 16 : 1126, 016 : 01126, 166 : 11266
26, 11	1 : 1126, 01 : 01126, 16 : 112, 016 : 0112
6, 11	12 : 1126, 012 : 01126, 126 : 112, 0112 : 0126
66	16 : 166, 126 : 1266, 1126 : 11266, 01126 : 011266
0, 66	016 : 166, 1126 : 011266, 0126 : 1266, 01126 : 11266
01, 66	026 : 1266
012, 66	026 : 166
0126, 66	0 : 1266
016, 66	0 : 166
02, 66	016 : 1266, 166 : 0126
026, 66	01 : 1266, 012 : 166
06, 66	01 : 166, 012 : 1266, 112 : 011266, 0112 : 11266
1, 66	6 : 166, 26 : 1266
12, 66	6 : 1266, 26 : 166
126, 66	2 : 166
16, 66	2 : 1266
2, 66	16 : 1266, 126 : 166
26, 66	1 : 1266, 12 : 166
6, 66	1 : 166, 12 : 1266, 112 : 11266, 0112 : 011266

Tables and Overviews

Boundary	Relations of Characteristic-types
1166	126 : 11266, 0126 : 011266, 1126 : 1266
0, 1166	126 : 011266, 0126 : 11266, 1266 : 01126
01, 1166	26 : 011266, 026 : 11266
012, 1166	6 : 011266
0126, 1166	+ or − : 011266
016, 1166	2 : 011266
02, 1166	16 : 011266, 016 : 11266, 166 : 01126
026, 1166	1 : 011266, 01 : 11266, 166 : 0112
06, 1166	12 : 011266, 012 : 11266, 0112 : 1266
1, 1166	26 : 11266, 026 : 011266
12, 1166	6 : 11266
126, 1166	0 : 011266
16, 1166	2 : 11266
2, 1166	16 : 11266, 016 : 011266, 166 : 1126
26, 1166	1 : 11266, 01 : 011266, 112 : 166
6, 1166	12 : 11266, 012 : 011266, 112 : 1266

VI. Symbols and abbreviations

⌣   Major triad as a component of a more complex chord: G B D F.

⌢   Minor triad as a component of a more complex chord: B D F A.

⌣ ⌢˙   Major or minor triad with the basic pitch indicated: D̰ G B E B♭, D Ė̲ A E♭.

⟵⟶   Indication of a symmetrical chord; §5.

∗   Indication of the lowest pitch in an orientation scheme: C∗ E G 43; §4.

+   Major triad; used independently or in conjunction with numerals and functional symbols.

−   Minor triad; used independently or in conjunction with numerals and functional symbols.

□   Characteristic maximum; §31 ff.

△   Characteristic nucleus; §32 ff.

○   Subordinate chord; §32.

⊕   Complete major or minor consonant triad; §110.

⌣   Basic pitch of a major or minor triad. The symbol appears beside the functional symbol: T ⌣ in C major indicates the pitch C; §110.

⌢   Supplementary pitch of a major or minor triad: in C major, D ⌢ indicates the pitch D, L ⌢ the pitch F♯, etc.; §110.

| Differentiating pitch of a major or minor triad: in C major, −S| indicates A♭; +D| in E minor indicates D♯; §110.

E——, F♯——   Duration and normal dying away of an imaginary pitch; §76, 78.

Tables and Overviews

E♭ ▬	Cancellation of an imaginary pitch; §76.
G♯ ▬ - - -	Slow dying away of an imaginary pitch; §78.
F ▬⌐	Accelerated dying away of an imaginary pitch; §78.
⌒→	Delayed resolution of a non-harmonic tone; §85.
╱	Indication of a counter-canceling pitch; §85.
1, 2, 3, etc.	Intervals; §2.
12, 313, etc.	Orientation schemes of chords; §3.
(5), (7), etc.	Complements to the octave in orientation schemes; §3.
11	Semitone clash of intervals 1; §24.
66	Semitone clash of intervals 6; §24.
0	Augmented triad 44; e.g. C E G♯.
$\frac{131}{1111131}$	Joint orientation scheme for negative and positive; §10.
12, **126**, etc.	Characteristic maxima; §31.
[1], [2], etc.	More detailed identification of a characteristic maximum: **12**[2] is the second maximum of the characteristic-type 12; §36 ff.
I, II, III, IV	Combination categories; §52.
+3−, −4+, etc.	Combination harmonies of category II. The number between the symbols of the component triads is the interval between their basic pitches: +3− represents C E G − E♭ G♭ B♭; §54.

$\widehat{+1-}$, $\widehat{-3+}$, etc.	Partial combinations with two components. The number of curved lines joining the triadic symbols indicates the number of pitches they have in common: $\widehat{+1-}$ represents G♯ C♯ E G C (C E G – C♯ E G♯), $\widehat{-3+}$ represents C E♭ G B♭ (C E♭ G – E♭ G B♭); §55.
–2–2+, –2+2+, etc.	Triadic combinations of categories III and IV; §56, 57.
T	Tonic triad: in C major, C E G.
D	Dominant triad: in C major and minor, G B D.
d	Altered (minor) dominant triad: in C major and minor, G B♭ D; §118.
S	Subdominant triad: in C major, F A C and F A♭ C; in C minor, F A♭ C.
s	Altered subdominant triad, major in a minor key: in C minor, F A♭ C; §118.
P	Phrygian harmony – the consonant triad a semitone higher than the tonic: in C major and minor, D♭ F A♭; in C minor also D♭ F♭ A♭; §108.
L	Lydian harmony – the consonant triad a semitone lower than the tonic: in C major and minor, B D F♯; in C major also B D♯ F♯; §108.
+T, +L, etc.	Major tonic: in C major, C E G; major lydian triad: in C major, B D♯ F♯.
–T, –S, etc.	Minor tonic: in C minor, C E♭ G; minor subdominant triad: in C major, F A♭ C.
Pr	Primary functions: T, S, D.
Aux	Auxiliary functions: P, L.

Tables and Overviews

(D), (L), $\begin{pmatrix}D\\P\end{pmatrix}$	Secondary function or functional combination; §117.
——(d)——	Altered secondary functional triad (here the dominant) that does not disturb the pitch-system of the main tonality; §118.
$\dfrac{\text{S T D D}}{\text{D I}^2\text{ T D}}$	Bitonal progression of functional triads; §116.
Ṫ, S̈, Ḍ	Complication of a functional triad by foreign pitches: in C major, Ṫ indicates C E G B or C E G A or C E G D♯, etc. A dot below indicates that the added pitch is at the bottom; thus we show D♯ G B D in C major as Ḍ. The number of dots indicates the number of added pitches; §110.
T·, S:, L·	One dot beside the functional symbol means one pitch of the corresponding triad, two dots, two pitches; In C major, T· means C or E or G; S: means F A or F C or A C; §110.
IN	Interfunction – a consonant harmony consisting of components of different functions. A more detailed intervallic identification must always be included: IN² is the consonant triad an interval 2 higher than the tonic (in C major, D F A or D F♯ A); IN₄ is the consonant triad an interval 4 below the tonic (in C major, A♭ C E♭ or G♯ B D♯); §110.
inv.	Inversion; §5.
neg.	Negative; §10.
$\begin{matrix}\text{D}\\\text{S}\\\text{T}\end{matrix}\ \begin{matrix}\text{T}\\\text{S}\end{matrix}$	Functional combinations; §110, 111, 112.

Bibliography

Bibliography and music examples correspond with titles stated in Karel Janeček's original *Foundations of Modern Harmony*.

Achtélik, Josef. *Der Naturklang als Wurzel aller Harmonien: Eine aesthetische Musiktheorie* [2 vols.]. Leipzig: C. F. Kahnt, 1922.

Bairstow, Edward C. *Counterpoint and Harmony*. 2nd ed. London: Macmillan, 1945.

Blažek, Zdeněk. *Dvojsměrná alterace v harmonickém myšlení* [Bidirectional Alteration in Harmonic Thought]. Brno: Rovnost, 1949.

Branberger, Jan. *Rhythmus a ton: Nástin theorie hudební* [Rhythm and Pitch: Outline of Music Theory]. Praha: Zemský Ústř. spolek jednot učitelských v král. Českém, 1909.

Carner, Mosco. *A Study of Twentieth-century Harmony. Volume Two: Contemporary Harmony*. London: J. Williams, [1944].

Dubovskij, I., S. Jevsejev, I. Sposobin and V. Sokolov. *Učebnik garmonii* [Harmony Text]. Moskva – Leningrad: Gosudarstvennoe Muz'ykal'noe Izdatel'stvo, 1947.

Dunk, John L. *The Structure of the Musical Scale*. London: John Lane, The Bodley Head, 1940.

Dyson, George. "Harmony." In *Grove's Dictionary of Music and Musicians*, 3rd ed., edited by George Grove and Henry Cope Colles. London: Macmillan, 1929.

Emmanuel, Maurice. *Histoire de la Langue Musicale* [2 vols.]. Deuxième édition. Paris: Renouard, 1928.

Foerster, Josef. *Nauka o harmonii* [Theory of Harmony]. 3., částečně přeprac. vyd. [3rd, partly rev. ed.]. Praha: nákl. vl. [by the author], 1909.

Hába, Alois. *Harmonické základy čtvrttónové souslavy* [Harmonic Foundations of the Quarter-tone System]. Praha: Hudební Matice Umělecké besedy [The Music Association of the Artistic Society], 1922.

——— *Neue Harmonielehre des diatonischen, chromatischen, Viertel-, Drittel-, Sechstel- und Zwölftel-Tonsystems*. Leipzig: Kistner & Siegel, 1927.

––– *O psychologii tvoření, pohybové zákonitosti tónové a základech nového hudebního slohu* [Regarding the Psychology of Creating, the Kinetic Principles of Tones, and the Foundations of New Musical Style]. Praha: Hudební Matice Umělecké besedy [The Music Association of the Artistic Society], 1925.

Hindemith, Paul. *Unterweisung im Tonsatz I–II*. Neue, erw. ausg. Mainz: B. Schott's Söhne, 1939–1940.

Honegger, Arthur. *Zaříkání zkamenělin* [Exorcizing Fossils]. Přeložil [Translated by] Jaromír Fiala. Praha: SNKLHU, 1960.

Hradecký, Emil. *Úvod do studia tonální harmonie* [Introduction to the Study of Tonal Harmony]. Praha: SNKLHU, 1960.

Hůla, Zdeněk. *Nauka o harmonii I+II* [Theory of Harmony I+II]. Praha: SNKLHU, 1956.

Hutter, Josef. *Harmonický princip* [The Harmonic Principle]. Praha: Česká akademie věd a umění [Czech Academy of Sciences and Arts], 1941.

D'Indy, Vincent. *Cours de composition musicale* [2 vols]. Paris: Durand, 1902, 1909.

Janáček, Leoš. *Úplná nauka o harmonii* [Complete Theory of Harmony]. 2. vyd. [2nd ed.]. Brno: A. Píša, 1920.

Janeček, Karel. *Otakar Šín*. Praha: Česká akademie věd a umění [Czech Academy of Sciences and Arts], 1944.

––– "Základní harmonické problémy a jejich řešení" [Fundamental Harmonic Problems and their Solutions]. *Musikologie: Sborník pro hudební vědu a kritiku* [Musicology: Annual for Musical Science and Criticism], 87–129. Praha: SNKLHU, 1955.

––– *Harmonie rozborem* [Harmony Through Analysis]. Praha: Státní hudební nakladatelství [State Music Press], 1963.

Kofroň, Jaroslav. *Učebnice harmonie* [Textbook of Harmony]. Praha: SNKLHU, 1958.

Kohoutek, Ctirad. *Novodobé skladebné teorie západoevropské hudby* [Modern Compositional Theories of Western European Music]. Praha: SHV, 1962.

Kulakovskij, L. *O russkom narodnom mnogogolosii* [The Many Voices of the Russian People]. Moscow – Leningrad: Muzgiz, 1951.

Kurth, Ernst. *Romantische Harmonik und ihre Krise in Wagners Tristan*. Zweite Auflage. Berlin: Hesses Verlag, 1923.

Lobe, Johann Christoph. *Katechismus der Kompositionslehre*. 7. verm. und verb. Aufl. Leipzig: J. J. Weber, 1902.

Louis, Rudolf and Ludwig Thuille. *Harmonielehre*. 9. Aufl. Stuttgart: Klett, 1942.

Maksimov, S. E. *Upražnenija po garmonii na fortepiano I–III* [Harmony Exercises on Piano I–III]. Moscow: Gosudarstvennoe Muz'ykal'noe Izdatel'stvo, 1951–1954.

Modr, Antonín. *Harmonie v otázkách a odpovědích* [Harmony in Questions and Answers]. Praha: Panton, 1960.

Morris, R. O. *The Oxford Harmony, Vol. 1*. London: Oxford University Press, 1946.

Neumann, Friedrich. *Synthetische Harmonielehre*. Leipzig: Breitkopf & Härtel, 1951.

von der Nüll, Edwin. *Moderne Harmonik*. Leipzig: Kistner & Siegel, 1932.

Ogolevec, A. S. *Vvedenic v sovremennoje muzykalnoje myšlenije* [Introduction to Contemporary Musical Thinking]. Moscow – Leningrad: Muzgiz, 1946.

von der Osten, Elisabeth. *Der musikalische Satz: Harmonie- und Melodielehre*. Leipzig: Breitkopf & Härtel, 1955.

Pícha, František. *Stručná a přehledná harmonie* [Brief and Easily-surveyed Harmony]. Praha: Melantrich, 1949.

Rejcha, Antonín. *Corso di composizione musicale ossia Trattato completo e ragionato d'Armonia pratica*. Trad. dal francese, con pref. ed annot. critiche di Luigi Felice Rossi. Milan: Ricordi, [1930].

Reuter, Fritz. *Praktische Harmonik des 20. Jahrhundert: Konsonanz- und Dissonanzlehre nach dem System von Sigfrid Karg-Elert*. Halle: Mitteldeutscher Verlag, 1952.

Riemann, Hugo. *Anleitung zum Generalbaß-Speilen. Harmonie-Übungen am Klavier*. 5. Auflage. Berlin: Max Hesse, 1917.

——— *Handbuch der Harmonie- und Modulationslehre: Praktische Anleitung zum mehrstimmingen Tonsatz*. 7. Aufl. Berlin: Max Hesse, [s. a.].

——— *Geschichte der Musiktheorie im IX.–XIX. Jahrhundert*. Zweite, vermehrte und verbesserte Auflage. Berlin: Max Hesse, 1920.

——— *Große Kompositionslehre. I. Band. Der homophone Satz: Melodielehre und Harmonielehre*. Berlin – Stuttgart: Verlag von W. Speamnn, 1902.

Rimskij-Korsakov, N. A. *Traité d'harmonie: Théorique et Pratique*. Traduction française de Félix Dorfmann. Paris: Alphonse Leduc, 1910.

Risinger, Karel. *Nástin obecného hudebního funkčního systému rozšířené tonality* [Outline of the General Musical Functional System of Expanded Tonality]. Praha: Svaz čs. skladatelů [Union of Czechoslovakian Composers], 1957.

——— *Přehledná nauka o harmonii* [Easily-surveyed Theory of Harmony]. University course texts. Praha: SPN, 1955.

——— *Vůdčí osobnosti české moderní hudební teorie: Otakar Šín, Alois Hába, Karel Janeček* [Leading Personalities in Modern Czech Music Theory: Otakar Šín, Alois Hába, Karel Janeček]. Praha: SHV, 1963.

——— "Výběrová bibliografie z oboru české hudební teorie mezi léty 1948–1960" [Selected Bibliography from the Field of Czech Music Theory from 1948–1960]. *Hudební věda* [Musical Science Quarterly] 4 (1961): 127–137.

——— "Vývoj českých harmonických systémů po roce 1948" [The Evolution of Czech Harmonic Systems After 1948]. *Hudební věda* [Musicology] 1/1 (1964): 44–82.

——— *Základní harmonické funkce v soudobé hudbě* [Fundamental Harmonic Functions in Contemporary Music]. Praha: SNKLHU, 1958.

Schönberg, Arnold. *Harmonielehre*. 3. verm. u. verb. Aufl. Wien: Universal Edition, 1922.

Skrebkova, O. L. and S. S. Skrebkov. *Chrestomatija po garmoničeskomu analizu* [Manual of Harmonic Analysis]. Moskva – Leningrad: Muzgiz, 1948.

——— *Praktičeskij kurs garmonii* [Practical Course in Harmony]. Moskva – Leningrad: Gosudarstvennoe Muz'ykal'noe Izdatel'stvo, 1952.

Skuherský, František Zdeněk. *Nauka o harmonii na vědeckém základě ve formě nejjednodušší se zvláštním zřetelem na mohutný rozvoj harmonie v nejnovější době* [Theory of Harmony with Scientific Foundations in its Simplest Form with Special Consideration of the Impressive Development of Harmony in the Most Recent Age]. Praha: Urbánek, 1885.

Šín, Otakar. *Úplná nauka o harmonii na základě melodie a rytmu* [Complete Theory of Harmony on the Basis of Melody and Rhythm]. 2. vyd., přepracované a rozšířené [2nd ed., revised and expanded]. Praha: Hudební Matice [The Music Association], 1933.

Vojtěch, Ivan (ed.). *Skladatelé o hudební poetice 20. století* [Composers on Musical Poetics in the 20th Century]. Praha: Československý spisovatel [Czechoslovakian Writer], 1960.

Volek, Jaroslav. *Novodobé harmonické systémy z hlediska vědecké filosofie* [Modern Harmonic Systems from the Perspective of Scientific Philosophy]. Praha: Panton, 1961.

——— *Teoretické základy harmónie z hľadiska vedeckej filozofie* [The Theoretical Foundations of Harmony from the Perspective of Scientific Philosophy]. Bratislava: Vydavateľstvo Slovenskej akadémie vied [Slovak Academy of Science Press], 1954.

Sources of Examples from Contemporary Music

Bořkovec, Pavel. *Quintet for Flute, Oboe, Clarinet, French Horn, and Bassoon*. Praha: Hudební matice [Musical Association], 1936. §148, Ex. 249.

——— *Suite for Piano*. Praha: Hudební matice [Musical Association], 1931. §135, Ex. 204; §144, Ex. 241; §145, Ex. 242; §150, Ex. 251.

Debussy, Claude. *Prélude à l'après-midi d'un Faune*. Paris: Jobert, 1922. §120, Ex. 166.

Hindemith, Paul. *Trio No. 1 for Violin, Viola, and Violoncello, Op. 34*. Mainz – Leipzig: Schott, 1924. §146, Ex. 244.

Honegger, Arthur. *Pacific 231*. Paris: Sénart, 1924. §149, Ex. 250.

——— *Prélude, Arioso et Fughette sur le nom de BACH*. Paris: Salabert, 1933. §150, Ex. 253; §151, Ex. 256.

——— *Symphonie pour cordes*. Paris: Salabert, 1942. §147, Ex. 247.

Krejčí, Iša. *Trio-Divertimento for Oboe, Clarinet, and Bassoon*. Praha: vl. nákl. [by the author], [1939]. §151, Ex. 257; §153, Ex. 260.

Martinů, Bohuslav. *Julietta*. Praha: Melantrich, 1947. §146, Ex. 243; §152, Ex. 258.

Novák, Vítězslav. *Serenade in D major for Small Orchestra, Op. 36*. Wien: Wiener Philharmonischer Verlag, [1913]. §122, Ex. 176.

——— *Slovak Songs*. Praha: Hudební matice [Musical Association], 1913–1936. The skeleton of the harmonization of one song is included in §120, Ex. 167.

——— *Third String Quartet, Op. 66*. Leipzig: Breitkopf und Härtel, 1939. §150, Ex. 254.

Pícha, František. *Suite for String Orchestra and Gong, Op. 18*. Praha: Hudební matice [Musical Association], 1933. §152, Ex. 259.

Roussel, Albert. *Quartet in D major, Op. 45*. Paris: Durand, 1932. §147, Exx. 245 and 246.

Scriabin, Alexander. *Prélude, Op. 74, No. 4*. Leipzig: Forberg [formerly Jurgenson], [s. a.]. §73, Ex. 76.

Stravinsky, Igor. *Three pieces for String Quartet*. New York et al: Édition Russe de musique, 1922. §135, Ex. 202.

Zusammenfassung

Karel Janeček's german summary published in *Foundations of Modern Harmony* (p. 357–379). In original conception of the book *Chapters III* and *VI* are not divided in sub-chapters *IIIa, IIIb* and *VIa, VIb, VIc*. We maintain original author's structure of chapters in german summary.

In den *Grundlagen der modernen Harmonie* wird systematisch das gesamte harmonische Material behandelt, welches das stabilisierte Tonsystem der europäischen Musik, die *temperierte Chromatik*, bietet. Aus dem Material sind einerseits die allgemeinen Gesetzmäßigkeiten, anderseits die teilweisen praktischen Erkenntnisse abgeleitet, die insbesondere die neuzeitige Kompositionstechnik betreffen.

Durchforscht wird hier die Zusammensetzung aller existierenden Zusammenklang-Gattungen (Kap. I). Ferner sind hier zusammenfassend die Klangeigenschaften der Zusammenklänge in isolierter Stellung beschrieben (Kap. II). Auf dieser Grundlage werden dann die Zusammenklänge übersichtlich nach zwei sich ergänzenden Methoden je nach der Toncharakteristik und kombiniert klassifiziert (Kap. III). Die lebendige Kompositionsarbeit betreffen die Kapitel über Anordnung und Ausdruck der Zusammenklänge (Kap. IV und V). Hier geht es insbesondere um die Applikation der Erkenntnisse, welche die imaginären Töne betreffen. Außer der statistischen Forschung ist auch der harmonischen Kinetik systematische Aufmerksamkeit gewidmet (Kap. VI). Aus den klassischen harmonischen Vorgängen sind die allgemeinen kinetischen Gesetze abgeleitet (das Prinzip der reinen Tonik, das Prinzip des Leittons und das Funktionsprinzip), deren Geltung sich markant auch in der modernen Musik durchsetzt. Das Ganze ist vervollständigt durch das Kapitel über die allgemeine Problematik der modernen Harmonie (beispielsweise: was die brennende Frage des Verhältnisses zwischen Konsonanzen und Dissonanzen anbelangt, Kap. VII).

Dem theoretischen Teil der Schrift sind endlich noch zwei Kapitel angefügt, in denen der Autor praktische Winke für die kompositorische und analytische Arbeit gibt (Kap. VIII und IX).

Der Inhalt der ersten 6 Kapitel, die den Kern der Schrift darstellen, ist folgender:

Kapitel I. Das harmonische material der temperierten chromatik

§ 1. *Die temperierte Chromatik.* Die temperierte Chromatik ist das praktische Tonsystem unserer Musik. Darin können in größtmöglichem Ausmaß die praktischen Konsonanzen zur Geltung kommen, das sind solche Konsonanzen, welche zwar nicht gänzlich vollkommen sind, aber doch den Anforderungen der musikalischen Praxis vollauf entsprechen.

§ 2. *Die Voraussetzungen für die Erforschung des harmonischen Materials.* In der temperierten Chromatik gibt es nur 12 unterscheidbare Intervalle, von denen der kleinste – Halbton – eine Einheit darstellt. Alle Intervalle kann man als ein Vielfaches der Einheit, des Halbtons, ausdrücken. Wir unterscheiden verschiedene Klassen von Zusammenklängen nach der Anzahl der verwendeten verschiedenen Töne. Das Wesen des Zusammenklangs (seine Gattung) wird weder durch Transposition noch durch seine Anordnung (verschiedenartige Umstellung seiner einzelnen Töne) verändert.

§ 3. *Das Orientierungsschema der Zusammenklang-Gattungen.* Im Orientierungsschema, womit die Gattung des Zusammenklangs eindeutig bestimmt werden kann, fassen wir alle beteiligten Töne in kleinstem Umfang zusammen. Haben einige Formen denselben kleinsten Umfang, so halten wir für das Orientierungsschema jene Form, in der die Intervalle von unten hinauf von den kleineren zu den größeren geordnet sind. Das Orientierungsschema läßt sich ziffernmäßig ausdrücken, zum Beisp. *c d e g* = 223, *c d g* = 25 u. ä.

§ 4. *Das harmonische Schema der Zusammenklänge.* Zum Unterschied vom Orientierungsschema erfaßt das harmonische Schema anschaulich das harmonische Wesen des Zusammenklangs. Bei den komplizierteren Zusammenklängen erweist es sich als notwendig, dichte Tongruppen auseinander zu stellen (Nachbar-Intervalle 1 und 2).

§ 5. *Inversion des Zusammenklanges. Symmetrische und asymmetrische Zusammenklang-Gattungen.* Durch Inversion des Vierklanges *c e fis h* 142 erhalten wir den Vierklang *c f g h* 241. Eine gattungsmäßig verschiedene Inversion kann man nur zu einem asymmetrischen Zusammenklang machen. Symmetrische Zusammenklänge sind von sich aus Inversionen. Ein symmetrischer Dreiklang ist z. B. der übermäßige Dreiklang *c e gis* 44.

§ 6.–9. *Gattungen der Zweiklänge bis Fünfklänge.* Es existieren 6 Gattungen von Zweiklängen, 19 von Dreiklängen, 43 von Vierklängen und 66 Gattungen von Fünfklängen. Es sind Notenbeispiele und Orientierungsschemata aller dieser Zusammenklang-Gattungen angeführt. Manchmal war es der Anschaulichkeit wegen notwendig, ein erweitertes Schema zu verwenden, d. i. mit beigefügter Ergänzung bis zur Oktave, z. B. (3) 2223 u. ä.

§ 10. *Das Negativ der Zusammenklang-Gattung.* Die Zusammenfassung der Töne der temperierten Chromatik, welche nicht im gegebenen Zusammenklang enthalten sind, stellt das Negativ des Zusammenklanges dar. Z. B. ist das Negativ des symmetrischen Dreiklangs *h d f* 33 der symmetrische Neunklang *g b cis e as c es fis a* 11112121.

§ 11. *Gattungen der Sechsklänge.* Es existieren 80 Gattungen von Sechsklängen. Einige sind von sich aus Negative. Siehe Beisp. 4.

§ 12. *Harmonische Möglichkeiten der temperierten Chromatik.* Die Zahl der Zusammenklang-Gattungen in den höheren Klassen zeigt wieder eine sinkende Tendenz: Siebenklänge gibt es 66 (wie deren Negative: Fünfklänge), Achtklänge 43 (wie Vierklänge) usw. Siehe die Übersichtstabelle.

§ 13. *Gattungen der Vielklänge.* Die Vielklänge sind nicht angeführt, weil es Negative niedrigerer Zusammenklänge sind. Beisp. 5 zeigt die symmetrischen Anordnungen des Elfklangs, Beisp. 6 wieder die Anordnung des Zwölfklanges.

§ 14. *Die in der temperierten Chromatik enthaltenen Tonsysteme.* Jedes Tonsystem können wir durch ein Orientierungsschema ausdrücken (ähnlich wie die Vielklänge). Es ist interessant, sich zum Bewußtsein zu bringen, daß die reine Diatonik, die anhemitonische Pentatonik und einige weitere Systeme symmetrisch sind.

§ 15. *Ergebnisse und Aussichten.* Das gesamte harmonische Material, welches die temperierte Chromatik bietet, kann man in der Komposition verwenden. Die Unterschiede zwischen den Zusammenklängen sind umso kleiner je komplizierter die Zusammenklänge selbst sind.

Kapitel II. Klangeigenschaften des Harmonischen Materials

§ 16. *Konsonanzen – Dissonanzen.* Die Konsonanz ist eine solche Art des Zusammenklangs, die unter günstigen Umständen auf den Zuschauer so einwirken kann, daß sie in ihm keine Spannung erzeugt. Es gibt nur zwei Grund-Konsonanzen: den Dreiklang Dur 43 und den Dreiklang Moll 34. Die Dissonanz ist eine solche Art des Zusammenklangs, daß sie im Zuschauer unter allen Umständen ein Gefühl der Unruhe und Spannung bei jedweder Anordnung und Folge der Zusammenklänge erzeugt.

§ 17. *Dissonante Elemente.* Es existieren vier dissonante Elemente: der Halbton (1), der Ganzton (2), der Tritonus (6) und der übermäßige Dreiklang (44), der auch als 0 bezeichnet wird. Jede Dissonanz enthält wenigstens irgendein dissonantes Element.

§ 18. *Das Prinzip harmonischer Inversion.* Es existieren Zwillingsklänge gleicher Dissonanz-Stufe und gleichen Dissonanz-Charakters. Es sind das die wechselseitigen Inversionen (z. B. *h d f a* 233 — *g h d f* 332, *c es g h* 134 — *c e gis h* 314 und ähnl.). Symmetrische Zusammenklänge haben keine konsonanten oder gleich dissonanten Gegenstücke. Sie stehen isoliert. So existiert kein Vierklang, den man als ebenbürtige Gattung dem verminderten Vierklang *h d f as* oder dem übermäßigen Dreiklang *c e gis* beiordnen könnte u. ä.

§ 19. *Dissonanz-Charakteristik der Zusammenklänge.* Beisp. 7 zeigt alle Gattungen von Zusammenklängen, in denen immer nur ein Dissonanz-Element zur Geltung kommt. Das Element selbst ist eingerahmt.

§ 20. *Der Einfluß konsonanter Bestandteile.* Mit fortschreitender Zunahme konsonanter Bestandteile wird die dissonante Prägnanz des Zusammenklanges, die durch die Wirkung des dissonanten Elements gegeben ist, gedämpft. Durchdringende gedämpfte Wirkung haben die vollen konsonanten Bestandteile. Die leere Quint-Konsonanz (7 = 5) wird kenntlich nur in Verbindung mit vollen Konsonanzen gedämpft.

§ 21. *Geschlechtscharakter der Zusammenklänge.* Außer durch das Vorhandensein (oder Nichtvorhandensein) dissonanter Elemente sind die Zusammenklänge auch charakterisiert durch das Vorhandensein von konsonanten Dreiklang-Elementen (43, 34). In der Tabelle ist die Anzahl der Zusammenklang-Gattungen in den einzelnen Klassen derart in vier Kolonnen angeführt, daß die erste Kolonne keine geschlechtscharakteristischen Bestandteile, die zweite Kolonne nur die Bestandteile Dur (+), die dritte Kolonne nur die Bestandteile Moll (−) und die vierte Kolonne beide Bestandteile vermischt enthält.

§ 22. *Steigerung der dissonanten Charakteristik.* Zusammenklänge, welche zwei oder mehrere charakteristische Dissonanzen derselben Gattung enthalten, sind nur etwas ausdrucksvoller als die Zusammenklänge mit einer einzigen solchen charakteristischen Dissonanz. Die Anhäufung dissonanter Elemente derselben Gattung im Zusammenklang nennen wir Steigerung. Die Möglichkeiten der reinen Steigerung zeigen die Beispiele 8, 9, 10 und 12. Beim Element des übermäßigen Dreiklangs (44) läßt sich die reine Steigerung nicht verwirklichen.

§ 23. *Die Verschmelzung dissonanter Charakteristiken.* Die gemeinsame Wirkung verschiedener dissonanter Charakteristiken im Zusammenklang bezeichen wir als deren Verschmelzung. Im Zusammenklang können dissonante Elemente immer je zwei (12,

16, 01, 26), je drei (126, 012, 016, 026) oder alle vier (0126) verschmelzen. Die einzelnen Elemente wirken durch die nur ihnen eigentümliche Weise in allen Zusammenklang-Gattungen, an deren Bildung sie einfach oder gesteigert teilhaben. Die dissonante Charakteristik ist ausdrucksvoller bei Zusammenklängen niedrerer Klassen als bei Zusammenklängen höherer Klassen. Eine besonders durchdringende Wirkung hat das Element des Halbtons (1). Die Mitwirkung des Tritonus rundet den Klang ab. Diese Meliorationsfähigkeit des Tritonus ist sehr wichtig. Siehe die Beispiele 14 und 15.

§ 24. *Das Halbtonzusammenprallen der Halbton- und Tritonus- Elemente*. Bei der Steigerung der Elemente 1 oder 6 kommt es manchmal zu einem qualitativen Sprung in der Wirkung. (Siehe die eingerahmten Zusammenklänge in den Beispielen 18, 19, 20.) So ein Zusammenprallen der Halbtöne werden wir mit 11, der Tritoni mit 66 bezeichnen.

§ 25. *Zusammenfassung*. Die Geschlechtscharakteristik und Dissonanzcharakteristik kann als Grundlage bei der Klassifikation der Zusammenklänge dienen. Die erste Tafel zeigt das Auftreten der vier dissonanten Elemente und Zusammenprallen der Halbtöne und Tritoni in allen Zusammenklängen der temperierten Chromatik. In der 2. Tabelle ist stets die Zahl der existierenden Zusammenklänge mit Beteiligung der verschiedenen kombinierten dissonanten Charakteristiken angeführt.

Kapitel III. Klassifizierung des Harmonischen Materials

§ 26. *Der Begriff des Akkords in der klassischen Harmonie*. Den Begriff des Akkords kann man allgemein so definieren: es ist ein harmonisch verständlicher, im Verhältnis zu tonlich ärmeren harmonischen Gebilden übergeordneter und im Verhältnis zu seiner Umgebung selbständiger Zusammenklang. Die Forderung der harmonischen Verständlichkeit wird verschieden beurteilt und ergibt verschiedene Ergebnisse je nach dein Entwicklungsgrad, zu dem das Schaffen und musikalische Denken der Musiker gediehen ist. Für einen Akkord halten wir nicht einen einfacheren Zusammenklang, falls wir ihn von einem komplizierteren (übergeordneten) Zusammenklang derselben Klangsubstanz ableiten können. Die Selbständigkeit eines Akkords äußert sich in Bezug auf seine harmonische Umgebung in der Komposition durch seine größere Einfachheit und dadurch auch Verständlichkeit. Ausdrücklich machen wir auf folgenden Unterschied aufmerksam: 1. Der Akkord an sich ist das komplizierteste Gebilde bestimmter harmonischer Qualitäten. Seine Ableitungen derselben Klangsubstanz sind einfacher (tonlich ärmer). 2. Dagegen ist der Akkord in Beziehung zu seiner harmonischen Umgebung das einfachste Gebilde in der Reihe der melodisch von einander abhängigen Zusammenklänge.

§ 27. *Durchgangsharmonien.* Neben den Akkorden machen sich in der Komposition unselbständige harmonische Gebilde geltend, die wir allgemein als Durchgangsharmonien bezeichnen. Es sind zeitweilig deformierte oder komplizierte Akkorde. Zu Deformationen oder Komplikationen der Akkorde kommt es in der Komposition durch Geltendmachung von Vorhalten, Durchgangstönen, Wechseltönen, Antizipationen und Orgelpunkten.

§ 28. *Unvollständige Akkorde.* Zweiklänge werden in der klassischen Harmonik als unvollständige Akkorde erklärt. Durch Unterscheidung von Zusammenklängen in Akkorde und in Durchgangsharmonien und durch Einführung des Begriffs der unvollständigen Akkorde wurde das System der klassischen Harmonik übersichtlich gemacht und vereinfacht.

§ 29. *Entstehung neuer Akkorde.* Beispiel 22 zeigt, wie es zur Entstehung neuer (moderner) Akkorde kommt (A = Akkord, P = Durchgangsharmonie).

§ 30. *Der Begriff des Akkords in der modernen Harmonik.* Die Unterscheidung von Akkorden und Durchgangsharmonien ist im Bereich der modernen Harmonik gleich wichtig und für das Begreifen der harmonischen Substanz konkret fließender Musik gleich unerläßlich wie im Bereich der klassischen Harmonik. In der modernen Harmonik muß man damit rechnen, daß der moderne Akkord sich nicht nur tonlich auf einen unvollständigen Akkord verärmern, sondern auch auf einen tonlich verdichteten Akkord aufreichern läßt (Terminologie von Leoš Janáček). Repräsentant des bestimmten Charakters (= Akkord) muß dann nicht immer der komplizierteste Zusammenklang, sondern gegebenenfalls auch ein weniger reicher Zusammenklang sein.

§ 31. *Der Begriff des charakterisierenden Maximums.* Das charakterisierende Maximum ist ein Zusammenklang der höchsten Klasse, also tonlich der reichste Repräsentant mit genau bemessener Dissonanzcharakteristik.

§ 32. *Der Begriff des charakterisierenden Kerns.* Der charakterisierende Kern ist das einfachste Grenz-Gebilde der bestimmten dissonanten Charakteristik. Es gibt Fälle, wo Maximum und Kern zusammenfließen (z. Beisp. beim übermäßigen Dreiklang 0, ferner bei Zusammenklängen mit der Charakteristik 012, 016, 166).

§ 33. *Konsonante Akkorde als Maxima mit negativer dissonanter Charakteristik.* Beide konsonanten Akkode 43 und 34 sind geeignet, Zusammenklänge niedrigerer Klasse (d. i. Zweiklänge) ohne dissonant Charakteristik (3, 4, 5) zu repräsentieren. Anstelle der Orientierungs-Schemata können wir auch für konsonante Akkorde einfachere Zeichen (+ für den Dur-Akkord, – für den Moll-Akkord) setzen.

§ 34. *Das charakterisierende Maximum* **6**. Der verminderte Vierklang 333 stellt das einzig existierende charakterisierende Maximum **6** dar. Ihm sind der verminderte Dreiklang 33 und der Tritonus 6 untergeordnet; es sind unvollständige Akkorde (in Beziehung zum Vierklang 333 als vollständigem Akkord).

§ 35. *Das charakterisierende Maximum* **2**. Die Gruppe der Zusammenklänge mit der Charakteristik 2 ist reicher. Sie wird einerseits durch das symmetrische Maximum 2232 und anderseits durch den charakterisierenden Kern 2 repräsentiert. Das Maximum **2**, da es voll harmonisch verständlich ist, kann man mit Recht als modernen Akkord betrachten. Die übrigen Zusammenklänge – soweit sie selbst nicht die Bedeutung eines klassischen Vollakkords oder unvollständigen Akkords haben – stellen dann denselben modernen unvollständigen Akkord dar.

§ 36. *Die charakterisierenden Maxima* **1** *und* **01**. Die Kerne des charakterisierenden Typs 01 (134 und 314) sind klassische Akkorde. Das Maximum $\mathbf{1}^{3)}$ (= 143) ist gleichfalls ein klassischer Akkord. Die übrigen Maxima ($\mathbf{1}^{1)}$ = 131 und $\mathbf{1}^{2)}$ = 313) sind in der modernen Musik so gang und gebe, daß man sie als moderne Akkorde betrachten kann.

§ 37. *Die charakterisierenden Maxima* **0**, **26** *und* **026**. Das Maximum **0** (der übermäßige Dreiklang 44) ist zugleich ein Kern. Der Typ 26 wird durch zwei Maxima repräsentiert: 2223 und 242. Beide sind zugleich klassische Akkorde. Die Zusammenklänge 332 und 233 sind zwar dem Maximum 2223 (wie die Abbildung zeigt) untergeordnet, es sind aber bekannte klassische Akkorde (dominanter Vierklang und vermindert kleiner Vierklang). Im Bereich des Typs 026 stellt der Kern 224 einen klassischen Akkord dar – man kann dann auch alle komplizierteren Zusammenklänge dieses Typs als Verdichtung dieses Akkords auffassen.

§ 38. *Die charakterisierenden Maxima* **16** *und* **016**. Aus den Notenbeispielen ist der enge Zusammenhang des Vierklang-Maximums **16** und des Fünfklang-Maximums **016** klar ersichtlich, besonders wenn im Vierklang 1331 (= **016**) die Charakteristik 0 durch konkrete Anordnung nicht betont ist. Alle angeführten Maxima treten in der modernen Musik so oft auf, daß mam sie als moderne Akkorde betrachten kann.

§ 39. *Die charakterisierenden Maxima* **12** *und* **012**. Zwischen den Maximen **12** und **012** hören wir eine enge Klangverwandtschaft heraus. Alle Maxima können wir als moderne Akkorde ansehen.

§ 40. *Die charakterisierenden Maxima* **126**. Dieser Typ umfaßt 42 Zusammenklang-Gattungen. Die Abbildung zeigt alle Maxima (sechs) und Kerne (zehn). Die Tafel macht auf den Zusammenhang der einzelnen Zusammenklänge (erste Kolonne), Kerne (zweite Kolonne) und Maxima (dritte Kolonne) aufmerksam. Von allen diesen Maximen kann man wie von modernen Akkorden sprechen. Untergeordnete Akkorde niedrigerer Klassen sind dann unvollständige Akkorde. Die Maxima **126**[3)] (12132) und **126**[4)] (12321) stellen zugleich Vollakkord-Kombinationen dar. (Darüber später im § 51.)

§ 41. *Die charakterisierenden Maxima* **0126**. Dieser Typ nähert sich sehr dem vorhergehenden Typ **126**. Er hat drei Maxima und sechs Kerne (siehe Abbildung). Das Paar 13121 und 12131 stellt Vollakkord-Kombinationen dar, welche heute schon eingelebte moderne Akkorde sind. Die Maxima **0126**[2)] und **0126**[3)] sind dann durch einen weiteren Ton verdichtete Akkorde. Die harmonischen Qualitäten des Maximums **0126**[1)] (angenehme Klangfülle, Verständlichkeit) treten besonders in der Anordnung hervor, in der der niedrigere Dreiklang-Bestandteil (bei unserem Muster *c e g*) gemeinsam mit der Dominantseptime (b) real unten klingt.

§ 42. *Charakterisierende Maxima* **166** *und* **1266**. Das Gebilde 151 ist vereinzelt (stellt das Maximum und auch den Kern **166** dar). Durch Bereicherung um einen ganzen Ton (2) gelangen wir zu einem einigermaßen reicheren Typ 1266. Zwecks theoretischer Untersuchung der Beziehungen zwischen den komplizierteren Zusammenklängen direkt aus den Orientierungsschemas machen wir auf folgende Gesetzmäßigkeit aufmerksam: Der niedrigere Zusammenklang ist im höheren enthalten, falls das Negativ des höheren im Negativ des niedriegren enthalten ist.

§ 43. *Charakterisierende Maxima* **112** *und* **0112**. Beide charakterisierenden Typen sind sich nahe besonders darin, daß die schrille Zuspitzung, die duch das Zusammentreffen der Halbtöne bewirkt wird, durch den Tritonus nicht gemildert wird. Als einen modernen Akkord kann man eher den Kern 3113 als beide Maxima (beim Typ 0112) ansehen. Bei den Zusammenklängen mit der Charakteristik 112 werden wir als Akkorde eher beide Maxima betrachten.

§ 44. *Charakterisierende Maxima* **1126**. Dieser Typ umfaßt im Ganzen 57 Zusammenklang-Gattungen. In Anbetracht dessen, daß alle Maxima schon zu den höheren Klassen gehören, wird es nicht ratsam sein, sie als Akkorde anzusehen. Aber auch nicht die Kerne – zu einfach und im Klang zu schrill – eignen sich nicht sehr dazu. Hier wird es besser sein, sich zu einer kombinierten Erklärung zu entschließen. (Siehe weiter § 51 und folgende.)

§ 45. *Charakterisierende Maxima* **01126**. Die Gesamtzahl der hierauf entfallenden Zusammenklang-Gattungen ist 56 (siehe die Tafel im § 25).

§ 46. *Charakterisierende Maxima* **11266**. Zusammenklänge dieser Type (es sind deren im Ganzen 29) nähern sich einerseits den Zusammenklängen des Typus 1126, anderseits den Zusammenklängen mit der möglichst kompliziertesten Charakteristik 011266.

Die einfachsten Zusammenklänge sind hier zwei Fünfklänge. Es sind Kerne, auf die sich sechs existierende Maxima reduzieren lassen (siehe Schema und Tabelle).

§ 47. *Charakterisierendes Maximum* **011266**. Hier ist nur ein Maximum: der Zwölfklang. Kerne sind 2 Sechsklänge: 11231 (Negativ 21311) und 13211 (Negativ 11312). Im Hinblick darauf, daß der Zwölfklang nicht transponierbar ist, lassen sich hier alle Transpositionen jedes Kerns plazieren. (Siehe Notenbeispiel.)

§ 48. *Das System der charakterisierenden Typen.* Alle Arten von Zusammenklängen, wie sie im § 33 bis § 47 aneinandergereiht wurden, stellen ein System charakterisierender Typen dar. Darin ist das gesamte Zusammenklang-Material der temperierten Chromatik zusammengefaßt. Grundlegende Bedeutung hat die Unterscheidung der Zusammenklang-Gattungen nach der Zugehörigkeit zu den einzelnen charakterisierenden Typen, nicht aber zu den einzelnen Maximen oder Kernen. (Hier macht sich eine reiche Vieldeutigkeit geltend.)

§ 49. *Zusammenhänge zwischen Zusammenklängen mit unterschiedlicher dissonanter Charakteristik.* In den Abbildungen, zu denen Notenbeispiele beigefügt sind, werden die Zusammenhänge zwischen den charakterisierenden Maximen der benachbarten Zusammenklang-Klassen demonstriert.

§ 50. *Grenzen zwischen den charakterisierenden Typen.* Die Unterschiede in der dissonanten Charakteristik zwischen den Zusammenklang-Gattungen bezeichnen wir als Grenzen. Z. B. die Grenze zwischen den Typen 6 und 16 drücken wir durch das Symbol 1 aus, die Grenze zwischen den Typen 1 und 2 durch das Symbol 12 u. ä. Die Grenze ist umso ausdrucksvoller, je niedriger die Klasse ist, zu der die verglichenen Zusammenklänge gehören.

§ 51. *Das System der Akkord-Kombinationen.* Die dissonanten Mehrklänge kann man als Verbindung verschiedener grundlegender einfacher Akkorde (konsonanter Dreiklänge) betrachten. Das System der Akkord-Kombinationen ist ein Konfrontations-System; dadurch wird das System der charakterisierenden Typen ergänzt.

§ 52. *Echte und unechte Kombinationen. Die Kategorien der Kombinationen.* Bei den echten Kombinationen haben die beteiligten Dreiklänge keine gemeinsamen Töne, bei den unechten zeigen sich gemeinsame Töne. Nach der Anzahl der beteiligten Dreiklänge unterscheiden wir 4 Kategorien der echten Kombinationen (Kombinationsakkorde): 1. Nicht kombinierte Grundakkorde, 2. echte Kombinationen mit zwei Gliedern, 3. echte Kombinationen mit drei Gliedern, 4. echte Kombinationen mit 4 Grundakkorden.

§ 53. *Grundakkorde (Akkorde I.).* Es sind die Dreiklänge Dur und Moll. Darin ist die Prim der Grundton (repräsentative Ton), die Quint Ergänzungston und die Terz Unterscheidungston.

§ 54. *Kombinations-Akkorde* **II**. Echte Kombinationen der II. Kategorie sind einerseits symmetrische (A im Beisp. 46), anderseits asymmetrische (B im Beisp. 46). Am einfachsten bezeichnet man sie so, daß man zwischen die Symbole für den Dreiklang Dur (+) oder Moll (–) die Bezeichnung der Intervall-Distanz zwischen den Grundtönen der beteiligten Dreiklänge einlegt. Einige Kombinationsakkorde II sind zugleich charakterisierende Maxima (+2–, –2+, +3–, –4+). Tonlich ärmere Zusammenklänge kann man als unvollständige Akkorde II ansehen (siehe Tabelle).

§ 55. *Unechte Kombinationen mit zwei Gliedern.* Das sind Fünfklänge und Vierklänge (siehe Beisp. 47, 48, 49).

§ 56. *Akkord-Kombinationen* **III**. Es existieren 8 solcher Kombinationen (siehe Beisp. 50), wobei man aber die Negative 34 und 43 auf dreierlei unterschiedliche Weise zusammenstellen kann. Die einzelnen Akkord-Kombinationen III kann man als moderne Akkorde bezeichnen. Mit Rücksicht auf ihre Kompliziertheit gebrauchen wir aber lieber die Bezeichnung Akkord-Kombinationen anstatt des Terminus: Akkord. Zusammenklänge, welche den Kombinationen III untergeordnet sind, betrachten wir auch als verdichtete Akkorde II.

§ 57. *Akkord-Kombination* **IV**. Die echte Kombination IV ist ein Zwölfklang. Die Möglichkeiten der Zusammensetzungen aus Dreiklängen zeigen die Beispiele 51 und 52. Aus dem Vergleich geht hervor, daß die Kombination IV nur auf zweierlei Weise zusammengesetzt werden kann: –2–2+2+ oder +2–4+2–.

§ 58. *Einordnung der Zusammenklänge in die Kombinations-Kategorien.* In den Kategorien II und III besteht eine große Vieldeutigkeit, soweit es um die Zugehörigkeit der einzelnen unvollständigen Kombinationen zu einzelnen Akkorden geht. Deshalb ist es besser, nur von der Zugehörigkeit zu einer bestimmten Kategorie zu sprechen, nicht aber zu einer bestimmten Kombination in dieser Kategorie.

§ 59. *Repräsentation der Akkord-Kombinationen.* Jeder Teilakkord (Dreiklang) hat in der Kombination seinen Grundton. Diese Grundtöne sind in der Kombination gleichwertig. Erst durch konkrete Anordnung gewinnt mancher von ihnen ein größeres Gewicht auf Kosten der übrigen und wird zum Haupt-Grundton. Größere Gewichtigkeit hat immer der Teilakkord (und damit auch sein Grundton), welcher im Tonraum niedriger angesetzt ist.

§ 60. *Bedeutung der Kombinations-Akkorde.* Zusammenklänge, deren Klasse zu entfernt von der entsprechenden höheren Akkordkombination ist, insbesondere die geschlechtslosen Zusammenklänge, teilen wir lieber nach der dissonanten Charakteristik ein; die Kombinationsmethode kommt hier nur in Betracht bei unechten Kombinationen II. Dagegen teilen wir aber die Zusammenklänge, welche schon von sich aus echte Kombinationsakkorde sind oder die sich einigen Kombinationsakkorden sehr nähern, mit Hilfe der Kombinationsmethode ein; die charakterisierende Methode verwenden wir dann, wenn die Kombinations-Zusammnensetzung verhüllt ist.

Kapitel IV. Anordnung der Zusammenklänge

§ 61. *Begriff der Anordnung.* Unter dein Begriff der Akkord- oder Zusammenklang-Anordnung fassen wir hier alle Tonraumarten oder Vorgänge zusammen, durch welche der wirklich tönende Zusammenklang sich in seiner Tonwirkting verärdert, soweit der ursprüngliche Toninhalt unberührt bleibt.

§ 62. *Form, Lage und Ausmaß der Zusammenklänge. Vervielfachte Töne.* Bei der Anordnung der Zusammenklänge entscheiden wir über die Form dadurch, daß wir irgendeinem Ton die Aufgabe des untersten Tons (Baß) zuteilen. Die Lage ist gegeben durch den höchsten Ton in der konkreten Anordnung. Das Ausnaß ist gegeben durch die Verteilung der Töne zwischen den Randtönen. Bei der Anordnung kommt es auch zur Verdopplung (oder Vervielfachting) einzelner Töne des Zusammenklanges. Dagegen fällt die Auslassung der Töne nicht in die Kompetenz der Anordnung.

§ 63. *Klangbewertung der Anordnung.* Die Wirkung der bestimmten Zusammenklang-Gattung kann man modifizieren. Das geschieht eben durch die Anordnung. Die Klangbewertung der Zusammenklang-Anordnungen geschieht durch Abschätzung. Hilfsmittel ist dabei die lebendige Schöpfung, durch deren kritische Analyse man fast mit Sicherheit die kompositorischen Tonabsichten erfassen kann. Die Komponisten sind meist um eine gute und abgerundete Zusammenklang-Anordnung bemüht. Das Bestreben nach barbarisch rauher Anordnung ist durch besondere Umstände bedingt. Auch die modernen Komponisten wollen eine klanglich schöne Musik schaffen, auch wenn sie sich dabei schriller Dissonanzen und übermäßig komplizierter Zusammenklänge bedienen.

§ 64. *Anordung der Grundakkorde.* Hier wird auf die Unterschiede der Anordnung der Konsonanzen aufmerksam gemacht, wie sie die Klassiker gefühlt haben.

§ 65. *Klangwerte der Inversionen und inversen Anordnungen.* Durch Analyse der Anordnungen von Grundakkorden, wie sie bei Klassikern auftreten, erkennen wir, daß –

obwohl es sich um gegenseitig inverse Gattungen (Dur – Moll) und deshalb um qualitativ gleichwertige Gattungen handelt – die Inversion konkreter Anordnungen doch Ergebnisse verschiedenartiger Werte ergibt. Der niedrigste Ton verwandelt sich in den höchsten Ton, das Ausmaß kehrt wieder, einzelne verdoppelte Töne bekommen eine andere Bedeutung. Es ist deshalb notwendig, ausdrücklich darauf aufmerksam zu machen, daß das Prinzip der Inversion (§ 5) für die Zusammenklang-Gattungen gilt, nicht aber für deren konkrete Anordnungen.

§ 66. *Anordnung konsonanter Bestandteile in dissonanten Zusammenklängen.* Bei Terzen (Intervallen 3 und 4) ist es im großen und ganzen gleichgültig, wie sie angeordnet sind. Der Intervall 5 als Quint wirkt gut zu unterst, abgeteilt tritt er in der Höhe zu sehr hervor (Vergl. Beisp. 55).

§ 67. *Anordnung dissonanter Elemente.* Von den dissonanten Elementen 1, 2, 6 reagiert auf die Anordnung empfindlich nur der Halbton (1). Das Element 1 klingt besser als große Septim als kleine Sekund oder kleine None; dabei macht sich der untere Ton des Elementes 1 (in *h c* also der Ton *h*) am besten als höchster Ton geltend. Nicht jedes Element 1 ist gleich reagierend auf die Änderung der Anordnung: im Zusammenklang 313 kommt es sehr auf die Anordnung gerade des Elements 1 an, dagegen im Zusammenklang 213 kommt es im großen und ganzen nicht auf die Anordnung des Elements 1 an. (Vergl. Beisp. 57 und 58.) Ähnlich verhält es sich bei Zusammenklängen, welche sich den Zusammenklängen 313 und 213 nähern (d. h. in denen diese Vierklänge enthalten sind). Schlecht klingen die Häufungen der Elemente 1 und 2.

§ 68. *Anordnung der Akkord-Kombinationen.* Wir unterscheiden Kombinations-Anordnungen (in denen die Kombinations-Zusammensetzung klar ersichtlich ist) und nicht kombinierte. Die kombinierte Anordnung macht die Akkordstruktur der Zusammenklänge sichtbar, während die nicht kombinierte diese Struktur verhüllt. Im Beisp. 63 sind einzelne Anordnungen analysiert (dobře [well] = gut, špatně [bad] = schlecht). Nur Töne von annähernd gleichem Gewicht kann man in ein harmonisches Ganze vereinigen. (Darum sind kombinierte Anordnungen vorteilhafter.) Für die Gesamt-Anordnung von Akkord-Kombinationen gilt, daß der unterste Teilakkord in der konkreten Anordnung der Bestimmer (bestimmende Faktor) der ganzen Kombination ist.

§ 69. *Anordnung der Akkorde* **II**. In der Tabelle sind die Kombinations-Anordnungen aller existierenden Akkorde **II** angeführt, wobei auch die Halbton-Elemente (1) im Hinblick darauf untersucht werden, ob sie Bestandteile der Teilzusammensetzungen 313 und 213 sind. Bemerkenswert ist die Feststellung bei der Kombination +6+, bei der alle kombinierten und nicht kombinierten Anordnungen durch wegs gut sind.

§ 70. *Anordnung unechter Kombinationen mit 2 Gliedern. Verdoppelte Töne in den Elementen 1.* Die Tabelle gibt eine Übersicht über die Möglichkeiten der Kombinations-Anordnungen. Bei den unechten Anordnungen, falls sie kombiniert angewendet werden sollen, ist es manchmal notwendig, die Töne zu verdoppeln. Bei der Verdopplung kann es zur Kreuzung gegenteiliger Wirkungen kommen. Hier gilt dann: die Anordnung klingt gut, wenn das im Zusammenklang enthaltene Element 1 in guter Position ohne Rücksicht darauf ist, ob vielleicht dasselbe Element auch in unvorteilhafter Position ist. Kurz gesagt: die gute Position des Elementes 1 hebt die verschlechternde Wirkung der schlechten Position dasselben Elements 1 auf.

§ 71. *Anordnung der Akkord-Kombinationen* III. Alle Kombinations-Anordnungen der Akkord-Kombinationen III sind klanglich schlecht. Die Kombinationen III lassen sich im Klang gut nur auf unkombinierte Weise anordnen. (Man kann allerdings auch eine besonders schrille unkombinierte Anordnung schaffen.)

§ 72. *Anordnung der Akkord-Kombination* IV. *Milderung des Halbton-Zusammentreffens der Elemente 1.* Alle Kombinations-Anordnungen der Kombination IV sind klanglich schlecht. Bei nicht kombinierten Anordnungen läßt sich eine gewisse Milderung der durchdringenden Wirkung des Halbton-Zusammentreffens dadurch erzielen, daß sich ihre Bestandteile mehr ausdehnen und gegenseitig durchschießen. Darnach werden die einzelnen Anordnungen des Zwölfklanges im Beispiel 70 bewertet (von der ziemlich guten Anordnung – A, B, C – über die schlechte – D – zu der sehr schlechten Anordnung – E, F –).

§ 73. *Anordnung von Zusammenklängen in harmonischer Bewegung.* Ein konkret angeordneter Zusammenklang, der in der zusammenhängenden Reihe der Zusammenklänge nur eine durchlaufende Harmonie darstellt, wirkt weniger auffallend, als wenn er einen Akkod darstellt. (Vergl. Beisp. 71.) Der Zusammenklang eines schrillen Klanges ist weniger auffallend, wenn die Stimmen von ihm und zu ihm auf möglichst direktem Wege (d. i. in den Intervallen 0, 1 oder 2) fortschreiten. (Vergl. Beisp. 72 und 73.) Eine geringfügige Milderung tritt ein, wenn ein schlecht angeordneter Zusammenklang nach einer guten Anordnung derselben Transposition derselben Zusammenklang-Gattung folgt (Beisp. 74). Ein schrill angeordneter Zusammenklang kehrt in der Komposition gewöhnlich wieder oder wird verlängert, damit der Komponist die Zuhörer überzeugt, daß es sich nicht um einen Irrtum handelt. (Beisp. 75.) Schlecht angeordnete Zusammenklänge wirken nicht so störend, wenn sie sich absichtlich häufen (Beisp. 76).

§ 74. *Anordnung von Zusammenklängen und die Kompositionspraxis.* Die Suche nach Zusammenklang-Gattungen ist beim Komponisten untrennbar verbunden mit der Suche nach einer geeigneten Anordnung; beide Verfahren verlaufen fast gleichzeitig.

Trotzdem bleiben Anordnung und Zusammenklang-Gattung klar unterscheidbar durch genau definierte Begriffe ohne Rücksicht darauf, daß ihre Verbindung (angeordneter Zusammenklang) sich auch auf einmal verwirklichen läßt.

Kapitel V. Ausdruck der Zusammenklänge

§ 75. *Reale und imaginäre Töne.* Einen Ton, der tatsächlich klingt, nennen wir einen realen Ton. Einen Ton, der real ausgeklungen ist, aber noch weiter wirkt, nennen wir einen imaginären Ton. Die Existenz der imaginären Töne ist durch die Faktur der Komposition gegeben. Harmonisch imaginäre Töne haben die Fähigkeit, harmonische Gebilde zu schaffen oder mitzuschaffen. Tonale imaginäre Töne haben diese Fähigkeit nicht, aber sie sind fähig, das tonale Aussehen eines Kompositionsabschnittes oder der ganzen Komposition zu beeinflussen. Der harmonische imaginäre Ton verklingt früher und wird leichter aufgehoben als der tonale imaginäre Ton.

§ 76. *Entstehung und Aufhebung des imaginären Tones.* Jeder reale Ton kann von sich aus eine Spur wie der imaginäre Ton hinterlassen. Den imaginären Ton kann man harmonisch auflösen. (Beisp. 77.) Die Auflösung kann auch nachträglich erfolgen (Beisp. 79 und 80).

§ 77. *Der kritische, die Auflösung verhindernde Ton.* Die Auflösung des imaginären Tons kann man kompositorisch verhindern durch den kritischen, die Auflösung verhindernden Ton (nur im Falle, wenn die vorausgesetzte Auflösung durch einen Ganzton-Schritt durchgeführt wird). Die überlebenden imaginären Töne verklingen dann beschleunigt. (Siehe Beisp. 81, 82 und 83, wo auf die kritischen, die Auflösung verhindernden Töne ein Pfeil hinweist.)

§ 78. *Verklingen des harmonischen imaginären Tons.* Jeder imaginäre Ton verklingt. Wir unterscheiden ein langsames (Beisp. 84), ein normales (Beisp. 85) und ein beschleunigtes Verklingen (Beisp. 86).

§ 79. *Künstliche (kompositorische) Beschleunigung des Verklingens des harmonischen imaginären Tons.* Zum beschleunigten Verklingen der imaginären Töne trägt das gemeinsame Auftreten einer Gruppe realer Töne bei, welche einen konsonanten Akkord bilden (Beisp. 88).

§ 80. *Harmonische Bedeutung imaginärer Töne.* Die in größeren Intervallen fortschreitende Melodie stellt nicht nur die einfache Folge einzelner Töne dar, sondern auch die Folge von Zusammenklängen (Beisp. 89). Ähnlich stellt die zweistimmige Komposition nicht nur die Folge von Zweiklängen, sondern die Folge reicherer Zusammenklänge dar

(Beisp. 90). Aus der ergänzenden harmonischen Wirkung imaginärer Töne ergeben sich die Möglichkeiten des Ausdrucks der Zusammenklänge. Zusammenklänge lassen sich auf dreierlei Weise ausdrücken: 1. durch reale Töne, 2. durch imaginäre Töne, 3. gemischt.

§ 81. *Zusammenklänge, ausgedrückt durch reale Töne.* Wenn Zusammenklänge in einer Reihe nacheinanderfolgen, ist es notwendig, dafür zu sorgen, daß in den neuen Zusammenklang keine harmonischen imaginären Töne aus den vorhergehenden hineingreifen, soweit sie nicht beiden Zusammenklängen gemeinsam sind (Siehe Beisp. 91). Einzelne überlebende imaginäre Töne haben noch keine Bedeutung (Beisp. 92). Erst Gruppen imaginärer Töne haben gegenüber den real ausgedrückten Zusammenklängen eine ausdrucksvollere Widerstandsfähigkeit; hier kommt es zu einer zeitweilig harmonischen Komplikation in Gestalt eines gemischt ausgedrückten Vielklanges (Beisp. 93, besonders aber 95).

§ 82. *Zusammenklänge, ausgedrückt durch imaginäre Töne.* In der Pause nach einem früher erklungenen Zusammenklang wirkt dieser Zusammenklang ausgedrückt durch imaginäre Töne. (Beisp. 96.)

§ 83. *Gemischter Ausdruck von Zusammenklängen in einstimmiger Komposition.* Zusammenklänge lassen sich gemischt durch eine bloße Melodie ausdrücken (Beisp. 98, 101, 102, 103), wenn dafür gesorgt ist, daß die einzelnen sich geltend machenden Töne sich fortschreitend nicht aufheben (wie die Beisp. 99 und 100 zeigen).

§ 84. *Gemischter Ausdruck von Zusammenklängen in mehrstimmiger Komposition.* Das Beispiel 105 zeigt einige Zusammenklänge mit Vorschlag für gemischten Ausdruck. Die Beispiele 106, 107 und 108 zeigen, daß die Klangqualität durch die Gesamtanordnung gegeben ist, nicht aber erst durch die Realisation beim Ausdruck. Es ist Sache der vernünftigen Wirtschaftlichkeit, daß die beteiligten Stimmen am Ausdruck des beabsichtigten Zusammenklangs ohne überflüssige Verdopplung der realen Töne teilnehmen.

§ 85. *Unharmonische Töne in gemischt ausgedrückten Zusammenklängen.* In einer Melodie haben die unharmonischen (nichtakkordischen) Töne eine bedeutsame Rolle (Beisp. 111), besonders dort, wo sie nicht unmittelbar gelöst werden (Beisp. 112). In mehrstimmigen Komposition verdunkelt erst die übermäßige Verwendung unakkordischer Töne gleichzeitig in verschiedenen Stimmen die ursprünglich geplante Harmonie. Besondere Aufmerksamkeit ist den unharmonischen Tönen zu widmen, deren Lösung durch Eingriff kritischer, die Auflösung verhindernder Töne gestört wird (wie wir es am Beisp. 115 sehen).

§ 86. *Zeitliche Grenzen zwischen gemischt ausgedrückten Zusammenklängen.* Die Begrenzung einer fließenden Reihe von Zusammenklängen im gemischten Ausdruck ist durch die Faktur der Musik gegeben. Wenn es möglich ist, eine Stelle der Komposition als Folge zweier einfacherer Zusammenklänge oder als einen komplizierteren Zusammenklang zu erfassen, muß man der ersten Auffassung den Vorzug geben. Wenn es möglich ist, die Begrenzung benachbarter Zusammenklänge auf mehrfache metrische Weise zu erfassen, dann ist es notwendig, sich für die einfachere Weise zu entscheiden. Abgeteilte rhythmische Gebilde führen auch zur harmonischen Teilung. Bei komplizierten tonreichen Harmonien, welche offenkundig keine herausragenden Dreiklänge enthalten, kann man sich nicht nach eingelebten Akkoden orientieren; die Erklärung kann dann mannigfach sein, besonders wenn auch eine Stütze in der Rhythmisierung fehlt (wie im Beisp. 120).

§ 87. *Tonale imaginäre Töne*. Tonale imaginäre Töne haben nicht die Fähigkeit, harmonische Gebilde mitzuschaffen. Sie haben aber tonale Bedeutung darin, daß sie konsonante Akkorde insoweit beeinflussen, daß sie nicht als verläßliche Tonika wirken können. Bedeutung haben hier vor allem solche tonale imaginäre Töne, welche zu den Konsonanzen tritonische Beziehung haben (vergl. Beisp. 127).

§ 88. *Unvollständiger Ausdruck von Akkorden*. Das Weglassen von Tönen aus einem Akkord beziehen wi nicht in die Manipulation ein, womit wir die Anordnung der Zusammenklänge durchführen (siehe § 62). Die Erscheinung des unvollständigen Akkords paßt besser in den Zusammenhang mit der Erklärung über den Ausdruck von Zusammenklängen. Tonarme Zusammenklänge inklinieren gleichsam selbstwillig dazu, daß sie weitere, sie bereichernde Bestandteile aufnehmen. Zu den tonarmen dissonanten Zusammenklängen (z. Beisp. Zweiklängen) fügen wir dann konsonante Bestandteile dazu, welche die dissonante Charakteristik nicht komplizieren, zu den tonarmen konsonanten Bestandteilen (3, 4, 5) geben wir nur solche weitere konsonante Bestandteile dazu, welche den unvollständigen Akkord zu einem vollen komplettieren. Dabei machen sich vor allem zur Hand befindliche, aus dem Kompositionskontext hervorgehende tonale imaginäre Töne geltend. (Siehe Beisp. 129 und 130.)

Kapitel VI. Harmonische Bewegung

§ 89. *Die Möglichkeiten der Bewegung in der Musik*. Wir sprechen von einer rhytmischen, harmonischen und melodischen Bewegung. Dabei kommt die melodische Bewegung mit Hilfe von rhythmischen und melodischen Mitteln, die harmonische Bewegung mit Hilfe von rhythmischen, melodischen und harmonischen Mitteln zustande.

§ 90. *Möglichkeiten harmonischer Bewegung*. Die harmonische Bewegung kann dreierlei sein: a) eine Teilbewegung, b) eine Grundbewegung, c) eine übergeordnete (tonale) Bewegung.

§ 91. *Bindung einer Zusammenklang-Folge.* Der gemeinsame Ton zwischen Zusammenklängen stellt die Bindung dar. Die Existenz dieser Bindung in der Zusammenklang-Folge bewirkt die Annäherung beider Zusammenklänge. Die Bindung kann man dadurch abschwächen, daß der wiederholte Ton bei der Verbindung zweier Zusammenklänge in eine andere Oktave übertragen wird, wobei der übertragene Ton den Sekund-Schritt in einer anderen Stimme durchschneidet (oder ihn wenigstens dicht berührt); wir sehen das am Beisp. 133 b). So eine abgeschwächte Bindung können wir als eine unterbrochene oder indirekte Bindung bezeichnen (zum Unterschied von der direkten (siehe Beisp. 133 a). Die direkte Bindung stellt ein wesentlich stärkeres Band zwischen den Zusammenklängen als die unterbrochene (indirekte) Bindung dar. Die Bindung ist umso wirksamer, je tonärmer die Zusammenklänge in der Zusammenklang-Folge sind. Die Bindung ist umso wirksamer, je niedriger sie realisiert wird.

§ 92. *Harmonische Teilbewegung.* Die harmonische Teilbewegung entsteht durch den melodischen Fortgang in Intervallen, wodurch die harmonischen imaginären Töne aufgehoben werden. Der Fortgang in anderen Intervallen ergibt nur eine melodische Bewegung (Beisp. 135). Durch mehrere Teilbewegungen kommt die Grundbewegung zustande. (Beisp. 134a und 134b.) Bei der harmonischen Teilbewegung handelt es sich nicht um eine Folge von 2 Akkorden, sondern um den Fortgang vom Akkord zur Durchgangsharmonie (oder umgekehrt), gegebenenfalls um das Fortschreiten von einer Durchgangsharmonie zu einer anderen gleichfalls Durchgangsharmonie.

§ 93. *Harmonische Grundbewegung.* Die harmonische Grundbewegung kann auf einmal realisiert werden (von Akkord zu Akkord) oder fortschreitend mit Hilfe von mehreren Teilbewegungen.

§ 94. *Intervalle in der harmonischen Grundbewegung. Imaginäre Bindungen.* Zwei Zusammenklänge, die so aufeinanderfolgen, daß die realen Töne des ersten Zusammenklangs von den realen Tönen des zweiten Zusammenklangs ersetzt werden, stellen die harmonische Grundbewegung in einer besonders ausdrucksvollen Gestalt dar (Beisp. 140). Bei periodischem Auftreten größerer Intervalle im melodischen Fluß kommt es zur Entstehung einer imaginären Bindung (Beisp. 141), welche die Bedeutung und Wirkung einer direkten Bindung hat.

§ 95. *Reale Bindungen in der harmonischen Grundbewegung.* Die direkten Bindungen bewirken eine sehr wesentliche Annäherung zwischen den Zusammenklängen. Durch absichtliche Häufung direkter Bindungen entsteht der Eindruck der Stagnation (d. h. die absichtliche Grundbewegung äußert sich nur als Teilbewegung). Bei indirekten Bindungen kann man den Eindruck einer harmonischen Grundbewegung auch bei verschiedenen Anordnungen derselben Zusammenklang-Gattung in derselben Transposition hervorrufen, wie das Beisp. 143 zeigt. Belehrend ist auch die Konfrontation der

Verbindungen im Beisp. 144. (In der obigen Notenzeile handelt es sich nur um die melodische Bewegung, in der unteren um die harmonische Grundbewegung.)

§ 96. *Nachbarschaft von Teil- und harmonischen Grundbewegungen.* Das Zusammenklang-Gebilde, zu dem wir nur durch harmonische Teilbewegung gelangen, gegebenenfalls nur durch melodische Bewegung, erscheint als metrisch weniger bedeutsames Gebilde als das Zusammenklang-Gebilde, zu dem wir durch harmonische Grundbewegung gelangen. Die Zerlegung der Grund- und Teil-Bewegungen begrenzt dann (außer anderem) die metrische Struktur der fließenden Musik. Die Beziehungen zwischen Harmonie und Metrik zeigen sich in der Musik jedes Stiles, in welchem Harmonie überhaupt zur Geltung kommt.

§ 97. *Übergeordnete harmonische Bewegung oder tonale Bewegung.* Als übergeordnete harmonische Bewegung bezeichnen wir ein besonders auffallendes Fortschreiten von einem Zusammenklang zum anderen (im Vergleich zu anderen benachtbarten). Es ist das zugleich eine harmonische Grundbewegung, aber eine solche, die sich von anderen (benachbarten) Grundbewegungen durch erhöhte Intensität unterscheidet. Eine übergeordnete harmonische Bewegung läßt sich nicht unter allen Umständen hervorrufen. Wenn wir uns nicht gleich vom Anfang an bestimmte Grenzen bei der Wahl der aneinandergereihten Zusammenklänge setzen und wenn wir immerwieder durchgängig harmonische Grundbewegungen von bedeutender Schwingungsweite verwenden, können wir nicht mehr die bisherige, „Übertreibung" überwinden. In der atonalen Musik kann man die übergeordnete Bewegung nicht anwenden.

§ 98. *Die Bedeutung der Schlußfolge der Zusammenklänge in der Komposition.* Von den Zusammenklangfolgen, die in der Komposition auftreten, ist besonders die Folge von dem vorletzten zum letzten Zusammenklang, der Eintritt in die Tonika, wichtig. Aus den Schlußfolgen der Zusammenklänge, wie sie in den Kompositionen zu Tage treten, kann man dreierlei Prinzipien ableiten: 1. das Prinzip der reinen Tonika, 2. das Prinzip des Leittons, 3. das Funktionsprinzip. Das 1. Prinzip ist die allgemeine Grundlage. Das 2. Prinzip des Leittons stellt ein Hilfs- bzw. Ergänzungsgesetz dar. Endlich das Funktionsprinzip ergibt sich als reale Synthese beider vorhergehender Prinzipien.

§ 99. *Das Prinzip der reinen Tonika.* Das Prinzip der reinen Tonika ist gegründet auf der Existenz der imaginären Töne. Man kann es so ausdrücken: der harmonische Satz gravitiert natürlicherweise zu so einem konsonanten abschließenden Zusammenklang, in den die unvollkommen aufgehobenen oder überhaupt nicht aufgehobenen harmonischen imaginären Töne, gegebenenfalls auch solche tonale imaginäre Töne, welche in einem Tritonus-Verhältnis zu Tönen der abschließenden Tonika stehen, nicht hineinwirken. Diesem Prinzip kann man bei der Suche nach einer bislang unbekannten abschließenden Tonika entsprechen. Dem Prinzip der reinen Tonika kann inan allerdings nicht Genüge leisten, wodurch in verschiedenem Maße absichtlich unbefriedigende Schlüsse entstehen. Durch das dem Prinzip Nichtentsprechen wird allerdings das Prinzip selbst nicht verneint. Das Prinzip der reinen Tonika gilt als Grundlage und Maß des kinetischen harmonischen Denkens auch dort, wo das tatsächliche Fortschreiten der Zusammenklänge davon abweicht oder sich geradezu entgegenstellt. Man kann es als allgemeines Gesetz betrachten, als Gesetz des Naturcharakters.

§ 100. *Verwendung des Prinzips der reinen Tonika in der temperierten Chromatik.* Im wirkenden (d. h. die Tonika nicht untervühlenden) vor der Tonika stehenden Zusammenklang kann man nicht Töne verwenden, welche die Tonika als fremde (überflüssig komplizierende) tonale imaginäre Töne beschädigen können. Für C-Dur sind es die Töne *b* (dieser besonders), *fis, des*, für c-Moll sind es die Töne *a, fis, des*, teilweise auch *b*.

§ 101. *Anwendung des Prinzips der reinen Tonika in der Diatonik.* Das Tritonus-Verhältnis *h–f*, welches in der grundlegenden Diatonik auftritt, kann vom Eingreifen in die abschließende Tonika sicher dadurch ausgeschaltet werden, daß keiner seiner Töne Bestandteil der Tonika sein wird. Es existieren eigentlich nur zwei solche Toniken: *c e g* und *a c e*.

§ 102. *Das Prinzip des Leittons.* Das Prinzip des Leittons ist gegründet auf dem melodischen Fortschreiten im Intervall 1. Unter einem Leit-Ton verstehen wir im allgemeinen jenen Ton, welcher einen Intervall 1 von irgendeinem Bestandteil des in Aussicht genommenen gezielten Zusammenklangs, der Tonika, entfernt ist. Einen Leitton betrachten wir als den Träger der bewegenden Kraft des Zusammenklangs. Es ist eben der Leitton, welcher bewirkt, daß der vor der Tonika stehende Zusammenklang zur Tonika gravitiert. Wenn es sich auch um eine kinetische Erscheinung handelt, ist es notwendig, als Ausgangspunkt eine statische Erscheinung zu betrachten, nämlich tiie Tonwirkung des Verhältnisses 1 im Zusammenklang.

§ 103. *Das Funktionsprinzip.* Aus dem Prinzip der reinen Tonika und aus dem Prinzip des Leit-Tons geht durch Verbindung beider Prinzipien das Funktionsprinzip hervor. Gegen die Tonika stehen nichttonische Zusammenklänge. Diese treten notwendigerweise in Paaren auf (als übertonische und ihnen entsprechende untertonische Zusammeklänge). Die Tonika ist die Achse des gesamten tonalen Funktions-Systems (siehe Abbildung). Die Funktionalität (Nichttonik) setzt notwendig das Bewußtsein von der Existenz einer bestimmten Tonika voraus; mit dem Verlust dieses Bewußtseins verschwindet das ganze Funktions-System. Jeder konsonante Zusammenklang kann zur Achse des Funktions-Systems werden. Das einmal gaschaffene Funktions-System kann sich im Verlauf der Komposition ändern, das heißt durch ein anderes ersetzt und aufgehoben werden. Durch Abweichungen und Kombinationen kann man erreichen, daß die ursprüngliche Ebene der Tonika verlagert wird, gegebenenfalls daß das Bewußtsein von der Existenz einer bestimmten Tonika verloren geht; das Funktions-System ist dann entweder verlagert oder aufgehoben (wenn auch zeitweilig).

§ 104. *Stabilisierung der Tonika.* Bedingung für das Erreichen der Stabilisierung der Tonika ist, daß sie konsonant ist. Der vereinsamte konsonante Akkord kann zum Träger der Funktion der Tonika werden. Wenn er ein Bestandteil der Zusammenklangreihe ist, kann seine Funktion als Tonika durch das Zusammenspiel der übrigen Zusammenklänge unterstützt werden. Ist dieses Zusammenspiel ein solches, daß die Tonika dem Prinzip der reinen Tonika und dem Prinzip des Leittons Genüge leistet, so ist die Stabilisierung der Tonika gesichert.

§ 105. *Die Gattung vor der Tonika stehender repräsentativer Akkorde.* Unter den mannigfaltigen nicht als Tonika wirkenden Akkorden kann man repräsentative Akkorde finden (d. s. solche, von denen die anderen abgeleitet sind). Die repräsentativen, nicht als Tonika wirkenden Akkorde sind notwendigerweise konsonante Dreiklänge, wie die Toniken. Daraus leitet man erst kompliziertere funktionsmäßig kombinierte Zusarmmenklänge ab.

§ 106. *Feststellung möglicher repräsentativer, vor der Tonika stehender Akkorde.* Sollen zwei repräsentative, vor der Tonika stehende Akkorde streng abgeteilte Gegenstücke sein, können sie nicht gemeinsame Töne haben. Ein Akkord, dessen Gegenstück irgendeinen seiner Bestandteile enthalten würde, wäre nicht ein reiner vortonischer Akkord; sondern schon eine Ableitung. In Beziehung zur Tonika muß beim repräsentativen, vor der Tonika stehenden Akkord die Möglichkeit zum Eintritt in die Tonika durch harmonische Grundbewegung bestehen. Deshalb kann ein solcher Akkord mit der Tonika höchstens einen gemeinsamen Ton haben. Aus dem Zusammenspiel dieser Forderungen und im Hinblick auf die Prinzipien der reinen Tonika und des Leittons geht ein einziges Paar möglicher repräsentativer, vor der Tonika stehender Akkorde, die Dominante und Subdominante, hervor.

§ 107. *Das dreigliedrige klassische Funktionssystem.* Unsere Forderungen und unsere allgemeinen Prinzipien wurden selbstverständlich nicht durch verstandesmäßige Vorschriften aufgestellt, sondern als etwas Natürliches erfühlt, dem man Genüge leisten muß. Die Richtung der historischen Entwicklung wurde mit elementarer Notwendigkeit eingeschlagen. So entstand das dreigliedrige Funktions-System. Andere Akkorde konnte man in Beziehung zur Tonika (nach dem tschechischen Theoretiker Otakar Šín) als mannigfaltige Kombinationen repräsentativer, vor der Tonika stehender Akkorde und der Tonika erfassen. Nach der Auffassung Šíns war es möglich, funktionsmäßig auch solche Zusammenklang-Gebilde zu erklären, welche man nicht in Terzen einreihen kann (also moderne Akkorde).

§ 108. *Šíns fünfgliedriges Funktions-System*. Die Subdominante und die Dominante sind neben der Tonika die Hauptfunktionen. Sie entsprechen dem Prinzip der reinen Tonika wie auch dem Prinzip des Leittons. Sie erschöpfen aber nicht alle Möglichkeiten, welche die temperierte Chromatik bietet. Durch die Einführung eines weiteren Paares nichttonischer Funktionen und zwar des phrygischen Akkords (in C-Dur *des f as*) und des lydischen Akkords (in C-Dur *h dis fis*), durch deren Kombinierungn mit den bisherigen Funktionen bei gegenseitigem Anschmiegen der Tonarten Dur und Moll, kann man dann alle Möglichkeiten der temperierten Chromatik decken (siehe Beisp. 153). Das neue Funktionspaar, angedeutet von Šín, entspricht zwar nicht dem Prinzip der reinen Tonika, dafür aber entspricht es in erhöhtem Maße (dreifach) dem Prinzip des Leittons. Von diesem Paar können wir wie von Hilfsfunktionen sprechen. Zu den traditionellen Zeichen für die Dominante (D) und Subdominante (S) fügen wir dann neue Zeichen für die Hilfsfunktionen hinzu: F [P] (für den phrygischen Akkord) und L (für den lydischen Akkord).

§ 109. *Stabilisierung der Beziehungen zwischen Akkorden des Funktions-Systems durch Tradition. Die Moll-Dominante.* Ausgangspunkt der Harmonik war das klanglich sinnliche Wesen der Zusammenklänge, woraus erst nach langem Prüfen und Suchen und das eher durch intuitive als durch kombinierende Kunst die Zusammenhänge und funktionellen Beziehungen aufgespürt wurden. Oft gebrauchte Zusammenklang-Folgen wurden zuletzt zur Gewohnheit, ein Vorgang, zu dessen Realisation nicht mehr Wachsamkeit notwendig war. Die so gefundene Folge D T ist der Prototyp eines solchen Vorganges. Die Gravitation der Dominante zur Tonika empfinden wir als Richtlinie, wonach wir auch andere Zusammenklang-Folgen vergleichen. Bei dem eingelebten Verhältnis ist es dann ganz gut möglich gewesen, daß durch irgendeine Abweichung selbst das führende Prinzip verletzt wurde, nach welchem dieser Vorgang ursprünglich gesucht und gefunden wurde. So eine Änderung stellt z. B. die Erniedrigung des unterscheidenden Tons (Terze) in der Dominante (in C von *h* auf *b*) dar. So entstand die Moll-Dominante. Mit dieser Moll-Dominante rechnen wir in Funktions-Kombinationen in Moll und Dur, soweit wir nicht eine andere geeignetere Erklärung zur Hand haben.

§ 110. *Konsonante Kombinationen von Funktionen (Zwischenfunktionen).* Konsonante Akkorde, welche nicht einfache Funktionen darstellen, nennen wir Zwischenfunktions-Akkorde (Zwischenfunktionen). Eine Übersicht darüber (für C-Dur, c-Moll) geben die Tabellen. Darin wird eine dreifache Bezeichnung verwendet.

§ 111. *Dissonante Funktions-Kombinationen.* Alle dissonanten Zusammenklänge sind – funktionsmäßig beurteilt – Kombinationen. Ihre Dissonanz ist zugleich ihre Spannung und zwar eine innere, nicht zu beseitigende Spannung. Dissonanzen können niemals absolute Ruhe erlangen, die für die Tonika bezeichnend ist. Wenn es möglich ist, durch zwei aufeinanderfolgende Konsonanzen das Bewußtsein von der Existenz einer bestimmten Tonika zu bilden, kann man dasselbe Resultat durch Zusammenklang derselben Konsonanzen im funktionsmäßig kombinierten dissonanten Zusammenklang erreichen. Wenn aber durch zwei derart aufeinanderfolgende Konsonanzen die Tonika nicht eindeutig bestimmt ist, ergibt nicht einmal ihr Zusammenklingen in einem Zusammenklang ein eindeutiges Ergebnis.

§ 112. *Funktionelle Mehrdeutigkeit dissonanter Kombinationen.* Die verläßliche Untersuchung der Mehrdeutigkeit kann man mit Hilfe allgemeiner Orientierungs-Schemas durchführen (Siehe § 3). Die Übereinstimmung der Schemas bedeutet, daß die entsprechenden Funktions-Kombinationen, nach welchen die Orientierungs-Schemas berechnet wurden, vertauschbar und damit mehrdeutig sind. Die Übersicht der mehrdeutigen dissonanten Funktionkombinationen gibt die Tabelle am Ende des § 112.

§ 113. *Bewertung der Funktions-Bestandteile gemäß ihrer tonalen Bedeutung, Anordnung und Vertretung.* Schon die Unterscheidung der Funktionen in Haupt- und Hilfsfunktionen zeigt, daß es hier keine Gleichheit gibt. Und nicht einmal die Hauptfunktionen treten untereinande gleich oft auf und haben also auch nicht den gleichen Wert. Dasselbe ist der Fall bei Hilfsfunktionen. Verminderte Bedeutung haben dann auch die im untersuchten komplizierteren Zusammenklang unvollständig vertretenen Funktionen. Schließlich entscheidet auch die Plazierung der Funktions-Bestandteile in der konkreten Anordnung (ob niedriger oder höher) über ihren Wert. Auch wenn dann schließlich die Erkenntnis möglich wäre, daß eine Vieldeutigkeit eigentlich nicht existiert, sagt doch die Kompositionspraxis, daß sie existiert: sie wird verwendet. Der Komponist kann eben die selbstverständliche Funktionsauffassung neglegieren und anders im weiteren musikalischen Fluß fortschreiten „gegen alle Erwartung".

§ 114. *Harmonische Bewegung zwischen Funktionen.* Wir können, von einer Qualität und Richtung der harmonischen Bewegung sprechen. Der Qualität nach stellen die Fälle *a)* im Beisp. 154 mäßigere Bewegung dar, die Fälle *b)* sind dagegen angespannter. Es sind Qualitäts-Unterschiede. Bedeutsam sind schon in der klassischen Harmonik die Unterschiede in der Richtung der Bewegung (zum Beisp. gegenüber dem natürlichen Vorgang S D offenbart sich der umgekehrte Vorgang D S als unnatürlich). Beim Fortschreiten zur Tonika sprechen wir von einer Lösung, beim Fortschreiten in eine andere als tonische Funktion von einer Verbindung. Ein besonderer Fall von Verbindung ist das Fortschreiten von komplizierteren Zusammenklang (zum Beisp. *g h d des f as*) zum einfacheren Zusammenklang, welcher Bestandteil des vorhergehenden ist (zum Beisp. in *g h d*).

§ 115. *Der funktionelle Aspekt der Zusammenklänge in der Zusammenklang-Folge.* Wenn wir manchmal nicht erklären können, daß durch eine bestimmte Reihe von Zusammenklängen ein ganz bestimmtes eindeutiges Bewußtsein von der Existenz einer bestimmten Tonika geschaffen wurde, müssen wir uns mit der Feststellung zufrieden geben, daß die verwendeten Zusammenklänge in sich eine Bewegungsspannung bergen, daß sie zu einer uns unbekannten, objektiv nicht bestimmbaren Tonika gravitieren. Daß es sich so oft verhält, zeigen die Zusammenklang-Folgen, die man vor dem Abschluß gleich gut in verschiedene Toniken hinleiten kann (siehe Beisp. 156).

§ 116. *Monotonale, bitonale und polytonale Kombinationen*. Bisher haben wir nur von monotonalen Kombinationen gesprochen. Bitonale sind solche, bei deren Bildung verschiedene (d. s. gegenseitig transponierte) Funktions-Systeme verwendet wurden. Zur bitonalen Erklärung kehren wir zurück, wenn die monotonale Erklärung allzu kompliziert ist und man im konkreten musikalischen Fluß zwei unterschiedliche oder unterscheidbare Reihen aufspüren kann. Die polytonalen Folgen sind dann schon selten.

§ 117. *Stellvertretende Toniken und außertonale Funktionen*. Jeder konsonante Akkord oder konsonante Bestandteil eines komplizierteren dissonanten Akkords kann zeitweilig als Tonika betrachtet werden, zur der dann (zeitweilig) die Akkorde in Beziehung gebracht sind, welche im Hauptfunktions-System nicht erklärbar sind. So entwindet sich im Beisp. 159 der Bestandteil *fis ais cis* (= *ges b des*) der Tonart C dur, hat aber eine einfache Beziehung zu *h dis fis* als Bestandteil der vor der Tonika stehenden Kombination aus *C* dur.

§ 118. *Deformation der Funktionen*. Deformierte Funktionen entsprechen nicht dem Prinzip der reinen Tonika. Es handelt sich vor allem um die Moll-Dominante, aber auch um die Dur-Subdominante in moll.

§ 119. *Modulation*. Bei der Modulation handelt es sich vor allem um die Schaffung eines neuen tonalen Zentrums, einer neuen Tonika. Die Modulation im eigentlichen Sinn des Wortes tritt nur in der funktionell klaren Musik auf. Wo die Funktionsverhältnisse zwischen den Akkorden nicht hinreichend klar sind, kann man nicht von Modulation sprechen.

§ 120. *Lockerung der tonalen Funktionsbeziehungen*. Eine wichtige Aufgabe des Komponisten ist nicht nur, das Bewußtsein von der Existenz einer bestimmten Tonika zu schaffen, nicht nur ein bestimmtes Tonsystem auszumessen, sondern auch das geschaffene Bewußtsein der Tonika aufzuheben, das Funktions-System zu vernichten. Negative oder destruktive Aufgabe haben dabei: außertonale Funktionen, Hilfsfunktionen, Zwischenfunktionsakkorde, Bitonalität und Polytonalität. Am Ende der romantischen Epoch in der historischen Entwicklung der Musik beobachten wir eine steigende Vorliebe für tonale Destruktion, was sich nach außen dadurch kundgibt, daß die Phasen der Lockerung sich in der Komposition öfters wiederholen, länger sind und oft selbst in das Ende der Komposition eingreifen. Im Beispiel 165 ist der Schluß aus Debussys „Nachmittag eines Fauns", im Beispiel 166 eine Probe aus den „Slowakischen Gesängen" von Vítězslav Novák angeführt.

§ 121. *Funktionslose (atonale) Musik.* Vom tonalen Funktionsstandpunkt aus können wir dreierlei Arten von Musik unterscheiden: *a)* mit eindeutiger Funktionsbedeutung der Akkorde, *b)* mit gelockerten Funktionsbeziehungen, *c)* ohne objektiv und zuverlässig feststellbare Funktionsbeziehungen. Im Falle *c)* handelt es sich um funktionslose atonale Musik. Bei der funktionslosen Auffassung helfen: konsequente Parallelismen, volle Ausnützung der Chromatik, unkombinierte Anordnung der Zusammenklänge, Beschränkung der diatonischen Vorgänge in den einzelnen Stimmen auf das Mindestmaß.

§ 122. *Kompositionsordnung und allgemeine Kompositions-Stilisation.* Der hypertrophische harmonische Reichtum der modernen Musik läßt sich stilistisch viel schwieriger bewältigen als dies in der klassischen Musik der Fall war. Die Komponisten konzentrieren sich oft auf ein beschränktes harmonisches Material, auf eine absichtlich ausgesuchte Auswahl. So eine absichtliche Auswahl des harmonischen Materials läßt sich im Wesen auf dreifachem Wege verwirklichen: 1. durch Beschränkung auf bestimmte Zusammenklang-Gattungen, 2. durch Beschränkung auf ein bestimmtes Tonsystem, 3. durch Bestimmung einer allgemeinen Kompositions-Stilisierung. Besonders die dritte Art ist in der modernen Musik beliebt (vergl. die Beisp. 176, 177, 178).

§ 123. *Horizontales Denken, Führung der Stimmen.* Führender und entscheidender Faktor bei der Schaffung einzelner Zusammenklänge und deren Folgen pflegt nicht nur, die konsequent durchgesetzte bestimmte Stilisierung zu sein, sondern auf höherer Stufe auch das freie melodische Denken in den gleichzeitig verlaufenden Linien (Polyphonie). Die Zusammenklang-Gebilde und die gesamte harmonische Struktur der Musik sind in der polyphon gedachten Komposition das bloße Ergebnis von melodisch frei entwickelten Stimmen. Das melodische Denken bezeichnen wir auch als horizontales Denken. Besonders in der Polyphonie, welche mit ausgeklügelten Imitationen arbeitet, kann man nur schwer eine selbständige harmonische Gesetzmäßigkeit durchsetzen. Es erscheint dann als überflüssig, im Verlauf einer derart geschaffenen Musik Funktionbeziehungen zwischen allen geschaffen Zusammenklängen zu suchen (siehe Beisp. 180 aus meiner II. Symphonie).

Additional Notes to Some Phenomena of Harmonic and Tonal Thinking

Karel Janeček

Originaly published as "Doplňující poznámky k některým jevům harmonického a tonálního myšlení" [Additional Notes to Some Phenomena of Harmonic and Tonal Thinking], *Živá hudba: Sborník prací hudební fakulty AMU* [Living Music: Collection of Works by the Music Faculty of AMU] (Praha: SPN, 1976) 21–29.

1. On Imaginary Pitches

The evidence for the existence of imaginary pitches is not found directly, but only through their impact. Their impact is convincing, demonstrated in musical pieces and compositions. From them we can deduce how composers hear and think harmonically, and what their assumptions may be about the hearing and thinking of their audience.

Imaginary pitches appear and die away, participating in the formation of concrete harmonic percepts. Certain compositional procedures can cancel imaginary pitches, cross them out of context, and possibly, they can continue (even after being harmonically cancelled) to function in their weaker form as tonal imaginary pitches. I wrote about all this in an older article *The Significance of Imaginary Pitches in Harmony* (1932), then in the *The Foundations of Modern Harmony* ((written in the years 1942–49, and published in 1965), and published in 1965), and most recently in the study *Fundamental Harmonic Problems and their Solutions* (around the turn of the year, 1953–54). Now, allow me to add one more note (a rather important one, I think): *imaginary pitches are cancelled* – becoming therefore also crossed out of the harmonic context – *even if they continue to sound as real pitches*. I have in mind those instances when music is played on an instrument with real reverb (such as a harp, or a piano played with the sustain pedal pressed), or when the music sounds in a space with a piercing and conspicuously prolonged acoustic echo. The ear, by itself, is able to isolate these real reverberations and to not hear them if they have been cancelled by proper (i.e., compositional) means. Otherwise, we would find the same music performed differently to be *substantially* different. We know it is not so. These reverberating real pitches do not belong in the momentarily ruling harmony, and after having been duly cancelled, represent a perhaps unpleasant but still only subsidiary complication of the sound. They do not change its essence. They do not enrich it with equivalent components; they only make it less lucid, less "clean". Refined musicians suppress, restrain, and shorten these reverberations according to circumstances, but it is done for the sake of culture and refinement. For instance, harpists use pedals to instantly retune the strings to a different pitch, pianists use the sustain pedal sparingly, conductors adjust tempos to the acoustics of the concert space, and so on.

Finally, one can still add that the cessation of a compositionally uncancelled imaginary pitch has an incomparably more striking impact on the forming of a harmony than a real tone reverberating that does not belong to that harmony and which has been compositionally cancelled. Imaginary pitches have full harmonic impact even if they do not really sound; real reverberating pitches, after cancellation, do not have any harmonic impact, in spite of actually (even weakly) sounding.

This phenomenon warns (however indirectly) of the fact that weaker and, at the same time, foreign components are of negligible significance to a chord. Especially weak components – such as harmonics – are then completely inconsequential, and therefore their participation or non-participation bears no implications. This means that a minor triad is completely equal to a major triad, regardless of the fact that the interactions of harmonic series differ radically within each.

2. The Dialectics of Chord-types, Transpositions and Dispositions

In the twenties, walking down Spálená Street, I would often meet a man, impeccably dressed with a top hat on, who would cause people to glance back in surprise as they passed him. It was Adolf Krösing, a famous Smetanian "Vašek".[1] In 1923, he sang the role for the last time, as by then only a guest performer at the National Theatre. The stage-Vašek and the man with the top hat are the self-same Adolf Krösing, just in different *dispositions*. Krösing's Vašek in 1923, and before that his Vašek of 1892, for example, when the opera company of the Prague National Theatre travelled for a memorable tour to Vienna, are also the same, only in different temporal transpositions: earlier in the strength of his best years, and later, delivering his definitive farewell to the stage.

With chord-types, it is the same. They can be used in various *transpositions*, and the most varied *dispositions*. An untrained ear will be hard-pressed to admit that the rejoicing fanfare of three trumpets playing D F♯ A, and the delicate broken chord of a harp

---

[1] Editor's note: Vašek is a comic yet unfortunate character from *Prodaná nevěsta* (The Bartered Bride), a comic opera by Bedřich Smetana. The stock character of the buffoon or simpleton, Vašek is a staple of Czech culture.

where A♭ C E♭ alternate, represent the same chord-type (major), only in a different transposition and disposition to each other. Music theory has the merit of systemizing this. As far as classical material is concerned, all the battles have been won. In modern harmony however, every once in a while we face the claim that two chords essentially differ (i.e. as *chord-types*), if their impact greatly differs. Here it becomes necessary to remind one of the fact that the impact of different chord-types can sometimes be very similar (to such a degree that they can even substitute each other), while at other times identical chord-types can appear in extremely dissimilar roles, opposing one another – at once as a man with a top hat, and at another, as Vašek.

Excuse me for using such a primitive metaphor. I did so because I know, from various discussions as well as from literature, how frequently people may be misled regarding this issue.

3. On Harmonic Functions

Historians of music theory point out two crucial findings in the field of harmony by Zarlino and Rameau, enriched later by Riemann. We can rightfully use the terms 'pre-Zarlinian' and 'post-Zarlinian' or 'pre-Rameauesque' and 'post-Rameauesque' (acknowledging, however, that even after Zarlino and Rameau, conservatives comfortably maintain the prior positions, allowing themselves to be discussed as pre-Zarlinists or pre-Rameauists). Both findings have one thing in common: they *generalize*, summarizing particulars as groups of unified elements. There are only two perfectly suitable chords (i.e., chord-types) appearing in various modifications (i.e., dispositions, transpositions). There are only three functions that can be asserted in various forms (i.e., as discernible chord-types diversely distributed in tonal space).

Each limit – the theoretical included – is provocative, raising objections or at least questions. The same is true about limitlessness: it calls for classification, some definition of limits. Can there really be only two fully satisfactory (i.e., consonant) chord-types? Even if we admit that there are more of them (as one often hears), Zarlino's most important finding maintains its validity – *that modification-particulars are convertible to a basic, representative form for each chord-type.*

So, as far as functions are concerned (i.e., Rameau's finding, enlarged upon by Riemann later), it follows that it is also possible to doubt that there are really only three. Aren't there more? However, even if their number were increased, the most significant differentiations would remain valid: above/under the axis, above/under the tonic, and dominant/subdominant. Thus, an innovation concerning functions would be thinkable only as a *pair*. The functional systems potentially possible are therefore: three-membered, five-membered, seven-membered… But hold on! Functionality signifies *generality*. There are certain transpositions of certain chord-types characterized by their *dominant quality*, represented by the dominant. There are others whose main feature is the *subdominant quality* and they are represented by the subdominant. If the number of functions was increased unduly, each transposition of any particular chord-type would become its own representative. A swollen officer corps of numerous ostentatious terms would arise, but no soldiers. Therefore, Rameau's system continues to be valid up to now because it relies on *three primary functions*. It might be possible to enrich this strictly limited number of functions, but only with a fourth and fifth as *auxiliary* and complementary (the primary functions would remain as they were, numbering only three). It turned out to be necessary to make his extension was made, and it was necessary because the compositional practice became enriched. Dominant and subdominant qualities were joined by something special: *phrygian* and *lydian qualities.*

It isn't necessary, perhaps, to even mention that a surplus of functions actually entails a denial of functionality as such, and thus also the theoretical return to a pre-Rameauesque idyll.

Recognition of dominant, subdominant and tonic features and the appointment of certain chords to represent those features has necessarily raised the question of the functional features of harmonies which are not representative. What is the functional meaning of harmonies that are, in the given tonality, neither pure tonic, nor pure dominant, nor pure subdominant? Pre-Rameau theorists (so-called even if living long after Rameau) would have spoken of the harmony built on the second, third, and sixth degree. However, this was only an orientational registration. As regards functional *explanations*, they were threefold:

a) as a pitch *enrichment* or *impoverishment* of the respective representatives (such as B D F = G B D + F − G);
b) as a temporary *loan* from elsewhere, irrespective of whether it is strictly a loan or adjusted to the primary tonality (such as A C E, in C major taking over from the relative A minor; A♭ C E♭, from the parallel C minor; D F A, from the dominant tonality G major, adjusted to the primary tonality of C major);
c) as a functional *hybrid* or even *combination* (G B D F is the hybrid of the full dominant G B D with the subdominant component F).

It is interesting that of these three possible explanations, the last one (*c*) is historically the youngest, even though it is also the most readily apparent. It is the most convincing because it does not have to deal with the randomness of added subordinate pitches (as in *a* above) which is difficult to justify, or with a fluctuating or possibly temporarily invalid main tonal center (as in *b* above). At the same time, both older explanations *a* and *b* are "worth something" – it is not necessary to dismiss them. It does happen sometimes that subordinate pitches enrich the chord (if they are in the position of auxiliary tones) and the tonal center does sometimes fluctuate – vanishing, moving. Nevertheless, the third explanation is universal – it always fits. There is no need to wonder at its relative recentness. It became necessary only after even the theorists had had to enrich the system and to reach for auxiliary functions. In that new situation, remaining within the limits of the two older explanations (*a* and *b*) was no longer possible.

4. On the Path to the Antitonic

Nobody is taken aback by the enriched functional system of five members with regard to its *older components* or their names (tonic, dominant and subdominant). With the newly introduced *auxiliary functions*, it is different. Heads are shaking over the names as well as the placement of the representatives in tonal space. I will leave the issue of the names aside, as it is a trivial matter. However, I must comment on the placement of the chords that represent the phrygian and lydian qualities.

The introduction of auxiliary functions was justified by the *fact that the distinct features of the lydian and phrygian qualities could not be fully converted to their respective dominant and subdominant qualities*. It was only partially possible. In C major or c minor, the pitches D♭ (phrygian) and F♯ (lydian) resisted explanation. If these pitches are conceived of as equal to the others, they resist the most basic tonal principle, i.e. the *principle of the pure tonic*. If despite that, they should appear to be acceptable, their relation to the tonic must manifest in a different manner, under the auspices of a different principle. This other principle is given – in the same way as with the principle of the pure tonic – by the relation of the non-tonic main functions to the tonic. It is the *principle of the leading tone*. I have explained all this sufficiently clearly in *The Foundations of Modern Harmony*. I would now like to supplement the explication with reference to the way that awareness of the tonal center arises, is strengthened, and perishes, and to a peculiarity in the hierarchy of non-tonic chords as related to a particular tonic.

The awareness of a tonal center as a reference point for orientation results predominantly from the *real sound presented* (pitch, harmony). Whoever comes first sets the rules for everything to follow. The first sound is the determinant. It is completely natural. If a sound void precedes the composition, we anchor at its first sound. According to it, we judge and measure what follows. Indeed, it is the *primary presentation of the tonic*. For a sound to become the central measure (the tonic), it is enough at first to simply present it – to make it sound. But as it can potentially be any sound (pitch, harmony, consonance as well as dissonance), it is also necessary to allow for the possibility that some other sound could, in turn, "take the chair". Why, it is quite common in music! And for that to happen, there is no need for the situation labelled above as a "sound void". It is sufficient to "push" the tonic out, to subvert its position, thus freeing its place for another referential center, for another tonic. Therefore, we must allow for the following possibilities:

1. the tonic being introduced by simple *presentation*;
2. an additional *strengthening* of an introduced tonic, by supporting compositional means;

3. *disproving* the tonic introduced formerly, by negating the means of composition;
4. *defining* the tonic – usually a new, hitherto unknown one – by compositional means.

In the possibilities here enumerated, "compositional means" are bandied around. It is not a case of simply presenting the phenomenon. It is a *manipulation*; intentional, considered, and tested; manipulation through sounds, harmonies, and functions; a choice between them, preferring one to the detriment of others. This is possible due to the fact that, relative to a particular center, other sounds, non-central ones, lie at different distances; they can be close, farther, or far; adjacent, relative, supportive; distant, even suppressing. Having said that, it is still possible for each to take the steering wheel – as well as to be dragged from it.

Translated into the language of music theory, this means that there are *functionally close* chords which can be used to *strengthen* the center (tonic), and *functionally distant* ones whose introduction *subverts* the center. According to our momentary position, the same chord can appear at once functionally close, and at another functionally distant. This implies that in strengthening one center we simultaneously subvert another, and vice versa – by subverting one, we strengthen another.

And now, permit me to return to an above-mentioned peculiarity in the hierarchy of non-tonic functions. Certainly the dominant and subdominant are functionally close. They reliably define their tonic. But each of these harmonies, dominant and subdominant, can take the wheel and become the tonic itself. Its closest functional companion will be the former tonic; the other one, however, will be more distant – it will be the so-called *second dominant* (D F♯ A in C major) or the *second subdominant* (B♭ D F in C major). Proceeding in this manner (i.e., round the circle of fifths), we get to the third, fourth, fifth, and finally to the sixth dominant or subdominant. We would find ourselves most distant from the tonic, on the opposite side of the circle (In C major, the path based on the dominant would lead to the harmony F♯ A♯ C♯; the path based the subdominant to the harmony G♭ B♭ D♭). Proceeding from there, we would start getting closer again to the original tonic.

At first glance, the matter appears to be simple: going up or down by fifths, we move away from the original tonic until we get to a single harmony which is, relative to the original tonic, simultaneously its *sixth dominant* and *sixth subdominant*. (We can label this harmony, which lies opposite the tonic and resists its rule the most, the *antitonic*.) However, immediately before this most distant point, we pass through two harmonies (in C: B D♯ F♯, D♭ F A♭) which, in spite of being in close harmonic relation with the distant harmonies and therefore being themselves distant too, *lie in close proximity to the original tonic, as regards the tonal space*. This proximity in tonal space might differ from its harmonic relation, however, in essence it is only a *deflection*,[2] in some aspects quite alike the deflection of the individual dominant or subdominant tones from

---

[2] Editor's note: David Copp defines this term as the *SLIDE*, see *Chromatic Transformations in Nineteenth-Century music* (Cambridge: Cambridge University Press, 2011).

the closest tones of the relevant tonic. Furthermore, it is the proximity of a *semitone*, i.e. with an especially strong tendency to continue. Therefore, the fifth dominant and subdominant are special in the sense that they can be conceived of as *very distant* and *tonally estranged* harmonies, but simultaneously also as close harmonies, elegantly shifted. Obviously, they are auxiliary functions. I think the peculiarity that I point out here is precisely the reason that these two harmonies should be considered the *representatives* of the lydian and phrygian qualities respectively, instead of others which may not be so very distant (e.g., D F♯ A, B♭ D F in C major), but neither are they close. (Other reasons are discussed in *The Foundations of Modern Harmony*.)

5. On Atonality

Finally, I would like to mention the phenomenon known as *atonality*. It is very common to encounter the naïve, simplistic opinion that in atonality, the principles of harmonic functions *do not hold*. It is simply supposing that "they do not hold" which is naïve. Does a mere claim, a mere dismissal, suffice here? A principle valid in one case but not in another is not a principle, it is a convention. The thinking and feeling of harmonic functions, however, is rooted deep, in the manner of perceiving and thinking as such. It was not without reason that I earlier emphasized the possibility of presenting the center merely by sounding it. Atonality makes use of the mechanism of hearing in such a way that *it nips any suggestion of a potential center in the bud*. However, nipping or rather subverting one usually comes hand-in-hand with establishing another (I refer to those four alternatives enumerated above). Therefore, the subversion must be *persistently maintained*. It is necessary to preclude any center from asserting itself. This means that the simple statement, "it does not hold", does not suffice; unrelenting effort is necessary to suppress tonal centers from arising. In essence, the only difference between atonal music, and music in which tonal centers alternate and possibly also permeate, is qualitative; *in atonal music, the nascence of individual centers*, which always requires time (because it takes place in time), *is compressed into a time span as short as possible*. However, this time span is not nil. Therefore, in terms of functionality as generally conceived, there exists only "music", singular: not tonal music on the one hand, with atonal music on the other. Nevertheless, manifestations of personalities, styles, and historical periods exist. These do differ. Additionally, it is well-known that the latest development likes to distance itself as radically (i.e., as exaggeratedly) as possible from the previous – and history provides many examples of this. From a critical distance, then, it is obvious that what has been claimed about atonal music does not dovetail into what is, in practice, implemented.

Order, System, Structure, Function and Mutual Interplay of Theory and Practice.
On the Primary Attributes of Music-theoretical and Pedagogical Thinking of Karel Janeček

Vladimír Tichý

1. On Music Theory

Let us start with a question: what does the term "music theory" mean to us?

If we set out to define the discipline of music theory, determine its subject and delimit its boundaries, we do not imagine that the task could be problematic. But as soon as we attempt to create such a definition, we realise that the general notions of music theory are in practice inaccurate and ambiguous, even among music experts. Everyone who deals with music on a professional level, everyone who studies or has studied music of any form and at any level, and even everyone who is involved with music only at an amateur level has sooner or later come in contact with music theory and has their own notion of what it is. Music theory can appear to be, variously, a summary of concepts and terminology directly related to musical practice; a summary of terms related to certain specific elementary musical skills (hearing and rhythmic skills); a description of a musical piece (or pieces) and the possibilities of its (their) interpretation; a summary of working rules, once respected as a part of compositional and interpretational practice and rejected today; or as a summary of working rules respected as a part of compositional and interpretational practice today, and formerly unheard of. In a more general approach, music theory is often understood as the sum of music knowledge with which we "ought to" be equipped if we are to pursue music professionally (be it in the artistic sense, or in the musicological, pedagogical, popularisation or critical fields, etc.), or as everything that is written about music (thus everything from scientific treatises in the musicological field to popular and critical texts), or even as any verbal expression concerning music. We often encounter music theory being seen as identical to musicology: music theory and musical sciences are mistakenly understood as synonyms in this case.

As you can see, there is a relatively rich palette of standpoints and opinions about the exact nature, purpose and specific practical benefits of the field of music theory. This richness of standpoints is likely related to their various perspectives: the field appears differently to a musicologist and to a practising musician. In the latter case, a composer will view music theory completely differently from, for example, a singer. A student at a conservatory will likely have a different idea of music theory than a music university student or a musician with rich experience in the field. We must not forget that there are several other fields related to music theory: for example, music pedagogy or musical acoustics. Of course, even the layperson has their own idea of what music theory is. All of these groups have (despite their differences of opinion) something in common: their relationship with music theory, which is only that of a user, not that of a creator. This "user" position is the primary source of their perspective. They approach music theory as something that is more or less developed *a priori* and something established that they can get to know in various levels of depth and then use in practice. Yet, those who feel the need to further develop music theory and come equipped with the necessary set of suitable skills are a dime a dozen.

Due to the nature of the matter, music composers are more inclined to study the field of music theory and apply it in practice: part of their field of work (profession) lies in breaching the boundaries of normative rules during their work, and in searching for a new order. Some do so purely intuitively (without being fully aware of all the internal structural relations in the music they are creating, or have created); others do so intuitively with the aid of rational thought; they are fully or mostly aware of their music's internal structural relations, without feeling the need to verbalise these relations. The third group of composers are those who also do so intuitively with the aid of rational thought – with the exception that they share some (or all) of the relations they are aware of through commentaries or in the form of publications. Out of this third group, there sometimes emerges a creative music theorist, either a theorising composer, or – after filling the gaps necessary for scientific work – an actual musicologist, a music theory specialist.

So what actually is music theory? *Music theory is the term used to describe a practice-oriented musicological discipline, closely related to the problems of musical composition and interpretation, aimed at the examination of musical structure, its facets, its internal relations, principles by which it is organised, etc., and that is either in the compositionally technical aspect (i.e., theory of composition), or with the goal of a deeper understanding and formulation of its general regularities.* It is a field with a legacy spanning many centuries. Out of practical needs, traditional music theory disciplines (or rather in relation to the defined field – sub-disciplines) have crystallised in the European environment: melodics, harmony, counterpoint, musical forms, organology, tuning and instrumentation theory, as well as more recent additions such as tectonics, kinetics and genre theory. Music theory can generally be divided into multiple parts: systematic theory, which gives us a complete and logically sorted summary of terms; analytical theory, which entails studying the regularities of musical expression in different times and places; and compositionally technical music theory disciplines, which attempt to create models for musical expression. A defining trait of actual music theory is its utmost exactness of thought (in this regard it is often similar to mathematics, logic, physics, etc., while at the same time being none of those disciplines). The subject of music theory is then the structure of music in general, i.e., a unit for which structured sound (by pitch, dynamics, timbre and time) is the material. The subject of music theory research is, then, everything ranging from the elements of a given musical structure, through all relations by which it is organised, up to general regularities of the musical language and the formation methods that a given structure displays. In a way, music theory, which examines the structure of musical expression, can be compared to linguistics, which examines the structure of language. In this respect, we can characterise the relationship between music theory and musicology as being comparable to the relationship between linguistics and literary science.

The exact subject of music theory research changes over time, depending on the development of music itself. Thus, for example, in the era of vocal polyphony the main subject of interest used to be the voice-leading in polyphonic parts, analysis of the intervals between the individual voices in terms of distinguishing consonances and dissonances (and defining the terms themselves), and imitative and invertible counterpoint techniques. In the tonal harmony period, it used to be the harmonic sentence, consisting of a sequence of functional harmonic devices, represented as a series of chords as a part of a tonally arranged whole (including defining the terms such as chords, diatonic function, tonic). 20th century music theory reflects not only the existence of compositional methods of 20th century composers – e.g., composers of the Second Viennese School and their successors – but also the existence of the possibilities of modern tonality, represented by classic composers of the first half of the 20th century, and modern modality as we know it from, e.g., the works of Messiaen (including determining and clarifying more terms necessary to understand the matter from a theoretical standpoint). Music theory also always investigates the degree to which the latest subject of music structure study can be described using traditional theoretical tools, or whether it is necessary to search for new tools in order to describe it, in other words, whether it could once more (as has happened many times in history) be a transformed subject of music theory research. During the time of the rise of harmonic thought, after the vocal polyphony epoch, the contemporary goal was to develop the theoretical understanding of figured bass. The next such step was the transition to a sophisticated functional harmony-oriented line of thought accompanied by the need to let go of the figured bass technique and once more to search for a new method of theoretical understanding, with the goal of not only creating a simple set of technical instructions but also primarily of understanding the inner workings of the internal relations in both the vertical and horizontal planes.

Thus, let us ask ourselves this question: which specific tasks was 20th century music theory solving in one of the historically most often developed music theory disciplines – the field of the theory of harmony? Even a brief survey of the rapid and rich development of European musical expression at the end of the 19th century and the beginning of the 20th century reveals the wide array of new problems and tasks waiting to be tackled through music theory research, be it the analytical understanding of harmonic devices brought about by contemporary music, or the realisation, systematic understanding and formulation of regularities and principles by which such devices have been organised, in situations where the principle of triadic construction of chords can no longer always be applied, when the tonal material loses its dependence on a primarily diatonic arrangement (either in the case of pure or altered diatony), and when various forms and variants of disruption, relativisation or outright negation of classical tonal hierarchy, based on the "planetary" principle of hierarchic relation of all harmonic events to one tonal centre. As can be seen, the development of musical expression in this period, and in the following years, brought about a large number of questions, incentives and challenges for music theory.

One of the most important attempts at creating a personal approach to the issues mentioned above was the music-theoretical publication by Paul Hindemith, *Unterweisung im Tonsatz*.[1] Hindemith bases his theoretical reasoning on natural order – the existence of the overtone series. From this he deduces the argument for his processes and constructions.[2] As a basis and foundation for further reasoning he constructed two series, the so-called series I and II. The method he used is interesting, yet it also raises questions.

The first series

C – G – F – A – E – E♭ – A♭ – D – B♭ – D♭ – B – F♯/G♭

illustrates a degree of affinity of each of the individual notes of the twelve-tone chromatic scale towards the root note (C), which represents the tonal centre. The highest affinity towards the root note is exhibited by the perfect fifth (G), and the furthermost position is then taken by the tritone (F♯/G♭). Hindemith derives the construction of the series I from the overtone series, specifically its first six notes. The foundation of this construction is the root note C ("father"). To each of his six overtones he serially assigns: a) lower serial degrees starting with the number 2, which creates the 2.–6. notes

---

[1] Paul Hindemith, *Unterweisung im Tonsatz I–II*, neue, erw. ausg (Mainz: B. Schott's Söhne, 1939–1940).
[2] Quote based on Ctirad Kohoutek, *Novodobé skladebné směry v hudbě* [Compositional Styles in the New Era], 2nd ed. (Praha: SHV, 1965).

of the series (G, F, A, E, E♭ – "sons"); and b) higher serial degrees through which he discovers additional new notes, which must, however, be transposed into the octave of the previous notes. The additional notes ("grandsons") D, B♭, D♭, and B are then derived from the "sons" in this manner. The last note (the furthest note from the root centre), "great-grandson" F♯/G♭ is derived from the "grandsons".

This undoubtedly peculiar attempt at a solution raises a number of questions. Why are only the first six overtones chosen as a source for the above-mentioned construction? After all, the overtone series is continuous and nature knows no boundaries between the individual notes! What is the reason for assigning lower serial degrees up to a certain degree and from this degree onwards assigning higher serial degrees? What is the actual reason for basing this construction on redistributing the serial degrees of individual notes?

The second series (intervallic) in its sequence represents individual intervals as a foundation for creating harmonic units:

perfect unison / perfect octave	C–C
perfect fifth / perfect fourth	C–G / G–C
major third / minor sixth	C–E / E–C
minor third / major sixth	C–E♭ / E♭–C
major second / minor seventh	C–D / D–C
minor second / major seventh	C–D♭ / D♭–C
tritone	C–F♯ / G♭–C

in its sequence represents individual intervals as a foundation for creating harmonic units. The harmonic effectiveness of an interval is determined by how pronouncedly is one of its notes (the root note) supported by combination notes (notes created in this manner are underlined in the above list). The root manifests the strongest in perfect fifths / perfect fourths, and this manifestation gradually weakens in the further intervals – in the case of the tritone neither of the tones asserts itself as the root note anymore. The individual intervals manifest these attributes in chords, consisting of three or more notes in which they figure.

Hindemith was aware of the fact that, under the conditions of 20th century harmony, he could no longer count on contemporary techniques in order to further develop chord theory: the possibilities of enhancing triadic constructions of chords by layering additional thirds had been exhausted, as had been the possibilities of altered chords, not to mention the fact that, due to the replacement of diatonic arrangement with the tonal system of the equally tempered twelve-tone chromatic scale, chord alteration lost its meaning. Assuming that the function of a harmonic unit can be taken by any (and altered in any way) combination of tones up to twelve note chords, he searched for a suitable method of categorisation of chord material, and that is by sorting every possible combination of chord options into a total of six groups.

One of the guiding elements for Hindemith is the presence or absence of the tritone in a given chord, and similarly the presence or absence of a minor or major second (individually or in tandem with the tritone). Furthermore, there is also the presence (strong or weakened) or absence of the root note, determined by the strongest of present intervals. As the most determinate he poses the chords of the I group (without the tritone and the second – exclusively major and minor triads), and as indeterminate the chords of the V and VI groups (without the root note).[3] Once again, this topic (chord conception) gives rise to several questions. How do the outlined attributes manifest in perception of the chords? What role does alteration of a specific interval play in their perception, or in the context within the boundaries of the musical stream over the course of time?

Despite these questions, it is necessary to state that Hindemith's publication was a very important step for music-theoretical reflection on 20th century harmony, and served as a valuable inspiration for future researchers and also an impulse for individual research.

---

[3] We can label the chords of the groups V and VI mentioned by Hindemith as centrically-nonhierarchic chord units using the terminology of Karel Risinger, *Hierarchie hudebních celků* [The Hierarchy of Musical Wholes] (Praha: Panton, 1969).

2. Karel Janeček – the Key Figure for Czech Music Theory

Karel Janeček is one of the leading figures of Czech modern music theory. In his music-theoretical and music-pedagogical work he is a direct successor of the series of Czech music theorists of the 19th and 20th centuries: Bedřich Diviš Weber, Karel Knittl, Karel Stecker, Josef Foerster, František Zdeněk Skuherský and Otakar Šín. Most of them were connected to the Prague Conservatory, founded in 1811. A very specific approach is presented in the works of Leoš Janáček. Specific examples of the continuity in the works of Karel Janeček in regards to the thoughts of his predecessors will be elaborated below (as a part of commentary of his work). Other Prague figures (the contemporaries and colleagues of Karel Janeček in the field of modern Czech music theory) were Alois Hába (micro-interval music specialist), Karel Risinger and Jaroslav Volek. Brno of course also had its share of influential figures – Miloslav Ištvan, Alois Piňos and Ctirad Kohoutek, to mention a few. These circles (contemporaries of Karel Janeček) were characterised by spirited discussion. Published and ready-to-be-published works and other music-theoretical topics went through the cleansing fire of critical yet inspirational discussion in their lively debates. In all of these contexts, Karel Janeček was perceived as a highly respected figure.

Janeček's point of view is derived from three correlated pillars. The first is his deep knowledge of the works of the great master composers of the past and present, analytical research of their masterpieces and experiences from his own composing work, which started with his studies in the composing class of Vítězslav Novák at the Master School of the Prague Conservatory. Janeček expressed his deep respect for and admiration of Vítězslav Novák throughout his life.

The second pillar of Janeček's point of view is his lifelong interest and care for the scientific field of music theory, especially in the areas directly related to the actual practice of music composition. Janeček expressed this interest not only through his deep knowledge of the topics, subject and methodology of this field but also through his conviction of his purpose and calling, and especially through his specific systematic research and publishing endeavours – starting with concise early music-theoretical studies, published most often in the pages of the journals *Tempo, Musical Horizons*, later *Living Music* (a yearbook, founded by his initiative, of theoretical studies of the Music Faculty of the Academy of Performing Arts in Prague), up to significant literary publications *Musical Forms*,[4] *Study of Melodics*,[5] *Foundations of Modern Harmony*,[6] *Tectonics*,[7] *Compositional Practice in the Field of Classical Harmony*.[8] Opuses of their own are the first part

---

[4] Karel Janeček, *Hudební formy* [Musical Forms] (Praha: SNKLHU, 1955).
[5] Karel Janeček, *Melodika* [Study of Melodics] (Praha: SNKLHU, 1956).
[6] Karel Janeček, *Základy moderní harmonie* [Foundations of Modern Harmony] (Praha: Nakladatelství ČSAV [Czechoslovak Academy of Sciences Press], 1965).
[7] Karel Janeček, *Tektonika* [Tectonics] (Praha: Supraphon, 1968).
[8] Karel Janeček, *Skladatelská práce v oblasti klasické harmonie* [Compositional Practice in the Field of Classical Harmony] (Praha: Academia, 1973).

of the generous team project *The Oeuvre and Life of Bedřich Smetana* (dedicated to the analysis of Smetana's chamber works)[9] and the methodically original workbook *Harmony Through Analysis*.[10]

The third important pillar – or, to be precise, differentia – of Karel Janeček's point of view is his mathematically exact way of thinking, undoubtedly connected to his original technical education, which manifested itself in the logical and systematic concept of his theoretical work and in specific work operations, especially in the field of modern harmony. The aptitude for systematic organisation of the material enabled him to shift the form of music-theoretical disciplines dramatically from mere description of musical phenomena and stating the sum of individual information towards the logically organised structure of a scientific discipline, capturing and reflecting not only the facts but also their mutual functional relations, both apparent and hidden connections and regularities of their function in the organism of a musical whole.

The connecting element between the three pillars of Karel Janeček was his pedagogical work and the unusual methodical inventions related to it (his method of so-called activated analysis comes to mind), as well as the search for a convincing and generally comprehensible verbal expression, by which his texts are characterised.

All of these factors undoubtedly contributed to Prof. Janeček's being asked to prepare the proposal for the conception of the music-theoretical component of the study of musical majors at the Music Faculty of the Academy of Performing Arts in Prague at the time of its founding in 1946, and to bring the proposed study programme to life. Prof. Janeček was one of the first educationalists of music theory in the Faculty, and, by virtue of his title as Leader of the department of Music Theory, he was in charge of all theoretical education (both conceptually and organisationally) and guaranteed its professional level.

Pedagogical considerations led Prof. Janeček to divide his music-theoretical disciplines into two groups – the so-called lower and higher disciplines. In the lower music-theoretical disciplines belonged all of the existing traditional conservatory disciplines: study of harmony, study of musical forms, counterpoint studies, rhythm, intonation and study of musical instruments. For the academic study of interpretational disciplines Prof. Janeček devised a two-year group seminar of piece analysis, synthesising and developing the knowledge and skills acquired at the conservatory degree of study and preparing the foundation for the following seminar on aesthetics. For the education of composers, conductors and opera theatre directors, Prof. Janeček implemented the subject of *Composition theory* as part of the so-called higher music-theoretical disciplines. This subject consisted of the study of melodics, modern harmony foundations, tectonics and planned genre and style study. As mentioned above, he prepared

---

9 Karel Janeček, *Dílo a život Bedřicha Smetany I. Smetanova komorní tvorba* [The Oeuvre and Life of Bedřich Smetana I. Smetana's Chamber Works] (Praha: Editio Supraphon, 1978).
10 Karel Janeček, *Harmonie rozborem* [Harmony Through Analysis] (Praha: Státní hudební nakladatelství [State Music Press], 1963).

a literary publication for the first three disciplines. A more demanding form of piece analysis called *Study of compositions* serves as a supplement and counterpart to the disciplines of composition, conducting and opera theatre direction.

During his formulation of the proposal and realisation of the theoretical part of the study of artistic disciplines, Janeček firmly respected two necessary requirements:

a) music theory must serve the needs of music practice;
b) in terms of quality and quantity the requirements for the music-theoretical study must fall in line with the generally applied and respected requirements for academic education.

It can be said with utmost certainty that the role played by Karel Janeček in the formulation of the theoretical part of the new study of artistic music disciplines was exceptional and undeniable.

An important chapter in Janeček's academic pedagogical activity was the formation and development of the Music Theory study subject, which was a part of the study programme at the Music Faculty of the Academy of Performing Arts in Prague. The establishment of this scientific discipline promised a close connection to the music practice of composition and interpretation, which is exactly what he expected of it. Sadly, before this project could bear fruit, the subject was cancelled through an administrative decision in 1948, and for many decades it survived only in the form of a partial replacement – a two-year postgraduate course, professionally and organisationally led by Prof. Janeček. After he passed away in 1974, Prof. Risinger took this duty upon himself. During the 1990's the department of Music Theory and History managed to justify and assert the subject back into the curriculum of the Academy of Performing Arts in Prague, thus fulfilling the half-a-century-old dream of Prof. Janeček.

The book *Foundations of Modern Harmony*, released in 1965, was a summary of thoughts that had been ripening for the preceding 30 years, and it represented a generous attempt at a theoretical interpretation of harmonic phenomena. This was a characteristic of the work of composers of the first half of the 20th century, who worked and pondered in conditions that resulted from the absolute equalisation of all the twelve tones in equal temperament. As mentioned earlier, Paul Hindemith had taken on this task a quarter of a century earlier with *Unterweisung im Tonsatz*. However, Janeček managed to avoid the systematic inconsistencies of Hindemith's publication (to avoid any misunderstanding, the critical comment is in regards to Hindemith as a theorist, not as a composer). Janeček was able to exactly identify and formulate the regularities of the general harmonic system, which Hindemith was only vaguely aware of, without it leading to any conflict between the system and empirical data and actual compositional practice. The system devised by Janeček classified all of the chords possible in the equal-temperament chromatic scale into groups depending on the number of notes involved, classifying their sound properties based on the so-called dissonance characteristic. The task of altering the chord-type, systematic and compositional technical operations with chord inversions and negatives, the concept of the imaginary tone and its application in harmonic parts, differentiating the terms "chord" and "simultaneity", systematic conception of consonances and dissonance with the application of dissonant characteristics and the principle of harmonic inversion, the system of triadic combinations, the system of functional combinations, viewing traditional and modern tonality through the lens of the principle of the pure tonic and the principle of the leading tone – all of the above are proof of the originality and exactness of Janeček's thought, as well as being of significant benefit to the topic of modern harmony in the context of Czech music theory.

Tectonics, published in 1968, presents a general overview of the subject of musical piece structure. This publication was created as a continuation of the earlier *Musical Forms*, which was characterised by systematic logic and purity (e.g., in the attention given not only to describing individual forms but also to the dynamics of the function of internal structural relations, applying internal completion means, identity, contrast and differentiating the terms "musical form" and "musical genre"). The tectonic view of the musical whole is, in a certain sense, a continuation of the musical form view; in a different sense, it is its counterpart and a plastic supplement of it, while form in the classical sense is divided into parts differentiable by the application of the possibility of thematic and tonal contrast, or by the applied compositional method (mutual contrast of the expositional and evolutionary presentation of the material). Tectonics respects the anthropological predispositions for perceiving music (they are de facto psychological) and it regards the whole as divisible and thus divided into so-called blocks, which are characterised by immediately perceivable sound qualities, i.e., timbre, dynamics, position in the sonic space, the frequency span of the sonic range, single- or multilayeredness of the sonic stream, facture, momentum, tempo, meter, articulation and other qualities that are immediately perceivable, i.e., at the moment of first listening. All of these qualities (and others) become (or can become) the subject of motivic creation and take part in the creation of the whole. In the sequence and progression of musical blocks Janeček takes notice of the placement of peaks in the piece, how they were constructed, and the gradation leading towards them, and, vice versa, the following descent. During his analysis of the time progression of a piece, he takes into consideration the fact that the objective "scientific" passing of time can be perceived subjectively (depending on the specific structure of the perceived music), and thus created the category of "musical time", which respects this actuality. In terms of approaching the time progression of a piece, he also invented the categories speed and momentum, the limits of motion of differentiation and motion stagnation, time minimum and maximum. In summary, we can state that sound and time are the two primary dimensions delimiting the general "space" and "substance" of musical events occupying it. In this delimited range Janeček searches for, and states, the general regularities whose function can be seen in the works of Bach, Beethoven and Brahms, as well as in the work of Penderecki, Lutosławski or Ligeti. Classical musical forms are only a specific historically and stylistically predisposed crystallisation of those general principles. In the case of compositions that appear to use the so-called loose form, it is not a case of their not having any form; such a case can (and must) be analysed as individual, unique and independent from classical forms, as the realisation of general tectonic principles.

Summary: both publications (*Foundations of Modern Harmony* and *Tectonics*) are to be considered, in regards to Czech music theory of the 1960's (in relation to the composition practice and from the aspect of its benefit for the actual field of systematic and analytical music theory), as a completely unique and exceptional step towards the essential deepening of scientifically driven, purely rational – and at the same time creative, inspired and inventive – thought in music, through music and about music.

After half a century, have further developments in music and music theory surpassed some of Janeček's ideas? Which of his points should we be critical of? From his large body of publications, *Study Melodics* needs to be mentioned in this regard. The publication, released in 1956, reflected the time of its creation and the origins of Janeček's views. Due to its focus on melodics of the tonal classical-romantic provenance, it certainly couldn't cover the entirety of what we would expect from such a publication today.

However it is necessary to view *Foundations of Modern Harmony* as an exceptionally successful attempt at creating a study of harmony in the conditions of equally tempered chromatic scale of the 20th century. Is this problem still relevant today? In addition, is Janeček's theoretical approach always fully understood and worked through? Based on repeated experience it can be stated, with a certain level of pity, that with a post-pinnacle approach, sometimes only a "numbered catalogue" of chord-types is appreciated in *Foundations of Modern Harmony*, without the adequate realisation of the fact that this "catalogue" is only an introduction – an entry point into the reflection on the subject of modern harmony.

If we were to agree that the theoretical approach devised by Janeček is no longer relevant to the latest trends in composition practice, the approach should not be simply "shelved". It should be critically reflected upon as being a result of the period of its creation, and thus a document of a certain epoch of harmonic thought. And it should also be seen as essential and of great benefit to Czech music-theoretic thought of the 20th century.

In the context of *Tectonics* today, it needs to be stated that the historical existence of the moment form, minimalism, conceptual composition and the growing influence of non-European musical cultures on our musical thought shed new light on the subject of perception and musical time perception (and the concepts of time minimum and maximum that arose from the subject), which was the subject Janeček was researching. These new developments, however, do not invalidate the thesis presented in *Tectonics*, for it is necessary to realise the relativity and conditions of their validity (a situation comparable to the situation of classical Newtonian physics in the circumstances of new empirical knowledge in physics at the turn of the 20th century, which found their formulation in Einstein's theory of relativity).

It is interesting that Janeček did not include the systematic research of the kinetic component of music (with the exception of a short and rather essayistic study *New and Old Rhythm* from 1933)[11] into his sophisticated work plan, even though it was precisely the subject of rhythm, meter and time that brought many new insights for music in the 20th century. Out of the topics he had planned, he was not able to realise his intentions to compile the system of musical styles and genres, which was intended to be the fourth of the higher theoretical disciplines).

At this point, let us also briefly mention Janeček's two late publications dedicated to the subject of harmony, that is, the textbook *Harmony Through Analysis* from the year 1963, and the publication *Compositional Practice in the Field of Classical Harmony*, released in 1973.

In *Harmony Through Analysis* Janeček proves to be an excellent and experienced pedagogue. His lifetime of pedagogical experience led him to realise the need for a specific methodical grasp of the explanation and teaching of harmony, aimed primarily (but not exclusively) at the students of interpretational majors, and that is in the form of analysing specific musical examples. The standard method of teaching this subject is primarily through solving practical assignments – most often on paper or with the use of a piano. For a performer, however, it is important to understand the complete (therefore also the harmonic) structure of the musical piece they are studying. Such skills are best developed precisely through the analysis of examples taken from real, live music. In *Harmony Through Analysis* Janeček also applies many of the discoveries and concepts that he found through his music-theoretic research.

In the book *Compositional Practice in the Field of Classical Harmony* Janeček presents his view of the function of his systematically formulated principles in solving specific composition tasks when working with consonances, dissonances, figuration, working with alterations and stylistic work. In the methodology supplement, he gives attention to the prerequisites of composition work. In the preface, he states that his goal was not to write a treatise, but to create and present a text serving as a guide for the subject with a focus on compositional practice.

---

11 Karel Janeček, "Rytmus starý a nový" [New and Old Rhythm], *Tempo* 12 (1932–33): 357–365.

3. The Path to *Foundations of Modern Harmony*

As mentioned above, *Foundations of Modern Harmony* summarise the thoughts of Karel Janeček, which had been maturing for the previous 30 years. Thus, it is not a one-off, but rather a summarising climax of a long-term process of perpetual searching, creative thinking and building. From the 1930's onward, he constantly devoted his attention to the subject of harmony in numerous studies and articles, published in professional journals and yearbooks such as early as the beginning of the thirties of the 20th century. He searched for, and found, new paths, without interrupting the continuity of the development and the continuation of the great works of preceding generations. Throughout this period, he gradually searched for, found and formulated, numerous topics and methods for problem solving, which then found their place in *Foundations of Modern Harmony*. These were organically integrated into the structure of this title, which brought the entire process to a conclusion.

The first published study, an article entitled *Modern Harmony. A General Outline*, appeared in 1931 in the magazine *Tempo*.[12] In it, Janeček presents his view on modern harmony as a constant expansion of chord possibilities. We can observe and assess a dual mode of action in chords: either separate (in isolation) or in context (in mutual relations). In this regard, we can then distinguish between stabilised and non-stabilised chords. Non-stabilised chords are the carriers of kinetic energy that are ambiguous in terms of direction: e.g. the dominant seventh G B D F can normally be diatonic to the key of C major, or, after being enharmonically modified, as an altered chord G B D E♯ in the key of F♯ major or D major, or as G B C✕ E♯ in the key of B major. Furthermore, Janeček states that the creation of new chords is facilitated by expanding and enriching existing chords with new notes, and also by their deformation resulting from alteration. One of the possible steps towards modern harmony is also the application of un-resolving non-chord tones (suspensions, passing tones and neighbouring tones), which, over time, begin to appear as chord tones, and the resulting harmonies start to become perceived as new chords. This is, after all, nothing new, for example in the past the seventh chord also became an accepted chord-type through the emancipation of the seventh (originally a non-chord tone, used e.g. as a passing tone) as a full-fledged chord tone. This study also mentions the imaginary tone, a topic that Janeček elaborated upon in more detail in other studies and that plays an important role in *Foundations of Modern Harmony*.

Janeček paid close attention to the topic of imaginary tones in 1932 in the study *The Significance of Imaginary Pitches in Harmony*, published in the journal *Music Education*.[13] Here, the imaginary tone is defined as a melodic tone, which remains in the

---

12 Karel Janeček, "Moderní harmonie. Souhrnný náčrt" [Modern Harmony. A General Outline], *Tempo* 11 (1931–32): 46–52.
13 Karel Janeček, "O významu imaginárních tónů v harmonii" [The Significance of Imaginary Pitches in Harmony], *Hudební výchova* [Music Education] 13 (1932): 8–9, 22–25.

mind of the listener even after it stops sounding and is cancelled by the following tone, if it passes stepwise by the interval of a second, especially the minor second. In the case of intervals greater than the second, it remains undisturbed. Thanks to the effects of imaginary tones, it is possible to express harmony in linear form, in the context of a single real voice, making possible the existence of the latent harmony phenomenon. In the context of the consideration of the harmonic effect of imaginary tones, Janeček argues that a perfect connection of two consecutive chords occurs only in the cases of absolute cancellation of imaginary tones. In this context, it is also possible to find the explanation for the specific effect of the resolution of leading tones. It can be stated that the discovery and formulation of the characteristics of the behaviour and function of imaginary tones is one of the greatest of Janeček's discoveries, allowing us to understand some of the harmonic phenomena of modern harmony in general. Let it also be noted that we sometimes encounter the interchangeable usage of the terms "imaginary tone" and the term "pacit",[14] invented by Leoš Janáček. In this regard, Janeček warns that using the terms interchangeably is erroneous, and that the terms describe two differing phenomena: while the effects of Janáček's pacits are physiological in nature, Janeček's imaginary tones are psychological phenomena, occurring only in our minds.

The third of Janeček's texts dedicated to the subject of harmony is *The Foundation, Structure, and Nature of New Chords*, published in 1933 in the journal *Tempo*.[15] In this text, Janeček ponders the questions of mutual inferiority and superiority between harmony and melody, contemplates the historical development of harmony and polyphony in general and also considers the influences that projected out of polyphony into harmonic thought. Janeček reminds us of the process of development of harmonic thought from Rameau to the present day:

"Harmony can be *independent*, i.e. its meaning can be in its existence itself. We must put extra emphasis on this truth, due to the fact that musicians trained by classicism tend to see harmony as mere 'accompaniment', a mere support for the musical thought. Their limited experience partially proves them right: cases of harmony appearing in isolation are rare […] I cannot resist quoting Rameau's opinion of this matter (from *Traité de l'harmonie*): 'At first it might seem that harmony originated from melody, that is, through individual melodic voices intertwining to create harmony, but for each of the voices *a path had to be created* first for them to appropriately harmonise […] Thus it is harmony that leads us, not melody.' […] We can assume that the first harmonic units were created indirectly, i.e. they were not searched for – they were a result of primitive polyphonic efforts. Experience (more than speculation) classified such created chords and chose some of the especially useful ones, which then became the foundation for

---

14 "Although *pocit* is an often-used word which refers to sensation, *pacit* is a very rarely used term. I felt that *illusion* would be the best English word, even though it does not give quite the same sense of peculiarity conveyed by Janáček's term." Michael Brim Beckerman, *Janáček as Theoretist* (Stuyvesant, NY: Pendragon Press, 1994), 38.
15 Karel Janeček, "Vznik, stavba a ráz nových souzvuků" [The Foundation, Structure, and Nature of New Chords], *Tempo* 12 (1933): 164–172.

the most primitive independent harmonic thought. (In the advancing Middle Ages, those were only perfect fourths and fifths). Vague experimentation was made obsolete by *discovered regularities*; melodic principles which used to be the only authority were seized and subordinated to *harmonic principles*. Safely understandable chords became the foundations; their absolute harmonic effects were naturally most independently applied where the effects of other forms ceased to be sufficient, mainly at the end of a melodic phrase. Conclusions are the main domain of independently intended harmony – harmony of this type shall be called *essential harmony*. In places intended in way other than harmonic, the purpose of harmony is secondary – such harmony shall be called *passing harmony*. […] This arrangement of matters created the possibility of *further development*. The principle of absolute clarity of the initial foundation harmonies did not apply to passing harmony. Passing harmonies, as the result of other formative elements, were not thus as restricted in their construction, and there could be more of them. Their colour could be considerably different, due to the fact that they drew less attention. Similar to the first essential harmonies resulted from the harmonies created through polyphonic experiments, i.e. from passing harmonies, the later essential harmonies were also created in this manner: *passing harmonies became the model for creating new essential harmonies*. This is still being applied to this day […] The gap between possible (= understandable enough) essential harmonies and passing harmonies has always been considerably wide, especially in the times of increased interest in polyphony. After all, even the possibilities for passing harmonies were limited by the applied tonal system."[16]

Furthermore, Janeček gives attention to the terms "consonance" and "dissonance". He talks about two principles of interpreting the perception of consonance and dissonance: the characteristic of the first principle is based on the psychological interpretation of the acoustic existence of the overtone series: the series smoothly transitions from consonant intervals to dissonant intervals, given that the consonant intervals manifest themselves most strongly (due to their position in the series) and the effect of the intervals gradually weakens as we get to the dissonant intervals. In discussing consonance and dissonance, Janeček held the view that the barrier between consonances and dissonances shifts over time – former dissonances become consonant. It must be said that he later reconsidered his standpoint, though he did not change his opinions on historical development: in the context of the many challenges of naming the problems of modern harmony and the search for their solution, the terms consonance and dissonance later receive a new interpretation reflecting the musical language of the 20th century. This will be discussed further below. The second principle of perceiving consonances and dissonances is based on the combination of two or more overtone series: the closer both series are to each other, i.e. the more tones they share, the more consonant is the resulting interval. Janeček devotes further consideration to the question of the relation between the degree of chord complexity and the degree of consonance and dissonance; in this context, he also ponders the problems related to triadic combinations.

---

16 Ibid., 164–165.

As a conclusion to this study, Janeček presents a proposal for the classification of harmonies, as suggested by contemporary developments:

"Let me add a few practical questions. The deliberate use of the extensive material of today's harmony is impossible without clear classification. The study of the old 'strict' harmony is pedagogically necessary, it is a necessary preparation and foundation, on which, after all the entirety of today's harmony has been built. Development brought by modifications and substantial changes of old principles, in certain directions the changes were so significant, that it can be called a complete collapse of old patterns. Thus, it is not sensible to insist on the validity of those principles by expanding them or creating aberrant definitions. Where it is needed, it is necessary to build anew, even if it means from the ground up. On the other hand, a mere abolition without a replacement would create chaos where there is none. If the context is only the harmonic material, with no regard to its possible relations, we certainly cannot make do with classifying only by a single variable. As with historical harmonic material, we consider the *structure* and *character* (colour) of harmony. The old Rameau structure, for long considered to be the only possibility, became merely one of the classes (harmonic triads), besides which other construction principles arose, even of higher order (polychords). Colour is defined by the structure (whether it is major or minor, which are much more complex terms today), the complex tonal relations (degree of consonance, resp. dissonance). Especially this delicate part of modern harmonic mechanism deserves more complex classification than before. Of course, the colour is a *quality*. Classifying qualities qua *immeasurable* phenomena might be merely a matter of *agreement*."[17]

Janeček goes on to present the actual proposal for practical classification into: a) three tone consonances constructed by thirds; b) dominant consonances without the semitone; c) consonances by fourths and non-dominant consonances by thirds without the semitones; d) dominant consonances containing the semitone; e) non-dominant dissonances with major sevenths; f) dissonances with semitone intervals; expressed by minor ninths; and g) clusters (groups of minor seconds). His approach is a specific case and a testament to his persistent search. It is not intended to be an end in itself; its goal must always be to respond to practical needs, in this case the full specifications and possibilities of modern musical language. As a footnote, Janeček states: "Allow me to highlight that by the terms 'consonance' and 'dissonance' I mean the static colour of harmony. I am not referring to the harmonic progression, therefore neither their relations given by their surroundings nor their internal kinetic forces."[18] One further comment: it is worth comparing Janeček's proposal for practical classification, both in the approach and the result, to the system of chord classification presented by Paul Hindemith in *Unterweisung im Tonsatz*.

Hereby let it be stated again that, in the approach presented three decades later in *Foundations of Modern Harmony*, Janeček adopts a completely new, ground-breaking

---

17 Ibid., 171–172.
18 Ibid.

standpoint regarding the sensible classification of harmonies and the questions of interpreting the phenomena of consonances and dissonances. This standpoint is general, systematically pure and diligent, and at the same time it respects all the needs and expectations of musical practice, in the form they were set by the contemporary development of musical language. The thoughts expressed in the conclusion of the above-mentioned study are both the first steps towards this goal and a testament to Janeček's constant and relentless research.

In the study *The Breakdown of the Diatonic System*, published in 1935 in the journal *Tempo*,[19] Janeček focuses his attention on the gradual transformation of diatony into chromatics in European music. Similarly, as the birth and development of diatony occurred by increasing the number of notes from the original five (pentatonic) into seven, so was the further development towards chromatics accompanied by further increasing their number – until the final limit of twelve notes was reached, which divide the octave into the same number of equal (tempered) semitone steps. The historical process of chromatisation is closely related to the gradual development of tonal thought, especially in the various forms of deforming pure diatony into altered diatony, with the gradual culmination into modern twelve-tone equal temperament. Janeček mentions three methods through which this occurred: 1) chromatisation through intermediate tones or deformation by altered melodic tones; 2) the creation of foreign passing harmonies through such chromatisation; and 3) the application of deliberately chosen unrelated (sharing no notes) harmonies, which are, however, not the result of the melodic chromatisation of leading voices. Janeček also warns that this development does not the mean the end of diatony. The statement does not, of course, anticipate the possibility of a return to pure diatony.

The last study, published before he began working on *Foundations of Modern Harmony*, is the study *The Principle of Harmonic Inversion* published in the journal *Rhythm* in 1943.[20] Here, Janeček evidently assumes the views that form one of the important standpoints presented in *Foundations of Modern Harmony*, that is, his view on the question of consonance and dissonance, which can be expressed as follows: it is true that for any consonance, its mirrored inversion carries the exact same degree of consonance. This standpoint is also in perfect accord with the practically verified consonance of the minor triad with the major triad, which is its inversion. (The question of the consonance of the minor triad caused many sleepless nights to the proponents of harmonic monism in the context of the historical discourse between the proponents of harmonic dualism and proponents of harmonic monism; the proponents of monism based their argument for assessing the question of consonance/dissonance on the structure of the overtone series, which is perfectly consonant with the major triad, while the minor tri-

---

19 Karel Janeček, "Rozvrat diatoniky" [The Breakdown of the Diatonic System], *Tempo* 14 (1935): 151–154, 191–195, 227–231.
20 Karel Janeček, "Princip harmonické inverse" [The Principle of Harmonic Inversion], *Rytmus* [Rhythm] 8 (1942–43): 54–57.

ad is in conflict with the series.) With his standpoint, Janeček clearly assumes a dualistic point of view.

Further studies – *The Harmonic Possibilities of the Chromatic System*[21] and *The System of Characteristic Chords*[22] – were published in 1947, i.e. when he was already working on *Foundations of Modern Harmony*. In the period before the release of *Foundations of Modern Harmony* in 1965, Janeček also produced a number of studies on the subject of harmony: *Fundamental Harmonic Problems and their Solutions* (1955)[23] and *The Harmonic Material of the Tempered Chromatic System* (1961).[24] During the same period, two chapters of the yet-to-be-published *Foundations of Modern Harmony* appeared: *The Expression of Chords* (1958)[25] and *Sonic Characteristics of the Harmonic Material* (1962).[26]

---

21 Karel Janeček, "Harmonické možnosti chromatiky" [The Harmonic Possibilities of the Chromatic System], *Rytmus* [Rhythm] 11 (1947): 21–23.
22 Karel Janeček, "Systém charakteristických akordů" [The System of Characteristic Chords], *Rytmus* [Rhythm] 11 (1947): 66–69.
23 Karel Janeček, "Základní harmonické problémy a jejich řešení" [Fundamental Harmonic Problems and their Solutions], *Musikologie: Sborník pro hudební vědu a kritiku* [Musicology: Annual for Musical Science and Criticism] (Praha: SNKLHU, 1955), 87–129.
24 Karel Janeček, "Harmonický materiál temperované chromatiky: Kapitola ze Základů temperované harmonie" [The Harmonic Material of the Tempered Chromatic System: Chapter of Foundations of Tempered Harmony], *Hudební věda* [Musical Science Quarterly] 4 (1961): 81–119.
25 Karel Janeček, *Vyjádření souzvuků: Kapitola ze Základů temperované harmonie* [The Expression of Chords: Chapter of Foundations of Tempered Harmony] (Praha: Svaz čs. skladatelů [Union of Czechoslovakian Composers, 1958).
26 Karel Janeček, "Zvukové vlastnosti harmonického materiálu: Kapitola ze Základů temperované harmonie" [Sonic Characteristics of the Harmonic Material: Chapter of Foundations of Tempered Harmony], *Živá hudba: Sborník prací hudební fakulty AMU* [Living Music: Collection of Works by the Music Faculty of AMU] (Praha: SPN, 1962), 69–93.

4. *Foundations of Modern Harmony* –
General Overview and Characteristics of the Main Questions

As Janeček states in the introduction (in his commentary on the intention and circumstances of the work's creation), he began working on *Foundations of Modern Harmony* since 1942 and he completed it in the May of 1949. On top of that, during 1948–1949 he worked on making the older text more concise and even reworked what was needed. Let it be said here that the preparation of the text for publication was complicated by obstacles created by the ideologies of the time: we can see their influence in, for example, some of the changes in terminology that accompanied the process of preparing and reworking the text, for example the multiple changes of the title of the publication: instead of the intended title, *Foundations of Modern Harmony*, he considered such titles as *Foundations of New Harmony* or *Foundations of Tempered Harmony*. In this respect, Janeček states:

"I had temporarily given up the designation modern for reasons resulting from the abnormal state of Czech culture in the 1950's. (Instead of 'modern' one could equally well say 'new'; the designation 'tempered' refers to the European tempered chromatic system, seen as the general foundation of all our music.) Today the term 'modern' has had its original meaning restored, without the derogatory connotations that accompanied it in the 1950's, when anything even remotely connected with avant-garde attempts in the arts was indiscriminately condemned. Therefore I have returned to the original designation. The reason for returning to my original term 'imaginary pitch', rather than continuing to use the later term 'thought pitch', is similar: today such a term will no longer lead anyone to suspect it of being a disguised remnant of idealist philosophy."[27]

In relation to the conceptual intent, Janeček strongly warns that it is not intended to be a textbook: "Knowledge of textbook harmony is expected of the reader. The book is not, however, intended only for composers, but for all musicians who come in contact with new music."[28] In this approach as well, the novelty and specific originality of Janeček's work is clear: while older harmony textbooks, intended as "manuals" for mastering the "correct" technical composition procedures, were characterised by their normative character, which manifested itself as e.g. a system of binding working rules – prohibitions, orders and recommendations, compliance with which was a necessary requirement for "correctly" solving the specific assignments of every practical exercise

---

27 Janeček, *Foundations of Modern Harmony*, 37 (pages refers to english translation of Janeček's text). Evidence of what has been said could be, for example, the names of studies published by Janeček from 1958 to 1962, through which he informed the academic community about chosen parts of the upcoming publication: *The Expression of Chords* or *Sonic Characteristics of the Harmonic Material*. The testimony of Karel Risinger also attests to this situation. In a text published in 1963 he mentions the existence of "never before published (Janeček's) study *Foundations of New Harmony*, which was created in 1942–1949 and its manuscript is already completed." See Karel Risinger, *Vůdčí osobnosti české moderní hudební teorie: Otakar Šín, Alois Hába, Karel Janeček* [Leading Personalities in Modern Czech Music Theory: Otakar Šín, Alois Hába, Karel Janeček] (Praha: SHV, 1963), 141.

28 Janeček, *Foundations of Modern Harmony*, 34.

– from elementary tasks, regarding the structure of chords and connecting them into a meaningful compositional unit, up to the absolute mastery of more complex tasks related to, for example, the subject of modulation and alteration. However, Janeček did not at all strive for a normative manual of any kind. As can be seen even today – with the hindsight of half a century – such decision is necessary to get a music-theoretical grasp of harmony and other expressions of the musical language of the first half of the 20th century. Compared to preceding epochs, the 20th century is characterised by not one, but multiple instances of musical language (we need think only of the diversity of individual styles, and the technical composition tools stemming from them, in the works of composers such as Schönberg, Stravinsky, Prokofiev, Bartók, Webern, Berg, Shostakovich, Honegger, Hindemith and Martinů. Thus, to find and formulate generally valid mutual rules is impossible, primarily because the general approach to musical expression is changing, which is after all true even for the artistic, literary and dramatic fields …). The meaning of communication is therefore found in a different plane, in a disproportionately larger area than mere control over the tools of the craft. It can, therefore, be asked: how does Janeček intend to present the matters of modern harmony? It is a musicological understanding, characterised by all of the attributes of scientific research, however directly aimed at musical practice. Instead of being a traditional "manual", it is intended to be a set of incentives and inspirations for developing one's own skills of observation, generalisation, setting one's perspective towards the perception of musical language, observing not only "how it's made" but also "why it's made", towards individual creative thinking, filling in the details of what's observed, and searching for, finding and discovering not only the phenomena itself, but also the principles through which they were created and are supported.

The initial considerations of *Foundations of Modern Harmony* are oriented towards the questions of creating and classifying harmonic material (chords). As historical experience shows, the subject of creating harmonic material and its classification tends to be, in the music-theoretical literature devoted to harmony, the standard entry point to the study of the issue. The traditional approach to harmony, with its roots in the soil of diatony (either pure or altered), as a continuation of Rameau,[29] derives the principles for creating harmonic material (chords) based on the application of the principles of layering thirds to create the basic shape (triads, seventh chords, ninth chords …) and then the alterations derived from it (inversions, different positions, open and closed voicing, doubling or omitting specific tones that are a part of its structure). However, modern harmony which takes the tonal system of twelve-tone equal temperament for granted, does not have a similar template available to it. Within the framework of the twelve-tone equal temperament, it is not possible to work with the classical interpretation of

---

29 This remark reminds us of the fact that Jean-Philippe Rameau interpreted chord inversions as modifications of their basic shape and thus made a step towards a new view of chords as harmonic units, freed from previous rules and the conventions of figured bass practice, opening the way for further development of harmony and harmonic thought.

intervals – being measured by the number of diatonic steps they consist of. No distinction is made between the diatonic semitone (C–D♭) and the chromatic semitone (C–C♯), and each tone in the twelve-tone equal temperament is equal, not defined by the chromatic alteration (raising or lowering) of any of the other tones. In this situation, it is, for example, no longer meaningful to think about any alteration or chromatic relation of chords or other related phenomena. The possibility of creating any chord shape consisting of at least two tones, and up to a maximum of twelve tones, can therefore be assumed. These and other actualities must be taken into account during the invention of a systematically pure conception of creating and classifying harmonic material with the requirement of its being closely related to musical practice. It is necessary to redefine the terms "chord", "simultaneity" and "tone cluster". As can be seen, the intent of and the decision for grasping the principles of creating and classifying harmonic material brings about a number of problems and incentives for solutions. Janeček further states:

"Although I originally intended to deal only with static harmony [*harmonic statics* refers to the research and classification of chords in isolation, assessed individually outside of context], I had laid the foundations for kinetic harmony a long time before beginning systematic work on the book [*harmonic kinetics* refers to the function of chords in harmonic motion, i.e. in the context of the progression of chords in time – both preceding and following, thus, we can also say, in the functional effects of chords]. Already in 1932 I had published an article entitled *The Significance of Imaginary Pitches in Harmony*. For me, the concept of the imaginary pitch links static and kinetic conceptions of harmony. [...] The discourse on the expression of chords (*Chapter V*), founded on the phenomenon of the imaginary pitch, is placed between the chapters on static and kinetic harmony. A knowledgeable reader will recognize that the concept of the imaginary pitch as I have defined it is entirely different from Janáček's 'pseudo-sensed tone' [pacitový tón]; [...]"[30]

Having explored the intent and the crucial default thoughts of Karel Janeček, let us turn our attention to the author's main discoveries and theses, which were made and formulated in this study. Much is said by the sequence of the individual chapters. The first seven chapters can be described as the systematic section: I – *The Harmonic Material of the Tempered Chromatic System*, II – *Sonic Characteristics of the Harmonic Material*, IIIa – *Classification of the Harmonic Material*, IIIb – *Triadic Combinations*, IV – *Disposition of Chords*, V – *Expression of Chords*, VI – *Harmonic Motion* (IVa – *Concepts and Principles*, VIb – *Functions and their Combinations*, VIc – *Function in Harmonic Progression*), VII – *Problems*. The two final chapters (VIII – *Compositional Practice*, IX – *Analytical Practice*) elaborate on the application of the results of the preceding systematic thoughts on the practice of music composition and practice. The text concludes with a set of supplementary tables, summaries and indexes.

---

30 Janeček, *Foundations of Modern Harmony*, 32.

During his research on harmonic material, Janeček pays close attention to the term *chord* and the broader term *simultaneity*.[31] Even in classical harmony we deal with chords and non-chord simultaneities. While we understand the term simultaneity as the simultaneous sounding of any given set of tones, a chord needs to fulfil certain requirements. Emil Hradecký describes the term chord as a *harmonic unit*.[32] As such, a chord is capable of being the *carrier of the harmonic element* of the musical stream. Classical harmony study largely connects the definition of a chord with the number of included tones (at least three) and with the structure of layered thirds. The default unit is then the three-tone chord – triad, created by stacking two thirds, adding another third then creates the tetrad-seventh chord, and adding yet another third creates the pentad-ninth chord, eventually even more complex chords through further triad stacking. By creating such basic chord shapes, we can derive alterations (such as inversions, different positions and open and closed voicings) by rearranging the individual notes, doubling them, or omitting some of the less important ones. Simultaneity that fulfils those conditions – chords – can easily fulfil the above mentioned role of the carrier of the harmonic element of the musical stream, however, we also encounter non-chord simultaneities – the so-called *passing harmonies* – as the result of the horizontal, i.e. melodic progression of the involved voices, manifesting through the presence of non-chord tones (passing tones, suspensions, and neighbouring tones). This does not mean that any harmonic unit fulfilling the given conditions must be a chord; for example, the cadential six-four chord (even though it fulfils the mentioned conditions) is not seen as an individual chord in classic harmony: it is perceived as a double suspension from above. During the examination of this subject in historical context it can also be stated that e.g. the seventh chord, which is a commonly accepted chord today, received this privilege after a long period of historical development, after it had acted as a passing harmony in the musical stream: the presence of the seventh as a chord tone in this harmonic unit was not implicit; the seventh had been gradually introduced into this position, most often as a passing tone, and only later was it emancipated as a proper chord tone (see also Janeček's commentary in *The Foundation, Structure, and Nature of New Chords* from 1933; and see above: "*passing harmonies became the model for creating new essential harmonies*"). As can be seen, to assess whether the analysed harmony is a chord or only a passing harmony, it is not sufficient to analyse it in isolation; it is necessary to analyse it in the context of what came before and after in the progression of the musical stream, as well as with regard to the horizontal (melodic) progression of voices, through whose interplay the given harmony occurs. A role can also be played even by imaginary tones and their effects.

---

31 In the English translation of Janeček's *Foundations of Modern Harmony* term "simultaneity" have been replaced by "chord" (meaning any group of simultaneous pitches) and term "harmony" is used for a harmonically intelligible chord – see Editor's note on p. 42; in this text the generally used terms are left for the sake of comprehensibility even for those who have not yet read the Janeček's book.

32 Emil Hradecký, *Úvod do studia tonální harmonie* [Introduction to the Study of Tonal Harmony], 2nd ed. (Praha: Supraphon, 1972), 200.

Anyone who seeks a music-theoretical understanding of harmony in the system of twelve-tone equal temperament is therefore faced with this question: how can we, under the given circumstances, define a chord in cases when we cannot rely on the support of the usual structure of stacked thirds, nor in e.g. the traditional understanding of the root note, when dissonance manifests differently than it does in traditional harmony, or when there is no reason to set a limit for the maximum number of tones?

In the *Chapter IIIa – Classification of the Harmonic Material* Janeček defines chords in a general manner: "[…] it is a *harmonically intelligible* group of pitches, *ranked higher* than formations containing fewer pitches, and it is *independent* of its surroundings."[33] To the listed requirements for harmonic comprehensibility, superiority and independence he adds a general commentary from which it is apparent that, without assessing the context, it is impossible to assess and with certainty decide whether the analysed harmony is a chord or a non-chord unit. The assessment criteria tend to be ambiguous; subjective factors also play a role. The only option for an objective and exact understanding of harmonic material thus remains to investigate the general harmonic material. This is what Janeček does in the *Chapter I – The Harmonic Material of the Tempered Chromatic System*. As the unit of measurement, replacing the intervals derived from traditional diatony, he sets the chromatic semitone, and individual intervals are then designated with numbers expressing the distance of the interval.[34] Through the interval structure, defined by the sequence of interval distances expressed by numbers, is then defined the specific *simultaneity-type*, e.g. the traditional major triad is defined as the number 43 and the minor triad as 34. Simultaneity-types can be handled in a similar manner to how traditional chords used to be: they can be altered by rearranging the notes, or by their doubling or tripling, or they can also be transposed. The designated number defining the specific simultaneity-type is referred to as the *orientation scheme*. The orientation scheme is not, however, equivalent to the root position of the traditional chord. While the root position of the traditional chord represented its optimal harmonically representative form, which then allowed the derivation of further also harmonically applicable modifications (inversions, position changes, changes of disposition) and

---

33 Janeček, *Foundations of Modern Harmony*, 93.
34 The principle of using a numbering system, tied to the equal-temperament semitone as the basic unit of measurement of the interval distance between notes, chosen with the goal of characterising, defining, cataloguing and registering multiple tone units (so-called *tone groups*), through the choice of tonal material and interval structure independent from diatonic quantification, found its application in 20th century music theory through many authors: see, for example, Allen Forte, *The Structure of Atonal Music* (London: Yale University Press, 1973), and in the Czechoslovakia Alois Piňos, *Tónové skupiny* [Tone groups] (Praha: Editio Supraphon, 1971). It is a general principle with a variety of possibilities for application. As is mentioned by Piňos in the introduction to his book, tone groups can be the ancient Greek tetrachords, diatony, modes both medieval and modern, simultaneities, various slices of the total of twelve tones… Janeček's classification of harmonic material and all operations on it also fully adheres to the characteristics mentioned. The choice of specific operations with material grasped in this manner is then driven by the goal pursued by the author; in Janeček's interpretation, this goal is the search for, and the finding of, the characteristics and classification of harmonic material, i.e. harmony types, applicable as essential harmonic units – chords.

transpositions, the aim of the orientation scheme is not the optimal harmonic representation of a given simultaneity-type, it only serves as a cataloguing tool during simultaneity-type classification and comparison. To avoid accidental duplicates (in terms of mistaking any alteration for the basic shape) in the categorisation, Janeček sets further conditions for its derivation: the orientation scheme must be derived from the closest possible disposition of a given simultaneity-type, and if a given simultaneity-type allows two or more possibilities for the closest alteration, then the valid alteration for creating the orientation scheme is the one with the lowest numerical value of its orientation scheme. This measure rules out any accidental duplicates, and ensures that every simultaneity-type is assigned exactly one orientation scheme and vice versa.

Janeček classifies all of the simultaneity-types that can be created within the scope of the twelve-tone equal temperament into groups based on the number of involved tones (two-tone, three-tone, four-tone, etc. groups). The group of the highest order is the twelve-tone class. He supplements the orientation scheme for individual examples with the so-called *harmonic scheme*, i.e. a disposition which allows – especially with simultaneities of higher order – to present the given simultaneity-type in the form of an example of a harmonically intelligible modification, serving as one of the multiple possible possibilities of such dispositions, which the given simultaneity-type allows. The purpose of the harmonic scheme is thus to serve only as an aid; the essential component for classifying harmonic material is then the orientation scheme.

Let us summarize: while traditional theory of harmony employed classification based on the system and terminology used to define the root position (major triads, minor triads, diminished triads, augmented triads, sixth chords, diminished-seventh chords, augmented-major seventh chords, etc.) to catalogue the individual harmonically applicable simultaneity-types, modern theory of harmony uses the above-mentioned orientation scheme to catalogue simultaneities that are potentially harmonically applicable within the scope of modern musical language. In the above lies the only difference in approach between traditional and modern harmony, necessitated (as mentioned earlier) by the transformation of the historical diatonic tonal system (pure or altered) into the tonal system of twelve-tone equal temperament as a part of the procedural changes that accompanied the development of harmonic events in European music in the late 19th and early 20th centuries. With regard to the application of further classification criteria (dispositions, transposition), no real difference exists between the approaches of traditional and modern harmony.

During the examination of the primary attributes of harmonic material, it is possible to find, as a part of the classes groups, attributes of individual simultaneity-types such as symmetry/asymmetry and inversion, and it is possible to find negative mirrored versions of the individual simultaneity-types. It is possible to examine their sonic properties – based on the presence of the so-called dissonant elements, i.e. the intervals 1 (semitone), 2 (whole-tone), 6 (tritone) and the triad 44 (augmented triad). It is necessary to highlight the fact that Janeček assumes, with regard to the question of consonance and dissonance, a completely different standpoint than he did in the study *The Foundation, Structure, and Nature of New Chords* (1933). He considers the listed dissonant elements as a stable fact, and does not anticipate any historical shifting of the boundary between consonances and dissonances. He perceives the presence of dissonant elements as a method for diversifying the sound of simultaneities: each of the elements has a different character, which manifests itself in the sonic character of the simultaneities of which it is a part. Dissonances cannot be quantified; each represents a specific sound quality. Janeček metaphorically characterises the effects of the individual dissonant elements: "The semitone (1) is *obtrusively piercing* […] The whole-tone (2) is generally *insipid, unobtrusive* […] The tritone (6) is pleasantly stimulating […] The augmented triad (44) is *noticeable without being piercing*."[35] Based on the dissonant elements present in the individual simultaneity-types, he then derives the so-called dissonant characteristic (e.g. the dominant seventh chord G B D F displays the dissonant characteristic 26, through the presence of the dissonant element 2 – the whole-tone between F G – and the dissonant element 6 – the tritone between B F) for each simultaneity-type. Among the simultaneities with the same dissonant character, natural sonic relations can be observed (with regards to the above-mentioned example, let us compare, for example, the altered dominant seventh chord G B D♭ F from this perspective). This logically applies for every pair of simultaneities harmonies that are the inversions of each other. The stated fact also relates to the historical conflict between harmonic dualism and monism: while orthodox monists attempt to, inter alia, classify the minor triad as a dissonance, their argument being its incompatibility with the overtone series (even though such an argument is in opposition to practical hearing experience), Janeček's standpoint is simple: neither the minor nor the major triad contain any dissonant elements, and thus the minor triad, as the inversion of the consonant major triad, is also consonant. In this regard, Janeček presents and formulates the *principle of harmonic inversion*, thus expressing his categorical dualistic proponence.

As a part of his exploration of harmonic material, Janeček presents one more option for creating and classifying specific simultaneity-types, and that is by creating triadic combinations. He refers to simultaneities created by combining consonant triads (the only consonant triads are the major and minor triads; all other harmonies of higher order are dissonant).

The major and minor triads serve as the primary units for this method. Indeed, even the traditional simultaneities consisting of four and more notes could be interpreted as combinations,[36] e.g. the major ninth chord can be interpreted as an true combination of the triads G B D and D F A (overalapping in the tone D). Again, Janeček takes a very

---

35 Janeček, *Foundations of Modern Harmony*, 74–75.
36 In Czech music-theoretical literature, see the approach of Otakar Šín, *Úplná nauka o harmonii na základě melodie a rytmu* [Complete Theory of Harmony on the Basis of Melody and Rhythm]. 2. vyd., přepracované a rozšířené [2nd ed., revised and expanded]. Praha: Hudební Matice [The Music Association], 1933.

exact approach to the classification and cataloguing of triadic combinations. He distinguishes between complete and incomplete, and true and partial triadic combinations. Depending on the number of consonant essential chords involved in a complete combination, he distinguishes between four categories: 1. uncombined basic triads; 2. true combinations of two basic triads; 3. true combinations of three basic triads; 4. true combinations of four basic triads. It can be stated that each of the simultaneity-types described in the chapter *Chapter I – The Harmonic Material of the Tempered Chromatic System* can be transformed into a combination via changes in disposition; the necessary requirement is the need for audible comprehensibility of the disposition: e.g. the hexad 12132 – C C♯ D♯ E G A – can be transformed into a partial combination of the basic chords C E G – C E♭ G – A C♯ E. This simultaneity is referred to as a partial combination because the basic chords involved in the combination contain shared notes. Out of interest, let us present an example of transforming a twelve-tone simultaneity into a complete true combination of four basic chords: C E G – D F♯ A – F♯ A♯ C♯ – G♯ B D♯.

To make sure the combination is comprehensible, in the disposition it is necessary to present the individual involved chords independently, and with adequate distance between each other in the tonal space (see e.g. the introduction in *Symphony No. 5 Di tre re* by A. Honegger). During the examination and classification of combinations Janeček distinguishes between *triadic combinations*, described here, and *functional combinations* – see below in relation to the treatise on harmonic function.

It is also necessary to emphasise the fact that all of the above considerations are a part of his examination and assessment of static harmony.

In the next part let us mention the most important of Janeček's discoveries and harmonic phenomena and principles formulated by him, which however function in the realm of harmonic kinetics (harmonic motion). Here we can mention his explanation of the existence and effects of *imaginary tones* (he elaborated on this subject in 1932 in the study *The Significance of Imaginary Pitches in Harmony* – see above).

Of utmost importance and validity is the *principle of the pure tonic, principle of the leading tone* and the *functional principle* stemming from these, which were discovered and exactly formulated by Janeček. The principle of the pure tonic is formulated by Janeček as follows: "*A harmonic phrase gravitates most naturally to a final consonant chord that is disturbed neither by uncancelled or incompletely cancelled harmonic imaginary pitches, nor by tonal imaginary pitches that form a tritone with the real pitches of the final tonic.*"[37] A historical example of the function of the principle of the pure tonic is the creation and early development of European tonal thought, the abolition of some of the medieval church modes and the preservation of the ionian and the aeolian modes as the foundations of the newly born major and minor tonalities. Careful examination of the individual church modes reveals that the very tones that characterise each of the modes – the dorian sixth, phrygian second, lydian fourth and mixolydian seventh – are at the distance of a tritone from one of the tones of the final tonic. Only the ionian and aeolian

---

37 Janeček, *Foundations of Modern Harmony*, 246.

modes contain no notes that would form the tritone interval with any other notes contained in the tonic, and thus do not weaken its effect. The other modes either abolish or alter the "interfering" characteristic notes, which is essentially the same thing. The principle of the pure tonic is intended as a statement of a certain functional fact; it is absolutely not intended to be a normative "manual". Quite the opposite! Janeček adds: "The principle of the pure tonic can be *ignored*, resulting in cadences that are to varying degrees intentionally unsatisfying, partially or even fully open-ended."[38] The tonic can be dissonant, it can be interfered with by the directly preceding or even simultaneously sounding *antitonic* (the term antitonic refers to the chord which is a tritone away from the tonic, and thus creating the state of the highest degree of functional remoteness, inter alia, due to the effects of the multiple tritone intervals between its tones and the tonic. Janeček does not directly define the term in *Foundations of Modern Harmony*, he establishes it later in the 1976 study *Additional Notes to Some Phenomena of Harmonic and Tonal Thinking*).[39]

Janeček supplements the effects of the principle of the pure tonic through his explanation of another principle, which is applied in tandem with the principle of the pure tonic. This is the principle of the leading tone. His discovery and formulation is supported by historical experience with the subject of the leading tone and its purpose of strengthening and anchoring the final tonic:

"If a closing chord progression is to give the impression of coming to rest and reaching its destination, there must be at least one possiblity of the progression by melodic interval 1. If there is no *interval 1*, either one of the chords is incomplete or the progression was not *sufficiently* directed to make a true conclusion. *The principle of the leading tone* is founded on melodic progression by interval 1. By *leading tone* in a general sense, we mean a pitch distant by an interval 1 from a component of the terminal chord, the tonic. It can be either an upper or a lower pitch. By *leading tone* in a narrower sense, we mean only the pitch situated an interval 1 lower than the root of the tonic. [...] We see the leading tone as the vehicle of the chord's kinetic energy of the impetus in the chord, as its tendency to flow into the tonic."[40]

Through the merging of the principles of the pure tonic and the principle of the leading tone, which co-participate in stabilising the tonic as the tonal centre, Janeček is able to formulate the *functional principle*:

"The *functional principle* arises from the merged principles of the pure tonic and the leading tone. Application of both these principles results in a particular distribution of

---

38 Ibid., 246.
39 Karel Janeček, "Doplňující poznámky k některým jevům harmonického a tonálního myšlení" [Additional Notes to Some Phenomena of Harmonic and Tonal Thinking], *Živá hudba* [Living Music] (Praha: Akademie múzických umění v Praze [Academy of Performing Arts in Prague], 1976), 21–29 (english translation of this study: pp. 453–459 in this publication).
40 Janeček, *Foundations of Modern Harmony*, 250.

tonal functions. We are looking for pre-tonic chords that could serve as a standard for perceiving or judging all other practically possible chord relations."[41]

The synergic cooperation of both principles can be illustrated with the cadence: Neapolitan sixth chord (F A♭ D♭) – dominant (G B D) – tonic (C E G). What we can state about this example is that the tone D♭, a tritone away from the fifth of the tonic – the note G, interferes with the function of the principle of the pure tonic in this context. Although at the same time, through the effects of the leading tone principle, it strengthens the tonic C, because it is a semitone above the root note. It seems that the functions of both principles cancel, or equalise, each other. But that is not all: while the tone G, which D♭ is a tritone away from, serves as the fifth of the tonic, it also serves as the root note of the dominant. Through a more detailed analysis we can then state that between the tones of the Neapolitan sixth chord and the dominant manifests its presence of not just one, but three simultaneous tritone intervals: D♭–G, F–B, A♭–D. This relation creates functional tension, through which both chords mutually prevent each other from being functionally interpreted as the tonal centre (both of them simultaneously assume the roles of potential tonic and antitonic) and thus the only guaranteed tonic in the circumstances of this context can be the unaffected chord C E G, which is also strengthened by the presence and resolution of three descending leading tones.[42] This example shall be seen as an illustration of the effects of the functional principle. In actual musical practice, however, further factors come into play, such as the specific rhythmic/meter situation, the presence of non-chord tones, passing harmonies, stylisation…

Janeček elaborates on an interesting circle of thinking by regarding the term *harmonic function*. Harmonic function and its interpretation have their own history, starting with Zarlino and Rameau, through Riemann's interpretation, up to the present day, which is distinctively represented in Czech music theory, for example by the music-theoretical works of Otakar Šín. Janeček builds upon the initiatives presented by his predecessors, and further develops their thoughts and applies them in the research of modern tonality of the 20th century. The initiatives mentioned are summarised below.

An important historical milestone is the year 1558, when Gioseffo Zarlino (1517–1590) discovers and becomes aware of the phenomenon of the basic harmonic unit – the chord: "The diversity of harmony does not stem only from the diversity of intervals, but also in the diversity of chords, which is given by the position of the tone, which serves as the third in the chord […]"[43] This discovery represents the birth of harmony on the "mycelium" of previously valid principles of polyphonic techniques, in the realm of harmony based only on the control over the intervals between individual voices without being aware of the harmonic unit – the chord – and its role as an indivisible homo-

---

41   Ibid., 251.
42   For more information see below – Šín's *triple-subdominant* and Janeček's *phrygian function*.
43   Gioseffo Zarlino, *Institutioni harmoniche* (Venezia, 1558) – quoted by Hradecký, *Úvod do studia tonální harmonie*, 94–95.

geneous harmonic unit. Becoming aware of chords therefore represents a crucial qualitative breakthrough in the process of development leading to harmony as we know it.

The consecutive contribution from Jean-Philippe Rameau (1683–1764) consists of the selection of a representative triple of chords, built on three tonic degrees privileged with tonal harmonic significance: first (tonic), fifth – a fifth above tonic (dominant), and fourth – a fifth below tonic (subdominant). Rameau understood that this triple of chords contains all of the notes of the key, and, most importantly, that it unambiguously defines the key. Through this realisation Rameau in essence laid out the foundations of the traditional three-function harmonic system, even though he did not use the term "function"; this term was used later by Hugo Riemann (1849–1919).

Further steps in classifying harmonic material brought consideration as to how chords, built on the other 4 notes of the key (the second, third, sixth and seventh degrees) should be integrated into the system of functional harmonic relations. There were various approaches to finding the solution. Hugo Riemann viewed those chords as *substitutions* of the three essential harmonic functions, based on which chord shares the majority of tones (in the case of triads therefore two) with the given essential chord. As a result of this, each of the three essential functions can have two third-relation substitutions, one above and one below: the tonic can be substituted by the triads built on the degrees III and VI degrees of the key, the subdominant can be substituted by the degrees VI and II and the dominant with the degrees VII and III. As can be seen, some of the substitutions (the degrees VI and III) can substitute two different chords. The final expression and functional interpretation is influenced by the specific context in such a case, and in some cases the final harmonic aural perception can be functionally ambiguous. The Czech music theorist Otakar Šín (1881–1943) solved this question by integrating the four auxiliary chords into the functional harmony system through the application of the principle of functional combinations: in particular, the triad built on the degree III was viewed by him as the combination of the incomplete tonic and the incomplete dominant. He interpreted the triad built on the degree VI as the combination of the incomplete subdominant and the incomplete tonic. Like Riemann, Šín's solution also takes into account the fact that the final harmonic aural perception and interpretation can be in favour of one of the two elements involved in the combination. Again, an important role is played by the context and dispositions. An important and impossible-to-miss element in Otakar Šín's thoughts concerns the pair of chords that are a semitone away from the tonic and that create three simultaneous semitone intervals towards the tonic from below (B D♯ F♯ towards C E G) and from above (D♭ F A♭ also towards C E G), both in minor and major keys. Through this construction, two artificial triads of the same type are created in relation to the tonic, consisting of three leading tones, in the first case ascending (as in the case of the dominant – Šín refers to this unit as the *triple-dominant* or the *lydian chord*, the lydian element is the tone F♯ – the raised fourth degree, typical for the lydian mode) and in the second case – out of three descending leading tones (as in the case of the minor subdominant – to this unit Šín refers as the *tri-*

ple-subdominant or the *phrygian chord*, the phrygian element is the note D♭ – the lowered second degree, typical for the phrygian mode). Thanks to the culmination of three leading tones, each of the above-mentioned chords carries great tension, waiting to be resolved into the tonic. Let us note that not all of examples given above carry the same tradition of application in music of the classical-romantic era. The lydian chord was applied very rarely. However, the phrygian major chord in the first inversion, i.e. the *Neapolitan sixth chord*, saw an extraordinary amount of application in the musical thinking of this period.

All of the above-mentioned constructs served great inspiration to Karel Janeček, and challenged him to create his own theoretical understanding, during the development of the reflection of the functionally harmonic arrangement of harmonic material, under the circumstances of musical thinking of the 20th century. Šín's concept of chords consisting of three leading tones was developed by Janeček into the theory of the so-called *auxiliary harmonic functions* – the *phrygian* and *lydian functions*. By this undertaking he accepted both of Šín's chords into the "family" of traditional harmonic functions and expanded Rameau's functional system of three members into the *functional system of five members*. The descriptor *auxiliary* function is established by Janeček for the purposes of differentiating and quantifying the weight and significance towards the traditional primary harmonic functions.

Establishing the auxiliary phrygian and lydian functions, together with linking to Šín's concept of functional combinations, enabled Janeček to, inter alia, base his interpretation of altered chords on the definition of chord units, created through the functional combination of one (or both) of the auxiliary functions: e.g. the tetrad D♭ F A♭ B as the combination of the phrygian function and the incomplete dominant (resolving to the tonic of C major), or the tetrad A♭ C D♯ F♯ as the combination of the incomplete minor subdominant and the incomplete lydian function (resolving to C major as well), etc. This approach towards Šín's legacy enabled Janeček to create a completely new, very well arranged, illustrative and clear interpretation of the phenomena of alteration. Its clarity and illustrative interpretation completely surpassing the traditional methodical approach to interpreting alterations, commonly used in older textbooks, often starting with a chaotic assortment of enumerations of types of altered chords. Its clarity and illustrative interpretation completely surpassed the traditional methodical approach towards interpreting alterations, commonly used in older textbooks, often starting with a chaotic assortment of enumerations of types of altered chords – using very complicated designations for the chords which were, however, merely describing their structure, qualifying each member (third, fifth, and seventh) of the chord extra.[44] For example, with B as the root note, the alterations would be: B D♭ F; B D♭ F♭; B D♯ F; B D F♭; B D♭ F A; B D♭ F A♭; B D♭ F♭ A♭; B D♯ F A; B D♯ F A♭; B D F♭ A♭; B D♯ F♯ A♭; B D F♯ A♭; B♭ D F♯ A♭. As can be seen, Janeček's solution is absolutely elegant and systematically pure in comparison, and easily comprehensible at first glance. Janeček also fully and

---

44 Zdeněk Hůla, *Nauka o harmonii I+II* [Theory of Harmony I+II] (Praha: SNKLHU, 1956), 331–333.

meaningfully employed his take on the interpretation of the subject in his publication with a didactic-methodical focus – the textbook *Harmony Through Analysis*, widely respected as an example of a modern inventive approach to interpreting the subject of harmony (see above).

Janeček was also interested in the question of whether the harmonic function fulfils the same or similar role in the musical language of the 20th century (considering the usage of the twelve-tone equal temperament) as it did in previous time periods. This is also connected to the question of the number of harmonic functions: does Rameau's functional system of three members (tonic, subdominant and dominant) still apply, or is it possible and necessary to work with a higher number, reflecting the richness and diversity of options provided by the material of the twelve-tone equal temperament? With these thoughts, together with the above-mentioned decision to adopt a functional system of five members, Janeček enters the discussion of this topic, which was ablaze in the Czech music theory community from the 1950's to the 1980's.

Various opinions and arguments for different approaches were voiced as part of the discussion. As an example of an extreme solution, let us mention the standpoint of Karel Risinger, published in 1957,[45] which assumes 15 harmonic functions. Their proportion towards the tonic is defined by the principle of the proportion of the root note to the root note of the tonic and the principle of outlining the diatonic unison, fifth and eventually the third, with the notes of a given function. The following harmonic functions result from applying these principles (towards the tonal centre C): tonic (C E G, C E♭ G), dominant (G B D, G B♭ D), subdominant (F A C, F A♭ C), phrygian function (B♭ D♭ F), mixolydian function (B♭ D F), lydian function (D F♯ A), dorian function (D F A), hyper-phrygian function (E♭ G B♭, E♭ G♭ B♭), hyper-lydian function (A C♯ E, A C E), upper tertian function (E G♯ B, E G B), lower tertian function (A♭ C E♭, A♭ C♭ E♭), upper leading tone function (D♭ F A♭, D♭ F♭ A♭), lower leading tone function (B D♯ F♯, B D F♯), tritone function on a diminished fifth (G♭ B♭ D♭, G♭ B♭♭ D♭), tritone function on an augmented fourth (F♯ A♯ C♯, F♯ A C♯). As can be seen, the functions in this approach are based on every tone of the twelve-tone equal temperament through the application of the above principles. Due to the impulses created by the above-mentioned discussions, Risinger would reconsider his standpoint a year later, reducing the total number of functions to 5: tonic, dominant, subdominant, phrygian function, lydian function. Thus he came to agree with Janeček's standpoint in terms to the number of functions, however not in the case of interpreting the lydian and phrygian functions.[46] In Risinger's interpretation of the lydian function (D F♯ A) and the phrygian function (B♭ D♭ F) the lydian F♯ and phrygian D♭ act not as the fifth and unison of the given functions, but

---

45 See Karel Risinger, *Nástin obecného hudebního funkčního systému rozšířené tonality* [Outline of the General Musical Functional System of Expanded Tonality] (Praha: Svaz čs. skladatelů [Union of Czechoslovakian Composers], 1957).

46 See Karel Risinger, *Základní harmonické funkce v soudobé hudbě* [Fundamental Harmonic Functions in Contemporary Music] (Praha: SNKLHU, 1958).

instead as their third. In discussions, Risinger justified his interpretation with historical arguments – by referring to harmonic material used in final harmonic progressions in the lydian and phrygian church modes.

Jaroslav Volek presents a critical view and a series of questions about increasing the number of harmonic functions. Volek's thoughts revolve around the actual number of harmonic functions, and he presents questions related to the matter of which additional tonal degree can be used for the fourth and further harmonic functions. In the study *Chromatic Mediants as the Fourth Primary Function in Traditional Harmony*,[47] he offers a critical view of the functional system of five members presented by Karel Janeček; if it were found necessary to expand the functional system of three members, he proposes the chromatic mediant as the fourth harmonic function, i.e. chords that are in chromatic tertian relation to the tonic, both from above and below (for example in the key of C major the chords would be E G♯ B, E♭ G B♭, E♭ G♭ B♭, A C♯ E, A♭ C E♭, A♭ C♭ E♭; in C minor then E♭ G♭ B♭, E G B, E G♯ B, A♭ C♭ E♭, A C E, A C♯ E). As can be deduced from these examples, the term "chromatic median" can – compared to the traditional harmonic functions T, D, S – describe a considerably large number of specific triads, which fulfil the stated condition: all of the above-mentioned mediant triads (both major and minor) are in tertian relation to the tonic, that is, tertian relation of the root note of the given chord to the root note of the tonic and at the same the chromatic relation of at least one tone towards a tone of the tonic. Regarding the second variable (chromatic relation), Volek distinguishes between chromatic mediants of the first degree – one tone is in chromatic relation to the tonic – and the second degree – two tones are in chromatic relation to the tonic. Yet it is true that if the mediant of the first degree is major (minor), then the tonic must also be major (minor); in the case of the second degree, however, the opposite is true. (For the sake of thoroughness, let us also mention the diatonic tertially related chords introduced by Volek, which are however not considered to be mediant functions; he refers to them as mediants of the null degree: in the key of C major the chords would be E G B, A C E, in C minor then E♭ G B♭, A♭ C E♭. In those cases, none of the tones are in chromatic relation to the tones of the tonic, and they are minor if the tonic is major, and vice versa.) The above makes it obvious that, due to the number and diversity of the chromatic mediants, a necessary condition for recognising their function – besides the tertian relation to the tonic – is the presence of the chromatic relation. This is their primary characteristic, by which they significantly differ from the primary functional triple (tonic – dominant – subdominant) as well as the so-called supplemental functions (phrygian and lydian functions). As we saw earlier, Volek was dismissive about the increase of the number of harmonic functions:

"If we base our reasoning, as is required by the principle of unity of induction and deduction, on empirical data [...] simultaneously with the firm realisation of the conse-

---

[47] Jaroslav Volek, "Chromatické medianty jako čtvrtá základní funkce v tradiční harmonii" [Chromatic Mediants as the Fourth Primary Function in Traditional Harmony] In Jaroslav Volek, *Struktura a osobnosti hudby* [Structure and Personalities in music] (Praha: Panton, 1988), 70–102.

quences of the philosophical tenet 'essence – phenomenon', then I believe the only correct path for the attempts to expand the original number of three functions is the following: we shall decide to establish a new function *when and only when* it is absolutely certain that a certain group of commonly used and mutually connected similar chords absolutely *cannot* be described by any current function or functional combination [...] Such a case occurs with the *mediant functions*."[48]

Karel Janeček addressed the question of the number of harmonic function in his last published text, *Additional Notes to Some Phenomena of Harmonic and Tonal Thinking*, published in 1976 – after the publication of *Foundations of Modern Harmony*. Due to the crucial significance of this study, a lot of attention is devoted to it in this text. The study provides a number of clarifications, new insights and ideas on the subject that he elaborated upon in Základy. On the number of harmonic functions, Janeček adds:

"So, as far as functions are concerned (i.e., Rameau's finding, enlarged upon by Riemann later), it follows that it is also possible to doubt that there are really only three. Aren't there more? However, even if their number were increased, the most significant differentiations would remain valid: above/under the axis, above/under the tonic, and dominant/subdominant. Thus, an innovation concerning functions would be thinkable only as a *pair*. The functional systems potentially possible are therefore: three-membered, five-membered, seven-membered... But hold on! Functionality signifies *generality*. There are certain transpositions of certain chord-types characterized by their *dominant quality*, represented by the dominant. There are others whose main feature is the *subdominant quality* and they are represented by the subdominant. If the number of functions was increased unduly, each transposition of any particular chord-type would become its own representative. A swollen officer corps of numerous ostentatious terms would arise, but no soldiers. Therefore, Rameau's system continues to be valid up to now because it relies on *three primary functions*. It might be possible to enrich this strictly limited number of functions, but only with a fourth and fifth as *auxiliary* and complementary (the primary functions would remain as they were, numbering only three). It turned out to be necessary to make this extension, as by it, compositional practice became enriched. Dominant and subdominant qualities were joined by something special: *phrygian* and *lydian qualities*."[49]

As can be seen, Janeček does not rule out the possibility of increasing the number of functions, yet he warns of possible excessiveness ("functionality is a *generality*"), an argument presented by Volek as well. Furthermore, the dualistic foundation of Janeček's thinking is apparent "above/under the axis [...] only as a *pairs*"), another sign of the continuation of Rameau's and Riemann's thoughts.

Additional Notes to Some Phenomena of Harmonic and Tonal Thinking is characterised by its close relation and connection of thought to *Foundations of Modern Harmony*, and the significance of its content certainly justifies its being integrated into the context

---

48 Ibid., 73.
49 Janeček, *Foundations of Modern Harmony*, 455–456.

of Janeček's other studies, which are also characterised by incredible music-theoretical inventiveness. We do so with the note that, while the preceding studies represent the search for and finding the path towards a specified goal – a systematic understanding of the subject of modern harmony – Janeček's last text can, in this context, be described as a peculiar epilogue containing crucial concepts. The study is a published report presented by Janeček at the symposium held in 1973, on his 70th birthday. It consists of five chapters: 1. *On Imaginary Pitches*, 2. *The Dialectics of Chord-types, Transpositions and Dispositions*, 3. *On Harmonic Functions*, 4. *On the Path to the Antitonic*, 5. *On Atonality*. As will be apparent below from a commentary on *Foundations of Modern Harmony*, Janeček returns in this report to certain chosen topics elaborated upon in *Foundations*, a special status is however given to *Chapter 4 – On the Path to the Antitonic*. The harmonic phenomenon called the *antitonic* represents both a brilliant insight and an ingenious and elegant design: the functionally most distant chord to the tonic is the one built on the note that is a tritone away from the root note of the tonic (e.g. to the tonic C major – the antitonic F♯ major). This insight is, inter alia, in absolute accordance with, for example, the arrangement of the circle of fifths: the maximum amount of contrast, resp. the maximum distance from the tonic, is displayed by the chord reached by six leaps by fifths from the root note of the tonic – both ascending and descending. This note is also the furthest one from the root note of the tonic in the circle of fifths. A further (seventh) leap by fifths would mean heading back towards the tonic again through the opposite side of the circle of fifths. It is necessary to highlight the fact that the presented concept of the antitonic is supported by modern tonal harmonic practice (see, for example, its use in the conclusion of *Symphony No. 5 Di tre re* by A. Honegger or the conclusion to the second part of the vocal-instrumental suite *Seven Romances on Poems by Alexander Blok, Op. 127* by Dmitri Shostakovich), and it serves as a testament to Janeček's brilliant music-theoretic inventiveness and insight. However, let us also highlight an interesting parallel between Janeček's concept and the result of the research of Paul Hindemith (see above, in the chapter *On Music Theory*, for commentary on Hindemith's first series: the first series illustrates a degree of affinity of each of the individual notes of the twelve-tone chromatic scale towards the root note, which represents the tonal centre. The highest affinity towards the root note is exhibited by the perfect fifth; the furthermost position is then taken by the tritone).

If we refer back to the above-mentioned discussion on the number of harmonic functions, we might wish to ask the question: which of the participants was actually right? Who is right – from today's perspective? In this regard, it is necessary to note that the question cannot be asked in this manner. The standpoints presented by the individual participants arose from different perspectives. Due to the fact that musical structure is a multilayered, amply internally functionally connected, truly living organism, it is apparent that the result of a different perspective, directed towards a multitude of facets of the structure of this organism, must therefore also be a different picture, accenting different attributes or traits in each case. It is this diversity of perspectives that enables us to perceive the subject in all of its richness and multilayeredness. Karel Janeček plays a significant role – together with the other figures mentioned – in the field of music theory.

We should also like to add an attempt at our own standpoint on this subject, informed by study, comparison and contemplation of the incentives provided by the above discussion, through the confrontation of individual standpoints. Equal temperament, within which the tonal thought of the 20th and 21st centuries is realised, enables the creation of a significantly wider array of simultaneity-types and dispositions – which finds its application in atonal harmonic functions – than in the case of the diatonic major and minor systems. The function of a chord in the harmonic phrase can be safely deduced from the relation of its root note to the root note of the tonal centre. We base our reasoning on the assumption that on *any tone of the twelve-tone equal temperament, a chord can be built (harmonic function)* – see Karel Risinger's concept from 1957. Based on the relations between tones, which are given by the mutual ratio of their frequencies, a sequence ("ranking") of the individual degrees of the twelve-tone equal temperament is *based on how they are functionally related or unrelated to the tonal centre*. From the perspective of functional relation, the perfect fifth manifests as the strongest (as the interval which defines the position of the authentic function – dominant), and its (in the tonal space) opposite plagal functions – subdominants. The next in the sequence are the substitutions of the plagal and authentic functions – the major and minor third above and below (mediants), the major and minor second above and below (adlegates), while the last-mentioned intervals function as the phrygian and lydian functions in tonal music. And, last but not least, the tritone, as the interval that is the most distant to the tonal centre (Janeček's antitonic). As can be seen, the order of the individual mentioned intervals corresponds to the sequence of the overtone series: the Pythagorean (and Aristoxenus's) perfect fifth – 3:2, Aristoxenus's major third – 5:4, Aristoxenus's minor third – 6:5, the Pythagorean whole-tone (resp. Aristoxenus's major whole-tone) – 8:9, Aristoxenus's major semitone – 16:15.[50]

This can be summarised and illustrated by the following diagram, which displays both the grading of the chords of the individual degrees in the twelve-tone equal temperament based on their closeness/distance to/from the centre – the tonic. The centre chosen for the diagram is C (begging the comparison to Hindemith's construction of the so-called first series); the harmonic plagal functions (subdominant substitutions) are assigned the left column and the authentic functions (dominant substitutions) the right column (dualistic concept). In a general sense, plagal functions can be referred to as *subdominants in a broader sense* and to authentic functions as *dominants in a broader*

---

[50] The exact same goal – looking for and finding the key to establishing the order of harmonic relation and distance of individual tones in the twelve-tone equal temperament towards the tonal centre – was pursued by Hindemith; see the first section of this study. Compared to our standpoint, which takes into account also the consistent mutual antagonism of the individual plagal and authentic functions (and thus the symmetry of the entire diagram – we can refer to it as a dualistic view), Hindemith only takes the distance into account, without accounting for functional authenticity and plagalness (his view is therefore monistic).

sense. In this context, Rameau's triplet (tonic – dominant – subdominant) remains the core of the system. The most distant to the centre is then the function, based on a tritone relation towards the centre – the above-mentioned antitonic:

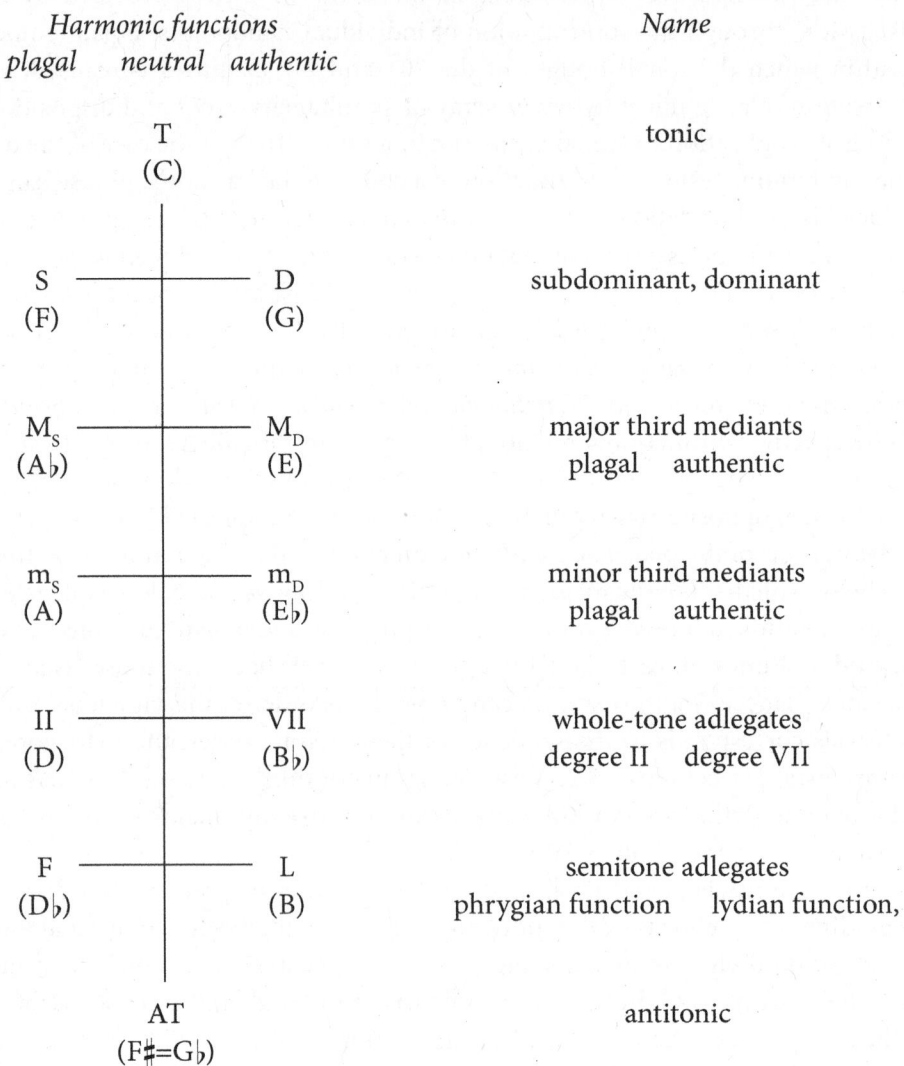

Harmonic functions			Name	
plagal	neutral	authentic		
	T (C)		tonic	
S (F)		D (G)	subdominant, dominant	
M_S (A♭)		M_D (E)	major third mediants plagal authentic	
m_S (A)		m_D (E♭)	minor third mediants plagal authentic	
II (D)		VII (B♭)	whole-tone adlegates degree II degree VII	
F (D♭)		L (B)	semitone adlegates phrygian function lydian function,	
	AT (F♯=G♭)		antitonic	

Let us remind ourselves of the fact that the above diagram and the expressed thoughts take into account only the direct relations of the individual degrees towards the centre. Applying the mediated relations, as represented by the world of applied functions, greatly expands the diversity of the entire functional harmony "universe". To our interpretation of mediants, let us also add that (unlike Volek's view) we do not distinguish between chromatic and diatonic mediants: we consider the above-mentioned interval distance from the root note of a given chord to the root note of the tonic (which represents the tonal centre) to be of great significance for functional relations.

For the sake of thoroughness, let us also mention that in modern tonality any function can be either major or minor (this attribute is significant for its perceptual outcome, which is assessed from the perspective of aesthetics – e.g. the "hard" character of major and the "soft" character of minor. The mentioned actualities do not affect the actual centre, as a significant attribute of tonality, in any way), it can also be neither of them (it does not contain the third above the root, which defines this quality of the chord and the key). If the major/minor quality is not clearly specified, it can be designated by its root note – without the major/minor descriptor (e.g. "in E♭" as can be seen in, for example, the description of fugues in the instance of Hindemith's designation of keys, resp. tonal centres of the individual fugues in *Ludus Tonalis*). This perspective does not affect the tonality, which is based on the presence of the centre and the hierarchical relations towards it.

Conclusion

There is no doubt that, from today's perspective, Karel Janeček slowly but steadily "resettled" from the present into the past. It must be realised that, at the time, when his life was heading towards its coda, that is, when he was already a senior citizen and thus had the right to summarise his experiences, to look back and reflect, Janeček still managed to cover many of the phenomena brought by music development after the Second World War, and which were only an implication of the direction of further development, rather than being a safe and mastered territory. At the same time, however, he could not deny his roots, which were, as has been mentioned, the school of Vítězslav Novák. Those of Janeček's students who had the opportunity to meet him in person during the last few years of his life must have perceived him as the overlap of, on the one hand, his lifetime of lived experience and, on the other hand, his search for himself with the sensations of infinite possibilities and infinite time and space before him. It is apparent that such moments and experiences are not transferrable, and if we are to present Janeček's thoughts to our generation of students, it cannot be through mere quotation, as if it was one truth set in stone (against such an interpretation, Janeček himself would protest the most). Since that time many things have changed and many new things have been brought by music itself.

Music theory too has advanced in many regards. It seems that it is necessary to view Janeček as a classic authority in his field, as we view Descartes in philosophy, Newton in physics and Kepler in astronomy: it is necessary to elaborate upon and convey Janeček's point of view to our students, hoping that at least some of them are lucky enough to experience it and take away insights from his work, about subjects that are generally applicable and indefinitely valid, not only in regards to the actual content of his works but also with respect to his work methods. Regarding those aspects of his work which seem obsolete today (for various reasons), it is necessary to become aware of their positive impact, as challenges for one of his successors – us included – to search for their own paths and finally to accept as a model his work ethos as a scientist burning with love for his field and for scientific research in general. The greatest tribute we can make to Janeček is by moving forward on the path he started with his work. The possibilities are endless: as a reminder, let us list the topics we went through, additional topics that have already established themselves in our debates, topics that provoke and inspire us, topics on which we are working, topics that we dream of covering: the application of Risinger's concept of the *hierarchy of musical wholes* and Volek's *main form-bearing component* during expanding musical tectonic concepts; assessing internal connecting elements applied in music as a structure of Wittgenstein's family resemblances; the application of chaos theory and fractals; the concept of the so-called third or transcendental time; finding new, yet-to-be-discovered parameters of musical structure; applying information theory and the theory of probability during organisation of musical structure; research on the procedurality of the musical stream; viewing the musical stream as "open", i.e. not limited by time in either direction; structure; approaching the analytical understanding of musical phenomena as ambiguous; the questions of tonal space in the perspective of modern music; the subject of the so-called harmonic field; applying the analytical tools of logic and linguistics; applying the theory of sets; a more detailed systematic and analytical development of musical kinetics, especially in areas yet to be developed in this manner (i.e. composition works of the late 20th century); music of cultures distant to our modern European culture both temporally and spatially; finding and formulating the functional interpretation of stated actualities; questions of theoretical terminology, solved face to face to the mentioned topics and thematic circles of thinking ...

The point of view of the musical theorist Karel Janeček is not only a passive description of musical phenomena. It is also the result and manifestation of a highly active search for, and discovery of, principles, organising and motivating – through rich internal functional relations – the shape and procedural development of the musical organism in time and space, its "live breath", and at the same time carefully building a logically structured theoretical system, in the end formulated through the application of eminently exact arguments and with an exceptional degree of comprehensibility. All of the above was done by Janeček, however, not as "science for science's sake" but as an aid and service for musical practice. His teachings should be seen as an integral part of general music-theoretical knowledge. We have attempted, through our attention to the development of Janeček's interest in the subject of harmony, to capture the ripening of Janeček's point of view over his lifetime (which culminated in the publication of *Foundations of Modern Harmony*) as authentically as possible.

References

Beckerman, Michael Brim. *Janáček as Theoretist*. Stuyvesant, NY: Pendragon Press, 1994.

Forte, Allen. *The Structure of Atonal Music*. London: Yale University Press, 1973.

Hindemith, Paul. *Unterweisung im Tonsatz I–II*. Neue, erw. ausg. Mainz: B. Schott's Söhne, 1939–1940.

Hradecký, Emil. *Úvod do studia tonální harmonie* [Introduction to the Study of Tonal Harmony]. 2nd ed. Praha: Supraphon, 1972.

Hůla, Zdeněk. *Nauka o harmonii I+II* [Theory of Harmony I+II]. Praha: SNKLHU, 1956.

Janeček, Karel. "Doplňující poznámky k některým jevům harmonického a tonálního myšlení" [Additional Notes to Some Phenomena of Harmonic and Tonal Thinking]. *Živá hudba* [Living Music]. Praha: Akademie múzických umění v Praze [Academy of Performing Arts in Prague], 1976, 21–29.

--- "Harmonické možnosti chromatiky" [The Harmonic Possibilities of the Chromatic System]. *Rytmus* [Rhythm] 11 (1947): 21–23.

--- "Harmonický materiál temperované chromatiky: Kapitola ze Základů temperované harmonie" [The Harmonic Material of the Tempered Chromatic System: Chapter of Foundations of Tempered Harmony]. *Hudební věda* [Musical Science Quarterly] 4 (1961): 81–119.

--- "Moderní harmonie. Souhrnný náčrt" [Modern Harmony. A General Outline]. *Tempo* 11 (1931–32): 46–52.

--- "O významu imaginárních tónů v harmonii" [The Significance of Imaginary Pitches in Harmony]. *Hudební výchova* [Music Education] 13 (1932): 8–9, 22–25.

--- "Princip harmonické inverse" [The Principle of Harmonic Inversion]. *Rytmus* [Rhythm] 8 (1942–43): 54–57.

--- "Rozvrat diatoniky" [The Breakdown of the Diatonic System]. *Tempo* 14 (1935): 151–154, 191–195, 227–231.

--- "Rytmus starý a nový" [New and Old Rhythm]. *Tempo* 12 (1932–33): 357–365.

--- "Systém charakteristických akordů" [The System of Characteristic Chords]. *Rytmus* [Rhythm] 11 (1947): 66–69.

--- "Vznik, stavba a ráz nových souzvuků" [The Foundation, Structure, and Nature of New Chords]. *Tempo* 12 (1933): 164–172.

--- "Základní harmonické problémy a jejich řešení" [Fundamental Harmonic Problems and their Solutions]. *Musikologie: Sborník pro hudební vědu a kritiku* [Musicology: Annual for Musical Science and Criticism]. Praha: SNKLHU, 1955, 87–129.

--- "Zvukové vlastnosti harmonického materiálu: Kapitola ze Základů temperované harmonie" [Sonic Characteristics of the Harmonic Material: Chapter of Foundations of Tempered Harmony]. *Živá hudba: Sborník prací hudební fakulty AMU* [Living Music: Collection of Works by the Music Faculty of AMU]. Praha: SPN, 1962, 69–93.

--- *Dílo a život Bedřicha Smetany I. Smetanova komorní tvorba* [The Oeuvre and Life of Bedřich Smetana I. Smetana's Chamber Works]. Praha: Editio Supraphon, 1978.

--- *Harmonie rozborem* [Harmony Through Analysis]. Praha: Státní hudební nakladatelství [State Music Press], 1963.

--- *Hudební formy* [Musical Forms]. Praha: SNKLHU, 1955.

--- *Melodika* [Study of Melodics]. Praha: SNKLHU, 1956.

--- *Skladatelská práce v oblasti klasické harmonie* [Compositional Practice in the Field of Classical Harmony]. Praha: Academia, 1973.

--- *Vyjádření souzvuků: Kapitola ze Základů temperované harmonie* [The Expression of Chords: Chapter of Foundations of Tempered Harmony]. Praha: Svaz čs. skladatelů [Union of Czechoslovakian Composers, 1958.

--- *Tektonika* [Tectonics]. Praha: Supraphon, 1968.

--- *Základy moderní harmonie* [Foundations of Modern Harmony]. Praha: Nakladatelství ČSAV [Czechoslovak Academy of Sciences Press], 1965.

Kohoutek, Ctirad. *Novodobé skladebné směry v hudbě* [Compositional Styles in the New Era]. 2nd ed. Praha: SHV, 1965.

Piňos, Alois. *Tónové skupiny* [Tone groups]. Praha: Editio Supraphon, 1971 (English Translation: Piňos, Alois. *Tone groups*. Translated by Eva Horová. Brno: Janáčkova akademie múzických umění, 2001).

Risinger, Karel. *Hierarchie hudebních celků* [The Hierarchy of Musical Wholes]. Praha: Panton, 1969.

--- *Nástin obecného hudebního funkčního systému rozšířené tonality* [Outline of the General Musical Functional System of Expanded Tonality]. Praha: Svaz čs. skladatelů [Union of Czechoslovakian Composers], 1957.

--- *Vůdčí osobnosti české moderní hudební teorie: Otakar Šín, Alois Hába, Karel Janeček* [Leading Personalities in Modern Czech Music Theory: Otakar Šín, Alois Hába, Karel Janeček]. Praha: SHV, 1963.

--- *Základní harmonické funkce v soudobé hudbě* [Fundamental Harmonic Functions in Contemporary Music]. Praha: SNKLHU, 1958.

References

Šín, Otakar. *Úplná nauka o harmonii na základě melodie a rytmu* [Complete Theory of Harmony on the Basis of Melody and Rhythm]. 2. vyd., přepracované a rozšířené [2nd ed., revised and expanded]. Praha: Hudební Matice [The Music Association], 1933.

Tichý, Vladimír. "Hudebněteoretický odkaz Karla Janečka ve světle hudební skutečnosti roku 2003" [Music-theoretical Legacy of Karel Janeček Viewed Through the Musical Reality of the Year 2003.]. *Živá hudba* [Living Music]. Praha: Akademie múzických umění v Praze [Academy of Performing Arts in Prague], 2003, 7–15.

--- "Tonalita/atonalita?" In: Vladimír Tichý et al. *(A)tonalita* [(A)tonality]. Praha: AMU, 2015.

--- *Harmonicky myslet a slyšet* [To Think and Hear Harmonically]. Praha: AMU, 2011.

Volek, Jaroslav. "Chromatické medianty jako čtvrtá základní funkce v tradiční harmonii" [Chromatic Mediants as the Fourth Primary Function in Traditional Harmony] In Jaroslav Volek. *Struktura a osobnosti hudby* [Structure and Personalities in music]. Praha: Panton, 1988, 70–102.

Subject Index

alteration 39, 289–90
alteration of functional triads 289–292
anhemitonic pentatonic system 65
anticipation 95, 235
atonality (non-functionality) 300
bitonality 265, 296
boundaries between characteristic-types cadence 134–136
cadence 360
cadential passage 385–388
cancellation of an imaginary pitch 196–198
characteristic
    disposition 374–376
    dissonant 74, 90–92, 130, 328
    family 77–80, 328
    functional 394–396
characteristic maximum 36, 101–102, 103
characteristic nucleus 102–103
characteristic-type 128, 134–136, 326, 339–342
chord-type 31, 43, 46–47, 325, 336–339
    applied 287
    asymmetrical 46–47
    belonging to both families, with a composite family characteristic 78
    belonging to neither family, of indefinite family 78
    pre-tonic 251, 355–356
    symmetrical 46–47
chord-class 42
church mode 249, 298–299
clash
    of semitones 83, 86–89, 185–190
    of tritones 83, 86–89
classification of the harmonic material (93–156)
combination
    bitonal 284

consonant 260–264
dissonant 264–266, 267–273
monotonal 284
of functional triads 260–264, 264–266
partial 138–139, 146–148, 179–184
polytonal 284–285
pre-tonic 355–356
triadic 115, 116, 118, 137–138, 148–150, 150–151, 169–174, 183–185, 185–190
true 138–139
combination categories 138–139, 152–153
combination method 138, 155–156
component
    consonant 76–77, 164–165
    functional 274–275
composition 333, 362–367
compositional order 305–309, 383–385
compositional technique 317–319
concordance 330
connection 279, 280
    compound 280
    of a higher (the second) degree 280
    of a lower (the first) degree 280
    simple 280
consonance 30, 39, 69, 159, 206, 330, 336–337
counterpoint 313, 334
cross-relation 207, 286, 338, 381
destruction of tonality 296
determinant triad of a combination 171
diatonic system 39, 249, 320–321, 381
    modified 65, 67
    pure 64, 249, 381
direction of harmonic motion 278
discordance 330
disposition
    combination 169, 174–176, 181, 183

non-combination 169, 177, 182
   of a chord 31, 33, 35, 43, (157–194), 159–160, 322–323, 324
disrupting the tonality 296
dissonance 30, 69–70, 159, 327, 330, 339
dissonant element 30, 70–72, 81–89
dominant 256
   altered 289
   applied 287
   minor 259–260, 289
dominant ninth chord 110
   dominant minor ninth chord 115, 166
dominantization 35
doubling 158
dying away
   of a sense of the tonic 282, 391–394
   of an imaginary pitch 198–202
   of outer tension 260
eight-note chords 63
eleven-note chord 63
experience
   direct 321, 324
   indirect 321, 324
expression
   composite 208–221
   incomplete 224–226
   of a chord 35, (195–226)
finalis 249
five-note chords 53–54
five-three chord 160
form of a chord/harmony 158
four-note chords 51–53
function
   altered 289–292, 296
   applied 286–289, 292, 296
   auxiliary 259, 296
   harmonic (functional triad), functionality 328–329
   primary 259
functional ambiguity 267–273
harmonic analysis 369–370
harmonic material 41–43, 67–68, (39–68)
harmonic symbol 33, 326
harmonizing a melody 345–349
harmony
   classical 96, 329
   functional 328
   latent (hidden) 336, 345, 361
   modern 315, 323, 325, 334
harmony (traditional chord) 36, 93–94
   applied 257, 287
   altered 257

   basic 139–141, 160, 164
   classical 96, 106, 108, 110, 115
   combined 139, 141–146
   consonant 104, 139–141
   incomplete 96–97, 100
   interfunctional 261–264
   lydian 258, 325
   modern, new 97–98, 98–100, 107, 108, 111, 112, 115, 116, 120, 141, 150
   phrygian 258, 325
   pre-tonic 254, 255–256
   quartal 106
   thickened 100, 120, 150
   uncombined 139
horizontal thinking 309–313
imitation 311
increasing the dissonant characteristic 80–82
inflection/bending 35
inner disposition of a chord 158, 161
interfunction 260–264, 296
interval 41, 236–237
inversion 46–47, 72–73, 140, 163
key 249
kinetic harmony 326–331
law
   artistic (conventional, stylistic, having to do with custom) 316–317, 318, 324–326
   universal (natural) 316–317, 318, 324–326
leading tone 250
link
   direct 229, 238
   imaginary 236–237
   indirect 229, 238
   interrupted 229, 239
   of a chord succession 229–230
   real 238–241
local tonic 286–289
lydian fourth 258
merging of dissonant characteristics 83–86
mode 249
modern melody 334–336
modulation 292–295, 296
monophony 200, 202–203, 208–211, 249
motion
   harmonic (227–313), 228–229, 227–281
      fundamental 228, 235–242
      higher-ranked 228, 242–244, 292, 295
      partial 228, 231–235, 241–242
   melodic 227
   rhythmic 227
   tonal 227, 242–244, 292
multi-note chords 63–64

music theory 319–321, 333–334
mutual negatives 62
negative of a chord-type 31, 54–58, 118
new formations (harmonic, chordal) 315, 369–371
nine-note chords 63
non-tonic quality 328–331
non-functional (atonal) music 252, 299–304, 310, 331
open fifth 140
scheme
    harmonic 38, 45–46
    orientation 31, 38, 43–45, 326
        expanded 44
        of the negative 54–58
ostinato 307
pedal point 95, 307
passing harmony, passing tone 95
phrygian second 258
pitch
    auxiliary 95
    basic 140, 153–154, 262
    counter-cancelling 198–199, 215, 216
    differentiating 140, 262
    doubled 158
    imaginary 32, 36, 37, 195–197, 202–203, 325, 330, 371–374
        harmonic 195–196
        tonal 195–196, 221–224
    multiplied 158
    non-chord, non-harmonic 95, 214–215, 377–381
    omitted (in a chord) 158
    pseudo-sensed 32
    real 195–196, 204–207, 371–374
    supplementary 140, 262
polyphony 211–214, 249, 311
polytonality 265, 284, 285, 296
position of a chord 158, 160
    basic 160
    of the fifth 161
    of the third 160
positive of a chord-type 56
practice
    analytical (369–396)
    compositional (333–367)
principle
    functional 245, 251–252
    of the leading tone 237, 245, 250, 258
    of the pure tonic 245–249, 325
problems (315–331)
progression
    passing 234

    suspended/appoggiatura 234
quality of harmonic motion 277
representation of triadic combinations 153–154
resolution 95, 214, 279, 280, 351–355
    compound 279
    harmonically imperfect 279, 286
    of a higher (the second) degree 279
    of a lower (the first) degree 279
    simple 279
    weakened 279
rotation 46–47
    of a harmony 157, 158
scale
    gypsy 65
    harmonic 66
    melodic 65
semitone 42, 71, 74, 165–169, 321
sense of the tonic 252, 282, 295, 391–394
seven-note chords 63
seventh chords
    augmented-minor seventh chord 110
    augmented-major seventh chord 107
    diminished-seventh chord 104
    diminished-minor seventh chord 110
    dominant seventh chord 110
    dominant with a sixth instead of a fifth 115
    major-major seventh chord 108
    major-minor seventh with diminished fifth 110
    minor-major seventh chord 107
    minor-minor seventh chord 106
six-note chords 58–61
six-four chord 160
six-three chord 160
sixth
    added 297
    dorian 299
    Landini 318
sonic characteristics (69–92)
static harmony (a static conception of harmony) 326–328
style, stylistic characteristics 316–317, 396
styling, styling resources/devices 349–351
compositional (styling studies) 305–309, 342–344
subdominant 257
    altered 290
    applied 287
subdominantization 35
succession
    applied (outside the key) 286–289, 292
    of chords 229, 281–284, 356–362, 385–388
suspension/appoggiatura 95, 235

system (pitch)
   asymmetrical 64, 67
   symmetrical 64
   tempered 39
   twelve-tone 39
   whole-tone 66, 321
system (harmonic, compositional)
   bichromatic (quarter-tone) 321
   dualistic 139
   functional
      of three members 256–257
      of five members (Šín's) 257–259
   pitch 319, 320, 321
tempered chromatic system 39, 64, 247
ten-note chords 63
tension
   chordal 328–331
   inner 260, 286, 329
   kinetic 282
   outer 260, 286
three-note chords 48–51
tonal decentralization 264, 292

tonal center 292
tonally functional plan 394–396
tonic [triad], tonic quality 244–252, 256, 329, 388–391
tonicization 35
transfer 279, 280
transient chord 95–96, 191, 330, 377–381
transposition 35, 42, 48, 50, 52–53, 59, 62–63
triad
   augmented 71, 75, 108–109
   diminished 104
   major 70, 77
   minor 70, 77
tritone 71, 74, 249
twelve-note chord 64, 127–128, 150, 188–190
two-note chords 48, 96
two-voice (texture) 203, 349–351
vertical thinking 310
voice-leading 206, 309–313, 385
weight of a pitch 171
whole-tone 71, 74

Name Index

Bořkovec, Pavel 343, 370, 371, 382–383, 386
Debussy, Claude 297, 299
Foerster, Josef 334
Fux, Johann Josef 334
Hába, Alois 35, 40, 194, 323, 376
Helmholtz, Hermann Ludwig Ferdinand 79
Hindemith, Paul 31, 376
Honegger, Arthur 40, 383–384, 386, 388
Hradecký, Emil 37
d'Indy, Vincent 41
Janáček, Leoš 32, 100, 171
Krejčí, Iša 389, 394
Martinů, Bohuslav 375, 392
Novák Vítězslav 298, 308, 387
Obukhov (Obouhow), Nicolai 40
Oettingen, Arthur Joachim von 79

Pícha, František 35, 393
Riemann, Hugo 79, 257, 287, 318, 334
Rimskij-Korsakov, Nikolaj Andrejevič 253
Risinger, Karel 36, 38
Roussel, Albert 378
Sérieyx, Auguste 41
Schoenberg, Arnold 40
Scriabin, Alexander 193
Skuherský, František Zdeněk 97, 194, 323
Stravinski, Igor 342
Strouhal, Čeněk 73, 79
Stumpf, Carl 330
Šín, Otakar 32, 34, 138, 257, 258, 259, 264, 280, 287, 325, 334
Toch, Ernst 40
Volek, Jaroslav 37